APR 24 2002

Nominalism and Literary Discourse
New Perspectives

Critical Studies

Vol. 10

General Editor
Myriam Díaz-Diocaretz

Editorial Assistant
Margarita de Bourbon Parme

Amsterdam - Atlanta, GA 1997

Nominalism and Literary Discourse

New Perspectives

Edited by
Hugo Keiper
Christoph Bode
Richard J. Utz

Gedruckt mit Förderung des Bundesministeriums für Wissenschaft und Verkehr in Wien.

∞ The paper on which this book is printed meets the requirements of "ISO 9706:1994, Information and documentation - Paper for documents - Requirements for permanence".

ISBN: 90-420-0288-3 (bound)
ISBN: 90-420-0278-6 (paper)
©Editions Rodopi B.V., Amsterdam - Atlanta, GA 1997
Printed in The Netherlands

CONTENTS

Acknowledgements	iii
Preface	v
Introductory Essay: A Literary 'Debate over Universals'? New Perspectives on the Relationships between Nominalism, Realism, and Literary Discourse *Hugo Keiper*	1
Signs of a New Literary Paradigm: The 'Christian' Figures of Chrétien de Troyes *Gerald Seaman*	87
The Dialectic of Divine Omnipotence in the Age of Chaucer: A Reconsideration *William J. Courtenay*	111
'As Writ Myn Auctour Called Lollius': Divine and Authorial Omnipotence in Chaucer's *Troilus and Criseyde* *Richard J. Utz*	123
Chaucer's Clerks and the Value of Philosophy *William H. Watts*	145
Literary Nominalism and Medieval Sign Theory: Problems and Perspectives *Stephen Penn*	157
Self, Action, and Sign in the Towneley and York Plays on the Baptism of Christ and in Ockhamist Salvation Theology *William F. Munson*	191
Charity and the Singular: The Object of Love in Rabelais *Ullrich Langer*	217
Semiotic Slippage: Identity and Authority in the English Renaissance *William C. Carroll*	227
Sign, Cause or General Habit? Towards an 'Historicist Ontology' of Character on the Early Modern Stage *James R. Siemon*	237

Don Quixote, Hamlet, Foucault—Language, 'Literature', and the Losses of Analogism *Andreas Mahler*	251
The Emancipation of the Sign: The Changing Significance of Beauty in Some English Renaissance Romances *Susanne Fendler*	269
John Locke and the Tradition of Nominalism *Nicholas Hudson*	283
A Modern Debate over Universals? Critical Theory vs. 'Essentialism' *Christoph Bode*	301
Bibliography	315
Contributors	345
Index of Major References *(Compiled by Hugo and Anita Keiper)*	349

ACKNOWLEDGEMENTS

The editors wish to point out and acknowledge that earlier versions of the contributions of Christoph Bode, William C. Carroll, Susanne Fendler, Andreas Mahler, and James R. Siemon were presented and discussed at a workshop on '"Realist" vs. "Nominalist" Semiotics? Shifting Paradigms in Literature: Medieval, Early Modern and After' (Chair: Hugo Keiper), which was held under the auspices of The International Society for the Study of European Ideas (ISSEI) at their conference 'The European Legacy: Toward New Paradigms', Graz (Austria), August 22-7, 1994. Abridged versions of the following workshop papers were published in the selected workshop proceedings, in *The European Legacy*, 2.2 (1997): Christoph Bode, 'A Modern Debate over Universals? Critical Theory vs. "Essentialism"', 229-37; William C. Carroll, 'Semiotic Slippage: Identity and Authority in the English Renaissance', 212-6; James R. Siemon, 'Sign, Cause or General Habit? Towards an "Historicist Ontology" of Character on the Early Modern Stage', 217-22. Copyright © 1997 by The International Society for the Study of European Ideas. The permission of MIT Press to print enlarged and revised versions of these papers is hereby acknowledged. William C. Carroll's contribution is adapted from William C. Carroll, *Fat King, Lean Beggar: Representations of Poverty in the Age of Shakespeare*, 39-47. Copyright © 1996 by Cornell University. Used by permission of the publisher, Cornell University Press. Acknowledgement is further made that some arguments of Hugo Keiper's 'Introductory Essay' were published in: Hugo Keiper, '"I wot myself best how y stonde": Literary Nominalism, Open Textual Form and the Enfranchizement of Individual Perspective in Chaucer's Dream Visions', in Richard J. Utz (ed.), *Literary Nominalism and the Theory of Rereading Late Medieval Texts: A New Research Paradigm* (Lewiston, NY: Edwin Mellen Press, 1995), 205-34, and 'Introduction: "Poohness", or Of Universals, Paradigms, and Literature', *The European Legacy*, 2.2. (1997), 199-205. Finally, we would like to acknowledge that some of the arguments of Nicholas Hudson's contribution are more briefly presented in: Nicholas Hudson, 'Locke's Nominalism and the "Linguistic Turn" of the Enlightenment', *The European Legacy*, 2.2 (1997), 223-8.

PREFACE

The impetus for a volume on 'nominalism' and 'literature' arose from a workshop on '"Realist" vs. "Nominalist" Semiotics' which the present writer conceived and organized for ISSEI's 1994 biannual conference at Graz (see Acknowledgements). However, as it is now submitted to our readers, the present collection of essays is not a workshop proceedings. It does contain some contributions that were presented and discussed at the Graz workshop, all of them in expanded, revised form, but more than half of the essays were specifically commissioned and written for this volume—some by participants in the workshop, some by scholars who could be convinced that their expertise in the field would be an asset to our project.

If there was any consensus at the Graz workshop, it was the conviction that a fundamental re-orientation of our enquiry into nominalism and realism as literary and cultural phenomena was needed, from an historical point of view as well as in theoretical and methodological terms. The shared impression among participants was that we had reached a cross-roads, because it was felt that a research program which had started off in recent decades as the study of the relationships between late-medieval literature and scholastic philosophy was now on its way to move into new and different directions, asking questions of a more comprehensive nature. An important task of those participating in our mutual project, therefore, was seen in the attempt to open up and consolidate such new perspectives for an emergent research paradigm and to suggest theoretically adequate, methodologically convincing ways to address literary discourse in its relation to what might be termed the 'nominalism/realism-complex'.

It is partly in response to that situation that a substantial introductory essay has been supplied, which aims to provide a thorough theoretical and methodological grounding for the new paradigm, as well as attempting an in-depth exploration of the present issue from a more general perspective. At the same time, this essay seeks to give a comprehensive introduction to a highly abstract problematic that is not easy to pinpoint in any definitive ways, but which is perhaps still less easy to grasp for the non-specialist. Indeed, a main consideration has been to offer an overarching framework and to suggest common points of reference for the essays to follow; for one of our aims right from the beginning has been to emphasize the common purpose of our joint efforts to arrive at a better understanding of 'literary nominalism' as a cultural and discursive phenomenon. Subsequent contributions have been arranged in roughly historical sequence, with some overlapping in terms of chronology, which, however, was less unavoidable than intended. It should finally be mentioned that the editors have as far as possible sought to allow contributors the space they needed to develop their argument, which would account for considerable variations in the lenght of individual articles.

It is with pleasure that the editors pay their debt of gratitude to a number of individuals and institutions for the help and support they received at various stages of the present project. We would like to thank ISSEI for providing us with the opportunity to meet and 'spawn' our ideas. Our sincere thanks go to all of our contributors for their most helpful cooperation and gracious forbearance in coping with any queries that might have arisen during the editing. We would also like to thank our publisher, Mr Fred van der Zee of Editions Rodopi, and Dr Myriam Díaz-Diocaretz, general editor of the Critical Studies series, for their belief in our project, and for their unflappable good humour, patience and help, all of which have been invaluable assets during the final stages of preparing this collection. We would like to extend our thanks to the Austrian Federal Ministry of Science and Transport for the subsidy they have given towards the publication of this volume. We are further grateful to Mr Wolfgang Schlinger of 'sw design' (Graz) for doing the layout and for the professionalism he showed in the process. The present writer, moreover, would also like to thank his co-editors, Christoph Bode and Richard Utz, for their part in the work, but in particular for the special contributions they made for this project to come into being. Richard did a great job in convincing a number of contributors to participate, but he also commented most helpfully on some aspects of the introductory essay. Heartfelt thanks also to Christoph for sharing his expertise as a literary theorist, but especially for his encouragement at various points during the laborious gestation of that essay. Needless to say that any shortcomings in that contribution are still my own. My very personal thanks, finally, are due to Anita Keiper for her unflagging support, not least in compiling the Bibliography and Index, and in preparing the layout of this volume, but also for just being around. It is to her and our children, Bernadette and Maximilian, that I would like to dedicate my share in this book, which has cost them a lot.

Graz, October 1997   Hugo Keiper

INTRODUCTORY ESSAY:
A LITERARY 'DEBATE OVER UNIVERSALS'?
NEW PERSPECTIVES ON THE RELATIONSHIPS BETWEEN
NOMINALISM, REALISM, AND LITERARY DISCOURSE

HUGO KEIPER

1. Words, Authors, and Authority: The Nominalism/Realism-Complex

'In the beginning was the Word, and the Word was with God, and the Word was God. The same was in the beginning with God. [...] And the Word was made flesh, and dwelt among us [...].' As is well known, these oft-quoted verses from one of the foundational texts of Christianity, the Gospel according to John (1:1-14), are not primarily a statement about literature; rather, they refer to the ultimate origins and foundations of our Universe, and to its essential relationship to the Creator, or Logos.[1] Yet it is entirely

---

[1] The Gospel is quoted from *The Bible with Apocrypha: Authorized King James Version* (Oxford Crown Edition), and one might stop for a moment to consider what, in the present context, that designation implies. In the following, bibliographical references are given mainly to sources cited and in order to document and illustrate less familiar or controversial points discussed. For further information, readers are referred to the Bibliography to the present volume and to the following essays, for which ample cross-referencing has been provided. Those of our readers who prefer a quick overview might first want to read section 8. of this essay ('About the Present Collection'), which includes a brief survey of individual contributions. I would like to acknowledge that some of the general ideas on which my essay is based were already presented at the 1994 Graz workshop: see Preface, and Hugo Keiper, 'Introduction: "Poohness", or Of Universals, Paradigms, and Literature', *The European Legacy*, 2.2. (1997), 199-205 (cf. esp. parts of sections 2. and 3. below); see also the published version of my workshop contribution, '"I wot myself best how y stonde": Literary Nominalism, Open Textual Form and the Enfranchizement of Individual Perspective in Chaucer's Dream Visions', in Richard J. Utz (ed.), *Literary Nominalism and the Theory of Rereading Late Medieval Texts: A New Research Paradigm* (Lewiston, NY: Edwin Mellen Press, 1995), 205-34 (cf. esp. the first part of section 6.3.). I would further like to thank my colleagues and friends Philip J. Keegan and Volker Horn for checking on the English of my essay and for the many valuable suggestions they made.

possible, and no doubt intended, that we discern profound analogies between the evangelist's statement about the universe at large and textual universes of human making: our text not only envisages the world's beginnings in terms of some original, creative 'word', 'sound' or 'language'; or even of some primordial Script or Ur-Text author(iz)ed by God, just as God, in turn, is author(iz)ed by it—if the references to 'God' in our quotation are supplanted by 'author(s)', the Gospel's words are equally applicable to any man-made text, but especially so to literary fictions.

At first glance, this would merely be stating the obvious: Surely no one in his right mind will deny that texts are made of, and thus originate in, words. Likewise, to common sense, it is perfectly reasonable to suppose that texts have authors; in any event, they will have some point of origin, regardless of whether that ultimate source is known to us or not. However, as the Gospel's strangely paradoxical phrasing, its multiple, curiously entangled layers of reference and meaning might warn us, the whole issue is in fact full of complexities. Nor is the precise relationship between words and authors, or God and the Word—or, indeed, between authors, words, the Word, and God—quite as simple or clear-cut as might initially appear, but rather takes the form of a bewilderingly complex dialectics, or even of a 'strange loop' or 'tangled hierarchy',[2] that is not easily resolved. Besides, if we suppose, like most cultures before us have done as a matter of course, that there is a Creator, it may still be hard to imagine,[3] although nevertheless quite possible, that some kind of immensely powerful, inherently creative Sound or Word acted as the primary instrument of creation—a claim, incidentally, that is made not only by the Gospel, but by many other such myths of creation, within and outside the Judaeo-Christian tradition. Witness, moreover, the many religious or semi-religious texts that lay claim to divinely inspired authorship, thus insisting—just as the Gospel's introductory verses do in their self-consciously reflexive, yet at the same time entirely self-assured manner—on a special, quite immediate relationship between the words they use, and the Word.

Those few observations, then, may lead us to ask very fundamental questions indeed: What precisely are words? How do they mean or signify? What do they refer to? What is it that guarantees their ability, or power, to signify? What is the relationship between word(s) and author(s)? Or be-

---

[2] For literary applications of these concepts, which gained currency mainly through Douglas R. Hofstadter's books, see Brian McHale, *Postmodernist Fiction* (New York and London: Methuen, 1987), esp. ch. 8.

[3] Obviously, this would chiefly apply to us Westerners, and here perhaps mainly to those unimpressed by New Age thinking, or indeed by various indigenous traditions. For the inherent power of words, or some words at least, as a fundamental aspect of most Eastern traditions, see John Blofeld, *Mantras: Secret Words of Power* (London: Unwin Paperbacks, 1977).

tween the Word and the words we use in our natural languages? In short, what is the ultimate nature of words and their exact ontological and epistemological status? On the other hand, we might ask ourselves: What is the status of an author? What precisely is it he or she[4] author(ize)s and thus gives authority to? What kind of authority does he convey to his creations? What gives authority to him, and what kind of authority, if any, are we dealing with? What is an author's position vis-à-vis whatever we choose to term 'reality', and how can we define his relationship to Nature or to the Creator himself, if we suppose there is one?

Naturally, his or her position and status as an 'author' will be of fundamental concern to any serious artist. Moreover, in their role as artificers they will also take an essential interest in the nature, properties and constraints of the material they use to create their artifacts. Obviously, then, such questions are of crucial importance, directly and indirectly, to all writers and poets. They are of equal pertinence, though, to philosophers, theologians, linguists, semioticians, literary theorists and many others, not least among them the 'common' reader. As a matter of fact, it is precisely questions of this sort that have troubled a good many (and eminent) thinkers before us, from Plato to Derrida, just as they have kept cropping up, over and over again, in the works of many creative writers of all ages: from Chaucer and Shakespeare to Lewis Carroll, A.A. Milne or J.R.R. Tolkien. To pursue such issues as well as possible connections and repercussions, in the areas thus staked out, between literature and other fields of knowledge, will be of considerable interest, therefore, not only to literary critics and other specialists, but also from the broader perspective of cultural history and its underlying dynamics.

2. Nominalism vs. Realism: Systematic and Historical Perspectives

As regards the general nature of words, there are few authorities throughout the history of European thought who would seriously object to the notion that words, as basic building blocks of language and thus, ultimately, of any discourse, are signs. As such, they represent part of an important, perhaps the single most important, sub-system of that vast, intricate web of signification, or signifying practices, which we have come to term 'culture'. (According to some, even Nature itself is to be seen as an extremely complex, all-encompassing network of signs authored by the Creator himself—the 'book of nature', which to decipher or 'read' properly can be regarded as one of humanity's foremost tasks.) However, while writers as

---

[4]Nearly all of the authorities and writers discussed in this essay are men. Hence, I will generally use the male forms of pronouns, with the obvious exceptions. But then, what might that tell us about the gendering of authority in European intellectual history?

diverse as St Augustine, St Thomas Aquinas, William of Ockham, John Locke, Ferdinand de Saussure, Roland Barthes, Jacques Derrida or Richard Rorty would surely agree that words, generally speaking, are to be considered as signs, there was, and is, strong disagreement and heated debate as to the exact nature and status one should ascribe to such signs, about how precisely they signify and what they actually refer to; in other words, about how they relate to language, thought, or any reality beyond—if they do in fact relate to any extra-linguistic or extra-mental reality—and what kind of reality we have to reckon with. In the final analysis then, these issues are inextricably bound up with questions about the general nature of language, perception, representation, signification, generalizing statements, and so forth, but also, ultimately, about the fundamental structure and make-up of 'reality' and the universe at large.

As a consequence, attempts to theorize such problems have been numerous and manifold, in both their approaches and results. Whilst, as a rule, they have been guided by basically semiotic orientations or frameworks, they have also been made within a wide variety of different disciplines and traditions which, more often than not, are only loosely connected in any formal sense. Thus, to name but a few, they have traditionally fallen into the domains of such diverse disciplines and fields of knowledge as poetics (or literary theory), philosophy, linguistics, psychology, theology, and even cosmology. Until well into our own century—which also saw the rise of semiotics and systematic linguistics as disciplines in their own right—poetics and literary theory, by and large, have mainly concerned themselves with the status of the literary text as a *fictum*, i.e. with its moral, theological, psychological, social or political effects, whereas the status of verbal signs as such has only recently received close attention (and, accordingly, has had more or less systematic treatment). Much the same can also be said of most of the other disciplines, whose interest in questions of semiosis has chiefly been governed by their primary objects of investigation.[5] Philosophy, on the other hand, has taken a long-standing, central interest in precisely that problem, focussing especially on the theory of universals, viz. of general terms. It is primarily in the latter context, then, that the terms 'nominalism' and 'realism' have come to signify two contrary and more or less extreme positions, or views, that can be taken on the nature of universals.

---

[5]For a useful general survey, see Tzvetan Todorov, *Theories of the Symbol*, tr. Catherine Porter (Oxford: Blackwell, 1982), but see also Paul Perron's informative article 'Semiotics', in *The Johns Hopkins Guide to Literary Theory and Criticism*, eds. Michael Groden and Martin Kreiswirth (Baltimore, MD, and London: Johns Hopkins University Press, 1994), 658-65.

If at this point we turn to works of reference on philosophy, we will be told that '[t]hings are particulars and their qualities are universals. So a universal is the property predicated of all the individuals of a certain sort or class.'[6] Especially in scholastic philosophy, someone who holds the 'view that universals [...] have a real substantial existence, independently of being thought',[7] is called a realist, while a nominalist holds 'that universals have no existence independently of being thought and are mere names, representing nothing that really exists.'[8] Moreover, as is often claimed, there were (and still are) 'conceptualists': occupying an intermediate position between realists and (extreme) nominalists, they 'grant universals reality only as categorial concepts within the mind'.[9] On the most abstract, generalized level then, we can differentiate between realists and nominalists (and, if one so chooses, conceptualists), depending on whether or not they accord to universals some sort of real, substantial existence outside the mind; in other words, depending on whether—and in what ways exactly—they hold that general terms represent some extra-mental or extra-linguistic order of reality.

No doubt, such general definitions are useful in terms of positioning a specific thinker or theory in a systematic or typological sense. In many respects, though, they also imply a crude simplification of the actual state of affairs. Thus, for one thing, the perennial debate over the status of universals has a highly intricate historical dimension to it, which is furthermore often obscured by the contingencies of textual tradition, the fact that quite a few important works by influential thinkers have not been edited as yet, or are just in the process of being edited or rediscovered.[10] Therefore, it is not an easy task by any account to (re)construct properly, or do justice to the many and various brands of realism and nominalism that evolved over the centuries, let alone to trace out with any degree of accuracy the

---

[6]*A Dictionary of Philosophy*, eds. Antony Flew et al. (Pan Reference Books) (London: Pan, 1979), s.v. 'universals *and* particulars'.

[7]Ibid., s.v. 'realism. 1.'.

[8]Ibid., s.v. 'nominalism. 1.'.

[9]*Encyclopædia Britannica, Fifteenth Edition* (Chicago, IL: Encyclopædia Britannica, 1988), vol. 9, s.v. 'Realism' (974).

[10]Jan P. Beckmann, *Wilhelm von Ockham* (Beck'sche Reihe, 533) (Munich: Beck, 1995), 190, points out that a complete critical edition even of Ockham's philosophical and theological writings has only recently been available, and that still no such edition exists of Ockham's political writings (see 10). For a useful selection of sources, with German translation, see *Texte zum Universalienstreit*, 2 vols., ed. and tr. Hans-Ulrich Wöhler: *Band 1—Vom Ausgang der Antike bis zur Frühscholastik: Lateinische, griechische und arabische Texte des 3.-12. Jahrhunderts*; *Band 2—Hoch-und Spätmittelalterliche Scholastik: Unter Einschluß von zwei erstmals kritisch edierten Texten W. Burleys und J. Buridans* (Berlin: Akademie-Verlag, 1992-4). See further William J. Courtenay's contribution to the present volume.

complex interrelations and lines of influence that prevailed between them, which are in some ways still quite obscure.[11]

Such difficulties notwithstanding, let us attempt a brief overview of the debate's most important historical stages and developments, as they have been perceived by cultural history. Broadly speaking, the debate—like most major issues in the history of European ideas—originated with ancient Greek philosophy, specifically with 'the ancient Greek theory of Forms or Ideas, which Plato held to have a real existence distinct from their manifestation in individual objects'.[12] Plato's theory, which had itself been developed, inter alia, in opposition to the 'nominalist' tenets of Sophists like Gorgias,[13] was contested, and modified accordingly by Aristotle and his followers, who held that universals did not exist 'before the thing' (*ante rem*), as Plato's somewhat more extreme realism contended, but 'in the thing' (*in re*).[14] Such altercations in turn were a powerful influence on succeeding generations of philosophers, right into Late Antiquity, but most momentous perhaps was the impact they had—partly through the mediation of writers like Boethius or St Augustine—on the thinking of the scholastic philosophers of the Middle Ages. In their majority, these schoolmen upheld a more or less pronounced realism, predominantly of the more moderate sort. Yet there were others, such as Roscelin, Abelard and, later, Ockham and his at times more radical 'followers' among the *moderni*, who developed views on the status of universals that can be, and were in fact, termed 'nominalist', thus giving rise to the famous Medieval 'debate over universals'.[15]

---

[11]See Courtenay's and Penn's contributions to the present collection, but especially the impressive work of Courtenay and Heiko J. Oberman (see Bibliography for a representative selection).

[12]*Encyclopædia Britannica*, vol. 12, s.v. 'universal' (162).

[13]See ibid., vol. 11, s.v. 'Sophist' (17), and vol. 25 (Macropædia), s.v. 'Philosophical Schools and Doctrines' (603ff.).

[14]See ibid., vol. 12, s.v. 'universal' (162). For the present purposes, the information to be gleaned from the sources cited is rather more to the point than the pertinent entries in more recent works of philosophical reference, such as *The Cambridge Dictionary of Philosophy*, ed. Robert Audi (Cambridge: Cambridge University Press, 1995), or *The Oxford Companion to Philosophy*, ed. Ted Honderich (Oxford: Oxford University Press, 1995). But see the useful discussion of technical detail especially in *The Oxford Companion*'s entries on 'realism and anti-realism' and 'universals'. For in-depth reference, see also *The Encyclopedia of Philosophy*, 8 vols., ed. Paul Edwards (New York and London: Macmillan, 1967), and *Historisches Wörterbuch der Philosophie*, 9 vols. (A to St), eds. Joachim Ritter and Karlfried Gründer (Darmstadt: Wissenschaftliche Buchgesellschaft, 1971-95) which, however, is incomplete as yet.

[15]For further details, see Christoph Bode's account in the present collection. For the designation 'nominalists' (*nominales*), see Beckmann, *Wilhelm von Ockham*, 176-81, and Richard J. Utz, *Literarischer Nominalismus im Spätmittelalter: Eine Untersuchung zu Sprache, Charakterzeichnung und Struktur in Geoffrey Chaucers* Troilus and Criseyde (Frankfurt a.M. et al.: Lang, 1990), 27f.

The Medieval debate then, which extended over several centuries, flaring up with renewed vigour every now and then, involved nominalists of all shades, a majority of quite moderate realists, but also a Neo-Platonic realism that, in its reception of an incomplete and heavily mediated version of Plato's thought,[16] and with particularly Christian fervour, hatched an extreme form of realist epistemology and ontology—as seen, for example, in Roscelin's adversaries. Coming to a head, apparently,[17] in late-medieval times, the debate seems to have reached a crucial stage in the process, 'critical mass' so to speak. Some such course of events, at any rate, is suggested by several of the most influential accounts of European cultural history:[18] notwithstanding the powerful resurgence of Platonism in the Renaissance, and despite other minor 'set-backs' in the centuries to follow, nominalism, the story goes, was gathering culturally transformative momentum at this point—to a degree, it is said, which was to prove decisive in the long run. Hence, it is often claimed that the rise of nominalism and its ultimate victory over 'realist' (or 'essentialist') positions are among the decisive factors underlying the formation of Modern Europe since the later Middle Ages,[19] but particularly since the Reformation. It is sometimes even alleged, therefore, that everybody is a nominalist nowadays, more or less.[20]

---

[16]For the reception of Plato, and generally the development of Platonism, see Theo Kobusch and Burkhard Mojsisch (eds.), *Platon in der abendländischen Geistesgeschichte: Neue Forschungen zum Platonismus* (Darmstadt: Wissenschaftliche Buchgesellschaft, 1997), but see also *The Oxford Companion to Philosophy*, s.v. 'Platonism' (686-8).

[17]One should stress here that not all recent historians agree on the precise nature, but especially on the extent of the impact which Ockham, and nominalism in general, had on fourteenth- and fifteenth-century intellectual culture. See William J. Courtenay's contribution to the present collection (esp. section B.), and Richard J. Utz, 'Negotiating the Paradigm: Literary Nominalism and the Theory and Practice of Rereading Late Medieval Texts', in Utz (ed.), *Literary Nominalism*, 1-30, esp. 13f. For a detailed survey of scholarly opinion, see also Utz, *Literarischer Nominalismus*, chs. 2 and 3.

[18]For details, see notes 38 and 39.

[19]In order to direct attention to the fact that such concepts as '(late-)medieval', '(early) modern', or 'post-modern' will often have an inherent tendency towards reification, or might contain a strong essentializing element, I have capitalized such words throughout, except where they are used neutrally as indicating rough historical periodization.

[20]For examples, see Stephen Knight's claim that '[a]part from Christian theologians, we are all nominalists nowadays', and Jorge Luis Borges's similar observation: 'No one [today] says that he is a nominalist, because nobody is anything else'. (See Stephen Knight, 'Chaucer—A Modern Writer?', *Balcony*, 2 (1965), 37, and Borges's essay 'From Allegories to Novels', in *Borges: A Reader*, eds. Emir Rodriguez Monegal and Alastair Reid (New York: Dutton, 1981), 231.)

Yet this is not really the end of the story, no matter what we would make of the after-effects of the scholastic debate or in what ways we would construe its evolutionary dynamics, for most of the questions it raises are still far from having been finally settled. Nor is it quite so clear, even from a Eurocentric perspective, that ours is indeed a thoroughly nominalistic age, i.e. an era entirely given to anti-essentialist thinking. Consider, for example, the enormous general impact that holistic or New Age thinking has recently had, or the late, unsettling upsurge of nationalist, even racist sentiments throughout Europe.[21] Thus, while the terms of the debate may indeed have shifted in some respects (just as the terms 'nominalist' and 'realist' are now rarely applied to post-medieval or post-Renaissance philosophers[22]), many of the issues at stake in the earlier debates are still with us and have continued to occupy, and divide, thinkers up to our own day: from the ongoing debates in mathematics over its 'true'—nominalist or realist—foundations, to philosophy, linguistics, or cultural studies. One need only think of the outcry against some of the more daring 'universalist' hypotheses on the 'innateness' of language acquisition, or of Derrida's and many other poststructuralists' struggle against 'essentialism', or the sometimes bitter altercations over essentializing tendencies in feminist and postcolonial studies.[23]

---

[21] As regards the general public's considerable susceptibility to heavily ideologized versions of 'realism', the most striking recent instance of an essentializing statement and a successful attempt at mystification is perhaps Elton John's revamped version of 'Like a Candle in the Wind', which was written for Lady Di's funeral service, September 1997, and immediately became an all-time megaseller. For a further example, however, note also the conflicts that may arise in some multicultural societies, as in July 1997, when the stylized script 'Air' on Nike's latest model of track shoes—understandably—hurt the sensibilities of fundamentalist American muslims because of its resemblance to the Arabic lettering of 'Allah', and had to be withdrawn. (This incident was covered on TV but, to my best knowledge, did not make it into international printed media, not even the US-edition of *Time Magazine*.)

[22] But see Frederick Jameson's chapter on 'Deconstruction and Nominalism', in *Postmodernism: Or the Cultural Logic of Late Capitalism* (Durham, NC: Duke University Press, 1991), 217-59, or Karl R. Popper's section on 'Essentialism *versus* Nominalism', in *The Poverty of Historicism* (London: Routledge & Kegan Paul, 2nd corr. ed. 1961), 26-34. Significantly, Popper had his intellectual roots in the 'Wiener Kreis' (Vienna Circle), whilst Jameson has been strongly influenced by Theodor W. Adorno (see also Adorno's remarks on nominalism in *Noten zur Literatur* (Frankfurt a.M.: Suhrkamp, 1977), 495ff.). See further Nicholas Hudson's and Christoph Bode's essays in the present volume, and D.M. Armstrong, *Universals and Scientific Realism I: Nominalism and Realism* (Cambridge: Cambridge University Press, 1978).

[23] For the debate in mathematics, see the compact articles on 'mathematics, history of the philosophy of', and 'mathematics, problems of the philosophy of', in *The Oxford Companion to Philosophy* (532-9). For the controversies about language acquisition, see David Crystal, *The Cambridge Encyclopedia of Language* (Cambridge: Cambridge University Press, 1987), 234. For linguistics in general, see most recently John E.

3. Nominalism and Realism as Competing Paradigms of Semiosis

What we have sketched in here, of course, is merely a skeleton outline of the debate's most important historical parameters and general development—or rather, as regards the latter point, of one influential version of it. And even though the overall trend thus captured may well be accurate (as certainly it reflects, by and large, the prevailing opinion of many cultural historians), it is once again based on sweeping generalizations, on wholesale interpretations of history which, we would submit, are in urgent need of close scrutiny and in-depth reconsideration, a point to which we shall return.

All the same, even the most detailed, sophisticated, and carefully balanced of historical accounts would hardly suffice to satisfy those historians of philosophy who, in growing numbers, have invested a life-time's labour and acumen in the precise understanding of the systems and positions of thinkers whom the less initiate trade, in a problematic shorthand, as 'nominalists' or 'realists'. This is so for several reasons. First of all, the philosophical or historical reconstruction of any system of thought is ever a precarious interpretive effort,[24] all the more so since most philosophical

---

Joseph's critique of twentieth-century linguistic theory in 'The End of Languages as We Know Them', *Anglistik*, 8.2 (1997), 31-46; Joseph claims: 'as soon as [the adjectives] "English" [or] "French" are turned into nouns, meaning "the English language" and so on, reification occurs, and we have the myth of a system, a "fixed code", that has set modern linguistics on a chimerical quest.' (35) As regards poststructuralism, feminism and cultural theory, one need only take a look at recent surveys of literary or cultural theory, as e.g. Peter Barry, *Beginning Theory: An Introduction to Literary and Cultural Theory* (Manchester: Manchester University Press, 1995), chs. 3, 4, 6, 9, 10. In this area, it is particularly apparent, perhaps, that 'the "mystifications" that recent theory seeks to transcend', such as essentialism, metaphysics, idealism, or authorship, go 'all the way back to Plato'—as in fact do many of Derrida's own ideas. Nonetheless, and despite the efforts of critical theorists, it seems that such so-called mystifications are still going strong. (See Howard Felperin, *Beyond Deconstruction: The Uses and Abuses of Literary Theory* (Oxford: Clarendon Press, 1985), 36f., but see also Christoph Bode's attempt to explain that state of affairs in his contribution to the present collection.) For a fascinating recent example of 'scientific realism', finally, see Rupert Sheldrake's much-discussed theory of morphogenetic fields. As Sheldrake himself points out, his approach to evolution rests largely upon concepts that might be construed as modernized—or dynamized—versions of Platonic Ideas, yet especially of Aristotle's 'formal causes' (*eidos*); see *The Presence of the Past: Morphic Resonance and the Habits of Nature* (1988; repr. London: Harper-Collins, 1994), esp. 102-9.

[24] Just how precarious it is in the case of nominalism/realism can be seen, for example, from Heiko A. Oberman's monumental study, *The Harvest of Medieval Theology: Gabriel Biel and Late Medieval Nominalism* (Cambridge, MA: Harvard University Press, 1963). But see also Courtenay's, Penn's and Bode's contributions to the present collection.

systems are not the static or stable affairs we would make them out to be, but are subject to development and change over time. Consequently, it is rarely possible to establish once and for all even a single philosopher's positions on certain issues (and this is not to speak, for the moment, of the vagaries of their reception at different times and ages). Plato's theory of Ideas, for instance, was not only modified throughout the philosopher's career; his peculiar dialectical method would also serve to dynamize, and thus subtly undermine, many of the tenets he, or rather the Platonic Socrates, proposes in some of his dialogues.[25] Secondly, as has been suggested, semiotics was not normally seen as an independent field of enquiry; rather, its traditional position was as a part or aspect, albeit often an important one, of much more extended, elaborate philosophical and/or theological systems. Alternatively, since semiotics, by its very nature, was associated in fundamental ways with the various divisions of the trivium, it was intimately bound up with such basic disciplines as logic, grammar and rhetoric, thus also serving a largely propedeutic function within the medieval and early modern system of the *artes*.[26] Thirdly, and closely connected with the second point, philosophy in the Middle Ages was primarily viewed as the 'handmaiden of theology'. As such, it was almost entirely subordinate to much larger issues at stake. Indeed, even Ockham, who is often credited with introducing a quintessential separation between the two fields of enquiry, always saw himself as both a philosopher and theologian.[27]

Historically speaking, then, 'nominalism' and 'realism', if we define them in terms of their underlying theories of universals, were rarely 'pure' in themselves, but have in actual practice—and this would especially apply to the Middle Ages and the (early) Renaissance—always been connected, and even subordinated, to larger concerns: to highly complex and much more inclusive as well as ideologically policed systems of

---

[25]For Plato's overall development as a philosopher, see the useful synopsis in *The Oxford Companion to Philosophy*, s.v. 'Plato' (683-6). For Plato's dialectical method, and generally its influence on philosophical discourse, see Jürgen Mittelstraß, 'Versuch über den sokratischen Dialog', in Karlheinz Stierle and Rainer Warning (eds.), *Das Gespräch* (Poetik und Hermeneutik, 11) (Munich: Fink, 1984), 11-27.

[26]See Beckmann, *Wilhelm von Ockham*, 16f. For the *artes*, see also D. Luscombe, 'Trivium, Quadrivium and the Organisation of Schools', *Miscellanea del centro di studi medioevali*, 12 (1989), 81-100. For the general situation and development of (late-)medieval universities, see Johannes Fried (ed.), *Schulen und Studium im sozialen Wandel des hohen und späten Mittelalters* (Sigmaringen: Thorbecke, 1986), and William J. Courtenay, *Schools and Scholars in Fourteenth-Century England* (Princeton, NJ: Princeton University Press, 1987), but see also the copiously illustrated book by Franco Cardini and M.T. Fumagalli Beonio-Brocchieri, *Universitäten im Mittelalter: Die europäischen Stätten des Wissens*, tr. Annemarie Seling (Munich: Südwest Verlag, 1991).

[27]See e.g. Beckmann, *Wilhelm von Ockham*, 13f.

thought that extended far beyond the more limited reaches of semiotic enquiry. In that sense, even if it were possible to definitely allocate particular philosophers to one of the two basic positions, and thus to classify them beyond doubt as either nominalists or realists,[28] their views on universals, in their manifold ramifications, cannot be finally disengaged from their notions in other areas, or of certain key issues which, at first glance, might appear largely unrelated to their stance in semiotic matters—questions, that is, ranging from the power of God, or necessity and contingency, to problems of authority, subjectivity, and so forth.[29]

Yet conversely, it is equally true that a philosopher's or any thinker's position on universals is indicative not only of his fundamental epistemological and ontological tenets but, most importantly, will also reflect his general semiotic orientation. In many respects, then, it can be regarded as the keystone of his entire thinking, and therefore as paradigmatic of his system at large. Semiotics, it has been suggested, 'can be defined broadly as a domain of investigation that explores the nature and function of signs as well as the systems and processes underlying signification, expression, representation, and communication'.[30] A paradigm, on the other hand, can be described as 'a central overall way of regarding phenomena, within which a scientist' or any other person 'normally works', and thinks.[31] In other words, paradigms function to underpin, shape, and ultimately prejudice the basic *gestalt* of our perception and construction of reality. Usually, moreover, paradigms are thought to operate in ways that are understood implicitly, tacitly, but which are nevertheless of a powerfully fundamental nature. Since, then, we cannot at any given moment escape thinking in terms of single, specific paradigms, they 'may dictate what type of explanation will be found acceptable'.[32] A paradigm is thus both an enabling thing and a limiting one: enabling because it provides the ultimate foundation, or conceptual grid, for any coherent act of reasoning, model-building or theorizing, and consequently for any systematic enquiry; limiting because it puts certain inescapable constraints on our ways of perceiving and thinking about

---

[28] The dividing line between nominalists and realists is precariously thin on occasion (see Beckmann, *Wilhelm von Ockham*, 180f., using the example of Ockham and the 'realist' Burleigh). But see also Christoph Bode's contribution to the present collection (esp. section II) for an incisive critique of the tendency, in some accounts, to turn 'nominalists' into 'conceptualists', or even 'realists'.

[29] For an overview of issues involved, one could do worse than taking a look at just the Contents of Oberman's magisterial *Harvest of Medieval Theology*.

[30] Perron, 'Semiotics', 658.

[31] See *A Dictionary of Philosophy*, eds. Flew et al., s. v. 'paradigm.'.

[32] Ibid.

reality, and thus 'of necessity [...] excludes a range of possibilities'.[33] Hence, in times of crisis, there may be 'paradigm shifts'.[34]

From this, we may conclude that 'nominalism' and 'realism' in the 'narrow', strictly semiotic sense of the terms can be construed as paradigms, or more precisely, as an opposition of conflicting, competing paradigms that are grounded in incompatible, even incommensurable[35] concepts of semiotics and semiosis. And that insight, again, might provide us with a handy epistemological meta-perspective on our issue, both in terms of a typological and of an historical approach to it.[36]

---

[33] See Jeremy Hawthorn, *A Concise Glossary of Contemporary Literary Theory* (London: Arnold, 1992), s.v. 'Paradigm shift'.

[34] For Thomas S. Kuhn's view of paradigms/paradigm shifts, see *The Structure of Scientific Revolutions* (1962; Chicago, IL: University of Chicago Press, 2nd ed. 1970). However, the actual complexity of Kuhn's notions can best be seen from the fierce controversies that arose in the wake of that book (see also Kuhn's 'Postscript' of 1969, included in the second edition). For a highly pertinent critique and important modifications of Kuhn's concepts, see Paul Feyerabend, *Against Method: Outline of an Anarchistic Theory of Knowledge* (1975; repr. London: Verso, 1978), but especially the revised and enlarged German edition, *Wider den Methodenzwang: Skizze einer anarchistischen Erkenntnistheorie* (Frankfurt a.M.: Suhrkamp, 1976), which also gives detailed documentation of the early controversies. For a convincing application of Feyerabend's theories to cultural studies, see his *Wissenschaft als Kunst* (Frankfurt a.M.: Suhrkamp, 1984). An interesting historical perspective on the term and concept 'paradigm' is provided by Hans Blumenberg's *Wirklichkeiten in denen wir leben: Aufsätze und eine Rede* (Stuttgart: Reclam, 1981), 157-62, in the essay 'Paradigma, grammatisch' [1971].

[35] For a 'strong' interpretation of paradigms and good reasons for insisting on their incommensurability, see especially Feyerabend, *Wider den Methodenzwang*, 368f. and 389-91.

[36] In terms of endowing us with a large-scale map of the territory we wish to explore, the proposed opposition is clearly useful, indeed indispensable. In the final analysis, though, it can—and probably should—be deconstructed, and this in fact is what often happens in literary texts. (See the following, but see also Christoph Bode's contribution, esp. section III, for a deconstructive reading of cultural history.) In order to avoid misunderstandings, one should further point out that the notion of paradigms underlying the present essay is mainly based on Feyerabend's theories and modifications of Kuhn. That is to say, paradigms are here seen as specific, structured ways of organizing our perception and construction of reality, and they are also seen as incommensurable in the sense that particular paradigms will absolutely determine the *gestalt* of such constructions at any given moment in time. In that respect, then, paradigms are regarded as radically exclusive of one another. On the other hand, however, they are not seen as absolutes that are mutually exclusive in terms of their *existence* at any given moment in history, or within a specific cultural configuration, nor are they considered as binding in any absolute sense even for single individuals, except at particular points in time. Hence, we do not conceive of paradigms as all-comprehensive, 'water-tight' systems of organizing an entire culture's perception of

4. Realism, Nominalism, and Literature: Methodological Issues and Perspectives

4.0. Preliminary Remarks: Cultural History, Literary Criticism, and the Realism/Nominalism-Complex

The debate over universals, then, has numerous momentous repercussions in many areas, inside and outside philosophy, and highly intricate implications that go way beyond a 'mere' theory of general terms. At the same time, it is not just an inconsequential historical episode either, however pertinent in itself. As has been shown, many of the issues it raises are of no slight importance even today. Moreover, influential commentators of European cultural history have argued that the ever growing ascendancy of 'nominalism' and the concomitant defeat of 'realism' were instrumental in the shaping of Modern European thinking, and thus, in the final analysis, of our own world-picture. Admittedly, this is probably an over-simplification of a situation that ought, perhaps, to be construed not so much in terms of a steady, straightforward evolutionary development, but rather as a complex dialectical movement, or even a see-saw-dynamics, that is in fact infinitely more evasive and ambiguous, indeed tortuous, than many such accounts would have us believe.[37]

Nonetheless, for a start, we are surely entitled to assume that there may be some fundamental truth in such a proposition, which has after all been made by such leading scholars in the field as F. Heer, R. Assunto, E. Panofsky, and H. Blumenberg,[38] and which several influential post-

---

reality in the ways Foucault's concept of *episteme* is often used—which has been rightly criticized for its 'monolithic' implications—and would therefore insist on a clear differentiation between the terms 'paradigm' and *'episteme'* as fundamentally different descriptive categories. (For a discussion and critique of Foucault, see also Andreas Mahler's contribution to the present volume, section I.)

[37] See also Christoph Bode's contribution to the present collection, esp. section III. Incidentally, in our discussions of papers presented at the Graz workshop, the most controversial points were precisely such issues. What remained contentious throughout, though, was the question of how one ought to interpret our findings in terms of a broader historical or 'developmental' perspective (see further sections 7. and 8. below).

[38] See, for example, Friedrich Heer, *Mittelalter: Vom Jahr 1000 bis 1350, Teil 2* (= vol. 10 of *Kindlers Kulturgeschichte Europas*) (1961; rev., expanded ed. 1977; repr. Munich: dtv, 1983), 562ff.; Rosario Assunto, *Die Theorie des Schönen im Mittelalter* (1963; repr. Cologne: Dumont, 1982), 119ff.; Erwin Panofsky, *Gothic Architecture and Scholasticism* (Latrobe, PA: The Archabbey Press, 1951), 11ff., esp. 15ff. and 69ff. Note, however, that in his *Early Netherlandish Painting: Its Origins and Character* (1953; repr. Cambridge, MA: Harvard University Press, 1964) Panofsky makes a clear distinction between 'northern Late Gothic', with its tendency 'to individualize', and 'the resurgence and enthusiastic acceptance of [...] Neoplatonism' in 'Italy and, more

structuralists like M. Foucault and J. Kristeva[39] have also subscribed to. It does in fact capture a powerful, or at any rate a pertinent general trend within (Early) Modern history. Hence, we have reason to believe that literary texts also responded and in turn contributed, in a variety of ways, to this process of cultural transformation. And it will clearly be of consequence to our current image of European cultural history, as well as to our (re-)construction of its underlying dynamics, if we can test this hypothesis and tackle some of the problems it poses by a close scrutiny and analysis of literary texts that can be read as 'representative' of such 'developments', but also by taking a fresh, unprejudiced look at their cultural and theoretical co(n)texts. In any event, whatever historical view we take of our problematic, there can be no reasonable doubt that literature will have interacted, in some ways, with the issues at stake.

This, however, raises further questions, about literature's position as well as its functions within such processes of cultural negotiation, or struggles for social, religious, ideological and political hegemony. Yet everything outlined so far does not tell us a lot about how precisely literature as a fundamentally symbolic mode of signification would interact with other cultural constituents, but especially about how it would respond to our problematic—which, beyond the manifold questions relating to the status of universals or signs, might include nominalism and/or realism as more comprehensive philosophical positions or 'movements', or indeed any of the other issues connected with them. Moreover, the concomitant question of how, in this context, literary discourse relates to other discursive domains and their specific signifying practices is an issue that has found little

---

specifically, in Florence' (8). For the need to distinguish between several different 'schools and currents' in Renaissance thought, see also Paul Oskar Kristeller, *Renaissance Thought and the Arts* (Princeton, NJ: Princeton University Press, 1964; expanded ed. 1990), 111. See further Hans Blumenberg, *The Legitimacy of the Modern Age*, tr. Robert M. Wallace (Cambridge, MA, and London: MIT Press, 1981), esp. Part II (125-226), and Utz's discussion of Blumenberg in 'Negotiating the Paradigm', 6f. But see also Umberto Eco's influential study *Kunst und Schönheit im Mittelalter*, tr. Günter Memmert (Munich: Hanser, 1991), esp. 146f., and Robert Weimann's sophisticated approach to the issue in *Shakespeare und die Macht der Mimesis: Autorität und Repräsentation im elisabethanischen Theater* (Berlin and Weimar: Aufbau-Verlag, 1988).

[39]See Michel Foucault, *The Order of Things: An Archaeology of the Human Sciences* (New York: Vintage, 1973), passim, but esp. 17ff., 46ff. and 58ff.; Julia Kristeva, *Le Texte du roman: approche sémiologique d'une structure discursive transformationelle* (The Hague: Mouton, 1970), and repr. of excerpt: 'From Symbol to Sign', tr. Seán Hand, in *The Kristeva Reader*, ed. Toril Moi (Oxford: Blackwell, 1986), 63-73, esp. 64 and 68. For a discussion of Kristeva's arguments, see Richard J. Utz, 'Literary Nominalism in Chaucer's Late-Medieval England', *The European Legacy*, 2.2 (1997), 206-11.

serious attention, let alone systematic treatment, at the hands of cultural historians and, until recently, even less so among literary historians, theorists and critics—whose business, after all, might be thought to consist mainly in dealing with the specifically literary modes of producing cultural meaning.

Previous research, then, with few exceptions, doesn't offer us a great deal in terms of a reliable or even a consistently argued groundwork that we, as literary critics or theorists, could build upon, either in the way of theoretical or of practical approaches to the matter.[40] However, as will be seen later, it is precisely in that area that we are faced with a whole range of serious—and highly controversial—methodological problems which, even if they cannot be solved once and for all, should at least be confronted. It is surely not amiss, therefore, to try and address some of those issues, in an attempt to sharpen our awareness of them and, if possible, to provide some kind of general framework within which they can be theorized.

4.1. Fundamental Types of 'Literary' Response to the Nominalism/Realism-Complex: Explicit vs. Implicit Engagement

4.1.1. Explicit Literary Responses

In order to establish and convey their 'meaning', literary texts typically make use of multiple modes of encoding, yet particularly so of formal, symbolic or 'aesthetic' codes. 'Literary meaning', in other words, could be said to emerge from the interplay between the formal and the 'contents' levels of a text and would thus reside in the interface, as it were, between these different textual dimensions. It may be primarily in that respect, then, that literature, but especially literary fictions, most characteristically differ from other types of discourse, such as philosophical, scientific, or other

---

[40]Of the few exceptions to that rule one might especially point out Ullrich Langer's exemplary book, *Divine and Poetic Freedom in the Renaissance: Nominalist Theology and Literature in France and Italy* (Princeton, NJ: Princeton University Press, 1990). But see also Utz, *Literarischer Nominalismus*, which was one of the first studies to suggest a systematic approach to the issue. See further Paule Mertens-Fonck, 'The *Canterbury Tales*: New Proposals of Interpretation', *Atti della Accademia Peloritana dei Pericolanti*, 69 (1993), 5-29, which gives a perceptive analysis of implicit markers of contingency, and Keiper, '"I wot myself best how y stonde"', which attempts a first, preliminary outline of a nominalist/realist literary aesthetic by referring to Chaucer's dream visions. From the camp of those critics who remain unconvinced about Chaucer's 'literary nominalism', Robert Myles stands out because of his considered methodological approach: see *Chaucerian Realism* (Woodbridge: D.S. Brewer, 1994). For a critical survey of pertinent Chaucer criticism, see William H. Watts and Richard J. Utz, 'Nominalist Perspectives on Chaucer's Poetry: A Bibliographical Essay', *Medievalia et Humanistica*, n.s. 20 (1993), 147-73, but see also Stephen Penn's contribution to the present volume. For further details, see section 5. of the present essay.

16   *Hugo Keiper*

referential text types, or at any rate, from what might be called most representative about such texts. In dealing with specifically 'literary' or 'aesthetic' responses to the nominalism/realism-complex, one might therefore attempt to differentiate between various fundamental types of literary treatment or assimilation of our problematic. In particular, though, it might appear helpful to distinguish between (1) an author's or text's explicit (or direct) treatment of such issues, and (2) different kinds of implicit (or indirect) responses to them,[41] which may then be inscribed in the very form of composition of a text as a whole or of certain parts of it, or in its basic conception and constructive principles, so that in that case a text's engagement or preoccupation with our problematic will have to be inferred from the specific ways it handles and organizes certain of its elements or structures, or—on the most general level—textual form as such.

As for the first option, it is clearly possible that a text picks up and deals with each and any of our issues in quite outspoken, direct ways—either by thematizing and representing them within its fictional world, i.e. at an intradiegetic level, or by addressing them in its textual universe at large, at the extradiegetic level of narratorial comment, for example, or even in an author's preface, prologue, or the like. Moreover, all of these elements may of course work together to draw the reader's attention to such subject-matter. Even the quickest, most superficial survey of literature, say of the English tradition, will immediately muster numerous memorable instances of such explicit treatment, from Chaucerian narrative to certain plays by Shakespeare (one need only think of Juliet's notorious question, 'What's in a name?'); from Marlowe's *Doctor Faustus*, or Swift's account of Gulliver's voyage to Laputa and his visit to the Academy's school of languages, right 'down' to so-called children's literature, such as Lewis Carroll's *Alice*-novels, A.A. Milne's *Winnie-the-Pooh*, or indeed J.R.R. Tolkien's *Lord of the Rings*.[42]

---

[41] In terms of an heuristic approximation to the analysis of literary texts, there is ample proof of the pertinence of differentiating between explicit and implicit textual features, provided, of course, that the distinction is not taken in absolute terms or handled in undialectical ways. (For a convincing example, see Manfred Pfister, *The Theory and Analysis of Drama*, tr. John Halliday (Cambridge: Cambridge University Press, 1988).) However, considering the overall drift of previous critical altercations about 'literary nominalism/realism', it seems even more important to make that distinction, because it will provide us with theoretical and methodological backgrounds that will help to arrive at a better understanding, and hopefully at solutions, of several highly contentious issues (see esp. sections 5. and 6. below).

[42] In Chaucer's works, one might pick up on the Eagle's hilarious disquisition on 'speech, or noise, or sound' (783) in Book II of *The House of Fame* (see *The Riverside Chaucer*, gen. ed. Larry D. Benson (Oxford: Oxford University Press, 1988), 357f., esp. lines 765-883). Shakespeare's *Romeo and Juliet* is an exceptionally fitting example, since the heroine's desperate outburst (2.2.43) neatly summarizes the pertinent

To get a better idea of what such explicit 'literary' handling of the matter might look like, let us consider just two of these examples—*Winnie-the-Pooh* and *Lord of the Rings*—which, to the present writer's mind, are quite instructive for our purposes. Since they are rarely discussed in the given context, moreover, we may approach them in a less prejudiced way than if we chose any of the other texts, some of which are hotly debated by critics of different convictions. Furthermore, being historically as well as generically removed from the texts discussed in this volume, they will allow us to generalize our observations, besides testifying to the fact that the issue of universals, in its manifold implications, continued to hold the interest of writers of fiction long after its alleged historical hey-day.

In Tolkien's *Lord of the Rings*, there are many passages that are preoccupied with the significance of naming, the nature and power of names, of language, and so forth, and would thus serve to address, in a fairly consistent manner, central aspects of our topic. When Frodo arrives at Bree, for instance, we are told that the local hobbits took him 'to their hearts as a long-lost cousin', because 'they could not imagine sharing a name without being related'.[43] In other words, these simple folk find it hard to believe that names might be identical just by accident and that, therefore, persons or things might have a name in common without simultaneously sharing some sort of substantial connection, such as blood relations. However, in a different chapter, much the same point is made by an initiate, when the wizard, Gandalf, gives a clear indication that in former times, names were not 'given only in idle fancy' (ibid., 573). Later on, the hobbits meet the Ent, '*Fangorn* [...] according to some, *Treebeard* others make it.' (Ibid., 485) Bewildered by their 'hasty', careless behaviour, he warns them to guard against giving away their true names too rashly:

> 'For I am not going to tell you *my* name, not yet at any rate.' [...] 'For one thing it would take a long while: my name is growing all the time, and I've lived a very long, long time; so my name is like a story. Real names tell you the story of the things they belong to in my language, in the Old Entish as you might say. It is a lovely language, but it takes a very long time to say anything in it [...]'. (Ibid., 486)

---

dimension of the entire play. As for Marlowe's *Faustus*, the A-text in particular would seem relevant because of its extensive treatment of the problematical, ultimately intractable status of signs. For Gulliver's unsettling visit to Laputa's Academy, see also note 60. *Alice in Wonderland*, finally, but especially *Through the Looking-Glass*, are a virtual mine of pertinent passages. (For a broadly 'nominalist' reading of *Faustus-A*, see also Hugo Keiper, 'Ikarus im Labyrinth der Zeichen: Überlegungen zu einer Neuinterpretation des A-Textes von Marlowes *Doctor Faustus*', in Peter Csobádi et al. (eds.), *Europäische Mythen der Neuzeit: Faust und Don Juan*, 2 vols. (Wort und Musik, 18) (Anif/Salzburg: Verlag Müller-Speiser, 1993), vol. 2: 373-96.)

[43] J.R.R. Tolkien, *The Lord of the Rings* (London: Allen & Unwin, 1968), 171.

Indeed, as T.A. Shippey states in his discussion of Goldberry's rain-song (which the hobbits understand without recognizing the words), and of Tom Bombadil's giving names to their ponies, to which the beasts respond for the rest of their lives: 'There is an ancient myth in this feature, that of the "true language", the language in which there is a thing for each word and a word for each thing, and in which signifier then naturally has power over signified—language isomorphic with reality once again.'[44]

Many more examples might be given of the strangely evocative, at times outright magical power, for good or ill, of certain names or languages in Tolkien's world, as when Gandalf's reciting of the spell on the Ring in the language of Mordor—itself a name which it is dangerous to say out loudly—conjures up a dark moment indeed, even in the secluded Elf-sanctuary of Rivendell: 'The change in the wizard's voice was astounding. Suddenly it became menacing, powerful, harsh as stone. A shadow seemed to pass over the high sun, and the porch for a moment grew dark. All trembled, and the Elves stopped their ears.'[45] However, beyond such bits and pieces, suggestive as they may be, or brief hints and allusions, no details are discussed or explanations given—either by the narrator or any of the figures, not even by those who should know, like Gandalf—of the true nature and function of names and languages, so that their actual status in the universe of the novel remains shrouded in mystery.

Such a state of affairs, though, is in perfect accordance with the fact that our common experience of life is replete with vagaries and contradictions, with unaccountable, even paradoxical intricacies and ambiguities, and thus, more often than not, is intractable rather than transparent, and altogether quite recalcitrant to full, let alone exhaustive rational explanation. Yet in so far as literature, as a rule, is centrally concerned with (re)presenting, or (re)creating, all sorts of human experience, be it of an ordinary kind or completely exceptional in nature, we have to reckon that literary texts will not normally provide us with any clear-cut answers to our issues. Instead, by refraining from such answers and ready-made solutions, or indeed by questioning or deconstructing them, literary discourse would rather tend to defy the strict but—to the poet's eye—somewhat simplistic

---

[44]T.A. Shippey, *The Road to Middle Earth* (1982; London: Grafton, 2nd ed. 1992), 97. See further George Steiner, *After Babel: Aspects of Language and Translation* (Oxford: Oxford University Press, 1975), but especially Umberto Eco, *The Search for the Perfect Language*, tr. James Fentress (Oxford and Cambridge, MA: Blackwell, 1995), even though Eco explicitly excludes 'fictitious languages' from closer consideration (cf. 3). On 'words' and 'things', see also below, note 60.

[45]Tolkien, *Lord of the Rings*, 271.

logic of philosophy or scholastic theology.[46] And while the ways it does so might themselves appear unsophisticated at first glance, or even inadequate to the matters at stake, they are in fact incredibly complex, and fraught with an inexhaustible wealth of implications (not to mention the occasional, engaging touch of highly-strung emotion). Indeed, it may well be the case that this kind of approach, by virtue of its verisimilitude, or homology, to the very stuff of experience, lies at the heart of what is specifically *literary* about such handling of our problematic.[47]

That assumption, at any rate, is borne out by our second example, *Winnie-the-Pooh*. Like Tolkien, Milne displays a clear awareness of the complexity of the question, 'What's in a name?', and of course conveys this to his young or not quite so young readers, thereby providing them with a powerful stimulus to reflect on the issue and, possibly, to turn either nominalists or realists (or, indeed, conceptualists). However that may be: in his 'Introduction', the author/narrator reminds us that the name, 'Pooh', originally belonged to Christopher Robin's swan:

> That was a long time ago, and when we said good-bye, we took the name with us, as we didn't think the swan would want it any more. Well, when Edward Bear said that he would like an exciting name all to himself, Christopher Robin said at once, without stopping to think, that he was Winnie-the-Pooh. And he *was*.[48]

Milne then tells us that, in the Zoo, Christopher Robin always goes to where the Polar Bears are; he has the 'special cage' opened,

> and out trots something brown and furry, and with a happy cry of 'Oh, Bear!' Christopher Robin rushes into its arms. Now this bear's name is Winnie, which shows what a good name for bears it is, but the funny thing is that we can't remember whether Winnie is called after Pooh, or Pooh after Winnie. We did know once, but we have forgotten [...].[49]

---

[46] For a typically ironic, offhand juxtaposition of the poet's world and preoccupations to those of 'clerkys' (i.e. philosophers and theologians), see the Proem to Chaucer's *House of Fame*, esp. lines 52ff. (*The Riverside Chaucer,* 349). See further William Watts's concluding remarks in his contribution to the present volume.

[47] In point of fact, it is quite probable that the manifold fundamental implications which such questions have for human existence as a *lived* experience—as opposed to 'mere' ratiocination—would also play an important part in making the nominalism/realism-complex an exceedingly attractive topic for literature. At the same time, though, that state of affairs will be also largely responsible for the fact that literary discourse would tend to treat such issues in contradictory, emotionally charged ways, and in a predominantly implicit manner, rather than explicitly discussing them. In that respect, then, it might seem difficult to overemphasize the idiosyncracy of literature's engagement with these questions.

[48] A.A. Milne, *Winnie-the-Pooh* (1926; repr. London: Methuen, 1965), ix (emphasis mine).

[49] Ibid., ixf.

On closer reflection, the playfully enigmatic assertions, mock-proofs and loose ends this riddling little passage confronts us with, turn out to be truly mind-bending (if only we could, we would surely like to know what exactly it is that constitutes 'Poohness'). More to the point, though, it illustrates quite graphically once again that, outside the philosophical or scientific realms of pure, logical reasoning, our attitudes to such issues are rarely fully consistent nor, as a rule, neatly resolved. Even more importantly, we have here also a hilarious demonstration of what may happen when linguistic games or, more generally, a playful attitude towards language take precedence over rational argument or logical, scientific proof. And this, of course, together with an innovative or experimental approach to language, or indeed the ways it is commonly used in referential discourse, is another key feature of many literary or fictional texts.

If, then, it is true that most typically it is the experiential dimension of our problematic which—often in conjunction with specifically 'aesthetic' uses of language—has proved of primary interest to writers of literary texts, we may assume that this will have had a considerable, even decisive impact on the particular ways our issues have found expression in literature. Even in those cases where we are faced with direct, explicit responses to the problem of universals or its concomitant issues, we have to expect, therefore, that it is less in rigorously discursive (let alone logically cogent) ways that literary texts will handle such topics. Much rather, they will approach them through quick hints or allusions, by indirections, or in a vaguely contradictory or dialectical manner; or they may be touching briefly on them, without going into full detail, or appear to gloss over their deeper implications, so that, ultimately, much is left open and to the surmise of the reader. Consequently, as often as not, such texts would appear to evade a precise pinpointing of their author's position[50] and will thus not normally lend themselves (even less so than is the case with philosophical or theological treatises) to immediate, easy classification in terms of 'nominalism' or 'realism'.

This, of course, is not to say that any definitive or extended handling of our issue, or of any of its aspects, is excluded from literature.[51] We all know that literary texts are capable of assuming almost any stance, and of integrating virtually anything, so that it is entirely possible that a specific

---

[50]For a more detailed discussion, see below, section 6.3.

[51]This point might appear self-evident, were it not for the fact that quite a few historians, and even critics of literature, have tended to accept as relevant only such instances of 'literary nominalism' for which it is possible to demonstrate beyond doubt that a text's explicit engagement or response occurred in more or less exact correspondence with specific philosophical or theological sources. See also below, section 5.

text gives a clear, authoritative statement of a writer's or character's attitude, or enters a detailed, perhaps even conclusive discussion of our problematic. Indeed, it might even contain a prolonged, historically faithful account or an accurate rendering of, say, a dispute between proponents of nominalist and realist positions, respectively.[52] But we have to be aware that such cases—which, in terms of identification, do not confront us with serious problems anyway—are the exception, not the rule. Moreover, there will always be *some* difference between literary and other discursive modes of treating our problematic, which might reside, for instance, in the different contexts provided for such discussions of the issue, but also, more generally, in the distinct functions such discursive modes are meant to fulfill.

Nor is it that the features we have uncovered so far are representative merely of particular literary genres or text types, such as children's literature or fantasy fiction. Try to assess, for example, the precise meaning of Juliet's rhetorical question in its immediate context, let alone in the context of *Romeo and Juliet* as a whole. And one might even speculate that she, and her lover, are ultimately 'done to death' because they appear in a play that its author chose to term a tragedy, and which, accordingly, he modelled on his or even 'the' idea of tragedy. Here, however, we touch upon an aspect which we are not now going to pursue, since it is not immediately pertinent to the present course of argument. Suffice it to say that the metafictional dimension of a text, directly or indirectly, may certainly have a bearing on our subject, not least in connection with postmodern literary theory and practice, and would thus deserve the attention of critics.[53]

4.1.2. Implicit Literary Responses

Let us turn, then, to our second category which, as we have said, may relate to almost any formal aspect or feature of a text or, indeed, to its overall

---

[52] As might chiefly be found in historical or pseudo-historical fictions, the most pertinent recent instance being Umberto Eco's *The Name of the Rose*. For Eco's novel, see also Utz, 'Negotiating the Paradigm', 8f.

[53] For medieval implications, see Gerald Seaman's and Richard Utz's essays in the present collection, and Keiper, '"I wot myself best how y stonde"'. For pertinent metafictional strategies in Post-Modern(ist) texts, see especially McHale, *Postmodernist Fiction*, who also pursues a convincing constructivist approach to the phenomenon of 'post-modernism' (see further his *Constructing Postmodernism* (London and New York: Routledge, 1992)). For constructivism generally, which has obvious affinities with nominalism, see Gebhard Rusch, *Erkenntnis, Wissenschaft, Geschichte: Von einem konstruktivistischen Standpunkt* (Frankfurt a.M.: Suhrkamp, 1987), and Humberto R. Maturana's classical study *Erkennen: Die Organisation und Verkörperung von Wirklichkeit*, tr. Wolfram K. Köck (1982; Braunschweig and Wiesbaden: Vieweg, 2nd ed. 1985).

conception and constructive principles. And one should add that here we encounter an area of possible response to the nominalism/realism-complex that may be a particular characteristic of literary fictions, or even their exclusive domain, because very likely no other type of discourse would rely, in part or wholly, upon implicit means to convey important aspects of its meaning. That is to say, no referential text would normally deal with such issues without explicitly stating and discussing them.

As might be expected, things get still more complicated here. For in the case of implicit or indirect literary responses, but especially in the absence of explicit pointers or other unmistakable clues as to its pertinence, how can there be ultimate 'proof' that a text is in fact concerned with our problematic? Furthermore, since literary fictions will often have a strong tendency to imply their themes and topics, rather than openly stating them as such, what sort of pointers out of the multiplicity of clues given might qualify as relevant? In other words, we have to confront the question of how we can establish, in convincing ways, that a text's structural make-up and formal features, or certain aspects of them, do indeed reflect its preoccupation with specific questions or key issues, or that they function to foreground that text's engagement with such topics.

In that area, obviously, much will depend on the reader's or critic's willingness and ability to perceive and admit such connections, on their expectations and their basic approach to a particular text, as well as on the specific ways they conduct their reading or analysis of it. And of course, the more alert and sensitive they are to the issues at stake, as well as to specifically aesthetic modes of creating meaning, the more easily will they be convinced that such textual features may indeed be functional.[54] All one can do in the abstract, then, is to try and sharpen that sort of critical awareness and sensibility by pointing out certain key topics or areas that may be relevant in the present context, and to encourage critics to take a close look at whether and how a specific text engages with such issues, which may relate to each and every of the points we have sketched in at the beginning of this paper. Thus, the question of how a text handles the matter of authorship or, more generally, of authority may be equally important as its authorizing strategies, its conception and treatment of character, of individuality and the subject, its manipulation of plot and events, or of textual perspective. Moreover, its use of such elements as symbol, allegory or analogy will be also indicative of a text's fundamental attitude towards signification.[55] Indeed, any or all of these features—and many more—may interact,

---

[54]In the critics' case in particular, such acceptance will depend, to a considerable degree, on the historical and critical paradigms they adhere to (see section 7. below for further discussion of this point).

[55]As a matter of fact, virtually all of these aspects are discussed and analyzed in the essays to follow. For an exemplary extended reading of allegorical modes against a

both synergistically and by cancelling out or deconstructing one another, to establish a text's individual position(s) in the area of tension between 'nominalism' and 'realism'. Still, precisely because such aspects may prove to be quite evasive and difficult to pinpoint or to define with any certainty before a text is analyzed in some detail, it is hardly surprising that the question of whether and how we can maintain that such implicit features are in fact pertinent to our problem—if and when it is discussed at all in terms of methodology—is still largely a matter of dispute, not to mention that other scholars might find it easy to take issue with conclusions based on such observations, easier at any rate than when a text explicitly points out such a connection, or even gives a clear, univocal statement of its basic position.[56]

On the other hand—and this point warrants repetition—it is a truism few theorists and critics of literature would deny, namely that the 'meaning' of literary texts as well as their underlying themes are not always, or even primarily explicitly stated but would tend to reside to a considerable degree, if not exclusively, in their formal features, i.e. in their very structure and mode of composition. Or, because that strategy will secure that the reader's attention is drawn to such phenomena, they may emerge from a combination of explicit thematization and formal design. In point of fact, if we define 'explicit' in the above, rather loose sense, this is presumably the form of literary response we are most likely to encounter, as surely it is the form that has most consistently attracted the attention of literary critics. In the second case, moreover, we are on comparatively safe methodological ground, since here our analysis of particular formal features can be anchored in explicit textual clues, which will support our findings.

It would nonetheless be a mistake if one decided to neglect, or even exclude beforehand, the possibility of primarily implicit responses: while the analysis of such textual phenomena might be more precarious in methodological terms, it may still carry conviction, depending on how we manage to support such readings and, possibly, on what kinds of additional proof we can adduce. Indeed, a good deal of current research, including many of the contributions to the present volume, shows an increasing awareness of all of these aspects and has, accordingly, begun to re-direct its efforts by seeking to identify and analyze the whole range of potentially pertinent textual features and strategies relating to our problematic. And

---

nominalist background, see Michael Randall, *Building Resemblance: Analogical Imagery in the Early French Renaissance* (Baltimore, MD: Johns Hopkins University Press, 1996), but see also Keiper, "'I wot myself best how y stonde'", for an attempt to analyze literary nominalism in terms primarily of textual perspective.

[56]See also note 51. For an account of such critical altercations, see Watts and Utz, 'Nominalist Perspectives', but see also Keiper, "'I wot myself best how y stonde'", 232-4, for a critique of the somewhat defeatist conclusions drawn in that essay.

this may be a promising course to pursue, for not only does it widen the scope of enquiry to include phenomena which, though they were largely neglected for a long time, are still worth close scrutiny; it may also help us to gain deeper insights into, and thus to get a firmer grip on what is specifically aesthetic about the ways literary texts might engage with our issues.

4.2. *Methodological Consequences and Questions*

In methodological terms, then, it would appear that the proposed distinction between explicit and implicit forms of literary engagement with the nominalism/realism-complex makes sense. Not only does it provide a reasonably firm basis for classifying various types of textual elements and features, such as are likely to pertain to a 'literary debate over universals' and, consequently, to its critical appraisal: even more importantly, that distinction would also serve to enhance our awareness of the specific forms of expression such engagement may take, as well as of their respective nature and functions. Thus, finally, it might enable us to pinpoint and address some of the more fundamental theoretical problems connected with our issue, and to seek viable ways of solving them.

However, we would also stress that the distinction is not an absolute one, but rather a matter of degree or emphasis. Explicit references, as we have seen, may be little more than occasional, even isolated hints or allusions that imply more than they actually state, i.e. they may—sometimes deliberately—be imprecise, ambiguous or implicative. Conversely, implicit textual elements and strategies may be arranged and employed in such consistent ways, and with such obstinate foregrounding, that it might appear almost impossible that their thematic implications for a text should be overlooked. In Chaucer's *House of Fame*, for example, the terms 'author' and 'authority' occur only once, albeit at strategically important points in the text.[57] Yet the way the entire text manipulates its elements is such that the overriding centrality of these concepts to the text and its 'meaning' as a whole might seem hard to miss.[58] Moreover, as we have argued, explicit

---

[57] See *The Riverside Chaucer*, 352 and 373, lines 314 ('auctour') and 2157 ('auctorite', this being the very last word before the text breaks off rather unexpectedly).

[58] Provided, once again, that a reader is ready to recognize and acknowledge the overall impact and importance of such features. That this need not necessarily be the case can be seen from the highly contentious critical history of that poem, of which Alastair J. Minnis gives an illuminating account in his chapter on *The House of Fame*, in *Oxford Guides to Chaucer: The Shorter Poems* (Oxford: Oxford University Press, 1995), 161-251. See further section 7. of the present essay.

and implicit textual elements will frequently work in conjunction, complementing or reinforcing each other, so that the discovery of explicit references or hints to our issue, even if they are sparse and scattered far and about, may lead to the identification of corresponding implicit features; and this, in turn, may point the way to the discovery of comparable phenomena, of either sort, in other texts. Ultimately, then, we may assume a dialectic of sorts between explicit and implicit textual features, both as regards the make-up and coding strategies of many texts themselves, and with respect to the discovery of such features through critical analysis—a dialectic which, in the second case, would naturally tend to enhance our sensitivity to such features as are not entirely obvious.

At the same time, our distinction would also highlight a different set of questions which, in the final analysis, comes down to the much-disputed problem of whether and where one should draw the line, i.e. which criteria of inclusion or exclusion—if any—one should apply to the various types and aspects of potential literary response to the nominalism/realism-complex, and which of those, therefore, one should accept as pertinent.[59] In the case of explicit responses, to begin with, should we include as relevant any literary reference, discussion, or representation of events pertaining to the nature and status of signs, such as the episode we have mentioned from *Gulliver's Travels*,[60] or Rabelais's hilarious parodistic account of the dispute between Panurge and his English adversary,[61] which relies entirely upon the use of signs without words? Or should we allow only those instances which may be firmly connected with specific historical forms or expressions of nominalism and/or realism, i.e. where the philosophical

---

[59] A recent example of varying opinion on that matter can be found in the divergent points of view expressed in Utz (ed.), *Literary Nominalism*.

[60] See Jonathan Swift, *Gulliver's Travels*, eds. Peter Dixon and John Chalker (Penguin Classics) (1967; repr. Harmondsworth: Penguin, 1985), Part III: 'A Voyage to Laputa [...]', ch. 5, with its famous account of the Academy's 'scheme for entirely abolishing all words whatsoever; [...] since words are only names for *things*, it would be more convenient for all men to carry about them such *things* as were necessary to express the particular business they are to discourse on' (230). For contemporary backgrounds to Swift's satire, which include Locke's *Essay Concerning Human Understanding*, see the editors' note to the passage cited (357); for Locke, see especially Nicholas Hudson's essay in the present collection.

[61] François Rabelais, *Gargantua and Pantagruel*, tr. J.M. Cohen (Penguin Classics) (Harmondsworth: Penguin, 1955), bk. II, chs. 18-20 (230-9). Significantly, the episode ends with the narrator's confession to the reader that he would have gladly expounded the meaning of the signs used in the dispute—'but I am told that Thaumaste has made a great book of them, printed in London, in which he explains everything without exception.' (239) For convincing reasons why one should include these works of Rabelais, see Ullrich Langer's contribution to the present volume.

debate over universals serves as a direct, readily identifiable source for its literary treatment? In that case, would the fact that Panurge's opponent comes from Ockham's native country, which can be read as a palpable allusion to late-medieval (English) nominalism, suffice to establish such a connection, or would Rabelais's exaggerated, reductive, and altogether light way of treating the matter—which, however, is part of the very strategy of literary parody—speak out against such a view? Likewise, should we limit our scope to the problem of universals in the strict sense? Or should we also include some or any of the other issues involved in the debate—which, after all, are both logically and historically intimately connected with, and in many cases directly derived from it? Finally, if the pertinence even of explicit references might be contentious, what about the whole range of implicit responses, especially in those cases where a specific text would appear to function primarily on that level of signification?

If such criteria of exclusion are strictly applied, we may not only miss the point—and relevance—of what literary texts set out to achieve in dealing with such issues; we may also be excluding issues that are centrally important to our topic in particular historical situations, even though at first glance that connection might be anything but conspicuous. If, on the other hand, we decide to include all and anything that might be linked with our problematic, there is, as various critics have warned, surely the contrary danger of diluting the issue or of missing the specific points that certain historical forms of nominalism and realism—as e.g. fourteenth-century Scholasticism—were out to make.[62] Neither does it appear that reliable criteria of exclusion can be found if one tries to distinguish between varying degrees of conspicuousness—and therefore of pertinence—in terms of textual features or elements, because in individual texts, entirely different aspects or levels of their structural make-up may be more or less equivalent in their functions, so that despite their structural or even conceptual diversity, each of them may yet be fundamentally engaged with our problematic.

Similarly, it may be the case, for specific historical or cultural configurations, that some issues or topics are in fact more central to the principal questions of the debate than others. Indeed, it may happen that a particular conjunction of topics, or even of textual features, can be identified as uniquely characteristic of a specific historical situation, or of a particular literary genre at a certain stage of its development—as for instance in Post-Modernist narrative fiction, where the metafictional dimension will generally be of greater centrality than a text's use of allegory, whilst

---

[62] For in-depth explorations of the late-medieval philosophical debate(s), see William J. Courtenay's survey in the present collection, but especially the works of Courtenay and Oberman listed in the Bibliography.

in Late-Medieval narratives this might be the other way round. But here again, it is by no means easy to draw the line. For if we decide to include the problem of 'authority', for example, can we really find any convincing reasons for excluding, say, the question of the individual and its ontological status, which may, from a different perspective, be just as relevant as the first issue? And much the same, of course, also holds true for specific forms of literary expression. Clearly, as a minimum consensus one might demand that a text should be centrally concerned with the issues at stake. Yet once more, for the informed reader, even a single, passing reference might suffice to place a text in the relevant context and thus to influence or shape its entire reception in decisive ways, which might—for that reader—change its entire *gestalt*.[63]

It seems, then, that we are here caught between the Scylla of too great and the Charybdis of too little specificity, both in terms of the textual features under consideration and of possible feedback between different discursive domains—a dilemma, incidentally, which has beset scholarly discussions of 'literary nominalism' and 'realism' from almost their very beginnings. Yet we would suggest that the problem can be solved, in part at least, by taking a close look at its actual origins, which lie less perhaps in the very nature of such issues themselves than in the history and presuppositions of earlier research in that area.

However, one should be clear about the fact that an answer to any of the above questions cannot be given once and for all, because it will depend on what exactly one's purposes are, and what one ultimately wishes to achieve by enquiring into our problematic. If, as has been the aim of many scholars so far, we are primarily interested in the impact which the Late-Medieval philosophical debate over universals had, directly or indirectly, on roughly contemporaneous literature, our approach will naturally be different than if we are interested in the problem from a more general, or an aesthetic point of view, because from that perspective the question of nominalist or realist influence on literature will be only one among many important aspects—one, moreover, that is restricted to just one stage or episode within the historical unfolding and cultural negotiations of the problematic. Both approaches, of course, are tenable and have their respective merits, but they will differ in the starting points chosen to tackle the problem and the overall view they take of it, as well as in the criteria of inclusion one may wish to apply. Considering the present state of the art, it may be more sensible, though, to opt for the second approach, since it is

---

[63]For an example, see Richard Utz's contribution to the present collection and the conclusions he draws regarding Chaucer's 'Lollius', but see also Mertens-Fonck, '*The Canterbury Tales*'.

here that we may hope for decisive advances, which may eventually open up new horizons and thus help to establish fresh conceptual frameworks for the study of 'literary nominalism' and 'realism'. This can be demonstrated by examining the principal directions which previous research in that field has taken.

5. Previous approaches to 'Literary Nominalism'

So far, the questions we have broached, if they were discussed at all, have been mainly of concern to Medieval and—very occasionally—Renaissance scholars, but especially so to the proponents, as well as critics and opponents, of a comparatively recent research program that has been tentatively termed 'literary nominalism'—a term that has also come to be applied to the subject thus scrutinized.[64] As it is commonly understood, this new, emergent paradigm can be described as the attempt to establish and analyze the relationship and possible connections between Late-Medieval/Early Modern literature and the Late-Medieval debate over universals, but especially the philosophical nominalism of Ockham and other *moderni*. Furthermore, since Medieval nominalism itself was generally viewed as an emergent paradigm posing a radical challenge to the long-established and well-intrenched realist tradition of thought, which was seen as culturally still dominant, primary interest was naturally invested in studying the formation of the—supposedly—ascendant discourse(s). Even so, the relationship between philosophical realism and literature has also received considerable attention in the wake of such enquiry, so that the study of 'literary realism' can in fact be seen as a complementary, if somewhat marginalized research program.

The chief focus of research on literary nominalism, then, has rested almost entirely on a particular historical and cultural configuration, namely the Late Middle Ages as basically a transitional era, whereas the aftermath and later development of those cultural negotiations were rarely looked into in any detail.[65] Much rather, the growing ascendancy of nominalism

---

[64]See Utz, 'Negotiating the Paradigm', and 'Acknowledgments', in Utz (ed.), *Literary Nominalism* (no page).

[65]It could thus be claimed as something of an innovation that the present collection includes not only studies on Renaissance literature and culture, but also on the aftermath of such developments. Among Renaissance scholars, Ullrich Langer is one of very few to have dealt with such issues in any detail (see especially *Divine and Poetic Freedom in the Renaissance*). Otherwise, the nominalism/realism-complex has of course been discussed—under headings such as 'subjectivity', 'authority' or 'language games', or in terms of 'iconoclasm'—but except for passing comments, this has mostly been done without acknowledging or even perceiving the connection. (However, see James R. Siemon, *Shakespearean Iconoclasm* (Berkeley, CA: University of California

was accepted without further questioning as historically given. Moreover, most proponents of literary nominalism have tended to act on the assumption that Late-Medieval culture was characterized by a high degree of general public awareness of and interest in the philosophical debate which, according to some historians, was engendered by the sometimes heated academic altercations of the day.[66] Hence, most previous efforts to establish a connection between literature and nominalism/realism are not only historically limited in their interest, but have often also placed strong—perhaps unduly strong—emphasis on the strictly philosophical side as well as roots of our problematic.

It may be a consequence of that situation that critics, more often than not, have failed to address some of the more fundamental theoretical issues connected with such research: either because it was virtually taken for granted—by supporters of the new paradigm—that almost any analogue or homology between philosophical nominalism and literary discourse reveals a more or less direct influence of nominalism, but especially so of Ockham, who soon came to hold the stage in quite lop-sided ways;[67] or—on the side of their critics—because any efforts to establish such links were downright rejected as questionable, since they were allegedly based on mere surmise and flimsy evidence. Still, over the years there has been a fair amount of critical reflection, and various dominant approaches have emerged. In an important recent attempt to survey the methodological ground, Richard Utz has grouped such trends under three headings, according to the kind of relationship they propose between philosophy (or theory) and literature: (1) 'nominalism or a nominalist thinker as direct (textual) source in the philological sense'; (2) 'nominalism as coeval philosophical superstratum representing a typical late-medieval Zeitgeist'; (3) 'nominalism

---

Press, 1985), esp. chs. 1 and 2, for an insightful analysis which does take note of the medieval situation.) For post-Renaissance developments, see Nicholas Hudson's and Christoph Bode's essays in the present volume, but see also Werner Wolf, 'The Language of Feeling between Transparency and Opacity', in Wilhelm G. Busse (ed.), *Anglistentag 1991 Düsseldorf: Proceedings* (Tübingen: Niemeyer, 1992), 108-29, and Matthias Waltz, *Ordnung der Namen—Die Entstehung der Moderne: Rousseau, Proust, Sartre* (Frankfurt a.M.: Fischer, 1993). For a well-founded general survey, see further Günther Mensching, *Das Allgemeine und das Besondere: Der Ursprung des modernen Denkens im Mittelalter* (Stuttgart: Metzler, 1992).

[66]See Utz, 'Negotiating the Paradigm', 11-5. Against a somewhat different ideological background, the Renaissance, of course, also took a central interest in quite similar issues, ranging from the nature and position of miracles to the question of predestination and free will to problems of (re-)presentation at all cultural levels. But that is a different story from the one to be told right now. (For examples of Renaissance perspectives and preoccupations, see William J. Carroll's, James R. Siemon's, Andreas Mahler's and Susanne Fendler's contributions to the present collection.)

[67]See also Stephen Penn's essay in the present volume.

as historical reassertion for prevalent modern/postmodern perceptions of literary critics'.[68] Once they are closely considered, however, all of these approaches would appear to run into quite serious conceptual problems or, in any event, would raise fundamental questions that need to be answered. Let us, therefore, discuss each of them in turn.

(1) As for the first approach, it might—at first glance—indeed seem to provide neat guidelines for tackling the issue. For if, in our study of literary nominalism or realism, we limit ourselves to strictly those cases of literary response for which a readily and definitely identifiable source may be found in the writings of Late-Medieval nominalists or realists, we may surely hope to have solved the problem of establishing a clear-cut criterion of relevance, viz. of inclusion or exclusion. However, if that sort of criterion is rigorously applied, we will not only miss or exclude, by definition, a host of potentially pertinent literary responses of a more indirect or mediated kind which, as we have argued, may nonetheless be equally, or even more relevant to our question than some direct references we might be able to identify; since there is also a notorious 'paucity of writers who actually mention a late medieval philosopher or text',[69] the resulting dearth of examples fulfilling such a criterion would probably, in actual practice, do away altogether with the very idea of a literary nominalism—regardless, that is, of whether such a project is in fact viable or not.

Moreover, what precisely do we mean by 'direct source', and what sort of literary or textual evidence might qualify as admissible in that respect? Do we accept just direct citations, or should we also include salient topics, issues, philosophemes, and the like? Let us take the hotly debated question of Ockham's epistemological and ontological scepticism as an example: Until recent decades, Ockham was seen even by specialists as a fundamentally sceptical thinker and this, it was thought, was evidenced by many passages from his work, which might then, presumably, qualify as direct sources in the above sense. More recently, though, such readings of Ockham's philosophy have been subject to radical revision, and he is now seen, especially by American historians of philosophy, as a reliabilist thinker who cannot in fact be termed a sceptic at all. As a consequence, readings of literary texts focussing on their sceptical epistemological or ontological stance—which had frequently been taken as indicative of Ockhamist influence—are now regularly denounced as beside the point, and hence as altogether irrelevant to the question of nominalist influence.[70]

---

[68]Utz, 'Negotiating the Paradigm', 10.

[69]Ibid., 14.

[70]By contrast, Beckmann seems rather more reticent about accepting the conclusion that such revisions of historical interpretation will also necessitate a complete revision of previous estimates regarding the overall impact which Ockham or Ockhamism may

Yet the problem here is not as simple as it seems. For it lies not merely in the fact that, even in the case of direct sources, the applicability of such criteria will to a decisive degree be subject to continual re-evaluation and revision of the primary evidence, and would thus inevitably depend on the inherent dynamics of textual and historical interpretation. It would also seem that any heavy, let alone exclusive reliance on philosophical reconstructions by twentieth-century historians of philosophy is quite off the mark in more fundamental ways. First of all, regardless of whether or not they do get ever closer to what Ockham 'actually' thought, such modern reconstructions do not really tell us a great deal about how a philosopher's work, or certain aspects of it, were received in his own day. Indeed, there are hints that many contemporaries, for whatever reasons, were strongly interested in the sceptical implications of Ockham's ideas,[71] not to mention that he had more radical followers among the *moderni*;[72] and even if those are usually marginalized by an over-emphasis on Ockham alone, they are just as pertinent to the question of nominalist influence. What's more, research based on contemporary philosophical reconstructions also tends to neglect the fact that nominalist thinking may have been influential in heavily mediated or, from a present-day historian's perspective, even in seriously distorted forms.[73] That is to say, there are many ways in which a contemporary might have read or (mis)understood Ockham or any other philosopher, whether as a direct source or, still more likely, through second- or third-hand information.

To argue from an analogous case, in many twentieth-century novels, for example, it is easy for us to detect traces and elements of psychoanalysis, or of Einstein's theory of relativity, and while it is true that some such literary representations may appear distorted or downright misleading to the informed reader, and yet more so to the specialist, still no one, not even the most meticulous expert, could seriously deny that Freud or Einstein— or modern physics or Freudian psychology—will have had an influence on these texts, or might even have been a direct source. Similarly, to most contemporaries, the nominalists' writings and methods of argumentation

---

have had on late-medieval culture at large (see *Wilhelm von Ockham*, esp. ch. VIII). For detailed discussions of some such revisions, see Penn's, but especially Courtenay's contribution to the present volume. For Ockham as a reliabilist thinker, see Marilyn McCord Adams's article 'Ockham', in *The Oxford Companion to Philosophy*, 633 (cf. also the entry on 'reliabilism', ibid., 759), but see also her monumental *William Ockham*, 2 vols. (Notre Dame, IN: University of Notre Dame Press, 1987).

[71] See Utz, 'Negotiating the Paradigm', 14f., and Beckmann, *Wilhelm von Ockham*, 20f., and ch. VIII.

[72] See Utz, 'Negotiating the Paradigm', 14, and Beckmann, *Wilhelm von Ockham*, 177.

[73] See Beckmann, *Wilhelm von Ockham*, 172-81.

will have appeared just as difficult, enigmatic, or arcane as Einstein's to us non-physicists, and there will inevitably have been a host of more or less momentous distortions, some of an involuntary, some of a deliberate nature. Nonetheless, all of those 'readings' will have contributed to make up the general public image—as well as impact—of a thinker or school, which, predictably, will have been highly contradictory.[74] In fact, to accept this, one need look no further than to contemporary critical theory and practice, i.e. the occupation of a rather highly specialized intellectual community. Although many of us will claim the direct influence of Derrida, for example, not quite so many will have read and fully absorbed the original, while many more will rely on secondary or tertiary sources. However, such sources will not just interpret Derrida's arguments; sometimes they will simplify and popularize them, or wrench certain ideas from their context or misrepresent them. Thus, as often as not, they might produce mere caricatures of the original, which are then frequently bashed by the opponents of deconstruction. Still, one would have to admit that any such claims to Derrida's intellectual sponsorship will largely be justified; indeed, it is well-nigh impossible today *not* to be influenced by Derrida in one way or another.[75]

The first approach, then, is much too narrow and lop-sided to account adequately for the multifarious, highly intricate phenomenon of literary nominalism. Moreover, it is mistaken in some of its basic assumptions: for not only would it exclude beforehand many potentially important ways in which literary texts may have responded to and engaged with contemporary philosophical discourse; since the very concept of source or influence is itself precarious, it is not even able to provide clear, reliable guide-lines as to what, in the end, might qualify as a direct source, or how such a source might be safely identified. At the same time, using this kind of approach, the question of which aspects of our problematic we should include in our research cannot really be solved in theoretically satisfactory ways, because any answer given would be contingent upon the writings of the philosophers alone, and thus, eventually, upon their individual predilections and emphases.[76]

---

[74]As for the considerable potential for deliberate distortions or misrepresentations in the immediate reception of Ockham's thought, see e.g. Beckmann, *Wilhelm von Ockham*, 20f. For varying twentieth-century representations of Ockham's nominalism, see Stephen Penn's contribution to the present collection (section 'Versions of Nominalism').

[75]For Derrida and the (mis-)use of some of his more pithy statements as mere slogans by later proponents of textualism, see e.g. Barry, *Beginning Theory*, 68.

[76]It is of course true that there was a set of more or less standardized *quaestiones* in medieval scholasticism, many of which go back to Peter Lombard and the numerous commentaries that were provoked by his *Four Books of Sentences*, which was used as

A Literary 'Debate over Universals'? 33

(2) The second approach, as Utz points out, 'has so far proven the most successful path toward establishing correspondences between literature and philosophy'.[77] Indeed, the notion of nominalism as a 'philosophical analogue', or rather as 'the academic [...] expression of a more general, typically late-medieval mentality, mindset, or Zeitgeist',[78] has the obvious advantage of being able to accommodate all of the potentially relevant aspects and types of literary response we have discussed, including specifically literary ways of engaging with our problematic. In that respect, it is certainly quite adequate from the point of view of the literary critic, and it may also help to 'historicize and comprehend', and perhaps even to account for 'what may seem problematic or inconsistent' in Late-Medieval literature.[79] Yet again, if the theoretical implications of this approach are scrutinized, there are problems with some of its basic assumptions and presuppositions.

To begin with, if we consider philosophical nominalism as primarily a response to a Late-Medieval Zeitgeist, we fail to do justice to, in fact bracket off, the complex inherent dynamics and historical development of the philosophical debate itself, but especially so of nominalism which, as has been shown, does have a history extending—in both directions!—far beyond the Late Middle Ages, and which cannot, therefore, be adequately conceptualized as exclusively an offshoot, let alone a mere by-product of that era.[80] Secondly, if we play down or even deny any direct causal

---

the official textbook in the universities until the sixteenth century. But apart from the fact that the answers given and the solutions offered within 'Scholasticism' were at great variance with one another—this being one of the factors behind the medieval debate over universals—the regulation and containment of academic discourse thus achieved would have mainly applied to the schools and universities themselves, or to their immediate spheres of influence. Not necessarily, however, would they have also been binding to medieval discourse at large. For a fascinating account of post-Reformation alternative discourses, see Carlo Ginzburg, *The Cheese and the Worms: The Cosmos of a Sixteenth-Century Miller*, tr. John and Anne Tedeschi (1980; repr. Harmondsworth: Penguin, 1992).

[77]Utz, 'Negotiating the Paradigm', 15.
[78]Ibid.
[79]See ibid., 16.
[80]However, this is exactly what Sheila Delany, to give a prominent example, attempts in her influential essay, 'Undoing Substantial Connection: The Late Medieval Attack on Analogical Thought' [1972] (repr. in *Medieval Literary Politics: Shapes of Ideology* (Manchester: Manchester University Press, 1990), 19-41). In the following, I shall single out Delany as being both representative of that particular trend and sophisticated in terms of her theoretical approach. In doing so, my chief interest, though, lies in the methodological implications of this sort of approach, not in Delany's actual application of it—which is at times strangely at odds with her more general claims, perhaps indicating that Delany herself may have had a hunch that such claims were riddled with inherent shortcomings and unresolved contradictions.

connections between philosophy and literature—and it would appear that that is precisely what is finally implied in this kind of approach[81]—we fall into the opposite extreme from the first one, because we will tend to neglect, or cut off, a potentially important, perhaps causally productive aspect or constituent of that relationship,[82] which is then construed as mediated in the extreme, hence as utterly loose, if not contingent. Paradoxically, moreover, since the roots of that relationship are thus transferred to a quite generalized, substructural level of universal cultural or social experience, any such relationships may, in effect, emerge as almost devoid of any conceptual or historical specificity—beyond mere catch-phrases, that is, such as 'class struggles', 'cultural change', or 'modernization'. Consequently, the explanatory power of such an approach will be poor. For an 'uncertain theological [or cultural] milieu', which Delany and comparable authors use as a spring-board for their arguments and historical reconstructions,[83] can be claimed not just for the fourteenth century, but for every transitional period—perhaps for any historical phase, if only one picks the right examples.[84]

Furthermore, as far as our issue goes, there is also an inherent danger of short-circuiting what is construed as a 'common field' of experience on the one hand,[85] and particular forms of its cultural expression, on the other. For by reducing the motivating forces and formative processes of history to no more than a universalized mentality or Zeitgeist, this approach will also tend to neglect the precise connections of that mentality to specific forms of cultural and discursive expression, but in particular to the concrete traditions and constraints governing and 'channelling' such modes of expression—which will therefore evade explication.[86] In the final analysis, then, it would appear that this sort of historical 'explanation' can do no better than postulate a vaguely mysterious, substructural undercurrent that is determined, as it were, by a loose, shifting, and altogether uneasy configuration of generalized cultural responses and constituents. In short—on

---

[81]For an example, see Delany's contention: '[...] nor is it possible to establish a direct causal connection between, say, late-medieval political theory and poetic practice, or between scientific method and political theory.' (Ibid., 19)

[82]For examples of such productive relationships, see Gerald Seaman's, William F. Munson's and Richard Utz's contributions to the present volume.

[83]See Utz, 'Negotiating the Paradigm', 16, which also gives a brief summary of Delany's arguments.

[84]Indeed, one might ask if there are any historical moments that are not experienced as transitional by those living through them.

[85]See Delany, 'Undoing Substantial Connection', 19 (quote) and 35f.

[86]Delany, it is true, tries to bridge—or gloss over—that gap by relying on her version of marxist analysis; yet if the concept of class struggle is used as no more than a substitute standing in for otherwise anonymous forces of history, this will clearly not do in terms of providing the 'missing link' lacking in that approach.

this theory, significantly, there is not just a gap, or some sort of black box, between what might be termed base (or substructure) and superstructure; since it is also claimed that correspondences between various constituents of that superstructure can be defined, not in terms of any direct causality or even interrelation, but only with reference to the very base structures that are said to generate these correspondences, there is no other choice than taking recourse to the logically weak concept of analogy to describe such relationships.

Yet if the relationship between literature and philosophy is conceptualized in terms of a mere analogy—that is to say, if it is viewed as just a homological relation that is rooted in little else than a set of comparable responses to a shared historical and cultural situation, or in the type of mindset and problem-solving which that situation is supposed to engender— one has to reconsider the appropriateness of using the term 'literary nominalism' at all. In any event, we need to discuss its precise meaning and significance in such a context. For in that case, to speak of 'literary *nominalism*' can hardly be more than metaphorical parlance. Besides, such usage is altogether fuzzy, since it would serve to identify no more than a universal trend in Late-Medieval literature that would tend to respond, not to a clearly defined or circumscribable problematic, but to a general type of experience inscribed in that unique cultural configuration—and to the intellectual, ideological and institutional challenge it poses. Hence, the concept of 'literary nominalism' would rather refer to a variety of corresponding conclusions from that fundamental situation than to a particular, coherent set of issues that are logically interrelated and co-dependent. However, since the term 'nominalism' has traditionally, and aptly, been used to denote a specific semiotic paradigm—as opposed, that is, to an indistinct range of ultimately contingent responses to epistemological or ontological uncertainties—if we subscribe to such an approach, the coinage 'literary nominalism' may be misleading, or in fact a misnomer. Indeed, we would be better off if we summarized the phenomena thus described under a different heading, such as 'Late-Medieval scepticism', 'challenges to traditional authority, assumptions and institutions', or perhaps even 'signification in an age of crisis'. But here, of course, one immediately notes the paradoxical lack of specificity which, in many respects, is the bottomline of this sort of approach.

Lastly, because it grounds nominalist thinking—and even its very genesis—in a typically Late-Medieval Zeitgeist, and therefore in historical preconditions it considers unique, this approach would definitely appear to confine such thinking to a particular historical and cultural situation (and, just possibly, its immediate aftermath). Thus, absurdly, it is not in a position to explain or theorize, in any convincing ways, the existence of comparable trends and developments in other periods. And while this might be no great matter to some medievalists, it would seem to impose undue boundaries and limitations on a cultural phenomenon, but especially on a literary one, which is in fact much more widespread in historical terms. At best, then, the second approach is able to account for the foregrounding of nominalist tendencies in that age of transition from Medieval to Early Modern culture, and consequently—if indeed that estimate can be maintained—for the considerable prominence which the debate over universals acquired at that time.

(3) The third approach, finally, confronts us with yet another extreme,[87] though this time it is related to the perennial question of whether and how literary texts can or should be read and interpreted in historically adequate terms, an issue to which we shall return. Let us just say at this point that any approach treating literary texts, or indeed the interpretive parameters it adduces, as mere historical reassertions of current critical perceptions, is of course exceedingly lop-sided. In that sense, it calls upon us to strike a sensible balance in our readings between the attempt to strive for the highest possible degree of historical faithfulness and the (legitimate!) interest of critics to recognize themselves gazing into that 'distant mirror'. Yet it may also help to sharpen our awareness of the limits there are to such efforts, as well as of the constraints governing them: for in so far as it compels us to acknowledge the historicity and precarious dynamism of our very positions as 'readers' of history, it is a healthy reminder that any historical research or (re)construction of past events, including that of individual texts, will inevitably be guided by the interests and preoccupations of scholars themselves, but also by the critical paradigms they use. Ultimately, therefore, the questions critics will ask, and the features of past cultures they would tend to foreground in their work, are ineluctably constrained by how they construe themselves as historical beings, and are in their turn construed as such by their own culture.

Having said that, we should nonetheless beware of indulging in historically unsupported, arbitrary reassertions or backwards projections of present-day positions and issues. In doing so, we may not only overstep the boundaries of legitimate historical interpretation and end up in patent misreadings or distortions of what may actually have been thought or felt in the Middle Ages (or in any other age); we will also fail to do justice to the radical alterity of past cultures and discourses. What's more, by levelling or altogether erasing their fundamental otherness, we might ultimately also forego the possibilities this otherness offers for a deeper, more comprehensive recognition and understanding of ourselves which, perhaps, requires less of a streamlining or adapting of the past to our own sensibilities than our admitting its alterity, both as a value in itself and as

---

[87]For examples, see Utz, 'Negotiating the Paradigm', 27f.

a suppressed, largely unacknowledged part of our very being as historical subjects.[88] Yet again, it is by no means easy in that respect to draw the line; for, in the final analysis, any decision as to which readings should be marked down as arbitrary and which as historically legitimate, will always be a matter of interpretation. As such, however, it will hinge upon a host of mutually dependent determining factors, but especially so upon the paradigms we bring to bear upon our (re)constructions of history.[89]

6. Literary Nominalism and Realism: Towards a Nominalist and Realist Aesthetics

6.1. Nominalism, Realism, and Literary Discourse: Suggestions for a New Theoretical Framework for a 'Literary Debate over Universals'

Each of these prevalent approaches to 'literary nominalism', then, is hampered by severe conceptual limitations as well as theoretical shortcomings. To be sure, they all manage to highlight important, even crucial methodological aspects of our issue, and we would also grant that few of their proponents, in their actual critical practice, will let themselves be fully restricted by the theoretical presuppositions of their chosen approach. In certain respects, moreover, some of the weaknesses we have uncovered may well be a matter of misplaced emphasis, rather than of principle.[90] Nonetheless, to the extent that these approaches can be viewed as theoretical attempts to come to grips with the problem of literary nominalism or realism as such, they have to be judged by their fundamental preconceptions, as well as their ultimate implications. From that perspective, though, they do not offer any satisfactory solutions, nor are they able to provide a firm methodological fundament, let alone a sufficiently comprehensive theoretical framework for coping with the issue. It appears, therefore, that an altogether different approach is required—one that would place equal emphasis on both the conceptual, in the widest sense 'philosophical' side of the issue, and on the specifically discursive, or 'aesthetic' component of its literary treatment, while at the same time it would also be able to accommodate and theorize its historical dimension, yet particularly so the complex interconnectedness and dialectics of discourses and cultural negotiations which, at any given moment in time, make up the specific co(n)texts of 'literary nominalism/realism'.

---

[88]See also Christoph Bode's contribution to the present collection.
[89]See further below, section 7.
[90]Some shifts in critical emphasis, in fact, may have even occurred as a result of fending off or giving in to all manner of attacks on the idea of a 'literary nominalism'.

We would suggest that such a fresh approach can in fact be found if the whole problem is rethought from a *typological* point of view—that is to say, if it is conceptualized within a frame of reference which would include, as its basic constituents, a 'discursive' and a 'transdiscursive' dimension, as well as the various transformational processes occurring between them.[91] Simultaneously, we would propose that the issue be located, for the moment, on the more general level of a *'literary debate over universals'*, rather than in terms of a simple, straightforward opposition between 'literary nominalism' and 'realism'. As our springboard, then, we would take the notion that the literary debate on the one hand, and the philosophical, theological, scientific or any other debates, on the other hand, can be regarded as *related but separate cultural phenomena*.[92] More specifically, in as much as all of these 'debates over universals' are equally engaged in a shared underlying problematic involving the status of universals and its concomitant issues, it is possible to view them as fundamentally *related*—on a level, that is, to which one might ascribe some sort of 'transdiscursive' status. Conversely, though, they are yet to be seen as *separate* phenomena, in the sense that on the discursive levels, the respective terms of such engagement, as well as its specific functions, will be essentially different, since each type of discourse or discursive genre will deal with our issues in its very own, idiosyncratic ways. Their crucial difference for us, therefore, lies neither in the principal nature of the issues such various

---

[91] In the following, the terms 'discourse' and 'discursive' are used in a roughly Foucauldian sense, i.e. as relating to a set of rules, conventions, and systems of mediation and transposition which govern the way a subject is talked or written about—'when, where, and by whom' (see Hawthorn, *A Concise Glossary*, s.v. 'Discourse' (49)). For Foucault's notion(s) of discourse, see *The Archeology of Knowledge*, tr. A.M. Sheridan Smith (London: Tavistock Publications, 1972), esp. Part II; for the term 'transdiscursive', and generally for Foucault's understanding of transdiscursivity, see especially 'Qu'est-ce qu'un auteur?', *Bulletin de la Société Française de philosophie*, 63.3 (1969), 73-104; English translation: 'What is an Author?', tr. J.V. Harari, in Josue V. Harari (ed.), *Textual Strategies: Perspectives in Post-Structuralist Criticism* (Ithaca, NY: Cornell University Press, 1979), 141-60, esp. 153f. But see also note 36 above.

[92] Against a somewhat different analytical background, Ullrich Langer has made a comparable observation. See his *Divine and Poetic Freedom in the Renaissance*, 20-4, but especially his seminal statement: 'Yet an emphasis on certain concepts, rather than on the impact of an individual's or a school's entire thought, seems heuristically more valid and more faithful to what literature is about. A literary text does not attempt to represent truthfully contemporary figures or their thought, but reworks key attitudes, experiences, sensations, and concepts into an imaginative whole that is in a sense incommensurable with the initial givens (though not unrelated to them).' (10f.) But see also Delany, 'Undoing Substantial Connection', 39: 'Naturally, a writer will not approach this problem [allegory] as the professional philosopher does. Instead, s/he will think of its aesthetic manifestations: does a particular mode render experience and meaning as fully as s/he would like?'

debates might engage with, nor in their underlying problematic 'as such'—not even in the conclusions they might be seen to draw. Rather, it would reside in their discursive components, i.e. in the fact that different types of discourse are indeed cultural constituents *sui generis*, in so far as their particular forms of expression or their specific manifestations of certain themes or topics are informed at base, and in decisive ways, by their respective modes of signification, their 'rules', as well as constraints and functions—both on the levels of discursive or 'generic' structures and of individual texts.[93]

At the same time, and on very fundamental levels indeed, such different types of engagement in the problematic will in turn be informed, governed and shaped—to a greater or lesser degree, and in more or less pronounced ways—by the conceptual frameworks and constraints of either a realist or a nominalist paradigm, or in fact by both. What's more, while some such 'paradigmatic underpinning' (which, we would suggest, is chiefly of a 'pre-' or 'subdiscursive' nature) will generally be operative in the very processes of constituting individual texts and discourses, these paradigms, by the same token, will themselves also be subject to a sizable inherent dynamics, even dialectics, whose precise nature and extent will ultimately depend upon the kind of relationship, in terms of expression and dominance, that would prevail between them in such texts or discourses. For what we have to bear in mind is not only that the two paradigms have in themselves to be conceived as dynamic, 'evolving' systems of reference, but also that each of them, once it begins to establish and unfold itself in individual discourses and texts, will inevitably enter a dialectical, mutually defining relationship with its 'counterpart'. In other words, on the discursive and textual levels, its very opposite will be inscribed, in one way or other, in each of the paradigms themselves.[94]

This, incidentally, is also the point where the intrinsic development of the various debates over universals comes in, and hence one important aspect of their historical dimension can be located. Furthermore, in the case of literary texts we may venture the surmise that their authors, as often as not, will feel less obliged to assume a partisan stance towards either position than writers of text types which strive for clear-cut answers and whose very *raison d'être* might depend upon providing neat, definitive

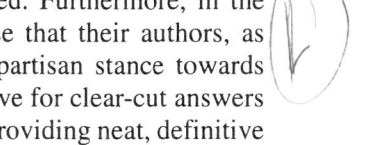

---

[93]Eventually, of course, the inherent dynamics of such formative processes and transformations will feed back upon the precise ways the problematic or certain of its aspects are conceptualized, (re)presented and 'worked out' in the context of various discourses and texts. Consequently, pace approach number one, such differences in terms of 'expression' cannot, to the present writer's mind, be construed as proof that the phenomena under consideration are in fact unrelated on a deeper, 'transdiscursive' plane.

[94]See also Christoph Bode's contribution to the present collection, esp. section III.

conclusions. Therefore, we have to reckon that literary discourse will regularly set in motion a yet more complex dialectics between the two basic positions, which will often be 'dramatized' rather than brought to a definitive solution. In some cases, moreover, a text may remain inconclusive altogether.[95] As a matter of fact, since literary texts, as a rule, will tend to throw into relief any of the fundamental positions they embrace, they might be generally expected to gravitate towards the nominalist pole rather than its realist opposite—as compared, that is, to most other types of discourse, and depending on how exactly one would define 'literary nominalism' and 'realism'.[96] Ultimately, though, such questions can only be answered with reference to individual texts. Indeed, while it is easy to see that there must be fundamental differences between various types of discourse, it might be much harder, in actual practice, to establish the precise relationships as well as patterns of exchange or interaction that would hold between them.

Yet it is not just the complex, dynamic nature of the boundaries between different types of discourse—as well as their underpinning paradigms—that we have to take into account, nor will it suffice to trace possible negotiations between such discursive domains or transactions between their constituents. We would further stress that the very relationship between the 'transdiscursive' dimension of the nominalism/realism-complex and its 'discursive' manifestations, likewise, is anything but a simple, straightforward affair. Neither is it static or one-sided in the sense that we may assume the existence of a fully independent, 'transcendent' problematic, or of a stable, immutable complex of issues which is merely 'worked out' on a discursive level and would thus seem to give rise—spontaneously, as it were—to any number of textual manifestations that are expressions, in the strict sense, of 'one and the same' problematic. For not only is it impossible to grasp that underlying problematic 'as such'—i.e., except with reference to its specific manifestations in individual texts and discourses—so that it has to be (re)constructed, indeed 'translated', in terms of a different text or discourse, from one or several of them, and might then be described in the way we have attempted at the beginning of this essay. It would also appear, for those very reasons, that there is a fundamental, ineluctable interdependence, a continual give-and-take, flux and feedback, between such individual textual, generic and discursive manifestations of 'the problematic' and the ways it can be articulated and defined at—or for—a specific point in history. In other words, even though

---

[95] In fact, lack of resolution might itself be taken as an index of a text's fundamentally nominalist orientation; see section 6.3. below, and Keiper, "'I wot myself best how y stonde'", passim.

[96] For an attempt to do so in terms of relational categories, see below, section 6.3.

it is possible to isolate the essential constituents of our issue—and thus to construct, formulate, and eventually to take recourse to the basic terms of the debate—we have to be aware that this will inevitably involve some process of translation. Hence, each individual description or manifestation of the nominalism/realism-complex will necessarily contribute towards its further unfolding, development or 'evolution'. At the same time, however, this will also alter, to a greater or lesser extent, the very terms of the debate.[97]

In important ways—and in many cases perhaps primarily—such transactions will occur within the boundaries of specific discourses, but especially of individual genres and sub-genres. For the particular manner in which the problematic is or has once been articulated and given shape in them may easily function to establish well-defined traditions and sets of conventions which, in turn, would tend to govern the specific terms and modes of subsequent engagement with it. In addition, though, we have also to reckon with a variety of 'cross-over' processes and determinations that are more of an 'interdiscursive' nature. Thus, one type of discourse might bring about certain manifestations or formulations of the problematic which, in their turn, might influence, in fact shape its precise terms as well as forms of 'expression' in other discourses. Alternatively, a specific discourse might bring into play its very difference *qua* discourse to throw an entirely fresh light on the problematic itself, which might then affect its further manifestations, within the bounds of that discourse and in others. Eventually, therefore, this might even bring about radical reformulations or reconceptualizations of the entire issue. Moreover, it would probably be a mistake to assume, for certain discourses at least, that any engagement with the nominalism/realism-complex need necessarily result from an entirely abstract interest in it 'as such'; rather we may suppose, in some cases, that such engagement will be a spin-off, directly or indirectly, of specific problems that are inherent in a particular type of discourse itself, or in the writing, conception and constitution of a particular text. In short, what we have to expect is a multiple, highly intricate interplay of various cultural traditions and discursive or generic conventions, which would occur within specific discourses or genres as well as between different types of discourse. And again, such interplay may be especially complex in all types of literary discourse, because of their singular ability to draw on almost any other discourse or text type, and to transform and adapt their features to their very own means and ends.

---

[97]This, presumably, is also a point where the idea of 'progress' might be usefully applied, i.e. as descriptive of an ever-increasing diversification of the issues involved and a concomitant awareness of that very complexity. Note, however, that such diversification will of course also lead to mounting contradictions. For the notion of progress in historiography, see further section 7. below, esp. note 134.

6.2. Methodological Implications

The general framework outlined so far, we would contend, is able to accommodate and theorize any type of 'debate over universals', and hence of 'nominalism' and 'realism', including their specifically literary forms of 'expression' or manifestation. At the same time, it puts us also in a position to conceptualize the discursive properties as well as dynamics of these various debates, and thus to arrive at a deeper, more extensive understanding of their elusively complex relationships to one another. In theoretical terms, then, the suggested approach takes a decisive step beyond previous notions of 'literary nominalism' or 'realism', and may ultimately even point the way towards a comprehensive textual as well as cultural theory of nominalism and realism. Yet we would further claim that an approach of this kind has considerable advantages, too, in terms of its actual applicability, but especially so with respect to our core issue. What remains to be done, therefore, is to discuss the most important methodological implications of our approach, and to develop them with an eye to the specifics of a 'literary debate over universals'.

The key point here, to begin with, is that the proposed theoretical framework—which, in effect, is a-hierarchical in its design—is conceived so as to preclude the a-priori privileging of any one debate over universals, or of a single brand of nominalism or realism, over others. Hence, literary nominalism and realism are no longer seen as derivative 'secondary discourses' that are fundamentally parasitical upon the philosophical or theological debates. Instead, they are regarded as cultural and discursive phenomena in their own right, which have to be treated accordingly. By the same token, their interrelationships and possible interplay with various non-literary intertexts and traditions, or with extra-literary contexts and circumstances, are no longer viewed as competing—or even mutually exclusive—factors, nor are they placed within any pre-defined hierarchical order of discourses, or prioritized in terms of causal relationships.

On the one hand, then, the present approach enables us to account for the literary debate's specifically aesthetic aspects, and would even emphasize them as essential features of its discursive dimension, while simultaneously it is yet sufficiently open and dialectical in its overall conception to integrate, in a suitable manner, the full range of intertextual, cultural and historical contexts and affiliations of literary nominalism/realism. As a result, our perception of the entire issue will change in quite radical ways, and so will the frames of reference, historical and otherwise, that are brought to bear upon its analysis. And this change of outlook, in turn, is full of consequences for how we may confront our subject in practical terms.

Thus, if the problem of universals is regarded as a genuine, altogether authentic issue, not just of philosophy or theology, but of literature or any other field of knowledge as well, we are now fully entitled to speak of a *'literary* debate over universals'—hence of *'literary* nominalism' and 'realism'—in the true sense of the word. On this premise, furthermore, we are completely justified—even obliged, from a methodological point of view—to scrutinize literary texts and their engagement in the debate on the basis of their specifically aesthetic, literary grasp and handling of the underlying problematic, or of certain aspects of it, which is to say that we may now approach and analyze them *'on their own terms'*, *qua* literary/aesthetic artifacts. Indeed, we would submit that only such an approach will enable us to establish in entirely adequate ways whether, and how precisely, writers of literature have engaged with and participated in the debate. Ultimately, then, we are now in a viable position to discover and formulate what could be termed a nominalist and a realist literary aesthetic. In fact, it may be only a short step from there to relating such principles of literary aesthetics to comparable tendencies in the arts as well.[98] Moreover, once the literary debate is studied as essentially an aesthetic phenomenon, it will also be granted a greater measure of autonomy than has hitherto been the rule. For evidently, from that angle of vision, it is quite unneedful, indeed amiss, to construe literary nominalism and realism as dependent as such, and in any exclusive or strictly causal understanding, on either the philosophical debate or on a particular, unique historical situation; or, for that matter, to treat the processes underlying their historical manifestations as mere functions of extrinsic circumstances—claims, incidentally, that have in the past conveniently served to dismiss or marginalize a wide range of potentially relevant factors, but especially such as are intrinsic to literary discourse itself, as unlikely or insufficient motivating causes of that specific debate.

As a first corollary, therefore, there is no cogent reason any longer to uphold the traditional, limiting notion that the literary debate, yet specifically literary nominalism, ought to be viewed as predominantly (Late-) Medieval phenomena, and hence to keep up the all-too narrow historical boundaries that critics themselves have so far imposed upon research in

---

[98]In that regard, one should point out the auspicious beginnings that have been made by Assunto, *Die Theorie des Schönen im Mittelalter*, and Panofsky, *Gothic Architecture and Scholasticism* (see also above, note 38). Yet beyond that, it might be well worth the effort to take a close look at Mannerism—as both an historical movement and an aesthetic orientation, in the arts as well as in literature—in order to determine the relationships between such trends and nominalist tendencies in particular. For a wealth of pertinent literary material, see Gustav René Hocke, *Manierismus in der Literatur: Sprach-Alchimie und esoterische Kombinationskunst* (Rowohlts Deutsche Enzyklopädie, 82-3) (Reinbek: Rowohlt, 1959); for the arts, see especially Werner Hofmann's excellent exhibition catalogue, *Zauber der Medusa: Europäische Manierismen*, ed. Wiener Festwochen (Wien: Löcker Verlag, 1987).

that area. Consequently, the historical scope of critical enquiry, as well as its potential range of subject-matter, can now be justifiably extended—much in the sense we have argued before—to include the whole of Western literature, from Antiquity right up to the Present (and, quite probably, the literatures of non-Western cultures as well). In terms of analytical procedure, on the other hand, we need no longer rely solely upon our finding of exact philosophical analogues, or even of direct sources, for every single text or aspect we might want to consider. Likewise, then, our criteria of inclusion will not hinge any more upon a painstaking, highly precarious cross-referencing of literary and philosophical or theological discourse, but will rather have to be found in and developed from the literary texts themselves. In other words, such criteria will have to emerge, first and foremost, from the close *literary-critical* analysis and interpretation of our primary textual material, and it will be only in a second or parallel step that an attempt would be made to relate such findings—where possible and appropriate—to pertinent non-literary co(n)texts or extra-literary circumstances.[99]

To be sure, our intention is not to play down the significance in itself of 'extrinsic' or contextual considerations. Obviously, to the extent that literary texts—arguably more so than most other text types—have to be seen as potential areas of intersection with any number of 'extraneous' cultural constituents and discourses, the respective historical moment or certain non-literary intertexts, such as the philosophical debate, will still be relevant, even as possible factors of direct influence. Nor, naturally, would we deny that literary texts will be responding to, and thus bear the stamp of specific historical or cultural configurations, or that they will tend to pick up on themes and issues that are prominent at a certain time and age. We would certainly take issue, though, with any attempts to give precedence to such factors over literary or aesthetic concerns, yet in particular with the all but pervasive tendency of previous critics to construct literary nominalism and realism in terms primarily of extrinsic determinants: for on the discursive levels, the emergence and historical unfolding of the literary debate cannot in fact be separated from the history and intrinsic evolution of specific literary genres, sub-genres and traditions. In so far, however, we might expect the discourse of literary nominalism and realism to be governed by the inherent 'principles' and dynamics of literary and generic evolution—rather, perhaps, than it would depend upon extrinsic, extra-literary factors, whose relationship to literary developments will generally be more mediated in kind.[100]

---

[99] See also sections 7. and 8. below.

[100] As a parallel case one might point out that the historical reconstruction and explanation of literary 'series', but particularly of their evolutionary dynamics, have tended to run into quite serious difficulties whenever their interrelation with other

In order to arrive at an historically adequate understanding of the literary debate, then, we will need to disentangle the specific conventions of literary nominalism and realism from other discursive and cultural practices and traditions pertaining to the debate over universals, and this, eventually, will also lead us to a clearer conception of their intricate transactions with various extraneous constituents. Such cultural negotiations, as we have argued, might involve all sorts of highly complex feedback and interplay between discourses and texts, covering a wide range of possibilities, from various types of direct influence (or opposition) to more oblique relations of mutual support, or of questioning and subversion. Simultaneously, however, they will also be subject to considerable variation, at any given moment in history as well as between different historical periods. In view of the shifting, composite character of such transactions, and bearing in mind that their ultimate site—hence our ultimate point of reference—will ever be the individual literary text (which in turn has to be seen as a particular historical manifestation of literary discourse), our analytical approach will thus need to be flexible in the extreme, even ad hoc. Only then will we be able to grasp the complex dialectics of transcoding and transposition that is of the very essence of such interdiscursive processes of cross-fertilization and appropriation: for once they enter and are absorbed into the domain of literary discourse, any such 'extrinsic' elements will inevitably be displaced, in terms of context and function, and will thus be adapted to its peculiar modes of expression as well as signification.

Among other things, but most importantly perhaps, an approach of this kind would also imply a radical reconceptualization of prevalent notions of influence and causation, with the consequence that many apparent problems that have so far beset the methodology of research in our field will disappear, or at least lose their edge. Such problems, more often than not, have resulted from the fact that previous criticism and theory have tended to think in sharp, uncompromising alternatives where some sort of 'both/and logic' might have been more appropriate to the issues at stake. For an example, let us turn to the much-disputed question of the drifting apart of signifier and signified, and the resulting split, in some texts, between sign and referent, which quite a few critics have read as a clear indication of nominalist influence on literary discourse. Up to now, the chief issue here was whether and how that split, once it has been diagnosed in a particular text, might in fact be connected to nominalist, yet especially

---

cultural systems or domains was conceived not as a problem of literary aesthetics but primarily in terms of direct, causal influences or interdependences. For examples, see the fierce altercations about such issues in Marxist theory and criticism, but also the still pertinent attempts of Tynianov and the Prague School, Mukařovský in particular, to define the relationships between literary systems and other 'historical series'.

to Ockhamist concepts of the sign and signification, or whether there may have been other, more plausible factors at work in precipitating that specific effect—such as, for instance, the influence of certain types or uses of rhetoric.

The suggested approach, by contrast, would no longer demand a definitive decision in favour of any one of these conceivable causes, nor indeed—unless, of course, a specific source can be safely identified—would this even be a matter of primary interest to us. For to the present writer's mind, the mere 'fact' of such semiotic slippage, if it is foregrounded and consistently supported by the overall dynamics of a text, would be sufficient in itself as a potential marker of '*literary* nominalism'. Thus, it is now possible to read particular uses of rhetoric—which might of themselves lead to the described effects—as genuinely literary ways of engaging with the nominalism/realism-complex, while on the other hand, this would still not exclude the simultaneous influence of certain trends or developments within school rhetoric or philosophical nominalism as additional, perhaps even enabling factors of such literary uses of rhetoric. And much the same, obviously, would also apply to other such seeming alternatives, as for example the allegedly absolute oppositions, in terms of influence or 'causation', that are sometimes asserted to hold between philosophical nominalism *or* (e.g.) mysticism *or* (e.g.) specific historical or social circumstances (alternatives which in their turn are often set in stark contrast to any factors intrinsic to literary discourse itself).[101]

On theoretical and methodological grounds, then, we are now in a position at last to avert our gaze from the all but hypnotic attraction of extrinsic factors 'per se', and thus from unending speculation about their relative importance, focussing instead on the specific functions they would assume *within* a literary discourse of nominalism and realism. In that respect, however, our approach is historically more adequate, too: although we would admit a multiplicity of motivating factors, of both extrinsic and intrinsic provenance, as contributing towards the 'genesis' and specificity of literary nominalism and realism in particular historical situations, we would not view them in isolation, nor indeed would we regard it as sufficient for a comprehensive understanding of these phenomena to consider merely the interaction of such factors with one another. For in the final analysis, we would construe the literary debate less as the product or 'outcrop' of any such particular impulses, but rather as attesting to an inherent tendency or endeavour of literary discourse to locate and assert itself in the area of ideological tension between nominalist and realist

---

[101] The actual intricacy of such relationships and their recalcitrance to conceptualization in terms of straight oppositions can perhaps best be grasped from Oberman's circumspect discussion of them in *Harvest of Medieval Theology*, esp. 323ff.

positions that is created by the totality of cultural negotiations about the 'true' nature of signification, as well as by the concomitant struggles of these contradictory paradigms for hegemony.

6.3. A Realist and Nominalist Literary Aesthetics

Against this background, we may now also venture an informed guess at what realist and nominalist literary texts might 'ideally' look like, and proceed to form some general hypotheses about the outlines of a realist and a nominalist literary aesthetic—which, in some respects, may be just two sides of the same coin. Considering the peculiarly slanted dialectics of interdependence and mutual definition that we have observed to prevail between the elements of explicit statement and representation on one hand, and the implicit, formal dimension of literary texts on the other, the weight of evidence in assessing a text's fundamental attitude in relation to realist and nominalist paradigms, as well as the degree of its involvement in the debate, has now clearly shifted towards the pole of implicit, indirect semiosis, and hence to the specific discursive and textual strategies employed. In particular, though, we will have to direct our attention to the overall conception of literary texts, and to the ways they deploy and manipulate individual structural elements and features in terms of such superordinate structural levels and discursive functions as textual perspective, framing, closure, and the like: for eventually, the concrete meaning and functions of any single elements or substructures will always depend upon the overriding context that is provided for them, which in effect may either function to emphasize or establish a realist frame of reference or, alternatively, a nominalist one.[102]

Thus, if literary authors believe—or choose to project the belief in particular texts—that verbal signs and language in general are capable of reflecting, and therefore of faithfully representing, the actual structure and set-up of reality, or of certain fundamental aspects of it, and if they see it as their task to lay down and convey to their readers this 'essential' order of things, they will probably tend to design and manipulate the various elements and structural levels of such texts in ways that would hierarchize—and ultimately appear to fix or even arrest—textual meaning. That is to say, they would probably seek to privilege certain concepts and ideological positions, or particular figures, events, modes of signification, etc, by investing them with greater authority, or a higher degree of 'truth' and significance than others—even if, as has been suggested, such attempts might never be quite successful: for contradictory or 'dissenting' voices (which in most cases, however, are part of the very 'drama' of literary

---

[102]The following juxtaposition of realist and nominalist tendencies in literary texts has been adapted from Keiper, "'I wot myself best how y stonde'", 229-32.

texts) can certainly be discredited or suppressed, yet never entirely cancelled, and may thus form the springboard for dissident or deconstructive readings.

A realist literary text, therefore, might want to use any means to check the undue, 'unruly' proliferation of the dissenting viewpoints it incorporates, doing its utmost to contain any dissident attitudes voiced. Moreover, it would probably introduce such voices precisely in order to measure and redress them according to the superior, absolute standards of whatever it posits as its 'ideal', 'essential' truth(s). Embarking on an 'archaeological' quest of sorts to reveal or unravel such essential, stable, or transcendent truths behind phenomena or concepts, it might proceed to re-focus the heretical voices to which it allots a certain, limited sway within its precincts, gradually adjusting them to its ideals, so that ultimately all perspectives within the text would seem to converge towards a semantic Omega point, so to speak, of an objectively 'given', authoritative, and guaranteed truth. In order to do so, such a text would presumably seek to mask its precarious status as an act of signification—in those parts, at any rate, which would seem to support its fundamental ideological tenets. Assuming absolute authority over its multiple voices, then, it might attempt to disclaim any sense of perspective, or to suspend and gradually absorb the unavoidable heterogeneity of its voices in the one privileged discourse it proclaims as true. The views of irredeemable dissenters, who would always be regarded as a dangerous presence in such a hypothetical text, would of course be branded as irrecoverable and finally disposed of accordingly.

Hence, realist texts might be expected to espouse a static, or in any case an essentialist, universalizing view of reality as it is or should be—a reality they will (re)present as unequivocally 'reason-able', and therefore as entirely accessible and transparent to human understanding. In other words, they would probably be strictly monologic or 'closed' texts, whose overall effect on the reader might be likened to that of a collecting lense bundling the text's various perspectives towards a clearly defined vanishing point of textual semiosis. Something like this, we would submit, is what one finds in many didactic or doctrinal fictions, or generally in many texts that are staunchly supportive, even uncritically affirmative of a stable, univocal world-view, and which might thus, ultimately, be regarded as firmly centered (or logocentric) discourses that gravitate towards a supreme transcendental signifier/d.

If, on the other hand, literary writers see verbal signification, and language in general, as contingent and its referents—if indeed they believe in the pertinence of that notion—as no more than concepts in the human mind, their texts might exhibit a pronounced tendency to emphasize their precarious character as mere human constructs which need not necessarily correspond to the 'actual' order of things, or refer to any ultimate or 'solid' reality 'out there' that can be recuperated through language in any reliable or binding ways. Such texts, therefore, might tend to foreground and highlight the inevitable relativity of the various voices and positions they (re)present, revealing them as more or less haphazard interpretations of a multifaceted, shifting 'reality' whose 'true', essential nature is ineffable, or may be altogether impossible to discover. Hence, such texts would probably stress undecidability and the opacity of discursive self-reference rather than a transparent concept of reality, or epistemological or ontological certainty.

Presumably, then, the ideal nominalist text would underscore, even loudly proclaim its impugnable status as an event or open-ended, self-referential process of signification,[103] and in that sense it would be self-deconstructive. Judging from what earlier critics and historians have identified as typically nominalist notions and areas of preoccupation, such a text might be expected to display a pervasive interest in the individual and contingent, the experiential and 'real' (as opposed to 'ideal'), thus bringing into sharp focus the tangible and idiosyncratic, the earthly and even down-to-earth. In one word, it would emphasize 'thisness'. Almost certainly, therefore, such texts would be disposed to project a dynamic and dialectical, sometimes even a paradoxical conception of an ineluctably perspectivated, heteroglossic reality, which they might seek to present as fundamentally intractable to human understanding, and hence as radically contingent upon judgment from individual experience, or from the limited, ephemeral perspective of subjective perception. They would no doubt exhibit a profound distrust in the reliability, even the pertinence of absolutes, or of ideals and truths as normative concepts or 'entities' that might be construed independently of an observer and his or her particular situation. Thence, they might show a marked tendency to focus on the doubtful nature of human, earthly knowledge, but especially on the limits of such knowledge.

Consequently, such texts would probably be seen to refrain from—or to abandon as futile—the quest for any ultimate source and authority, or for an authorizing, pristine moment of privileged insight or revelation. Very likely, moreover, by taking a questioning stance towards ideological absolutes and hypostasized cultural norms, they would seek to define and locate themselves in iconoclastic opposition to the essentializing drift towards reification of culturally stabilizing, ideologically affirmative discourse formations, and might thus be fantastically heterogeneous, inconclusive and open-ended compounds of plural, a-hierarchically organized discourses, flaunting, as it were, the deconstructive, subversive brand of intertextuality they espouse. In their aesthetic conception, they might

---

[103]Such tendencies, of course, will often be connected to a text's use of metafictional modes and strategies.

therefore be highly idiosyncratic, so that such tendencies might manifest themselves less in positive terms—i.e. as a readily identifiable presence of particular textual elements, or through explicit statement—but rather as an absence of characteristics that may be envisaged to define a 'realist' text. Nominalist literary texts, then, might most readily be found among the many 'interrogative', 'subversive' texts of the Late Middle Ages,[104] yet particularly of the Renaissance, as well as of Modernism and Post-Modernism. But obviously, in other periods, too, there will be many more texts—such as *Tristram Shandy* or *Gulliver's Travels*, for example—that would similarly epitomize an aesthetic of that kind.

All of this, of course, is not just a function of divergent concepts of authorship or textuality, but will also affect, and even determine, the fundamental position and role of the reader, who may be construed either—in the case of realist texts—as primarily a passive receptacle for taking in their 'proper', 'intended' meaning, or else—in the case of nominalist texts—as an active, emancipated participant in the construction of textual meaning who is encouraged to engage, on more or less an equal standing with the author, in a mutual, open-ended process of interpreting the world and universe of the text, and of fathoming their 'true' nature. In individual texts, moreover, the described tendencies may be actualized to a greater or lesser extent, and with varying degrees of prominence, so that a particular piece of literature might occupy virtually any position on a scale between both extremes.

Indeed, since in actual practice there are almost no limits to the combination of such textual features and elements, on both the explicit and the formal levels, we have to reckon with all sorts of interplay between them, ranging from their neat correspondence and synergistic agreement to a wide variety of discrepant or contradictory relationships—on top of the fact, that is, that there will usually be some unresolved residual tension between the two paradigms. For even extremely realist texts, as has been argued, will often be haunted by the nagging suspicion that what they (re)present and endorse as reliable, guaranteed truths may ultimately be no more than figments of the imagination, while conversely even the most radically nominalist texts might yet imply the possibility or hope, however faintly, of some epiphany that could eventually turn the tables on their epistemological and ontological relativism, indeed scepticism.[105]

---

[104]For readings of Chaucer's dream visions as 'interrogative texts', see Keiper, "'I wot myself best how y stonde'", but see also Alastair Minnis's brilliant explorations of these poems in *Oxford Guides to Chaucer: The Shorter Poems*, 73-321.

[105]In fact, this might be seen as another crucial factor underlying the inherent dynamics and mutual determination of the twin paradigms in terms of their historical unfolding. At the same time, the virtual unavoidability in literary discourse of that sort

Thus, although many literary texts will plainly fall into one of these categories—and there may be a surprisingly large number of these, given the cautious reticence of many earlier critics in ascribing any such labels—others might rather be found to vacillate between discrepant features. Or they might be characterized by a strong pull of disparate elements into different directions, or by a largely unresolved clash between them, and may therefore be much harder to categorize. In point of fact, some texts—predominantly perhaps of an experimental or aesthetically 'advanced' kind—might even seem to suspend, or in fact to transcend any such straight, clearcut oppositions. One need only think of such extreme specimens of Modernism and Post-Modernism as Joyce's *Finnegans Wake*, or certain works by Gertrude Stein or Christine Brooke-Rose,[106] with their radical disruption of conventional uses of language and of traditional modes of verbal signification and representation. Consider, furthermore, the inconclusive, pastiche-like design and incongruous aesthetics underlying other post-modern texts, more recent in origin mostly, such as Peter Ackroyd's *Hawksmoor* (1985), for example. Despite the intense, indeed paramount efforts this novel invests, on the level of manifest, explicit contents, in attempting to unravel its central enigma and to penetrate its final implications—thereby whetting the reader's appetite for a solution pointing in either a realist or a nominalist direction—it still remains indecisive about the matter. For it is cunningly designed so as to strike an impregnable (hence all the more unsettling) balance between the two positions and the possibilities for interpretation they offer. But comparable effects, no less radical in terms of decidability, can also be found in earlier texts, such as Keats's *Endymion* or the A-text of Marlowe's *Doctor Faustus*.[107]

Such pieces—like any other texts that are deeply involved in our problematic—might often belong to periods of cultural transition, or to phases of ideological upheaval, and thus of intense, even fierce struggles between different semiotic paradigms. For naturally, any such obvious tensions within specific historical configurations, or onslaughts upon prevalent paradigms will serve to sharpen an author's—and the readers'—awareness of and sensibility to problems of signification and their con-

---

of dialectical drift makes it seem even less probable that literary texts will merely 'react' or 'respond' to developments in other discursive domains. On the contrary, it may well be the case that an important social and cultural function of non-literary discourses consists in stemming the 'anarchic' drift of 'semiotic slippage' in literature—just as in actual reality. (For the latter point, see also William C. Carroll's contribution to the present collection.)

[106] For Stein, see especially *Tender Buttons* (1914) and *The Making of Americans* (1925); for Brooke-Rose, see *Such* (1966), *Between* (1968), and *Thru* (1975).

[107] See Christoph Bode, *John Keats: Play On* (Anglistische Forschungen, 242) (Heidelberg: Winter, 1996), ch. II: 'Endymion' (37-85); for *Faustus*, see Keiper, 'Ikarus im Labyrinth der Zeichen'.

comitant issues, while at the same time they would no doubt also enhance the ideological pressures for engaging in the debate, as well as the subjectively felt urge for open intervention, or even for taking sides in it.

On the other hand, there will be a good deal of literary texts which, on the face of it, would create the impression of being unruffled, more or less, by any of these issues, and therefore of being largely 'neutral' or altogether 'detached' in that respect—even if those, too, can be positioned on our 'scale': someplace near the middle, presumably, and tending rather towards the realist pole. Such texts, by contrast, might often be working safely within the limits of firmly established literary and generic conventions, or of certain 'naturalized' practices of literary representation and semiosis, but in particular they might belong to various traditions and types of 'representational' or 'mimetic' realism.[108] That is to say, they would pertain to specific sets and configurations of historical circumstances or to ideological and cultural formations which would either allow or coerce them to mask, or indeed to deny, their ultimately inescapable involvement in these matters.

This, of course, does not exclude the possibility that such texts might manifest an advanced, even revolutionary aesthetics and that, at any given cultural moment, they might be at the forefront of literary developments—in which case a reader might take their aesthetic conception in itself as a challenge to wonted modes of writing as well as perception, and might thus be quite sensitive to markers, however submerged, hinting at their status as something 'made'. Yet beyond that, and perhaps in the majority of cases, if a text strives to bracket off any reflections on its character and status as a verbal artifact, or if it attempts to suppress any hints as to that state of affairs, this would mainly tend to satisfy 'normal rather than intensified perceptions of reality'.[109] Hence, by and large, texts of that kind would tend to affirm and naturalize the assertions and claims to hegemony of specific, culturally or ideologically prevalent constructions of reality, and in that sense they might primarily function to perpetuate and buttress—unquestioningly as it were—such constructions as well as their corresponding modes of discursive constitution. The bulk of such texts might therefore be rather on the epigonic, or in fact the 'trivial' side, in that they would merely continue, in more or less 'automatized' (and sometimes crudely reductive) ways, literary conventions suggesting the allegedly

---

[108] The relationships between 'mimetic' and 'semiotic' realism have long been a largely neglected field of enquiry which would be worth exploring in some detail; however, see Wolf, 'The Language of Feeling between Transparency and Opacity', for an instructive discussion of such issues.

[109] See *The New Princeton Encyclopedia of Poetry and Poetics*, eds. Alex Preminger and T.V.F. Brogan (Princeton, NJ: Princeton University Press, 1993), s.v. 'realism' (quote: 1016).

untrammeled transparency of literary discourse and representation, and their underlying ideologies. As such, they are no doubt important in terms of studying a culture's or period's general literary set-up, but from the present point of view, their relevance would mainly lie in their providing a broad 'background', so to speak, to the culturally advanced literary phenomena and negotiations that are of primary concern to us.

For the most part, then, the degree to which a particular text would realize and foreground some or all of the features outlined, together with—but perhaps beyond—any explicit, sustained treatment of our problematic, will be a sufficiently reliable measure of the depth and intensity of that text's engagement with the nominalism/realism-complex. At the same time, to the extent that we succeed in establishing detailed, historically differentiated inventories of pertinent textual features and strategies, this will help to determine a text's contribution to the development of the literary debate at a particular historical stage, but it will also assist in getting a clearer image of the part a text had in extending the aesthetic modes and possibilities for expression that literary discourse holds in store at specific moments in time: for at any given cultural moment, authors may of course look to the entire literary and cultural tradition available to them. However, in order to arrive at an accurate estimate of a text's fundamental position in these matters, and of the individual stance or orientation it projects, we will need to analyze the peculiar dialectics and types of interplay that would hold between such textual features and elements. In particular, though, we will have to pinpoint and describe the overriding dynamics of the relationships between them, and this, as has been argued, will require close attention not just to pertinent detail, but even more so to a text's overall aesthetic conception. What we need, in other words, are convincing ways and reliable methods of theorizing and describing a literary work's overall economy as a dynamic system of signification, both in itself and in relation to the role it accords to the reader.

In that regard, it is surely no disadvantage that the proposed juxtaposition between a nominalist and a realist literary aesthetic should, in a number of ways, tie in with, and even take recourse to such well-established typologies of literary discourse as the oppositions between 'monologic' and 'polyphonic' writing, or 'open' and 'closed' or 'writerly' and 'readerly' texts,[110] or indeed the now-popular notion of the 'interrogative text'. This might enable us to cross-reference and correlate our findings, and perhaps even to dovetail important aspects of our enquiry with at least some of the results that the application of these categories has brought forth over the last few decades—which have revolutionized our

---

[110] See also below, especially notes 113 and 116.

understanding of literary texts and their aesthetic functions in quite radical ways. As a matter of fact, it might turn out in the end that such a limited convergence of perceptions and categories might even be helpful in advancing our own theoretical claims because—for all we know from the history of the sciences and humanities—the negotiating and establishing of any new research paradigm is dependent to no small degree on the amount of evidence one is able to accumulate in support of its fundamental tenets and hypotheses. Therefore, the success of any research program will largely depend on whether and how it is able to accommodate both new and familiar evidence, and on how such evidence will fall into place and can be explained in terms of its general framework ('Give us fitting "facts" and the paradigm will look after itself!').[111]

At the same time, though, despite a considerable amount of overlap between them, and even far-reaching correspondences, perhaps, in their underlying notions of literary aesthetics, none of the categorizations we have mentioned are in fact co-extensive in the strict sense of the term, as each of them addresses somewhat different aspects and problems of literary discourse. In the interest of theoretical accuracy, therefore, one should beware of conflating any of these typologies with one another, but even more so of rashly equating or collapsing them with our own categories. This would merely result in a blurring of the theoretical contexts they stand for, as well as of critical paradigms whose precise relationships will need to be looked into with great care.[112] Hence, for the moment at least, we would insist that all of these categories be regarded as no more than heuristic tools, conceptual approximations that may guide us in our textual analyses. Their precise theoretical status, however, especially in relation to the paradigm we propose, must remain open for now, since any in-depth clarification of such differences, obviously, is beyond the scope of the present paper and will thus have to be left to future critics to undertake.

Rounding off our general discussion and outline of a nominalist and realist literary aesthetic, it might nonetheless be helpful to sketch in some of these differences—not in order to prejudice the possible directions of future enquiry, but in an attempt to highlight the specificity and distinctive peculiarities of the present project. In this way, moreover, it will also be possible to accentuate more clearly its underlying theoretical assumptions,

---

[111] See Kuhn, *The Structure of Scientific Revolutions*, but especially Feyerabend, *Wider den Methodenzwang*. For the humanities, see Christoph Bode, *Den Text? Die Haut retten! Bemerkungen zur 'Flut der Interpretationen' und zur institutionalisierten Literaturwissenschaft* (Graz: Droschl, 1992), esp. 30ff., and Pierre Bourdieu, *Homo academicus* (Paris: Editions de Minuit, 1984).

[112] For a detailed discussion of such issues, see especially Feyerabend, *Wider den Methodenzwang*, 368f. and 389-91.

as well as their methodological implications. Thus, above all, it should be recalled that our interest in the aesthetic conception and properties of literary texts is not for their own sake primarily, nor even in their assumed effects on readers, but that such interest proceeds from addressing literary texts and their discursive functions from a more fundamental point of view which, at the same time, is also more inclusive than most previous approaches to literary aesthetics. For our principal endeavour is the attempt to ground issues of literary representation at the deeper levels of a text's underpinning semiotic paradigms, and to theorize them in more comprehensive terms—that is to say, in terms of the multivarious relationships and feed-back in literary discourse between textual semiosis and our constructions of reality at large, but also of the larger cultural and discursive mediations and dialectics underlying and shaping such processes.

Hence, notwithstanding the central importance we would accord to the aesthetic dimension of our problematic, particularly at the level of textual analysis, we would regard nominalist and realist literary aesthetics mainly as manifestations, in terms of literary discourse, of such larger cultural issues and their discursive negotiations. As a consequence, we would conceive of literary nominalism and realism primarily in terms of textual functions, and would thus construe them as *functional categories* rather than as descriptive categories in any strict sense of the term, or as solid taxonomic categories being comprised of clearly definable or limited sets of textual features and elements. 'Literary nominalism' and 'realism', therefore, are indeed to be seen as 'master categories' that are meant to subsume certain fundamental aspects and tendencies of literary aesthetics in terms of their underlying discursive as well as cultural functions—in terms, that is, which are at least partly anterior to literature and operating outside and beyond the closed circuit and economy of mere author-text or text-reader transactions. An extended theoretical framework of that sort, however, would in its turn require an in-depth re-orientation, or reconversion, of prevalent concepts of literary aesthetics to include functions and determinants preceding and shaping the very conditions of both literary production and reception—and it may be here, in fact, that an important difference to the other typologies can be located, in so far as such functions are now viewed as an integral part of aesthetic theory.

To the extent, then, that textual categories such as Barthes's 'writerly/readerly', Eco's 'open/closed', or even Bakhtin's 'monologic/polyphonic'[113] can be fruitfully adapted to fit the context of such an aesthetic—

---

[113]For succinct discussions of these categories, see the pertinent entries in Hawthorn, *A Concise Glossary*. It should also be mentioned that with Bakhtin, in particular, there has been some controversy among specialists about whether such concepts as 'monologic' and 'polyphonic' can in fact be construed in terms of categories. But see James Diedrick's article on 'Heteroglossia', in *Encyclopedia of Contemporary Literary Theory:*

presumably by redefining them as purely descriptive, analytical categories—they will obviously assume somewhat different functions within that new frame of reference, which at the same time, however, might also give them a fresh edge and an enhanced sense of theoretical purpose and definition.[114] For it has to be borne in mind that all of these oppositions were conceived, right from the beginning, as both typological and historical categorizations,[115] and have accordingly been used—indiscriminately, sometimes, or with questionable historical accuracy—to characterize and conceptualize particular types of literary writing *as both exemplifying and defining* specific developmental stages in what was seen as the more or less steady evolution of (literary) aesthetics. At any rate, only such a reading might lend plausibility, theoretically at least, to Barthes's and Eco's claims that the categories they propose are not just able to comprehensively theorize the crucial factors distinguishing the 'traditional' aesthetics of 'classical' works from certain advanced types of 'modern(ist)' aesthetic, but that they are also descriptive, in an exclusive sense, of those particular phases of literary and aesthetic evolution.[116]

Approaches, Scholars, Terms, ed. Irena R. Makaryk (Toronto: University of Toronto Press, 1993), 551-2, which endorses precisely that interpretation: 'Heteroglossia provides Bakhtin with a conceptual scheme for categorizing—and judging—individual authors, schools and genres. [...] [he] identifies two traditions in the history of the novel, one of which suppresses heteroglossia. This "monologic" tradition is typified by such forms as the Greek romance, the chivalric romance [...]. [...] Beginning with Rabelais and Cervantes another tradition emerged in which prose narrative foregrounds, intensifies and dramatizes heteroglossia. For Bakhtin, Dostoevsky is both heir and supreme master of this "polyphonic" tradition.' (552) For Eco, see note 116.

[114]In as much as the new paradigm rests upon a re-orientation towards semiotic analysis, it may also help to initiate a return to more considered, precise uses of semiotic concepts and terms than, regrettably, has become the hallmark of a good deal of recent cultural criticism.

[115]Even if the following argument focuses on Barthes and Eco—who are more explicit in these points than Bakhtin—it might similarly apply to Bakhtin's juxtaposition of 'monologic' and 'polyphonic' discourse.

[116]For Barthes, see especially 'The Death of the Author' and 'From Work to Text', in Roland Barthes, *Image-Music-Text*, tr. Stephen Heath (London: Fontana, 1977), 142-8 and 155-64. For Eco, see *Das Offene Kunstwerk*, tr. Günter Memmert (Frankfurt a.M.: Suhrkamp, 1977), 7ff. (esp. 'Vorwort zur zweiten Auflage'), and Christoph Bode's perceptive discussion of Eco in *Ästhetik der Ambiguität: Zu Funktion und Bedeutung von Mehrdeutigkeit in der Literatur der Moderne* (Konzepte der Sprach- und Literaturwissenschaft, 43) (Tübingen: Niemeyer, 1988), 99-106. In a characteristic move, Eco himself denies that he ever conceived of the 'open/closed work' as 'critical categories' (see 'Vorwort zur zweiten Auflage', 11f.), but in fact, that is precisely how he uses these concepts in actual practice—as certainly do most of his followers. For Eco's seemingly paradoxical understanding of 'open' and 'closed' and its customary reversal in later usage—to which the present writer also subscribes—see Hawthorn, *A Concise Glossary*, s.v. 'Open and closed texts' (137f.).

The sort of categorization we are suggesting, by contrast, besides being function-oriented, is conceived as a purely typological means of classification, and is thus not intended *per se* to carry any specific historical associations. In principle, therefore, our categories are, between them, applicable to any literary text, independent of its historical and even its cultural provenance. When such categories are applied to describe the general semiotic orientation of literary texts, as well as their overall conceptional and aesthetic bias, they are fundamentally ahistorical, then, and perhaps even transhistorical, as long as one moves at the level of textual analysis only (and to the extent, of course, that this is at all possible).[117] This is not to say, however, that they can be taken as absolutes in historical terms, because at that level of analysis a strong relational element comes in too, which also has to be given due consideration. For in order to ascertain the exact historical position as well as functions of literary texts, and to judge their probable impact on contemporary readers, it will clearly not be enough to look at them in isolation, but we will also have to take into account and determine their peculiar relationships to the specific literary traditions and generic 'series', as well as to the particular cultural moment and general historical context they originally belong to.

On the one hand, then, a specific literary text will often display a more or less clear tendency in the direction of either nominalism or realism, and that tendency is likely to be realized in terms of the fundamental aesthetic and discursive functions we have suggested (which in their turn will be constrained by the specific literary and generic traditions of which that particular text is a part). On the other hand, though, the precise historical position of that text, as well as its impact on the majority of contemporary readers, is an entirely different matter—different, that is, from locating that text on our scale, which as a rule may indeed be done in broadly 'absolute' terms. Hence, two moderately 'nominalist' texts, for instance, might display more or less the same overall conception, and might even employ quite similar textual strategies to attain much the same general effect, but each of them may nonetheless have to be judged quite differently in historical (as well as contextual) terms, depending on the precise backgrounds against which the text scrutinized was written. If it was written against the background of, say, Medieval realism, or Renaissance neo-Platonism, it will probably have to be read as questioning or countermanding prevalent realist tendencies, or even as introducing some sort of 'nominalist turn'. By contrast, if it has to be evaluated against a background of, say, Post-Modernist writing, it might be seen even to mark a (re-)surfacing of realist tendencies, or indeed to initiate a 'realist turn' of sorts.[118]

---

[117]For a detailed discussion of such issues, see section 7. below.

[118]Chaucer's use of multiple embedding in his dream visions, for example, could be taken as one such feature which makes these poems appear as distinctly, even radically

Vice versa, of course, two texts that might be judged as quite different in 'absolute' terms might yet be comparable in terms of their historical functions, for the simple reason that our sensibilities, and hence the limits of our perception of what constitutes more or less extreme forms of nominalism or realism, are dependent on context and will thus change over time (though not necessarily in just one direction).[119] In much the same way, moreover, we will also have to consider the particular genre or sub-genre a text belongs to—for here, again, we may encounter quite striking differences even for roughly the same time span.

In order to arrive at a comprehensive evaluation, then, in aesthetic and historical terms, of any particular text in relation to 'literary nominalism' and 'realism', we shall need to combine a typological approach at the level of textual analysis with adequate methods of historical analysis, i.e. with a relational, context-oriented approach to its historical functions, and we would further submit that it is only through a procedure of that kind that we may hope to arrive at a more precise understanding (and reconstruction) of the actual dynamics of change and cultural development in that important area of literary aesthetics. For while it is true that the means of literary expression, and even the discursive strategies at the writers' disposal, are subject to continual evolution (in the sense that such means and strategies would enable writers to choose from an ever growing variety and range of aesthetic possibilities), it would at the same time also appear that literary writing—except for very special cases, or developments unforeseen as yet—is ever confined within the boundaries staked out by nominalism and realism, and cannot therefore go beyond the fundamental possibilities and choices implied by these principal semiotic paradigms. In any case, it would hardly seem possible that any such transcendence might

---

nominalist texts in their immediate literary-historical context, but presumably beyond. On the other hand, the mere use of multiple textual framing of the type we encounter in Chaucer, would quite probably not be enough to warrant that extreme sort of classification against the background of Post-Modernist writing. For in that case, 'stronger' means of creating a sense of contingency or *mise-en-abyme* might be required, as for instance the possibility of infinite regress that is suggested through William Burroughs's wholly confusing deployment of repetitive nested framing in the chapter 'Wind Die. You Die. We Die' from *Exterminator!* (1973), or the still more unsettling strategies of *mise-en-abyme* one finds in John Barth's 'Life Story'. (For details, see Keiper, "'I wot myself best how y stonde'", 217f., and McHale, *Postmodernist Fiction*, 114-21.)

[119]For an example, compare the sense of pervasive contingency that is projected through Shakespeare's uncompromising use of multiperspectivism in *Henry VI* or *Troilus and Cressida*, for instance, and the quite similar, if perhaps milder effects that are created in some of Iris Murdoch's novels, as opposed to the radically abysmal pull exerted by some Post-Modern fictions, such as Burroughs's *Naked Lunch* or Muriel Spark's *The Comforters*.

establish itself in any decisive, definitive ways, or as an irreversible literary trend or practice, because in that area writers will always find themselves confronted with some sort of either/or quandary. Therefore, even if they should decide to project some kind of synthesis, or attempt to suspend the uncheckable dialectics between the two basic positions, they will nonetheless remain within the dialectics between nominalism and realism, and will thus still be moving within their domain (the limits of which cannot perhaps be transcended except by a complete disintegration of language, signification and reference, which might be seen as constituting the very pillars supporting these paradigms; but this, in effect, would also mark the end of writing as we know it[120]).

Bound up as it is with the very nature of linguistic, but especially textual semiosis, this paradox, moreover, might in fact also go a long way towards explaining why, despite what seems a consistent expansion over the centuries of the aesthetic inventory of literary writing, there appears simultaneously to have been a perennial struggle between the two paradigms—some sort of see-saw dynamics, giving rise to an unending series of cycles, or to a spiral movement, as it were, which would ever appear to be thrown back on that basic choice, notwithstanding the fact that the conditions for such enagagement will always be different, and in that sense 'developing'. Yet this raises the difficult question of historical reconstruction and of how our findings might fit in with various competing ideas of historical development and cultural 'evolution'—an issue on which a few words need to be said in conclusion.

7. History, Interpretation, and Historical Reconstruction

It is chiefly in two ways that 'history' and historical considerations have a central, immediate bearing on our project. For in addition to the historicity of our subject-matter itself, we have also to acknowledge the ineluctable historicity of our own interpretive approaches. That is to say, the discovery of potentially pertinent properties of the texts we scrutinize, as well as the ascription of historical validity to such features, will fundamentally depend upon what we view as admissible methods of analyzing and interpreting texts that are, as often as not, historically far removed from the present (and this, in fact, is one of the reasons why such issues are especially

---

[120] Moreover, if a writer tries his or her hand at a complete disintegration of conventional linguistic means or semiosis, such attempts will regularly be countermanded by the inherent tendency of language to 'signify', i.e. by the readers' unquenchable urge to project meaning and reference—even where none might be intended. Paradoxically then, the less apparent the 'meaning', the greater the efforts to extract some, as can be seen, for example, from the unflagging struggles of Joyce's exegetes to 'read' and re-read a text like *Finnegans Wake*.

contentious in the field of Renaissance Studies, but even more so in methodological altercations among medievalists).[121] Moreover, since all of these aspects have to be seen as part of a hermeneutic circle, or spiral, governing the procedures of discovery as well as of validation, they cannot be finally disentangled or disengaged. While, on the one hand, the analysis and interpretation of individual texts will elicit—and in many ways create—the 'facts' on which our historical (re)constructions are based, previous or prevalent (re)constructions and interpretations of history will, on the other hand, influence and even determine, to a more or less decisive degree, our approaches to specific texts, which in turn will condition the interpretive categories we use, and so on and so forth.

The issue (and feasibility) of historically adequate interpretation, therefore, is of paramount importance for us, with respect both to the assumptions and analytical methods we bring to bear upon individual texts, and to the historical evaluation (and ultimate integration) of the evidence thus produced. What is more, we have further to take into account that the interpretation—hence also the 'meaning'—of individual texts, or of the work of individual authors, is anything but a stable affair. Nor will it do to view 'textual meaning' as simply a cumulative process converging towards some ultimate truth about a text, i.e. towards some sort of coherent, consistent master-reading that is able to smoothly accommodate all previous interpretations. Much rather, a text is subject to continual and divergent re-readings, re-interpretations and re-assessments, so that, even if we strive for historically 'faithful' readings, our notions of what and how a text 'means' will inevitably change over time, often in such radical ways that many of them are fundamentally incompatible, or indeed incommensurable, with one another.

For an example of such shifting perspectives and assessments, let us take a quick glance at some prevalent twentieth-century images of Chaucer. Second only to Shakespeare, this pre-eminent Late-Medival writer has served as the very icon of English cultural and national identity, from virtually his lifetime to the present day. As such, however, it is not only his writings that were turned into a chief testing ground for various theoretical and critical approaches, but the man himself has become a prime test case for varying constructions of English cultural history, many of which were biased by a strong, nostalgically tinged longing to view positions of cultural and ideological integrity as constituting the very roots of 'the English tradition'.[122] It is thus quite in keeping that mainstream criticism,

---

[121] For Renaissance Studies, see also the introductory paragraphs of Christoph Bode's essay in the present collection; for some aspects of the medievalists' debate, see Richard Utz's contribution.

[122] Anne Rooney, *Geoffrey Chaucer: A Guide through the Critical Maze* (State of the Art series) (Bristol: The Bristol Press, 1989) provides a quick overview of such

until well into the second half of our century, tended to construe 'Chaucer' as *the* prototypical representative of Merry Old England, and that his works, too, were interpreted much along the lines thus suggested.

The prevailing image, then, was one of a jolly, humorous man—independent and critically-minded, no doubt, and with a strong penchent for irony, but one whose basically affirmative ideological stance and unfailing orthodoxy as a Christian writer were never seriously questioned. Consequently, Chaucer was largely seen as a mild, good-natured ironist at best, and as a writer who could be safely associated with the very beginnings of a long-standing tradition of 'typically' English humour, i.e. of a homely or well-meaning 'humanistic' variety, rather than of caustic, let alone radical subversion. In recent decades, by contrast, such images of Chaucer, ideologically slanted as no doubt they were, have come under increasing pressure from critics of various orientations. In particular, though, they were challenged—and are gradually being supplanted—by the conviction of a growing number of Chaucerians that he may in fact have been a profoundly sceptical, trenchantly ironical author who can even be read, at least in some of his poems, as a deconstructionist *avant la lettre*.[123] Accordingly, critics of Chaucer have more and more begun to read his poems as interrogative texts—i.e. as questioning, in more or less radical ways, the dominant ideologies of his time—thus painting his image in varying shades of subversion.

Regardless of which of these assessments, if any, is actually 'true', or closer to 'reality'—and current interpretation, despite its extreme theoretical self-consciousness, may just as much be a mythmaking in its own terms as earlier approaches were in theirs—such changing views of authors and their texts do shape, to a considerable extent, our views of history, just as they, in turn, are informed by received ideas of what is historically 'given'. If, then, one chooses to construe Chaucer as an affirmative, entirely orthodox Christian author writing in the 'exegetical' tradition of Patristic discourse(s), one will feel wholly justified in subjecting his works to consistently allegorized, enclosed and univocal readings.[124] Indeed, one might be tempted to distort or even suppress what is now perceived—and appreciated—as the unsettling, disruptive features of his texts, or to read such elements in ways that will make sure to blunt their potentially radical, subversive edge. What is more, that kind of approach—which was propagated with particular fervour by D.W. Robertson and his many followers—was not merely the product of an uncompromisingly orthodox

---

changing constructions, but see especially the detailed surveys of criticism in the *Oxford Guides to Chaucer* series.

[123]See e.g. Keiper, "'I wot myself best how y stonde'".

[124]For a discussion of 'exegetical' criticism, see also the final section ('Theory, Practice and Influence') of Stephen Penn's contribution to the present collection.

hermeneutic tradition in the critical interpretation of Medieval literature, or of its conjunction with an ideologically charged nostalgia for the 'good old days' (as was rampant a few decades ago). Its premises were also reinforced—and in fact largely enabled—by the then dominant historical view of the Middle Ages as adhering, virtually without exception, to a solidly unified, monolithic Christian world picture which simply did not allow for the possibility of an author—still less a prominent writer who appears to have never got himself into trouble over his writings—as being radically questioning, or indeed subversive of the prevalent world view. Naturally, then, all sorts of evidence could be produced to support precisely such readings as the only adequate ones.

Obviously, for critics working from that particular set of assumptions, but especially for the many critics influenced by the tenets of Robertson's exegetical approach, it would have been well-nigh impossible to see, and even theoretically unthinkable to suggest, that Chaucer and Ockham—or indeed some of the more radical Late-Medieval nominalists—may have been engaged, each in his own way, in much the same general 'project' of cultural, ideological and philosophical critique, or that they may have had comparable theoretical interests, perhaps even ideological leanings. Partly, of course, this would also have been due to the fact that, until recent times, the Late-Medieval nominalists were predominantly seen as radical sceptics, whereas Chaucer was not. Hence, even if a critic or historian should have noted traits in Chaucer's works that might have pointed to his interest (or partisanship) in the debate over universals, s/he would probably have failed to make the connection.

But there is yet another, perhaps more important reason for such oversights, which might well be termed 'systematical'. Until well into the 1940s, as Utz has shown in some detail,[125] there was an overpowering tendency among historians of philosophy (and culture) to marginalize, or at least to play down nominalism in its general cultural and historical impact. In particular, though, and for a variety of reasons, it was Late-Medieval nominalism which was construed as a more or less ephemeral episode that was historically inconsequential and quite haphazard in nature. Indeed, even from the 1950s, when an increasing number of historians began to reconsider that assessment, recognition of the late-medieval debate over universals as one of the potentially most momentous transforming factors in European intellectual history was fairly slow. Hence, little attention was given to questions concerning the emergence and possible ascendancy of nominalism—or, more generally, of nominalist orientations and ideologemes. Even today, in fact, there are some quite influential historians, especially of philosophy, who believe that the

---

[125]See 'Negotiating the Paradigm', 3-10, and *Literarischer Nominalismus*, ch. 3.

general repercussions and culturally transformative momentum of Medieval nominalism are being overestimated or misconstrued, and it has to be conceded that they may have a point in cautioning us against hypostasizing *philosophical* nominalism as the single most important factor underlying such processes of transformation.

Nonetheless, what we are currently observing is a growing interest in and valuation of 'nominalism'—and that change in outlook and attitude finds a quickly spreading reflection in many areas of literary and cultural studies which might be said to result from a major (and still quite contentious) paradigmatic shift, both in the general orientations of cultural historians and in our entire construction of European intellectual history. However, since all of this has taken its full effect only after the heyday of Robertsonian criticism (and partly, moreover, on quite different tracks from the other factors we have mentioned), adherents of that approach, naturally, would have been unable to acknowledge the potential importance of nominalism for the study of Medieval and Early Modern literature. In point of fact, even among those critics who were first to pursue the possibility of such a connection, there was initially a strong tendency to preserve the image of 'orthodox Chaucer' by firmly limiting the interrogative aspects of his texts and their discursive and ideological 'faultlines' to the realm of earthly mutability, which was juxtaposed to a domain of divine immutability that could be 'known' only intuitively, or rather believed by some sort of deistic 'leap of faith'.[126]

Conversely, many of today's critics are prepared to emphasize—indeed to generalize—the subversive, disruptive dimension of Chaucer's oeuvre and its carnivalesque, anti-essentialist features. If then, among other things, they seek to relate such 'interrogative' tendencies to a 'nominalist turn' in Late-Medieval/Early Modern thought and notions of reality, this might well be a re-assertion, in part at least, of present-day theoretical assumptions and predelections, or a backwards projection that may ultimately go back to what we conceive as the increasingly unsettling ideological dynamics, insecurity and fragmentation of our own age. And depending on whether we judge that situation as historically unique, or rather as a characteristic type of response in phases of cultural upheaval or historical transition,[127] that sort of approach can be considered as more or less adequate in historical terms.

---

[126]This is true even of Sheila Delany's influential book, *Chaucer's 'House of Fame': The Poetics of Sceptical Fideism* (Chicago, IL: University of Chicago Press, 1972; repr. Gainesville, FL: University Press of Florida, 1994).

[127]In a still more generalized sense, however, responses of that sort might be even construed as universal ways of coming to terms with the confusion of lived experience and might thus be seen as largely independent of specific historical settings.

Still, even though we may think it possible to give viable 'proof' of the existence of such textual features in works by Chaucer—e.g. by means of our most sophisticated methods of structural, functional or cultural analysis—there remains yet the question of whether, and to what extent, such features would have actually been perceived and recognized by Chaucer's contemporaries, i.e. whether they could not have been suppressed, or simply skipped over, by a fundamentally different mindset or aesthetic sensibility and might thus, for a majority of such readers, not have been operative at all, or in any case not in the ways we would ascribe to them today. From an historical point of view, then, the question is perhaps less whether any or all of Chaucer's works *can* be read as subversive, but whether they *were* in fact understood in such terms by their original readers, or at least by some (which?) of them.[128] But apart from direct reception documents—which are few and far between, however, and need not necessarily be representative—the answer to that question, again, will largely depend on how we construct the specific historical situation and cultural ambience of Chaucer's writings and of their reception, as well as on the specific focus and sort of context we would select as the basis and point of reference for such reconstructions.[129]

Moreover, what we have said about Chaucer would, by and large, also apply to most other writers. For even where we may assume a comparatively homogeneous contemporary setting,[130] there is never just one way of reading a text or oeuvre, and the idea of the 'ideal' or 'informed reader', or of anything like a univocity of response, is largely a convenient fiction espoused and promoted by critics in order to authorize their readings as well as historical reconstructions.

In the final analysis, then, there is no denying the historicity and conditional nature of our positions as literary critics, which are, on the one hand, contingent upon the mere fact of our being situated in history and on the specific vantagepoints this would offer us to perceive the past and its relations to the present, whilst on the other hand, and even more decisively, they are conditioned by the choices we make—actively and on a conscious level, as well as subconsciously or from mere habit—among such competing

---

[128]For a more detailed discussion of such issues, see Richard Utz's contribution to the present collection, but see also Gerald Seaman's contribution for the pertinence of distinguishing between different contexts and modes of reception, i.e. audience/listeners and readers, in particular.

[129]For such varying points of reference in the history of recent Chaucer criticism, see especially Alastair Minnis's instructive surveys in *Oxford Guides to Chaucer: The Shorter Poems*.

[130]For the considerable historiographical problems and contradictions involved in any assumptions of cultural homogeneity, compare especially the discussions provoked by Foucault's notion of *episteme* (see note 36).

interpretive frameworks and presuppositions as are available to us or can be constructed at any given moment in time. Primarily, therefore, it is such choices which will prejudice and shape the assumptions we make about the functions and meanings of individual texts, including the very freedom we would allow them to signify in particular ways. For at any level of analysis, the interpretive paradigms and theoretical models we rely upon will operate not only to focus our perspectives on a text, but also to filter our very perception of its features and production of meaning. Any act of textual analysis and interpretation is thus dependent upon a complex dialectical feedback between dynamically interacting presuppositions or mutually defining frames of reference. At the same time, paradoxically, it would appear to be founded on little else than variously intersecting webs of assumptions that are, in a sense, self-validating and self-supporting—a precariously insecure, shifting grounds for any critical statement, and a predicament that cannot be solved except by acknowledging that state of affairs and by sharpening our awareness of it.[131]

Yet if it has to be accepted that whatever we perceive or say about individual texts, or the work of single authors, is inescapably provisional and of a conditional status, i.e. if the very 'facts' underpinning our assessment of a text's cultural 'meaning' and significance are subject to continual and often quite radical revisions or shifts of perspective, and are thus of a highly protean, ephemeral character, what about the infinitely more complex task of (re-)constructing and interpreting the larger-scale processes and dynamics underlying the unfolding of history (or rather, of what—in a dangerously seductive, essentializing simplification—has come to be termed 'History')? As the etymology of the word might remind us, 'history' not only 'tells a story, but [...] passes judgment on it, puts it in order, and gives it meaning.'[132] History, in other words, can be seen as a narrative of sorts and hence, in the last analysis, as a discursive phenomenon in the widest possible sense. However, since there is never just one way to select and arrange the 'facts of history', or to describe the sequence of events or configuration of facts thus given, it would be more adequate to switch to the plural and conceive of 'history' in terms of competing conceptualizations and constructions of historical processes that are based on, and simultaneously generate, a variety of *grands récits*—master-narratives that are variously distilled from a range of more or less heterogeneous smaller-scale narratives describing specific areas and phases of what is perceived as historical or

---

[131] See also Christoph Bode's argument in his contribution to the present collection.
[132] Sister Wendy Beckett, *The Story of Painting* (London: Dorling Kindersely, 1994), 9. See further: 'Our word "history" comes, by way of Latin, from the Greek word *historien*, which means "to narrate", and that word comes from another Greek word, *histor*, "a judge".' (Ibid.)

cultural difference, change or 'evolution'. And such narratives, of course, are themselves distillations—as well as abstractions—from even more localized, mostly conflicting accounts of events or phenomena. Thus, any kind of 'history', or historical account, will necessarily rest upon a multi-layered series or nested hierarchy of ever larger, more generalized abstractions from the actuality of what is historically 'given' or 'experienced'.

Narrative, in turn, has recently been described as 'by-and-large [...] a technique for getting coherence'—a deliberately vague phrasing that is intended to leave 'open [...] the issue as to whether the process alluded to is the *discovery* or the *production* of coherence'.[133] Yet in fact, these two sides of the issue cannot really be disentangled. For even though it is surely possible to speak of the discovery of particular historical traces, facts or sources, and even though such discoveries may indeed happen by accident, when one is actually dealing with them, but specifically in the case of textual sources, the evaluation and interpretation of 'significant facts', and even their 'discovery', will always and necessarily be directed and prejudiced by the questions we ask and the issues we wish to address. With textual sources in particular, therefore, such discoveries will never be a neutral or disinterested thing, but much rather the product of the hypotheses and preconceptions we hold about the nature and significance of 'history' in any or all of its aspects, and of our attempts to structure the unstructured and thereby to endow it with causality, coherence and followability. In that sense, then, all of history, on any level, is a 'reading of history' that is produced—by our selection and foregrounding of certain 'facts' that have come down to us through tradition (or, indeed, through personal experience), as well as by our structuring and interpretation of such facts; and it is only at those levels and as a result of our specific interests and perspectives that they are given significance and meaning.

In many respects, therefore, our 'reading' of history is not altogether dissimilar from the interpretation of individual texts (and still less disconnected from it), in that it will always and necessarily be some kind of circular, self-referential process that is dependent upon the interpretive frameworks we employ and the models we adduce to make sense of 'history'. Moreover, while such shapegiving is perhaps not of an entirely arbitrary nature, in so far as it would appear to rest upon the comparatively secure basis of historical 'facts', the models used to arrange and contextualize those facts, as well as to select them in the first place, comprise a wide variety of possibilities indeed—from various patterns of 'upward'

---

[133] See 'Foreword', in Christopher Nash (ed.), *Narrative in Culture: The Uses of Storytelling in the Sciences, Philosophy, and Literature* (Warwick Studies in Philosophy and Literature) (London and New York: Routledge, 1994), xiii (emphasis added).

evolution and progress to 'Edenist' visions of the decline and fall of human civilization(s), including combinations of them in sundry patterns of rise and decline (or vice versa) that would in turn generate any number of cyclic views of historical development. As a matter of fact, there are virtually no limits to the combinations of such fundamental patterns, which are usually based on some kind of teleology or the idea of directedness in history.[134] Moreover, in varying degrees of complexity, the application of such patterns may range from apparently simple large-scale 'laws' of historical change, as are chiefly known from speculative systems of history, to quite intricate smaller-scale applications to specific phases or developments within history, such as the evolution of single cultures or civilizations, or of particular areas or aspects within them. At the same time, the dynamism and mechanisms of change within any such systems and sub-systems may be construed in terms of linear developments, and therefore of gradual, cumulative processes, or rather as some sort of dialectical movement that is said to be driven by revolutionary upheavals or radical epistemic shifts. Alternatively, though, there is of course also the possibility of rejecting any such models and of viewing history as a an utterly fortuitous, contingent sequence of happenings and events, in which case history is seen as little else than a 'blind', meaningless process without inherent significance, which cannot be interpreted in terms of any overarching patterns or of meaningful causality, but simply described for what it is.

This is clearly not the place to embark on an extensive discussion of the problems of historiography, or of the recent altercations among historians and philosophers of history about the role of narrative in historiography. Nonetheless, in view of the fact that the historical dimension and long-term evolvement of nominalism and realism—in all of their varieties—do have a central bearing on our project and on how one might go about it, we should at least take a closer look at those aspects and issues of historical reconstruction that are of particular and immediate importance for us.

Let us begin with a concept that is frequently adduced to counter the relativist claims and epistemological scepticism of narrativist historiography, namely the suggestion to establish 'causal fertility' as a criterion to

---

[134]For in-depth discussions of such historiographical patterns, see Sidney Pollard, *The Idea of Progress: History and Society* (1968; repr. Harmondsworth: Penguin, 1971), and Popper's trenchant critique of speculative and 'essentialist' history in *The Poverty of Historicism*, but see further the useful article on 'history, history of the philosophy of', in *The Oxford Companion to Philosophy*, 360-4. For a critical recent view of the value of such notions in literary and cultural studies, see Lee Patterson, 'On the Margin: Postmodernism, Ironic History, and Medieval Studies', in Stephen G. Nichols (ed.), *The New Philology* (special issue of *Speculum*, 65 (1990)), 87-108, but see also Christoph Bode's and Andreas Mahler's contributions to the present collection.

differentiate between more and less pertinent historical 'facts'.[135] Indeed, at first glance, that criterion might offer a viable solution to some of the problems we have encountered in that it might help us to define and isolate particularly crucial, momentous phases in any area of historical development, or even historical turning points and watersheds, by working our way backwards from the effects we wish to explain to their probable causes. On closer inspection, however, one notes that the concept might work fine to explain changes in some areas of historical development—such as constitutional or political changes, or the evolution from feudal types of economy to more 'modern' forms—but that it might be much less well-suited for the adequate description of developments in other areas, yet especially so, perhaps, in philosophy, literature and the arts, where it is much more difficult to pinpoint precisely the ultimate purpose or 'aim' of historical 'evolution' and change. Moreover, since the selection, interpretation and valuation of 'causally fertile' facts will once again depend upon the models and paradigms we employ, the application of that criterion is ultimately also contingent upon the specific perspective on history and the type(s) of historical reconstruction we subscribe to, and thus, eventually, on our particular interests and inclinations as historians. For the very idea of 'causal fertility' surely makes sense, and can be defined, only with respect to the specific aspects or issues we address, which in turn will depend upon what we deem important or culturally dominant within a specific context of discovery.

Analogously, notions such as 'the emergent', 'the dominant' and 'the residual', which are often used to conceptualize and explain the fact that certain cultural and historical phenomena are co-existent in time, even though they appear to belong to different and discrete stages of historical development,[136] are also applicable and useful only in relation to the specific narratives of cultural and historical evolution we choose to tell, because

---

[135]For a concise definition of 'causal fertility' and arguments in favour of this concept, see *The Oxford Companion to Philosophy*, s.v. 'history, problems of the philosophy of' (366), but see also ibid. (366f.) for a discussion of 'narrative and interpretation'.

[136]Against a different ideological and theoretical background, these three terms would seem to cover between them much the same set of circumstances as the earlier German concept and term 'Koexistenz des Gleichzeitigen und des Ungleichzeitigen', which was apparently coined by Siegfried Kracauer (see Hans Robert Jauß, 'Literaturgeschichte als Provokation', in *Literaturgeschichte als Provokation* (Frankfurt a.M.: Suhrkamp, 1977), 146). In Britain, the 'triadic' conceptualization of such phenomena appears to have gained currency mainly through Raymond Williams: see his *Marxism and Literature* (Oxford: Oxford University Press, 1977), ch. 8 ('Dominant, Residual, and Emergent'), 121-7, but especially *Keywords: A Vocabulary of Culture and Society* (1976; London: Flamingo-Fontana, rev. and exp. ed. 1983). See further the 'Epilogue' to Andreas Mahler's essay in the present collection.

otherwise they could just as easily be interpreted as mere signs of the contingency of history, or as indicating that certain historical developments will tend to run along parallel tracks instead of following any clearly defined sequence of evolutionary stages. If, finally, in the face of such difficulties we should decide to redirect our efforts from the 'factual' side of historical 'actuality' to studying the significance and functions which 'history' and various historical constructions have had for the members of particular societies, we are bound to come up against much the same sort of difficulties once more. For in doing so, all we will have achieved, in fact, is shifting our focus of interest from an essentialist or realist reading of history and its underlying processes to a constructivist or nominalist one. In itself, however, this will not do away with the fact that there are many ways of reading history and that one might still feel the need to uncover their factual basis or relation to 'actuality'. Lastly, moreover, it should be borne in mind that most readings of history cannot be discounted beforehand, or in any offhanded manner, since in at least some areas, and to some extent, each of them would appear to capture pertinent aspects of the historical process—in terms, that is, of the perception of such processes or, indeed, of historical 'reality'.

If, then, one's aim is to outline and reconstruct the 'history' of a neglected phenomenon such as the literary debate over universals, and if one strives to do so in ways that are fully adequate to the phenomena one wishes to describe, where should one start? In point of fact, the only thing we may take for granted is that there have been differences over the centuries and an enormous amount of variety in the ways literary texts have engaged with the nominalism/realism-complex, as well as in the positions they have taken in that matter. In order to determine, however, whether such changing responses and attitudes have followed any particular directions, whether there have been specific patterns to such developments, or whether some of these developments have proved irreversible in terms of the historical evolution of literary aesthetics, one will first of all have to make sure about the 'facts', regardless of how precarious in itself that business may be. In other words, we will have to provide as reliable as possible a 'factual basis' for the particular type of historical reconstruction(s) we wish to undertake. Indeed, this is another reason why the kind of typological approach we have been suggesting in this essay is of advantage here. Using the best, most advanced analytical tools and methods available, such an approach may help us to establish the relevant interpretive data in a first step, which allows as independent an evaluation of them as feasible, while at the same time it would still leave open various possibilities for constructing the historical evolvement of the phenomena we find, and of accounting for them, so that the historical evaluation and 'slotting' of such findings in terms of large-scale developments may, to some extent, be taken as an additional, quite independent step.

If our reconstruction of the cultural and historical dynamics of literary realism and nominalism is thus made to rest upon 'localized' readings of texts[137] that can be shown to be pertinent in that context, we might also be able to avoid a mere rehashing of established patterns of historical interpretation, or an uncritical re-affirmation of previous attempts at periodization[138] (which in turn might slant our perception of those texts). Instead, we might actually be able to liberate our perceptions and historical sense, and thus to arrive at fresh, perhaps more accurate insights into the processes and dynamics underlying cultural change in this perennially important area of literary aesthetics. Yet in order to do so, we will have to be very careful about any rash hypostasizing of the historical impact or transformative momentum of individual texts or authors, and about projecting onto them more than can be actually proven. In particular, though,

---

[137] For thought-provoking 'localized' readings of Shakespeare, see Richard Wilson, *Will Power: Essays on Shakespearean Authority* (New York et al.: Harvester Wheatsheaf, 1993).

[138] A pet concept of many a cultural historian is of course the widespread notion that the Renaissance or Early Modern period (as it is now preferably called) functioned as *the* decisive 'watershed' or 'threshold' to Modernity. However, it is perhaps significant that this idea has been propagated with particular fervour by Renaissance scholars. For a medievalist's critical view of such attempts at periodization, see Lee Patterson's unconvinced response and convincing counter-arguments in 'On the Margin', esp. 93ff., but see also Richard Wilson's illuminating account of the genesis and underlying ideology of such notions in his 'Introduction' to *Will Power*. Furthermore, Philippe Ariès has argued that one should altogether abandon the simplistic evolutionary view that 'the history of Western society or culture was foreordained and that progress toward modernity was steady and uninterrupted, with perhaps an occasional pause, an abrupt reversal, or even a momentary regression'. Any such view, Ariès claims, only 'obscures the diversity and complexity that must be counted among the leading characteristics of Western society in the sixteenth, seventeenth and eighteenth centuries.' Perhaps, then, as Ariès suggests, a periodization that 'comes [...] closer to the reality of the situation [...] requires us to modify the usual periodization, arguing instead that from the central Middle Ages to the end of the seventeenth century there was no real change in people's fundamental attitudes (*mentalités*)'. (See Philippe Ariès, 'Introduction', in *A History of Private Life*, gen. eds. Ariès and Georges Duby, Vol. III: *Passions of the Renaissance*, ed. Roger Chartier, tr. Arthur Goldhammer (Cambridge, MA, and London: Harvard University Press, 1989), 2.) In our particular context, however, even that attempt at a more adequate periodization would appear doubtful. Not only are there many striking examples—from nineteenth-century developments of the novel to the relationships between Modernism and Post-Modernism—that might cast serious doubts upon the assumption that nominalism was fully ascendant from about 1800; as has been shown, some versions of realism are still going strong, perhaps even themselves gaining ascendance today—all of which would require us to be careful in accepting the confident slogan, 'nominalism rules OK'. (For nineteenth-century fiction, see Wolf, 'The Language of Feeling between Transparency and Opacity', esp. 128f.; for 'Modernism and Postmodernism', see Hawthorn, *A Concise Glossary*, 49.)

we will have to be wary about such concepts as historical or cultural 'turning points', 'thresholds' or 'watersheds', which are often used quite indiscriminately, and are in fact sometimes misused,[139] to suggest the alleged irreversibility of specific literary trends and developments. For obviously, the overall historical significance we would ascribe to specific cultural moments or phenomena will always depend upon the sort of questions we ask and on the specific context(s) to which we choose to relate them. Hence, even if it were possible, from one point of view, to describe a particular text as suggesting a 'turning point', or perhaps even as initiating an irreversible trend, one may well arrive at entirely different conclusions if only one assumes a different, historically more comprehensive angle of vision. Indeed, as Mr Spock has recently reminded us, we may then find that 'history is replete with turning points'.[140]

8. About the Present Collection

It is against this broad background that our readers are invited to consider the present collection of essays. In an attempt to provide reasonable historical focus for our joint efforts to understand literary nominalism (and realism), but also in order to keep the volume within manageable proportions, the general idea has been to limit its historical scope to late-medieval and early modern developments. On the one hand, this implies an important, in fact seminal extension of historical perspective, in as much as the overwhelming majority of previous studies have concentrated mainly on late-medieval literature, but especially on Chaucer, while at the same time it would nonetheless serve to secure a sufficient measure of historical continuity, perhaps even coherence, not least because we have also made a point of focussing chiefly on English literature and its cultural and historical contexts. Moreover, since it is the transitional phase from Medieval to (Early) Modern which is commonly viewed as the decisive, or even the implemental stage in the historical emergence and evolution of nominalist orientations on a broader cultural scale, it might well be here that one is able to glean fundamental new insights into the underlying dynamics of such developments—if indeed there are any clear-cut patterns to such evolutionary processes, and provided that it is at all possible to pinpoint the emergence and purported rise of nominalism to cultural hegemony. In

---

[139] For a well-founded attack on such misuses, especially by critical theorists working in Early Modern studies, see Patterson, 'On the Margin', 93 ff.

[140] In *Star Trek VI*, this is what the detached analyst replies when confronted by his Vulcan opponent's challenge: 'Sir, I address you as a kindred intellect. Do you not recognize that a turning point has been reached in the affairs of the Federation?' (see *Star Trek VI: The Undiscovered Country* (Paramount Pictures, 1991)).

fact, this widening of perspective to include the Early Modern situation as well might help to avoid misconceptions or misrepresentations of such changes and types of development as may have occurred between the Middle Ages and the blending and petering out of Renaissance paradigms into so-called Modernity. Thus, if it should turn out that any obvious, directional patterns of change will emerge from analyzing significant moments within a relatively compact historical phase, this would also be helpful in reconstructing and evaluating subsequent developments, right up to the present. In any event, it might provide a reasonably firm basis to form valid hypotheses about such developments and could thus create a springboard of sorts for future attempts to synthesize the overall historical evolvement of literary nominalism and realism. In this way, then, it might help us to get a clearer picture of their evolutionary dynamics.

Among other things, it was with an eye to such overarching developments that a few exceptions to the above rules have been made. As we have seen, the history of literary nominalism as a counterdiscourse to—and even within—realism neither starts with the late Middle Ages, nor does it end with the Renaissance, regardless of whether one believes that nominalist orientations attained well-nigh complete ascendancy during modern times, or whether one assumes an unquenchable dialectics between the twin paradigms and, consequently, their continual, unabated competition to the present day. Furthermore, it would be also misleading to suggest that the developments we are interested in are specifically English phenomena, even if England may in fact have played an important, and quite possibly a seminal part in inaugurating such processes on a European level as well. It is for such reasons, then, that we have included two contributions—by Gerald Seaman and Ullrich Langer—that specifically deal with French literature, which was undoubtedly of considerable influence on English developments in both medieval and early modern times, if perhaps to a lesser degree in the latter case. Both of these essays, therefore, seek to highlight decisive moments in the evolution of French literary culture which were at the same time of some consequence for the English situation—Langer by taking a close look at Rabelais, a writer of European stature who has been not without influence on the English tradition, especially in the context of Renaissance humanism and its aftermath; Seaman by analyzing Chrétien des Troyes's striking concept of authorship as inaugurating a new, indeed revolutionary paradigm of literary writing. Simultaneously, Seaman's essay also serves to enhance the historical depth of our collection by affording important glimpses of the high-medieval literary context in general, and thus at the 'pre-history', as it were, of the phenomena with which we are centrally concerned. In fact, findings such as Seaman's may finally prove of no little significance for the historical reconstruction of literary nominalism and realism, because they may help to put into perspective what might otherwise be considered—and perhaps misconstrued—as genuinely new, revolutionary developments, if seen in an exclusively Late-Medieval or Early Modern context.

On the other hand, it is at least equally important to look at the 'aftermath' of the medieval and early modern debates. Hence, Nicholas Hudson and Christoph Bode have provided essays in which they address aspects and stages of post-Renaissance developments to which special historical significance can be demonstrably ascribed. Here, any predominantly literary focus might easily have created the impression of arbitrary selection, and this is why Hudson and Bode have chosen to analyze developments within the realms of philosophy and literary/cultural theory that can be said to exemplify, indeed epitomize, the uninterrupted continuity of the debate; for after all, it is precisely this continuity which makes our issues so fascinating from a contemporary point of view.

It should finally be mentioned that contributors were asked to place primary emphasis on the nominalist side of our issue, but in particular to trace the emergence of phenomena that can be seen as representative of nominalist orientations in literature and/or culture. Yet here again it turned out, quite significantly, that practically all of the essays also give due consideration to the realist 'counterdiscourses' to nominalism, and that special attention is directed to the intricacies and fundamentally dialectical nature of the transactions between the two paradigms. This, we believe, can be taken as a strong indication that the two sides of the issue cannot in fact be separated, but have to be analyzed in terms of their mutual dependence and interactions.

Apart from such necessary restrictions, contributors were given free range in their choice of subject, as well as in their selection of texts and cultural moments they consider as particularly pertinent or representative in the present context. Least of all, however, it has been our intention to suggest any preferences in terms of critical approach or analytical method. Given the present state of criticism, with its unprecedented degree of methodological scope and diversification, any such attempts would have been futile anyway, but they would have been counterproductive also in relation to a research paradigm that is still looking for its theoretical bearings, and which is therefore of particular volatility in its methodology. More importantly, though, any attempts to achieve paradigmatic unity, or indeed closure, in such ways cannot in any case be the answer to the problems we are facing in the study of literary nominalism and realism. In point of fact, our aim in the preceding has never been to privilege any particular critical approaches to our problematic or any single type of analytical methodology, but—and this point should be stressed in conclusion—to draw attention to the specifically aesthetic dimension of nominalist and realist literary discourse, and to theorize that particular type of discursivity. For it is this dimension of literary texts which, after all, makes literary nominalism and realism the phenomena they are: *sui generis*.

It is significant, therefore, that contributors to the present collection not only tend to stress the need to develop fresh, convincing approaches to our issues, and that many of them end up pointing out promising new directions for such fundamental re-orientations, but that virtually all of them are of one mind in emphasizing the specifically literary modes of expression and aesthetic side of literary discourse as pivotal to their arguments and as irreducible points of departure for the successful analysis and understanding of literary nominalism/realism. Hence, most of our contributors seek primarily to describe and/or theorize the literary dimension and aspects of the texts they discuss, and it is those features which, in many cases, are placed in relation to pertinent philosophical and theological contexts, as well as to a variety of other backgrounds. It turns out, moreover, that in the majority of essays special attention is given to a number of recurrent key issues, topics or aspects, and one might suspect that it is this limited range of issues that would eventually also function as chief focal points for future research. Most prominent among these are (1) the problem of subjectivity and individuality, particularly in relation to the literary representation of character (see especially the essays by Munson, Langer, Siemon and Fendler); (2) the question of authorship and of the status and authority of literary writers (cf. Seaman, Utz, Carroll); (3) the issue of necessity and contingency, especially in its relation to the creation of fictional worlds and to the characters' position and standing within them (see Courtenay, Utz, Munson, Mahler, Fendler), and (4) the obvious problem of a specifically literary semiotics—as expressed, for example, in questions centering around the readability or transparency of textual signs or of textual worlds in general, or in various historical politics of the sign and signification as a background or co-text to literary discourse (see e.g. Munson, Seaman, Carroll, Siemon, Mahler and Bode). It is through the close, perceptive analysis of literary texts, then, as well as of their varying contexts, that we may finally hope to arrive at a better understanding of how exactly one might define the 'nominalism/realism-complex' in our particular context of discovery, but also of how it may be analyzed with a sufficient degree of focus as well as reliability.

But let me now try and give brief introductions to the individual contributions, which, by and large, have been arranged in historical sequence.[141] Hence, GERALD SEAMAN leads off with his essay on the so-called 'Christian' figures in Chrétien de Troyes, who is indeed shown to have been a seminal figure of the establishing of a genuinely European tradition of (romance) writing. Considering Chrétien as an author and poet, not as a rhetorician or

---

[141]Throughout the following, I have as far as possible attempted to give voice to our contributors themselves. For this reason, quotes from essays in the present collection have not been specifically marked, as a rule.

theologian, Seaman contends that Chrétien's notion of authorship was informed by a nominalist theory of universals and a textually-based tradition of knowledge that permitted him to mediate the *texte-œuvre* dichotomy without remaining indebted to discourses of authority from religious and rhetorical traditions. Seaman's analysis of the prologues to Chrétien's works demonstrates that this writer was preoccupied with establishing a new literary paradigm, not with perpetuating or mimicking others. As Seaman suggests, Chrétien's intense concern with his status as a vernacular poet in a world of competing, contingent literary modes led him to deploy his Christian figures as part of an attempt to secure paradigmatic identity for his work, and for romance authorship in general. In this setting, therefore, the rhetorical and poetic features of Chrétien's prologues can be read as culturally encoded poetic phenomena that set out to challenge discourses of former authority, rather than remaining passively beholden to them. Drawing on Abelard's anti-realist philosophy—a project, as Seaman points out, that can be said to support the 'truth' of fiction rather than the truth of philosophy—Seaman goes on to demonstrate its successful incorporation into early medieval romance poetics. He concludes that, paradoxically, where Abelard's nominalism failed for philosophy, it succeeded tremendously in literature since it helped romance composers such as Chrétien de Troyes to redefine the literary culture of their day, and in so doing to found principles for authorship and the written text that have prevailed well beyond their lifetimes and into ours.

WILLIAM J. COURTENAY has long been a prominent critic of any naive or rash attempts to establish direct connections between late-medieval philosophical nominalism and literature which, in his view, are often based on ill-informed or out-dated readings of the philosopher-theologians themselves. Focussing on a key concept of fourteenth-century nominalism, the 'dialectic of divine omnipotence' (i.e. the distinction of divine power as absolute or as ordained), Courtenay gives a much-needed update on the latest historiographical developments concerning that topic which, he admits, 'has proved far more complex and shifting than any of us realized a decade ago'. Moreover, as Courtenay points out, the changes in interpretation he sets out to describe have not occurred because of shifts in scholarly taste, but because new evidence has been discovered, revealing that there was not just one model but two, with some blending between them throughout the fourteenth century. Although the new picture is still developing, Courtenay nonetheless concludes that the 'mixed success of the early efforts in tracing the influence or application of that theological distinction should not dissuade present-day scholars from looking at fourteenth-century literary texts against the background of the schools and of an educated society aware to some degree of the philosophical and theological content of the instruction provided there'. He goes on to suggest some promising areas to pursue in our attempts to establish such links, among which he names the issue of miracles and the development of allegory in the wake of Ockham's 'campaign against reification'. Of greatest consequence, however, may be Courtenay's suggestion that 'wherever the realm of human events interacts with the realm of divine will [...], one should be attuned to the possibility that the dialectic of divine power may be an operative motif, a framework within which an author sets his characters to play out their parts'. For it is in this area that one might seek to locate important continuities between medieval philosophy and literature, on one hand, and crucial aspects of Renaissance culture, on the other, especially in the context of Protestant doctrines of predestination and free will.

RICHARD J. UTZ's study of literary nominalism in Chaucer's *Troilus and Criseyde* can in some ways be read as an 'informed' response to Courtenay, because it is precisely the concept of God's absolute power which for Utz provides the pivotal point for his argument. Utz starts off with the much-disputed identity of 'Lollius'—whom Chaucer gives as the putative source of his *Troilus*—in a critical examination of the most important theories that have been advanced on that vexing question ever since Kittredge put forth his ingenious philological hypothesis in order to exonerate Chaucer from having simply fabricated the name 'Lollius'. This, in turn, leads Utz to propose his own hypothesis, namely that 'Lollius' was part of a poetic strategy which Chaucer devised in order to draw attention to the possibly absolute power (*potentia absoluta*) that the fourteenth-century author perceived to hold over the microcosm of his literary creation. Utz, then, uses the concept of God's absolute power to suggest a structural analogy with the power wielded by the author of *Troilus and Criseyde*, and this, he contends, will assist in understanding several of the premises of literary representation in Chaucer's text. Utz's detailed analysis of narrative strategies in that epic poem reveals the narrator as only second in a three-layered hierarchy of fictionalizers, from which he concludes that the introduction of 'Lollius' was intended, on the one hand, to lead Chaucer's general audience to believe the intuitive cognition of a non-existent (i.e., the creation of the linguistically authenticated apprehension of Lollius as a physically real master source). Chaucer's informed readers, by contrast, must have recognized the invention and parodic insertion of Lollius as representing the most manifest verbal marker of their friend's growing selfconsciousness as an author. Much like Seaman, then, Utz demonstrates that nominalist concepts and orientations may have helped medieval authors in asserting and re-defining their authority and position as writers of fiction as against established traditions of authorship, and that this may also provide an important matrix for our reading and understanding of such texts.

It is indeed plausible that Chaucer's informed circle of readers and friends should have included such leading contemporary figures as Gower, or in fact the somewhat shadowy figure of Strode, as Utz suggests. What is much less clear, though, is the exact nature of the influence which philosophers like Strode, Bradwardine or Holcot may have had on Chaucer, or whether we may count on any such influence at all. Among other things, it is this much-disputed issue which WILLIAM H. WATTS sets out to reexamine in his essay on 'Chaucer's Clerks and the Value of Philosophy'. Indeed, Watts concludes, one would be hard-pressed to identify passages in Chaucer's poetry that necessarily depend upon the thinking of any particular philosopher of the period, and in his view this would apply even to Holcot, whose acceptance as a source for *The Nun's Priest's Tale* has been near-universal. Furthermore, as Watts goes on to demonstrate, Chaucer's representation of philosophizing clerks in his works reveals that the poet appears to have taken a dim view of such figures of contemporary life, whom he tends to portray as either devious or irrelevant. This, Watts finally suggests, should give us pause as we try to relate the poet to the philosophical disputes of his contemporaries in any direct way, because there may well be more *game* than *ernest* in the poet's response to the *greet disputisouns* of the fourteenth century.

STEPHEN PENN's contribution on 'Literary Nominalism and Medieval Sign Theory' contends that 'nominalism and literature were never parts of a single, seamless discourse and that, therefore, the influences between them would at best have been complex and indirect'. Penn's theoretically oriented essay offers a careful analysis of nominalist sign theory (as exemplified in Ockham's semiological and linguistic theory) which demonstrates the often intractable nature of the subject matter itself, whose recalcitrance to accurate historical analysis, as Penn goes on to show, has given rise to some erroneous assumptions about the relationship between philosophical theory and literary practice in the Middle Ages, yet specifically the inappropriate assumption that Ockham's nominalist language theory can be described in terms of split signs. This, in turn, leads him to conclude that literary nominalism in the Middle Ages need not necessarily be the direct product of contemporary philosophical developments. Rather, he points out, there may have been other influences at work that contributed to such literary developments. Starting from that insight, Penn then proceeds to present the case for an alternative methodology which would take into account other possible sources than nominalist philosophy in order to explain ambiguity, linguistic play and suchlike symptoms of 'nominalist' tendencies in late-medieval literature. As conceivable alternatives to a sceptical nominalism, we are invited to consider certain 'subversive' developments in late-medieval rhetoric, and even sceptical realism which, paradoxically, might have given rise to developments that could be seen as expressions of *literary* nominalism. In conclusion, Penn suggests that Wyclif's writings, for instance, might provide an indication of how the precepts of nominalism could be exploited and exaggerated by its opponents.

Thus, by attending to works of this kind, 'we should feel better prepared, both from a theoretical, and from a literary-historical point of view, to speculate about the effects of nominalism on literary practice'.

WILLIAM F. MUNSON's essay on 'Self, Action, and Sign in the Towneley and York Plays on the Baptism of Christ' straddles the line between cultural expressions that are generally perceived as 'late-medieval' and developments that might well be classed as 'early modern'. Throughout the Middle Ages, as Munson points out, the baptism of Christ by John was a richly cultivated locus for the topic of humble service, which was also fundamental to religious definitions of man as creature of God and sinner in the process of salvation. Against this background, then, the two mystery plays he discusses acquire considerable significance in the present context. Munson develops his argument from a close analysis of characterization, action, spectacle and other stylistic resources in order to demonstrate that the Towneley play constructs an importantly different relation of self to others and to God from that of York. In particular, John the Baptist's conception as a dramatic figure and its underlying notions of selfhood and individuality in the two plays are shown to differ in highly significant ways, and such differences are further underscored through Towneley's use of localized, interactive signs, which results from its understanding of sacraments as contingent vehicles—signs—that are used in interactions, rather than as realist vessels for universals. In a parallel move, Munson contextualizes such differences in philosophical nominalism, especially of the Ockhamist theological wing, which are shown to provide discursive context for Towneley's emphasis on concrete localization and the positive, active role for man in an interactive salvation process. Simultaneously, though, such discursive backgrounds can also be used to explain that cycle's specific type of dramatic causality and its characterization of John as autonomous and reflexive individual, and this in turn helps to locate its accommodation of the play's psychological action. Thus, the Ockhamist theologians of the *via moderna* are shown to supply a rationale not only for Towneley's distinctive thematic emphasis on man's role in salvation, but for a dramatic form, too, which makes distinctive contribution to an early modern selfhood. It is in exemplary ways, then, that Munson's essay demonstrates how links, even direct links, between philosophical nominalism and literary discourse can be established in a convincing manner—without losing sight, that is, of literature's distinctive modes of discursive expression.

ULLRICH LANGER's paper on 'Charity and the Singular: The Object of Love in Rabelais' once more takes us on an excursion into French literature. At the core of his essay, as Langer points out, is the problem of individuality and its literary representation which, in the final analysis, can be seen as a problem of literary mimesis. Langer starts off by demonstrating that the relationship of charity, as defined by Rabelais's contemporary

Erasmus and the evangelical humanists in general, presupposes a 'realist' perspective on the understanding of the love of one person for another. In that view, when you love an individual, you love her or him fundamentally as a creature of God, i.e. as a member constituting the body of Christ. It follows that when you love a sinner, you do not love that sinner because of the fact that he or she sinned, but because he or she is a creature of God. Hence, a sinner—say, an infidel or an adulterer—can be hated or even killed, yet not *qua* creature of God but only as infidel or adulterer, for in this case that person is not seen under the light of sameness that charity sheds equally on all of God's creatures. Recent Rabelais criticism, Langer goes on to argue, has insisted with some justification on the central role that Christian charity plays in the evangelical thematics of *Pantagruel* and *Gargantua*, as well as on the notion that the Rabelaisian fictional universe is one governed by the relationship of charity. It is against this background, then, that Langer sets out to show that it is precisely the realist perspective on charity which the narrative of Pantagruel's and Panurge's relationship refuses. For in order to understand Pantagruel's love of Panurge, he argues, we must understand not the nature of Christian love, or the essence of either Pantagruel or Panurge as creatures of God, but instead we must perceive *this* character, Pantagruel, in his singularity, and *this* character Panurge, in his singularity, and take notice of the great love of the giant Pantagruel for the trickster Panurge. In other words, by far the most likely interpretation of that relationship is that it is precisely the singular nature of Panurge that provokes the often excessive love of Pantagruel. Concluding his observations, Langer points out that charity is an inherently *mimetic* relationship, and that this is again both suggested and refused in these works of Rabelais. That observation, though, leads to a troubling question: 'if love in the Rabelaisian context absolutely refuses the copying of the other that is the model of charity; i.e., if love is the action of one singular on another singular, how can one then love *oneself?*'

As one moves into the Renaissance, different contexts than the background of scholasticism, obviously, gain in importance for the study of nominalism, in literature and elsewhere. WILLIAM C. CARROLL draws an intriguing sketch of one such background in his perceptive analysis of 'semiotic slippage' in the Tudor authorities' attempts (and continual adjustments of such attempts) to mark and banish vagabonds, yet specifically the so-called 'sturdy beggar'. And this context, of course, is of considerable importance in relation to contemporary literary discourse as well. Carroll finds his point of departure in Foucault's *Discipline and Punish*, which describes an elaborate theory of 'penal semiotics', but which also observes that the necessary presence of an audience—at whom all the juridical signs were pointed—guaranteed the subversion of the regime's semiotic intentions. In Tudor England, Carroll goes on to argue, we witness precisely the same dialectic in what can be fairly described as a 'war of signs' which the various organs of local and national government waged against the country's vagrants and criminals before the 'audience' of the general populace. It is in this context, then, that the figure of the vagrant or 'sturdy beggar' acquired special significance, for a sturdy beggar was by definition a paradox of deceit: not a real beggar—stricken by disease or mischance—but a man or woman whose body was whole and unmarked who 'counterfeits' disease and mutilation in order to escape detection, evade work, and prey upon our sympathies. However, the sturdy beggar also represented a particularly subversive threat to the prevailing ideology of authority because his actual physical wandering replicated his destabilized social position; in a world in which, ideally, identity and relationship were constituted and fixed within a hierarchy, the vagrant thus became a chief instance of disorder of all kinds. Finally, since the sturdy vagrant was understood to be a virtuoso of histrionics, a master dissembler, he also served to expose the signifier/signified relation in the realm of status as something constructed rather than 'natural'. Drawing on historical and literary evidence, Carroll demonstrates that the ideology of order and authority engaged in various futile efforts to recuperate a purity of signification, always pitted against (and lagging behind) the vagrants' enactment of what Baudrillard's distinction differentiates as 'dissimulation' and 'simulation'. This led to paradoxical results: the more strenuously civil authorities attempted to control the means and methods of social signification, the more slippage there was, for in the case of judicial markings of beggars' bodies, the actors themselves either refused to cooperate, or rewrote the scripts altogether, thus demonstrating a sophisticated, ultimately subversive understanding of the cultural codes of punishment. Therefore, Carroll concludes, 'no program of semiotic confinement succeeded, or could succeed, in the English Renaissance'.

In an attempt to define aspects of a semiotics implicit in early modern stage representations of character, JAMES R. SIEMON combines methods of textual and dramaturgical analysis with terms and arguments derived from the work of two thinkers who stand at either end of modern European social analysis—Francis Bacon and Pierre Bourdieu. Specifically, Siemon's study on 'Sign, Cause, or General Habit?' focuses on William Shakespeare's highly stylized characterization of King Richard III, which is considered in the light of recurrent themes in the historical debates between nominalism and realism while, on the other hand, it is read against the background of Bacon's essay 'Of Deformity' and of Bourdieu's arguments for a social analysis that would transcend nominalist/realist oppositions in describing agency and identity. Siemon's analysis of *Richard III* demonstrates that the modes of realist iconism (as instanced by the emphasis given to the meaning of Richard's various deformities) and nominalist semiotic voluntarism (as exemplified in the self-conscious theatricalism of Richard and others who repeatedly 'counterfeit') are both contained within the play's representation of a larger matrix of culturally produced schemata that organize action and perception. Comparing Bacon's employment of the term 'general habit' to Shakespeare's treatment of Richard's social environment, both of which, in turn, he places in relation to Pierre Bourdieu's notion of 'habitus', Siemon concludes that the signs of such shared 'substantial' identity are everywhere apparent in *Richard III*, with virtually everyone sharing aspects of Richard's ostensibly individualizing characteristics.

In recent times, Michel Foucault's semiologically oriented account of a Renaissance *episteme* in *Les mots et les choses* has been one of the most influential reformulations of the premodern analogical world-view. ANDREAS MAHLER's essay on Don Quixote, Hamlet, Foucault, and 'the losses of analogism' begins with a concise outline and critique of Foucault's version of a Renaissance semiotics and proceeds to modify it by taking into closer account the roles of subject and language in the early modern acquisition of 'truth'. Mahler goes on to illustrate the epistemological function of language by giving a non-literary example, Thomas Drant's and John Dryden's respective attempts to define the word and thing 'satire'. His comparison shows that Dryden, as opposed to Drant, is obsessed with the correct etymology, the 'true' origin of the word and thing 'satire', in order to fix it eternally in a system of identities and differences. This, Mahler argues, also explains why Dryden is no longer occupied with the question of what satire is *like*, as Drant was, but with what it *is*. Turning to Cervantes's *Don Quixote* and Shakespeare's *Hamlet*, Mahler then demonstrates that both of these texts explicitly thematize the losses of analogism—*Don Quixote* by placing an analogist character in an open world, *Hamlet* by confronting analogical inauthenticity with a scepticist subject. He concludes that Don Quixote still uses language to build up a providentialist universe, but that the truth he finds remains unratified by his surroundings, whereas Hamlet explicitly discards the topical knowledge of similitude in order to find truth outside language, in empirical evidence. Looking back at 'the passing era of analogism', and foreshadowing 'the new age of transparency', both texts thus thematize the slow but conclusive early modern epistemological 'death' of language. The essay ends with a brief look at the early modern question of 'realism' vs. 'nominalism' and the divergent histories of England and Spain after *Hamlet* and *Don Quixote*. Thus, Mahler not only highlights an issue—analogism—which both Penn and Courtenay define as a promising area for the study of literary nominalism, but he also provides revealing insights into what 'nominalism', 'realism', 'transparency' and suchlike concepts may mean for a seventeenth- and perhaps even an eighteenth-century context. It is through studies like this, then, that we should eventually arrive at a more accurate estimate of how realist and nominalist orientations evolved over the centuries, as well as within different cultural contexts.

SUSANNE FENDLER rounds off our Renaissance 'section' by taking a close look at the changing meaning and significance of beauty in English Renaissance romances, specifically in a tradition or sub-genre which was initiated by Sir Philip Sidney's new *Arcadia* and found its continuation in various seventeenth-century imitations of and variations on that 'prototype'. Fendler's comparison of these texts shows that the development of this particular generic tradition led to ever more radical re-evaluations and, finally, to a complete dismantling of the original, conventionalized semiotics of beauty, which can be observed as still largely 'intact' in Sidney's text. Such developments, Fendler argues, might be seen as related to the introduction of individualized characters, and generally of the idea of the individual, into the texts scrutinized, for any such tendencies would presuppose that beauty be freed from its religious associations. Hence, what started off with a comparatively firm belief in a significance of beauty that stretches beyond mere external, earthly beauty, is seen to end with a clear emphasis on external appearance alone, at the expense of whatever may lie beyond. In a sense, then, and in a secularized context, the evolutionary dynamics described here would seem to replay, from almost square one, a development that had already taken place, in not entirely dissimilar ways, about a century earlier, in the mystery pageants discussed in William Munson's essay.

This leaves two more contributions, both of which aim to point up the still unabated relevance of the 'historical' debate over universals. In the context of the present collection, therefore, they can be read as attempts to negotiate the gap between Renaissance developments and the contemporary situation. In his essay on 'Locke and the Tradition of Nominalism', NICHOLAS HUDSON observes that Locke was an important bridge between the past and the future because, until this century, he was among the last philosophers to deal explicitly with the scholastic problem of universals. At the same time, he was also widely recognized by later philosophers of the Enlightenment as the figure who had launched a new and vigorous movement in the study of language, thus inaugurating, as it were, the 'linguistic turn' of the Enlightenment. Strangely, Locke's background in the tradition of nominalism has been little studied because, as Hudson points out, philosophers have considered his linguistic thought almost solely in the light of twentieth-century developments. Hudson, therefore, begins by placing Locke in a tradition of nominalist thought leading from Ockham to Hobbes, whom he regards as a major predecessor to Locke in the development of nominalist theories. However, Locke's insistence that our general ideas, formed by the mind, only vaguely reflect the real (and inaccessible) order of nature, led him further down the road of scepticism than either Ockham or Hobbes. This, Hudson argues, is of major and largely unrecognised significance, for Locke's position in that point does not seem consistent with the modern reading of Locke as a 'mentalist' who insisted on the absolute independence and primacy of mental discourse. In the final part of his essay, Hudson goes on to examine how Locke's thought inspired a wave of interest in general terms and in the interrelations between language and reason. The pivotal figure here is Condillac, who went much further even than Locke in questioning the existence of species and genera. The legacy of Condillac, in turn, is shown to have been a seminal influence on the *idéologues* of the early nineteenth-century, as well as on linguistic thought in Germany, as exemplified in Süssmilch, Herder, and Wilhelm von Humboldt. It is here, in fact, that Hudson locates 'the flourishing heritage of the nominalist tradition'. But it was Locke 'who opened a debate on the relationship between language and thought, and on the nature of universals, that still continues today'.

Last but not least, CHRISTOPH BODE's deftly dialectical argument in 'A Modern Debate over Universals?' seeks to bridge the ostensible chasm between the contemporary situation and the medieval beginnings of the debate. Bode starts off by suggesting that today's critical altercations between what might be termed 'essentialist' approaches to the meaning of texts, on the one hand, and a 'rainbow coalition' of 'anti-essentialist' orientations that can be lumped together under the tag of 'critical theory', on the other hand, could be seen as a replay of sorts of the realist vs. nominalist controversy of the European Middle Ages. In view of the 'conspicuous structural analogies' he uncovers between the two debates, Bode asks: 'Can we learn something from history?' His answer is in the affirmative because, as he goes on to show, each of the apparently incompatible positions of realism/essentialism and nominalism/anti-essentialism can not only be said to have 'swallowed up its opposite', but to have been 'inwardly taken over by its Other', thus 'allowing its parasite discourse to influence if not govern its metabolism and critical practice'. The meaning and message we may derive from history, Bode concludes, is 'that our critical discourses are defined by the way in which they take cognizance of the share of the Other in themselves, thus acknowledging the reciprocal containment and preservation of the submerged Other'.

As this brief survey demonstrates, the present collection provides a considerable range of perspectives on a variety of aspects and topics that may be safely associated with literary nominalism/realism. Within the limits we have set ourselves, moreover, as wide as possible a ground has been covered in terms of literary genres, discursive contexts, and historical developments. At the same time, there is a common focus of interest not just in so far as attention is chiefly directed towards the literary, discursive dimension of our problematic, but also in that virtually all of the essays offer 'localized' readings of nominalism and realism by providing 'snapshots' of phenomena and cultural moments whose significance in the given context is amply substantiated. Thus, even though at present we may not yet fully understand the overall historical 'script' and 'plotlines' which such particularized cultural processes are parts of—mainly, we would submit, because it is still too early for any successful attempts to give a synthetic overview of that kind—the frameworks developed for the textual analysis and historical description of literary nominalism/realism do suggest viable ways in that direction.

In other words, what this volume attempts is not to write *the* 'story' of literary nominalism and realism—be it for the 'transitional era' from Medieval to Early Modern that has been our main concern, or for European intellectual history at large—but to take the necessary first steps towards the construction of that particular 'history' by breaking it down into several 'stories': of varying discourses and literary genres, traditions and conventions, as well as of their intricate transactions with one another. Still, it may happen that certain overarching patterns of change, perhaps even of historical evolution, begin to suggest themselves to the reader. If so, so much the better! We would nonetheless warn against jumping to conclusions, as further investigations might yet lead to discoveries that could affect any such assumed outcome, but in fact any inclusive pictures that might be seen to emerge from our arguments. What seems fairly predictable even now, though, is that such findings will be at odds, in part at least, with most accounts that have so far been given. For the history of literary nominalism (and realism) seems anything but a foregone conclusion, nor does it appear to have followed any definitive patterns of historical development, still less any directional or linear evolutionary dynamics that would tend towards supreme nominalist ascendancy. On the contrary, that particular story might rather give the impression of having been a tortuously intricate dialectical process that is in many ways contingent, but possibly altogether haphazard. In point of fact, it may eventually turn out that its underlying dynamics of change can be better understood if it is cast in terms of chaos theory and other recent theories of complexity,[142] rather than of prevalent teleological models of historical evolution, which would appear to follow mainly the script of 'Progress' so many of us have all too willingly succumbed to in the past.

Our collection, then, is clearly not intended to supply ready-made solutions to our issues, and even less to foreclose discussion about literary no-

---

[142]For applications of chaos theory and related theories of non-linear or self-organizing systems to cultural and literary studies, see e.g. Eve Tavor Bannet, *Postcultural Theory: Critical Theory after the Marxist Paradigm* (London: Macmillan, 1993), 192f., and N. Katherine Hayles, *Chaos Bound: Orderly Disorder in Contemporary Literature and Science* (Ithaca, NY: Cornell University Press, 1990). For useful general introductions, see James Gleick, *Chaos: Making a New Science* (New York: Viking, 1987), and Edward Lorenz, *The Essence of Chaos* (1993; repr. Seattle, WA: University of Washington Press, 1995).

minalism and its history. Indeed, it might rather be read as an invitation to reconsider and re-engage with these issues that seeks to encourage further research in that area. Such research might well include a close, critical sifting of available literary and cultural studies, as much of what is already 'known' about some of the phenomena discussed may certainly acquire a fresh kind of significance against the background provided, and might thus be seen to fall into place in a critical paradigm whose ultimate aim could be described as an attempt to relate and synthesize certain crucial aspects of literary semiosis which, as often as not, have been looked at as largely unconnected so far. In that sense, we would suggest, the notions and terms 'literary nominalism' and 'realism' should rather be taken as key concepts that would help us to define and address such fundamental problems of literary discourse, and to observe them with greater clarity of focus, but not as offering by themselves clear-cut answers to any such questions. It will be a rewarding task, therefore, to further develop the solutions proposed in this volume and, if possibe, to find even better ones. In doing so, future research may be able to open up yet other exciting perspectives upon the history of literary semiotics, and generally the development of literary aesthetics, in an important area that has somewhat escaped the attention of critics for a long time.

SIGNS OF A NEW LITERARY PARADIGM:
THE 'CHRISTIAN' FIGURES OF CHRÉTIEN DE TROYES

GERALD SEAMAN

In the opening lines of the prologue to *Le Conte du graal*, Chrétien de Troyes invokes the biblical parable of the sower as a kind of literary, historical and poetic emblem. This ostensibly 'Christian' figure has mystified interpreters to the point of generating a polarization of opinions on its author's purpose and intention. On the one hand, there are those such as Holmes and Klenke, whose work contends that the prologue reveals Chrétien as a 'Christian poet' bent on writing an 'allegorical tale with a serious moral, filled with the popular liturgical symbolism of the day and calculated thereby to please Philip of Flanders',[1] himself a Crusader who died overseas. On the other hand, there is Tony Hunt, who believes there is nothing particularly religious about Chrétien's opening verses and that 'Chrétien's prologue remains solely an encomium of Philip and exemplifies the Ciceronian method of obtaining the *benevolentia* of the audience by the *ab iudicum persona* approach'.[2]

Our understanding of this prologue, then, is bounded by two mutually exclusive views which either reduce Chrétien de Troyes to a simple servant of his feudal patron or raise him to the idealized ranks of those who serve the Christian God. It is my contention, however, that this opposition is unnecessary, and that it results from a false assumption about paradigms of medieval vernacular literature. Indeed, by obliging Chrétien's text and its guiding principles to conform to discourses of authority from other and past cultures, the positions given above necessarily presuppose a fundamental paradigmatic incoherence for Old French romance, one which compels the reader to buttress interpretation with the structural overlays of the Church or rhetorical tradition. As the Hunt-Holmes/Klenke case shows, although romance composition staged itself against rhetorical and

---

[1] Urban Tigner Holmes and Sister M. Amelia Klenke, O.P., *Chrétien, Troyes, and the Grail* (Chapel Hill, NC: University of North Carolina Press, 1959), 91-2.

[2] Tony Hunt, 'The Prologue to Chrestien's *Li Contes del Graal*', *Romania*, 92 (1971), 362-79.

exegetical backdrops, these settings can in fact impose restrictive hermeneutic limits on researchers. Followed too closely, they distract us from what is most important: the cultural and poetic context of vernacular writing itself. As Chrétien de Troyes was not a theologian, nor a rhetorician, but rather a poet, there is ample justification for this point of departure. From *Erec et Enide* to *Le Conte du graal*, the prologues to his works convincingly demonstrate that he was concerned with establishing a new literary paradigm, not with perpetuating or mimicking others. For these reasons, I maintain that Chrétien, preoccupied with his status as a vernacular poet in a world of competing and contingent literary modes, deployed his Christian figures as part of an attempt to secure paradigmatic identity for his work and for romance authorship in general. In this setting, therefore, the rhetorical and poetic features of his prologues are to be read as culturally encoded poetic phenomena that did not remain passively beholden to discourses of former authority, but that rather challenged them. In so doing, Chrétien gave voice and form to early medieval romance production, elevating Old French fiction beyond art and performance into the realm of what would become the immutable, integral and historically valid written text.

Paradigms of Authorship: Jongleuresque and Romanesque

While it is extremely likely that Chrétien de Troyes was a Christian, and it is certain that he wrote under the patronage of Philip of Flanders, it is not, however, necessary that either dedication to God or subordination to the Count compelled him to be an author. With an extant corpus dating from approximately 1170 to 1190, a period of emerging literacy and evolving textual communities,[3] Chrétien wrote at a time when the intellectual climate of France stood on the brink of Aristotelianism, but still retained a mixture of Augustinian realism and the conceptualist-nominalism of Abelard. Obviously well-educated and well-read, and perhaps a member of minor orders, Chrétien has left us only conjecture for his biography. Concerning his works, however, the seminal writings of F. Douglas Kelly have thoroughly explored and impressively elucidated the link between romance composition and medieval arts of poetry.[4] Without ignoring this link, or Professor Kelly's magisterial scholarship, I propose to examine in this first section the question of authorship in early medieval romance according to the following conceptual model: Supported by Zumthor, and

---

[3]Brian Stock, 'History, Literature, and Medieval Textuality', in Kevin Brownlee and Stephen G. Nichols (eds.), *Images of Power: Medieval History/Discourse/Literature* (special issue of *Yale French Studies*, 70 (1986)), 10-2.

[4]Cf. most recently, F. Douglas Kelly, *The Art of Medieval French Romance* (Madison, WI: University of Wisconsin Press, 1992).

at least some of the suggestive conclusions of oral-formulaic theory,[5] this model conceives of 'authorship' in twelfth-century literary culture as a phenomenon that crossed boundaries of the oral and the written (and hence of the literate and illiterate). Though it greatly expands the field of inquiry, such a conception has a specific functional merit in that it permits the community of twelfth-century authors to express a level of complexity that was once evidently original to it, even if it is only partially communicated in the textual testimonials of the period. Given this complexity, when one makes conceptual allowance for a literary environment that is free of modern assumptions that arrogate the title of authorship to the 'written' work alone, the specifically medieval and innovative character of Chrétien's writing comes to the foreground, and in this light the impetus behind his poetic project becomes all the more necessary, urgent and compelling.

To treat authorship in the twelfth century as an authentically medieval *episteme* is to acknowledge a cultural context that is, for modern readers, by no means fixed in texts or already known because of them. Indeed, to the extent that it can be localized as part of a medieval textual legacy, the sustained enigma of authorship expresses itself in romance composition as both a mediation of a textual past and as a reaction to a literary present where vernacular transmission and reception are commonly associated with the oral activity of the jongleur. This erstwhile literary paradigm is known to us only by means of authorial inscription, perhaps self-conscious, of a system of inter-modal (oral vs. written) cooperations and contingencies, rivalries and competitions. Zumthor's opposition between *texte* and *œuvre* is descriptive of this system in medieval literary culture, and it challenges the certainty of purely textual interpretation by asking us to acknowledge that the objects of our study have been effectively stripped of many layers of their signifying substance (specifically those pertaining to the sight, sound and feel of literary performance).[6] As Zumthor claims, 'chaque performance [était] une œuvre d'art unique dans l'opération de la voix' (ibid., 269), and the authentically medieval expression of these individual works is therefore irretrievable. Nevertheless, signs of such expressions are clearly latent in early medieval romance prologues (and elsewhere), and they are especially evident in texts whose authors depict conflicting performative scenarios as a cause for reflection, mediation, and concern.

The first of these scenarios generally involves texts or stories that have become the instruments of the jongleur who, through an application of his 'comportement global' (ibid., 272), constitutes himself as a system of signs, a physical matrix through which the text or story, in the totality of

---

[5]Cf. Albert B. Lord, *The Singer of Tales* (Cambridge, MA, and London: Harvard University Press, 1960).
[6]Paul Zumthor, *La lettre et la voix* (Paris: Editions du Seuil, 1987), 246.

its signifying structure, must pass (ibid., 256). The second concerns the relationship between author, text and reader. This scenario differs from that of the jongleur to the extent that the 'gestus' (ibid., 272) of the performance is mediated by a text that endeavors to communicate an author's presence, and, consequently, his purpose, message and indeed even his property. An attempt to create a complete aesthetic experience without third party intervention, this literary gesture finds the author conceiving of the written word as autonomous unto itself, a signifier that discovers its property and identity at the level of its form: the letter, transcribed on parchment.[7] In this case, even as it assures, through the jongleur, the accomplishment of the aesthetic experience in the first scenario, *œuvre* presumes a disruption of the autonomy of *texte*, and seems to allow it to be wrenched away from its original voice and appropriated by another. The author in the second scenario, then, must assert himself as someone who is able to recognize (even facilitate) these modalities of performance and at the same time to overcome them, almost to the point of erasing the performer from the stage.[8] In this operation, *texte* would finally become marked with the echoes of an historical consciousness.[9]

---

[7]For more on this concept and Chrétien, see Sandra Hindman, *Sealed in Parchment: Rereadings of Knighthood in the Illuminated Manuscripts of Chrétien de Troyes* (Chicago, IL: University of Chicago Press, 1994).

[8]On these points, see Paul Saenger, 'Silent Reading: Its Impact on Late Medieval Script and Society', *Viator*, 13 (1982), 367-414; Martin Stevens, 'The Performing Self in Twelfth-Century Culture', *Viator*, 9 (1978), 193-212; Evelyn Birge Vitz, 'Chrétien de Troyes: Cler ou ménestrel. Problèmes des traditions orale et littéraire dans les cours de France au XIIe siècle', *Poétique*, 8 (1990), 23-42; and Joseph P. Duggan, 'Oral Performance of Romance in Medieval France', in Norris J. Lacy and Gloria Torrini-Roblin (eds.), *Continuations: Essays on Medieval French Literature and Language in Honor of John L. Grigsby* (Birmingham, AL: Summa Publications, 1989), 51-61.

[9]See Hans-Georg Gadamer, *Truth and Method*, tr. Garret Barden and William G. Doerpel (New York: Seabury Press, 1975). For Gadamer, this is the essence of historical consciousness: the self finds itself in history as a product of this same history. History, however, is not conceived of as a series of individual events with fixed meanings supposed to speak to every generation with univocality. It is rather a chain of discourses, a multiplicity of voices and tones, which surrounds events in an effort to situate their significance in relation to other events which are dependent on discourse as well. As an individual with historical consciousness, one attains primarily an apprehension of the past through the memory of an other. This apprehension is necessarily incomplete, since one can never assume the aspect of the other in an immediate way. It is interesting to note, nevertheless, that reception of the other, for Gadamer, is in a way a product of his speech. He writes, 'historical consciousness is always filled with a variety of *voices* in which the echo of the past is *heard*' (252, emphasis added). To the extent that it is 'spoken', the past, therefore, is a kind of imperfectly formed presence, resonating like echoes in the ears of the historically conscious, necessarily incomplete but nevertheless granted the status of information which influences our knowledge of our own present.

And, for writerly romance, these echoes would implicitly acknowledge that literacy supersedes the modalities of a performance whose temporality is finite since, although a method of transmitting *œuvre*, it cannot guard it from the flow of time, nor rescue it from the vicissitudes of memory.

Knowing this, the modern reader must accept without hesitation the disappearance of what Zumthor calls *le poème*: 'le texte (et, le cas échéant, la mélodie) de 'l'œuvre', sans considération des autres facteurs de la performance',[10] that system of performative order and structure never expressed in writing. A fundamental question to address in Chrétien and in early medieval romance generally, then, is the following: How did these authors mediate the *texte-œuvre* dichotomy of their culture and so establish authorship as a value prevailing in writing even as their epoch waned and the 'texte de l'œuvre' disappeared? Historical distance may hinder, rather than help, in our answer. For, in retrospect, we know that although the *poèmes* of Chrétien have slipped the bonds of their original and defining cultural context to join a textual history, their significance, although diminished, has stabilized in time and secured for their author a place in our own traditions. But how did this first occur? Without being overly teleological, one can assert that an elemental gesture in the establishment of the writerly romance paradigm was the insistence on associating texts with authors and names. In modern terms, this may sound remarkably banal, almost naive. But the anachronistic risk here would be to assume a perfect correspondence between this medieval innovation and its commonplace contemporary usage.

For us today, as the name of a producing subject behind a printed work, the author is defined by a reader's system of values, a system that is influenced partly by an author's personal ability, partly by the commercial success of the work on the open market and partly by the social and intellectual success of the work within the reader's cultural sphere. As Michel Foucault puts it, the author's proper name is ultimately situated between the poles of description and designation,[11] each of which operate in the modern world as signs of his monetary and literary worth. Further, for Foucault, the author's name also serves to delimit a certain literary stock. In this way, the proper name has a discursive role.[12] Much of this, as we know, coincides nicely with the extant textual testimony of Chrétien de Troyes. Chrétien 'signs' each of his five romances in a particular way, beginning with *Erec et Enide* where the importance of his signature is underscored by the repetition of Chrétien's name (in full or in part, or as

---

[10]Zumthor, *La lettre et la voix*, 246.

[11]Michel Foucault, 'Qu'est-ce qu'un auteur?', *Bulletin de la Société Française de philosophie*, 63.3 (1969), 81.

[12]Ibid., 83.

part of a pun) in three of the opening 26 lines, including the final line of the prologue ('tant con durra crestïantez'). The author's name is also highlighted in manuscript BN f fr. 1376 by a hand sketched into the margin at line 9 of the *Erec et Enide* prologue, alerting the reader to the importance of identifying Chrétien with the work and of remembering them both as an inseparable unit of literary significance. In Chrétien's second romance, *Cligés,* the classificatory function of the author's name is undeniable. As is well known, in the prologue to this romance Chrétien names himself in line 23 (in four of the six extant *Cligés* manuscripts; there is a seventh, but according to Micha it is severely damaged), but only after providing a list of his works that begins with *Erec et Enide* and includes translations of Ovid and a tale of Mark and Yseut.[13] In the *Chevalier de la Charrette,* Chrétien's name appears in both the prologue and epilogue, with Godefroi de Leigni's deference to the original writer and defense of his poetic charge to *parfaire* a work begun by Chrétien serving to underscore the importance of linking authorial identity and property to textual integrity and perfection. In the *Chevalier au Lion* Chrétien 'signs' his name in the final verses rather than in the prologue. Chrétien, finally, does not fail to 'sign' his *Conte du graal,* either, where he places his name in verses 7 and 62.

Thus, the discursive function of Chrétien's name, and its role in establishing an authorial status for the romance writer, are visibly supported by extant prologue and epilogue manuscript evidence. Indeed, there is no doubt that we can consider Chrétien as engaging in what might be called a poetics of the proper name and so inaugurating Zink's period of literary subjectivity.[14] However, because his works have been distributed, read, and studied within our contemporary system of textual production and intellectual and monetary values, Chrétien's authorship and subjectivity risk being all too easily misunderstood.[15] For Foucault's question 'Qu'est-ce qu'un auteur?' also carries with it a set of psychological and psychologizing overtones that are indicative of modern prejudices about the status and meaning of the author's proper name. In fact, as literary scholars have looked at the Middle Ages, they have typically resolved the question 'What is an author?' by naming an example: Chrétien de Troyes. And, according to 'rules of the game' common to the biobibliographical strand of criticism, the original question ('What is an

---

[13]Cf. Michelle A. Freeman, *The Poetics of 'Translatio Studii' and 'Conjointure': Chrétien de Troyes'* Cligés (Lexington, KY: French Forum Publishers, 1979).

[14]See Michel Zink, 'Une mutation de la conscience littéraire: Le langage romanesque à travers des exemples français du XIIe siècle', *Cahiers de Civilisation Médiévale,* 24 (1981), 3-27; and *De la subjectivité littéraire* (Paris: Presses Universitaires de France, 1985).

[15]Cf. David F. Hult, 'Reading it Right: The Ideology of Text Editing', *Romanic Review,* 79 (1988), 74-88.

author?') has therefore traditionally been reformulated as 'Who is Chrétien de Troyes?'

Recalling Zumthor, however, who referred to authorship as 'an organization of forms',[16] and who reiterated the difficulties of recovering across vast historical space an authentic image of the author in the twelfth century,[17] one could argue that the attempt to identify Chrétien *the man* with and from his *work*[18] has participated (ironically) in a process of fragmenting and fracturing rather than assembling and completing his portrait. Indeed, from idealized psychologies to imagined identities of Chrétien, the question 'Who is Chrétien de Troyes?' has elicited an anthropomorphic fantasy that personifies internal evidence and literary testimony. Rather than impose authority and property on his text, then, Chrétien's name has been passed down to us as little more than a moniker for an insubstantial hybrid form: a great poet of high genius, a converted Jew, a world traveler, a herald at arms, a servant of the church, or a canon of a medieval abbey—which one of these, if any, was Chrétien?[19] Still, such an eclectic gallery of portraits, even in its potential inaccuracy, bespeaks the enduring power of Chrétien's name and might even suggest that our poet was aware of the historical effects of willfully and visibly resisting anonymity. For Foucault, indeed, such anonymity would signal the absence of an author.[20] In Chrétien's case, this potential absence seems to have been operative in his poetics, and he seems to have forecast the profound cultural impact of attribution even from a context where lack of an authorial name was commonplace in written works.

Realism, Nominalism and Literary Culture

The concept of literary subjectivity nonetheless goes beyond the borders of the simple authorial name.[21] As Zink's model makes clear, authorship

---

[16]Paul Zumthor, *Speaking of the Middle Ages*, tr. Sarah White (Lincoln, NE, and London: University of Nebraska Press, 1986), 61.

[17]Ibid., 60-1.

[18]Cf. Jean Frappier, *Chrétien de Troyes: l'homme et l'œuvre* (Paris: Hatier-Boivin, 1957).

[19]Cf. Foster Erwin Guyer, *Chrétien de Troyes: Inventor of the Modern Novel* (New York: Bookman Associates, 1957), 16-21; Urban Tigner Holmes, *Chrétien de Troyes* (New York: Twayne Publishers, 1970), 22-5; Gaston Paris, '[Cligés]', in Mario Roques (ed.), *Mélanges de littérature française du moyen âge*, 2 vols. (Paris: Champion, 1912), vol. 1: 252-60; L.T. Topsfield, *Chrétien de Troyes: A Study of the Arthurian Romances* (Cambridge: Cambridge University Press, 1981), 17.

[20]See Foucault, 'Qu'est-ce qu'un auteur?', 83.

[21]Zink, 'Une mutation', 8. When the question of anonymity and romance literary subjectivity arises, Zink resolves it by opposing the culture and education of romance authors to that of authors operating in the oral-aural mode of the *chanson de geste*. The

from Chrétien forward is linked to a specific function: producing a written text with authority, integrity and historicity. Prior to the emergence of vernacular literary subjectivity, however, these attributes of authorship were the exclusive domain of the *auctor*, 'someone who was at once a writer and an authority, someone not merely to be read but also to be respected and believed'.[22] Moreover, '[t]he writings of an *auctor* contained, or possessed, *auctoritas* in the abstract sense of the term, with its strong connotations of veracity and sagacity. In the specific sense, an *auctoritas* was a quotation or an extract from the work of an *auctor*' (ibid.). We should remember, however, that *auctor* was a posthumous title, one 'bestowed upon a popular writer by those later scholars and writers who used extracts from his works as sententious statements or *auctoritates*, gave lectures on his works in the form of textual commentaries, or employed them as literary models' (ibid.). In this respect, medieval romance authorship and the activity of the *auctor* are distinct both in terms of their historical status and in terms of their place in intellectual tradition.

Though they are not *auctores* per se, romance composers like Chrétien can be said to establish an historical link between modern and medieval notions of authorship on the level of their personal investment in the written text. As we have seen, the first stage of this investment is the insistence on attribution. Recalling the *texte-œuvre* dichotomy, however, I would like to emphasize that the historicity of romance is a secondary effect of a more basic poetic gesture that one might call the poetics of exclusion and whose purpose is to redefine the values of twelfth-century literary culture according to the notions of the inviolability and immutability of the poetic word. In this connection, early medieval romance and Chrétien's literary project situate themselves within the limits of a greater medieval inquiry on universals and find a certain affinity with Abelard's conceptualist-nominalism. Though an admirer of Plato and Augustine, Abelard shaped a critique of their concepts of universals that was not unlike Aristotle's critique of his own master, especially to the extent that he considered it impossible for universals to exist as entities separate from and independent of particulars. In theology, Abelard observed, such a realist theory of universals would invite a perverse and, indeed, heretical duplication, insofar as it would require us to conceive of the Trinity as connoting three separate entities rather than expressing the unified and universal concept of one God. To resolve this dilemma, Abelard surmised that the Trinity had no objective existence, but that its status as a universal

---

romans antiques are thus viewed as the work 'sinon d'érudits, du moins de bon latinistes, de traducteurs' while the epic—even if it does refer to a written Latin source—proceeds in a manner that is both 'désinvolte' and 'prolixe'.

[22] Alastair J. Minnis, *Medieval Theory of Authorship: Scholastic Literary Attitudes in the Later Middle Ages* (London: Scolar Press, 1984), 10.

was a function of its expression in words that were in turn mediated by the human mind. Thus, for Abelard the Trinity was an 'abstraction', but not in the Platonic or Augustinian sense whereby its essence dwelled in the realm of the Forms, or in the mind of God. Instead, the words of the Trinity were thought to abstract from their particulars and therefore to express a reference or 'mental image' that was universal, or common to them all. In such wise, Abelard's brand of nominalism concluded that God was a conceptual and linguistic reference that unified for us the separate expressions of the Father, the Son, and the Holy Spirit, assuring for each a unique theological potency without insisting that all three connote individual essences.[23]

Despite this brilliant theological treatment, Abelard's anti-realist philosophy was soon to be eclipsed by Aquinas who, like Aristotle, discovered universals in things rather than in composite reference images or mental existence. Ironically, the realist critique of nominalism, that it proceeded from radical subjectivity rather than common reference, provides insight into what I contend to be its successful incorporation into early medieval romance poetics. For, as Abelard's nominalism supposed that 'there are more true sentences than there are truths'[24] (such that the universal God is not diminished or altered by its multiple enunciations), so too did it assume that all writing conduced to the expression of a unified and perduring verbal presence outside of and independent from things. On a personal level, Abelard made this clear in a letter to his son Astralabius:[25]

> Qui pereunt in se, vivunt per scripta poetae
> Quam natura negat, vita per ista manet.
> Per famam vivit defuncto corpore doctus
> Et plus natura philosophia potest.
>
> [Those who perish in themselves live on through the writings of poets
> As nature denies, life through that abides.
> Through report the learned man lives with a dead body,
> And philosophy is able to do more than nature.]

---

[23] For selections from Abelard's work in English, see *Abelard's Christian Theology*, tr. J. Ramsey McCallum (Oxford: Blackwell, 1948). I have also found the entries on 'Abelard' (Thomas Gilby, O.P.), 'Medieval Philosophy' (Desmond Paul Henry) and 'Universals' (A.D. Woozley) in *The Encyclopedia of Philosophy*, 8 vols., ed. Paul Edwards (1967; repr. New York: Macmillan, and London: Collier Macmillan, 1972) to be very useful.

[24] Calvin G. Normore, 'The Tradition of Mediaeval Nominalism', in John F. Wippel (ed.), *Studies in Medieval Philosophy* (Studies in Philosophy and the History of Philosophy, 17) (Washington, DC: Catholic University of America Press, 1987), 207.

[25] Quoted in Ernst Robert Curtius, *European Literature and the Latin Middle Ages*, tr. Willard R. Trask (Bollingen Series, 36) (Princeton, NJ: Princeton University Press, 1983), 477. The translation from Latin to English is my own.

Ostensibly a theory of universals based on words, Abelard's nominalism, here expressed in human terms, founds itself in this letter not simply on enunciations, but on *written text*—the 'scripta poetae'—and in so doing could be said to obviate the realist critique by fixing common references in cultural artifacts rather than solely in individual mental existence. Although, for philosophy, this move toward textuality does not suffice to eliminate the arbitrary and subjective nature of these enunciations (text must still pass through the mind), it does, for poetry, establish an epistemological basis that associates truth with text and text with history and authorial legacy.

Abelard's conceptualist-nominalism, therefore, is a project that can be said to support the 'truth' of fiction rather than the truth of philosophy. Since, in this system, words, as universals, do not create or refer to entities outside of the mind or the text, they are indeed of most beneficial service to the poet's imagination. In fact, with nominalist poetics, referents can be created freely, without the burden of connoting entities but only mental references. The consequences for fiction are tremendous. If the illusion of truth must only maintain itself in verbum, not in factum, its very mode of expression guarantees that illusion and makes it self-authenticating. As Abelard's letter (perhaps unintentionally) makes clear, verbum expresses truth in and through the mind of the reader. And, as long as there are readers, that truth should prevail at some level in the material essence of the text, lasting well beyond (and indeed in spite of) the author's or his subject's historical presence.

The 'scripta poetae' of Abelard, however, assume a textually-based epistemological tradition in Latin that had yet to gain currency in the literary culture of the Old French vernacular, though it existed and was recognized by writers of early medieval romance, especially Chrétien de Troyes.[26] In order to establish its own preeminence in the complex literary climate of the twelfth century, romance had to create a self-perpetuating epistemology for its fictions and its texts. It did so by playing off Abelard's nominalism to create a poetics of authorship and exclusion that asserted the historical and intellectual prominence of *texte*. In a first gesture, romance utilized the prologue to introduce its author, thereby excluding the jongleur from the stage and creating the potential for a complete aesthetic experience free of performative intervention. On this point, there is ample testimony both in romance prologues and in rhetorical tradition. Writers as early as Evanthius acknowledged that in the prologue 'it is

---

[26]For more, cf. R. Howard Bloch, 'Genealogy as Medieval Mental Structure and Textual Form', in *La littérature historiographique des origines à 1500* (= vol. 11/1 of *Grundriß der Romanischen Literaturen des Mittelalters*, eds. Hans Ulrich Gumbrecht et al.) (Heidelberg: Winter, 1986), 135-56.

permissible to say something extrinsic to the argument, addressed to the audience and for the benefit of the poet or the drama or an actor'.[27] Donatus contended that the prologue 'is first speech, so called from Greek *proto logos* ['first word' or 'first speech'] preceding the complication of the plot proper'.[28] Further, the prefatory function of the prologue is outlined in medieval rhetorical tradition dating from Cicero and Quintilian.[29] This moment of the *proto logos* was indeed crucial to the historical development of vernacular literature. For, rather than permit the ensuing verbum to be appropriated by *œuvre*, the author here would deploy his proper name and/or other rhetorical devices to assure that the written work would remain attached to a specific cultural artifact: a manuscript *texte* could thus be proffered as a universal and timeless nominalist reference, abstracted from the particulars of an author (such as Chrétien, the man) and yet independent of his life. In the end, the nominalist insistence that universals were to be found in mental images (preserved by texts) rather than in physical entities served a fruitful poetic purpose in that it established the historicity of the written work and of its author and thereby guaranteed for both a quality of timelessness not found in *œuvre* and hitherto absent from Old French literary culture.

The poetics of exclusion and authorship were practiced with great skill by Chrétien de Troyes in each of his five Arthurian romances. In verses that have been cited in support of a variety of claims on Chrétien's authorship, Chrétien delivered perhaps the most famous blow to jongleuresque performance and authorship in the prologue to *Erec et Enide*:[30]

d'Erec, le fil Lac, est li contes,	[The tale is about Erec, son of Lac,
que devant rois et devant contes	Which, before kings and counts,
depecier et corronpre suelent	Those who wish to make a living at storytelling,
cil qui de conter vivre vuelent[.]	Are prone to fragment and corrupt.]
(19-22)	

Chrétien's negative tableau of the jongleurs is remarkable both in its vocabulary and in the type of performative and discursive space within which the jongleurs' stories and Chrétien's text coexist. Literature of the court and for the court, the story of Erec son of Lac is judged in an

---

[27]Cited in O.B. Hardison, Jr. et al. (eds.), *Medieval Literary Criticism: Translations and Interpretations* (New York: Frederick Ungar, 1974), 45.
[28]Ibid., 47.
[29]Cf. Tony Hunt, 'The Rhetorical Background to the Arthurian Prologue: Tradition and the Old French Vernacular Prologues', *Forum for Modern Language Studies,* 6.1 (1970), 1-23.
[30]Quoted from *Erec et Enide*, ed. Mario Roques (Paris: Champion, 1983). All translations from Old French to English in this essay are my own. Here and elsewhere, references in the text (in parentheses) are to verse lines.

aristocratic setting according to standards of authorship set by Chrétien himself and which, as earlier lines of prologue indicate, result from a system of textual production and authentication grounded in 'pleisir' (8), 'reison' (10), beauty (14 cites the *bele conjointure*), 'savoir' (15-6), and 'science' (17, 's'escïence'). Taken together with the verb forms used to define the activity of Chrétien's rivals, this vocabulary foregrounds the antinomies inherent in the poetics of writerly and jongleuresque performance and authorship, and thus allows Chrétien to assert his proper place as the author of *Erec et Enide*. Indeed, by placing them before the court, and literally inscribing on their works the poetic verdict of neglect, fragmentation, and corruption, Chrétien uses his prologue to present himself as judge and jury of his peers. In a single, and essential, poetic gesture, then, Chrétien invokes and excludes jongleuresque authorship from the space of the court and from the romance profession. In this way, he occupies and refuses to relinquish the middle space of the court, that definitive space within which authorship reveals itself as such according to either jongleuresque or writerly modes.

Chrétien's opening verses mediate poetic relationships between the author and his literary peers, his listening (and eventually reading) public, and his literary predecessors. Like the authors of the *romans antiques*, Chrétien defines his authorship in terms of both writerly and jongleuresque modes of textual transmission. This nominalist wrinkle in the poetics of exclusion is most clear in lines 39-42 of the prologue to *Cligés* where Chrétien dismisses the *matière antique* as no longer pertinent to his model of authorship:[31]

> Car des Grezois ne des Romains   [For, of the Greeks and the Romans,
> Ne dit an mes ne plus ne mains,   One says no more,
> D'ax est la parole remese   Talk of them has ceased
> Et estainte la vive brese[.]   And their vital flame has been extinguished.]
>   (39-42)

Although it is unclear whom Chrétien is targeting with these remarks (i.e. is his dismissal of the *matière antique* also a criticism of writerly romancers whose names we know, such as Benoît?), it is nevertheless apparent that these judgments are charged with meaningful literary and historical overtones. Indeed, with these few lines the space of Chrétien's model authorship is rendered all the more concise, delimited in specific terms of subject matter and historical geography. The poetics of exclusion, then, carry with them a powerful expression of literary triumphalism depicted in the *Cligés* prologue by the image of the extinguished flame of the ancient past.

---

[31] Quoted from *Cligés*, ed. Alexandre Micha (Paris: Champion, 1982).

The poetics of exclusion, however, operate not only on a literary level but on a social level as well. Nowhere is this more evident than in the bitingly ironic Christian isotopy of the final lines of the *Erec et Enide* prologue. To grasp the power of this isotopy, it is perhaps productive to recall that, in the *Roman de Thèbes* and Benoît de Sainte Maure's *Roman de Troie*, the jongleurs are simply described as lacking in education and social graces. In *Thèbes*, the jongleur is a jackass harper performing for a society of fools (13-6). In *Troie*, the entire jongleuresque literary class is a society of eructative authors who spew and belch forth stories of little value (30.095-106). In Chrétien's *Erec et Enide,* on the other hand, the opposition between Chrétien and his jongleur rivals takes on the form of a religious binarism that sets the memorable and enduring word of Chrétien/Christianity ('Des or comancerai l'estoire | qui toz jorz mes iert an mimoire | tant con durra crestïantez | de ce s'est Crestïens vantez (23-6)), against the fragmented and corrupted word, a word necessarily set to worldly purposes since used by the jongleurs to make a living. There is no doubt that 'corronpre' (21) shares secular and ecclesiastic semantic values which, when used ironically by Chrétien, collapse the literal fragmentation of the story of Erec son of Lac with a figurative destruction of the soul through sin. Thus, Chrétien places jongleuresque authorship in a light of eternal damnation cast not only on the story, but on its tellers, while he the romance author becomes the embodiment of *crestïantez.* In this way, Chrétien opposes writerly romance authorship to jongleuresque performance and authorship much as the *Chanson de Roland* opposes Christians and Saracens, where the former have God's grace (cf. verse 18 of *Erec et Enide,* 'tant con Dex la grasce l'an done') and the latter resist it in every way. Although it would be wrong, however, to claim that religious conviction and an aspiration to *caritas* are the touchstones of Chrétien's work, it is nonetheless intriguing that one of his fundamental gestures in the poetics of exclusion consists of appropriating the well-worn Christian-Pagan opposition and applying it to definitions of authorship. Indeed, in an ironic way, one could claim that Chrétien's denunciation of the performative literary class expresses a desire to grant supreme authority to romance by associating it with religious texts that are ineffable, immutable and inviolable.

The Seed and the Word: Death and Resurrection in the *Conte du graal*

Evidence of romance's poetics of exclusion is not limited to these examples. Chrétien condemns servile flatterers in the prologue to the *Chevalier de la Charrette* (1-15)[32] and sets up Calogrenant and Kay as

---

[32]The essay follows the edition by Mario Roques (Paris: Champion, 1983).

competing storytellers in the *Chevalier au Lion* (53ff.).[33] Finally, the prologue to the *Conte du graal*[34] contrasts the seed of Chrétien's romance with the 'bad seeds' of other romancers. This last extant and most ambitious (it is over 9.200 verses in Roach's edition) of Chrétien de Troyes's Arthurian romances is also perhaps the most peculiar. Notwithstanding its lack of ending, *Le Conte du graal* stands out among Chrétien's works both for its relatively lengthy prologue and for its conspicuous and abundant use of Biblical echoes in the 68 verses of its exordium. While no obvious quotations from the Bible are to be found in the prologues to *Erec et Enide, Cligés, Le Chevalier de la charrette,* and *Le Chevalier au lion*, in the *Conte du graal* 'nine-tenths of the prologue is given over to paraphrasing the Scriptures and to lauding a patron's many Christian virtues, particularly that of Christian charity'.[35] As is well known, this poetic and rhetorical innovation of the *Conte du graal* begins with the prologue's first phrase:

Ki petit semme petit quelt	[He who sows little reaps little
Et qui auques requeillir velt	And whosoever wishes to gather a little
En tel liu sa semence espande	Scatters his seed in such a place
Que Diex a cent doubles li rande[.]	Where God increases it one hundred fold.]
(1-4)	

Despite the objection of Hunt,[36] for partisans of the Judeo-Christian reading of the *Graal* (such as Klenke and Claude Luttrell) crucial keys to the interpretation of Chrétien's final romance are furnished by the Biblical allusions contained in the prologue, allusions which themselves announce exegesis grounded in and inspired by the historical understanding of twelfth-century France's profound interest 'in the spreading of Christ's kingdom on earth'.[37] For these partisans, *Le Conte du graal* represents a definite departure from the works of Chrétien's early poetic career. For them, it can be read as a 'deeply mystical narrative'[38] filled with a 'prominence of religious feeling'.[39] If one follows this hypothesis to its unstated but no less logical conclusion, Chrétien's break with his early career could be read as a literary and spiritual conversion. No longer the poet who once composed a tale of adultery for Marie de Champagne, Chrétien, with *Le*

---

[33]The essay follows the edition by Mario Roques (Paris: Champion, 1982).

[34]The essay follows the edition by William Roach (Paris: Librairie Minard, and Genève: Librairie Droz, 1959).

[35]Holmes and Klenke, *Chrétien*, 91.

[36]Cf. Hunt, 'The Prologue', 361.

[37]Holmes and Klenke, *Chrétien*, 91.

[38]Ibid., 100.

[39]Claude Luttrell, 'The Prologue to Crestien's *Li Contes del Graal*', *Arthurian Literature*, 3 (1983), 11.

Conte du graal is thought to redeem himself and to direct his poetry to the greater good of the Christian faith.

The boundaries of the debate on romance authorship and the prologue to *Le Conte du graal* need to be redefined, and I believe that one can do so productively by embracing the terms of authorship evoked above. For, to treat Chrétien as a 'Christian poet' is to collide inappropriately the divine Word with the poetic word. And to allow this collision is to trust, naively I think, that divine grace flowed through the poet and anointed him and his page with the favor of the Lord. By contrast, to subordinate Chrétien's poetics to his rhetorical training and to his ties to his literary patron is to inscribe the contents of his poetry within an economy where supply is generated solely according to the patron's demand. To accept this economy uncritically is tantamount to reducing authorship to a kind of dictation so obliged to remuneration that it abandons all claims to artistic agency or literary creativity. It is somewhat limiting to accept the notion that, even under medieval patronage, the author's sole and exclusive duty to his text resulted from his need and desire to please his patron.

In each of these approaches, the notion of authorship as a value appears to be diminished or ignored. Whether a Christian or a feudal servant, the poet comes to be viewed as an individual who peddles wares, one who plies a stock and trade whose value flees the author to become commensurate with the command of the patron or the Word of the Lord. According to my argument, however, authorship as a value itself transcends the conditions and contingencies of a text's original production and reception to imprint on the work a special property that allows it to endure the vicissitudes and hazards of history and memory. In the form of a signature or in the form of a basic poetic gesture, or significant codex structure, authorship stakes a claim to historical expression and textual responsibility which, again as a value, motivates and justifies literary composition.

When Chrétien de Troyes takes the stage for the final time as an author, he uses the image of the good seed ('bone semence') as a figure for romance composition and thus stakes his historical claim to authorship. Contrary to the arguments of Klenke and Luttrell, in the figure of the 'semence', the prologue to *Le Conte du graal* establishes a basic continuity with the expressions of authorship found in Chrétien's first four romances. In his final work, as in those previous, Chrétien de Troyes above all represents for us a poet who is conscious of the complex literary climate of his culture and of the value romance culture places on the textually-based epistemological tradition. Through this figure of the seed Chrétien highlights his condition as an author who has in the past both translated Ovid and presided over the literary silencing of 'les anciens', and who in his final romance uses a vernacular translation of the Gospels to compare his writing ironically to the writings of the New Testament Evangelists. By inviting a kind of exegetical attention normally afforded only to Western culture's greatest, most mysterious, and holy text of the Bible, the prologue and the text of *Le Conte du graal* indicate the greatest success of Chrétien de Troyes's authorship, one which has allowed him to place not only his text but his name in history, and thus to mark indelibly the cultural record.

In verses 7-10 of *Le Conte du graal* Chrétien combines in four lines a gesture of identity, poetics, and literary patronage whose interpretation has been skewed by the Christian-poet school toward a kind of literary evangelism with didactic intent.[40] Thus, according to Klenke, when the prologue announces that

Crestïens semme et fait semence	[Chrétien sows and makes seed
D'un romans que il encomence	Of a romance which he begins
Et si le seme en si bon leu	And so sows it in such a good place
Qu'il ne puet [estre] sanz grant preu[.]	That it cannot go without great reward.]
(7-10)	

its poetic statement has the equivalent value of making Chrétien a disciple of Christ who informs his public 'that he is about to sow the seed—"the word of God"—in good ground'.[41] Klenke's gloss on the passage, therefore, obviously results from a reading of the gloss Christ gives to his own parable of the sower in the books of the Evangelists. In Matthew, for example, Christ informs his disciples that the seed is the 'word of the kingdom' (Matt. 13:19). In Mark, similar information is conveyed by the phrase 'the sower sows the word' (Mark 4:14). In Luke, finally, Christ gives the following interpretation to the parable of the sower: 'Now the parable is this: The seed is the word of God' (Luke 8:11).

Given the connections between romance authorship and nominalism outlined above, is it possible to consider Chrétien's seed truly as the word of God? Can one argue, without the comforting buttress of faith, that it is imbued with that primal causality expressed by the first verse of the prologue to the Gospel according to John: 'In the beginning was the Word, and the Word was with God, and the Word was God'.[42] According to doctrine, this Word is the genesis of all things that can redeem all things. It is eternal and came to earth in the form of Jesus Christ who played the role of mediator between God and men. As Saint Augustine makes clear in Book X of his *Confessions*: 'as a man, he is our Mediator; but as the Word of God, he is not an intermediary between God and man because he is equal with God, and God with God, and together with him one God'

---

[40] Cf. Holmes and Klenke, *Chrétien*, 100-1.

[41] Ibid., 94.

[42] All quotes from the Bible are taken from: *The New Oxford Annotated Bible with the Apocrypha* (Revised Standard Edition), eds. Herbert G. May and Bruce M. Metzger (New York: Oxford University Press, 1977).

(X, 43).[43] The figure of Christ as embodiment of the divine Word, then, invites even more questions: Could Chrétien be considered a kind of poetic Christ? If so, can we, at a remove of over 800 years, claim that his poetry represents a kind of 'Christian eloquence' which could stand 'both literally and figuratively as vessel of the Spirit, bearing the Word to mankind, incorporating men into the new covenant of Christ and preparing them through its mediation for the face-to-face knowledge of God in the beatific vision'?[44]

In the absence of compelling proof of Chrétien's religious leanings (such evidence might include a text, in Latin or in the vernacular, with a clear Christian focus and intent), one cannot help but argue that in Chrétien's prologue the only word in question is the word of the poet. Therefore, the only seed sown is the seed of poetry. Because Chrétien is no Evangelist, but rather a vernacular poet, both his word and his seed can be understood only as they situate themselves at once in a history of sacred and secular texts and within a linguistic context bordered by the eternal Word of God and the words of mortal men. Augustine perhaps defines this linguistic field best when he claims in Book XI of his *Confessions* that God's Word is 'far different from these words which sound in time. They are far beneath me; in fact they are not at all, because they die away and are lost' (XI, 6). According to Augustine, human language, unlike the language of the divine, is a kind of 'speech in which each part comes to an end when it has been spoken' (XI, 7). Like human existence, human language sounds in time, follows a syntax of temporality and mortality that Augustine, inspired by the death of his friend in Thagaste spells out in Book IV:

> Not all reach old age, but all alike must die. Not all the parts exist at once, but some must come as others go, and in this way together they make up the whole of which they are the parts. Our speech follows the same rule, using sounds to signify a meaning. For a sentence is not complete unless each word, once its syllables have been pronounced, gives way to make room for the next. (IV, 10)

Thus, the linguistic field within which Chrétien's seed is sown is fertile with the following oppositions: temporal language versus the eternal Word; the redeemed speech of theologians versus the speech of the poets; memory versus eternity. These Augustinian dichotomies point up a fundamental distinction between on the one hand the eternal Word of God, the Word made flesh, and on the other a temporal language whose object was

---

[43] All quotes are taken from: Saint Augustine, *Confessions*, tr. R.S. Pine-Coffin (New York: Penguin, 1961).

[44] Marcia Colish, *The Mirror of Language: A Study in the Medieval Theory of Knowledge* (Lincoln, NE, and London: University of Nebraska Press, rev. ed. 1983), 26.

not God, but rather language itself. Although D.W. Robertson believed that all writing conduced to Charity,[45] more recent commentators have noted the difference between the divine logos and the poetic word. As Eugene Vance puts it: 'Medieval poetry is an art whose status as the embodiment of beauty in temporal language was a consequence of a chosen *dissimilitudo* from the *logos,* and therefore from God as the only proper object of human love and understanding'.[46] Following Vance, it therefore becomes possible to argue that, if Chrétien used Christian figures (either by punning on his own name in *Erec et Enide* or through biblical paraphrase in the *Graal*) to define and to idealize his status as author and his text's status as cultural artifact, he was not unaware that these figures functioned *as* figures, semiotic devices that suppressed a surface meaning to convey a deeper one. As a dominant cultural phenomenon, the doctrine of the Incarnation necessarily finds itself present in the semiotic system of Chrétien's text. For the same reason, Ciceronian rhetoric is present as well. Nevertheless (and this is a crucial point for understanding Chrétien), neither the Incarnation nor Cicero are *encoded* in Chrétien's text. Rather, they are part of its codes, meant to be broken. Once broken, these codes reveal that, with Chrétien, rather than an Incarnation, a Word made flesh, we have a manuscript verbalization, *a flesh made word on flesh.* The reality granted to the verbal structures of the prologue to the *Graal* and to the Christian figure of the prologue to *Erec et Enide,* therefore, would be trivial, if reduced to mere rhetorical boasting, or absurd, if understood in terms of a supposed Christian eschatological vision. If the Christian figures of Chrétien were to convey an ontological reality, finally, it would be completely without significance, since it would have no means of self-justification or self-definition other than the code of figurative language with which it is expressed.[47] In figuring his text, then, Chrétien cleverly and cryptically employs the discourse of the Church against itself, using irony and nominalist poetics as the touchstones of his new vernacular paradigm, and foreshadowing what will become the modern European notion of authorship and textuality.

Although Biblical echoes abound in Chrétien's prologue, they should be understood only as words which 'come as others go', hoping to reach old age, and yet literally incapable of serving 'as vessel of the Spirit' in me-

---

[45] See D.W. Robertson, 'Some Medieval Literary Terminology, with Special Reference to Chrétien de Troyes', *Studies in Philology,* 48 (1951), 687-8.

[46] Eugene Vance, *Mervelous Signals: Poetics and Sign Theory in the Middle Ages* (Lincoln, NE, and London: University of Nebraska Press, 1986), 49-50.

[47] John Freccero makes similar remarks on Dante and irony. See especially his *Dante: The Poetics of Conversion,* ed. Rachel Jacoff (Cambridge, MA: Harvard University Press, 1986); and 'Introduction to *Inferno*', in *The Cambridge Companion to Dante,* ed. Rachel Jacoff (Cambridge: Cambridge University Press, 1993), 172-91.

diating human knowledge of God. As a poet, Chrétien must have acknowledged that the eternal Word of God could not be accommodated by the fragile word of vernacular poetry, a word imbued with a polysemy unknown to the generative and redemptive logos. And so, when Chrétien claims that he 'makes seed of a romance', he provides the reader and interpreter with a trope on secular writing that, although it ostensibly takes its source from the Bible, is fundamentally linked to the world and to the word of the poet through polysemy. Indeed, when Jesus claims in the Gospel according to Mark that 'there is nothing hid, except to be made manifest; nor is anything secret except to come to light' (Mark 4:22, also Luke 8:17), he furnishes his own trope on the eternal and divine Word, a Word whose immutability and eternity are guaranteed precisely by its lack of polysemy. Thus, in every Gospel containing the parable of the sower, Jesus the omniscient teacher condemns the perceived polysemy of the Word of the Lord, blaming diabolical meddling and human frailty for the faulty reception of the logos. This blame resounds in the phrase 'He who has ears, let him hear' (Matt. 13:43), a phrase which in Mark and Luke is accompanied at once by a warning against the dangers of incorrect interpretation of the Word, and by a promise of reward for dutiful and correct interpretation: 'If any man has ears to hear, let him hear. Take heed what you hear; the measure you give will be the measure you get, and still more will be given you' (Mark 4:23-4). Finally, the caution against ascribing polysemy to the divine Word is even more marked in Luke: 'Take heed then how you hear; for to him who has will more be given, and from him who has not, even what he thinks he has will be taken away' (Luke 8:18).

Due to its mediated and mutable nature, then, the secular romance word of the prologue to *Le Conte du graal* should be understood in terms of its basic proliferation of meaning. According to this argument, the seed of Chrétien's opening lines could be read as a kind of literary celebration of linguistic and poetic polysemy. Because its dissemination invites (and has invited) a history of conflicting interpretations, the seed of this celebration therefore actually serves to commemorate the text and to assure its place in the secular cultural record long after the author's death. As medieval nominalism claimed, and modern European definitions of authorship and textuality attest, for this poetic commemoration and dissemination to occur, however, the invocation of the sacred is not necessarily required. Rather, it is simply necessary to portend that a continual multiplication of forms and meanings will result from sowing the seed of the story.

Still, as Chrétien sows the seed which gives to his romance a life and historical vigor equivalent to that of fruit multiplied one hundred times, he also acknowledges, with the very gesture that tosses the seed from the bag, a kind of unavoidable separation of author and text. This last poetic figure of Chrétien de Troyes, then, marks implicitly his compositional event with a complex sign of dissemination which points to prosperity and to finality.

Indeed, to make seed of a romance, and to scatter it on the ground of the good reader, is tantamount to making an eventual and triumphal exit from the stage of authorship. And yet, this exit must remain incomplete. Romance authorship, like modern authorship, tends to portray a preoccupation with leaving signs of its historical presence inscribed within the text. The letter from Abelard to Astralabius cited above helps elucidate this claim and also situates it within a nominalist, or anti-realist, poetic paradigm. As we have seen, Abelard's correspondence with his son points up a relationship between the individual and the letter where secular writing becomes the earthly haven of a soul dispossessed of human flesh. To the extent that this relationship signals a kind of secular concern for immortality, it also appears to invert—or even to subvert—the Judeo-Christian tradition of redeemed speech or of the divine Word. Indeed, rather than the Word made flesh, rather than an Incarnation whose purpose is to mediate the temporal and the eternal, the writing of the poet 'sounds in time', mediating knowledge and memory by taking on aspects of the flesh made word. Chrétien, therefore, could indeed be viewed as a kind of secular Christ figure, one that is wrapped in the poetic power of temporal language and free of any divine pretensions.

The progeny of Chrétien's seed is a text with the potential to survive historical obstacles and to create its own history as well as the history of its author. In the nominalist subtext of authorship, one discovers a tacit acknowledgment that, in the ensuing history of the text, the individual writer can be preserved and commemorated only as a figure described by the letter. In the retrospective glance of the interpreter, authorship emerges as a simple desire to write and thereby to live on as a figure. To be written is thus to acknowledge life through textual commemoration and dissemination. It is also to acknowledge death, that time when spoken words, like our human skin, die, fall away, and become lost. There is no absence of this kind of figure among the earliest composers of medieval romance. The *Thèbes* poet, for example, claimed in his short prologue that:

> Qui sages est nel doit celer
> ainz doit por ce son senz moutrer
> que quant il ert du siecle alez
> touz jors en soit ramenbrez[.]
> (1-4)

> [He who is wise should not hide it
> For this reason, he should therefore display his knowledge
> Such that, when he has departed from this world
> He may henceforth be remembered for it always.]

And the same topos is found in the opening lines of Benoît de Sainte-Maure's *Roman de Troie:*

Salemons nos enseigne et dit,	[Solomon teaches us and says,
Et si lit len en son escrit	And thus one reads in his writings,
Que nul ne deit son sen celer,	That no one should conceal his knowledge.
Ainz le deit len si demostrer	Therefore, one should reveal it
Que len i ait prou et enor;	Such that one derives honor and profit from it,
Car si firent li ancessor[.]	For thus did the ancestors.]
(1-6)	

Chrétien himself participated in this poetic tradition. Through an insistence on the importance of the 'estuide' (4), the danger of silence (7: 'teisir'), the need to 'bien dire et bien aprandre' (12) and the need to dedicate one's wisdom to the pursuit of knowledge (16-7: 'cil ne fet mie savoir l qui s'escïence n'abandone'), the exordial space to Chrétien's first romance makes a clear allusion to the 'qui sages est nel doit celer' topos, and thereby establishes a poetic continuity between *Erec et Enide* and the *romans antiques*.

It therefore becomes possible to contend that Chrétien's poetics of the seed planted in good earth, a seed sown in ground that will allow it to grow and to prosper, responds to a tradition of nominalism and romance poetics typified by the immortality topoi of the prologues to these *romans antiques* as well as to *Erec et Enide*. Since, in this poetic tradition, authorship defined itself as the activity involved in the revelation, continuation, and historical preservation of the self and of one's wisdom through writing, it seems clear that in *Le Conte du graal* Chrétien's seed rejoins this literary and poetic tradition by figuratively portending a harvest of potential literary wisdom. Thus, like the mustard seed from the second parable of the Gospel according to Matthew, this wisdom will grow and serve as a secular monument to Chrétien the author:

> The kingdom of heaven is like a grain of mustard seed which a man took and sowed in his field; it is the smallest of all seeds, but when it has grown it is the greatest of shrubs and becomes a tree, so that the birds of the air come and make nests in its branches. (Matt. 13:31-2)

It is also interesting to note that the prologue's invocation of 'bone semence' (7) actually constitutes 'an echo of *bonum semen (Matthew xiii 24)* in the parable of the harvest, which follows in the same chapter and also has a sower'.[48] According to Christ's gloss on this parable in the Gospel of Saint Matthew:

> He who sows the good seed is the Son of man; the field is the world, and the good seed means the sons of the kingdom; the weeds are the sons of the evil one, and the enemy who sowed them is the devil; the harvest is the close of the age, and the reapers are angels. Just as the weeds are gathered and burned with fire, so will it be at the close of the age. (Matt. 13:37-41)

---

[48]Luttrell, 'The Prologue', 1.

As the harvest represents the end of time, it also marks an apocalyptic moment when the truth of Christianity will descend on the world to gather its disciples and to grant them eternal life. If the age of Christianity were to come to a close, vengeance would be wreaked upon the detractors from the faith and they would be condemned to misery and to oblivion.

Through the harvest parable, therefore, we discover a unique and revealing subtext to Chrétien de Troyes's authorship. In particular, the notions of apocalypse, of the closing of the age, and of separating the wheat from the weed visibly rejoin Chrétien's poetics of authorship and exclusion as they are outlined most vividly in *Erec et Enide*. As I have previously described it, the Christian isotopy found in verses 21-6 of the prologue to Chrétien's first romance contains a trenchant irony that places competing authorships in a light of eternal damnation (theirs is indeed the word of the enemy) while transforming Chrétien into the embodiment of *crestïantez*. When read in relation to the harvest parable, and with respect to the seed of the romance, this Christian figure from *Erec et Enide* begins to find a new level of coherence. Chrétien's claim that his text will last until the end of time is accompanied in the final verse of this prologue by an even more boastful claim that, even at the literary apocalypse, when the age of human time and temporal language comes to a close, Chrétien de Troyes's text alone will be remembered:

Des or comancerai l'estoire	[Now I shall begin the story
qui toz jorz mes iert an mimoire	Which henceforth will always be remembered
tant con durra crestïantez	As long as 'christianity' endures
de ce s'est Crestïens vantez[.]	Of this Chrétien made his boast.]
(23-6)	

Indeed, although eight centuries have passed, this kind of literary 'Christianity' still endures in the texts of *Erec et Enide, Cligés, Le Chevalier de la charrette,* and *Le Chevalier au lion*. And, it has a special vigor in the text announced by one of Chrétien de Troyes's final exordial phrases: 'Le meillor conte I qui soit contez a cort roial I Ce est li Contes del graal' (64-6). As we have seen, although the profound religious statement of the Gospels cannot serve as a basic interpretative grid for the understanding of Chrétien's final text, the mystery of Christ's parables does in fact seem to inform Chrétien de Troyes's authorship in a way that is completely secular and remarkably ironic. It is, therefore, perhaps significant of a desire to lace poetic continuity with a certain amount of literary mystery that Chrétien, unlike Christ, chose to leave his own parables unexplained. With no history of manuscript marginalia or gloss to elucidate these parables, the modern reader is obliged to interpret Chrétien's literal and secular appropriation of the good seed as nothing more than a figurative gesture that rejoins the poetics of his prior romances to make a promise of a new literary paradigm.

In this new paradigm, authorship was informed by a nominalist theory of universals and a textually-based tradition of knowledge that permitted it to successfully mediate the *texte-œuvre* dichotomy without remaining indebted to discourses of authority from religious and rhetorical traditions. Thus, as has been suggested by the work of Michel Zink in particular, one promise of twelfth-century romance was to inaugurate a vernacular tradition where secular writing, as shared cultural artifact, expressed the historical value of authorship and thereby garnered for itself the prestige necessary for fiction's claim to validity and the poet's claim to literary jurisdiction. In the end, where Abelard's nominalism failed for philosophy, it succeeded tremendously in literature. By bestowing on the poetic word a referential quality that did not depend on any factual or essential underpinnings, nominalism at once justified fiction and liberated authors. That one could conceive of and describe universals without requiring their objective existence abundantly served the imaginations of poets who were free to create their own universe in texts, a universe unlike God's but no less true in its historical verbal expression. With such a theoretical and conceptual system at their disposal, romance composers such as Chrétien de Troyes redefined the literary culture of their day and in so doing founded principles for authorship and the written text that have prevailed, like Abelard's 'scripta poetae' and Chrétien's seed, well beyond their lifetimes and into ours.

THE DIALECTIC OF DIVINE OMNIPOTENCE IN THE AGE OF CHAUCER: A RECONSIDERATION

WILLIAM J. COURTENAY

The importance of the philosophical context and contacts of Chaucer and contemporary English poets has been acknowledged for almost a century, although their relation to the late medieval current of thought usually referred to as Nominalism has only been explored in the last few decades.[1]

---

[1] For the early work on philosophical background, see: Carleton Brown, 'The Author of the *Pearl*, considered in the Light of his Theological Opinions', *PMLA*, 19 (1904), 115-53; George G. Coulton, *Chaucer and His England* (London: Methuen, 1908); Ernest P. Kuhl, 'Some Friends of Chaucer', *PMLA*, 29 (1914), 270-6; Howard A. Patch, 'Troilus on Determinism', *Speculum*, 6 (1931), 225-43; and Robert M. Lumianski, 'Chaucer's *Parlement of Foules*: A Philosophical Interpretation', *Review of English Studies*, 24 (1948), 81-9. On the late medieval philosophical background, variously understood, see: Mary Edith Thomas, *Medieval Scepticism and Chaucer* (New York: William Frederick Press, 1950); Morton W. Bloomfield, 'Distance and Predestination in *Troilus and Criseyde*', *PMLA*, 72 (1957), 14-26; J. Mitchell Morse, 'The Philosophy of the Clerk of Oxenford', *Modern Language Quarterly*, 19 (1958), 3-20; Stephen Knight, 'Chaucer—A Modern Writer?', *Balcony*, 2 (1965), 37-43; John F. McNamara, *Responses to Ockhamist Theology in the Poetry of the 'Pearl'-Poet, Langland, and Chaucer*, PhD diss. Louisiana State University, 1968; Huling E. Ussery, 'Fourteenth-Century English Logicians: Possible Models for Chaucer's Clerk', *Tulane Studies in English*, 18 (1970), 1-15; Laurence Eldredge, 'Chaucer's *House of Fame* and the *Via Moderna*', *Neuphilologische Mitteilungen*, 71 (1970), 105-19; Laurence Eldredge, 'Poetry and Philosophy in the *Parlement of Foules*', *Revue de l'Université d'Ottawa*, 40 (1970), 441-59; Joseph Grennen, 'Science and Sensibility in Chaucer's Clerk', *Chaucer Review*, 6 (1971), 81-93; Gertrud Mary Jurschak, *Chaucer and Fourteenth-Century Thought*, PhD diss. Loyola University of Chicago, 1972; Sheila Delany, *Chaucer's 'House of Fame': The Poetics of Sceptical Fideism* (Chicago, IL: University of Chicago Press, 1972; repr. Gainesville, FL: University Press of Florida, 1994); Sheila Delany, 'Undoing Substantial Connection: The Late Medieval Attack on Analogical Thought', *Mosaic*, 5.4 (1972), 33-52; Geoffrey Shepherd, 'Religion and Philosophy in Chaucer', in Derek S. Brewer (ed.), *Geoffrey Chaucer* (Writers and Their Background) (London: Bell, 1974), 262-89; Winthrop Wetherbee, 'Some Intellectual Themes in Chaucer's Poetry', in George D. Economou (ed.), *Geoffrey Chaucer* (New

Among the themes of late medieval philosophy and theology that have been used as distinctive features or *mentalités* through which to interpret passages in works of Middle English literature, the dialectic of divine omnipotence, i.e., the distinction of divine power as absolute or as ordained, has played an important role. One thinks in particular of the contributions of Robert Stepsis, David Steinmetz, Larry Eldredge, Kathleen Ashley, Janet Coleman, and Richard Utz.[2]

York: McGraw-Hill, 1975), 75-91; Laurence Eldredge, 'Boethian Epistemology and Chaucer's *Troilus and Criseyde* in the Light of Fourteenth-Century Thought', *Mediaevalia*, 2 (1976), 49-75; Salatha Marie Griffin, *Chaucer's 'Troilus' from the Perspective of Ralph Strode's 'Consequences'*, PhD diss. University of Nebraska, 1978; Russell A. Peck, 'Chaucer and the Nominalist Questions', *Speculum*, 53 (1978), 745-60; Eugene Vance, *'Mervelous Signals*: Poetics, Sign Theory, and Politics in Chaucer's *Troilus*', *New Literary History*, 10 (Winter 1979), 293-337; Denise Baker, 'From Plowing to Penitence: *Piers Plowman* and Fourteenth-Century Theology', *Speculum*, 55 (1980), 715-25; Janet Coleman, Piers Plowman *and the 'Moderni'* (Rome: Edizioni di storia e letteratura, 1981); Marsha Siegel, 'What the Debate Is and Why It Founders in Fragment A of *The Canterbury Tales*', *Studies in Philology*, 82 (1985), 1-24; Holly Wallace Boucher, 'Nominalism: The Difference for Chaucer and Boccaccio', *Chaucer Review*, 20 (1986), 213-20; Linda Tarte Holley, 'Medieval Optics and the Framed Narrative in Chaucer's *Troilus and Criseyde*', *Chaucer Review*, 21 (1986), 26-44; William J. Courtenay, *Schools and Scholars in Fourteenth-Century England* (Princeton, NJ: Princeton University Press, 1987), 356-80; Jay Ruud, 'Chaucer and Nominalism: The Envoy to Bukton', *Mediaevalia*, 10 (1984), 199-212; Warren Ginsberg, 'Place and Dialectic in *Pearl* and Dante's *Paradiso*', *Journal of English Literary History*, 55 (1988), 731-53; Karl Reichl, 'Chaucer's *Troilus*: Philosophy and Language', in Piero Boitani (ed.), *The European Tragedy of 'Troilus'* (Oxford: Clarendon Press, 1989), 133-52; Richard J. Utz, *Literarischer Nominalismus im Spätmittelalter: Eine Untersuchung zu Sprache, Charakterzeichnung und Struktur in Geoffrey Chaucers* Troilus and Criseyde (Frankfurt a.M. et al.: Lang, 1990); Rodney Delasanta, 'Chaucer and Strode', *Chaucer Review*, 26 (1991), 205-18; Anna Baldwin, '"The Man of Law's Tale" as a Philosophical Narrative', *Yearbook of English Studies*, 22 (1992), 181-9; John Finlayson, 'The Knight's Tale: The Dialogue of Romance, Epic, and Philosophy', *Chaucer Review*, 27 (1992), 126-49.

[2] In the wake of Heiko Oberman's *Harvest of Medieval Theology: Gabriel Biel and Late Medieval Nominalism* (Cambridge, MA: Harvard University Press, 1963), which focused attention on the dialectic of divine power as the key to understanding late medieval nominalism, some authors tried to apply those insights to literary texts, e.g., McNamara, *Responses to Ockhamist Theology*; Kathleen M. Ashley, 'Divine Power in Chester Cycle and Late Medieval Thought', *Journal of the History of Ideas*, 39 (1978), 387-404, but see critique of James R. Royse, 'Nominalism and Divine Power in the Chester Cycle', *Journal of the History of Ideas*, 40 (1979), 475-6, and response of Ashley, 'Chester Cycle and Nominalist Thought', *Journal of the History of Ideas*, 40 (1979), 477. Others, however, remained largely untouched by the revised understanding of nominalism, e.g., Robert Stepsis, *'Potentia absoluta* and the *Clerk's Tale'*, *Chaucer Review*, 10 (1975), 129-46, and even Eldredge, 'Boethian Epistemology'. For a more informed approach, see: David Steinmetz, 'Late Medieval Nominalism and the *Clerk's Tale*', *Chaucer Review*, 12 (1977), 38-54; Laurence Eldredge, 'The Concept

It is certainly the case that if one wishes to explore parallels and contexts between Middle English literature and philosophical ideas and assumptions, it is either the ever-read early Christian authors, such as Augustine or Boethius, or the contemporary philosophical and academic scene of fourteenth-century England that one should be using for comparison, not the world of Albert the Great, Bonaventure, or Thomas Aquinas except insofar as their ideas and approaches remained viable in the schools a century later. Yet the task of identifying reliable guides to late medieval thought and understanding the intricacies of late scholastic argumentation has not been easy. For those who do not work primarily in the field of late medieval thought, the differences in interpretation found in the early work of such scholars as Gordon Leff and Heiko Oberman, especially on the distinction of absolute and ordained power, have not been fully appreciated, nor have the interpretive shifts that have taken place since 1970 been absorbed.[3] Moreover, since much of the research in late medieval thought, especially the work of Oberman, has focused on Continental authors, and on some, like Gabriel Biel, who wrote a century after Chaucer, there is always the question of what is precisely relevant to the situation in England and to the court circle of which Chaucer was a part.

The following remarks will be concerned with the new developments that have taken place in the understanding of the distinction of absolute and ordained power since Oberman's *Harvest of Medieval Theology*, my own articles on nominalism in the 1970s, and even since the approach taken in my *Schools and Scholars in Fourteenth-Century England*.[4] This is a topic that has proved far more complex and shifting than any of us

---

of God's Absolute Power at Oxford in the Later Fourteenth Century', in D.L. Jeffrey (ed.), *By Things Seen: Reference and Recognition in Medieval Thought* (Ottawa and Grand Rapids, MI: University of Ottawa Press, 1979), 211-26; Coleman, *Piers Plowman*; and Utz, *Literarischer Nominalismus*.

[3]For Leff's understanding of the implications of the distinction, see his *Medieval Thought from Saint Augustine to Ockham* (London: Merlin, 1959); *Bradwardine and the Pelagians* (Cambridge: Cambridge University Press, 1957); *Richard Fitzralph* (Manchester: Manchester University Press, 1963). For Oberman's interpretation, see his 'Some Notes on the Theology of Nominalism with Attention to its Relation to the Renaissance', *Harvard Theological Review*, 53 (1960), 47-76; 'Facientibus Quod in Se Est Deus Non Denegat Gratiam: Robert Holcot, O.P. and the Beginnings of Luther's Theology', *Harvard Theological Review*, 55 (1962), 317-42; *Harvest*, 30-56.

[4]William J. Courtenay, 'Covenant and Causality in Pierre d'Ailly', *Speculum*, 46 (1971), 94-119; 'Nominalism and Late Medieval Religion', in Charles Trinkaus and Heiko A. Oberman (eds.), *The Pursuit of Holiness in Late Medieval and Renaissance Religion* (Leiden: Brill, 1974), 26-59; both, along with 'The Dialectic of Divine Omnipotence', repr. in Courtenay, *Covenant and Causality in Medieval Thought: Studies in Philosophy, Theology and Economic Practice* (London: Variorum Reprints, 1984). See also *Schools and Scholars in Fourteenth-Century England* (Princeton, NJ: Princeton University Press, 1987).

realized a decade ago. These changes in interpretation did not occur because of shifts in scholarly taste, or because the conclusions reached in the 1970s and 1980s were rejected, or because the earlier interpretive model was overturned, but because new evidence revealed that there was not just one model but two, with some blending between them throughout the fourteenth century. The history of the distinction in the early fourteenth century has some surprising and fascinating turns that had not been anticipated. Although we have not yet sufficiently combed fourteenth-century scholastic texts to fill out the new picture that is emerging, we have a better idea today of what to look for and where to look. But in order to understand the newer evidence, it is necessary to be aware of the historiographical shifts that have taken place across the last generation of scholarship.

A. *Potentia absoluta*, 1960-1985

Discussions about what God could do, *de potentia absoluta*, have long been considered a distinctive feature of late medieval thought, both in England and on the Continent. Whether as far back as Carl Feckes and Erwin Iserloh, or in the early work of Gordon Leff and Francis Oakley, or in numerous recent articles by Leonard Kennedy, the distinction of absolute and ordained power, and the posing of arguments *de potentia absoluta*, were seen as arguments for occasional, arbitrary divine intervention that undermined certainty both in the physical order of nature and in the order of salvation.[5] God could, if he so chose, suspend the laws of nature through his absolute power, so that there would be causes without their normal effects, or effects without their normal causes. He could cause someone to have intuitive cognition of a non-existent (i.e., the perceptual apprehension of something as physically present that does not in fact exist). He could

---

[5]Carl Feckes, *Die Rechtfertigungslehre des Gabriel Biel und ihre Stellung innerhalb der nominalistischen Schule* (Münster, Westf.: Aschendorff, 1925); Erwin Iserloh, *Gnade und Eucharistie in der philosophischen Theologie des Wilhelm von Ockham: Ihre Bedeutung für die Ursachen der Reformation* (Wiesbaden: Steiner, 1956); Francis Oakley, *The Political Thought of Pierre d'Ailly: The Voluntarist Tradition* (New Haven, CT: Yale University Press, 1964); for the works of Leff, see above, note 3; and among Leonard Kennedy's numerous articles, see 'Late-Fourteenth-Century Philosophical Scepticism at Oxford', *Vivarium*, 23 (1985), 124-51; 'Philosophical Scepticism in England in the Mid-Fourteenth Century', *Vivarium*, 21 (1983), 35-57; 'Osbert of Pickenham, O.Carm. (fl. 1360) on the Absolute Power of God', *Carmelus*, 35 (1988), 178-225. It should be noted that both Leff and Oakley modified their interpretations of the distinction; see Leff, *William of Ockham: The Metamorphosis of Scholastic Discourse* (Manchester: Manchester University Press, 1975), esp. xiii, 455-68; Oakley, *Omnipotence, Covenant, and Order* (Ithaca, NY, and London: Cornell University Press, 1984).

reward with eternal salvation someone who did not possess the infused habit of grace, and could reject someone who did good works in a state of grace. Looked at from that perspective, arguments *de potentia absoluta* undermined confidence in the orders of nature and grace and disassociated the balance of faith and reason that had been achieved in the thirteenth century.

The appearance of Heiko Oberman's *Harvest of Medieval Theology* in 1963 altered the terms of discussion. Oberman accepted one aspect of the traditional view, namely that arguments *de potentia absoluta* were a distinctive feature of late medieval thought, and he argued that the distinction of absolute and ordained power was a foundation concept, perhaps *the* foundation concept, of late medieval nominalism. He stressed, however, that it had to be understood as an analytical tool in which the two parts worked together—a dialectic of absolute and ordained power that operated within the context of a pact or covenant. One side of the distinction, the side of *potentia absoluta*, expressed the freedom of God, the fact that God was not bound by external rules or laws, whether in nature or in the realm of salvation. The other side, always taken in combination with the first, namely the side of *potentia ordinata*, showed that God had bound himself to maintain the laws of nature he established as well as the order of salvation effected through the Incarnation and Crucifixion. The famous theological proposition that God will not deny grace and salvation to those who do their best ('Facientibus quod in se est, Deus non denegat gratiam'), epitomized in the expression 'facere quod in se est', as with so many other aspects of late medieval 'nominalist' theology, depended on the dialectic of absolute and ordained power. Although God remained free to accept or reject whomever he wished, *de potentia absoluta,* regardless of the presence or absence of the habit of grace, he had bound himself, *de potentia ordinata*, to reward with grace those who tried to do their best, and eventually to reward with eternal life only those who possessed and used that habit of grace. Viewed from this perspective, the distinction stressed *both* the omnipotence of God as well as his dependability or reliability. Although free, God never acted nor would ever act irrationally or arbitrarily. He observed the rules of the system he had ordained.

Since the appearance of *The Harvest* a generation ago, considerable attention has been given to this distinction, both its history and its meaning. There were two modifications on that picture that occurred in the 1970s.[6] The first was to establish (or re-establish, since a little-known German dissertation in 1925 had presented some of the evidence) that the distinction was not a late medieval distinction, nor one employed more by nominalists than by others, but that it went back to twelfth-century dis-

---

[6]See above, note 4.

cussions of divine volition developed in reaction to Peter Abelard's view that God could only have done what he did. The specific language of the distinction was created in the early years of the thirteenth century. It was therefore a much older distinction than was commonly thought, and its use and application in this earlier period, although not as frequent as later, was essentially identical with the usage found in Ockham and most late medieval theologians. The second point developed in the 1970s was to further document the fact that in the normal, theological use of the distinction, it was never a description of two forms of divine power, one absolute and the other ordained, but two ways of looking at or talking about *one* divine power. To talk about divine power and freedom *absolutely*, or simply, was to look at it as raw capacity without taking God's will, intention, or his ordained system into account. To talk about divine power and freedom *de potentia ordinata* was to understand divine power as the implementation of the divine will, according to the restrictions God has placed on himself. Originally, that is in the late twelfth century, *absolute* and *ordinate* were adverbs applied to the two ways we can consider or discuss one and the same divine power, not two forms of divine action. And even when the language shifted from adverbial to adjectival and was applied to *potentia* rather than *considerans*, the theological understanding and application of the distinction remained the same. It expressed two ways of looking at or talking about divine power, not two divine powers. This traditional theological understanding of the distinction was not only universal among thirteenth-century theologians from William of Auxerre to Thomas Aquinas; it was repeated and defended at great length by Ockham, Gregory of Rimini, and Pierre d'Ailly in the fourteenth century. On the basis of that body of evidence, it appeared that the interpretation of the distinction as an expression of two forms of divine action was a mistake of modern historical interpretation that had little or no foundation in the high and late Middle Ages.

In the course of the 1970s this revised understanding of the distinction was gradually accepted by most of those working in the field of late medieval thought. Appreciation of this shift was slower in coming among those seeking to apply this distinction to the interpretation of literary texts. Robert Stepsis' 1975 article on *potentia absoluta* in *The Clerk's Tale* made use of Oberman's 1960 article on nominalism but made no reference to the *Harvest* book of 1963, and Stepsis remained wedded to the older interpretation of the distinction found in Etienne Gilson, Gordon Leff, and Dom David Knowles.[7] Kathleen Ashley, in her 1978 article on the Chester Cycle, was aware of much of the recent literature on the distinction up to 1975, but she remained under the spell of the older interpretation of

---

[7] See Stepsis, '*Potentia absoluta*'.

Gilson, Leff, Knowles, and Oakley who saw *potentia absoluta* as absolutist action, perhaps because a one-sided emphasis on divine omnipotence, unchecked by any ordained plan, better suited the picture of God found in the Chester Cycle.[8] David Steinmetz's correction of Stepsis in *The Chaucer Review*[9] showed how a more informed understanding of the distinction, as uncovered in the 1960s and 1970s, could be applied to the *Clerk's Tale* with better results, but in the last decade and a half almost no one has followed his lead.[10] As recently as Rodney Delasanta's 1991 article on Chaucer and Strode, which includes a discussion of *potentia absoluta*, the old clichés and misunderstandings survive, untouched by decades of research in late medieval thought, despite the excellent treatment of Strode.[11]

B. *Potentia absoluta*, 1985-1994

Although the revised understanding of the distinction of divine power sketched out above made surprisingly little impact on the understanding of nominalism as it was applied to texts in middle English literature beyond *The Clerk's Tale*, now is not the time to move in that direction, since the understanding of the historical meaning and significance of that concept has become more complex in the last decade. At the time of writing *Schools and Scholars* I was only partially aware of the work of two other scholars, John Marrone, who had edited a previously unknown text of

---

[8] Ashley, 'Divine Power'. Without commenting on the validity of Ashley's interpretation of the 'nominalist' teaching on divine power, James Royse, 'Nominalism and Divine Power', observed, correctly I think, that the view of God presented in the Chester Cycle is biblical, not academic or nominalist. The fact that in the plays the potentiality of divine power is not linked to the self-limitations imposed by God's ordained plan is a clear indication that the so-called nominalist view of divine power is *not* being employed.

[9] See Steinmetz, 'Late Medieval Nominalism'.

[10] Eldredge, 'The Concept of God's Absolute Power', laid out some of the scholastic uses of the distinction in the fourteenth century, but did not go on to apply it to the interpretation of literary texts. Similarly, Utz, *Literarischer Nominalismus*, discusses the distinction at many points in his work, but does not actually apply it to *Troilus and Criseyde*. Both these works are *au courant* with the revisions in the understanding of nominalism, but the same cannot be said of Jay Ruud's 'Chaucer and Nominalism', which, although it does not touch on the distinction of divine power, presents a caricature of nominalist thought barely influenced by the research gains of the 1960s and 1970s. Caution also needs to be used with Thomas, *Medieval Scepticism and Chaucer*, and the widely-read article of J. Mitchell Morse, 'The Philosophy of the Clerk of Oxenford', both of which appeared before the revisions in the field of late medieval thought.

[11] See Delasanta, 'Chaucer and Strode'.

Henry of Ghent on divine power and human sovereignty, and a young Italian scholar, the now late Eugenio Randi, who had unearthed some interesting new material on the distinction of absolute and ordained power for the early fourteenth century.[12] Marrone pointed to the fact that canon lawyers in the third quarter of the thirteenth century adopted the theological distinction of absolute and ordained power, but adapted it (or understood it) to be a distinction between normal action according to the rule of law, and extraordinary action, outside of and above the law. Their model was not divine power but papal power that allowed the pontiff to grant dispensations from church law for the good of an individual or for the good of the Christian community. This form of the distinction was not two ways of looking at power but two forms of the exercise of power: one the normal or ordinary way in which a sovereign power supported the laws that he or his predecessors had instituted; the other, the ability occasionally to override or make exceptions to those laws—in short, to *act* absolutely.

The introduction of a new and conflicting definition of the distinction of absolute and ordained power led to a split in theological usage. Some theologians in the late thirteenth century, such as Peter de Trabibus, maintained the traditional definition as one between divine capacity (what God could have done or theoretically could do) and divine volition (what God actually does do and will do), and consequently they rejected the canonist interpretation and the analogy to papal power.[13] Other theologians, however, such as Henry of Ghent, followed the canonist definition and, because of the implications of that definition for the doctrine of the immutability of the divine will and the potential arbitrariness it would introduce, refused to apply the distinction, understood in that sense, to God.[14]

Henry of Ghent was apparently among the first theologians to adopt the canonist interpretation of the distinction. For him *potentia absoluta* was

---

[12]John Marrone, 'The Absolute and Ordained Powers of the Pope. A Quodlibetal Question of Henry of Ghent', *Mediaeval Studies*, 36 (1974), 7-27; Eugenio Randi, 'Il rasoio contro Ockham? Un sermone inedito di Giovanni XXII', *Medioevo*, 9 (1983), 179-98; 'Potentia Dei conditionata. Una questione di Ugo di saint-Chér sull'onnipotenza divina (Sent. I, 42, q. 1)', *Rivista di storia della filosofia*, n.s. 1 (1984), 521-36; 'La vergine e il papa. *Potentia Dei absoluta* e *plenitudo potestatis* papale nel XIV secolo', *History of Political Thought*, 5 (1984), 425-45; '*Lex est in potestate agentis.* Note per una storia dell'idea scotista di *potentia absoluta*', in M. Beonio-Brocchieri Fumagalli (ed.), *Sopra la volta del mondo: Onnipotenza e potenza assoluta di Dio tra medioevo e età moderna* (Bergamo: Lubrina, 1986), 129-38; and Eugenio Randi, *Il sovrano e l'orologiaio: Due immagini di Dio nel dibattito sulla 'potentia absoluta' fra XIII e XIV secolo* (Firenze: Cionini, 1987).

[13]See Gedeon Gál, 'Petrus de Trabibus on the Absolute and Ordained Power of God', in R.S. Almagno and C.L. Harkins (eds.), *Studies Honoring Ignatius Charles Brady, Friar Minor* (St. Bonaventure, NY: The Franciscan Institute, 1976), 283-92.

[14]Marrone, 'The Absolute and Ordained Powers'.

equivalent to the exercise of royal or papal *plenitudo potestatis*. For that reason Henry felt it was an inappropriate distinction when applied to God, even if it was a useful concept when applied to papal power. In theological contexts, therefore, Henry avoided using the distinction. John Duns Scotus, however, although he applied the traditional theological model throughout most of his work, repeated the canonistic analogy to papal power when he defined the distinction. It was essentially through Scotus, therefore, that a second and very different understanding of the distinction entered theological and philosophical discussion—a distinction between the way God normally acts and the way he might occasionally act. For Scotus such occasional action would never be capricious or despotic but always an implementation of a beneficent divine will. And such action, when it occurred, would be ordained, since God never acts *inordinate*.

The implications for late medieval thought of the Scotistic inclusion of the canonist interpretation into the distinction of divine power are considerable.[15] There was not one definition in use in the fourteenth century but two definitions, with a blending of usage in numerous authors. Wherever the Scotistic tradition was strong—and this covers most of the fourteenth century—we should expect to find elements of a canonistic interpretation of the distinction, while among those primarily influenced by William of Ockham, or for that matter by Thomas Aquinas, we find the traditional theological interpretation. As the influence of Ockham's thought waned at Oxford in the 1340s and 1350s—and it is now clear that it was never as strong as was believed[16]—it is likely that when theologians used the distinction in England in the second half of the century, it was more often to be either the canonist interpretation or some blend of the canonist and earlier theological definition. It is surprising that any potential destabilization produced by a theory of divine intervention through the exercise of absolute power came not with Ockham, who was adamantly opposed to it, but earlier with Scotus, and was associated with the Scotistic tradition. Yet the canonist definition of the distinction was more pervasive than the Scotistic tradition. We find traces of it in Robert Holcot, Thomas Bradwardine, and Stephen Patrington—none of whom could be described as a Scotist nor, for that matter, as an Ockhamist.

---

[15]See William J. Courtenay, *Capacity and Volition: A History of the Distinction of Absolute and Ordained Power* (Bergamo: Lubrina, 1990). The early history of the distinction is also covered in Lawrence Moonan, *Divine Power: The Medieval Power Distinction up to its Adoption by Albert, Bonaventure, and Aquinas* (Oxford: Clarendon Press, 1994).

[16]See Katherine H. Tachau, *Vision and Certitude in the Age of Ockham: Optics, Epistemology, and the Foundations of Semantics, 1250-1345* (Leiden: Brill, 1988).

C. Implications for thought and literature in fourteenth-century England

On the basis of that historiographical analysis, especially the recognition of two different definitions of the distinction of absolute and ordained power operative in fourteenth-century England, and two correspondingly different models of the created universe and the operation of the divine will, what should one be looking for in Middle English texts that might betray the shadow cast by these different interpretations of an important theological theme? The mixed success of the early efforts in tracing the influence or application of that theological distinction should not dissuade present-day scholars from looking at fourteenth-century literary texts against the background of the schools and of an educated society aware to some degree of the philosophical and theological content of the instruction provided there. Wherever the realm of human events interacts with the realm of divine will, be it on epistemological issues, or moral issues, or the freedom of the human will, one should be attuned to the possibility that the dialectic of divine power may be an operative motif, a framework within which an author sets his characters to play out their parts. Both interpretations of the language of divine power—whether it be the distinction between divine capacity and divine will, or the distinction between God's normal action and his occasional intervention—will employ the image of God as legislator, will speak in terms of a divine plan, and stress the goodness and reliability of the divine nature. None of the instability born of irrational, arbitrary divine action, attributed by earlier historians to fourteenth-century nominalism, can be found with either of these models or interpretations. Both interpretations stress the contingency of creation, divine transcendence, but also the self-binding, covenantal relation of God to the orders of nature and grace he established. Even those who see the *potentia Dei absoluta* as a form of divine action assume that miraculous divine intervention is always for the benefit of the people of God. Where the two definitions will differ will be in whether the dialectic is focused on legal and causal relationships and is used simply to underscore simultaneously both contingency and dependability, or whether it is focused on the divine nature and is used to express the dependability of normal processes alongside occasional divine intervention. Also critical will be where miracles are placed. In the traditional theological interpretation, miracles are part of the eternal plan of God, part of the total ordained order even if hidden and less comprehensible. In the canonist interpretation, miracles are those very moments in which God as sovereign power suspends the normal operations of the laws of nature and grace to benefit certain individuals or to reveal the divine majesty.

As the image of God as legislator suggests, late medieval thinkers, including those characterized as nominalists, did not eschew analogy as a major tool for expressing philosophical and theological truths.[17] Ockham's campaign against reification, against pre-existing forms or universals independent of existing substances and qualities, against arguments from the nature of the created order to the nature of God, or against a realist view of allegory should not blind us to the fact that Ockham also recognized the importance of figures of speech, metaphoric expression, and the usefulness of human analogies to describe God's relation to his creation. At the heart of the distinction of absolute and ordained power lies the belief that the omnipotent creator is identical with the wise legislator and the beneficent judge.

---

[17]Sheila Delany's perceptive 'Undoing Substantial Connection' overlooks areas of 'nominalist' thought in which analogy is not only retained but extensively used. Although her view of *potentia absoluta* (51) was understandably untouched by the revisions occurring at that time, her main point nicely anticipates Francis Oakley's important *Omnipotence, Covenant, and Order*.

'AS WRIT MYN AUCTOUR CALLED LOLLIUS': DIVINE AND AUTHORIAL OMNIPOTENCE IN CHAUCER'S *TROILUS AND CRISEYDE*

RICHARD J. UTZ

> Chaucer's Lollius has long been regarded by us critics and scholars as a mystery; and, to confess the truth, the thing has become a mystery indeed under our treatment. For in our discussions we have made so many mistakes about plain matters of record, and have emitted so many discordant conjectures, that the whole subject has become entangled to the verge of distraction and is now involved in a kind of druidical mist. Let us try to extricate ourselves from the fogbound labyrinth, and to that end let us examine certain obvious phenomena—for such there are—in an orderly and logical manner, in the light of reason and common sense and of what we know of the habits of literary men.[1]

This powerful statement is the introductory paragraph of George Kittredge's magisterial eigthy-five-page essay entitled 'Chaucer's Lollius'. The site and date of this publication, the *Harvard Studies in Classical Philology* in 1917, may be regarded as representative of the critical methodology which dominates scholarly work on the Latin-sounding, seven-letter name which Chaucer mentions only three times in all his texts, once in the *House of Fame* (see 1464-72) and twice in *Troilus and Criseyde* (I, 394; V, 1653).[2] Kittredge and numerous other critics, in a veritable flurry of historical scholarship, beginning in the second half of the nineteenth century and abating in the 1950s,[3] defended the medieval

---

[1] George Lyman Kittredge, 'Chaucer's Lollius', *Harvard Studies in Classical Philology*, 28 (1917), 47-132.

[2] All references to and quotations from Chaucer's texts in this essay are according to *The Riverside Chaucer*, gen. ed. Larry D. Benson (Boston, MA: Houghton Mifflin, 1987).

[3] For a fairly inclusive survey of opinions before Kittredge, cf. Eleanor P. Hammond, *Chaucer: A Bibliographical Manual* (New York: Macmillan, 1908), 94-8, and Rudolf Imelmann, 'Chaucers *Haus der Fama*', *Englische Studien*, 45 (1912), 406-9. It would be difficult to discuss all existing opinions on Lollius which appeared together with or

author against the insinuation that he might be guilty of the worst of all crimes a philologist can conceive of: plagiarism or, as Kittredge has it, 'fraud' or 'deceit'.[4] Although the philological effort to exonerate a genial Chaucer from having simply fabricated or invented the name 'Lollius' is not always as openly acknowledged as in Kittredge's essay, it can be perceived as the ruling paradigm behind practically all the investigations which have tried to provide historical Lollii to Chaucer studies (or, similarly, historical 'Kyots' to Wolfram von Eschenbach studies[5]).

To answer the vexing question of Lollius' identity, a variety of theories about medieval and Roman candidates—usually ones with some connection to the matter of Troy—have been advanced. Charles Hathaway's sug-

---

after Hammond and Imelmann. I list the following bibliographical references only to show the extent of interest in the question: James R. Kreuzer, 'An Alleged Crux in Chaucer', *Notes & Queries*, n.s. 4 (1957), 409; W. Morel, 'An Alleged Crux in Chaucer', *Notes & Queries*, n.s. 4 (1957), 238-9; M.L. Levy, 'As myn Auctour Seith', *Medium Aevum*, 12 (1943), 25-9; Catherine Carswell, 'Lollius Myn Autour', *TLS*, Dec. 28, 1935, 899; R.C. Goffin, 'Chaucer's Lollius', *TLS*, Aug. 26, 1926, 564, and 'Chaucer's Lollius', *TLS*, April 21, 1927, 280; Hertha Korten, *Chaucers literarische Beziehungen zu Boccaccio: Die künstlerische Konzeption der* Canterbury Tales *und das Lolliusproblem* (Rostock: Hinstorff, 1920), reviewed by Walther Fischer, *Die Neueren Sprachen*, 20 (1921), 172-3; Hubertis M. Cummings, *The Indebtedness of Chaucer's Works to the Italian Works of Boccaccio* (Cincinnati, OH: University of Cincinnati, 1916), 153-75; John E. Wells, *A Manual of the Writings in Middle English* (New Haven, CT: Yale University Press, 1916), 664-5; 872-3; Emil Koeppel, 'Chaucer and Cicero's *Laelius de Amicitia*', *Archiv*, 126 (1911), 180-2; John L. Lowes, 'Chaucer's "Etik"', *Modern Language Notes*, 25 (1910), 87-9; Eleanor P. Hammond, 'Two Chaucer Cruces', *Modern Language Notes*, 22 (1907), 51-2.

[4]Kittredge, 'Chaucer's Lollius', 52; 62. An even earlier warning against attributing to Chaucer any capricious intentions with respect to Lollius is John Koch's 'Ein Beitrag zur Kritik Chaucers', *Englische Studien*, 1 (1877), 249-93. Numerous scholars have attempted to explain Chaucer's silence about his main source for *Troilus and Criseyde*, Boccaccio's *Filostrato*, on the basis of biographical assumptions. Pietro Borghesi (*Boccaccio and Chaucer* (Bologna: N. Zanichelli, 1903)) maintains that Chaucer left Boccaccio unmentioned because the Italian poet was known as a man of loose habits and the English king would not have approved of Chaucer's celebrating him as his master source. More recently, Donald Howard has seen a disappointing personal meeting of both poets in Italy as the reason for Chaucer's ignoring of Boccaccio (*Chaucer: His Life, His Works, His World* (New York: E.P. Dutton, 1987), 192-3).

[5]Beryl Smalley, commenting on the philological search for Kyot's identity (*English Friars and Antiquity in the Early Fourteenth Century* (Oxford: Blackwell, 1960), 19-20), states that '[v]ernacular writers perhaps felt a need to imitate the schoolmen in arguing from authority, even to the point of inventing what they could not otherwise have put forward'. Cf. also W. Falk, 'Wolframs Kyot und die Bedeutung der "Quelle" im Mittelalter', *Literaturwissenschaftliches Jahrbuch*, n.s. 9 (1968), 1-63; Joachim Bumke, *Die Wolfram von Eschenbach Forschung seit 1945: Bericht und Bibliographie* (Munich: Fink, 1970), 243-50; C. Lofmark, 'Die Interpretationen der Kyotstellen im *Parzival*', *Wolfram Studien*, 4 (1977), 33-70.

gestion that Lollius might stand for the thirteenth-century philosopher and alchemist, Raymond Lull, sounds intriguing but is far-fetched and has been dismissed as such.[6] Lillian Herlands Hornstein, trying to defend Chaucer against commentators who assumed Lollius to be 'a literary hallucination',[7] detected a friend of Francis Petrarch, one Lellus Pietri Stephani de Tosettis, to whom Petrarch in his letters referred as 'Lelius', as Chaucer's 'auctour'. In her opinion, Chaucer, before he wrote the *House of Fame* and *Troilus and Criseyde*, received a manuscript of Boccaccio's *Il Filostrato* (the main source for his *Troilus*) without Boccaccio's name but with the statement (oral or written) that the begetter was Lollius. A Roman historian of the third century, a certain Lollius Urbicus, the elder, has also been advanced as a possible source by a whole host of scholars ever since the late seventeenth century. This theory, one which led astray such famous Chaucerians as Thomas Warton, Eleanor P. Hammond, and T.R. Lounsberry, was successfully dismissed by Kittredge who was able to follow back an amazing chain of 'information and misinformation' to its beginnings in Speght's list of authors appended to the 1598 Folio.[8] Hans J. Epstein, in his essay on 'The Identity of Chaucer's Lollius', suggested Bassus Lollius, a first-century Roman, as the probable Classical authority from which Chaucer claims to have translated his *Troilus*.[9] Several of Bassus' epigrams touch on the matter of Troy, and Epstein maintained that Chaucer may have had access to these texts either via a *compendium* or a *florilegium*, perhaps a yet unknown version of the *Greek Anthology*.

The most substantial theory on the historicity of Lollius has been proposed by Kittredge himself. Expanding on earlier indications made by R.G. Latham[10] and Bernhard Ten Brink,[11] Kittredge claimed that Chaucer's Lollius should be associated with Horace's student Maximus Lollius whose name and reputation as an 'auctor' on the Trojan War he encountered due to a careless or ignorant reading of the first line of Horace, *Epistolae* 1.2, a text which Chaucer might have stumbled upon while reading John of Salisbury's *Policraticus* VII, 9:

> Troiani belli scriptorem, Maxime Lolli,
> dum tu declamas Romae, Praeneste relegi [...].

---

[6]Charles Hathaway, 'Chaucer's Lollius', *Englische Studien*, 44 (1911), 161.

[7]Lillian Herlands Hornstein, 'Petrarch's Laelius, Chaucer's Lollius?', *PMLA*, 63 (1948), 64.

[8]Kittredge, 'Chaucer's Lollius', 83-9.

[9]Hans J. Epstein, 'The Identity of Chaucer's Lollius', *Modern Language Quarterly*, 3 (1942), 391-400.

[10]R.G. Latham, 'Chaucer', *The Athenaeum*, Oct. 3, 1868, 433.

[11]Bernhard Ten Brink, *Chaucer: Studien zur Geschichte seiner Entwicklung und zur Chronologie seiner Schriften* (Münster, Westf.: Russell, 1870), 87-8.

Chaucer or Chaucer's source, so Kittredge's argument, must have misconstrued 'Maxime' as a simple adjective (instead of a noun). Moreover, if one introduces the (mis)reading 'scriptor' or 'scriptorum' in place of the accusative 'scriptorem', one arrives at the phrase: 'Lollius, you great writer of the Trojan War' or 'Lollius, you greatest writer of the Trojan War'.[12]

Thus, according to Kittredge, when Lollius is mentioned in the *House of Fame*, Chaucer

> was not inventing: he was under a misapprehension. He believed that a work by Lollius had once existed, but, since neither he nor any of his acquaintances had ever seen it, that it was lost. [...] When Chaucer wrote the *Troilus*, his erroneous belief that one Lollius had written a (lost) work on Troy had not been corrected. [...] Accordingly, in the *Troilus*, as part of the fiction, Chaucer pretended to be translating faithfully the Latin work of Lollius. Lollius is not Boccaccio, nor Petrarch, nor Benoit, nor Guido: he is purely and simply Lollius—a supposed ancient writer on the subject. The fiction consists not in ascribing to Lollius a work on Troy (for that was merely an error) but in claiming to have this work in hand and to translate it faithfully.[13]

In 1950, Robert Pratt was able to substantiate Kittredge's hypothesis by providing evidence of two medieval manuscripts in which the assumed textual corruptions actually occur.[14] One of the misreadings/misspellings ('scriptorum' instead of 'scriptorem') Pratt found in a copy of John of Salisbury's *Policraticus* (1159), which cites various lines from the Horatian *Epistolae* while discussing the use of poetry in the teaching of moral philosophy.[15] The second and more important one Pratt detected in a French translation of the *Policraticus* which a fourteenth-century Franciscan, Denis Foullechat, undertook for Charles V. Unlike Chaucer, who might have misread 'lolli' as vocative, Foullechat seems to have interpreted 'lolli' as nominative and mistranslated the passage as if Horace was introducing the principal ancient authority on the Matter of Troy:

> Car il [scil. Horace] dit, que lolli fu principal escrivain de la bataille de troye.[16]

---

[12]Kittredge ('Chaucer's Lollius', 77) hypothesized that such a medieval version, without the facilitation of punctuation and enlightening capitals, might have looked like this:
>   Scriptorem belli troiani maxime lolli
>   dum tue declamas rome preneste relegi.

[13]Ibid., 71-2.

[14]Robert Pratt, 'A Note on Chaucer's Lollius', *Modern Language Notes*, 65 (1950), 183-7.

[15]For a discussion of Chaucer's possible knowledge and use of the *Policraticus*, see Pratt's 'A Note on Chaucer and the *Policraticus* of John of Salisbury', *Modern Language Notes*, 65 (1950), 243-6.

Kittredge's findings, together with Pratt's corroborating textual evidence, seem to have extricated Chaucerians from the pre-Kittredgian 'fogbound labyrinth' concerning Lollius. Consequently, Stephen A. Barney, in his 'Explanatory Notes' to *Troilus and Criseyde* in the 1987 edition of the *Riverside Chaucer*, expresses his complete confidence that—given Pratt's findings—'[n]o better evidence that Kittredge was right could be desired'.[17]

I am far from challenging the theoretical possibility of Chaucer's misapprehending a hypothetically existing version of John of Salisbury's *Policraticus* or his taking for factual information such a misapprehension by the author of somesuch manuscript. However, I do have serious problems with construing a relentless causal necessity out of Pratt's findings. After all, the misreadings which the dominant philological hypothesis attributes to Chaucer and/or his source are only supported by two relatively obscure manuscripts. Neither of them can be linked to Chaucer, and their existence certainly does not warrant Stephen Barney's universalizing statement that an error like this 'was current in Chaucer's time'.[18] Furthermore, I have a hard time believing that Chaucer, who had researched the earlier renderings of the Trojan War thoroughly enough to get intimately acquainted with Guido delle Colonne, Giovanni Boccaccio, and to know about the works or reputations of Homer, Dares, Dictys, Geoffrey of Monmouth, Josephus, Statius, Vergil, Ovid, Lucan, and Claudian would be willing to accept helter-skelter a certain 'Lollius' as the 'principal' authority on the Matter of Troy based on the evidence of one single (misapprehended) phrase.[19] Therefore, in the absence of irrefutable, hard-core textual proof, I would like to abandon Kittredge's ingenious philological

---

[16] Quoted from Pratt, 'A Note on Chaucer's Lollius', 186.
[17] *The Riverside Chaucer*, 1022.
[18] Ibid.
[19] John V. Fleming (*Classical Imitation and Interpretation in Chaucer's* Troilus (Lincoln, NE, and London: University of Nebraska Press, 1990), 179-200) has recently reopened the question about Chaucer's Lollius. Although Fleming has similar doubts about Kittredge's hypothesis because it reduces Chaucer—despite Kittredge's disclaimers—to a credulous 'dimwit' (191), he does subscribe to the assumption that the name Lollius (that of Maximus Lollius, that is) was indeed suggested to Chaucer in the opening lines of Horace's *Epistola* I.2. However, far from regarding this incident as one of misapprehension (on Chaucer's part or on the part of his source), he asserts that the name's inclusion presents an intentional act of his poetic imagination, one that consciously conceived and executed *Troilus and Criseyde* as 'a moral allegory in precisely the fashion that Horace found the *Iliad* to be moral allegory' (199). Thus, Fleming holds, bringing to literary fame an obscure Roman poet called Lollius served the author's own medieval classicism. Like the earlier philological readings, Fleming's learned and suggestive hypothesis depends on Chaucer's intensive knowledge of Horace for which there is no secure textual or historical evidence.

hypothesis to pursue my own—one which situates Chaucer in the intellectual milieu of late-medieval England and which assumes that the author invented 'Lollius' as part of a poetic strategy which draws attention to the possibly absolute power (*potentia absoluta*) the fourteenth-century author perceived to hold over the microcosm of his literary creation. While my intention with this essay is thus—on the one hand—to propose a historicizing variant to the philological *status quo* on the Lollius question, I would—on the other hand—like to introduce a powerful exception against the 'New' Philologists' claim that any interpretive approach by a medievalist based on authorship must be ill-informed because medieval authors did not share their modern counterparts' concern for copyright questions.[20]

In the preceding paragraph I invoked a term from late-medieval scholasticism to indicate a methodological assumption upon which the following deliberations depend. I will make use of the late-medieval nominalist concept of the absolute power (*potentia absoluta*) of God's free will in a structural analogy with the power Chaucer wields as the author of *Troilus and Criseyde*. In recent years, critics have made ample use of nominalist thought to explicate some of the cruces of fourteenth-century texts whose writers

> were less interested in restating moral and religious commonplaces than in investigating the possibilities and limitations of language. Responding to the developing nominalism of the time and the pervasive uncertainty as to exactly what one could know, storytellers joined schoolmen in focusing not on truth itself but on such epistemological matters as the essential ambiguity of signs and the inherent complexity of language. Along with speculative grammarians, poets explored processes of signification and modifications of meaning. And, along with semioticians, fiction writers investigated modes of signifying ways in which language altered concepts of reality. For those involved with the word, the emphasis was on inference, equivocation, and various kinds of conundrums or *aenigmata*.[21]

Among late-medieval English texts, Chaucer's have yielded most fruitful results for exploring potential correspondences with nominalist tenets, and Ralph Strode, the 'philosophical' (in two manuscripts 'logical')

---

[20]For the 'New' Philologists' claims about authorship, see Stephen G. Nichols (ed.), *The New Philology* (special issue of *Speculum*, 65 (1990)), especially the contributions by Suzanne Fleischmann, Stephen G. Nichols, Gabrielle M. Spiegel, and Siegfried Wenzel. This recent movement has been critically reviewed by Karl Stackmann, 'Neue Philologie?', in Joachim Heinzle (ed.), *Modernes Mittelalter: Neue Bilder einer populären Epoche* (Munich: Insel Verlag, 1994), 398-427 (esp. 403-5, on 'Autor, Werk').

[21]Edmund Reiss, 'Ambiguous Signs and Authorial Deceptions in Fourteenth-Century Fictions', in Julian Wasserman and Lois Roney (eds.), *Sign, Sentence, Discourse: Language in Medieval Thought and Literature* (Syracuse, NY: Syracuse University Press, 1989), 113-37, here: 114-5.

Strode to whom *Troilus and Criseyde* is dedicated, has been presented as a probable source from which Chaucer might have gleaned basic epistemological and theological concepts propagated by fourteenth-century nominalists.[22] For the purpose of this paper, I will apply the nominalist concept of divine omnipotence as a structural analogue, as a form of theological discourse which, not unlike literary discourse, participated in the negotiation of late-medieval and early modern human problems. I will attempt to suggest a correspondence between the divine creative act and Chaucer's act of creating his literary fiction. Postulating such a correspondence seems far-fetched, as high and late-medieval authors almost never presented their work as a free creation *ex nihilo* or *de potentia absoluta*.[23] Rather, readers are assured that texts are based on preexistent material, that the author is part of a well-established and clearly defined tradition of literary production and reception. As Ullrich Langer explains:

> Recourse to prior themes or elements was usually perceived as authenticating, as enabling, rather than disabling, for the fictional world was believed to celebrate the survival of human culture, not its original reinvention by an individual. Theologically speaking, the human author conceived of himself as an *artifex*, not as a *creator* or *prima causa efficiens*; he was caused to write by conditions outside himself. Human imagination, then, was not the freeing of the mind from the constraints of the existing world, but an ability

---

[22] For a survey of existing scholarship on Chaucer and nominalism, cf. William H. Watts and Richard J. Utz, 'Nominalist Perspectives on Chaucer's Poetry: A Bibliographical Essay', *Medievalia et Humanistica*, n.s. 20 (1993), 147-73. For Ralph Strode as Chaucer's possible connection to basic nominalist concepts, cf. Richard J. Utz, 'Negotiating the Paradigm: Literary Nominalism and the Theory and Practice of Rereading Late Medieval Texts', in Richard J. Utz (ed.), *Literary Nominalism and the Theory of Rereading Late Medieval Texts: A New Research Paradigm* (Lewiston, NY: Edwin Mellen Press, 1995), 10-4, and Rodney Delasanta, 'Chaucer and Strode', *Chaucer Review*, 26 (1991), 205-18. For a recent essay which reinforces earlier scholarship marginalizing nominalism and centering on Thomism as the central contemporary philosophical and theological current in late-medieval England, cf. Robert H. Boyer, 'Chaucer and Thomas', in Michael B. Lukens (ed.), *Conflict and Community: New Studies in Thomistic Thought* (New York et al.: Lang, 1992), 103-24.

[23] Cf. Alastair J. Minnis, *Medieval Theory of Authorship: Scholastic Literary Attitudes in the Later Middle Ages* (Philadelphia, PA: University of Philadelphia Press, 2nd ed. 1988), for an inclusive survey of high medieval and in-depth study of late-medieval authorial attitudes and mentalities. A different, highly perceptive reading of Chaucer's inclusion of the free will theme in his poetry has been advanced by Joerg O. Fichte ('Man's Free Will and the Poet's Choice: The Creation of Artistic Order in Chaucer's Knight's Tale', *Anglia*, 93 (1975), 335-60). He postulates that the poet was cognizant of the concept of the *poeta-theologus* in fourteenth-century Italian poetics and shaped his 'Knight's Tale' so as to have its perfect structure mirror that of divine creation. *Troilus and Criseyde*, especially in view of the contingency of its structure, demands a radically different view of God's (and an author's) role in his creation.

to reproduce images and spiritual constructs that were already contained in the created fabric of the world itself. The imagination allowed man to uncover the similitudes in the vast network of signs around him, not to produce an alternative to that perfect work. Imagination, thus, in a sense, belonged partly to the objects contemplated, partly to the person contemplating them.[24]

With most late-medieval authors, the preeminence of this tradition can hardly be overestimated.[25] For Chaucer, it is certainly palpable in the constructions of the narrators of his dream visions or the *Treatise on the Astrolabe*.[26] Even in his *Troilus and Criseyde*, the text in which narrative strategies are most openly a topic, the poet devises a narrator who presents himself as a mere *interpres*, a faithful translator, of the Lollian master fabric, who commences each of the five books with an invocation of various Muses, and who leaves no doubt that he is a faithful servant of the members of his audience, themselves servants of the God of Love. However, the existence of these and several other devices indicating external

---

[24] Ullrich Langer, *Divine and Poetic Freedom in the Renaissance: Nominalist Theology and Literature in France and Italy* (Princeton, NJ: Princeton University Press, 1990), 22. I am greatly indebted to the insights of this excellent study.

[25] For a critical investigation of Deschamps', Usk's, Gower's, Hoccleve's, Lydgate's, Henryson's, Douglas', Skelton's, Hawes' views on Chaucer's role as *auctour*, see Joerg O. Fichte, 'Quha wait gif all that Chauceir wrait was trew—Auctor and auctoritas in 15th Century English Literature', in Walter Haug and Burghart Wachinger (eds.), *Traditionswandel und Traditionsverhalten* (Tübingen: Niemeyer, 1991), 61-76.

[26] On the *House of Fame*, e.g., cf. Jaqueline T. Miller, *Poetic License: Authorship and Authority in Medieval and Renaissance Contexts* (New York and Oxford: Oxford University Press, 1986), 71: 'Throughout the poem the narrator has alternately asserted his superiority to and attempted to disappear behind previously authorized versions of trouthe, claiming and disclaiming his role as author as he tests and rejects all available authorities, including himself. No position—whether of self-effacing dependence, or assertive self-reliance, or even a more moderate middle position—has proven satisfactory. What results is an oscillation among inadequate options that constantly surface, call each other into question, and replace each other. The narrator's silence at the end acknowledges the limitations of his own voice but also recognizes and predicts the inevitable failure of the "man of gret auctorite" to maintain his status, and it recalls the evidence of similar failures that have occurred throughout the poem. No truly authoritative voice has been discovered; no authorial stance can be fully validated; and the poetic voice and enterprise end'. In his *Troilus and Criseyde*, however, Chaucer has found a solution for this problem, one that allows him to acknowledge openly his authority over the fictional text by attributing limited authority to Pandarus, the narrator, and himself.—The *locus classicus* for disclaiming authority about compiling the *Treatise on the Astrolabe* appears in lines 59-64, where Chaucer lets 'lyte Lewys' know that 'I ne usurpe not to have founden this werk of my labour of olde astrologiens, and have it translatid in myn Englissh only for thy doctrine'. In this text, Chaucer undoubtedly chooses the compiler's mask.

causes and determinants for Chaucer's fiction should not foreclose the simultaneous presence of alternative, more consciously authorial self-presentations. The traditional features may become, as Ullrich Langer has recently demonstrated for several early modern French and Italian poets, mere formal exercises which serve to challenge or caricature dominant masks of authorship and which are meant as a backdrop against which alternative definitions are rendered possible.[27] Langer contends that 'nominalist features of God can be seen in the way Renaissance authors construct their fictional worlds, and that these features often point to the most interesting aspects of those fictional worlds: the feeling of contingency, the feeling that things could easily be otherwise, and that they are dependent on an only partially motivated decision of their author'.[28] Although high medieval authors/compilers sometimes also stylize themselves as 'werltgot' (i.e., Lord of the fictional world created by them), they take pains in convincing their readers that their books are rationally plausible, solidly based on preexistent sources, and legible just like the book of God's creation.[29] In this sense, the choices some thirteenth-century Arthurian writers make in compiling their preexistent material become

---

[27]Langer, *Divine and Poetic Freedom*, 20-4. The deference to *auctores* as a 'shield and defence' for the personal opinions and prejudices by a compiler's choice and treatment of experts can be observed as early as with the *apologia* in Jean de Meun's *Roman de la Rose*, where the 'traditional protestation of the compiler is well on its way to becoming a "disavowal of responsibility" trope' (Minnis, *Medieval Theory*, 198). The playful extrapolation of this technique seems to develop with Chaucer; its abandonment is an early modern feature. Flora Ross Amos (*Early Theories of Translation* (New York: Columbia University Press, 1920), 29-46) observes that Chaucer is part of the transition period from the fourteenth to the fifteenth century in which authors/translators begin to insert more commentary on their work and techniques. However, Amos shows that in most cases the additional commentary is merely larger in quantity, not in the quality and consciousness of observation. That Chaucer knew full well how to follow both *verba et sententia* of his sources truthfully, if he only decided to do so, has recently been demonstrated by Alastair J. Minnis and Tim William Machan, 'The Boece as Late-Medieval Translation', in Alastair J. Minnis (ed.), *Chaucer's Boece and the Medieval Translation of Boethius* (Cambridge: D.S. Brewer, 1993), 167-91.

[28]Langer, *Divine and Poetic Freedom*, 22.

[29]See, e.g., Matthias Meyer's discussion of Heinrich von dem Türlin's stylization as 'werltgot' in his novel *Diu Crône*: '"Sô dunke ich mich ein werltgot": Überlegungen zum Verhältnis Autor-Erzähler-Fiktion im späten Artusroman', in Volker Mertens and Friedrich Wolfzettel (eds.), *Fiktionalität im Artusroman* (Tübingen: Niemeyer, 1993), 185-202, esp. 194-200. For further critical discussions of the medieval parallelization of author and God, see Thomas Cramer, '*Solus Creator est Deus*: Der Autor auf dem Weg zum Schöpfertum', *Daphnis*, 15 (1986), 261-76; Wladyslaw Tatarkiewicz, *Geschichte der Ästhetik, vol. II: Die Ästhetik des Mittelalters* (Basel and Stuttgart: Schwabe, 1980), 262-70; Ernst Robert Curtius, *Europäische Literatur und lateinisches Mittelalter* (Berne and Munich: Francke, 4th ed. 1963), 541-53; and Leo Spitzer, 'Note on the Poetic and the Empirical "I" in Medieval Authors', *Traditio*, 4 (1946), 414-22, esp. 415 and note 3.

more and more obviously theirs, but the source material still fully motivates the degrees of variation or self-involvement of the respective author.[30]

How can the nominalist stressing of God's absolute power result in new paradigms of thought which may facilitate more freedom for the individual in late-medieval England or early modern France and Italy? Nominalist thinkers (William of Ockham, Nicholas d'Autrecourt, Pierre d'Ailly, Gabriel Biel, to name only a few) stress the distinction between two aspects of God's power, the *potentia absoluta* (all the possibilities open to God, absolutely and hypothetically speaking) and the *potentia ordinata* (those possibilities He has chosen and are visible in the existing order of creation and salvation).[31] According to His absolute power, He could have chosen to create a different world, to incarnate Himself as an ass or a stone, or to cause someone to have intuitive cognition of a non-existent. For some of these thinkers, the only limitation to this power is the principle of non-contradiction—that is, God cannot do something logically contradictory. Of course, God has promised us that he will follow his own chosen order, so in fact God will not suddenly and arbitrarily exercise his absolute power in any way which might compromise the goodness and reliability of the divine legislator.[32] Still, even the merely hypothetical possibility of God's exercise of his *potentia absoluta* became a favorite tool for advancing

---

[30]Cf., e.g., Bonaventure's high medieval description of the relationship between God, Nature, and art in his *Commentary on the Sentences*: 'Cum enim sit triplex agentis, scilicet Deus, natura et intelligentia, ista sunt agentia ordinata, it quod primum praesupponitur a secundo, et secundum praesupponitur a tertio. Deus enim operatur ex nihilo; natura vero non facit ex nihilo, sed ex ente in potentia; ars supponit operationem naturae et operatur super ens completum; non enim facit lapides, sed domum de lapidibus' (*Doctoris Seraphici S. Bonaventurae S.R.E. Episcopi Cardinalis Opera Omnia, iussu et auctoritate R.mi P. Bernardini a Portu Romatino totius ordinis minorum S. P. Francisci Ministri Generalis edita studio et curia P.P. Collegii S. Bonaventurae*, vol. 2 (Ad Claras Aquas (Quaracchi): Ex Typographia Collegii S. Bonaventurae, 1885), 202).

[31]Brief late-medieval definitions of the *potentiae* and related terms can be found in Johannes Altensteig's *Vocabularius theologie complectens vocabulorum descriptiones, [...] compilata a Joanne Altenstaig Mindelhaimensi [...]* (Hagenau: Henricus Gran, 1517); cf. also Heiko A. Oberman's helpful glossary appended to his *Harvest of Medieval Theology: Gabriel Biel and Late Medieval Nominalism* (Cambridge, MA: Harvard University Press, 1963), 459-76. For a recent application of the dichotomy between the two powers to fourteenth-century English culture, see Lara Ruffolo's *Unison and Cacophony: Reflections of Skepticism in Fourteenth-Century English Poetry*, PhD diss. University of California at Irvine, 1993. Unfortunately, Ruffolo merely invokes the distinction as a vague cultural analogue without presenting textual correspondences.

[32]There is disagreement among experts in history, philosophy, and theology as to the consequences of the nominalist stressing of God's absolute power. A sizeable group of scholars, among them Heiko A. Oberman and William J. Courtenay, maintains that the dialectic between *potentia absoluta* and *ordinata* in fourteenth- and fifteenth-century thought demonstrated both the contingency and the reliability of the existing *ordo*. In

theoretical speculation among late scholastic thinkers. The questions these thinkers entertained severely challenged the high medieval Thomist synthesis between reason and faith, a synthesis only viable if God guaranteed the stability of the existing *ordo*. By stressing God's absolute power the nominalists demonstrated the inadequacy of human rational thought to plumb the mysteries of God's free will and rendered the world a contingent place to live and think in. As Sheila Delany has demonstrated, this hypothetical postulate severely challenged, perhaps destroyed what she calls 'substantial connection', the intimate analogical relationship which linked God's ideas and intentions (*invisibilia*) with the outcome of these intentions, i.e., the existing *ordo* (*visibilia*). The postulate had immediate repercussions on all forms of thought based on the stability of such epistemological analogy: its emergence provides potential explanations for the fourteenth-century attacks on analogical political theory (e.g., Jean Quidort, Marsilius of Padua), science (e.g., Jean Buridan, Nicholas Oresme), and for the aesthetic interrogation of analogical forms of literature (e.g., Geoffrey Chaucer's abandoning or, at least, interrogating of allegory).[33] As a final consequence, the postulate separated theological assertions about God and theoretical assertions about nature and led to the rise of two

---

his contribution for this essay collection, 'The Dialectic of Divine Omnipotence in the Age of Chaucer: A Reconsideration', William Courtenay states, e.g., that '[e]ven those who see the *potentia Dei absoluta* as a form of divine action assume that miraculous divine intervention is always for the benefit of the people of God'. Steven Ozment, *Mysticism and Dissent: Religious Ideology and Social Protest in the Sixteenth Century* (New Haven, CT: Yale University Press, 1973), even claims that the nominalist dichotomizing of both *potentiae* bolstered the security of the existing *ordo*, as this *ordo* is revealed and ordained by God. According to Ozment, it is the movement of mysticism which puts the *potentia absoluta* to more stringent use than the nominalist thinkers. On the relationship between mysticism and nominalism in fourteenth-century English texts, cf. Jay Ruud, 'Julian of Norwich and the Nominalist Questions', in Utz (ed.), *Literary Nominalism*, 31-49. For concise discussions of the contending critical theories about nominalism, see Langer, *Divine and Poetic Freedom*, 6-11, and Utz, 'Negotiating the Paradigm', 5-10. Judgment on the issue seems to depend on whether one tends to investigate the original, conservative, theological intentions of most late scholastic thinkers (i.e., to free God from too much human rationalistic speculation) or one is interested in a general cultural outcome analysis of late-medieval nominalist theses for the history of European ideas. Ruedi Imbach demonstrates how both diametrically opposed views of nominalism are intrinsic to the genesis and development of this late-medieval movement of thought and consequently characterizes it as one of the great paradoxa in the history of philosophy; see his 'Vorwort' in Wilhelm von Ockham, *Texte zur Theorie der Erkenntnis und der Wissenschaft: Lateinisch/Deutsch*, ed. and tr. Ruedi Imbach (Stuttgart: Reclam, 1984), 5-10.

[33]See Delany's chapters on 'Undoing Substantial Connection: The Late Medieval Attack on Analogical Thought' and 'The Politics of Allegory in the Fourteenth Century' in her study *Medieval Literary Politics: Shapes of Ideology* (Manchester: Manchester University Press, 1990), 18-60.

strictly separated levels of truth: a religious truth of revelation, which was the only secure truth and which could only be attained by faith alone; or, a contingent, secular truth which could be gained through human rational thinking. Such separation of truth resulted in a shift of interest from transcendence to immanence. Hans Blumenberg summarizes the general intellectual consequences of the nominalist assertions about God's absolute freedom and autonomy:

> The modern age began, not indeed as the epoch of the death of God, but as the epoch of the hidden God, the *deus absconditus*—and a hidden God is *pragmatically* as good as dead. The nominalist theology induces a human relation to the world whose implicit content could not have been formulated in the postulate that man had to behave as though God were dead. This induces a restless taking stock of the world, which can be designated as the motive power of the age of science.[34]

Although I do not want to claim the direct influence of any specific late scholastic text on *Troilus and Criseyde*,[35] I would like to contend that Chaucer, similarly, begins to take stock of his own fictional world in a way which may be unprecedented in late-medieval English literature but which has clear parallels in the coeval philosophical superstructure. This corresponding cultural constituent will assist in understanding several of the premises of literary representation in Chaucer's text.

Chaucer intends to tell a story in which a mood of contingency surrounds all characters. Consequently, his plot is ideally situated in the midst of pagan times and the Trojan war, and for years the changing luck of warfare has produced a general sense of calamity. If life outside the walls of Troy is insecure, it is similarly contingent for Criseyde inside the city walls. Her own father, Calkas, has left her behind and has become a traitor to his city by joining the enemy. Her remaining male relative, 'uncle'

---

[34]Hans Blumenberg, *The Legitimacy of the Modern Age*, tr. Robert M. Wallace (Cambridge, MA: MIT Press, 1983), 346. David C. Lindberg (*The Beginnings of Western Science: The European Scientific Tradition in Philosophical, Religious, and Institutional Context, 600 B.C. to A.D. 1450* (Chicago, IL, and London: University of Chicago Press, 1992), 240-4) and Amos Funkenstein (*Theology and the Scientific Imagination from the Middle Ages to the Seventeenth Century* (Princeton, NJ: Princeton University Press, 1986), 152-79), in contrast to Blumenberg, warn against postulating a simple causal connection between the theological doctrine of divine omnipotence and the emergence of modern experimental science.

[35]That Chaucer did see and react against the potential dangers of radical medieval realist thought can be deduced from his creation of the character 'Troilus' as a practical literary caveat against Wycliffite realism in the poem. See my '*For all that comth, comth of necessitee*: Chaucer's Critique of Fourteenth-Century Boethianism in *Troilus and Criseyde* IV, 957-958', *Arbeiten aus Anglistik und Amerikanistik*, 21 (1996), 29-31.

Pandarus, is not very reliable either, as the happiness of his friend Troilus seems to take clear precedence over his niece's well-being. Finally, like fathers and uncles, even the Greek Gods cannot be trusted. They speak 'in amphibologies I And for o sooth they tellen twenty lies' (IV, 1406-7).[36] Within this world of chance, Chaucer has strategically placed three well-developed fabricators (or *artifices*) of fiction—Pandarus, the Narrator, and Lollius—whose limited creative powers in the end all refer the reader to their *prima causa efficiens*, Geoffrey Chaucer himself.[37]

Pandarus is a truly Chaucerian creation. The author takes special care in transforming Boccaccio's Pandaro into his very own Pandarus when he attributes twice as many lines to this character as does *Il Filostrato*.[38] As John Fyler summarizes, 'Pandarus operates as love's strategist, the expert in the Ovidian *ars amatoria*. He is an artificer of situations, a deviser of fictions to bring Troilus and Criseyde together'.[39] Whatever his own intentions, brotherly friend or voyeuristic pander, on the level of the story Pandarus is the author of a web of rhetoric, mostly proverbial, which entices both Troilus and Criseyde to consent to a relationship.[40] At a decisive moment in the story, when he wants to underline the urgency of

---

[36]Cf. Richard Waswo, 'The Narrator of *Troilus and Criseyde*', *English Literary History*, 50 (1983), 1-25, who contends that some of the contingency in Chaucer's text might be due to his own sociological circumstances in the calamitous fourteenth century.

[37]Cf. Lee Patterson, *Chaucer and the Subject of History* (Madison, WI: University of Wisconsin Press, 1991), 26: 'Throughout his early poetry Chaucer had insisted upon subjectivity as the unavoidable condition of all discourse, that all writing, both that endowed with cultural authority and that which purports to render experience directly, is mediated by a historically specific human consciousness. The early complaints and the dream visions constantly call attention to the narratorial voice, while *Troilus and Criseyde* is both presided over by the go-between Pandarus and delivered by an unavoidable narrator, in effect defining itself as a study in mediation'.

[38]Cf. B. Sandford Meech, *Design in Chaucer's* Troilus (Syracuse, NY: Syracuse University Press, 1959), 9.

[39]John Fyler, 'The Fabrications of Pandarus', *Modern Language Quarterly*, 41 (1980), 115-6.

[40]On Pandarus' use of proverbs as an implicit 'nominalist' critique of a linguistic universal, cf. the critical summary of my chapter on proverbs in *Literarischer Nominalismus im Spätmittelalter: Eine Untersuchung zu Sprache, Charakterzeichnung und Struktur in Geoffrey Chaucers* Troilus and Criseyde (Frankfurt a.M. et al.: Lang, 1990), 77-108, in Paule Mertens-Fonck's review essay, 'Le nominalisme de Geoffrey Chaucer dans *Troilus and Criseyde*: A propos d'un ouvrage récent', *Le Moyen Age*, 101 (1995), 317: 'Bien que d'origine individuelle, le proverbe exprime une vérité générale. D'abord employé comme moyen d'argumentation juridique, il marque de son empreinte la méthode scolastique et se répand dans tous les milieux. R[ichard].U[tz]. constate en effet qu'au Moyen Age, ce n'est pas tant l'expérience de vie empirique de l'individu qui sert de critère de décision: ce sont des formes de langage cristallisées

Troilus' visit to Criseyde's bedchamber, he even invents a story about a Trojan with a fairly well-known, Greek sounding name, Horaste (Orestes), to whom she has—supposedly—promised her heart (III, 792-8). Although Pandarus does succeed in soothing Troilus' desires, his rhetorical ruses must fail at easing Troilus' pain when the young prince looses Criseyde to the Greek Diomede. After all, Pandarus' powers as a wielder of words are engendered, determined, and upheld by external causes, by the story line as presented in the master source, Lollius, and its rendering into English by the narrator. Deprived of linguistic means to carry the plot any further, his resigned 'I kan namore seye' (V, 1743) hands back the story line and its characters to the next higher level of creative authority.[41]

The narrator of *Troilus and Criseyde* presents himself in typical self-effacing fashion to his target audience of courtly lovers. As they are servants of the God of love, he intends to serve them 'As though I were hire owne brother deere' (I, 51). He poses as the 'sorrowful instrument | That helpeth loveres, as I kan, to pleyne' (I, 10-1) and for the longest time abstains from any claim to being the creator or originator of the story he is about to tell. Moreover, he renounces any ambition to potential personal

---

telle que l'exemplum, la parabole et surtout le proverbe qui déterminent la pensée, la parole et l'action de l'homme réel et des personnages littéraires. Le nominalisme met en question ce réalisme néoplatonicien puisque la théorie ockhamiste refuse les universaux, les idées générales comme point de départ de la connaissance. Pour ses adeptes, la connaissance vraie ne peut être atteinte que par le particulier saisi de façon immédiate par les sens. Ockham insiste par conséquent sur le caractère précaire de l'abstraction et sur l'importance que revêtent la clarté de la langue et la concision de l'expression (le fameux 'rasoir d'Ockham'), ainsi que sur l'univocité des concepts. La pensée d'Ockham sur la langue ébranle la confiance que l'on pouvait avoir dans les moyens linguistiques abstraits et dans l'autorité de la langue elle-même. Aux yeux d'un poète comme Chaucer, elle devait rendre suspects tous les procédés stylistiques fondés sur la généralisation ou l'abstraction avec, en première ligne, le proverbe. Dans l'usage qu'il fait de ce dernier, Chaucer opère une véritable transposition de la pensée nominaliste au domaine littéraire. Ce mode d'expression est celui que le poète a choisi d'attribuer à Pandare, l'entremetteur qui parvient à ses fins à force de ruse, de mensonges et de supercheries: les vérités générales exprimées par le proverbe, dont il fait largement usage, font miroiter aux yeux de ceux qui y croient une certitude qui n'a aucune existence réelle et qui est largement dépassée par l'expérience empirique'. Cf. also my forthcoming essay, 'Zu Funktion und Epistemologie des Sprichwortes bei Geoffrey Chaucer', *Das Mittelalter: Perspektiven mediävistischer Forschung*, 2.2 (1997) (forthcoming).

[41]Parallels between Pandarus and Chaucer's narrator are legion. For several successful discussions, see, e.g., Adrienne Lockhart, 'Semantic, Moral, and Aesthetic Degeneration in *Troilus and Criseyde*', *Chaucer Review*, 8 (1973), 117-8; E. Talbot Donaldson, 'Chaucer's Three "P"s: Pandarus, Pardoner, Poet', *Michigan Quarterly Review*, 14 (1975), 289-290; Rose Zimbardo, 'Creator and Created: The Generic Perspective of Chaucer's *Troilus and Criseyde*', *Chaucer Review*, 11 (1977), 287-8.

additions to or comments on his material. He stylizes himself as a mere translator—sometimes a compilator—with no expertise in the 'matere' of his text who will faithfully represent not only the facts but also the feelings as expressed in his source: 'Of no sentiment I this endite, | But out of Latin in my tonge I write' (II, 13-4). At first sight, these statements and about sixty others suggested to Kittredge—who does not distinguish between narrator and author—that Chaucer wants his audience to confide in their narrator's exact adherence to his Latin original.[42] However, even if the narrator of *Troilus and Criseyde* is a much better candidate for identification with Chaucer than the bookish pedant of the dream visions or the naïf of the *Canterbury Tales*, a closer look at his ambiguous statements and his changing involvement in his own story reveals that the narrator should be seen as just another playful level within a fictional world constructed to direct attention to and negotiate the absolute power of the author and free creator of this fiction.[43]

The narrator is far from being a mere 'instrument' through which his audience can reflect upon their own courtly loves. Rather, his numerous intrusions into the plot constitute the main source of contingency which permeates the poem. There is, for one, his increasing identification with the success and failure of the love relationship which, during Troilus' and Criseyde's first night together, makes him forget earlier and nobler intentions for his soul ('For so hope I my sowle best avaunce, | To prey for hem that Loves servauntz be'; I, 46-7) and to offer it in exchange for the least of the lovers' joys ('Why nad I swich oon with my soule ybought, | Ye, or the leeste joie that was there'; III, 1319-20). As with Pandarus, the audience realizes that this fictionalizer, too, has a personal interest in the story which makes him deviate from his supposed Latin source and demonstrate powers of appropriation and variation of his material which go above and beyond those expected from a mere translator or compiler. Knowing he must finish his increasingly sad story, his heart 'gynneth blede' (IV, 12) and his pen 'quaketh for drede' (IV, 13). The most conspicuous examples of the narrator's subjective tendencies are his confusing com-

---

[42]Cf. Kittredge, 'Chaucer's Lollius', 92-109.

[43]For a differing view, cf. Sherron E. Knopp, 'The Narrator and His Audience in Chaucer's *Troilus and Criseyde*', *Studies in Philology*, 79 (1981), 323-40. Knopp argues that *Troilus and Criseyde* 'does not depend upon a contrast between the *litel wit* of a naïf narrator and the God-like creating intelligence of the poet for its effect. Its power comes instead from the use which a superbly competent narrator makes of his matter to confront his audience with the essential inadequacy of human love. From the very beginning of Book I, his attitude illustrates the perspective which he will advocate in the Epilogue towards which he propels his audience even as he accepts them on their own terms as devotees of *kynde love*. Although the narrator may not be identical with the poet, he probably comes closer in temperament and philosophy than any other figure in Chaucer's works' (324-5).

mentaries concerning Criseyde: Did she have children or not (I, 132-3); how old was she (V, 826); did she or did she not recognize the obvious symptoms of Troilus' lovesickness (I, 492-7); did she believe Pandarus' protestations that Troilus had left town (III, 575-8); why did she not ask Troilus to rise when he was on his knees in front of her bed (III, 967-70); did she fall in love with Troilus too easily (II, 667)? 'He voices a suspicion, explains it away, but makes sure it lingers on our minds. [...] Characteristic are his whimsical digressions and benevolent explanations of things that are either self-evident or become problematic simply because they are explained'.[44] This *sfumato* of defense or potential innuendo reaches its peak when the narrator withholds judgment against Criseyde although all of his sources indicate—and Criseyde herself even foreknowingly extrapolates her future reputation ('Allas, of me, unto the worldes ende, I Shal neyther ben ywriten nor ysonge I No good word, for thise bokes wol me shende'; V, 1058-60)[45]—how easily the faithful translator can defy textual tradition, including that of the venerable Lollius. Unhappy with his mastersource, he seeks the reports of 'they that of hire werkes knewe' (IV, 1421), presumably actual observers of Criseyde's actions. The narrator refuses to accept external causation in all his sources which blame Criseyde for abandoning Troilus for Diomede; he exclaims that he simply is not sure: 'Men seyn, I not, she yaf him her herte' (V, 1050). However, he does know because 'the storye' (V, 1094) is positive about this piece of information, and it is his free decision to go 'Forther than the storye wol devyse' (V, 1094). The narrator, therefore, is pressured to adopt a final technique of saving his heroine: 'And if I myghte excuse hire any wise, I For she so sory was for hire untrouthe, I Iwis, I wolde excuse hire yet for routhe' (V, 1097-9); this he supports by claiming that sources are deficient or absent: 'Ther is non auctour telleth it, I wene' (V, 1088).[46] The narrator's obligation to follow the traditional storyline and morality is put to the test, and it

---

[44]Frans Diekstra, 'The Language of Equivocation: Some Chaucerian Techniques', *Dutch Quarterly Review*, 11 (1981), 276. On Chaucer's defending Criseyde against accusations of a 'sodeyn love' (II, 667), cf. E. Talbot Donaldson, *Speaking of Chaucer* (New York: Norton, 1970), 66: 'People who had never thought that there was any formal law governing the rate of speed at which a woman should fall in love may suddenly start believing that there is one, and go looking in Andreas Capellanus to find out whether Criseyde has exceeded the limit'.

[45]This textual passage indicates in how arbitrary a manner Chaucer's narrator places himself outside of existing and future readings of Criseyde. Cf. Gretchen Miezkowski's inclusive essay on the characterizations in these other readings, 'The Reputation of Criseyde', *Transactions Published by the Connecticut Academy of Arts and Sciences*, 43 (1971), 71-153.

[46]Cf. Hans Käsmann, '*I wold excuse hir yit for routhe*: Chaucers Einstellung zu Criseyde', in Arno Esch (ed.), *Chaucer und seine Zeit: Symposion für Walter F. Schirmer* (Tübingen: Niemeyer, 1968), 97-122.

becomes obvious to his readers that things could very easily turn out completely otherwise if someone with unlimited authority behind the narrator had only chosen to change them. These deviations are situated in starkest contrast with numerous occasions in the poem through which the narrator constructs the illusion of his own bookishness and close adherence to his source(s); for example: 'For as myn auctour seyde, so sey I' (II, 18); 'Myn auctour shal I folwen, if I konne' (II, 49); 'And treweliche, as writen wel I fynde' (IV, 1415).[47]

One of the most impressive of these many moments, when Chaucer's narrator seems to place complete trust in his Lollian mastertext, appears in Book III:

> But now, paraunter, som man wayten wolde
> That every word, or soonde, or look, or cheere
> Of Troilus that I reherce sholde,
> In al this while unto his lady deere—
> I trowe it were a long thyng for to here—
> Or of what wight tht stant in swich disjoynte,
> His wordes alle, or every look, to poynte.
>
> For sothe, I have naught herd it don er this
> In story non, ne no man here, I wene;
> And though I wolde, I kounde nought, ywys;
> For there was some epistel hem bitwene,
> That wolde, as seyth myn autour, wel contene
> Neigh half this book, of which hym liste nought write
> How sholde I thanne a lyne of it endite.
>
> (III, 491-504)

Although the narrator and Lollius seem to be presented as conscious and capable compilers of preexistent material, this passage (and similar ones) also introduces readers to a sense of insecurity because they must realize to which extent he relies on a whole series of arbitrary choices by a host of retellers of the 'real' story of Troilus and Criseyde. Lollius evolves as

---

[47] Barry Windeatt, *Oxford Guides to Chaucer: Troilus and Criseyde* (Oxford: Clarendon Press, 1992), 40-1, summarizes: 'The narrator mentions texts on twenty-nine occasions in the poem, and on twenty-two of these he asserts or implies his subjection to his sources. Expressions of deference to "myn auctour" occur when Chaucer is actually writing independently of *Filostrato* [...], and it is also noticeable that, when in Book V Chaucer's text begins to overlap with the narrative of the traditional accounts of the story of Troilus and Criseyde, references become especially frequent'. See also Lisa Kiser, *Truth and Textuality in Chaucer's Poetry* (Hanover, NH, and London: University Press of New England, 1991), 81; for her, the narrator 'is most like Criseyde when he begins his betrayal of Lollius, slowly but definitively abandoning the "true" text to which he was previously quite sincerely committed'.

only one element in a long chain of mediators each of whom made subjective decisions at least about inclusion and exclusion of information.

Interestingly, the unreliable narrator drops Lollius' name at the very moment when he relates to his audience Troilus' song about the paradoxical nature of love. He explains the following about this passage:

> And of his song naught only the sentence,
> As writ myn auctour called Lollius,
> But pleinly, save oure tonges difference,
> I dar wel seyn, in al that Troilus
> Seyde in his song, loo! eery word right thus
> As I shal seyn, and whoso list it here,
> Loo, next this vers he may it fynden here.
> (I, 393-9)

In one and the same stanza the narrator claims to follow slavishly, save for the differences between Lollius' Latin and his English, his master source, and promises to relate something which is not at all part of Lollius, namely the exact words of Troilus' song of which Lollius had only given the 'sentence', that is, a précis. Where did the narrator find the full citation? Does he have alternative sources?[48] Did he himself author these lines for Troilus? By directly contrasting his claims for faithful translation, conspicuously authenticated by the invented name Lollius, with the open question about the authority for Troilus' lyrics, a narrator's potential power to create as he wishes is once again revealed.

The name itself, Lollius, provides another helpful piece of the puzzle: the significant Latinizing of the native English verb *lollen*, which comprises such diverse meanings as 'to hang limply', 'to mumble', 'to sing indistinctly', or of the noun *loller*, which describes some kind of wastrel who relied on others for support, might again underline the thesis that Chaucer created this fictional 'auctour' to draw attention to his own role as as a late-medieval vernacular poet who arbitrarily combines and willfully juggles a large variety of available classical and postclassical materials.[49]

Despite some intentional ambiguity about who is speaking at the begin-

---

[48] Scholars agree that the so-called 'Canticus Troili' is based on Petrarch's Sonnet 'S'amor non è'. Cf. Robert O. Payne, *The Key of Remembrance: A Study of Chaucer's Poetics* (New Haven, CT: Yale University Press, 1963), 184-7 and 201-9; and Patricia Thomson, 'The *Canticus Troili*: Chaucer and Petrarch', *Comparative Literature*, 11 (1959), 313-28. Bella Millett, 'Chaucer, Lollius, and the Medieval Theory of Authorship', *Studies in the Age of Chaucer*, 1 (1984), 102, contends that Chaucer's authoritative hand becomes palpable at this point: 'His emphasis on the authenticity of Troilus' song is more explicable if we take it as a half-private joke, directed to those members of his audience who would have recognized its actual source'.

[49] This tendency toward the Latinization of medieval intertexts is noticeable especially in his adaptations of Boccaccio. See, e.g., David Wallace, 'Chaucer's *Ambages*',

ning of the poem, narrator/persona or author/Chaucer, there is a clear indication that the narrator is only second in this three-layered hierarchy of fictionalizers. When the narrator chooses the medieval popes' designation as 'servant of the servants of God' (cf. I, 15), he invokes for himself the position of a representative of someone outside of creation who is the originator of, possesses ultimate powers over, and guarantees that creation. The pope is as much subject to God's omnipotence over His creation as the pagan narrator of *Troilus and Criseyde* is subject to Chaucer's powers of selection and invention for his fictional world.[50] Living in their contingent worlds (the pope in the tradition of binding dogma and commentaries on commentaries; the narrator imprisoned by predetermined storylines and the tradition of compilers/translators), neither representative—at least according to coeval nominalist readings—can plumb the mysteries of their creators' free will and arbitrary intervention. This early parallelization between narrator/pope and author/God becomes even more palpable at the end of the poem when the author, not the narrator, finalizes the poem with a clarity of vision which the pagan narrator's involved perspective simply does not allow for. Shortly after Pandarus' fictional voice has fallen silent before the external forces of the plot, the narrator yields his power of

---

American Notes and Queries, 23 (1984), 1-4. The semantic history of 'lollen' and 'loller' is a contested one. Cf., e.g., the discussion of the terms by Malcolm D. Lambert, *Medieval Heresy: Popular Movements from Bogomil to Hus* (London: Arnold, 1977), 302; Helen Barr, *Signes and Sothe in the* Piers Plowman *Tradition* (Cambridge: D.S. Brewer, 1994), 110-5; and Wendy Scase, Piers Plowman *and the New Anticlericalism* (Cambridge: Cambridge University Press, 1989), 150-60. Cf. also Ruth Morse's suggestion (in her *Truth and Convention in the Middle Ages: Rhetoric, Representation, and Reality* (Cambridge: Cambridge University Press, 1991), 196-7) of Chaucer's potential pun on the plant named 'lolium' which is hard to distinguish from the true crop in the parable of the wheat and the tares in Matt. 13. Henry Morley, *English Writers: An Attempt Towards a History of English Literature*, vol. 5.2 (London: Cassell, 1890), 213-6, had already made that connection suggesting that the poet's use of 'lolium' expressed his sense of Boccaccio's wickedness. Finally, cf. W.G. East's suggestion ('Lollius', *English Studies*, 58 (1977), 396-8) that 'Lollius' may be an attempt to imitate Boccaccio's name ('boccaccio'='ugly mouth') in English.

[50]The narrator of Boccaccio's *Filocolo* presents himself also as a servant of Love's servants. He subsequently claims to follow the true testimony of one Ilario, the priest who received Florio and company into the Christian religion. David Wallace, *Chaucer and the Early Writings of Boccaccio* (Woodbridge: D.S. Brewer, 1985), 50, concludes that '[b]oth Ilario and Lollius are (almost certainly) imaginary. But their supposed existence allows each poet to take up a particular authorial posture. Each suggests that his modern vernacular narrative is supported by the backbone of ancient authority'. However, it is exactly the validity of this authority which Chaucer is interrogating in his text. Cf. also Millett, 'Chaucer, Lollius', 95, who holds that by using of the Pope's title, Chaucer seems to aim less at 'the traditional compiler's role than a mildly blasphemous parody of it'.

speech to the author. The stanza of transition is the one in which the narrator declares to have fulfilled his promise from the prologue to tell the 'double sorwe' (I, 1) of Troilus 'Fro wo to wele and after out of joie' (I, 4). That story, the Trojan 'tragedye' (V, 1786) has come to its end with Troilus' self-sought death. The prince's surprising ascension—guided by Mercury—to the 'eighte spere' (V, 1807) represents a moment of shifting perspectives from a partly determined and limited to an unlimited, undetermined power of narration. The medieval Christian author transcends the sadness of his fiction's worldly sense of what is tragic and intervenes suddenly, not unlike the Christian creator who was thought to interrupt the existing *ordo* in the case of miracles.[51] The poet positions himself above the breathing human passions of the pagan characters, the unreliable narrator, and that narrator's invented source, Lollius, and parallelizes himself thus with the 'stedfast Crist' (V, 1860) and 'the Lord' (V, 1862), who— 'Uncircumscript, and al maist circumscrive' (V, 1865)—rules supreme over the existing *ordo*.[52] As in his 'Retractatio' in the *Canterbury Tales*, Chaucer's Christian ending of *Troilus and Criseyde* closely connects orthodox Christianity and artistic intention. In the 'Retractatio', in a tongue-in-cheek statement which repeats the titles of all the texts for which he asks forgiveness, Chaucer subtly demonstrates his pride in his most demanding artistic creations as an 'auctour'.[53] At the end of *Troilus and Criseyde*, he denounces 'the forme of olde clerkis speche | In poetrie, if ye

---

[51] At this moment in the text, the pagan tragedy is transformed by the omnipotent Christian author/poet for whom all tragedy was comprised in Christ's tragedy. For Chaucer, this is not only an act of faith but his final demonstration of his *potentia absoluta* over his literary creation. On the impossibility of tragedy in the Middle Ages, cf. Erich Auerbach, *Mimesis: Dargestellte Wirklichkeit in der abendländischen Literatur* (Berne and Munich: Francke, 3rd ed. 1964), 296, and Rolf Breuer, 'Christian Tragedy/ Tragedy of Christianity', in Uwe Böker, Manfred Markus, and Rainer Schöwerling (eds.), *The Living Middle Ages: Studies in Mediaeval English Literature and its Tradition—A Festschrift for Karl Heinz Göller* (Stuttgart: Belser, 1989), 183-95.

[52] Cf. Robert M. Jordan, 'The Narrator of Chaucer's *Troilus*', *English Literary History*, 25 (1958), 237-57, who also sees a shift in the narrator's identity from fictional character to historical author in the so-called 'Epilogue'. I disagree, however, with Jordan's suggestion that the narrator suffers from a simple-minded hero worship because of his close identification with Troilus. He seems at least as involved with his female as with his male protagonist.

[53] See Howard, *Chaucer*, 501-2, about Chaucer's retraction at the end of the *Canterbury Tales*: 'We may see him here faltering, in a moment of confusion, possibly fear. He has, in his last hour, one eye on God and the other on posterity, one on salvation and the other on fame. The contradictions in the passage are not different from the contradictions in all his writings: with his ironic self-effacement he turns to meet his Maker, carefully reminding the reader of the exact titles of those works he would "retract", by which he means to ask for our best intentions in reading them; and they are the works for which, six centuries later, we do remember him. [...] The belief in

hire bokes seche!' (V, 1854-5). Directly after this warning to stay away from searching the informing principles of those 'olde bokes', Chaucer situates his dedication of his own book to 'moral Gower', 'philosophical Strode' (V, 1856-7), and 'Crist' (V, 1860), presumably three authorities who would have known immediately that the search for Lollius or his book would indeed lead nowhere. Gower and Strode, at least as well educated and knowledgeable about the matter of Troy as Chaucer was, must have recognized behind the invention of this 'auctour' Lollius their friend's own 'elvissh countenaunce' (*Canterbury Tales*, VII. 703), his playful hint at his own absolute powers of free literary creation. 'Verisimilitude [...] by means of an ancient and well-accredited device'[54] may indeed have been one of Chaucer's intentions causing the inclusion of Lollius' name in his fiction as far as his general audience was concerned. With his immediate circle of friends, actual readers of his written texts, however, Lollius underlines a parody of a confining tradition which obliged medieval authors (judged from a post-medieval point of view) to hide their own artistic light under the bushel and to go along with the predestined storylines of the proverbial *olde bookes*. Gower and Strode were aware of Chaucer's actual sources and that what was happening on the level of the story was dependent on an only partially motivated decision of the author, who used, changed, amplified, named and invented entirely arbitrarily if and when he willed to do so.[55] Chaucer is not yet capable of presenting himself wholeheartedly in the role of the omnipotent and arbitrary author of his own text as, for example, Rabelais does, who feels entirely free of any constraints that are prior to his original literary creation and who—in a more immediately palpable parallel with the omnipotent divine creator— stylizes himself as the *prima causa efficiens* who reenacts the creation of a completely contingent literary universe.[56] However, Chaucer, participat-

---

Chaucer's age that dying can be an art reveals, more than anything else, its new feeling about art. Death is no longer only the beginning of eternal life; it is one's last moment of artful glory in the world'. The retraction is as much a hint at the *prima causa efficiens* for the *Canterbury Tales* as Heinrich von Neustadt's less literary, perhaps more business-like mentioning of his name, his profession, and his home address at the end of his reworking of the *Apollonius* novel (see Neustadt's *Apollonius von Tyrland: Nach der Gothaer Handschrift*, ed. Samuel Singer (Berlin: Weidmann, 1906), vv. 20.600ff.).

[54] Kittredge, 'Chaucer's Lollius', 59.

[55] See Karla Taylor, *Chaucer Reads the* Divine Comedy (Stanford, CA: University of California Press, 1989), 227, and Winthrop Wetherbee, *Chaucer and the Poets: An Essay on 'Troilus and Criseyde'* (Ithaca, NY: Cornell University Press, 1984), 25, who indicate that the poet's use of Lollius may represent the partial and ambiguous transmission of the classics through the tradition of the commentary.

ing in the paradoxically revolutionary potential of late-medieval nominalist thought for his artistic enterprise, experiments toward such an early modern concept of authorship and fiction. While his general audience was made to believe the intuitive cognition of a non-existent (i.e., the creation of the linguistically authenticated apprehension of Lollius as a physically real master source),[57] his informed readers must have recognized the invention and parodic insertion of Lollius as representing the most manifest verbal marker of their friend's growing self-consciousness as an author.[58]

---

[56]Cf. Langer, *Divine and Poetic Freedom*, especially 102-10. It is important to note the difference between prenominalist analogy, which guaranteed the intimate connection between *visibilia* and *invisibilia*, and postnominalist analogy (God/Author) which signals the separation between the metaphysical and the human realms and can be seen to exemplify what Blumenberg (see note 34) called a 'restless taking stock of the world' in late-medieval and early modern times.

[57]I have carefully chosen the phrasing 'was made to *believe*' in this sentence to conform with Ockham's opinion on this problem in his *Quodlibeta* IV q. 14. There, he makes it clear that God cannot create the actual perceptual apprehension of a non-existent in human beings; he can only create the *belief* or *conviction* that something absent is present. In the earlier *Commentary on the Sentences* he had upheld a more radical position; see the concise discussion of this problem by Kurt Flasch, *Das philosophische Denken im Mittelalter: Von Augustin zu Machiavelli* (Stuttgart: Reclam, 1988), 452.

[58]Cf. Tim William Machan, 'Robert Henryson and Father Aesop: Authority in the *Moral Fables*', *Studies in the Age of Chaucer*, 12 (1990), 214: 'Writing at the end of the fifteenth century and in a tradition of vernacular self-consciousness established by Chaucer, Henryson evidently had very forward-looking conceptions of himself as a poet and of the potential for authoritative utterance in the vernacular, but at the same time he lacked cultural validation of these conceptions.' Cf. also Fichte, '*Quha wait gif all that Chauceir wrait was trew*', 63, who calls *Troilus and Criseyde* a 'comedy of *auctoritas*' in which Chaucer 'hides behind a fake authority in order to tell his own version of the Troilus story', and Paule Mertens-Fonck, '*The Canterbury Tales*: New Proposals of Interpretation', *Atti della Accademia Peloritana dei Pericolanti*, 69 (1993), 26-9, who discusses the poet's freedom of decision in correspondence with Ockham's thought.—It should be noted that Chaucer's mentioning of Lollius in the *House of Fame* is compatible with the parodic/artistic intentions outlined above. If the *House of Fame*, as Hugo Lange has indicated ('Chaucers "Myn Auctour Called Lollius" und die Datierung des *Hous of Fame*', *Anglia*, 42 (1918), 345-51), was written after *Troilus and Criseyde*, the poet's placing the invented *auctour* among the famous authorities of Dares Phrygius, Dictys Cretensis, and Homer must have amused his circle of friends and informed readers even more. For a dissenting view which predates the *House of Fame* on the basis of the Lollius passages, cf. Imelmann, 'Chaucers *Haus der Fama*', 406-9.

CHAUCER'S CLERKS AND THE VALUE OF PHILOSOPHY

WILLIAM H. WATTS

In relating Chaucer's poetry to the concerns of fourteenth-century philosophy, we find ourselves in a kind of 'dulcarnoun', to borrow the difficult word that Criseyde uses for a difficult and perplexing situation (III. 931).[1] On the one hand, Chaucer's engagement with philosophical issues throughout his career, from his translation of the speech of Raison in the *Roman de la Rose* to his adaptation of Boethian material in his later poetry, gives us reason to think that he might have taken an interest in the philosophical discourse of his own day. Even though Chaucer typically appeals to the authority of such venerable figures as Plato,[2] Tullius (Cicero),[3] Seneca[4] and Boece[5] for his excursions into philosophical matters, it is at least tempting to see in these passages indirect references to figures closer to home—both in time and in place—such as Duns Scotus, William of Ockham, Robert Holcot, Thomas Bradwardine, or John Wyclif. On the other hand, however, there are some very good reasons for hesitating before drawing a direct line between Chaucer's poetry and more contemporary thinkers. As Walter Clyde Curry cautions in his ground-breaking work on the poet's relation to contemporary thinkers, 'It must be remembered that Chaucer was in his poetical works first an artist and secondarily a philosopher or scientist'.[6] Moreover, while Chaucer shows a fondness for philosophical terms, even beyond the Boethian passages in his poetry,[7] there is little in either the

---

[1] All quotations from and references to works by Chaucer are from *The Riverside Chaucer*, gen. ed. Larry D. Benson (Boston, MA: Houghton Mifflin, 1987).
[2] *General Prologue*, I. 741; *Manciple's Tale*, IX. 207.
[3] *Tale of Melibee*, VII. 1165, 1176, 1180, 1192, 1202, etc.
[4] *Parson's Tale*, X. 467; *Wife of Bath's Tale*, III. 1168, 1184, 2018; etc.
[5] *Wife of Bath's Tale*, III. 1168; *Nun's Priest's Tale*, VII. 3294; *Legend of Good Women*, F. 425.
[6] Walter Clyde Curry, *Chaucer and the Mediaeval Sciences* (New York: Barnes & Noble, 2nd ed. 1960).
[7] To cite but two examples, both drawing on Aristotle, the Parson speaks of the 'cause final of Matrimonye' (X. 941) and Pandarus searches for the 'final cause of wo' that Troilus endures (I, 682).

language or the content of these passages that must necessarily derive from any particular thinker of the later Middle Ages. For this reason, Curry generally does not identify 'sources' for the scientific and philosophical ideas in Chaucer's verse, but instead speaks of parallels, analogues and commonplaces.

Until recently, the cautious approach we find in Curry's treatment of the sciences has also prevailed in the discussion of the metaphysical and epistemological implications of Chaucer's poetry. While there has been wide-spread recognition of the philosophical interests in Chaucer's work, these interests have generally been explained in terms of Boethius or Augustine, and when late medieval figures have been invoked, they have generally served as analogies rather than as probable sources or influences.[8] In the past twenty years, however, there has been a sea-change in philosophical approaches to Chaucer's poetry, and it has become increasingly common to place the fourteenth-century poet in the context of fourteenth-century philosophy. Russell Peck's 1978 article, 'Chaucer and the Nominalist Questions',[9] prepared the way for a great many subsequent discussions of Chaucer's poetry in the terms of fourteenth-century nominalism.[10] And, increasingly, critics have tended to see Chaucer as a partisan in the debate between the nominalists and realists in the latter half of the fourteenth century;[11] that is, they see him either as sympathetic to nominalist positions,[12] or as a realist who opposed the nominal-

---

[8]J.D. Burnley's *Chaucer's Language and the Philosophers' Tradition* (Cambridge: D.S. Brewer, and Totowa, NJ: Rowman & Littlefield, 1979), one of the few book-length treatments of philosophical issues in Chaucer's poetry, is a good example of this tendency. Burnley consistently finds sources in Boethius, Cicero, Seneca and Augustine for the philosophical language and ideas of Chaucer's verse.

[9]Russell Peck, 'Chaucer and the Nominalist Questions', *Speculum*, 53 (1978), 745-60.

[10]For a comprehensive account of such approaches, see William H. Watts and Richard J. Utz, 'Nominalist Perspectives on Chaucer's Poetry: A Bibliographical Essay', *Medievalia et Humanistica*, n.s. 20 (1993), 147-73.

[11]Note, however, that William Courtenay denies that any such debate was going on during Chaucer's career: 'The spirit of the age in England was clearly in the direction of realism. If there are any *contemporary* philosophical or theological influences, therefore, of the late fourteenth-century schools on the language and content of English literature, they should probably be sought in realism, simplified logic, and practical theology, not in the direction of Ockham or nominalism' (William J. Courtenay, *Schools and Scholars in Fourteenth-Century England* (Princeton, NJ: Princeton University Press, 1987), 379).

[12]Peck takes this position, as does Jay Ruud in 'Chaucer and Nominalism: The Envoy to Bukton', *Mediaevalia*, 10 (1984), 199-212, and, more recently, in his *'Many a Song and Many a Lecherous Lay': Tradition and Individuality in Chaucer's Lyric Poetry* (New York: Garland, 1992).

ists,[13] or as someone who tried to steer a middle course between the extreme positions of the nominalists and the realists.[14] Nor has this philosophical re-evaluation of Chaucer been confined to the terms of realism and nominalism. Lois Roney, for example, has argued that *The Knight's Tale* should be seen within the context of the late-medieval debate over faculty psychology. In her reading, Arcite represents 'the intellectualist theories of the Aristotelian Thomists', Palamon represents 'the voluntarist theories of the Augustinian Franciscans' and Chaucer himself develops a theory of psychology which Roney gives the problematic label of 'humanist'.[15] In making her argument, Roney overturns Curry's earlier assessment that Chaucer was a poet first and a philosopher secondarily; she writes, 'The Knight's Tale is a spirited defense of poesy, of the great poems of pagan antiquity and of figurative language use in general [...]. It is at the same time, *and equally*, a brilliant philosophical presentation of the later medieval theories about the three kinds of human nature'.[16]

The emerging view of Chaucer as a poet actively engaged in the philosophical and theological issues of his day has been both invigorating and productive. This re-assessment has been made possible by the editing, dissemination and reinterpretation of important texts of the fourteenth century, including those by William of Ockham and Robert Holcot, and it has been motivated by the laudable aim of historicizing the philosophical concerns of Chaucer's poetry. Moreover, this new approach to Chaucer's philosophy has led to innovative readings of his poetry. Recent nominalist readings of *The Clerk's Tale* provide but one example of this. Even if one does not accept the claim that the dialectic of God's ordained and absolute powers informs the structure of *The Clerk's Tale*, the readings by Robert Stepsis, David Steinmetz and Elizabeth Kirk which make use of this terminology have contributed to our understanding of the tale.[17] At the

---

[13]See, for example, the three articles by Laurence Eldredge: 'Boethian Epistemology and Chaucer's *Troilus and Criseyde* in the Light of Fourteenth-Century Thought', *Mediaevalia*, 2 (1976), 49-75; 'Poetry and Philosophy in the *Parlement of Foules*', *Revue de l'Université d'Ottawa*, 40 (1970), 441-59; 'Chaucer's *House of Fame* and the *Via Moderna*', *Neuphilologische Mitteilungen*, 71 (1970), 105-19.

[14]Rodney Delasanta takes this position in the article discussed below. John Michael Crafton takes a similar position when he argues that, in his early poems, 'Chaucer becomes more infatuated with nominalist thematics until he is finally disillusioned with them' ('Emptying the Vessel: Chaucer's Humanistic Critique of Nominalism', in Richard J. Utz (ed.), *Literary Nominalism and the Theory of Rereading Late Medieval Texts: A New Research Paradigm* (Lewiston, NY: Edwin Mellen Press, 1995), 123).

[15]Lois Roney, *Chaucer's Knight's Tale and Theories of Scholastic Psychology* (Tampa, FL: University of South Florida Press, 1990), xiv.

[16]Ibid., 3 (emphasis added).

[17]Robert Stepsis, '*Potentia absoluta* and the *Clerk's Tale*', *Chaucer Review*, 10 (1975), 129-46; David Steinmetz, 'Late Medieval Nominalism and the *Clerk's Tale*',

same time, however, despite the great amount of work that has been done in this area, there continue to be real problems with relating Chaucer in any direct way to the philosophical discourse of the fourteenth century. I will consider some of these problems, and I will also suggest that Chaucer's representations of philosophizing clerks throughout his poetry provide us with a useful perspective on his posture vis à vis contemporary philosophy.

An important point of departure for investigations of Chaucer's engagement with fourteenth-century philosophy lies in the two tantalizing references to fourteenth-century philosophers that he makes in his poetry. The first reference comes at the end of *Troilus and Criseyde*, where the narrator sends his work out first to 'moral Gower' and then to 'philosophical Strode' with the request that the two men correct the work 'ther nede is' (V, 1856-8). The precise identity of this 'philosophical Strode' and the significance of this gesture to him at the end of the poem have been the subject of a great deal of critical discussion. Despite some lingering reservations,[18] the current critical consensus holds that the Ralph Strode addressed at the end of *Troilus* was both fellow of Merton College who authored several important treatises on logic and, later in his career, Chaucer's neighbor at Aldersgate in London who served as Common Pleader for the city. There is, however, considerably less consensus about what this relationship with Strode meant for Chaucer, and one can, in fact, trace out a 500-year history of speculation on this score. A Latin colophon in a fifteenth-century manuscript of the *Treatise on the Astrolabe* states that Chaucer's son Lewis was a student of the philosopher Strode at Oxford.[19] But because Strode would have been a lawyer working in London by the time Lewis began his studies at Oxford, this explanation seems unlikely. As Derek Pearsall wittily comments, the author of the colophon 'seems to have been one of those enthusiasts who, knowing two facts, think they must be related'.[20] Yet Pearsall himself is not immune from such speculation, for he imagines that the philosopher might have left his academic career at Oxford in order to be married, and then goes on to say, 'If Strode did make the move to secular life in order to get married, it would be interesting to have heard his conversations with Chaucer, who by now may have been thinking that he had missed, through his earlier marriage, many of the opportunities for living comfortably and writing poetry that would have been available to him if he had taken holy

---

Chaucer Review, 12 (1977), 38-54, esp. 40; Elizabeth Kirk, 'Nominalism and the Dynamics of the *Clerk's Tale*: *Homo Viator* as Woman', in C. David Benson and Elizabeth Robertson (eds.), *Chaucer's Religious Tales* (Cambridge: D.S. Brewer, 1990), 111-20.

[18]See, for example, the note on Strode in *The Riverside Chaucer*, 1058.
[19]See ibid., 1092.
[20]Derek Pearsall, *The Life of Geoffrey Chaucer* (Oxford: Blackwell, 1992), 217.

orders'.[21] Alternatively, H.A. Kelly has proposed that Strode provided Chaucer with glosses for his translation of the *Consolation of Philosophy*.[22] Most recently, Rodney Delasanta has provided an extended discussion of the possible philosophical implications of Chaucer's address to Strode. Delasanta begins by noting Strode's importance and influence as a philosopher, and then goes on to say that the relationship 'could have meant for Chaucer a virtual ten- to fifteen-year tutorial in the company of a scholar intimately associated with the "disputisouns" that had engaged the best minds of his century'.[23] And through Strode, Delasanta suggests, Chaucer may have gained access to other leading thinkers of the period. In particular, acquaintanceship with Strode might have meant that Chaucer knew the philosopher's great adversary, Wyclif, 'at least in the scholastic sense' (ibid.). Likewise, Strode's connection with Merton College, which he apparently maintained even after moving to London, may have meant that Chaucer gained familiarity with the thinking of that other eminent Mertonian, Thomas Bradwardine. And finally, because of the realist positions of both Wyclif and Bradwardine, Chaucer may also have become acquainted with their nominalist adversaries who were associated with Oxford, including 'William of Ockham, Robert Holcot, Thomas Buckingham, and Adam of Woodham' (ibid., 206). In fact, Delasanta uses Chaucer's connection with Strode to suggest that the poet sought a middle position between the realists and the nominalists. For while Chaucer inherited a realist epistemology from Boethius, Delasanta also finds sympathies for nominalist positions in the poet's discussion of the relationship between word and deed, in his examination of processes of knowing, and in his apparent skepticism about the reality of abstract ideas. Given these two divergent tendencies, Chaucer may have found a sympathetic figure in Strode, whose moderate realism might have provided the poet with a middle position between the extreme realists and the nominalists (see ibid., 217).

In many ways, the address to 'philosophical Strode' in *Troilus* is emblematic of the very problem of relating Chaucer to the philosophy of his day, where so much is possible but so little is either proven or provable. Strode may have had a hand in the education of Lewis Chaucer, he may have discussed marriage with Geoffrey Chaucer, he may have worked with him on *Boece*, and he may have offered the poet a fifteen-year tutorial on current philosophical thought. Or he may have done none of these things; we simply have no means of knowing one way or another. Moreover, Chaucer's tribute to Strode could have been inspired by either personal or

---

[21] Ibid., 134.
[22] Henry Ansgar Kelly, 'Chaucer and Shakespeare on Tragedy', *Leeds Studies in English*, 20 (1989), 4.
[23] Rodney Delasanta, 'Chaucer and Strode', *Chaucer Review*, 26 (1991), 205.

professional considerations and need not suggest anything about the poet's philosophical leanings. In the end, Strode represents a very thin thread from which to hang any kind of philosophical interpretation of Chaucer's poetry.[24]

We face similar problems in interpreting the significance of Chaucer's reference to Bradwardine in *The Nun's Priest's Tale*. In the course of his discussion of Chauntecleer's destiny, the Nun's Priest speaks of the 'greet altercacioun' over the question of whether God's foreknowledge determines man's actions. He goes on to say,

> But I ne kan nat bulte it to the bren
> As kan the hooly doctour Augustyn,
> Or Boece, or the Bisshop Bradwardyn,
> Wheither that Goddes worthy forwityng
> Streyneth me nedely for to doon a thyng.
> (VII. 3240-4)

This passage is remarkable in Chaucer's poetry for the way in which it juxtaposes the name of a contemporary figure with more venerable authorities, and the rhyme of 'Bradwardyn' with 'Augustyn' would seem to emphasize the high honor accorded to the archbishop.

As with the tribute to 'philosophical Strode', the reference to Bradwardine has given rise to speculation about Chaucer's place among fourteenth-century philosophers. The fact that Bradwardine, like Strode, hailed from Merton College has been seen as further evidence that Chaucer enjoyed a special relationship either with that college in particular or with Oxford in general.[25] Frederick Powicke has pointed to this line as evidence both for Bradwardine's wide-spread influence and for Chaucer's responsiveness 'to the moods of his age'.[26] And, on the basis of this direct reference in *The Nun's Priest's Tale*, together with the philosophical and theological interests exhibited throughout the poet's work, Gertrud Mary Jurschak has claimed that Chaucer 'undoubtedly had personal recollections of Bradwardine'.[27] But Chaucer would have been nine years old when Bradwardine died in 1349, and there is little in either this passage or

---

[24]See, however, Richard Utz's careful attempt to relate Strode to a 'nominalist orientation' which might have guided Chaucer's thinking, in 'Negotiating the Paradigm: Literary Nominalism and the Theory and Practice of Rereading Late Medieval Texts', in Utz (ed.), *Literary Nominalism*, 10-3.

[25]J.A.W. Bennett, *Chaucer at Oxford and Cambridge* (Toronto: University of Toronto Press, 1974), 58.

[26]Frederick Powicke, *The Medieval Books of Merton College* (Oxford: Clarendon Press, 1931), 24.

[27]Gertrud Mary Jurschak, *Chaucer and Fourteenth-Century Thought*, PhD diss. Loyola University of Chicago, 1972, 66.

in the corpus of Chaucer's writing that would suggest such intimacy with either the thought or the person of the theologian. The controversy surrounding Bradwardine's *De causa dei* ensured that his name was well known and was attached to the question of free will in relation to divine omniscience. In the context of this passage, the Nun's Priest's purpose is not to lay out Bradwardine's position on God's foreknowledge and human free will, but to invoke a well-known name among the hundred thousand men who have taken up the problem.

The references to Bradwardine and Strode would be more significant in establishing Chaucer's relationship to fourteenth-century thought if there were textual support for such a relationship. Yet one would be hard-pressed to identify passages in his poetry that necessarily depend upon the thinking of any particular philosopher of the period. The one possible exception to this is the extended discussion of divination through dreams in *The Nun's Priest's Tale*. Just over 100 years ago, in 1892, Kate Petersen argued that Chaucer drew upon Robert Holcot's commentary on the Book of Wisdom both for the debate over the validity of dreams and for the substance of Chauntecleer's dream in *The Nun's Priest's Tale*,[28] and Robert Pratt has renewed the argument for Holcot's influence in an article published in 1977.[29] The claims of Petersen and Pratt have been widely influential and the notion that the *Wisdom Commentary* is an important source for Chaucer's tale has gained broad acceptance.[30] Delasanta, for example, states that Holcot is the only philosopher, among those with whom Chaucer may have gained acquaintance through Strode, who receives the poet's 'open attention'.[31] Moreover, the belief that Chaucer makes use of the *Wisdom Commentary* has led critics to speculate that the poet was also influenced by the metaphysics and epistemology of Holcot. Thus, both Russell Peck and Jay Ruud point to Holcot as the intermediary through whom Chaucer became acquainted with the nominalist ideas of William of Ockham.[32]

It would make sense for Chaucer to have drawn upon Holcot's *Wisdom Commentary*, given the great popularity of that work. In her essays on the tradition of Sapiential commentary, Beryl Smalley suggests that Langland may have made use of the work for his own representation of Sapience,

---

[28] Kate O. Petersen, *On the Sources of the 'Nonnes Preestes Tale'* (Radcliffe College Monographs, 10) (Boston: Radcliffe College, 1892).

[29] Robert Pratt, 'Some Latin Sources of the Nonnes Preest on Dreams', *Speculum*, 52 (1977), 538-70.

[30] See Grover C. Furr, 'Nominalism in the *Nun's Priest's Tale*: A Preliminary Study', in Utz (ed.), *Literary Nominalism*, 139-40.

[31] Delasanta, 'Chaucer and Strode', 207.

[32] Peck, 'Chaucer and the Nominalist Questions', 746-7; Ruud, 'Chaucer and Nominalism', 200.

and she quotes J.C. Wey's statement that Holcot's *Wisdom Commentary* 'made its author famous overnight and his fame held throughout the next two centuries'.[33] Likewise, William Courtenay identifies Holcot's *Sapientia*, together with Bradwardine's *De causa dei*, as one of the few works from the first half of the fourteenth century that found an 'extra- or supra-university' audience and thereby provided a model for such works in the latter half of the century.[34] Yet the case for Holcot's influence on Chaucer is less clear-cut than the near-universal acceptance of the *Wisdom Commentary* as a source for *The Nun's Priest's Tale* would seem to suggest. While Petersen and Pratt are able to point to parallels between the *Commentary* and the *Tale*, there is little in Chaucer's work that must of necessity come from Holcot. The argument for Holcot's influence rests largely on similarities in verbal choices, in the structure of argument, and in the narrative details Chauntecleer deploys in the exemplary tales that support his case for the prophetic value of dreams, but it would seem that these similarities can be accounted for without resorting to Holcot.

For example, Pratt points out that at the beginning of her argument against the validity of dreams, Pertelote, like Holcot, assembles and then dismisses the claims that run counter to her argument. But such a mode of argumentation would certainly not have been unfamiliar to a great many scholastic (and even non-scholastic) writers. Likewise, Pratt suggests that Pertelote's dismissal of dreams, 'ne do no fors of dremes' (VII. 2941), has its origin in Holcot's declaration, 'Somnia ne cures, nam fallunt sompnia plures'.[35] Yet Pertelote cites Cato as her authority, and the utterance can be accounted for equally well through a passage in the *Distiches*. Moreover, the sentiment was proverbial, and would have been available to Chaucer from any number of sources. Similarly, in his discussion of the tales Chauntecleer tells in which deaths are foretold through dreams, Pratt points to details in the story which could have come from Holcot. Yet it is not clear that these details could not have emerged from Chaucer's manipulation of versions of the story related by Valerius and Cicero.

But even if we accept Pratt's claim that Chaucer 'rifled Holcot [...] for Pertelote's discussion of the humors and for most of Chauntecleer's argument',[36] the evidence for the poet's engagement with fourteenth-century philosophy is still very slight. Moreover, Chaucer's persistent habit of deriding clerks who profess philosophy calls into question his reliance on

---

[33] Beryl Smalley, *Medieval Exegesis of Wisdom Literature*, ed. Roland E. Murphy (Atlanta, GA: Scholars Press, 1986), 131. Smalley's quotation is from J.C. Wey, 'The *Sermo finalis* of Robert Holcot', *Mediaeval Studies*, 11 (1949), 219.

[34] See Courtenay, *Schools and Scholars*, 369.

[35] Pratt, 'Some Latin Sources', 545.

[36] Ibid., 569.

Holcot or any of the other clerks. For we find in Chaucer's poetry a kind of anti-clericalism, focused not on the worldly abuses of the religious orders but on the hubris and misdirected studies of clerks which, I propose, invites us to reconsider Chaucer's attitude toward contemporary philosophers.[37] For Chaucer frequently portrays these contemporary clerks who practice philosophy in terms that suggest either criticism or derision. We see something of this attitude even in the portrait of the Clerk in the *General Prologue* to the *Canterbury Tales*, where Chaucer writes, 'al be that he was a philosophre, I Yet hadde he but litel gold in cofre' (I. 297-8). While this particular Clerk seems to be devoted to his 'Twenty bookes [...] I Of Aristotle and his philosophie' (294-5),[38] the clear implication of this description is that other clerks use their knowledge of philosophy for their own ill-gotten gain, either through alchemy or through other devious means. Certainly, the other clerks of Fragment I bear out this suggestion. 'Hende Nicholas', the clerk of *The Miller's Tale*, uses his knowledge of astrology and the Bible to dupe John and thereby gain a night in bed with Alison. In fact, we see Nicholas directly employ the 'subtlety' so essential to his profession when, we are told, 'As clerkes ben ful subtile and ful queynte; I [...] prively he caughte hire by the queynte' (I. 3275-6). Here, it is suggested that Nicholas's clerkly abilities directly aid his sexual ambitions. In *The Reeve's Tale*, when Symkyn the Miller confronts the two clerks from Oxenford, he resolves to dupe them despite their abilities as philosophers: 'by my thrift, yet shal I blere hir ye, I For al the sleighte in hir philosophye' (I. 4049-50). And while the young clerks are unable to match wits with the Miller in the bagging of newly milled corn, their philosophical slights do allow them to bed the Miller's wife and daughter. In his condemnation of the slights and subtleties of clerks, John the Carpenter says, 'Men sholde nat knowe of Goddes privetee' (I. 3454). If we look beyond the representation of clerks in the fabliaux of Fragment I, we continue to find clerks who delve into 'Goddes privetee'. In *The Franklin's Tale*, the clerk from 'Orliens' uses his talents as a philosopher

---

[37] Of course, clerks are not necessarily philosophers. In the basic meaning of the word in Middle English, a clerk was a member of the clergy, often in minor orders. But the word is often used for a student, especially a university student, and, by extension, sometimes refers to a learned person (see *MED*). Thus, for example, the Wife of Bath refers to Seneca as a clerk (III. 1184).

[38] But even the pilgrim Clerk may come under some criticism in the *General Prologue*. Jill Mann writes, 'The Clerk is an ideal representative of the life of study. Yet the phrase "the eternal student" aptly sums up our impression [...]. His conformity with the ideal is faultless, but it was an ideal even more likely in medieval than in modern times to be associated with an "ivory tower"'. Mann also notes the conspicuous lack of any suggestion of religious piety in the portrait of the clerk. (*Chaucer and Medieval Estates Satire* (Cambridge: Cambridge University Press, 1973), 74)

not only to aid Aurelius in his quest to win the love of another man's wife, but also to interfere with the order of God's created universe by concealing the black rocks; in the process he gains a thousand pounds for himself. It is only at the end of the tale that this philosopher realizes that clerks are also capable of 'gentilesse'. And perhaps most spectacularly, the canon, whom the Yeoman describes as being even 'gretter than a clerk' (VIII. 617), uses his claims as a philosopher in the most shameless way to defraud nearly everyone he meets of their cash and precious metals.

When Chaucer's clerks are not taking actions that are devious, they are often portrayed collectively as engaging in endless disputation that in the end yields little more than confusion and irresolution. Thus, Dorigen ends her examination of the difficult problem of why God permits evil in the world by saying:

> I woot wel clerkes wol seyn as hem leste,
> By argumentz, that al is for the beste,
> Though I ne kan the causes nat yknowe.
> But thilke God that made wynd to blowe
> As kepe my lord! This my conclusion.
> To clerkes lete I al disputison.
> (V. 885-90)

In a similar moment of perplexity, Criseyde enters into an extended consideration of the matter 'Which clerkes callen fals felicitee' (*Troilus and Criseyde*, III, 814) and arrives at a similarly inconclusive conclusion. And Troilus, 'Disputyng with hym self' in the matter of free will and predestination, also declares his inability to sort out the various opinions of the clerks, saying, 'O welaway! So sleighe arn clerkes olde | That I not whos opynyoun I may holde' (IV, 972-3). And the Nun's Priest expresses a similar bewilderment over the divergent views of clerks when, after surveying their opinions on free will, he declares, 'I wol nat han of swich mateere; | My tale is of a cok, as ye may heere' (VII. 3251-2). In this way, the Nun's Priest pointedly calls attention to the disparity between the lofty concerns of the clerks and the business of the barnyard.

Surely, we need not accept the views of the Nun's Priest or John the Carpenter as representing Chaucer's own opinion of clerkly knowledge. Chaucer attributes these views of clerks to various characters in his tales, and we cannot conclude from them that he himself held clerks in contempt. Nevertheless, these passages suggest that if we are to imagine a Chaucer who was actively engaged in the philosophical disputes of his day, we need also to imagine the possibility of a Chaucer who was aware of these disputes but saw them as largely irrelevant to his own concerns. It is in this light that I would like to propose an alternative reading of the direction of *Troilus* to Strode. One need not go so far as E. Talbot

Donaldson, who called the ending a 'nervous breakdown in poetry',[39] to see in the final stanzas of *Troilus* a series of efforts to find an adequate resolution to the poem. The address to Strode in the penultimate stanza is but one moment in a series of endings that leads to the ultimate truth of the Trinity in the final stanza. It is possible, therefore, to see the direction of the poem to Strode not as declaration of the poem's engagement with contemporary philosophical issues but as a gesture of futility. It is as if the narrator is saying, 'I have raised some difficult issues here, but will let you, Strode, who are an expert in these matters, resolve them'. In this sense, the narrator of *Troilus* joins Dorigen in saying, 'To clerkes lete I al disputison', as he moves on to the enduring truth of the Trinity.

In the end, then, Chaucer's tendency to portray philosophizing clerks as either devious or irrelevant should give us pause as we try to relate the poet to the philosophical disputes of his contemporaries in any direct way. It may very well be that Chaucer was conversant with the great philosophical issues of his day, including the ongoing debate between the nominalists and the realists; as John Michael Crafton has recently observed in making his argument for Chaucer's awareness of nominalism, very little escaped the poet's gaze.[40] It is even more clearly the case that the language and issues of fourteenth-century philosophy can be successfully deployed, either as a reconstruction of the Zeitgeist in which the poet operated or as a hermeneutical tool, to illuminate Chaucer's verse.[41] These facts do not, however, make Chaucer a partisan in the debates of the clerks or a proponent of any one position. In fact, Chaucer so often approaches weighty metaphysical and epistemological matters with a tone of bemused attachment and histrionic despair over the possibility of resolving thorny issues that there may very well be more *game* than *ernest* in the poet's response to the *greet disputisouns* of the fourteenth century.

---

[39] E. Talbot Donaldson, *Speaking of Chaucer* (New York: Norton, 1970), 91.
[40] Crafton, 'Emptying the Vessel', 117.
[41] See Richard J. Utz's incisive discussion in 'Negotiating the Paradigm'.

LITERARY NOMINALISM AND MEDIEVAL SIGN THEORY: PROBLEMS AND PERSPECTIVES

STEPHEN PENN

Literary attitudes towards nominalism have changed markedly since J. Mitchell Morse, in one of the first such articles on Ockhamist theology, complained that there was 'no more than a bare mention' of Ockham or Scotus in the criticism of his contemporaries.[1] Modern critics, given the profusion of nominalist readings over the past decade, might well find themselves longing for the lost age of ignorance Morse describes. The number of literary articles devoted specifically to nominalist issues is already sufficient to form a lengthy bibliography, and references to nominalism itself are repeated with an almost formulaic regularity in footnotes and parentheses.[2] The methodology of this kind of research, however, has been relatively neglected,[3] and critics have often been less than explicit about the theoretical approaches they have adopted. The purpose of the present study is to examine the methodological problems raised by the literary analysis of nominalist *sign theory*. This comparatively new area of interest has as yet been recalcitrant to accurate historical analysis, and has given rise to some erroneous assumptions about the relationship between philosophical theory and literary practice in the Middle Ages. It will be

---

[1] J. Mitchell Morse, 'The Philosophy of the Clerk of Oxenford', *Modern Language Quarterly*, 19 (1958), 3-20 (quote: 3, note 1).

[2] The most recent and comprehensive published bibliography is that of William H. Watts and Richard J. Utz, 'Nominalist Perspectives on Chaucer's Poetry: A Bibliographical Essay', *Medievalia et Humanistica*, n.s. 20 (1993), 147-73. For more recent studies, see Richard J. Utz (ed.), *Literary Nominalism and the Theory of Rereading Late Medieval Texts: A New Research Paradigm* (Lewiston, NY: Edwin Mellen Press, 1995).

[3] The most thorough methodological studies to date are those of William J. Courtenay and Robert Myles. Both, though they approach the problem from very different perspectives, are highly sceptical about the possibility of establishing direct links between literature and nominalism. See William J. Courtenay, *Schools and Scholars in Fourteenth-Century England* (Princeton, NJ: Princeton University Press, 1987), 374-80; Robert Myles, *Chaucerian Realism* (Woodbridge: D.S. Brewer, 1994), ch. 1.

argued that the reasons for this owe much to the state of modern criticism and history, as well as to the often intractable nature of the subject matter itself. Nominalism will therefore be considered both in terms of its modern historical definition, which will be taken as a point of reference, and in terms of the different theoretical approaches to the problems of nominalist sign theory. In the concluding section, the case will be presented for an alternative methodology.

Versions of Nominalism

Much of the confusion and contradiction that surrounds literary accounts of nominalism has arisen out of its uncertain historical status. Since the 1930s, the traditional view of a unified, coherent system of thought has been repeatedly challenged, and historians and philosophers alike have found themselves revising or even rejecting their earlier definitions. The most important ideas to come under scrutiny are those which associate nominalism with a radically sceptical and fideistic conception of knowledge, with an omnipotent and unknowable God, and with a particularised, atomistic view of reality. Many of the historical accounts written earlier this century, including those of David Knowles, Gordon Leff, and Meyrick Carré,[4] depend heavily on such ideas, and emphasize the discontinuities between nominalism and the older Scholastic tradition. Nominalism is presented in terms of an abrupt paradigm-shift, a break with established ways of thinking which threatens to render conventional forms of enquiry worthless, to sever the link between reason and faith, and to leave mankind at the mercy of an omnipotent and unknowable God.

Though this rather depressing view of nominalism was beginning to lose its hold on historians long before the accounts of Knowles, Leff, and Carré were being written, the old prejudices were slow to disappear. William Courtenay, in a survey of nominalist literature up to 1972,[5] attributes this delayed response to a reluctance to reinterpret the primary texts. Many of the mistakes that have been made, he suggests, are mistakes of *interpretation*, which are not obvious from the texts themselves.[6] The revised view of nominalism, which Courtenay describes as 'moderate' nominal-

---

[4]See David Knowles, *The Evolution of Medieval Thought* (London: Longman, 1962), 291-337; Gordon Leff, *Medieval Thought from Saint Augustine to Ockham* (London: Merlin, 1959), 255-305; Meyrick H. Carré, *Realists and Nominalists* (Oxford: Oxford University Press, 1946), 120-5.

[5]William J. Courtenay, 'Nominalism and Late Medieval Religion', in Charles Trinkaus and Heiko A. Oberman (eds.), *The Pursuit of Holiness in Late Medieval and Renaissance Religion* (Leiden: Brill, 1974), 26-59.

[6]Ibid., 32.

ism, is still developing,[7] but its basic principles, all of which have a direct or indirect bearing on Ockham's semiological and linguistic theory, may be summarized briefly according to a number of key themes. Firstly, there is the problem of universals, the logical aspect of nominalist philosophy against which all others are defined. According to Ockham, the reality attributed to universals, whether as immanent properties of individuals or as archetypes *ante rem,* is purely fictional, the result of a process of *abstractive cognition.* This process is always secondary to that of *intuitive cognition,* the act of knowing and conceptualizing individual entities, which are then represented by *natural signs* in the mind. As concepts, universals *are themselves singulars,* leading Ockham to the conclusion that 'quodlibet universale [...] non est universale nisi per significationem, quia est signum plurimum'[8] ('every universal [...] is not a universal, except by signification, because it is a sign of many things').

The second major area to attract the attention of historians and critics is the theological problem of the relationship between God and His creatures. Though Ockham's views on this problem were developed essentially independently of his ideas on the logic of universals, the two are fundamentally compatible, and are characterized in the early histories by the same scepticism. His insistence, for example, on preserving an absolute distinction between divine and human natures led to an exaggerated emphasis on the futility of thought and of rational enquiry. This was reinforced by a general misunderstanding of Ockham's use of the scholastic concepts of the *potentia dei absoluta* and the *potentia dei ordinata.* Rather than seeing the absolute power of God in terms of possibilities once available but now excluded, commentators saw the threat of supernatural intervention in the created order. According to Courtenay, this represented not only a misinterpretation of the nature of divine power itself, but of the purpose behind the distinction:

> The distinction is deceptive for the modern reader because it seems to be talking about possibilities and avenues for divine action when in fact it is making a statement about the non-necessity of the created order. Both parts

---

[7]Courtenay uses the term 'moderate' specifically to refer to William of Ockham, Pierre d'Ailly and Gabriel Biel, all of whose writings were carefully re-evaluated in the first revisionist histories. Elsewhere it is used in a more general sense to separate Ockham's philosophical doctrines from the more extreme nominalism of the twelfth-century thinker Roscelin and his followers. For a discussion of recent developments in nominalist historiography, see Courtenay's later article, 'Late Medieval Nominalism Revisited: 1972-1982', *Journal of the History of Ideas,* 64 (1983), 159-64, and his contribution to the present collection.

[8]William of Ockham, *Summa totius logicae,* I, c. xiv, in *Philosophical Writings,* ed. and tr. Philotheus Boehner (Indianapolis, IN: Hackett, 1957), 33. The translation here is my own.

of the dialectic, which must be taken together to be meaningful, face in the direction of creation, not God. Together they declare the contingent, covenantal character of the created world.[9]

A possible cause of the misunderstanding Courtenay describes is Ockham's doctrine of primary and secondary causes. According to the principle of primary causation, God, though he would never behave in a way which was unnecessary, could still produce supernatural effects, provided only that they were analogous to the effects produced by natural agency:

> 'Quidquid Deus producit mediantibus causis secundis potest immediate sine illis producere et conservare'. Ex ista propositione arguo sic: Omnem effectum quem potest Deus mediante causa secunda potest immediate per se; sed in notitiam intuitivam corporalem potest mediante obiecto; ergo potest in eam immediate per se.[10]

Ockham's suggestion that God would be capable, if he chose to do so, of producing an intuitive cognition of a non-existent, has often been taken as a further affirmation of his sceptical epistemology. Reason, it is argued, incapable of distinguishing between natural and supernatural, would be rendered futile as a means of enquiry. Again, however, the assumption that God can produce such effects miraculously is merely a guarantee of His omnipotence, and not an indication of the likelihood of their being brought into being.[11] For Ockham, as for the earlier Scholastics, reason was a sacred faculty, and remained an authority for Christian and philosopher alike.[12] God's existence, for faith and reason alike, could never be doubted,

---

[9]Courtenay, 'Nominalism and Late Medieval Religion', 39. Courtenay discusses the importance of the distinction in the later nominalist tradition in 'Covenant and Causality in Pierre d'Ailly', *Speculum*, 46 (1971), 94-119.

[10]"'Whatever God can produce by means of secondary causes, He can directly produce and preserve without them". From this maxim I argue thus. Every effect which God can produce by means of a secondary cause He can produce directly on His own account. He can produce intuitive sense cognition by means of an object; hence He can produce it directly on His own account.' (William of Ockham, *Quodlibeta*, VI, q. vi. Text and translation are those of Ockham, *Philosophical Writings*, ed. Boehner, 25-6.)

[11]On the problem of interpreting Ockham's idea of intuitive cognition of non-existents, see Philotheus Boehner, 'The *Notitia Intuitiva* of Non-Existents According to William of Ockham', in *Collected Articles on Ockham*, ed. Eligius M. Buytaert (St. Bonaventure, NY: The Franciscan Institute, 1958), 268-300. Boehner argues against the many sceptical interpretations, suggesting that for Ockham, as for the other Scholastics, intuitive knowledge was *infallible*. To know a non-existent intuitively, therefore, was always to be *aware* of its non-existence at the same time. The idea, moreover, was developed in response to a specific theological problem, and was not a general epistemological principle (275).

[12]On Ockham's use of the Scholastic concept of *recta ratio* ('right reason'), see David W. Clark, 'William of Ockham on Right Reason', *Speculum*, 48 (1973), 13-36.

despite the charges of agnosticism which have sometimes been made against Ockham and the later nominalists.[13]

A final area of concern, related closely to the second, is salvation and merit. Ockham has often been accused of voluntarism, given his prioritization of the will over the supernatural habit. Salvation in Ockham, however, always proceeds according to God's ordination, and would be impossible in the absence of God's will. Ockham's theology, despite what the early commentators were prepared to believe, was less extreme than most of the alternatives offered by contemporary theologians, and whilst it would be unwise to deny that many of his ideas *did* cause controversy, we should be cautious about identifying him with radicalism. The damage that has already been done by such naïve identifications will be only too clear from what follows.

Language, Signs and Signification: the Context

Critics and literary historians concerned with the problem of language have tended to portray nominalism as a disruptive, anti-authoritarian philosophy. Re-interpreting the radical scepticism of the early historical

---

Clark discusses the implications of the *ordinata-absoluta* distinction for the moral sense of the individual, concluding with an optimistic assessment of the function of reason. He points out, in particular, the error of seeing 'the contingent decrees of God [as] the sole basis of moral value and obligation' (19).

[13]Ockham raised some important objections to the accepted proofs of God's existence. Both the cosmological arguments of Duns Scotus and Thomas Aquinas (God as necessary first cause), and the famous ontological argument presented by Anselm, were rejected. Scotus's proof was held to be untenable because it overlooked the logical possibility of an infinite regression of causes. Anselm's was rejected on the grounds that it failed to establish God's existence *self-evidently*. For these Ockham substituted an argument based on *conservation*, casting God in the role of first conserver. Since all creatures in existence were necessarily conserved by an external agent, and since creature and agent existed simultaneously, there had to be an original conserver in order to prevent an actual infinity. On Ockham's treatment of the arguments of Scotus and Anselm, see Gordon Leff, *William of Ockham: The Metamorphosis of Scholastic Discourse* (Manchester: Manchester University Press, 1975), 382-98. See also Ockham, *Quaestiones in lib. I Physicorum*, q. cxxxii-vi (in Ockham, *Philosophical Writings*, ed. Boehner, 115-25). Anselm's argument is presented in the *Proslogion* (II.ii) (ed. with parallel English translation by M.J. Charlesworth (Oxford: Clarendon Press, 1965), 116-7). Scotus's proof appears in his *Ordinatio* (I, dist. II, q. i, a. 1). The text of this section of the *Ordinatio* can be found in John Duns Scotus, *Philosophical Writings: A Selection*, ed. and tr. Allan Wolter (Edinburgh: Nelson, 1962), 35-52. Aquinas' own version of the cosmological argument, which, though never directly challenged by Ockham, was implicitly rejected in the argument based on conservation, is to be found in the *Summa Theologiae* (1a.2, 1-3) (ed. and tr. Timothy McDermott (vol. 2 in the Blackfriars series) (London: Blackfriars, 1964), 5-17).

accounts and their literary offshoots,[14] they have found in nominalist sign theory a linguistic relativism equally inimical to stable and transcendent truths. Among the effects commonly listed are a tendency to separate, or at least to render unstable signifier and signified, a desire to explore and exploit verbal ambiguities, and an implied reversal of the order of signification (the sign now being seen as constitutive of the 'reality' it was once held to reflect). All of these are conspicuously modern ideas, and whilst it would be unfair to deny such continuities as exist between modern and medieval semiotics,[15] it would be as well to consider the contexts in which they have been used. Modern critical theory exerts its own demands on the sign, and we should be aware of these, as far as possible, if we are to do nominalism justice. To take the first example, it is not obvious what such terms as 'signifier' and 'signified', or even 'sign' and 'referent' actually mean in the context of nominalism. Nor is it clear, in most cases, what is meant by 'reality', a term which was always used in a very specific way by the philosophers themselves. To declare simply, then, that nominalist discourses force signifier and signified apart, or sever the link between sign and reality, is to leave many of the most important questions of medieval sign theory unexamined. At worst, it is to distort the concepts themselves beyond recognition.

A number of critics, observing Chaucer's indebtedness to Augustine, Boethius and Dante, have tacitly equated 'signified' with 'universal'. Holly Wallace Boucher, in an article on Chaucer and Boccaccio, contrasts the word games of the Canterbury pilgrims with an earlier tradition in which a poet's words, guaranteed by their relation to the Logos, 'possess[ed] the inalienable power of signs to signify the real'.[16] This Platonic aesthetic,

---

[14]Early literary studies influenced conspicuously by the sceptical interpretation of nominalism include Morse, 'The Philosophy of the Clerk of Oxenford'; Robert Stepsis, '*Potentia absoluta* and the *Clerk's Tale*', *Chaucer Review*, 10 (1975), 129-46; Kathleen M. Ashley, 'Divine Power in Chester Cycle and Late Medieval Thought', *Journal of the History of Ideas*, 39 (1978), 387-404. Ashley and Stepsis, though writing after the most important revisions to the historical understanding of nominalism had been made, continue to rely on an essentially sceptical outlook.

[15]The parallelism between modern and medieval sign-based approaches to epistemology has been pointed out by a number of commentators. See, for example, Anthony Kenny, *Wyclif* (Oxford: Oxford University Press, 1985), 5; Umberto Eco, 'The Return of the Middle Ages', in *Travels in Hyperreality*, tr. William Weaver (London: Pan, 1987), 59-85. See also the important articles by Hans Robert Jauß, 'The Alterity and Modernity of Medieval Literature' (181-230); Eugene Vance, '*Mervelous Signals*: Poetics, Sign Theory, and Politics in Chaucer's *Troilus*' (293-338); and Brian Stock, '*Antiqui* or *Moderni*?' (391-401), in *New Literary History*, 10 (Winter 1979). For a linguist's perspective on the subject, see Geoffrey Bursill-Hall's *Speculative Grammars of the Middle Ages* (The Hague: Mouton, 1971), 327-42.

[16]Holly Wallace Boucher, 'Nominalism: The Difference for Chaucer and Boccaccio', *Chaucer Review*, 20 (1986), 213-20 (quote: 214).

she argues, informed works as diverse as Dante's *Commedia* and *La Queste del Sainte Graal*. Poets shared a belief that their poetry 'bore a simple and intelligible relationship to the truth and was an image of the divine order'.[17] With the advent of nominalism, however, the link between poetry and the immutable truths of the universe had been broken. Language had become an opaque and potentially distorting lens:

> Concepts and the words which expressed them had become relative. The firm bonds between signifier and signified (*vox* and *conceptus*) had unravelled: so had the necessary tie between sign and reality (*res* and referent). Words could no longer be assumed to fit the shape of reality because of their origin in a real world of ideas beyond the mind. Language is no longer a shadow pattern of the real, but has become a skewed grid that may not fit the scheme of reality.[18]

Boucher is more explicit than many about what the split between signifier and signified implies for her. There is an apparent inconsistency, however, between the above account and the view of language and reality we find in Ockham. It is not obvious, for example, how the connection is made between the disappearance of 'a real world of ideas' and the epistemological problem of fitting language to the 'scheme of reality'. By depriving universals of their ontological status, Ockham was not casting doubt on the capacity of words to signify 'reality'. Rather, he was attempting to change the nature of that reality by confining it to the particular. The problem, therefore, was primarily an ontological one concerning the nature of the universal itself, and not an epistemological one relating to knowledge of reality in general. The fact that universals were to be considered concepts (*ficta* or *figmenta* in the mind) rather than things (*res*) did, it is true, have far-reaching consequences for Ockham's theory of signification,[19] but it did not result in the wholesale relativism Boucher describes. Words for Ockham, no less than for the Thomists and Scotists against whom he was reacting, were ultimately (to borrow the oft-cited phrase of Dante) the consequences of the things which they signified.[20] The relationship between the two was complicated by the rigour of Ockham's individualist logic, which translated what had been a simple link between sign and universal into a more complex relationship based on

---

[17]Ibid.

[18]Ibid., 215.

[19]See Leff, *William of Ockham*, 131-9; Ernest A. Moody, *The Logic of William of Ockham* (London: Sheed & Ward, 1935), 31-6.

[20]Cf. Dante Alighieri, *La Vita Nuova*, xiii, 4 (in *Tutte le opere: edizione del centenario*, ed. Fredi Chiappelli (Milan: Mursia, 7th ed. 1969), 375).

universal predication.[21] Nonetheless, linguistic signs could always be related to a real referent in the end, even if, as Gordon Leff has remarked, there was now a marked 'asymmetry' between the world of things and the world of language and logic.[22] Ockham is quite explicit about this relationship, which he describes in terms of a modified form of the classical *res-conceptus-vox* triad:

> [...] voces imponuntur ad significandum illa eadem, quae per conceptus mentis significantur, ita quod conceptus primo naturaliter aliquid significat, et secondario vox significat illud idem, in tantum quod voce instituta ad significandum aliquod significatum per conceptum mentis, si conceptus ille mutaret significatum suum, eo ipso ipsa vox sine nova institutione suum significatum permutaret.[23]

Though he avoids assuming a linear connection between words, ideas and things (things, it is argued, are signified directly by both concepts and words together), Ockham is adhering closely here to the traditional realist schema. In common with Aristotle and Boethius, whose influence he acknowledges,[24] and with grammarians and logicians up to the time of the *Modistae*, Ockham insists on preserving a relationship of dependency between *vox* and *conceptus* (Boucher's signifier and signified), and upon subordinating them to the real world of the *res* (Boucher's referent). There is not, then, strictly speaking, a split between any of the traditional elements in Ockham's theory of signification; signifier, signified and referent have merely been redefined. Moreover, there would appear to be a much weaker parallel between modern and medieval conceptions of the sign than their shared terminology implies. In the medieval view, for example, as the passage from Ockham shows, the signified represented an idea in

---

[21]Ockham's theory combined the principles of *conceptual* and *predicate* nominalism. The status of universals was ultimately conceptual, but the universality of the concept itself depended on its *predicability* of more than one particular. The most universal concepts were therefore those terms which could be predicated of the largest number of particulars. (See Leff, *William of Ockham*, 182.) On the different varieties of nominalism, see D.M. Armstrong, *Universals and Scientific Realism I: Nominalism and Realism* (Cambridge: Cambridge University Press, 1978), 11-56.

[22]See Leff, *William of Ockham*, 237.

[23]'[...] words are applied in order to signify the very same things which are signified by mental concepts. Hence the concept signifies something primarily and naturally, whilst the word signifies the same thing secondarily. This holds to such an extent that a word conventionally signifying an object signified by a mental concept would immediately, and without any new convention, come to signify another object, simply because the concept came to signify another object.' (*Summa totius logicae*, I, c. i; text and translation are those of Ockham, *Philosophical Writings*, ed. Boehner, 48.)

[24]See ibid.

the mind. As such, it acted as a sign of its referent (*res*), but was not, unlike the signified of the Structuralists of our own time, a part of the language system. This is significant, since it is only by virtue of its membership of such a system that the signified can be seen as a relative, rather than an absolute (or 'positive') term.[25] Philosophers and linguists of the Middle Ages were simply unaccustomed to thinking about language in this way,[26] and in spite of the many and far-reaching changes which Scholasticism and nominalism brought with them, clung to the essentially mimetic principles of their classical forebears.[27] Terms like 'signifier' and 'signified', therefore, with their unavoidable modern theoretical associations, should be carefully qualified if they are to be used at all in the context of medieval sign theory. Critics, likewise, should guard against perceiving parallels too readily.

Though there is no support for Boucher's claims in the writings of Ockham themselves, it is nonetheless possible to point to elements in his philosophy which may have encouraged such a reading. In an article on Chaucer's *Envoy to Bukton*, for example, Jay Ruud defines Ockhamism not primarily as a philosophy of particulars, but as a science of *terms*.[28] As such, he argues, it effectively separates the word from the real world altogether, leading inevitably to a sceptical assessment of the power of language in general. Though few would disagree with the first part of Ruud's definition, which is supported by Ockham's own assertion that logic and the 'real' sciences are 'de intentionibus' rather than 'de rebus',[29] it is

---

[25]'Qu'on prenne le signifié ou le signifiant, la langue ne comporte ni des idées ni des sons qui préexisteraient au système linguistique, mais seulement des différences conceptuelles et des differences phoniques issues de ce système' (Ferdinand de Saussure, *Cours de linguistique générale*, ed. Charles Bally and Albert Sechehaye (Paris: Bibliothèque Scientifique, 1955), 166).

[26]The closest pre-Renaissance analogue to the Saussurean signified is found in the philosophy of the Stoics, whose definition of 'thing signified' (the *lekton*), unlike that of Aristotle and the Scholastics, is linguistic rather than conceptual. See Tzvetan Todorov, *Theories of the Symbol*, tr. Catherine Porter (Oxford: Blackwell, 1982), 19-20.

[27]This is not to say, of course, that there was held to be a *perfect* correspondence between language, thought and reality. Ockham's critique of the *Modistae*, for example, is based on the assumption that not all linguistic forms (*modi significandi*) are matched by substances, accidents or processes in the real world (*modi essendi*). (See Alfonso Maierù, 'The Philosophy of Language', in *History of Linguistics, 2: Classical and Medieval Linguistics*, ed. Giulio Lepschy (London: Longman, 1994), 272-306, esp. 302-6.)

[28]Jay Ruud, 'Chaucer and Nominalism: the *Envoy to Bukton*', *Mediaevalia*, 10 (1984), 199-212.

[29]Logic is distinguished from the sciences by its concern with 'universales supponentes pro rebus' ('concepts standing for things'), rather than with 'intentiones supponentes pro intentionibus' ('concepts standing for concepts'). (See Ockham, *Philosophical Writings*, ed. Boehner, 12; the relevant passage is cited in full in Ruud's article, 102.)

important to be aware of the very specific context from which it has been abstracted. Given, for example, that Ockham is concerned primarily with the conditions of different kinds of knowledge, and is making no claim for the status of terms in general, it is difficult to see how the power of language itself is being undermined as Ruud suggests. Logic and the 'real' sciences take terms as their object not because terms *never* stand for things, but because terms, and not their referents, establish the truth or falsity of the propositions that contain them. Ockham illustrates the point as follows:

> [...] diversa suppositio terminorum bene facit ad hoc quod de termino aliquod praedicatum vere praedicetur vel vere negetur. Unde ad hoc quod haec sit vera, 'Res mutabilis est subiectum vel illud de quo scitur', bene facit suppositio istius termini, non consideratio rei extra. Nam si iste terminus 'res mutabilis' supponat simpliciter pro se, tunc haec est vera 'Res mutabilis, (hoc est, hoc commune "res mutabilis") est illud, de quo aliquid scitur'. Si autem supponat personaliter, tunc est falsa, quia quaelibet singularis est falsa.[30]

For Ockham, as for Aristotle, the truth-value of a proposition was more important than its content, since it was only by isolating propositions that were *necessarily* true (true, that is, in all possible contexts) that one could arrive at 'scientific' knowledge.[31] This is not to say, however, that other forms of knowledge were simply worthless, nor that propositions with external referents were in any way faulty or ambiguous. Existential propositions (i.e. propositions beginning 'there is/are...'), for example, could *only* be true if their terms 'supposited' for an external referent. Ruud's reading, by emphasizing Ockham's concern for scientific certainty, marginalizes cases such as these in the interests of preserving an essentially sceptical epistemology. His assumptions, though they are nowhere so explicitly stated, are almost certainly shared by a good number of commentators, a fact which might help to explain why Boucher and other critics have been so insistent on seeing Ockham's epistemology in

---

[30]'[...] it does certainly depend on the different *suppositio* of the terms whether a predicate is truly predicated or truly denied of a term. Hence, in order that this proposition be true, "The mutable thing is the subject or is that about which there is a science", what is important is not the consideration of the thing outside the mind but the *suppositio* of the term "mutable thing". For if it has simple *suppositio*, i.e. stands for itself, then our proposition is true: "'Mutable thing' (i.e. this common term 'mutable thing') is that about which something is scientifically known". If, however, it has personal *suppositio*, then it is false, because every singular proposition of this kind is false.' (*Prologus in Expositionem super viii libros Physicorum*; text and translation are taken from Ockham, *Philosophical Writings*, ed. Boehner, 14.)

[31]See Ockham, *Philosophical Writings*, ed. Boehner, xxiii-iv.

negative terms.[32] The arguments Ruud presents, then, though they appear to support Boucher's reading, ultimately highlight the inappropriateness of describing nominalist language theory in terms of split signs. We are at best resorting to an anachronistic metaphor if we are to apply such an image to fourteenth-century texts.

Literary Theory and the Rise of 'Sceptical' Nominalism

Boucher's article, in its use of the concepts of signifier and signified, is typical of the many nominalist readings influenced by current trends in literary theory. It represents more, however, in its portrayal of the split sign, than the simple appropriation of an idea. Underlying it is the assumption of a shared outlook, whose nature is defined by our own historical and critical biases. Among these, it is perhaps the tendency towards scepticism that has most obviously struck a chord with nominalism. Scepticism has been a discernible trait in British critical and cultural theory since the popularization of continental models in the 1970s, and has manifested itself most conspicuously in theories of language and semiotics.[33] The differential nature of the sign, the theory of 'language games', the politicized, ideological character of 'discourse' and the deconstruction of the signified are a few of the many ideas that have contributed to an increasingly chaotic understanding of reality. Long accustomed to a world of shifting and illusory truths, apologists for the new discursive methodologies have been only too ready to seize upon historical precursors to their condition. The perceived impact and scepticism of nominalism, a philosophy similarly preoccupied with signs and their relation to reality (albeit an *ideal*, rather than an empirical reality in many cases), has made it an attractive candidate. As Boucher's article has shown, however, the parallels that have been drawn between modern and medieval theory have tended to create a hybrid philosophy whose tenets might well have shocked our scholastic ancestors.

The critics themselves, of course, are not entirely to blame. It was the historians, after all, who brought the earliest and most extreme charges of scepticism against nominalism. One such charge, in particular, has had a profound effect on linguistic readings like Boucher's. This is the charge of

---

[32] The possible confusion of Ockham's opinions on the objects of knowledge with the more extreme views of Robert Holcot make this all the more likely, particularly given that Holcot saw linguistic, rather than mental terms as the objects of scientific knowledge. (See Ernest A. Moody, 'A Quodlibetal Question of Robert Holkot, O.P., on the Problem of the Objects of Knowledge and Belief', *Speculum*, 39 (1964), 53-74.)

[33] For a recent critical account of the retreat from 'Enlightenment' notions of 'truth' and 'certainty', etc. in modern theory, see Christopher Norris, *Truth and the Ethics of Criticism* (Manchester: Manchester University Press, 1994), ch. 1.

conceptual idealism, a charge which placed the nominalist's *viator*, already powerless to know God in any 'evident' way, entirely at the mercy of his own ideas (Ockham's *ficta* or *figmenta*).[34] The philosopher and theologian Philotheus Boehner, arguing for the 'realistic' nature of Ockham's conceptualism, is among a number of commentators who have attempted to dissociate the nominalists from this radical idea.[35] His arguments, however, have increasingly fallen on deaf ears, particularly in the literary establishment. Post-structuralist critics, always conscious of their utter dependence on the discourses that surround them, have found in nominalist idealism a tantalizing parallel to their own, equally disabling *linguistic* idealism.[36] Rather than a reality of transitory, potentially unreliable intellections (or 'terms', to make the parallel more explicit), they have discovered a world of sliding signifiers which, liberated from the centralizing force of the 'transcendent' signified, float free of particular signifieds in the language system. Reality is thus reduced to a kind of linguistic play.

Interestingly, Boucher mentions both conceptual and linguistic idealism together. Thought, she explains, has become 'an autonomous, limited sphere', lacking any stable foundation.[37] Language, likewise, now that signifier and signified have become separated, is the locus of that 'linguistic play' so beloved of the present generation of critics:

> [The poet] must now concern himself with the new ambiguity of symbol patterns, the new power of words to create autonomous worlds. The Logos is now only partially available through language, and the strict duality of sacred text and blasphemy has opened to create a space for linguistic play.[38]

In one sense, what Boucher says is right: the status of certain forms of biblical language was put in question by fourteenth-century logicians.[39]

---

[34] The tendency to perceive Ockham as an idealist, common in the early histories, was possibly perpetuated by a misunderstanding of the philosopher's views on the objects of knowledge (see also above, end of section 'Language, Signs and Signification: the Context'). For examples of historians who have succumbed to idealist prejudice, see Philoteus Boehner, 'The Realistic Conceptualism of William Ockham', *Traditio*, 4 (1946), 307-35, repr. in Boehner, *Collected Articles*, 156-74 (esp. 157-8).

[35] See ibid. See also the Introduction to Ockham, *Philosophical Writings*, ed. Boehner, xxiii-v.

[36] On the origins of this particular form of idealism in a philosophical misreading of Derrida, see Christopher Norris, *Derrida* (London: Fontana, 1987), ch. 6.

[37] Boucher, 'Nominalism', 215.

[38] Ibid.

[39] See Alastair J. Minnis, '"Authorial Intention" and "Literal Sense" in the Exegetical Theories of Richard Fitzralph and John Wyclif', *Proceedings of the Royal Irish Academy*, 75 (1975), 1-31.

Nonetheless, we may still ask whether 'linguistic play' and sliding signifiers are actually what we get if we remove God (the obvious candidate for the role of transcendent signified) from the sign system. Only, it seems, if we are twentieth-century literary theorists. For Ockhamist thinkers of the Middle Ages, the notion of reality being an 'autonomous' verbal construct of *any* kind would almost certainly have been a foreign and an unwelcome one.

Another image which Boucher borrows from contemporary theory is that of the infinitely regressing signifier. Like the idea of linguistic play, the regressing signifier is strongly suggestive of a kind of linguistic idealism, denying as it does the possibility of any final, stable referent. It is this idea, Boucher claims, which marks off Chaucer's contemporary, Boccaccio, as a nominalist. The pun on the name Frate Cipolla in Boccaccio's tale ('cipolla' is literally 'onion') is suggestive, she argues, of the character's empty rhetoric, which like the regressive signifier, never yields up truth:

> The onion does [...] have a centre, but it is composed of onion [...]. The image, then, suggests that Cipolla's words do not reveal a core of truth [...] but that they refer to words. Signifier uncovers signifier in succession, without any relation to truth or reality.[40]

Recalling Ockham's model of the sign, it is difficult to see how this idea relates to medieval nominalism at all. Signs in Ockham, it is true, did not always have to refer to things. The theories of 'simple' and 'material' supposition, which he used to account for self-referential terms and verbal fictions, were created specifically to free the sign of the necessarily significative function the realists had given it.[41] Nonetheless, Ockham nowhere suggests that signs can refer to signs in endless succession, even if, as in the cases of simple and material supposition, they do not have final external referents. Moreover, Boucher does not seem to have had either of these kinds of supposition in mind when she decided to link Boccaccio's rhetorical strategies with nominalism. All the more reason to locate her view of nominalism with certain historians and theorists of this century, and not with the philosophers of the fourteenth.

---

[40] Boucher, 'Nominalism', 216.

[41] Simple supposition occurs when a word or term stands for a concept, as in 'animal is a genus'; material supposition occurs when the word itself, as a graphic or phonic entity, is the referent ('"animal" is a word'). (See the discussion in Leff, *William of Ockham*, 131-9.) Simple and material supposition are also analysed in Philotheus Boehner, 'Ockham's Theory of Supposition and the Notion of Truth', *Franciscan Studies*, 6 (1946), 261-92, repr. in Boehner, *Collected Articles*, 232-67. See also Moody, *Logic*, 185-210.

Although it is not always possible to trace the influence of modern theory as closely as this, there has been a striking proliferation of readings, over the past decade in particular, which have concerned themselves with the epistemological implications of linguistic play and verbal ambiguity.[42] Much of the most recent work on the literary aspects of medieval sign theory, whether explicitly concerned with nominalist issues or not, has emphasized the sign's potential for ambiguity, its capacity to deceive or mislead, and its relative autonomy with respect to its referent.[43] According to Edmund Reiss, who devotes an entire paper to the problem of ambiguity, these were issues which intrigued storytellers and semiologists alike:

> Responding to the developing nominalism of the time and the pervasive uncertainty as to exactly what one could know, storytellers joined schoolmen in focusing not on truth itself but on such epistemological matters as the essential ambiguity of signs and the inherent complexity of language [...]. [A]long with semioticians, fiction writers investigated modes of signifying ways in which language altered concepts of reality.[44]

Reiss, like Boucher, portrays the later Middle Ages in terms which bear a striking resemblance to those of postmodernist literary theory. Once again, ambiguity in literary texts is simplistically associated with nominalist metaphysics, and authors and philosophers alike are seen to be adopting an essentially constructivist outlook. Reiss is not explicit about the assumptions he is making, yet we need not look far to find a more direct comparison with contemporary theory. J.M. Crafton, for example, in a reading much indebted to Boucher, suggests that we should resist the temptation to disregard philosophical influences, whose importance in Chaucer's day was as great as that of the theorists of our own:

---

[42]Before the 1980s, the emphasis of nominalist criticism was largely theological. In Lorrayne Y. Baird's *A Bibliography of Chaucer, 1964-1973* (Boston, MA: G.K. Hall, 1977), for example, the only entry for nominalism came under 'Ockhamist Theology'. This contrasts sharply with the five entries of the 1974-1985 edition, of which only two are specifically concerned with theological issues. (See Lorraine Y. Baird-Lange and Hildegard Schnuttgen, *A Bibliography of Chaucer, 1974-1985* (Hamden, CT: Archon Books, and Cambridge: D.S. Brewer, 1988).)

[43]This tendency has been particularly conspicuous in recent research on the *Gawain*-poet. See Robert Blanch and Julian Wasserman, 'The Current State of *Sir Gawain and the Green Knight* Criticism', *Chaucer Review*, 27 (1993), 401-12 (esp. 405-6). See also Ross Arthur's *Medieval Sign Theory and* Sir Gawain and the Green Knight (Toronto: University of Toronto Press, 1987).

[44]Edmund Reiss, 'Ambiguous Signs and Authorial Deceptions in Fourteenth-Century Fictions', in Julian Wasserman and Lois Roney (eds.), *Sign, Sentence, Discourse: Language in Medieval Thought and Literature* (Syracuse, NY: Syracuse University Press, 1989), 113-37 (quote: 114).

The dry rattle of Duns Scotus, Abelard and Occam, not the texts or terms necessarily but the effects of them, was doubtless as lively a reality for Chaucer as Derrida and Lyotard are for modern readers. Certainly, there has been much discussion of deconstruction by people who have never read a line of Derrida.[45]

Crafton's last point is perfectly true, but it should not be forgotten that Derrida and Lyotard, unlike Scotus, Abelard and Ockham, have the weight of the literary establishment behind them. Literary history would be incomplete without them, yet we cannot even be sure whether Scotus, Abelard and Ockham were known in literary circles. Crafton is not unaware of these difficulties, yet in the course of his reading creates further problems by assuming, like Boucher and Reiss, that ambiguity makes nominalist influence the more likely. Reworking Boucher's analysis in terms of Harold Bloom's theory of misreading, he attempts to show how Chaucer, in his shift from stability to linguistic diversity, 'misreads' Dante both as a philosopher and as a poet. Something like this may indeed be happening, but it would be wrong, as the analysis of Boucher's article has shown, to imagine that Chaucer the 'nominalist' was misreading Dante the 'realist'.[46]

The influence of modern theory on the portrayal of nominalist semiotics is perhaps most apparent in Peggy Knapp's Bakhtinian readings of the *Knight's Tale* and the *Miller's Tale*.[47] For Knapp, as for Boucher and Delasanta, nominalism engenders a split between the sign and its universal referent (identified as 'signifier' and 'signified', respectively). The *Knight's Tale*, she argues, represents an authoritative, aristocratic discourse (the 'dominant' discourse of Bakhtinian theory), and is informed, correspondingly, by a philosophical realism. Its point of reference is not the world of things, but the world of ideas, which must account, Knapp claims,

---

[45]John Michael Crafton, 'Emptying the Vessel: Chaucer's Humanistic Critique of Nominalism', in Utz (ed.), *Literary Nominalism*, 117-34 (quote: 118).

[46]The tendency in theory-oriented readings to perceive ambiguity and equivocation as the hallmarks of nominalist philosophy has some important precedents in earlier criticism. Rodney Delasanta, for example, whose article on Chaucer and universals is not obviously influenced by split signs or regressing signifiers, sees ambiguity as the poet's only certainty in a nominalistic world of particulars (see 'Chaucer and the Problem of the Universal', *Mediaevalia*, 9 (1986), 145-63, esp. 150-2). Russel Peck, likewise, in his ground-breaking study of Chaucer's nominalism, anticipates many of the points about ambiguity, deception and verbal trickery which were to be made in a more theoretical context by Boucher, Reiss, and Crafton (see 'Chaucer and the Nominalist Questions', *Speculum*, 53 (1978), 745-60).

[47]Peggy Knapp, *Chaucer and the Social Contest* (New York: Routledge, 1990), chs. 2 and 3. An earlier version of chapter 3 is published in Wasserman and Roney (eds.), *Sign, Sentence, Discourse*, 294-308.

for the particular system of correspondences in the tale. Each character, in effect, becomes a sign of the real:

> Arcite's link with the God Mars, the colour red, the fluid blood, the element fire, the quality brutal strength, and the champion Emetrius is matched by Palamon's association with the Goddess Venus, the colour white, the fluid milk, the element water, the quality gentle weakness, and the champion Lycurgus. As a result, the world of specific persons does not seem the Knight's real subject, although it is necessarily the medium through which the world of eternal forms must be glimpsed.[48]

The symmetry between the temporal and the eternal is matched, Knapp argues, by the assumptions of 'mainstream' (as Knapp herself characterizes it) medieval language theory, which insisted on a close correspondence between word and referent. The Knight's 'literal habit of mind' and formal narrative strategies (which yield their meanings univocally) imply a like respect for the efficacy of language. Nevertheless, in practice, 'the Knight cannot secure signifier to signified and arrest the shifts of significance which words [...] undergo'.[49] This is the result, Knapp claims, of an anti-authoritarian 'nominalist' discourse which seeks to subvert the 'realist' principles that underlie the narrative. She finds a similar principle at work in the *Miller's Tale*, but now it is nominalism itself, conspicuously ironizing the Knight's orderly system, that defines the story:

> The [*Miller's*] *Tale* should [...] be called nominalist because words—signifiers—are irreverently pried loose from what they signify. No guaranteeing order is assumed to prevail to keep everything in place. The story proceeds because Nicholas, in his con of the carpenter, plays fast and loose with the faith the dominant discourse had placed in the revelatory power of words.[50]

The difficulty with Knapp's reading, though illuminating in its own terms, is that it enlists nominalism wholly in the service of another idea. This would explain the fact that, as Watts and Utz have observed, she never explicitly defines nominalism, either historically or otherwise.[51] What she is concerned with, after all, is not nominalism itself but its putative ideological correlates. The split between signifier and signified, though repeatedly characterized as 'nominalist', is ultimately less important for her as a philosophical definition than it is as a literary theoretical concept. It certainly owes more to Mikhail Bakhtin than it does to William

---

[48] Knapp, *Chaucer and the Social Contest*, 19.
[49] Ibid.
[50] Ibid., 38.
[51] See Watts and Utz, 'Nominalist Perspectives on Chaucer's Poetry', 147.

of Ockham,[52] whose only real function in Knapp's reading is to ground what she says in a philosophical and historical context. Strictly speaking, neither nominalism nor realism as historical facts are necessary conditions for her interpretation, based as it is on a model originally applied to much more recent literature. As might be expected from a theoretically-oriented critic, she offers no textual support for nominalist influence.[53]

The chief problem with Knapp's approach is its tendency to place too great an emphasis on abstract details, so that she is always in danger of sacrificing historical content to ideological form. Nominalism and realism, as subjugated and dominant discourses respectively, become polarized, discontinuous entities. What we have, in other words, are not different parts of a shared philosophical outlook (which, in spite of their differences, is what medieval nominalism and realism were), but ideas which appear to have only a brief period of shared currency in common. What is worse, realism is forced into the position of an orthodox and authoritarian doctrine, whilst nominalism, in a way which can only reinforce the claims of the early 'sceptical' histories, is cast in a marginal and subversive rôle. Such drastic over-simplifications, as well as being noticeably artificial, are shown to be untenable by the course of history itself. Whilst it is certainly true that Christian orthodoxy has been upheld by many distinguished realist thinkers (Augustine, Aquinas, Bradwardine, etc.), it is equally true that realists have included notorious heretics among their number. John Wyclif, as Anthony Kenny has argued, would disappoint anyone who expected to find a necessary link between realism and orthodoxy.[54] Likewise the nominalists, once portrayed as the radical breakers of the 'Scholastic synthesis', or as sceptics for whom even the existence of God was not a certainty, are seen as less unorthodox figures in recent revisionist histories.[55]

---

[52]Knapp's reading is informed, in particular, by Bakhtin's *The Dialogic Imagination*, ed. Michael Holquist, tr. Caryl Emerson and Michael Holquist (Austin, TX: University of Texas Press, 1981).

[53]The opposition between the realist Knight and the nominalist Miller has recently been placed in a more specific intellectual and historical context by Edgar Laird, who analyses the two characters in terms of Robert Grosseteste's five 'levels' of Knowledge. What distinguishes the Knight from the Miller, Laird argues, is his ability to elevate his mind beyond the level of accidents or particulars (the lowest level), and to consider things according to their *causae formales* and *rationes causales*, as the structure of his tale demonstrates. This distinction does not imply, of course, that the Miller is *necessarily* a nominalist, though his views and narrative style would be compatible with nominalist epistemology. (See Edgar Laird, 'Cosmic Law and Literary Character in Chaucer's *Knight's Tale*', in Utz (ed.), *Literary Nominalism*, 101-15.)

[54]Kenny, *Wyclif*, ch. 1.

[55]See above, section 'Versions of Nominalism'.

An Alternative to Sceptical Nominalism: Rhetoric

Given that recent theoretical concerns have had such an impact on literary studies of nominalist semiotics, it remains to determine whether the claims that have been made so far regarding ambiguity, relativism and the relation between signifier and signified have any validity *outside* the context of the literary readings in which we find them. If they do, and are not simply figments of the modern theoretical imagination, we must ask what, if not nominalism, is a likely or reasonable cause of such effects. This is an important question, since it serves to highlight further those aspects of medieval philosophy and aesthetics that have appealed to literary critics and theorists. Moreover, if the described effects can be explained in terms of a *number* of philosophical causes, we must ask what is to be gained by prioritizing nominalism. We might also question further the extent to which nominalist sign theory stood apart from Scholastic semiotics more generally.

To begin with ambiguity, it is hardly possible to deny the fascination that a word's multiple meanings could hold for the fourteenth-century writer. Chaucer, Langland and the *Gawain*-poet, not to mention the dramatists of the fourteenth and fifteenth centuries, all experimented in their own way with ambiguous expressions, puns and rhetorical trickery. This can hardly be shown to have been a direct consequence of nominalism, although it would be fair to suggest that nominalism may have contributed to a more general concern with ambiguity. Reductive distinctions between the stable, unambiguous signs of the realist text and the shifting symbols of nominalist discourse, however, are untenable. In his discussion of the *Canterbury Tales*, Rodney Delasanta makes just such a distinction, apparently ignoring the fact that realists were as ready to admit ambiguity as nominalists.[56] Properly speaking, the theory of equivocal terms was a Scholastic one, and not a peculiarity of nominalist thought. Moreover, equivocation itself had been recognised since philosophers first began to think about language. Though it may well be true, as Eugene Vance has claimed, that interest in *ways* of signifying (which would have included ambiguous signification) became more intense in the fourteenth century, we should not be tempted to see this solely as the outcome of nominalism.[57] Equivocation would have interested anyone acquainted with the philosophy of the day, whether nominalist or not. John Wyclif, for example, includes a standard discussion of equivocation in his introductory tract on logic, and devotes great attention to it in the *De Veritate Sacrae Scripturae*.

---

[56] See Delasanta, 'Chaucer and the Problem of the Universal', 150-1.
[57] Eugene Vance, *Mervelous Signals: Poetics and Sign Theory in the Middle Ages* (Lincoln, NE, and London: University of Nebraska Press, 1986), 279.

Likewise, discussions of equivocation are found in realist writings of the previous generation, including those of Thomas Aquinas and Roger Bacon.[58] Interest in equivocation, then, is perhaps better understood as a consequence of the more general thirteenth- and fourteenth-century interest in terms (sometimes referred to as *terminism*)[59] than as a specific response to nominalism.

Another possible source of writers' interest in ambiguity, all the more likely for being less esoteric than speculative grammar or supposition theory, is rhetoric. Like dialectic, rhetoric is of interest because it deals with those aspects of language that signify *indirectly*, through tropes and figures. The core principles of rhetoric would have been known to writers like Chaucer through the works of the 'preceptive' grammarians, whose popularity in the thirteenth and fourteenth centuries is known to have been considerable.[60] Rhetorical principles also underlie much of the textual exegesis found in commentaries on the Bible and on secular writers; many of these would certainly have been familiar to fourteenth-century writers. For Chaucer, rhetoric encompassed both the high style of the scholar and the instrument of persuasion and deception (at the hands, for example, of Nicholas in the *Miller's Tale,* the Pardoner, or the friar of the *Summoner's Tale*). Robert M. Jordan has argued that Chaucer's poetry itself, with its close attention to verbal detail, might also be characterized as 'rhetorical'.[61] In all of these cases, rhetoric is clearly being understood as potentially deceptive and subversive. It grants to language a far greater freedom than either grammatical or logical analysis will allow (being the only one of the three that actually *relies* on principles of ambiguity and non-reference), and in many ways poses a greater threat. The scepticism

---

[58]John Wyclif, *De Logica,* 3 vols., ed. M.H. Dziewicki (London: Trubner, 1899), vol. 1: 2-3; *De Veritate Sacrae Scripturae,* 3 vols., ed. Rudolf Buddensieg (London: Trubner, 1905-7), vol. 1 (1905), ch. 1. On discussions of equivocation in the thirteenth century, see *The Cambridge History of Later Medieval Philosophy: From the Rediscovery of Aristotle to the Disintegration of Scholasticism, 1100-1600,* eds. Norman Kretzmann et al. (Cambridge: Cambridge University Press, 1982), 174-87.

[59]*Terminism* is sometimes used synonymously with *nominalism*. Here, however, its reference will be restricted to the general science of propositional terms. As such, it may be taken to include both nominalists and realists.

[60]On Chaucer and the preceptive grammarians, see C.P. Baldwin, *Medieval Rhetoric and Poetic* (New York: Macmillan, 1928), ch. 7 (esp. 187-8) and ch. 10. Baldwin's arguments for seeing Geoffrey of Vinsauf as a major influence on Chaucer's poetics have been re-examined by James J. Murphy in 'A New Look at Chaucer and the Rhetoricians', *The Review of English Studies,* n.s. 15 (1964), 1-20 (see esp. note 1).

[61]See Robert M. Jordan, *Chaucer's Poetics and the Modern Reader* (Berkeley, CA: University of California Press, 1987), 15. Jordan's assumption that this rhetorical style is a *correlate* of Chaucer's nominalism is, as Robert Myles has pointed out, a misguided one (see Myles, *Chaucerian Realism,* 12-6).

many have perceived in nominalism, then, might properly belong, albeit in a different way, here; it would certainly be at no greater risk of exaggeration to claim that it did. Paul de Man, in an article entitled 'The Resistance to Theory', has argued that rhetoric, as the component of the *trivium* exclusively concerned with language *in itself*, was always a potential threat to the stability of the medieval system of knowledge. Unlike grammar and dialectic, whose principles were always referable to the world of phenomena (since *res* ultimately determined *conceptus* and *vox*), rhetoric preserved an unsettling autonomy. Provided it was kept subordinate to grammar and logic, knowledge remained secure. When, however, discourse itself became the focus of enquiry, all claims to certainty were lost:

> Rhetoric, by its actively negative relationship to grammar and logic, [...] [undid] the claims of the trivium (and by extension, of language) to be an epistemologically stable construct [...]. [S]ince grammar as well as figuration [was] an integral part of reading, it follow[ed] that reading [would] be a negative process in which the grammatical cognition [was] undone, at all times, by its rhetorical displacement. The model of the trivium contain[ed] within itself the pseudo-dialectic of its own undoing and its history tells the story of this dialectic.[62]

Chaucer's poetry, if what Boucher, Crafton and Knapp have said is correct, would appear to encourage just such a 'negative' reading. If we assume that it does, and that the work of his contemporaries is similarly 'rhetorical', then we have an explanation which is at once more plausible and less anachronistic than readings which assume nominalist influence. Moreover, we have an analysis which is explicit about the relation between medieval and modern theory. Rhetoric, it is argued, poses a threat to the trivium precisely because, like contemporary critical theory, it takes language as its object. Nominalism, on the other hand, is ultimately rooted in empirical reality, and can only be distorted by such analogies with the modern critical enterprise.

A Second Alternative: Sceptical Realism

As a possible explanation for the preoccupation with ambiguity, rhetoric is not the only alternative to a sceptical nominalism. The tradition of philosophical realism itself, as it was inherited from Plato, Augustine, Chalcidius and Boethius, among others, contained the seeds of scepticism in its

---

[62]Paul de Man, 'The Resistance to Theory', *Yale French Studies*, 63 (1982), 3-20 (quote: 17). De Man's idea is elaborated by Rita Copeland, 'Rhetoric and the Politics of the Literal Sense in Medieval Literary Theory', in Piero Boitani and Anna Torti (eds.), *Interpretation Medieval and Modern* (Cambridge: D.S. Brewer, 1993), 1-23.

very fabric. Though the *Timaeus* would have been the only work of Plato familiar to Chaucer and his contemporaries, Plato's distrust of language, which received its most famous expression in the *Cratylus*,[63] would certainly not have escaped them. Theologians and philosophers would have learned from Augustine of the potential dangers of placing too great a trust in language, which whilst it could reveal, through Christ's incarnation, divine truths, could equally well confuse and deceive. The popular image of word as body and soul (*vox* and *verbum*) conveys precisely this ambiguous nature. Poets like Chaucer and Langland, perhaps even more than theologians, would have been aware of the problematic relation of language to truth, particularly given the uncertain status of fictional narrative. The Chartrian image of poetry as a veil of truth, after all, was not accepted by everyone, and poets of the fourteenth century, no less than grammarians and encyclopedists of the thirteenth, had to confront the doubts that Neoplatonism had brought with it.

Though the scepticism of the realist tradition is not a final explanation of fourteenth-century attitudes to literary language, it is in many ways the most useful account that can be offered. It is not incompatible, either, with the rhetorical explanation, since the dangers of empty rhetoric were only too well known to thinkers like Augustine and Boethius. Textual evidence for realist scepticism is comparatively strong, and if nothing else, provides a good reason to look elsewhere for signs of nominalist influence. Even if nominalism encouraged the kind of linguistic scepticism critics have attributed to it, it would be difficult, given the lack of evidence, to distinguish this from scepticism deriving from other sources. As it is, there are some important indications that the philosophical problems identified by Boucher, Knapp, Crafton and Delasanta belong properly to the realist tradition. The emphasis, noted earlier, on *knowing,* rather than being, for example, is strongly suggestive of a realist perspective: Given the existence of the universal, how can it be known? Though Boucher and Delasanta are both explicit about the ontological aspects of nominalism, their analyses are ultimately framed in epistemological terms. This is a conspicuous tendency in nominalist criticism in general, in which the problem of the universal has played a surprisingly minor rôle. Laurence Eldredge, for example, in an essay on nominalism and Boethian philosophy in *Troilus and Criseyde*,[64] sees the poem as a reaction against the epistemol-

---

[63] In the *Cratylus*, Plato ultimately abandons language, flux-ridden and transitory, as a philosophical tool. The real, it is argued, is better contemplated directly. See Plato, *Cratylus*, ed. and tr. H.N. Fowler (Loeb Classical Library) (London: Heinemann, 1926), 438-40 E. For a recent interpretation of the final section, see Timothy M.S. Baxter, *The 'Cratylus': Plato's Critique of Naming* (Leiden: Brill, 1992), 164-88.

[64] Laurence Eldredge, 'Boethian Epistemology and Chaucer's *Troilus and Criseyde* in the Light of Fourteenth-Century Thought', *Mediaevalia*, 2 (1976), 49-75.

ogy of fourteenth-century scepticism. Troilus' confused progression towards truth, he argues, is an ironic parallel to the nominalist's quest for empirical knowledge. Only by a slow process of realization, beginning with his earliest thoughts on the nature of love itself (divorced from its particular manifestations) (I, 400-15) is Troilus able to cast aside his naïve scepticism and embrace fully the principles of Boethian realism (culminating in his ascent to the eighth sphere in book V). This is by no means a controversial reading, but we must still ask why, given that the *Consolation of Philosophy* itself does not present knowledge as a goal easily won, we need to cast Troilus in the rôle of nominalist. If his confusion consists in mistaking the world for the true object of knowledge, he is not essentially different from Boethius in the *Consolation*, or from the *discipulus* figures of contemporary Christian literature. The problems he confronts are not those of the nominalist, who refuses on ontological grounds to admit the possibility of universals, but those of the man whose confused perceptions blind him to the true nature of things.

In an earlier paper by Eldredge, we are presented with a similar scenario. The theme again is the failure to achieve transcendent knowledge, and once again it is nominalism that is to blame. The poem under scrutiny this time is the *House of Fame,* whose narrator, Geoffrey, is seen caught between the conflicting worlds of the *Via Moderna,* represented by Ockham, and the *Via Antiqua,* which emphasized the old values inherited from the Neoplatonists.[65] The refusal of the narrator to accept any single theory of dreams (I, 1-63), his confused and incomplete thoughts on the love of Dido and Aeneas (Eldredge focuses on his final reaction to the story in Book I, 468-79), and his insistence on seeing his flight from the Earth in physical, non-transcendent terms (II, 896-909), are all suggestive, Eldredge argues, of his sceptical habit of mind. As an adherent of the *Via Moderna*, he places little trust in transcendent knowledge or abstract theories, preferring instead, like Troilus, to dwell in the world of particulars. For Eldredge, however, the answers he discovers there are never adequate, and he continues to strive, until the narrative breaks off in Book III, for knowledge of a different kind. Transcendence is never achieved in the poem, but if this is to be seen as a failure, as Eldredge sees it, we must ask what is to be gained from construing such a failure in nominalist terms. As in the case of *Troilus and Criseyde*, there are a number of alternative explanations available in Chaucer's immediate sources. The problems the narrator confronts are again problems of personal conviction and perception, and are not vastly different from those encountered by Boethius and Dante. Eldredge's radically sceptical version of nominalism, it would seem, is neither a necessary nor a useful explanation of the problems he discusses.

---

[65]Laurence Eldredge, 'Chaucer's *House of Fame* and the *Via Moderna*', *Neuphilologische Mitteilungen*, 71 (1970), 105-19.

A tacit affirmation of the potential for scepticism in the realist tradition is provided by Phillip Pulsiano. In an essay on language in *Troilus and Criseyde*,[66] Pulsiano lists a range of possible sources for Chaucer's verbal epistemology, drawing both on the realist and the nominalist traditions. Though he makes no attempt to identify Chaucer as either realist or nominalist, he is willing to admit that the poet's ideas on language 'are compatible with those of a wide range of writers' (ibid., 153). His own interests lie with the sign theory of Augustine, and with the potential of language to signify truth. *Troilus and Criseyde* is important in this respect because it 'explore[s] the breakdown of language as a vehicle for truth and the acquisition of knowledge' (ibid., 154). Throughout the poem, Pulsiano suggests, truth is continually undermined by illusion and ambiguity, as characters and narrator alike struggle against the inadequacies of word and symbol. The narrator's distrust of language is made explicit in the closing formula of the poem ('Go, litel bok [...]'), in which he prays that the 'gret diversite I in Englissh' (V, 1793-4) will not obscure his purpose. The solution to his problem, according to Pulsiano, comes with his final exhortation to the 'yonge, fresshe folkes' to love God and retreat from 'worldly vanyte' (V, 1835-49). Only here, with the assurance brought by the Incarnation, is the truth finally and unambiguously available:

> According to Augustine, man sees within himself a distant parallel to the Trinity; and though it is not an adequate image, it is nevertheless a reflection of the image of God (*De Civitate Dei*, 11.26). In calling to mind the Supreme Trinity, Chaucer affirms the Trinity within man; and in doing so in his role as poet, he also affirms the validity of the Word. (Ibid., 161)

Though Pulsiano never rules nominalism out as a possible influence, the sources of doubt and scepticism he mentions in relation to the poem all belong to the realist tradition of Augustine and Dante. As such, they mirror many of the concerns that poets and theologians in particular would have had over the status of poetic language, and of which writers like Chaucer, as we have argued, would certainly have been aware. Whether nominalism, with its conceptualist approach both to universals and to divine names, would have made these concerns any more pressing, must remain a matter for speculation. What is certain, however, as Pulsiano's article only serves to confirm, is that ambiguity and linguistic play are better seen as part of a more general anxiety about language than as a symptom of nominalist thought in particular.

---

[66]Phillip Pulsiano, 'Redeemed Language and the Ending of *Troilus and Criseyde*', in Wasserman and Roney (eds.), *Sign, Sentence, Discourse*, 153-74.

Signs, Words and Deeds

If ambiguity and linguistic play can tell us nothing of nominalist semiotics, they at least offer a caveat against taking the poets at their words. There have been a number of readings, nevertheless, which have sought to find nominalism or realism in the explicit statements of the poets themselves. Interest has focused primarily on the remarks contained in Chaucer's *General Prologue*, in which the pilgrim-narrator, having presented his apology for the 'pleyn' language of his narrative, reminds us that, if we are to be true to Plato, '[t]he wordes moote be cosyn to the dede' (I. 742).[67] These words have been variously interpreted, but are generally taken to be an affirmation of the narrator's—if not the poet's—philosophical realism. Similar points have been made regarding a near-identical passage in the *Manciple's Tale* (IX. 207-10), whose apologetic narrator is equally committed to a philosophy which equates poetry with truth. Likewise, Chaucer's short complaint-poem, *Lak of Stedfastnesse*, in which 'worde' and 'dede' are no longer seen in harmony, has been interpreted as a plea for us to get back to a 'Platonic' ideal of truth and fidelity. Recent critical theory is again a conspicuous influence in a number of these readings, whose words and deeds are easily translated into signifiers and signifieds. Nominalism is generally equated with anything not obviously Platonic, although the existence of scepticism and empiricism outside nominalist thinking is often tacitly acknowledged.

Among the earliest and most comprehensive studies of the relationship between 'word' and 'dede' is that of P.B. Taylor.[68] Taylor takes Chaucer's knowledge of nominalism for granted, but in spite of this, provides some of the best evidence that nominalism, in its fourteenth-century form at least, need not have been known to the poet at all. In a detailed reading of the apology passage in the *General Prologue*, Taylor reveals a discrepancy between the Platonic and the Boethian sources, which insist upon a close correspondence between word and thing (*res* in Boethius and Chalcidius), and the texts as Chaucer presents them, which apparently emphasize fidelity to *fact* ('wordes moote be cosyn to the *dede*'). The cause of this discrepancy, Taylor suggests, is a passage in Jean de Meun's *Roman de la Rose*, in which 'faiz' is substituted for the 'chosez' that appears in Jean's translation of Boethius. Jean attributes the passage to Sallust rather than Plato, emphasizing his concern for empirical detail rather than philosophical truth.[69] The mistaken attribution to Plato in Chaucer, Taylor

---

[67] All quotations from and references to works by Chaucer are from *The Riverside Chaucer*, gen. ed. Larry D. Benson (Oxford: Oxford University Press, 1988).
[68] P.B. Taylor, 'Chaucer's *Cosyn to the Dede*', *Speculum*, 57 (1982), 315-27.
[69] Ibid., 321.

argues, reveals a tension in the poet's mind between a nominalist concern with particulars and a realistic orientation towards universal ideas.[70] Whether by 'nominalist' Taylor intends 'fourteenth-century nominalist' is uncertain, but there is clearly no necessity, as the sources themselves indicate, to assume any connection with contemporary nominalist issues.[71]

The most important sign of nominalist influence for Taylor is the separation of word from thing or intent. The Pardoner, whose words continually belie his intent, is accordingly characterized as the archetypal nominalist.[72] There is a potential contradiction here, since Taylor's analysis of Plato and Boethius would appear to confirm the idea, discussed earlier, that proportionality of word and thing is a prescriptive *ideal*. As such, it can only reaffirm the view of language that Taylor finds in nominalism, namely that words are imperfect, potentially deceptive signs of things. In the face of his own evidence, then, Taylor opposes nominalistic relativism to a realism of perfect mimesis.

Taylor's exaggerated view of Platonism is shared by those who have equated the idea of linguistic fidelity in Chaucer with that of a former state of moral perfection. The fallen condition depicted in *Lak of Stedfastnesse*, for example, has been described by Liam Purdon and Rodney Delasanta, as well as by William Watts and Richard Utz, as the result of a decline from a former linguistic 'Golden Age':[73]

> Somtyme the world was so stedfast and stable
> That mannes word was obligacioun,
> And now it is so fals and deceivable
> That word and deed, as in conclusioun,
> Ben nothing lyk, for turned up-so-doun
> Is al this world for mede and wilfulnesse,
> That al is lost for lak of stedfastnesse.
> (1-7)

---

[70]Ibid., 323.

[71]The conflict between empirical and philosophical truths which Taylor identifies is by no means unique to the age of Ockham. Twelfth-century commentators, following the example of Macrobius, drew the distinction between *historia*, an account of real events of the past, and *fabula*, a fictional narrative which could nonetheless embody philosophical or moral truths. Variations on this division, moreover, had been recognized by philosophers since the time of Plato. See Alastair J. Minnis and A.B. Scott (eds.), *Medieval Literary Theory and Criticism c.1100-c.1375* (Oxford: Oxford University Press, 1986), 113-26; on versions of the distinction in Plato's aesthetics, see Monroe C. Beardsley, *Aesthetics from Classical Greece to the Present: A Short History* (New York: Macmillan, 1966), 31-9.

[72]See Taylor, 'Chaucer's *Cosyn*', 326.

[73]The phrase is Liam Purdon's. See his 'Chaucer's *Lak of Stedfastnesse*: A Revalorization of the Word', in Wasserman and Roney (eds.), *Sign, Sentence, Discourse*, 144-52. Rodney Delasanta's views are presented in 'Chaucer and the Problem of the Universal', 152-3. See also Watts and Utz, 'Nominalist Perspectives on Chaucer's Poetry', 152-3.

Of the three articles, it is Delasanta's which links the vision of corruption most explicitly with nominalism. Purdon, by contrast, mentions no philosophical movements by name. What each of the critics shares, however, is an insistence on seeing the poem in terms of contrasting epistemological theories. This is curious, since on the face of it, the poem has little to do with epistemological or linguistic issues. Even if it did, it would be difficult to see how the epistemological condition described could act as an index of moral or social perfection. Philosophical scepticism, after all, was not a consequence of any *moral* failure, despite what critics of Ockham and his followers may have wanted to think. Boethian 'scepticism' is also ruled out here, where the failure to match word with deed is entirely a human, rather than a linguistic shortcoming. Boethius' known influence on the poem, nonetheless, may be one explanation of the need to read it in epistemological terms.[74] Another is almost certainly modern literary theory, whose split-sign epistemology and broad linguistic emphasis are conspicuous influences on Purdon's reading in particular.[75]

There emerge from this selective survey a range of distinct historiographical problems. Besides the obvious precursorism of readings that borrow terms and images from modern literary theory, there is the conspicuous lack of attention to source material, particularly evident in the treatment of Plato and Boethius. This reluctance to engage rigorously with the primary philosophical texts has been the chief cause of confusion over medieval scepticism, and has only served to reinforce the anachronistic ideas imported from critical theory. Nominalism itself, though still recognizable beneath its literary historical glosses, has become an almost chameleonic entity, modifying its definition with the changing emphases of literary and historical scholarship.

Analogy and Allegory

Although the effect of nominalism on the theory of the sign was less profound than many would like to believe, there is one aspect of realist semiotics which bears the indelible mark of Ockhamist assault: the theory of *analogy*. As a principle inherited from the Church Fathers at the beginning of the Middle Ages, analogy exercised a profound influence on virtually all aspects of medieval thought. Logicians under the influence of Aristotle in the thirteenth century, no less than exegetes and theologians in

---

[74]*Lak of Stedfastnesse* is normally listed among Chaucer's 'Boethian' poems (see *The Riverside Chaucer*, 1083-6). For Chaucer's specific debts to Boethius see B.L. Jefferson, *Chaucer and the Consolation of Philosophy of Boethius* (Princeton, NJ: Princeton University Press, 1965), 136. Jefferson is possibly mistaken in his identification of Boethius as the source of the word and deed motif here.

[75]See Purdon, 'Chaucer's *Lak*', 146-8.

the fifth and sixth, were fascinated by the explanatory possibilities this ancient principle seemed to offer. The desire to make explicit the perceived harmony of the created order, as well as the correspondences between the human and the divine, led to much elaborate theorizing on the subject. Things, words and ideas could all be subjected to the rules of analogy, which as well as being a way of seeing the universe, soon became a powerful analytical tool. As in classical philosophy, it was the analogy of words (*analogia nominum*) and the analogy of things (*analogia rerum*) which were most often the subjects of discussion and debate. The problems analogy gave rise to, therefore, were largely to be solved within the framework of signification, as problems of linguistic epistemology. Like other aspects of realist philosophy, analogy was ultimately an optimistic doctrine, but it was also profoundly paradoxical. Though it guaranteed on the one hand the proximity of man to the divine, it emphasized on the other the imperfection of any such relationship between them. By the Thomistic definition at least,[76] analogy always fell short of identity:

> [...] non dicitur esse similitudo creaturae ad Deum propter communicantiam in forma secundum eamdem rationem generis et speciei, sed secundum analogiam tantum, prout scilicet Deus est ens per essentiam et alia per participationem.[77]

Aquinas' insistence on seeing analogy as a *participatory* ('per participationem')[78] relationship identifies him with the fundamental realism of Plato and Augustine. For all three thinkers, the analogy between nature and the divine, whilst 'partial' by definition, was also a guarantee of the symbolic relationship between them. The perceived similarity between their respective modes of being (God's perfect, man's 'participatory'), it was

---

[76]A discussion of the historical and philosophical background to Aquinas' theory of analogy is provided in E.J. Ashworth's article, 'Analogy and Equivocation in Thirteenth-Century Logic: Aquinas in Context', *Mediaeval Studies*, 54 (1992), 94-135. See also Marcia Colish, *The Mirror of Language: A Study in the Medieval Theory of Knowledge* (New Haven, CT: Yale University Press, 1968), 209-22.

[77]'[...] creatures are said to resemble God, not by sharing a form of the same specific or generic type, but only analogically, inasmuch as God exists by nature, and other things partake existence.' (*Summa Theologiae,* Ia. 4, 3, *responsio,* 3; text and translation from the *Summa Theologiae,* ed. McDermott.)

[78]On the notion of participation, see John Dunne, 'St. Thomas' Theology of Participation', *Theological Studies,* 18 (1957), 487-512; John F. Wippel, 'Thomas Aquinas and Participation', in John F. Wippel (ed.), *Studies in Medieval Philosophy* (Studies in Philosophy and the History of Philosophy, 17) (Washington, DC: Catholic University of America Press, 1987), 117-58.

argued, was a suggestion of their *proportional* likeness.[79] The principle of analogy could thus be invoked as a means of defending allegorical fictions, whose content could be glossed as an analogical representation of a higher truth or nature. For Augustine and Aquinas, as for most Christian exegetes, analogy could confer significance of this kind only on scriptural allegory, whose fictions were divinely sanctioned, but the possibility of discovering a 'spiritual sense' in ordinary fables and stories was defended by literary commentators throughout the period.[80]

For thinkers like Ockham, the analogical view of the universe was simply untenable. As well as conferring a false harmony on elements of the created order, it dissolved the absolute and necessary divide between the natural and divine realms. Essence and existence, the basis of Aquinas' doctrine of participation, were one and the same thing in Ockhamist theology, which posited a univocal, rather than an analogical relationship between human and divine being.[81] Univocity in Ockham did not imply identity or continuity, however. 'Being' could be predicated of God only as a concept abstracted from individual beings in the real world, since God was properly the first being. There was, nonetheless, no real similarity between God and creatures, nor did univocity imply any ontological connection between the term 'being' and God Himself. An individual possessed being only by virtue of his or her own existence, and signified nothing beyond the fact of individual existence itself. At best, then, allegorical fictions were dramas of abstractions rather than signs of divine ideas (the universal archetypes of particular beings) or of God himself. At worst, they were literally meaningless.

---

[79] This was known as analogy of *proportionality*—as distinct from analogy of *attribution*, in which the two analogates were related in different ways to a common attribute (as in the case of 'healthy man' and 'healthy urine', in which only the former is *intrinsically* healthy). Strictly speaking, analogy of proportionality was held to exist between *relations*: man's relation to being (imperfect) was analogous to God's relation to being (perfect). See Frederick Ferré, 'Analogy in Theology', in *The Encyclopedia of Philosophy*, ed. Paul Edwards, vol. 1 (New York and London: Macmillan, 1967), 94-7.

[80] See Peter Dronke, *Fabula* (Leiden: Brill, 1974); Beryl Smalley, *English Friars and Antiquity in the Early Fourteenth Century* (Oxford: Blackwell, 1960). On the 'spiritual sense' in vernacular literature, see Judson B. Allen, *The Friar as Critic: Literary Attitudes in the Later Middle Ages* (Nashville, TN: Vanderbuilt University Press, 1971), chs. 1 and 3.

[81] On being, see *Summa Totius Logicae*, I, c. xxxviii (in Ockham, *Philosophical Writings*, ed. Boehner, 90); on the distinction between univocity and analogy, see *Reportatio*, III, Q. viii (in Ockham, *Philosophical Writings*, ed. Boehner, 107-8). For a discussion of Ockham's metaphysics, see Philotheus Boehner, 'The Metaphysics of William Ockham', *Review of Metaphysics*, 1.4 (1947-8), 59-86, repr. in Boehner, *Collected Articles*, 373-97.

Despite the manifest importance of Ockham's rejection of analogy, there have been relatively few serious attempts to explore its consequences for literary theory and practice. Those studies which have been made have tended towards the general rather than the particular, often at the expense of theoretical and historical detail. Clifford Davidson, for example, in a paper on the York Passion Plays, offers an essentially intrinsic account of the dramatist's shift from allegory to realistic detail.[82] His work draws mainly on the comparative study of earlier liturgical drama, but though he makes no reference to primary philosophical texts, he is in no doubt that nominalist epistemology lies behind the changes he describes. Johan Huizinga, in his famous study of late-medieval culture, works at a more general level still, dismissing nominalism as a minor challenge to the dominant mode of realist allegory. The eventual decline of allegory is attributed to a broader and more protracted process of cultural change.[83] Similarly, in her two recent Marxist analyses of Chaucerian allegory, Sheila Delany identifies nominalism only as one possible cause among many of the tendency towards realistic detail rather than allegory in the *Canterbury Tales*.[84] Though she devotes an entire section of her paper on analogy to the nature of the relationship between allegory and analogy, she makes no attempt to relate Ockhamism or Thomism *directly* to the literary changes she describes. Chaucer, she admits, may well have known nothing of the work of scholars such as Ockham, but Ockhamism and Chaucerian realism were nonetheless equivalent expressions of the 'unusual complexity' and 'ambiguity' of the late-medieval period. Both served to express, in particular, the primacy of the will over traditional forms of authority:

> Allegory simplifies experience by systematising it. If one wishes to know why a lady is receptive, then it is merely tautological to say, as the *Roman de la Rose* says, 'Because she is under the influence of Belacueil.' If one wants to be sober, it is pointless to reply, as the *Psychomachia* does, 'Sobriety

---

[82] Clifford Davidson, 'The Realism of the York Realist and the York Passion', *Speculum*, 50 (1975), 270-83.

[83] Johan Huizinga, *The Waning of the Middle Ages: A Study of the Forms of Life, Thought and Art in France and the Netherlands in the Fourteenth and Fifteenth Centuries*, tr. Frederick Jan Hopman (London: Arnold, 1924), 182-94. This is the earliest study to draw an explicit connection between nominalism and allegorical decline. The first literary analysis, identified recently by Edgar Laird, is that of Raymond Preston, who at a similarly abstract level, points to the apparent connection between nominalism and the 'abandonment' of allegory. (See Preston, *Chaucer* (London: Sheed and Ward, 1952); Laird, 'Cosmic Law', 103, note 4.)

[84] See Sheila Delany, 'Undoing Substantial Connection: The Late Medieval Attack on Analogical Thought' and 'The Politics of Allegory in the Fourteenth Century', in *Medieval Literary Politics: Shapes of Ideology* (Manchester: Manchester University Press, 1990), 19-41 and 42-60.

always conquers Luxury.' Our sense of choice [...] is more involved than that, and so [...] was Chaucer's. The ambivalence of human will is his constant theme [...]. The nominalist theory of will expresses the same consciousness.[85]

Delany's ultimate concern is with politics rather than philosophy, and her reading is conspicuously shaped by her theoretical interests. This would apparently account for the broad cultural focus of her study, which like that of Peggy Knapp, ultimately subordinates ideas to their political base structure. The consequence, once again, is an artificial polarization of nominalism and realism at the expense of theoretical detail.

A more detailed account of the process of analogical decline is offered by Michael Randall, who in a recent article on the French poet Jean Molinet, shows how the conventional terms of analogy were actually being *reversed* in the later Middle Ages.[86] Ockham's concept of univocity, he argues, though it had rendered analogy ineffectual as a pathway to knowledge of the divine, had made it a far more flexible tool at the hands of poets and storytellers like Molinet. In the *Chappellet des dames*, for example, Molinet exploits this flexibility by using divine analogates (the Virgin Mary and Jesus Christ) to describe human subjects (Mary of Burgundy and the House of Burgundy), effectively overturning the normal order of perception.[87] Randall describes the nature of this analogy in detail, listing numerous correspondences between biblical history and the events and personages described in Molinet's poem. The evidence he presents is persuasive, though he is forced to admit that a firm connection between Molinet's poetic style and Ockhamist philosophy would be impossible to establish.[88] Nevertheless, his analysis is an important illustration of the complexity of the relationships that may exist between philosophical and literary discourses. All too often, the assumption has been that the latter is simply a passive reflection of the former. Randall's reading of Molinet, on the other hand, shows literary analogy flourishing (albeit in a modified form) in the wake of its philosophical decline.

The possibility that nominalism, far from rendering analogy and allegory unworkable in any direct way, may in fact have contributed positively to its development, has been hinted at by a number of other critics. Alastair Minnis, for example, though his concern is with logic in general rather than nominalism as such, points to the tantalizing coincidence between the 'modern' logicians' critique of allegorical exegesis and the rise of alle-

---

[85]Delany, 'Undoing Substantial Connection', 39.
[86]Michael Randall, 'Reversed Analogy in Jean Molinet's *Chappellet des dames*', in Utz (ed.), *Literary Nominalism*, 81-100.
[87]Ibid., 93-4.
[88]Ibid., 99.

gorized readings of pagan texts in the fourteenth century.[89] More recently, Grover C. Furr, who sees himself to be 'modifying' the work done by Sheila Delany, has attempted to show how this predilection for moral allegorization is combined with an essentially nominalistic realism in Chaucer's *Nun's Priest's Tale*.[90] Like Minnis, he turns to the example of moralized pagan tales to support his claim. Both of these critics, like Randall, see allegory in terms of a relatively complex process of change, and advocate a method of analysis which draws on a neglected form of evidence. The claims they make, though they do not constitute certainties, bring us much closer to a properly historical form of criticism, and are a strong suggestion of the need for a change in approach.

Theory, Practice and Influence

If any conclusion can be drawn from the problems discussed so far, it would appear to be that nominalist readings generally assume far more than is necessary or demonstrable. If we were to apply Ockham's razor to the logic of the critics themselves, there are few who would emerge unscathed. At best, their readings are interesting speculations on a complicated period of literary history. At worst, they are anachronistic or simply ahistorical. The problem, however, is not merely one of historical methodology. Closely related to it, though distinct in the kinds of relationship it presupposes, is the problem of linking theory to practice. The difficulty many of the critics have encountered in their attempts to do just this is a strong suggestion that they are looking in the wrong place. Ockham and Holcot were theorists, but their connection with literary practice, despite the numerous textual studies that have been made, remains a matter for guess work.[91] The modern assumption that theory (philosophical, lin-

---

[89]Minnis, '"Authorial Intention" and "Literal Sense"', 17.

[90]Grover C. Furr, 'Nominalism in the *Nun's Priest's Tale*: A Preliminary Study', in Utz (ed.), *Literary Nominalism*, 135-46.

[91]The most thorough study of philosophical sources remains Robert Pratt, 'Some Latin Sources of the Nonnes Preest on Dreams', *Speculum*, 52 (1977), 538-70. A recent study of Holcot's influence on the *Gawain*-poet (though no more decisive than those of Pratt and others) is that of Philip F. O'Mara, 'Robert Holcot's "Ecumenism" and the Green Knight', *Chaucer Review*, 26 (1992), 329-42, and 27 (1992), 97-106. Numerous critics have attempted to connect Chaucer with the philosophy of Ralph Strode (the 'philosophical Strode' of the *Troilus* (V, 1857)), but with little real success. Rodney Delasanta devotes an entire article to the Strode problem, arguing that Strode's position midway between the nominalism of Ockham and the realism of Wyclif would have had a significant effect on Chaucer's poetics. He fails to present any new evidence, however. (See 'Chaucer and Strode', *Chaucer Review*, 26 (1991), 205-18.) See also Richard J. Utz, 'Negotiating the Paradigm: Literary Nominalism and the Theory and Practice of Rereading Late Medieval Texts', in Utz (ed.), *Literary Nominalism*, 10-3.

guistic, literary) should be intimately connected or even indistinguishable from practice will simply not hold for Scholastic philosophy, whose principles and precepts were less widely disseminated than is often assumed. The rise of the so-called 'speculative' sciences in the twelfth and thirteenth centuries, for example, points to a progressive isolation of the more theoretical aspects of academic enquiry. Even if this were not the case, the fact that these theoretical disciplines were largely in decline by the later fourteenth century makes their influence on vernacular literature seem much less likely.[92]

Though we should not assume that the curricular changes of the later Middle Ages rule out the possibility of a 'literary' nominalism, we should at least be aware that nominalism and literature were never parts of a single, seamless discourse. At best, it would seem, the influences between them would have been complex and indirect. Any reading which assumes the self-conscious cultivation of a nominalist 'mode' or style, or which seeks to demonstrate that writers of the fourteenth century were dramatizing or allegorizing nominalist issues in their work, is almost certainly taking too much for granted.

One way of bridging the gap between theory and practice is to concentrate not on vernacular literature but on medieval literary theory itself. Interest in this area, made popular by D.W. Robertson's work in the 1960s,[93] has declined in recent years, largely in response to the growth in Bakhtinian and Foucauldian 'discursive' methodologies. Peggy Knapp possibly speaks for a good number of critics when she argues that Robertson's exegetical approach, which necessarily privileges patristic discourses, is inflexible and reductive.[94] Whilst it would be difficult to ignore this criticism, it remains a fact that the debates of Scholastic philosophy are more likely to have influenced commentators and exegetes than they are to have concerned literary practitioners. Though scriptural commentaries and traditional forms of exegesis were less fashionable when nominalist influence was at its height in the early fourteenth century, their

---

[92]William Courtenay has suggested that both logic and theology, despite the renewed interest in these areas in the preceding half-century, had become marginalized as university disciplines by the beginning of the Ricardian period. Among the philosophers and theologians who remained in the universities, few, he argues, would have been nominalists. (See Courtenay, *Schools and Scholars in Fourteenth-Century England*, 365-8.)

[93]Robertson's 'exegetical' criticism (sometimes referred to as 'exegetics') sought to apply the techniques of patristic biblical exegesis to the interpretation of vernacular texts. His technique is most fully elaborated in his classic study, *A Preface to Chaucer* (Princeton, NJ: Princeton University Press, 1962). On the application of patristic exegetical methods to secular Latin texts in the Middle Ages, see Smalley, *English Friars*.

[94]See Knapp, *Chaucer and the Social Contest*, 4-5.

later revival furnishes us with some important evidence. The writings of John Wyclif, for example, a contemporary of Chaucer and Langland, reveal a deep concern for the effect of nominalism on exegetical practice.[95] The status of allegory, the uses of symbolism and the dangers of attending too closely to the properties of signs are all discussed at length in Wyclif's work, and are related explicitly, in many cases, to the philosophical assumptions which underlie them. Here, moreover, we are able to identify a 'literary' scholar who was deliberately and unambiguously presenting the nominalists in a critical and satirical light. If nothing else, his writings might at least provide a better indication of how the precepts of nominalism could be exploited and exaggerated by its opponents. By attending to works of this kind, therefore, we should feel better prepared, both from a theoretical, and from a literary-historical point of view, to speculate about the effects of nominalism on literary practice.[96]

---

[95] I am at present preparing a doctoral thesis on theories of symbol and allegory in Wyclif's *De Veritate Sacrae Scripturae*, which I am considering primarily in the context of fourteenth-century nominalism. It is scheduled for completion in 1997-8.

[96] I should like to thank Professor Alastair Minnis, who read through an earlier draft of this article, for his invaluable comments and suggestions.

SELF, ACTION, AND SIGN IN THE TOWNELEY AND YORK PLAYS ON THE BAPTISM OF CHRIST AND IN OCKHAMIST SALVATION THEOLOGY

WILLIAM F. MUNSON

The play in the Towneley mystery play cycle which dramatizes John baptizing Jesus is titled *Johannes Baptista*, after its human agent.[1] Although the unique manuscript (c. 1500) has associations with Wakefield, a principal town and manorial seat during the time of this Yorkshire compilation, its civic ambiance is significantly less apparent than it is for that of the contemporaneous and related cycle from the ancient ecclesiastical and commercial center of York.[2] The manuscript of *The York Plays* (between 1463 and 1477) is an official register; the civic purpose of performance is described in the municipal *Memorandum Book* as being 'chiefly for the honor and reverence of our Lord Jesus Christ and for the profit of the citizens'.[3] The *Memorandum Book* entry for this baptism play also identifies the performing guild; and it suggests the confluence of social focus and emphasis on the divine which the text indeed confirms, where John and angels are subordinate to Jesus as ministering servants: 'Barbours: Jesus, Johannes Baptista baptizans eum et ij angeli administrantes'.[4] The Towneley text does also reflect its title and give a qualified

---

[1] *The Towneley Plays*, 2 vols., eds. Martin Stevens and A.C. Cawley (Oxford: Oxford University Press, 1994), vol. 1: 218-26, from which all quotations are taken. For dating and provenance, see ibid., xv; xix-xxii.

[2] It is not a civic register of acting texts (see *Towneley*, xxii-v). Martin Stevens makes a major case for Towneley's compilation (and partial authorship) by a single individual as a finished book in *Four Middle English Mystery Cycles* (Princeton, NJ: Princeton University Press, 1987), 88-180.

[3] 'Ob honorem precipue et reverenciam Domini nostri Jesu Christi, et commodum civium' (*York: Records of Early English Drama*, 2 vols., eds. Alexandra F. Johnston and Margaret Rogerson (Toronto: University of Toronto Press, 1979), vol. 1: 28). See also *The York Plays*, ed. Richard Beadle (London: Arnold, 1982), 10-2.

[4] *York: Records*, vol. 1: 19. The play text itself has no subject title in the manuscript. All quotations for the York Baptism are from *The York Plays*, ed. Beadle, 181-6.

centrality to John. Asserting his autonomy and agency, the Towneley play constructs an importantly different relation of self to others and to God from that of York. This essay seeks, first, to establish this contrast and then to contextualize it in the salvation theory of the late medieval theologians influenced by philosophical nominalism. The Ockhamist theologians of the *via moderna* supply not only a rationale for Towneley's distinctive thematic emphasis on man's role in salvation but, also, for a dramatic form which makes distinctive contribution to an early modern selfhood.

Paul Tillich construes the self in terms of a dialectic between the poles of individualized separation and of participation in a structured world.[5] In philosophical realism, medieval culture gives theoretical privilege to the pole of participation, while an emergent nominalism privileges the individual; the dialectic of the two can also be conceived to shape cultural history, with an increasing individualism reflected in 'the attack of nominalism on medieval realism and the permanent conflict between them' (ibid., 95). The characteristic form of the 'courage to be' for the medieval self is affirmation of the power of participation:

> The courage of the Middle Ages as of every feudal society is basically the courage to be as a part. The so-called realistic philosophy of the Middle Ages is a philosophy of participation. It presupposes that universals logically and collectives actually have more reality than the individual. The particular (literally: being a small part) has its power of being by participation in the universal. (Ibid., 94)

In this perspective, humility in willing subjection to, and participation in, a superior order—including the social order of the world—is the medieval form of 'courage', indeed of 'self-affirmation':

> The self-affirmation expressed for instance in the self-respect of the individual is self-affirmation as follower of a feudal lord or as the member of a guild or as the student in an academic corporation or as a bearer of a special function like that of a craft or a trade or a profession. (Ibid.)

Throughout the Middle Ages the baptism of Christ by John is a richly cultivated locus for the topic of humble service, fundamental to religious definitions of man as creature of God and sinner in the process of salvation. The York and Towneley plays on the baptism of Christ develop distinctive versions from the unique Gospel account of the encounter at the Jordan provided by Matthew 3:13-7:

---

[5] 'The self is self only because it has a world, a structured universe to which it belongs and from which it is separated at the same time' (Paul Tillich, *The Courage to Be* (New Haven, CT: Yale University Press, 1952), 87-8).

Then Jesus came from Galilee to the Jordan to John, to be baptized by him. John would have prevented him, saying, 'I need to be baptized by you and do you come to me?' But Jesus answered him, 'Let it be so now; for thus it is fitting for us to fulfill all righteousness'. Then he consented.[6]

Liturgy and Bible exegesis use this encounter as a model of man's dependent and cooperative relation to God. An Epiphany week antiphon employs the master-servant and king-knight models: 'Baptizat miles regem: servus dominum suum: johannes salvatorem aqua jordanis stupuit'.[7] The first interlinear gloss from the *Glossa Ordinaria* identifies the moral meaning of the relation: 'a knight imitates the humility of the king'.[8] The likeness of imitation, however, also contrasts God's ultimate and originary power with man's dependence on it for his own moral empowerment through baptism. Matthew 3:11 contrasts the action of John with the fulfillment in Jesus and in the Holy Spirit—a contrast central to the York play: 'I baptize you with water for repentance, but he who is coming after me is mightier than I, whose sandals I am not worthy to carry; he will baptize you with the Holy Spirit and with fire'. Nicholas of Lyra comments that Christ's baptism 'brings the grace of the Holy Spirit, which no man can do except God'.[9]

Rosemary Woolf has located in 'John's fearful reluctance to baptize the Lord' a distinctive devotional warmth shared by the Towneley and York plays.[10] The plays notably diverge, however, in their use of the Matthew interaction in respect to its bearing on critical places in medieval salvation theory where man's effort intersects God's grace. Where Towneley gives initial emphasis to man's power, the York John responds to an announcement by angels of Jesus' arrival with model praise and subordination to God's: 'I thanke hym euere, but I am radde [afraid] | I am noȝt abill to fullfill | Þis dede certayne' (59-61). York's version of the knight-king, servant-lord relation is beggar-rich man; it also privileges God's role in the way of the traditional norm where it is the blessing of sanctifying grace which makes man's deeds worthy of ultimate glory:

Lorde, þou arte riche and I am full poure,
Þou may blisse al, sen þou all wrought.

---

[6]This and the following quote from Matthew are taken from: *The New Oxford Annotated Bible with the Apocrypha* (Revised Standard Edition), eds. Herbert G. May and Bruce M. Metzger (New York: Oxford University Press, 1977).

[7]*Breviarium ad usum insignis ecclesie eboracensis: Vol. 1*, ed. Stephen W. Lawley (Surtees Society, 71) (Durham: Surtees Society, 1880), 188.

[8]*Biblia Sacra cum Glossa Ordinaria*, vol. 5 (Antwerp, 1617), cols. 77-8.

[9]Ibid., col. 76. Nicholas of Lyra gives the same general reading in respect to John's 'reverentia' and adds the specific doctrine of the hypostatic union used by Towneley (ibid., col. 77).

[10]Rosemary Woolf, *The English Mystery Plays* (London: Routledge & Kegan Paul, 1972), 218.

>   Fro heuen come all
>   Þat helpes in erthe, yf soth be sought,
>   Fro erthe but small.
>   (122-6)

John is confirmed in a broadly Augustinian emphasis in which the agency is decisively on the side of God's grace in matters of redemption—an emphasis importantly buttressed by association with God's primacy in creation. Jesus confirms this formulation ('Thou sais full wele John' (127)) and John immediately performs the baptism as the 'subject' who is recovering his identity as God's creature: 'Lord, I am redy at þi will, I And will be ay I Thy subgett lord' (137-9). It is in this full and model subjection that the climactic sacramental event, baptism in the Holy Spirit, can occur.

In Towneley, on the other hand, a climax comes when John does obediently exercise a power which radically qualifies the conventional call to awed reverence and humble service before God. The angel enjoins John, 'To do this dede haue thou none aw' (76), but John humbly demurs at his role as the superior: 'That shall neuer be, I traw' (78). There is fear, but it is an individually empowered obedience which at last takes the less accustomed form of a standing—not kneeling—as John becomes 'God's seruande' (178) at the baptism: 'I am ful ferd [very afraid] yit ay amang; I If I dyd right I shuld done knele' (203-4). The call to *unawed* obedience becomes the dramatic impetus of Towneley's action of human realization and divine blessing. Human nature, thereby, is not constituted as a self whose worth for salvation is defined in ethical and metaphysical subjection but rather in man's autonomous might interacting with God's will in a learning process. John, in fact, at first employs the traditional king and knight metaphor in a mistaken way: 'A knyght to baptyse his lord kyng— I My pauste [power] may it not fulfyll' (127-8), he protests. Jesus then makes explicit correction about man's power in Towneley's key thematic formulation of man in his relation to God: God the Father 'knayws mans hart, his dede, his thoght I He wotys [knows] how far mans myght may reche' (141-2). The Towneley *Johannes* thus readjusts York's theocentric Augustinian anthropology and soteriology to give John power and agency in a dramatic interaction.

1.

In the York Baptism of Christ, man relates to Christ in the vocabulary of a Christocentric mysticism in which God acts and the self is constituted by its participation in God and also in a universal Church. In an echo of neo-Platonic light metaphysics, John the Baptist announces Christ as the coming of a light in which each—and every—man participates through its indwelling presence:

> Þus am I comen in message right
> And be fore-reyner in certayne,
> In wittnesse-bering of þat light,
> Þe wiche schall light in ilka man
> Þat is comand
> Into this worlde [...]
>
> (15-20)

This paraphrases the announcement of Christ as Logos in the Gospel of John and sets a framework for the angels' 'tythandis [tidings] wondir gode' of the 'lorde Jesus' (51-2). John is instructed in the divine Word, receiving explanation why a sinless Christ needs baptism. Jesus' exposition is based on the theology of man's power as derivative from God. York's model for man, 'subgett nyght and day' (73) to God, is of a creature fallen into radical deficiency because of sin, to be remedied by God's infusion of the grace of the Holy Spirit. 'How schulde I þan, þat is a thrall, I Giffe þe baptyme, þat rightwis is [...]?' (115-6), John inquires. John asks for the power to escape bondage which comes through God, not from him: 'Now helpe me lorde, thurgh þi Godhede, I To do þis werk' (146-7). God's action in Christ overcomes sin by this heteronomous and universal empowering through the agency of baptism: 'The dragons poure [power] ilk a dele I Thurgh my baptyme distroyed haue I, I Þis is certayne, I And saued mankynde [...]' (157-60). So Christ's baptism has infused power into the baptismal water; it is available to general mankind through all time by imitation of Christ's baptism and by partaking of Christ's power through the water:

> My will is þis, þat fro þis day
> Þe vertue of my baptyme dwelle
> In baptyme-watir euere and ay,
> Mankynde to taste [...]
>
> (100-3)

The play's discursive exposition developing its concept of universal man constituted by taking within himself the baptismal power may be based on a source as specific as the *Vita Christi* of Ludolphus the Carthusian (d. 1377), where the chapter with the title 'De Baptismo Domini' includes a section, 'Reasons why Christ wished to be baptized'.[11] For Ludolphus, the baptism of Christ by John brings our salvation by

---

[11] Ludolphus de Saxonia, *Vita Jesu Christi*, 4 vols., ed. L.M. Rigollot (Paris: Victorem Palme, and Brussels: G. Lebrocquy, 1878), vol. 1: 182 (XXI.4). Woolf, *The English Mystery Plays*, 218, mentions the *Vita* for possible 'source or analogues of all the detail'.

sanctifying and constituting the sacrament of baptism.[12] The section in the *Vita* on the 'Inhabitation of the Word in Us' stresses the union of man and God effected by the sacramental Word. Man is, of course, not himself essence as the Logos or Light, giving light from itself; but the Logos is nevertheless inseparable from the nature of man, who is in the light by participation.[13] For this kind of difference *within* an inclusive and privileged unity, York employs especially the metaphor of container or vessel. Made clean by God's arrival, 'Oure bodis are Goddis tempyll þan, I In the whilke he will make his dwellyng' (37-8).[14] As sacramental vessels of God, we also participate in the universal Church. However individual the receiving 'bodies' are in baptism, the privileged reality is the participation in common social and metaphysical being. In the power of regeneration of the sacrament, Christ marries the universal church and all faithful souls to himself.[15]

The model participation in God and his universal Church is available to men through the otherness of the Holy Spirit, filling him with the fire of charity. This, man is not able to accomplish by himself; it comes only through grace.[16] The power he brings to the baptismal water, Christ explains, is for '[m]ankynde to taste, I Thurgh my grace þerto to take alway I Þe haly gaste' (103-5). The York play thus gives special and climactic emphasis to God's action in the Holy Spirit. At the conclusion of the

---

[12]'Operatur nostram salutem, tactu sacri corporis aquas mundans et consecrans, ac vim regenerationis et jus Baptismatis eis conferens, sacramentumque Baptismatis sanctificans et constitutuens, ac crimini nostra lavans et purgans' (Ludolphus, *Vita*, vol. 1: 185 (XXI.9)). Walter Baier, *Untersuchungen zu den Passionsbetrachtungen in der Vita Christi des Ludolf von Sachsen*, 3 vols. (Salzburg: Institut für Englische Sprache und Literatur, 1977), vol. 1: 450-74, treats Ludolphus' Christological salvation theology.

[13]'Verbum habitavit in nobis, id est in nostra natura inseparabiliter ut amplius nullatenus ab ea disjungeretur' (Ludolphus, *Vita*, vol. 1: 158 (XVIII.8)). '*Non erat ille lux*, scilicet vera per essentiam, et ex se naturaliter lucens [...]; sed lux per participationem, et a luce vera illa [...]' (ibid., 155 (XVIII.2)).

[14]Ludolphus develops the metaphysical nuance of the Incarnate Word and how it dwells inside minds, as in a building ('qua mansionem') (ibid., 159 (XVIII.83)), through God's grace, as distinct from the way Christ's humanity is one with his divinity in the unity of the carrier ('suppositi') or person (ibid., 158 (XVIII.7)). Linked to this devotional construction of how man relates to Christ, is Ludolphus' neo-Platonic exemplarism, which York also echoes. Christ is baptized so that 'men schall me þer myrroure make I I haue my doyng in ther mynde' (ms. reading 93-4); in Ludolphus, we are illumined by Christ, who is to us as a mirror, a 'clarissimum speculum et totius sanctitatis exemplar' (Ludolphus, *Vita*, vol. 1: 6 (Proemium 10)).

[15]Christ 'desponsat sibi universalem Ecclesiam, et omnes animas fideles; nam in fide Baptismatis desponsamur Domino nostro Jesu Christo' (ibid., 185 (XXI.9)).

[16]'Deinde Joannes subjungit: *Ipse vos baptizabit*, non solum in aqua, sed et *in Spritu Sancto et igne*, gratiam Spritus Sancti, et charitatis conferendo, quod non potest facere, nisi Deus' (ibid., 168 (XIX.13)).

baptism, the present availability to mankind of the grace of the indwelling Holy Ghost is rehearsed in the Pentecost hymn sung by angels: 'Come, Creator Spirit, visit the minds of your people; fill with supernatural grace the hearts which you have created'.[17] It is possible that the descent of the dove as emblem of the Holy Spirit occurs during the singing of the *Veni Creator*, which would make it coincide also with Jesus announcing that he takes baptism to bring for man's profit the destruction of the dragon's power. Although the manuscript shows revision and an incomplete patching, the angel anticipates such a descent, as in the Biblical narrative, by announcing, 'Þe heuenes schalle be oppen sene, | The holy gost schalle doune be sente' (66-7).[18]

The angels' supplication to the Holy Spirit in the *Veni Creator* poises man on the brink of the gracious indwelling by God which reconstitutes human nature as part of the universal church. The Towneley *Johannes Baptista* omits the descent of the Holy Spirit entirely. It constructs, instead, an interaction actively engaging John himself. The angels arrive to mediate a call from God the Father for John's immediate response and initiative:

> Harkyn to me, thou Iohn Baptyst!
> The fader of heuen, he gretys the weyll,
> For he has fon [found] the true and tryst,
> And dos thi dever euery deyll.
> Wyt thou well his will thus ist,
> Syn thou art stabyll as any steyll,
> That thou shall baptyse Iesu Cryst
> In flume Iordan, mans care to keyll.
>   (65-72)

On the one side, they bring God's greeting and call to action; on the other, John, 'true and tryst [faithful]' and 'stabyll [firm]' as steel, is given importance as general moral agent called to a specific task. The climax will be not the descent of the Holy Spirit but another interactive event, the handing over of a Lamb to John. The Lamb is the point of contact of two

---

[17]'Veni creator spiritus mentes tuorum[;] visita imple superna gratia que tu creasti pectora' (*Breviarium [...] eboracensis*, 503). The hymn links the fire of charity to York's metaphors of indwelling and light: 'Accende lumen sensibus[;] infunde amorem cordibus'.

[18]The existing York play emphasizes the Son-Holy Spirit instead of Father-Son relation, with the effect of stressing the reception of the Holy Spirit in the human heart instead of the intradeical relation. Ludolphus discusses the Holy Spirit's descent in the sign of the dove to emphasize that it is Jesus alone who gives baptism (XXIII.6). For the Holy Ghost linked with dove at Jesus' baptism, with its subsequent reception by all the baptized which effects the remission of sins and reconciliation with God, see Aquinas, *Summa Theologica*, III, q. 39, art. 6.

agents: a gift by God and occasion for man's understanding and response. John, possessed of power, must learn in the interaction that Jesus is man's 'fere' (164), a companion *with* him and *for* him instead of a presence *within* him constituting, completing, and empowering him.

This interaction is realized in the concrete and strongly localized world of hearing, sight and touch. Towneley's defining issue about John's own moral power is developed as the problem of the literal seeing of 'whatsoever he [God] sendys' (124). In the first exchange with the angel, John *hears* but does not *see* the speaker who calls for his action:

Iohannes.	A, dere God, what may this be?
	I hard a steuen, bot noght I saw.
1 Angelus.	Iohn, it is I that spake to the.
	(73-5)

Just as John's seeing and hearing are not coordinated in the angel as object, so the divine content of the message—obedience *without* awe—is, at this point, also separate from John's understanding: 'This bewteose lord to me to bryng, I His awne seruande, this is no skyll [reason]' (125-6). The gap between perception and obedience drives the subsequent interactions to shape a general action of error and recognition: a bringing together of sensory particulars with their correct meaning.

The play dramatizes the surprising immediacy, the particular localization, for this meaning. The particularity for John's task is at first opposed to the universality of God's ordinations which John expects: 'By this I may well vnderstand I That childer shuld be broght to kyrk I For to be baptysyd in euery land' (85-7). The angel, however, insists not on baptism 'in euery land' but, instead, on a divine task entailing physical immediacy:

> Iohn, this place it is pleassyng,
> And it is callyd flume Iordan.
> Here is no kyrk, ne no bygyng [building],
> Bot where the Fader wyll ordan,
> It is Godys wyll and his bydyng.
> (89-93)

Immediacy is constituted by God's will making a surprising intersection with man's task, the exercise of man's will. The combination produces unique particularity. Jesus commands, 'Bot com to me in this present' (118), where the phrase means both the present moment and the presence of Jesus in sensible form.[19]

---

[19]Cf. *OED*, s.v. 'present', sb. 1: 'the thing or person that is present', 'that which is before one' (2); 'in the present time' (4a).

Jesus in his physical presence is the vehicle by which John and God the Father complete their interaction. Touching Jesus becomes the thematic metaphor in the Towneley play for the climax of significant contact. John inappropriately denies his capacity in sacramental fulfillment due to a claimed deficiency of worth, knowledge, and the courage of touch:

> And if I were worthy
> For to fulfyll this sacrament,
> I haue no connyng, securly,
> To do it after thyn intent.
> And therfor, Lord, I ask mercy:
> Hald me excusyd, as I haue ment;
> I dar not towche thi blyssyd body,
> My hart will neuer to it assent.
> (129-36)

But John must make the act of will to touch which still seems a violation of his reason ('connyng') and his heart. Obedient humility and fulfillment of the sacrament, however, do entail his own sight, touch, worth, and power in response to God's call.

If John's side of the action is a surprising engagement of himself, God's side involves a 'law'—a divine rationale for a sequential order of events. This unexpected baptism without a church is indeed God's law ('To me this law yit is it myrk [obscure]' (88), John had said). Thus Jesus explains the action which rules it in terms of a divine decision which is a 'reprefe'— a 'rebuke', even a 'disproof' or 'refutation'—to John's understanding: 'For reprefe vnto mans rytt | The law I will fulfyll right here; | My Fader ordynance thus is it' (109-11). The law of God is an ordination involving God's will and John's engagement, in its full agency, touching Christ in a sacrament which is uniquely 'right here'.

In Towneley, therefore, the sacrament is 'worthi' because it is the place where God's willed ordination meets man's initiative in their surprising point of localized contact. In York the baptism is sacramental because of the presence of God as the Word and as the Holy Ghost in man; in Towneley the angels bring a 'word' which is not an indwelling presence but an external call upon John's own powers: 'Therfor to the this word I bryng: | My Lord has gyffen the powere playn, | And drede the noght of thi conyng' (158-60). This call to know without 'drede' is, specifically, to interpret the meaning of Christ. Towneley uses the semiotic vocabulary of 'token' to identify this signifying task in which John must actively engage in order to be obedient:

> Behold, he sendys his angels two
> In tokyn I am both God and man;
> Thou gyf me baptym or I go,
> And dyp me in this flume Iordan.
> (145-8)

Jesus himself, whom like the angels John has 'seen' without fully understanding what divine will demands, is only now near the point of being 'heard' by John with doctrinal understanding of the hypostatic union.[20] The initial disjunction between seeing and knowing thus moves at last into a mutually supportive conjunction. The Jesus, that is, whom John *sees* and touches in the unique situation at the Jordan, is the *same* unique Jesus who is also the second person of the Trinity whom John must recognize as such:

> And therfor, Iohn, do as thou awe,
> And gruch thou neuer in this degre
> To baptyse hym that thou here saw,
> For wyt thou well this same is he.
> (173-6)

The angels' words—at first a sound heard, then the physical presence seen—are finally an action linked to an understanding of the unity in the Godhead. John now 'knows well' and he makes his active reformulation of service in the gesture of baptizing Jesus.

Just as John approaches his own climactic act of faith by coming to understand the angels as token of God, God's climactic response also involves a token:

> This beest, Iohn, thou bere with the,
> It is a beest full blyst;
> Iohn, it is the lamb of me,
> Beest none othere ist.
> *Hic tradat ei agnum dei.*
> [Here he hands over to him the Lamb of God.]
> It may were [protect] the from aduersyte,
> And so looke that thou tryst [trust].
> (209-14)

The Lamb, John's emblem as saint, is given by Jesus, on the one hand, as a token of his divine promise, in his double role as God and man, to take away the sins of the world; on the other, it engages John's faith and will. Towneley's distinctive construction of the sacramental conjunction of God and man as an interactive event localized through tokens is realized in this exchange. The play presents an aetiological myth for the iconography of John with Lamb as witness to Christ; it furnishes an interactive *process* by

---

[20]The play presents the intradeical relation as interaction also: Jesus speaks out of union with the Father but in the distinctness of the Son through emphasis on his willed obedience (105-220), a parallel (despite creaturely difference) of John's willed relation to Jesus.

which signs take on meaning.[21] The Lamb as *token* given by God for man's understanding is Towneley's alternative to the full *presence* of the Holy Ghost in man which is anticipated at the climax of the York play.

The interaction of God and man in Towneley involves a distinct turn, but it is not a conversion—a reversal—in Augustinian terms where the perverse self-will of fallen man is informed by the indwelling presence of God's redirection. John has turned to a capacity of self interacting with God which is understood as instrumental and distinctly 'his own', made out of his own might. It also entails a reflexive *self*-awareness. John's motto in the traditional emblem projects forward onto the divine object of vision: Ecce agnus Dei. Here, however, the understanding of the Lamb as token of God becomes also a reflective moment about his own act of perception and about his individual error:

> For I haue sene the lamb of God
> Which weshys away syn of this warlde,
> And towchid hym, for euen or od—
> My hart therto was ay ful hard.
> (217-21)

An active subject, an 'I' with psychological subjectivity, has emerged from the concrete interaction with Jesus. John now has a reflexive relationship with his own past and his own might which is integrative: by seeing Jesus and knowing him as the same with God he thereby forges an identity with himself. John's 'I', that is, is psychological in the sense that it is reflexively self-aware.[22] The retrospective awareness of faulty self-understanding is itself an appropriation of one's own power efficacious toward salvation. The *theological* tension between man and God, between humility and grace in an action moved by God and centering in God—the terms of the York Baptism—here accommodates a *psychological* tension in an interaction in which man is agent in subjective fullness. The interaction

---

[21]Louis Réau, *Iconographie de l'art Chrétien*, 3 vols. (Paris: Presses Universitaires de France, 1956; repr. Nendeln and Liechtenstein: Kraus, 1979), vol. 2, pt. 1: 450-1.

[22]Augustine applies John the Baptist as witness to the light (John 1:8) to the soul of man achieving the inwardness which receives the Light or Logos (*Confessions*, tr. Henry Chadwick (Oxford: Oxford University Press, 1992), 123 (VII.10)). Charles Taylor (*Sources of the Self: The Making of the Modern Identity* (Cambridge, MA: Harvard University Press, 1989), 130-1) credits Augustinian inwardness with a modern kind of 'radical reflexivity' by its shifting focus from field of objects to the 'activity itself of knowing' (130), a 'kind of presence to oneself which is inseparable from one's being the agent of experience' (131). However, Augustinian inwardness is based on the dynamics of a *fallen* will, entailing a theocentric and dependent definition of self: as Taylor says, 'Healing comes when it [this reflexivity] is broken open [...] to acknowledge its dependence on God' (ibid., 139). See note 48.

occurs through angels and Lamb as tokens, or signs. The signs are points of contact for significant interaction in which a self is reflexively constituted.

2.

The English biblical drama, V.A. Kolve asserted in a generative and influential book, undertook 'to understand in his full empirical complexity the creature we shall call natural man'.[23] To formulate interpretation in terms of a divinely created 'natural man' is to engage a fundamental theological crux. Pelagian versus Augustinian emphases in respect to man's capacity in relation to God's role in the salvation process—nature's relation to grace—as well as the general relation of nature and supernature, were readdressed in high and late medieval theology with the impetus of Aristotle and then of 'modern', Ockhamist nominalism. In the end, Kolve frames a vigorous appreciation of the features of natural man in an Augustinian sense of fallen man's sinful powerlessness against which, and by means of which, God's redemptive purpose in universal history is established. In this light, John's demurral, his incomplete obedience, is seen to serve a *theological* irony—to emphasize and advance the overarching divine purpose centered in Christ. Philosophical nominalism and the Ockhamist theological wing provide discursive context for Towneley's emphasis on concrete localization and the positive, active role for man—John's might—in an interactive salvation process. This process contextualizes Towneley's use of localized, interactive signs by understanding sacraments as contingent vehicles—signs—used in interactions rather than as realist vessels for universals.

Although nominalism's 'razor' against universals in epistemology is often approached as a simplification and reduction of entities, its bearing on some, at least, of the religious plays is to bring into visibility a multipli-

---

[23] V.A. Kolve, *The Play Called Corpus Christi* (Stanford, CA: Stanford University Press, 1966), 207. Kolve uses theological formulation glancingly but revealingly to emphasize Augustinian emphases on man's fallen nature and the primacy of grace in salvation: the imaginative basis of the drama, he says, is not only man's *'categorical* severance [from God] deriving from man's identity as creature' but 'a severance that is *willful*, [...] an estrangement whose origin is not in creaturely definitions but in the perversity and rebellion of the individual human life' (209). Accordingly, the correction of John by the Towneley angels is a situation 'created for no other purpose than to demonstrate or advance' stages in Christ's 'larger purposes' (200-1). I read David Mills' provocative account, although it notes complexity 'resolved in a structure focussing on John, not Christ', similarly to contrast and privilege 'Christ's divinity' over the drama of John's reluctance (David Mills, 'Religious Drama and Civic Ceremonial', in A.C. Cawley et al., *The Revels History of Drama in English: Vol. 1: Medieval Drama* (London and New York: Methuen, 1983), 183-4).

cation of parts and complexity of interrelation. Nominalism distinguishes entities separated by distance instead of giving privilege to a substantial unity taking precedence over separation in space and time:

> Ockham's tendency, then, was to split up the world, as it were, into 'absolutes'. That is to say, his tendency was to split up the world into distinct entities, each of which depends on God but between which there is no necessary connection: the order of the world is not logically prior to the divine choice, but it is logically posterior to the divine choice of individual contingent entities.[24]

Historians interpreting the trajectory of Western intellectual history see the metaphysical pluralism of nominalism as a gain in both personal subjectivity and empirical world. Nominalism, Panofsky puts it, focuses on 'the multiplicity of particular things and psychological processes'; it throws 'the individual back upon the resources of private sensory and psychological experience'.[25] Charles Taylor employs the striking phrase 'strong localization' for the gain in presence of psyches and of things in nominalist division where 'subject and object are separable entities'.[26] Modern identity, he claims, is based in the greater looseness of metaphysical *similarity* among entities instead of their *identity*—instead of the tight linkage in structures given an essential ground by informing Logos:

> This is a profoundly nominalist conception: there is no identity criterion of a 'nature' other than the similarity of causes operating in a number of entities, and each identified 'kind' of thing is ontologically independent of all the others. It may causally depend on them, but its nature isn't defined by its place in a whole, as with a theory of ontic logos.[27]

This is a 'new subjectivism' whereby there is placed '"within" the subject what was previously seen as existing, as it were, between knower/agent and world, linking them and making them inseparable'.[28] This ontological independence applies not only to a perceiving subject, a subjective drift in models of knowledge and valuation as universals are understood to be

---

[24]Frederick Copleston, *A History of Philosophy, Vol. 3: Ockham to Suarez* (Westminster, MD: The Newman Press, 1953), 68.
[25]Erwin Panofsky, *Gothic Architecture and Scholasticism* (New York: New American Library, 1951), 14-5.
[26]Taylor, *Sources of the Self*, 188. Although 'strong localization' is developed here in the general context of the early modern identity of Descartes and the seventeenth century, it is the key element of separation—'exclusive localization'—which gives it important medieval nominalist affiliation.
[27]Ibid., 190.
[28]Ibid., 188.

localized within individual minds, but also to the independence of empirical objects.[29]

Nominalist demarcation of the independent psychological subject *and* the objectivity of the external world seems, perhaps, so comfortable to a modern as to blunt the force of tension between the two in late medieval culture.[30] One location of this tension is in the status of universals as intermediaries. Universals do not disappear when their privilege in the wholeness of Logos is modified; instead, the universal aspect of knowledge demands new accounting when there is a non-participatory *relation* of individual things to individual knowers, and of knowers to each other— where, that is, there is 'space between' subject and object. Signs emerge as elements in-between which allow relation and communication; instead of universal presences, they take on crucial functions in *inter*relations and *inter*actions.[31]

Nominalist relations in epistemology can carry over to the theological relation of God and man:

---

[29]The rise of observational science as secular knowledge is associated with the empirical, objective side, a 'hunger for reality in respect to the created world' because of its construction of direct, empirical perception of objects without the linking intermediary (Heiko A. Oberman, 'Some Notes on the Theology of Nominalism with Attention to its Relation to the Renaissance', *Harvard Theological Review*, 53 (1960), 62). See also William J. Courtenay, 'Nominalism and Late Medieval Religion', in Charles Trinkaus and Heiko A. Oberman (eds.), *The Pursuit of Holiness in Late Medieval and Renaissance Religion* (Leiden: Brill, 1974), 45.

[30]Jorge Luis Borges, remarking on implications for medieval allegory, says, 'No one [today] says that he is a nominalist, because nobody is anything else' ('From Allegories to Novels', in *Borges: A Reader*, eds. Emir Rodriguez Monegal and Alastair Reid (New York: Dutton, 1981), 231).

[31]Even Ockhamist epistemology of vision involved accounting for action at a distance between entities instead of linkage by means of 'species' in a medium: see Katherine H. Tachau, *Vision and Certitude in the Age of Ockham: Optics, Epistemology, and the Foundations of Semantics, 1250-1345* (Leiden: Brill, 1988), 131-3. Steven Ozment (*The Age of Reform 1250-1500: An Intellectual and Religious History of Late Medieval and Reformation Europe* (New Haven, CT: Yale University Press, 1980), 56-9) provides a succinct introduction to the mind's relation to terms, things, and other minds in nominalism. Paul Tillich (*A History of Christian Thought: From its Judaic and Hellenistic Origins to Existentialism*, ed. Carl E. Braaten (New York: Simon & Schuster, 1967), 200) remarks that when individuals have become independent, 'the substantial presence of God in all of them has no more meaning' and 'Augustinian community' is replaced by 'social relations' through the mediation of signs. Marilyn McCord Adams (*William Ockham*, 2 vols. (Notre Dame, IN: University of Notre Dame Press, 1987), vol. 1: 71-2) comments on implications for language signs and linguistic community in Ockham's conventional signification as the 'voluntary imposition' of language users.

> God himself has become an individual. As such he is separate from all other individuals. He looks at them and they look at him. God is no longer in the center of everything, as he was in the Augustinian way of thinking. He has been removed from the center to a special place at a distance from other things. The individual things have become independent. The substantial presence of God in all of them has no more meaning, because such a notion presupposes some kind of mystical realism. [...] God knows everything empirically from the outside [...].[32]

In the salvation process God knows man and makes initiatives toward him; man as an individual entity also knows and makes initiatives. And just as a sensory sign can be a means of contact between two different individuals having similar experiences but not sharing a virtual participatory 'identity', so in the theological relation, a sacrament can likewise be a point of fruitful exchange between God and man—but in a way which preserves separate freedoms and integrities.

The lamb as focus of a sacramental exchange in the Towneley *Johannes Baptista* is given rationale in the late medieval emphasis on the contingent status of sacraments as causes. Steven Ozment draws the parallel to universals in epistemology:

> For Aquinas, sacraments were instrumental causes of grace and salvation. They really contained and communicated grace [...]. [A]s Aquinas believed that universals were really in things and, as so-called intelligible species, also really in the mind so he believed that grace was really in sacramental rituals and elements and, as accidental form, also really in the soul. Scotus, by contrast, identified with a tradition that explained the efficacy of the sacraments in terms of a covenant made by God. Sacraments work not because they intrinsically contain and convey grace, as a cause intrinsically contains and conveys its effects (Aquinas), but because God has agreed to be present with grace when the sacraments are performed.[33]

The Scotist emphasis on this willed choice, this covenant, which God makes with the world Heiko Oberman places as a decisive fourteenth-century Franciscan reaction to the high scholastic Aristotelianism of 'a metaphysically fool-proof causal system which embraces the whole chain of being, including God as first and final cause.'[34] God, instead, is a 'free-willing person' making a promise, a 'reliable commitment' or pact in a 'metahistorical' and covenantal conception of causality:

---

[32] Tillich, *A History*, 199-200.
[33] Ozment, *The Age of Reform*, 35, calling this Scotus' 'soteriological razor'.
[34] Heiko A. Oberman, 'Fourteenth-Century Religious Thought: A Premature Profile', *Speculum*, 53 (1978), 84.

[T]hese two conceptions are *totaliter aliter*. Whereas in Thomas's metaphysical ontology the natural and supernatural realm are organically joined by the *Being* of God in whom we participate by reason and faith, the metahistorical alternative retraces nature and supernature, creation and redemption, to the *Person* of God [...].[35]

The sacraments limited in this way as functions of God's decision, do not have intrinsic power for man's salvation; they have a granted or ascribed, not an inherent, value.[36] 'The Word, Sacraments, and clergy of the Church', as Oberman explicates the distinction by a contrast employing the vessel metaphor, 'have undergone the metamorphosis from vessels for growing participation in God's being through justification to mere requirements for graduation to eternal bliss'. This new contingency founded on God's willed covenant in one way limits and distances man's accessibility to God through them: 'The supernatural world, instead of accompanying and nourishing the *viator*, has receded and has become a hemisphere, a dome'.[37] The vessel is a metaphor for the inclusive presence and completeness of ontic Logos, giving primacy to God either as vital, informing content or as enclosing form. Nominalist understanding of interrelations invites structural metaphors implying division and interacting parts. No longer vessels and intrinsically 'full', sacraments, instead, are vehicles for mutuality based on generous promise and trusting response.

Especially for the Ockhamist, or *via moderna*, theologians, however, this contingency of the sacraments as vehicles of God's promise gives man new possibilities: 'This dome shuts out the world of God's non-realized possibilities and provides room on the inside for man's own realm, in which he, as the image of God, thinks and acts'.[38] The sacraments are promised in a pact by which God chooses to be self-limiting, to make them available for man's use in his own domain.[39] The sacramental middle point

---

[35]Ibid., 84-5.

[36]See William J. Courtenay, 'Covenant and Causality in Pierre d'Ailly', *Speculum*, 46 (1971), 110-6. See also Courtenay, 'The King and the Leaden Coin: The Economic Background of "Sine Qua Non" Causality', *Traditio*, 28 (1972), 193, for the economic analogue of the sacramental exchange in which, as for sacraments, the value of the coin depends on the ascribed value given by the king, not the inherent value. For analogous dynamics of valuation applied to merit in the salvation process, see note 45.

[37]Oberman, 'Some Notes', 63. The hemisphere imagery, with its hint of both partition ('dome') and separation (a 'receding'), is a suggestive equivocation between a monism represented by a sphere (with single center) and a dualism of parts.

[38]Ibid. See notes 43 and 48 for the historiographical problem of terminology which enters here.

[39]See Alistir E. McGrath, *Iustitia Dei: A History of the Christian Doctrine of Justification, Vol. 1: From the Beginnings to 1500* (Cambridge: Cambridge University Press, 1986), 87-8, on the conditional necessity God 'imposed upon himself' to reward man's effort.

is still part of God's ordained order for the world, still a dependable requirement for salvation. But it is a part of a reliable order only because a trustworthy God has decreed it *and* because man has the freedom to respond to it in the 'room on the inside' of his own hemisphere. Where the York baptism play rehearses an identity for man as sacramental vessel receiving God, Towneley constructs man in a process of thinking and acting interaction with God through these sacramental middle points.

This interaction built upon a *volition* of persons instead of *ontological* causality requires new formulations for action and for the persons or selves involved in it:

> In this emphasis on covenantal and not-necessary relationship between God and his world, as well as between God and his Church, man is no longer primarily a second cause moved by the prime mover and first cause. In the nominalist view man has become the appointed representation and partner of God responsible for his own life, society and world, on the basis and within the limits of the treaty or *pactum* stipulated by God.[40]

With man's new agency in the causality of salvation—and thus with the accommodation of a *double* agency in the process—action becomes an interaction. Covenantal causality opens the door to what can be called interactive causality. Causality which is 'absolute' from its foundation in God as First Cause is distinguished from one which is 'looser', what the English Dominican Robert Holcot (d. 1349) called a 'necessity of consequence' in order to accommodate his great emphasis on man's freedom, his capacity to respond to God's call and even to initiate the approach to God. Holcot cites the verses, 'Behold I stand at the door and knock; if any one hears my voice and opens the door, I will come in to him [...]'.[41] Here God

---

[40] Heiko A. Oberman, 'The Shape of Late Medieval Thought: The Birthpangs of the Modern Era', in Trinkaus and Oberman (eds.), *The Pursuit of Holiness*, 15.

[41] Robert Holcot, *In Librum Sapientiae Regis Salomonis: Praelectiones CCXIII* (Basel, 1586), 492 (Lectio 146). The verses (Rev. 3:20-1) are used as argument for Holcot's form of the central *via moderna* position on man's and God's complementary roles in his qualified kind of necessity: 'qui disponit se faciendo id, quod in eo est, aperit sibi: ergo intrat necessario'. Holcot distinguishes 'compulsory necessity' (*necessitas coactionis*) which is 'absolute' (*absoluta*) from the 'looser' conditional 'necessity of consequence' (*necessitas consequentiae*). The latter, however, is infallibly secured by God's promise, pact and ordained law: 'necessitas vero infallibilitatis cadit in Deo ex promissio suo & pacto, siue lege statuta' (ibid., 492 (Lectio 146)). For justification itself understood, from the twelfth century onward, as process with inner structure, but with weakened linkage from Scotus onward, see McGrath, *Iustitia*, 40-51. See Heiko A. Oberman, 'Facientibus Quod in Se Est Deus Non Denegat Gratiam: Robert Holcot, O.P. and the Beginnings of Luther's Theology', *Harvard Theological Review*, 55 (1962), 328, for Holcot's solution accommodating man's free will to predestinarian causality and unmerited grace: without the 'gift of grace man is *helpless*; but it is just as true that without the full use of man's own natural powers, the offer of grace is *useless*'.

initiates an external call, with man given the choice and capacity to respond. Within God's ultimate covenant, there is thus an ordained pattern of units in each of which there is an act and a response. As in the Towneley *Johannes Baptista,* these together move a play's action forward to yield the pattern of God's call, man's response, and God's subsequent blessing. The York Baptism, on the other hand, announces the presence of God. It poises man as receptor for God's indwelling action, stressing comprehensive theocentric causality and ontological fullness through union with God. With an eye on the play texts which later criticism has come to call drama, one can speak of a 'dramatic causality' in the plays which do structure action with interactive causality.

In *via moderna* theology man's new agency is a decisive stage within the long-developing consolidation in high medieval salvation theory of what Alistir McGrath calls the 'subjective appropriation of justification'.[42] For theologians in the wake of Ockham (d. 1347), including Robert Holcot and Gabriel Biel (d. 1495), this agency in an interactive relation with God based on pact is a positive one, efficacious in the process of salvation.[43] The fundamental theological tension in God's role versus man's role centered in discussion of the formula *facienti quod in se est Deus denegat gratiam.* This is usually paraphrased, 'God will not deny grace to the man *who does his best'*, which stresses that man does have causal agency in a stage preparing for God's grace.[44] *Via moderna* theology not only allowed but insisted on merit for man's act. As a result of man doing his best, it was fitting by God's decision, out of his merciful liberality, to allow a qualified, appropriate merit *(meritum de congruo)* to morally good acts in this initial or preparatory stage of the salvation process. These acts are then rewarded by traditional sacramental grace which, in its turn, grants (by contract also) man's subsequent effort full merit and worth *(meritum condignum)* for

---

[42]See McGrath, *Iustitia,* 70-91, especially 87-90.

[43]The term 'semi-Pelagian' sometimes enters here. Using '*via moderna*' here does not violate usages in the specialized historiography charting the complex web of affiliations and divergences in philosophical and theological positions: the *via moderna* is associated with a theology where the idea of the pact and covenantal causality 'allows man to play a positive role in his own justification, without elevating that role to Pelagian proportions' (McGrath, *Iustitia,* 170). McGrath's cautious usage reserves 'nominalism' for epistemological positions, with soteriological teachings 'independent of this nominalism' (*Iustitia,* 166-70). See also Alistir E. McGrath, *The Intellectual Origins of the European Reformation* (Oxford: Blackwell, 1987), 70-81. Specialists in these areas will quickly recognize the influence on this literary essay by those who see fundamental connection between philosophical nominalism, *pactum* theology, and the *via moderna.*

[44]See McGrath, *Iustitia,* 83; Heiko A. Oberman, *The Harvest of Medieval Theology: Gabriel Biel and Late Medieval Nominalism* (Durham, NC: Labyrinth Press, 3rd ed. 1983), 132. For Holcot's formulation, see note 41.

heaven.[45] This first stage is dramatized in the major section of the Towneley *Johannes Baptista*, which is the focus of this essay. In response to the external call from God through the angels, John comes to do his best by which he and the sacrament thus have worth; through God's liberal promise this results in the gift of the Lamb of God. In this theological context, the Lamb can then be construed as the sanctifying grace in which by an act of acceptance God restores man to the status of 'friend', forgiving sin.[46]

But a literal rendering of the *facienti quod in se* formula is also crucial because it comprises an autonomous definition of self, structurally enclosed and reflexive: to do one's best is to do 'what is in oneself', *in se*. It is the combination of these two basics—interactive causality of action and an autonomous and reflexive anthropology—which the Towneley *Johannes Baptista* play also constructs. The *via moderna* emphasizes autonomy and differentiation by including the phrase *ex puris naturalibus* in the *facere quod in se* formula. Man does what is in himself out of his own natural powers where natural powers of knowing and willing are distinguished from, separate from, God's supernatural, informing grace.[47]

---

[45]Ozment, *The Age of Reform*, 233-4, gives a concise overview and useful diagram stressing the relations of man's moral effort and God's grace in the traditional process of salvation and in the extension 'backwards' to man's disposition, where the late medieval theological controversy on the relations of God's and man's roles gravitated. In the *via moderna* man's *own* purely human moral effort and merit precede the reward of sacramental grace which, in turn, is the basis for man's traditional moral co-operation. Man's purely human capacity has its positive role by the congrual merit which allows ascribed (*valor impositus*), rather than intrinsic value (*valor intrinsicus*) to it (see McGrath, *Iustitia*, 88; 170).

[46]John had asked, 'Thou blys me, Lord, hence or thou gang, I So that I may thi frenship fele' (205-6). Lines 152 ('And do it, Iohn, right as thou can') and 191-2 (quoted above) paraphrase the sense of the 'facere quod in se' formula. It is not possible here to discuss the play's handling of the second, traditional stage where the infused habit of grace is the basis for subsequent moral cooperation. This involves the difficulty about the role left for the high scholastic created habit of grace, given the *via moderna* critique of it based on demonstration of its radical contingency: see McGrath, *Iustitia*, 172; 145-54; Oberman 'Some Notes', 56-60, and *Harvest*, 160-70. Emphasis moves from the created habit of grace as a God-liberated power within man neutralizing the ennervation of sin (an ontological change) to grace as status conferred by God's external acceptance in which sin is forgiven.

[47]In the *via moderna*, things performed *ex puris naturalibus* include God's gifts in creation and his general rule of the world (the *concursus Dei*), and only exclude the supernatural, infused habits of grace (see McGrath, *Iustitia*, 172; Oberman, 'Some Notes', 65). See Oberman, *Harvest*, 135-41, for Biel's complex usages of 'gratia' terminology involving this sensitive boundary area of created nature and pre-sacramental grace. By free will *ex puris naturalibus* a man may choose a morally good act without the need for grace, avoid mortal sin, love God above everything else, and dispose himself towards the reception of sanctifying grace (see McGrath, *Iustitia*, 76).

Man's *in se* autonomy gives a new construction to the normative value of the 'natural': man's freedom is based in a self with a legitimate center within, not in a theonomous self founded in God.[48] Man's structural autonomy and his positive role as a factor in the salvation interaction thus comprise both a non-Augustinian anthropology and soteriology for 'natural man'. In York, man's individuality as created entity and as free agent in redemption is blurred by a theonomous and heteronomous relation to Christ as indwelling Word and to the Holy Ghost. There a normative, 'natural' self is a vessel informed by God in creation and empowered by God in sacramental restoration.[49] In Towneley, on the other hand, natural man is created with emphasis on God's will which makes him contingent but also autonomously empowered with a place of his own:

> God, that mayde both more and les,
> Heuen and erth, at his awne wyll,
> And merkyd man to his lyknes
> As thyng that wold his lyst fulfyll—
> Apon the erth he send lightnes.
> (1-5)

Created man in Towneley is 'marked' in the *via moderna* kind of 'likeness' to God: autonomous and interactive, not participatory in the way that a part is contained in the whole or the way a vessel is informed by indwelling spirit. The world of nature is willed by God in nominalist separation.

---

[48] A *via moderna Augustiniana* which generally followed the *via moderna* in nominalist philosophy and *pactum* theology diverged by denying congrual merit and the possibility of morally good acts without grace (McGrath, *Iustitia*, 87; 179; and see also McGrath, *Intellectual Origins*, 90). Man's freedom in the *scola Augustiniana moderna* is grounded in a 'theonomous anthropology which sees in God not the opponent but the creator, preserver, and cause of man's freedom' (Oberman, 'Some Notes', 63). But in the *via moderna* it is based in an autonomy granted by his contingent position in the world (ibid., 63-4). The more radical freedom in separateness, *ex puris naturalibus*, Oberman takes to be the place where 'the Nominalist break with medieval tradition takes place' (ibid., 65). Ozment, *The Age of Reform*, 244, sees in this Ockhamist theology the influence for Luther's reversal of the medieval norm of the *likeness* of man and God, insisting instead on 'unlikeness' as the 'unitive principle in religion' where God and man relate to each other 'by will and by words'.

[49] The *via moderna Augustiniana* increasingly emphasized the uncreated grace of the Holy Spirit (see McGrath, *Iustitia*, 179). The York Baptism by collapsing into one the roles of God as Creator and God as savior (see above) and by emphasizing the heteronomous indwelling of the Holy Spirit fits this context. In York, natural man, the created image of God, is defined by mystical participation, not autonomous difference. Thus Christ's instruction to John in York refers to 'kynd wyt' (natural knowing) in the context of an Augustinian, illuminationist epistemology. For the accommodation of *in se* natural knowledge in the *via moderna*, see especially Oberman, 'Facientibus', 317-25.

Light, in York a divinely informing and illuminating essence, is here an extrinsic, created feature of heaven and earth. Natural man is a volitional entity ('thing') with his own capacity to will to respond to God's wish in contingent sacraments.

A play with features of the Towneley *Johannes Baptista*—autonomy and efficacy of human agency in dramatic interaction through contingent tokens—is thus described by *via moderna* formulations. The *via moderna*, by heightening both the difference between, and the mutuality of, man and God—with bold claims both for God's sovereignty and man's autonomy—encourages an enhanced and explicit sense of tension. Theologically, God's freedom is exercised in the eternity of his absolute presence. The root tension in this presence is between God's 'absolute' and his 'ordained' power—what God is free to do absolutely versus the reliable order which God has actually ordained for the world in his willed promises.[50] Drama has resources to represent God's agency, however, not just as a pact constituted in eternity—as a theological, intradeical tension—but as a unique present, and presence, for natural man in the created world. From the underside, as it were, of man's hemisphere, from man's domain, the established and reliable *ordinata* of sacraments and clergy 'is never divorced from the possibilities of the *absoluta*'.[51] The interactive and autonomous anthropology of the *via moderna* opens the door for that tension of the possible to be psychologically reflexive. The 'divine immediacy'[52] of Towneley's theology is localized in space and time through an ironic psychological action of obedience. Here, that is, the counterpart to the theological dialectic of God's absolute and ordained powers is a highly charged dynamic possibility in human experience: there are, on the one hand, the normal, reliable ordinations of God's revealed law—anchoring man's expectations—and, on the other, the unique immediacy of events and the differentiated self in which he exercises his freedom.

Seen from within man's autonomous side of his own self-awareness, the theological tension involving divine reliability and the world's contingency means inescapable *surprise*. The dramatization of John's surprising

---

[50]McGrath, *Intellectual Origins*, 78. On 77-81 he provides a useful introduction for non-specialists to this dialectic of God's two powers, a concept central in the historiography of late medieval theology.

[51]Oberman, 'Shape', 12. 'This directness of God's acting, essentially belonging to the vertical aspect of the sphere of the *potentia absoluta*, when introduced to the given order, causes a short-circuiting' (Oberman, 'Some Notes', 62). McGrath, *Intellectual Origins*, 78-9, cautions, however, that these 'are not two different courses of action open to God at any given moment in historical time'—normal versus miraculous—but 'two quite distinct orders of existence'.

[52]Oberman's term for a basic characteristic (positioned between the 'sovereignty of God' and the 'autonomy of man') of the covenant theologians (see 'Some Notes', 61-3).

obedience accommodates *both* the contingency and the dependability—Holcot's unfailing necessity—of the sacraments in God's ordained order. Baptism is a necessary point where man and God come together—but unexpectedly in a way fraught with the tensions of dramatic causality in which man's subjective effort and self-awareness play a major role. We saw Towneley's distinctive formulation which captures this energizing disjunction in Jesus' explanation of the law's fulfillment as the Father's 'ordynance' in 'reprefe' to man's writ (109-11).[53] God has willed in the *ordinata* a dependable meeting point, but this dependability is founded on the radical uniqueness of responsive interchanges involving man's own power to act and his own faith. There is, finally, the shock of the confrontation of self and God culminating in self-discovery: when John acknowledges the 'I' who has seen the Lamb of God, he at the same time acknowledges that the angel has nearly destroyed him ('nerehand mard' (222)). The deep basis of sacramental dependability is the surprise of uniqueness in every sacramental interaction, the tension of expectation and actual event.

The play thus affirms God's absolute sovereignty, God's 'pauste' in the unmistakable, strong terms of Scotist theology generally; it also affirms in equally strong terms the area of man's autonomous 'might' which God knows and calls to from the outside in the particular manner of the Ockhamist *via moderna*. It shows man's power in full independence, although implicitly hedged by uncertainty in knowing that he *is* doing what he can—using his full natural powers—as well as by the ultimate mystery of God's absolute otherness.[54] Sacramental interactions through the localized and contingent tokens of space and time—the Jordan, 'here in this present'—are a rebuke to man's generalizations and expectations about the world: they defamiliarize the world and compel man to confront his freedom and power in its foundational contingency and foundational autonomy.

3.

Via moderna formulations about causality, self, and the divine dialectic of powers help describe Towneley's dramatic causality, its characterization of John as autonomous and reflexive individual, and to locate its accommo-

---

[53] See Courtenay, 'Covenant', 116-9, for the tension of contingency and dependability involved in covenant and covenantal causality. His explanation in terms of a child's relation to an affectionate parent whose unlimited power he knows, but need not fear, is strikingly parallel to Towneley's explanation of the ordained law as 'reproof': God's absolute power is 'in theology a reprimand to the child in man not to take the given order for granted' (118).

[54] On one side, that is, the uncertainty of knowing that one has done his own natural best; on the other, trust that God will keep his promise: see McGrath, *Iustitia*, 172, and note 23.

dation of the play's psychological action. They also suggest a theory of drama in which there is an individualized and dynamic relation of audience to the play's religious meaning. This relation reaches its climax and becomes explicit when John's newly adequate faith and his blessed, or graced, actions become the actions of the preacher teaching the very lesson he himself has learned: the relation of sacramental baptism to obedience. 'Thynk how in baptym ye are sworne | To be Godys seruandys withoutten nay' (285-6), he says in his concluding address to the audience. He is following Jesus' earlier instruction which occurs after John's self-discovery: 'Bot, Iohn, weynd thou furth and preche | Agans the folk that doth amys, | And to the pepyll the trowthe thou teche' (233-5). To what extent are 'the pepyll' here to be apprehended by the play's late-fifteenth or early sixteenth-century Christian audience as the specifically differentiated historical audience of Jews, and to what extent is the 'trowthe' addressed immediately to itself as a contemporary collective?

Traditional descriptions of the mystery plays in reference to their teaching function privilege the latter emphasis, with 'the trowthe' (235) and 'rightwys way' (236) having the force of direct didactic address to an audience affirming historical linkage with the past and affirming itself as a paraliturgical or civic community. For the Towneley play, however, to present John's encounter with Jesus at the Jordan as a temporally and spatially specific event is to emphasize not only John as individual but also the separation between an audience's historical placement and John's acts at the Jordan.[55] In the portion of the play insisting on particular localization for John's action, John *has* seen and touched Jesus as God; an early modern audience of the late-fifteenth or early-sixteenth century has 'seen' Jesus only at a remove, as an 'acted' re-presentation.

This latter, nominalist emphasis on a separation between the audience and God which must be mediated by signs is made overtly thematic in Towneley. At the very moment in which Jesus rewards John with the ultimate promise of glory, he also addresses us, in an audience, who have

---

[55]In a felicitous formulation about this central aspect of Biblical drama given detailed analysis throughout by Hans-Jürgen Diller, *The English Mystery Play: A Study in Dramatic Speech and Form*, tr. Frances Wesels (Cambridge: Cambridge University Press, 1992), the Towneley *Johannes Baptista* is cited as one of the most 'instructive examples' of 'a strong and unforced fluctuation between play-sphere and audience-sphere' (122). His analysis (175-7) of John's introductory address in Towneley and John's introductory prayer in York raises the crucial factors in respect to interrelations of speaker, audience and represented event. The Towneley interaction emphasized in this essay occurs after sixty-four introductory lines in which John speaks in a more traditional relation to an audience collectivity as Christian saint in the universal Church, precursor of Christ in universal history, and moral exemplar '*in persona generis humani*' (*Biblia Sacra*, col. 77).

neither seen Jesus literally in his unique presence in time and space nor in the eventual presence of heavenly glory:

> I graunt the, Iohn, for thi trauale,
> Ay-lastand ioy in blys to byde;
> And to al those that trowys this tayll
> And saw me not yit gloryfyde,
> I shal be boytt of all thare bayll
> And send them socoure on euery syde.
> (225-30)

The promise of 'bliss' is thus to us as well as to John: we must come to 'trow this tayll'—the dramatic presentation—in a way parallel to John's coming to know the angels as tokens of Christ.

The play itself is therefore overtly and self-consciously a certain kind of sign. It asks for audience understanding, with John's interaction with God as the mediating element. The culmination comes appropriately at the crucial moment when the Lamb of God is handed over to John: 'By this beest knowen shall thou be, | That thou art Iohn Baptyst' (215-6). The Lamb, that is, is *both* a response to John for his act of obedience and a summons to us for an act of knowledge and faith *through John* in a process structured by the play. Through attending to John's interaction, the Lamb becomes our sign that John is John the Baptizer, the learner who through an independent act of doing what is in himself has been rewarded by sacramental grace. As the Lamb is an interactive sign for John, the play itself is an interactive sign for each of us. The play's thematic self-awareness here is compelling in visually and verbally concrete ways, analogous to Towneley's strong localization of signs. The handing over of the Lamb, with the only 'stage direction' supplied in the manuscript, gives visual emphasis to the icon of John with Lamb. And the accompanying stanza is unique among the play's eight-line stanzas of four feet because of its three-foot b-rhyme lines.[56]

This break with expectation in the aural pattern of the climactic stanza is just one of the challenges to immediate audience perception analogous to the one presented to John in the dramatic interaction: actively to overcome expectation and engage one's individual power in a unique event. Through John's dramatic interaction, our knowledge, our cognition, of

---

[56] Lines 209-14, quoted above (Section 1), yielding $a^4b^3a^4b^3a^4b^3a^4b^3$. My reading, by invoking late-medieval kinds of theological and dramatic tension, attempts to rehabilitate the doctrinal and didactic to a modern ear. Peter Meredith hears the verse as 'flat and repetitive' and feels the play 'so lacking in dramatic power' that Towneley's potential in Christ handing over the Lamb to John is unrealized ('The Towneley Cycle', in *The Cambridge Companion to Medieval English Theatre*, ed. Richard Beadle (Cambridge: Cambridge University Press, 1994), 141).

John has become a re-cognition analogous to John's re-cognition of humble service. The familiar visual icon of John holding the Lamb and announcing God itself is being changed and defamiliarized by a play showing the foundation of its meaning in the dramatic action. Just as John began his exchange with God by 'knowing' the universal truth of child baptism, a medieval Christian audience 'knows' from the outset in an 'external' way the general importance of John as link to Christ and sacramental grace. The play is not itself a devotional icon or exegetical moralization to the considerable extent that it functions as a nominalist kind of *intermediary*—an interactive sign—to that familiar and accustomed knowledge. Direct didactic address in iconic and liturgical ways is interrupted and complicated by the representation of the localized particularity of John's drama of self-discovery. The play in this way energizes received faith through the particular presence of dramatic presentation. Just as John made his surprising discovery of what obedience was through the localized contingency of tokens, the play prompts a Christian audience to experience that contingency anew through a play.

The sensory uniqueness of spectacle and word is thus a sign analogous to an external call of God—like the call of God to John mediated by angels—to an audience whose members must individually answer its call with natural, reflective resources. The Towneley play invites an act of individual and reflexive self-appropriation by members of its audience based on implicit trust in familiar religious imagery and ritual resources.[57] These associations give common ground with others as well as with God. In John's lyric of personal, affectionate farewell to Jesus at the end of the play, each person is invited to join John in an affirmation of faith which shares with others—in a common 'we' as a member of a Christian audience. But it also acknowledges the surprise of the individualizing instance just witnessed through John:

> Farwel, gracyouse gome! Wherso thou gone,
> Ful mekill grace is to thy geyn [given];
> Thou leyne [lend] vs lyffyng on thi lone [loan],
> Thou may vs mende more then we weyn [expect].
> (269-72)

If the play, through characterization, action, spectacle and other stylistic resources, succeeds in energizing this self-discovery and affirmation of

---

[57] The official sacraments are conspicuously promoted: through the oil and chrism brought by John 'men may know' that the sacrament is 'worthy' and that 'ther ar vi other' (194-7). Towneley thus is not anabaptist in my reading—children *should* be brought to church, as John first thinks; but the full experiential meaning of that ordained law he must learn.

faith—'more than we expect'—through John, it will have succeeded also in forming of its audience reflective and autonomous selves. For the individualized self and in the individualizing event, John's own gesture of farewell, of separation, is important. For each person in the audience will be linked in a relation of sympathy with, but also distance from, John which mirrors John's own connection to, and difference from, Jesus. In that way—a way encouraged by nominalist difference and by the positive tensions of the late medieval *via moderna*—the play creates individual selves interacting in a world become meaningful by connections made within its separations.

CHARITY AND THE SINGULAR:
THE OBJECT OF LOVE IN RABELAIS

ULLRICH LANGER

The nominalism/realism debate in the late Middle Ages and the early modern period has consequences, I believe, not simply for logic, epistemology, and theology, but also for moral philosophy, and as many of us have been seeing, for the nature of literary representation.[1] In the following pages I would like to offer some thoughts on the status of the relationship of charity in Rabelais's *Pantagruel* and *Gargantua*, a status which is indissociable from the nominalist bent of much of the period's intellectual culture. I will argue that the relationship of charity itself, as it is inherited from Augustine and the scholastics, and as it is defined by Rabelais's contemporary Erasmus in the *Enchiridion militis christiani*, presupposes a 'realist' perspective on the understanding of the love of one person for another, and that it is precisely this realist perspective that the narrative of Pantagruel's and Panurge's relationship refuses. I will also argue that charity is an inherently *mimetic* relationship, which again is both suggested and refused in these works of Rabelais.

Recent Rabelais criticism has insisted with some justification on the central role that Christian charity plays in the evangelical thematics, and I

---

[1]See, on the French side, Michael Randall, *Building Resemblance: Analogical Imagery in the Early French Renaissance* (Baltimore, MD: Johns Hopkins University Press, 1996); François Cornilliat, *'Or ne mens': Couleurs de l'éloge et du blâme chez les 'Grands Rhétoriqueurs'* (Paris: Champion, 1994), especially 85-129; my own *Divine and Poetic Freedom in the Renaissance: Nominalist Theology and Literature in France and Italy* (Princeton, NJ: Princeton University Press, 1990). On the English side, see Richard J. Utz, *Literarischer Nominalismus im Spätmittelalter: Eine Untersuchung zu Sprache, Charakterzeichnung und Struktur in Geoffrey Chaucers* Troilus and Criseyde (Frankfurt a.M. et al.: Lang, 1990), and William H. Watts and Richard J. Utz, 'Nominalist Perspectives on Chaucer's Poetry: A Bibliographical Essay', *Medievalia et Humanistica*, n.s. 20 (1993), 147-73. I am not, in the present study, doing justice to the complexity of the nominalist/realist debates in the period. I wish to thank Susan J. Erickson and my colleague Jan Miernowski for their helpful criticism of this study.

emphasize *thematics*, of Rabelais's books.[2] Leaving aside for a moment Gargantua's device, 'Charity does not seek its own' (1 Cor 13:5) (ἡ ἀγάπη [...] οὐ ζητεῖ τὰ ἑαυτῆς), and concentrating on *Pantagruel*, we find in the letter of Gargantua to his son:

> [...] il te convient servir, aimer et craindre Dieu, et en lui mettre toutes tes pensées, et tout ton espoir. Et, par foi formée de charité, être à lui adjoint, en sorte que jamais n'en sois désemparé par péché. [...] Sois serviable à tous tes prochains, et les aime comme toi-même.[3]

This is not the only use of the New Testament commandment, *Diliges proximum tuum sicut teipsum* (Matt. 22:39, etc.), in the book: among other instances, Panurge cites it, as does the *haute dame de Paris* when she is being cornered by Panurge. It is taken to be the touchstone of Pauline humanist evangelical thought, at the heart of what a Christian life should be like, in these urgent times: leave all superfluous things aside, and concentrate, as Erasmus says, on ways in which we can exercise charity.[4]

It is on a text by Erasmus that I would like to reflect for a moment, in the light of the topic to which this volume is devoted. In Erasmus's *Enchiridion militis christiani* (1503) we find a sustained examination of the relationship of charity, in the 6th canon, in the section devoted to the *Opiniones christiano dignae*. Charity is the love of the pious in Christ, and the love of the impious because of Christ ('Pios amet in Christo, impios propter Christum').[5] All human beings should be loved as part of the body of Christ, which one should love when one loves any human being:

---

[2]See Edwin M. Duval, *The Design of Rabelais's* Pantagruel (New Haven, CT: Yale University Press, 1992), especially 33; also Jerome Schwartz, 'Scatology and Eschatology in Gargantua's Androgyne Device', *Etudes rabelaisiennes*, 14 (1977), 265-75; Michael A. Screech, *Rabelais* (London: Duckworth, 1980).

[3]François Rabelais, *Pantagruel*, ed. Gérard Defaux (Paris: Librairie Générale Française, 1994), ch. 8, 165. Page references in my text are to this edition. Defaux has chosen the 1534 edition as the basis for his text.

[4]See his note to 1 Tim. 1:7 in his translation and edition of the New Testament, in his *Opera omnia*, vol. 6 (Loudun: Petrus Vander Aa, 1705), 927F.

[5]Desiderius Erasmus, *Opera omnia*, 10 vols. (Loudun: Petrus Vander Aa, 1703-6), vol. 5 (1704): 44F. (Further references in the text are to this edition; translations given are my own.) This formula is derived from Augustine (*De trinitate* 8.6.9), perhaps as quoted by Peter Lombard: 'Qui ergo amat homines, vel quia iusti sunt, vel ut iusti sint amare debet, hoc est in Deo vel propter Deum' (*Sententiae in IV libris distinctae*, 3rd ed., vol. 2 (Grottoferrata (Rome): Collegium S. Bonaventurae ad Claras Aquas, 1981), III dist 27 cap 5 art 1). In Augustine's thought the love of the neighbor clearly represents a love secondary to and directed to the love of God. See P. Ruggero Balducelli, *Il concetto teologico di carità attraverso le maggiori interpretazioni patristiche e medievali di I ad Cor. XIII* (Washington, DC: Catholic University of America Press, 1951): 'L'amore del prossimo cessa di rappresentare nella concezione d'Agostino un valore morale autonomo, per diventare attraverso la morale d'intenzione

Hoc unum tibi obversetur ob oculos, & satis sit: caro mea est, frater[6] est in Christo: quod in membrum confertur, nonne in universum corpus redundat, atque inde in caput? Omnes sumus invicem membra: membra cohaerentia constituunt corpus: corporis caput Jesus Christus, Christi caput Deus: tibi fit, singulis fit, Christo fit, Deo fit, quidquid unicuilibet membro fit, seu bene, seu male: haec omnia unum sunt, Deus, Christus, corpus & membra. (45D)[7] [That this one thing be before your eyes and be sufficient: he is my flesh, and a brother in Christ: what happens to one member, does it not happen to the entire body, and from there to the head? We are all members of each other, in their coherence the members form a body, the head of the body is Christ, the head of Christ is God: what happens to any member, good or bad, happens to you, happens to individuals, happens to Christ, happens to God. That is all one: God, Christ, the body and the members.]

---

e dei riferimenti una manifestazione particolare dell'amore di Dio' (100). Erasmus defines charity as 'qua diligimus Deum super omnia, & proximum propter Deum', and 'vera charitas proximi non separetur a charitate Dei, ex qua nascitur' (see his note to 1 Cor. 14:13 in his edition and translation of the New Testament, in the *Opera omnia*, vol. 6: 727D). The scholastics say little else: according to Lombard, 'Caritas est dilectio qua diligitur Deus propter se, et proximus propter Deum vel in Deo' (*Sent* III dist 27 cap 2). See also Johannes Altensteig, *Opusculum de amicicia* (Hagenau: Anshelm, 1519), ch. 8 ('De amicicia christianorum'): 'Et qui recte diligit se vel proximum: quid diligit finaliter nisi deum. [...] Tunc vere diligimus deum cum deum super omnia et propter deum omnia nos ad deum promoventia volumus et efficaciter quaeri[m]us. Haec sunt Charitas, virtutes, et praeceptorum observantia' (n. p.). On Erasmus and charity, see Jacques Chomarat, *Grammaire et rhétorique chez Erasme* (Paris: Belles Lettres, 1981), especially 607 (on the *Paraphrases*).

[6]On the debates concerning the extension of 'frater' (Christians only or non-Christians as well), see Hélène Pétré, *Caritas: Etude sur le vocabulaire latin de la charité chrétienne* (Louvain: Spicilegium sacrum lovaniense, 1948), 118–40. Augustine's solution is to say that charity enjoins us to love our enemies as brothers in the sense that we *wish* for them to be brothers in Christ ('Non enim amas in illo quod est, sed quod vis ut sit. Ergo cum inimicum amas, fratrem amas', *In Epistolam Ioannis* 8.10, cited in Pétré, *Caritas*, 137).

[7]See also canon 5: '*Caritatem* Paulus vocat, *aedificare proximum*, omnes eiusdem corporis membra ducere, omnes unum in Christo putare [...]' (*Opera omnia*, vol. 5: 35F). See also his note to Matt. 22:39 in his translation of the New Testament: 'Magis placet mihi Paulina similitudo de membris corporis, in quo plus etiam honoris adhibemus iis, quae per se sunt infirmiora' (*Opera omnia*, vol. 6: 117D). Traditionally the metaphor of the body is applied to the Christian church only, not to humanity in general; however, see Augustine, *In Ioannis evangelium* 65.2: 'Ad hoc ergo [Deus] nos dilexit, ut et nos diligamus invicem; hoc nobis conferens diligendo nos, ut mutua dilectione constringamur inter nos, et tam dulci vinculo connexis membris corpus tanti capitis simus' (in *Patrologiae cursus completus*, vol. 35 (Paris: Migne, 1841), 1809). Erasmus does use the metaphor of the body of Christ to designate the Christian church alone (see *Paraphrases in Epist. Pauli ad Ephesios* 4:11-16, in *Opera omnia*, vol. 7: 1039F). Some of Erasmus's formulations recall Ambrose and Augustine (especially the commentary on the *Epistola Ioannis ad Parthos*); see Pétré, *Caritas*, 289-93.

When you love an individual, you love her or him fundamentally as a creature of God, as a member constituting the body of Christ. In this sense when you love one 'neighbor' and also another 'neighbor', you are loving these two different individuals *qua* the same thing, that is, their membership in the body of Christ. Erasmus's use of the *similitudo* of the body of Christ is functionally equivalent to the more Platonic solution of his contemporary Jacques Lefèvre d'Etaples, who explains that in the relationship of charity you love your 'neighbor' as an image of God, since God made man in his image.[8] Again, two different individuals are loved by virtue of the same thing, namely God whose image they are.

It follows that when you love a sinner, you do not love that sinner because of the fact that he or she sinned, but because he or she is a creature of God.[9] A sinner, say, an infidel or an adulterer, can be hated or even killed, but not *qua* creature of God, rather, as infidel or adulterer:

> Adulter est, sacrilegus est, Turca est: exsecretur adulterum, non hominem: Sacrilegum adspernetur, non hominem: Turcam occidat, non hominem. Det operam, ut impius pereat, quem ipse se fecit: sed ut servetur homo, quem fecit Deus. (44E-45A)[10]
>
> [He is an adulterer, a sacriligious person, a Turk: let the adulterer be execrated, not the man; let the sacrilege be rejected, not the man; let one kill the Turk, not the man. May one expend efforts so that the impious may perish, which he has become himself, but so that the man be saved, whom God made.]

Attributes, to the extent that they are the product of sin, can be separated out from the creature of God who is the same as any other creature of God

---

[8] 'Diliges dominum deum tuum. [...] Diliges proximum tuum sicut teipsum. Et est simile primo: quia ut primum de amore est, ita & hoc de amore. Primum de veritate, secundum de imagine. Faciamus (inquit deus) hominem ad imaginem nostram. & haec est ratio amandi proximum perinde ac seipsum: quia dei imago & similitudo est, & aeque quoque ut & ipse, quantum est ex natura' (*Commentarii initiatorii in quatuor evangelia* (Meaux: Simon de Colines, 1522), f. 85r [on Matt. 22:39]).

[9] See Augustine, *In Ioannis evangelium* 65.2: 'Qui sancte ac spiritualiter diligit proximum, quid in eo diligit nisi Deum?' (in *Patrologiae cursus completus*, vol. 35: 1809).

[10] See Augustine, *De doctrina christiana* 1.27.28: 'Omnis peccator, in quantum peccator est, non est diligendus, et omnis homo, in quantum est homo, diligendus est propter Deum' (in *Patrologiae cursus completus*, vol. 34 (Paris: Migne, 1841), 29). On the scholastic side, see Altensteig, *Opusculum de amicicia*, ch. 8 (citing Gabriel Biel): 'amicus connotat actum virtutis secundum dilectionem in amante: quo tendit in amatum propter virtutem amati: Inimicus connotat actum odii viciosum inimico: quo odit eum cui est inimicus propter bonum virtutis quod est in eo. Namque qui odit vicium alterius non est inimicus. Inimicus ergo inquantum talis est malus et vitiosus et per consequens nullo modo ut sic est diligendus. Hoc enim modo virtuose odivit inimicum qui dixit: Verte impios et non erunt [...]'.

as an object of Christian charity. In this sense sinful attributes tend to be the *meaningful, relevant* differences between creatures, as they are the ones that require work or effort (*Det operam, ut impius pereat [...]*). However, the relationship of charity constitutes its object as the same as itself, *qua* creature of God: *diliges proximum tuum sicut teipsum*, as yourself. (Erasmus would not draw precisely this conclusion; he encourages to love the other *more* than yourself, in a typically heuristic move.[11]) Charity overtly eliminates any substantial singularity in the object loved.

Erasmus insists on the nullity of individual and group differences when seen under the light of sameness that charity sheds on them:

> Quorsum enim dissensionum vocabula, ubi tanta est unitas? Non sapit Christianismum, quod vulgo aulicus oppidano, rusticus urbano, patricius plebeio, magistratus privato, dives pauperi, clarus obscuro, potens imbecilli, Italus Germano [...] & ne omnia discrimina referam, nugatoria in re dissimilis dissimili est iniquior. Ubi caritas quae & hostem diligit, quando cognomen commutatum, quando color vestis nonnihil diversus, quando cingulus, aut calceus, & similia deliramenta hominum, me tibi faciunt invisum?
>
> [For what purpose are the words of differences, where the unity is so great? That does not taste of Christianity, that commonly the courtier be different from the provincial city-dweller, the peasant from the bourgeois, the patrician from the plebeian, the functionary from the private man, the rich from the poor, the famous from the obscure, the powerful from the weak, the Italian from the German [...] and may I not recall all the differences, the dissimilar is unequal to the dissimilar in a vain thing. Where is charity that loves even the enemy, when a changed name, when the color of clothing slightly different, when the belt or the shoe and similar extravagances make me hateful to you?]

The silly differences between men cited by Erasmus are all differences between groups of people, e.g., the courtier and the provincial; even when these differences concern extravagantly trivial things such as the color of clothing, these trivial things presumably take their significance from the fact that they indicate a larger category (that is, a certain type of clothing may indicate a political party or family). The *cognomen commutatum* perhaps comes closest to a truly individual distinctness. But on the whole it is clear that Erasmus is preoccupied by the conventional differences designating social groups and by their incompatibility with the relationship of charity. They are not incompatible with charity because they neglect the individuality of the person loved, but *a contrario* because they neglect the

---

[11]See Lombard, *Sent* III dist 29 cap 1 art 3: 'expressum est nos amplius debere diligere Deum quam omnes homines vel nos ipsos, et amplius animum alius hominis quam corpus nostrum'.

fundamental sameness that objects of charity enjoy: a common status as creatures of God. Thus, when Erasmus says that one should kill the Turk, not the man, this is not a move beyond conventional attributes to the individual *propter seipsum*, but to the essential sameness of the creature.

The relationship of charity, as interpreted by Erasmus and, one might say, the evangelical humanists in general, is then a realization of an ethical principle that precedes Christianity and that on the surface seems incompatible with it. This is the Aristotelian maxim that 'affection is equality and similarity' (ἡ δ' ἰσότης καὶ ὁμοιότης φιλότης, *Nicomachean Ethics*, 1159b 2-3), repeated by Erasmus himself in his *De ratione studii* (1510): 'et simile gaudet simili; et aequalis aequalem delectat'.[12] Since our status as creatures of God is more important than anything else, and we all resemble each other in that way, we should all love each other, as what is similar attracts. The move from an explanatory statement (I love a person because she or he is similar to me) to a normative one (I *should* love this person because she or he is similar to me) is one that the modern period might find difficult, but in Erasmus it is more a matter of making Christians aware, or of reminding them, of the sameness that charity derives from. It is also important to point out the gap that separates, in one sense at least, Aristotle from Erasmus. For the statement that 'affection is equality and similarity' in the Philosopher implies that only good men can be loved by good men; in other words, it is a way of submitting affection to the ethical distinctions that allow for the definition of a good life in the city-state. For Erasmus, charity goes beyond those distinctions in a fundamental way: Christianity is universalist both in its political appeal and in its refusal of classical elitism. But charity, and ethical love in the Aristotelian tradition, are never conceived of as a love of an object *in its difference*.

If, then, the Rabelaisian fictional universe is one governed by the relationship of charity; if, as recent critics would have it, Rabelais is setting up a utopian society under the aegis of *caritas*, then the 'singular', as applied to the representation of persons, should be inimical to his project. Indeed, as I pointed out earlier, attributes of a person which seem to direct attention away from his or her status as creature of God, tend to be associated with sin, and also, paradoxically, tend to be *marked* attributes, the ones which deserve to be eliminated through effort. One can consider the abbey of Thélème to be precisely an attempt to represent the sameness of charity; the very non-individuality of the anti-monks is a sign of their status as subjects and objects of the relationship of charity. They have no attributes, other than being young, handsome and well-born, perhaps because any individual attributes would be a distraction from their

---

[12]Desiderius Erasmus, *Opera omnia*, vol. 1.2., ed. Jean-Claude Margolin (Amsterdam: North Holland Publishing Company, 1971), 139.

status as creatures of God. On the other hand, Thélème as anti-monastery is the product of rigorous selection: why not let Sorbonne theologians, usurers, etc. enter the abbey *as children of God*, not as theologians and usurers, just as Erasmus had recommended that we treat adulterers and Turks? The excluded are given strings of epithets, whereas the included are described much less than the buildings and grounds of the château-abbey.

We are coming up against two kinds of problems as we enter the fictional world of Rabelais. The first is the more theoretical problem of mimetic representation and its construction of the individual (in the sense of the singular). I will come back to this problem at the conclusion of this essay. The second is the representation by Rabelais of charitable relationships and the implications of these representations for the singularity of the persons involved.

Let us entertain for a moment the notion that the relationship between Pantagruel and Panurge, say in *Pantagruel*, is one of charity. The first observation one can make, and I will not dwell on this, is that the relationship is exclusive: Pantagruel loves excessively not all creatures of God, but only Panurge. As Erasmus says in his *Colloquies*, 'Christiana charitas se dilatat ad universos, familiaritas autem cum paucis habenda est' ('Christian charity extends to the whole world; intimate friendship should be restricted to a few').[13] The second feature of their relationship is the immense love, sympathy, and amusement which Panurge produces in Pantagruel:

— during their first meeting, Pantagruel conceives a love of epic proportions for the trickster;
— after the recounting of the Turkish adventure, Pantagruel expresses sympathy for Panurge's plight (and not, say, sympathy for the Turks' plight as creatures of God): 'Et que fis-tu, pauvret?' (229);
— after Panurge recounts how he would build the fortifications of Paris, Pantagruel laughs uncontrollably: 'Ho! ho! ha! ha! ha!' (235);
— after Panurge recounts how he knows that Parisian women are promiscuous, Pantagruel says: 'Vraiment, tu es gentil compagnon, je te veux habiller de ma livree' (241);
— Pantagruel is pleased to see the humiliation of the *haute Dame de Paris*, the spectacle of which he finds 'fort beau et nouveau' (317). The spectacle of humiliation is what produces the giant's reaction, not any eschatological subtext (in the order of 'the great will be humbled and the meek glorified'). The fact that this is all *mis en scène* by the trickster Panurge (and not, say, by Christ), seems not to bother but to amuse Pantagruel.

---

[13]From 'Amicitia' [1531], in *The Colloquies of Erasmus*, tr. Craig R. Thompson (Chicago, IL: University of Chicago Press, 1965), 527.

— Pantagruel is willing to assist Panurge personally in the war against the Dipsodes, whereas the reverse is not true when it may be harmful to Panurge's health.

All of these reactions can be interpreted as love of Panurge *qua* creature of God, but a far more likely interpretation is that it is precisely the singular nature of Panurge that provokes the often excessive love of Pantagruel. In other words, attributes of Panurge that in many cases strike us as entirely unrelated to the love of God are not only marked, but they do not produce in the giant the effort to remove them. Pantagruel spends little time trying to make Panurge into a more charitable person. Panurge is, quite simply, amusing, and he is amusing *not* as a creature of God. He is amusing as others are not amusing: the episodes dealing with his *moeurs et conditions* are the construction of differences between him and other characters, or simply other creatures.

To what extent is this not true, however, of any literary fiction? Any character, even if this is not a character in, say, a nineteenth-century sense, has to be distinguished from other characters. Any agent in a narrative by the very fact that he or she is an agent, is distinct from some other agent. A narrative is inconceivable without positing that whenever an action is performed, the agent of the action is in that very instance distinct from other agents: otherwise there would be no perceivable action. In addition, narratives usually derive at least part of their interest from the fact that it is assumed that the agent function cannot be filled by any creature of God, in other words, that we do not all do the same things all the time. (It may be true in a more profound sense that we all do the same things, but this is not the stuff of narrative.) Part of the interest of *Pantagruel* is surely that in the relationship between Pantagruel and Panurge, the Christ-like giant is not interchangeable with the trickster.

But seen from another perspective, literary fiction as mimesis does entertain connections to at least the structure of the relationship of charity. If charity is the love of another *sicut teipsum*, based on the similarity of all creatures of God and on the attraction of the similar, then it is not unlike the mimetic relationship between the thing imitated and its imitation. In other words, for an 'imitation' to be recognized as standing for something else, it must resemble that thing (be it a real or a fictional person). That is why Lodovico Castelvetro, commenting on Aristotle's *Poetics*, translates *mimesis* with *rassomiglianza*, and confirms Aristotle's categorization of poetry as a kind of mimesis: 'poesia è rassomiglianza, e la sua maniera generale è rassomiglianza'.[14] (Generally, however, *mimesis* is translated as 'imitatio', 'imitazione', by Scaliger, Bernardo Segni, etc.) In some ways to love someone through charity is to love the other *in imitation* of one's love

---

[14]*Poetica d'Aristotele vulgarizzata e sposta*, ed. Werther Romani, vol. 1, 1.2 (Rome and Bari: Laterza, 1978), 23.

for oneself; as creatures of God we are all representations of each other; conversely, in some deeper way to represent someone, to resemble someone is perhaps an act of love.

Indeed Panurge frequently *imitates* his master Pantagruel, as has been pointed out by many critics, including Gérard Defaux in his books and edition of *Pantagruel*.[15] Panurge imitates and represents his master during the disputation with Thaumaste. He imitates Pantagruel in his response to the approaching 660 *chevaliers*. In the victory celebration following the burning of 659 of them, Pantagruel proposes a 'trophée', a *carmen figuratum* celebrating human intelligence above brute force in the first stanza, and then God's *beneplacitum*, his good pleasure, in the second. Pantagruel's poem has an obvious ethical content to it: the praise of *ingenium* and by implication, prudence, points to the humanist critique of blind warrior violence and the superiority of letters over arms. Individual initiative is nothing without the support of God, in whose will one must (and can) have faith. Pantagruel is offering substantive moral-religious advice.[16]

When we get to Panurge's imitation of Pantagruel's *trophée*, we find a poem that resembles his master's in a purely formal way. That is, the poem's graphic shape is that of the cup, the rhyme scheme and even the rhymes themselves match the giant's poem. So the reader is given ample opportunity to savor the resemblance of the two poems, and, by implication, of the two persons. The problem is, however, that the content of Panurge's poem is radically different from his master's. Whereas Pantagruel emphasizes prudence and faith in God, Panurge emphasizes the consumption of hare, of wine, and the virtues of vinegar in the preparation and tastiness of meat.[17] In other words, the specifically ethical message of Pantagruel is what is left out, whereas what is retained is the rhyme scheme. This 'sophistic' imitation is then the sort of imitation that is most removed from an *ethical* resemblance, that is least likely to lead the reader to conclude a profound similarity of prudent agents of God's will. This anti-ethical *mimesis* of Pantagruel by Panurge is true of the other instances as well.

What Panurge has done, then, is to remove from imitation the resonances of charity (as the similarity of children of God), and to use imitation rather as a tool of *singularity*. Panurge sets up the comparison formally,

---

[15]See *Pantagruel*, ed. Gérard Defaux (e.g. 348, note 13). Defaux connects this mimetic obsession in Panurge with his sophistry.

[16]'[...] engin vaut mieux que force. | Car la victoire, | Comme est notoire, | Ne gît qu'en heur | Du consistoire | Où règne en gloire | Le haut Seigneur; | Vient, non au plus fort ou greigneur, | Ains à qui lui plaît, comme faut croire: | Donques, a chevance et honneur | Cil qui par foi en lui espoire' (*Pantagruel*, 347).

[17]'Car l'inventoire | D'un défensoire | En la chaleur, | Ce n'est qu'à boire | Droit et net, voire | Et du meilleur. | Mais manger levraut, c'est malheur | Sans de vinaigre avoir mémoire: | Vinaigre est son âme et valeur, | Retenez-le en point péremptoire' (*Pantagruel*, 349).

and then makes his own distinctiveness even more apparent than it would have been without the initial signs of resemblance. To return to Erasmus's analysis of personal difference, Panurge makes, as it were, the least important attribute into the one shared (rhyme scheme), whereas the most important one (the relationship to God and to each other) is the one not shared by the giant and his friend. What this emphasis on profound singularity means, then, is that the charitable relationship as a relationship of the profoundly similar is entirely marginalized.

In other words, in order to understand the proposition, 'Pantagruel loves Panurge', we must understand not the nature of Christian love, the essence of either Pantagruel or Panurge as creatures of God, but instead we must perceive *this* character, Pantagruel, in his singularity, and *this* character Panurge, in his singularity, and take notice of the great love of the giant Pantagruel for the trickster Panurge. Panurge and Pantagruel are not representations of each other, *qua* their love in the body of Christ, that is, through their common status the essence of Panurge is not present in Pantagruel, and vice-versa. In a further sense, then, the essence of Panurge is not captured by the words used to 'represent' him; these words point to him, designate him, refer to him, but they are not a 'copy' of a real Panurge. If the most important thing connecting the imitation and that which is imitated is not their resemblance, but an act of love based on their difference, then analogously the copy cannot resemble its model, or the thing represented, but only refer to it. I suspect that there is indeed an analogy between the refusal of love as representation of the other, that is, a refusal of charity, and a more general, nominalist refusal of the mimetic model of representation. It is, admittedly, a leap to pass from a relationship between two fictional characters to the relationship between the words and the 'persons' they refer to. But the insistence on singularity as the basis for the characters' relationship produces a momentum that moves towards the possibility of perception of the singular, and this perception on a linguistic level is equivalent to *reference*.

But there is another consequence to this sort of speculation. For if love is the paradigmatic relationship to the other, in its entire concentration on the other person, and if furthermore love in the Rabelaisian context absolutely refuses the copying of the other that is the model of charity, then this nominalistic critique would also attach itself to the second element of the proposition of charity, *diliges proximum tuum sicut teipsum*. For, if love is the action of one singular on another singular, how can one then love *oneself*? In other words, what is the object of the love of oneself? How is it possible to *diligere seipsum*?

SEMIOTIC SLIPPAGE: IDENTITY AND AUTHORITY IN THE ENGLISH RENAISSANCE

WILLIAM C. CARROLL

> It is in the Renaissance that the false is born along with the natural.
> —Jean Baudrillard, *Simulations*

Whether the English Renaissance is the period which *first* self-consciously registers the separation of the signified from the signifier is perhaps arguable, but there can be no doubt that the general crisis of authority in this period was simultaneously also a crisis of the sign, and especially a crisis of those semiotic systems designed to enforce and regulate social and class distinctions. As such, this crisis reflects one stage of the general shift from realism to nominalism in the early modern period.

Since self-identification requires other-exclusion, it was considered crucial in this period to be able to read, clearly and simply, the various signs—of language, behaviour, clothing, hygiene, etc.—which mark off low from high, deviant from normal. Thus Tudor sumptuary laws were designed to define and confirm—indeed, to fix immutably—the exact signifying correspondences between the representations of clothing and socio-economic status; e.g. no man under the degree of Baron was permitted to use any cloth of gold, cloth of silver, etc.[1] But just here, in the move toward a hegemony of signifying practices, the authorities in early modern England met some very surprising contradictions; likewise,

---

[1] See Barry Taylor, *Vagrant Writing: Social and Semiotic Disorders in the English Renaissance* (Toronto: University of Toronto Press, 1991) for an account of the semiotics of clothing as expressed in Renaissance conduct books and treatises on rhetoric, particularly Puttenham. The present essay is an expanded version of the paper I presented at ISSEI's 1994 Graz Conference (see Preface) which was published, under the same title, in the selected workshop proceedings: *The European Legacy*, 2.2 (1997), 212-6. It is adapted from William C. Carroll, *Fat King, Lean Beggar: Representations of Poverty in the Age of Shakespeare*, 39-47. Copyright © 1996 by Cornell University. Used by permission of the publisher, Cornell University Press.

attempts by judicial authorities to guarantee a particular reception of signs by the populace also met with failure.

Any account of the sign in the English Renaissance must acknowledge the disruptive static of historical texture which always interferes with the clear transmission and reception of signs; Marvin Carlson has recently called for such an analysis of history and reception of this kind.[2] Elizabethan sumptuary laws and public penal spectacles derive from a state-sponsored regimen of socio-semiotic control which promised to regulate the signs of status among the citizenry, on the one hand, and to insure their obedience through the signifying power of exemplary public punishments, on the other. Such a formulation assumes a complete and unimpeded mastery of sign systems on the part of the regime of authority, however—an assumption that the prescriptive is the descriptive, that semiotic intention coincides with semiotic reception. Yet such was frequently not the case.

In *Discipline and Punish*, Michel Foucault describes an elaborate theory of 'penal semiotics', particularly the spectacle of the public execution. Yet Foucault also observes that the necessary presence of an audience, at whom all the juridical signs were pointed, guaranteed the subversion of the regime's semiotic intentions, because the presence of large crowds—necessary to the political ends of the spectacle—inevitably turned the occasion into a 'momentary saturnalia [...] in which rules were inverted, authority mocked and criminals transformed into heroes'.[3] 'The terror of the public execution', he notes in a final irony, itself 'created centres of illegality'.[4] Thomas Laqueur, in examining English public executions 1604-1868, has recently confirmed Foucault's point with substantial archival documentation; echoing Foucault, he notes that the 'natural genre of [the] execution [scene] is carnival'.[5] Show trials, as modern states are always still discovering, rarely show what they are intended to show. When Thomas Platter, a Swiss traveller, visited London in 1599, he remarked, as virtually all visitors did, on the grisly spectacle of some thirty impaled heads of executed traitors stuck on tall stakes on top of London Bridge, swaying in the breeze to greet all those who crossed into the City—an admonitory spectacle of perfect semiotic clarity, one might think. And yet, Platter went on, the dead traitors'

---

[2] Marvin Carlson, 'Theatre and Performance', *Semiotica*, 92 (1992), 103.
[3] Michel Foucault, *Discipline and Punish: The Birth of the Prison*, tr. Alan Sheridan (New York: Vintage, 1979), 60-1.
[4] Ibid., 63.
[5] Thomas Laqueur, 'Crowds, Carnival and the State in English Executions, 1604-1868', in A.L. Beier, David Cannadine, and James Rosenheim (eds.), *The First Modern Society* (Cambridge: Cambridge University Press, 1989), 340.

descendants are accustomed to boast of this, themselves even pointing out to one their ancestors' heads on this same bridge, believing that they will be esteemed the more because their antecedents were of such high descent that they could even covet the crown, but being too weak to attain it were executed for rebels.

The ironic moral was clear: 'thus they make an honour for themselves of what was set up to be a disgrace and an example'.[6] Another foreign visitor records being shown the exact spot

> where the brave hero the Earl of Essex was beheaded, and lay buried in the chapel close by. How beloved and admired this Earl was throughout the kingdom, may be judged from the circumstance that his song, in which he takes leave of the Queen and the whole country, and in which also he shows the reason of his unlucky fate, is sung and played on musical instruments all over the country, even in our presence at the royal court, though his memory is condemned as that of a man having committed high treason.[7]

The various organs of local and national government waged what can fairly be described as a war of signs against the country's vagrants and criminals before the 'audience' of the general populace. As an exemplary instance of this conflict, and in an effort to narrow my focus considerably, I will take up for the remainder of this paper the figure of the vagrant or so-called 'sturdy beggar'—the man or woman fully capable of work but refusing to seek or accept it. A sturdy beggar was by definition a paradox of deceit: not a real beggar—stricken by disease or mischance—but a man or woman whose body was whole and unmarked who 'counterfeits' (in the favourite term of the period) disease and mutilation in order to escape detection, evade work, and prey upon our sympathies.

The authorities who so assiduously provided for the truly infirm at the same time pursued the sturdy beggar with relentless energy. Many official documents of the period as well as the popular literature of the day elevated sturdy beggars to near demonic proportions, inflating their numbers, exaggerating their powers of disguise and deception, and dramatically

---

[6]Thomas Platter, *Thomas Platter's Travels in England 1599*, tr. Clare Williams (London: Jonathan Cape, 1937), 155.

[7]'Diary of the Journey of Philip Julius, Duke of Stettin-Pomerania, through England in the Year 1602', ed. G. von Bulow, *Transactions of the Royal Historical Society*, n.s. 6 (1892), 15. George Whetstone, on the other hand, describing the executions of the members of the Babington Plot, observed that 'although the assembly were wonderful great, and the traitors all goodly personages, clothed in silks, and every way furnished to move pity, and that the order of their execution was a fearful spectacle, yet the odiousness of their treasons was so settled in every man's heart, as there appeared no sadness or alteration among the people at the mangling and quartering of their bodies: yea, the whole multitude, without any sign of lamentation, greedily beheld the spectacle from the first to the last' (*The Censure of a loyall Subject* (London: 1587), 13).

overstating the seditious threat they represented. Local historical documents, such as court and assize records, however, reveal that in most cases the truth has been highly inflated and in some cases simply invented. It seems evident, in retrospect, that the *genuine* phenomenon of the sturdy beggar—for there certainly were such people—was systematically demonized by the prevailing discourse. As with other forms of deviant behaviour during this period, preeminently witchcraft, the alleged threat to authority was used to legitimate authority; the need to control the threat is employed to justify the authoritarian repression already in place. Why the sturdy beggar prompted such harsh official and private persecution remains a difficult question. In part this vengeful attitude must derive from a failure of contemporary economic theory to understand the causes and nature of unemployment; still, with the establishment of bridewells, which were to provide work at state expense, this gap in theory (though certainly not in practice) seems closed. Anyone still without work could therefore be declared incorrigibly and willfully idle, beyond reformation. Other complex economic and social causes thus remained invisible.

The sturdy beggar represented as well a particularly subversive threat to the prevailing ideology of authority because his actual physical wandering replicated his destabilized social position; in a world in which, ideally, identity and relationship were constituted and fixed within a hierarchy, the vagrant was a chief instance of disorder of all kinds. Worse, beggars created their own language—canting—and became adept at counterfeiting the signs of the dominant culture: dressing like middle-class citizens, providing convincing but fictional narratives of personal history, carrying precisely forged documents, such as passports, which seemed to license their vagrancy. The sturdy vagrant was understood to be a virtuoso of histrionics, a master dissembler. The figure of the counterfeiting beggar, as we will see, exposed the signifier/signified relation in the realm of status as something constructed rather than 'natural'. As a result, the ideology of order and authority engaged in various futile efforts to recuperate a purity of signification.

Tudor authorities devised several ways, all equally ineffective in the end, by which to distinguish 'true' beggars from sturdy beggars so that the 'true' poor could be cared for, and the others properly punished. As a first move, the genuinely poor were to be officially certified. In 1517, the Court of Aldermen ordered officials in London to distribute specially-made tokens to licensed beggars (about 500 were given out): 'a pair of beads round with the arms of London in the middest [...] of pure white tin, and [...] to be set upon their right shoulders of their gowns openly to be seen, which persons having the said tokens upon them shall be suffered to beg and ask alms'.[8] Similar measures were attempted throughout the period—

---

[8]Frank Aydelotte, *Elizabethan Rogues and Vagabonds* (1913; repr. New York: Barnes & Noble, 1967), 140-1.

from York in 1515[9] and Lincoln in 1543[10] to Salisbury in 1638; in Salisbury even children were to wear badges and blue caps 'whereby they might be known the children of the workhouse and distinguished from all other children'.[11] In one ironic variation on this theme in Elizabethan Essex, all those poor people who received clothing under the terms of Henry Smith's will were to be given 'upper garments on the right arm of which shall be a badge with the letters H. S.'.[12]

Badging licensed beggars was ordered for the entire country in 1563; when poor relief later became nationally mandatory, there was even greater reason for the authorities to attempt to mark the licensed beggars with badges. As some observers noted, however, badging could be an odious cultural sign; John Howes remarked in 1587 that 'the shame of this badge will make some keep in and not to go abroad',[13] and thus not receive the alms they were entitled to. Counterfeiting was rampant, moreover. Thomas Dekker, for example, in 1612 described how vagrants created the 'Marke of Bedlam', in the (mistaken) belief that inmates of Bedlam Hospital had legal permission to beg: they 'have the letters E. and R. upon their armes: some have crosses, and some other mark, all of them carrying a blue colour'. The marks 'are printed upon their flesh' like a crude tatoo, and stick 'in the flesh a long time after. When these marks fail, they renew them at pleasure'.[14] As late as 1675, the governors of Bedlam would have to issue a warning that there was no such 'distinction or mark put upon any lunatic during their being there, or when discharged thence. And that the same is a false pretence'.[15] As a national policy, badging failed, and in any event badging could never eliminate the causes of vagabondage.

The next step beyond badging licensed beggars was to turn the semiotic arrow in the other direction and mark the unlicensed beggars. Since anything disposable was an unacceptable sign, the beggar's own body

---

[9]See A.L. Beier, *Masterless Men: The Vagrancy Problem in England 1560-1640* (London: Methuen, 1985), 154.

[10]See E.M. Leonard, *The Early History of English Poor Relief* (1900; repr. New York: Barnes & Noble, 1965), 41.

[11]Paul Slack, 'Poverty and Politics in Salisbury 1597-1666', in Peter Clark and Paul Slack (eds.), *Crisis and Order in English Towns 1500-1700* (London: Routledge & Kegan Paul, 1972), 192.

[12]Keith Wrightson, *English Society 1580-1680* (New Brunswick, NJ: Rutgers University Press, 1982), 182.

[13]*Tudor Economic Documents*, 3 vols., eds. R.H. Tawney and Eileen Power (London: Longmans, 1924), vol. 3: 426.

[14]Thomas Dekker, *O per se O* (London: 1612), M2v.

[15]Gamini Salgado, *The Elizabethan Underworld* (London: J.M. Dent, 1977), 198. For an analysis of the Bedlam beggar in relation to *King Lear*, see William C. Carroll, '"The Base Shall Top Th'Legitimate": The Bedlam Beggar and the Role of Edgar in *King Lear*', *Shakespeare Quarterly*, 38 (1987), 426-41.

would receive the mark of signification. The statute of 1547 (considered so harsh it was repealed a few years later) authorized the branding of vagrants, who were 'to be marked with an hot iron in the breast the mark of V'.[16] Branding was revived in the statute of 1604, however; this time, incorrigible rogues were to be 'branded in the left shoulder with a hot burning iron [...] with a great Roman "R" upon the iron [...] [to be] so thoroughly burned and set on upon the skin and flesh, that the letter "R" be seen and remain for a perpetual mark upon such rogue during his or her life'.[17] If a branding iron was not legally authorized or handy, a whip would be sufficient to inscribe the desired sign. Henry VIII's proclamation against vagabonds in 1531, for example, provided that anyone found guilty of vagrancy would be 'stripped naked, from the privy parts of their bodies upward [...] and sharpely beaten and scourged'. If a beggar is arrested again within a short time, he risks the same punishment again unless, being stripped naked before the law, 'if it may evidently appear unto them by the tokens on his body, that he hath been already scourged or beaten, they shall then suffer him to depart without other harm'.[18] The difficulty with this semiotic scheme was that the signs faded, and the incorrigible could go on; reading the signs also required an inquisitorial procedure. Permanent markings were superior, and the more easily visible the better. So the 1572 statute against vagrants authorized ear-borings, whereby the offender would be 'burned through the gristle of the right ear, with an hot iron of the compass of an inch about, as a manifestation of his wicked life, and due punishment received for the same';[19] second offenses led to boring the left ear, third offenses to death. Thus the semiotic mutilation of the vagrant's body became both the 'manifestation of', *and* the 'due punishment received for', his 'wicked life'—that is, his class status, in an eerie anticipation of Kafka's 'In the Penal Colony'. In the vicious bodily economy of marking, those sturdy beggars who had counterfeited broken limbs or horrible wounds to move pity in the onlookers might well have found the 'tokens' of authority permanently marked over their own false signs of impoverishment and suffering; the state could make real what had only been feigned, writing the true text of pain over the counterfeit one.

These attempts at marking the guilty are what Foucault means by 'penal semiotics', when the actual punishment for vagrancy has become its external physical sign, a bodily wound which is not life-threatening but which can never be separated from what it signifies; while this punishment

---

[16]*English Historical Documents*, vol. 5 (1485-1558), ed. C.H. Williams (London: Eyre & Spottiswoode, 1967), 1030.
[17]Beier, *Masterless Men*, 159-60.
[18]Aydelotte, *Elizabethan Rogues and Vagabonds*, 143-4.
[19]Raphael Holinshed, *Holinshed's Chronicles*, 6 vols., ed. Henry Ellis, vol. 1 (London: J. Johnson, 1807), 310.

eliminates the constant need to uncover and 'read' the sturdy beggar's body so as to reveal his fraudulence, it also insures that the vagrant can *never* escape his status, and thus ironically preserves the very condition which it purports to control and suppress.

The major effect of this semiotic program is therefore not on the guilty beggar, for whom one brand or mark is much like another, nor on the judicial authorities, who can always order a beggar stripped and examined. Rather, this penalty, like all punishment, is as Foucault says 'directed above all at others, at all the potentially guilty. So these obstacle signs [...] must therefore circulate rapidly and widely; they must be accepted and redistributed by all; they must shape the discourse that each individual has with others and by which crime is forbidden to all by all'.[20] In leaving its mark on the body of the guilty, the state establishes that that body is the King's property; the monarch ironically reasserts possession of his dispossessed inversion, the beggar. Nevertheless, it cannot be said that even this innovation had a noticeable effect on the general problem of vagrancy or on the specific phenomenon of the sturdy beggar. Moreover, the inequities in the policy of marking did not go unnoticed: in *Kind-Hartes Dreame* (c. 1592), Henry Chettle observed that 'The Rogue that liveth idly is restrained, the fiddler and player that is masterless is in the same predicament, both these by the law are burned in the ear, and shall men more odious scape unpunished[?]'.[21]

If civil authorities could not distinguish among the vagrants *qua* vagrants they wished to control, they had an even more difficult time in distinguishing some counterfeiting vagrants from the proper citizenry—at least, there were many claims that some vagabonds had mastered the codes of civil society, infiltrating the hierarchy from which they supposedly chose to be excluded. John Awdeley reported in 1561 that some vagabonds 'will go commonly well apparelled, without any weapon, and [...] they will bear the port of right good gentlemen, and some are the more trusted'. Others, he reports, take their place at the very center of London's social world, dressing and acting in such a way that no semiotic analysis can distinguish them from anyone else: 'scarcely a man shall discern, they go so gorgeously, sometime with waiting men, and sometime without. Their trade is to walk in such places, where as gentlemen and other worshipful citizens do resort'.[22] In remarking on those who 'sometime counterfeit the

---

[20] Foucault, *Discipline and Punish*, 108.
[21] Henry Chettle, *Kind-Hartes Dreame (1592)*, ed. G.B. Harrison (London: John Lane, 1923), 18.
[22] John Awdeley, *The Fraternitye of Vacabondes* [1561], in Edward Viles and F.J. Furnivall (eds.), *The Rogues and Vagabonds of Shakspere's Youth* (London: New Shakspere Society, 1880), 7-8.

possession of all sorts of diseases', William Harrison also describes their imitation of other vocations: 'Diverse times in their apparel also they will be like serving men or laborers; oftentimes they can play the mariners, and seek for ships which they never lost'.[23] One Justice of the Peace claimed in 1596 that there were counterfeit vagrants present as spies at 'every assize, sessions, and assembly of Justices' who 'will so clothe themselves for that time as any should deem him to be an honest husbandman'.[24] If marginality itself is understood as a role, if rogues and beggars can choose to become like 'serving men or laborers', 'mariners' or the 'honest husbandman', 'well apparelled', going 'so gorgeously [...] with waiting men', bearing themselves like 'right good gentlemen', then the sturdy beggar may be semiotically indistinguishable from the rest of society, no matter what schemes of punishment and marking the state attempts. The further the sturdy beggar was exiled toward the margins of society, ironically, the greater the threat he or she seemed to pose for the center.

These supposedly remarkable powers of simulation are occasionally borne out by documentary evidence, but for the most part they are fantasies of projection, a downward displacement of a general crisis of the sign. These vagrants thus enact Jean Baudrillard's distinction between dissimulation and simulation: 'To dissimulate', he notes, 'is to feign not to have what one has. To simulate is to feign to have what one hasn't. One implies a presence, the other an absence'. Thus the beggars' feigning of wounds and sores to gain sympathy is an annoying social fact, but dealing with such counterfeiting is primarily a matter of gaining control of the signifying systems: 'Thus', as Baudrillard concludes, 'feigning or dissimulating leaves the reality principle intact: the difference is always clear, it is only masked'. But the beggars' assumption of the clothing, speech, and role of the middling sort represents something far more threatening, since 'simulation threatens the difference between "true" and "false", between "real" and "imaginary"'.[25] The nature of representation itself thus comes under interrogation, and the arbitrariness of the sign is exposed.

The more strenuously civil authorities attempted to control the means and methods of social signification, the more slippage there was. The penal semiotic program undertaken by Tudor authorities was always one of reaction, invariably lagging a step or two behind the quicker wiles of vagrant counterfeitors, and, more generally, lagging far behind overwhelming and at the time inexplicable social and economic forces. Even bodily mutilations were subject to invention and dissimulation. In the case of judicial markings of beggars' bodies, then, the actors themselves either

---

[23] Holinshed, *Holinshed's Chronicles*, vol. 1: 309.
[24] *Tudor Economic Documents*, vol. 2: 345.
[25] Jean Baudrillard, *Simulations* (New York: Semiotext(e), 1983), 5.

refused to cooperate, or re-wrote the scripts altogether, thus demonstrating a sophisticated, ultimately subversive understanding of the cultural codes of punishment. No program of semiotic confinement succeeded, or could succeed, in the English Renaissance.

SIGN, CAUSE OR GENERAL HABIT?
TOWARDS AN 'HISTORICIST ONTOLOGY' OF
CHARACTER ON THE EARLY MODERN STAGE

JAMES R. SIEMON

Employing terms and arguments derived from the work of two thinkers who stand at either end of modern European social analysis—Francis Bacon and Pierre Bourdieu—the essay which follows seeks to define aspects of a semiotics implicit in early modern stage representations of character. Attention will specifically be directed to Shakespeare's highly stylized characterization of King Richard III, which will be considered in the light of recurrent themes in the historical debates between nominalism and realism: causality and ontology, truth conditions and common natures, willed covenants and natural affinities, relations and substances. These themes will be related to Bourdieu's arguments for a social analysis that would transcend nominalist/realist oppositions in describing agency and identity.

E.A. Moody has characterized historical nominalism as the application of logical analysis to philosophical and religious problems with the effect that these problems became questions of 'the meaning and reference of terms and the truth conditions of sentences'.[1] In this broadest of abstract definitions, one might be more or less 'nominalist' depending upon how far one pursued the Ockhamist repudiation of the 'common nature' asserted by realism to inhere in individuals of the same species.[2] Such a

---

[1] See 'Buridan and a Dilemma of Nominalism', in *Harry Austyn Wolfson Jubilee* (Jerusalem: American Academy for Jewish Research, 1965), vol. 2: 577; Moody is cited in William J. Courtenay, *Covenant and Causality in Medieval Thought: Studies in Philosophy, Theology and Economic Practice* (London: Variorum Reprints, 1984), 720. Cf. Moody's 'Ockhamism', in *The Encyclopedia of Philosophy*, ed. Paul Edwards, vol. 5 (New York and London: Macmillan, 1967), 533-4. The present essay is an expanded version of the paper I presented at ISSEI's 1994 Graz Conference (see Preface) which was published, under the same title, in the selected workshop proceedings: *The European Legacy*, 2.2 (1997), 217-22.

[2] See Courtenay, *Covenant and Causality*, 720.

broad, essentializing definition may be usefully sharpened by remarking certain social historical problems addressed by the Ockhamist movement and its linguistic turn. Steven Ozment has defined some of the intertwined religious and socio-political issues at stake in the rise of late medieval nominalism. According to Ozment, nominalism insisted that the relations of man to God and of man to the created world are 'covenantal and not ontological, based on willed agreements and conventions, not on common natures and necessary connections'.[3] The epistemology of historical nominalism, moreover, was '"revolutionary" precisely because it challenged the traditional assumption that only like can know like' and, in place of this assumption, emphasized the key role of contingent verbal relationships in constituting knowledge.[4] The truth of things and relationships, in other words, was not an eternal sameness and difference—the tautological certainty of an eternal 'system'—but lay in 'historical covenants' by which truth and the system of hierarchies and differences dependent upon it had been instituted. As Ozment puts it:

> In the final analysis, words are the connecting link between the mind and reality and between the soul and God. Man must come to grips with the world around him through 'signs voluntarily instituted'; and he must work out his salvation on the basis of 'laws voluntarily and contingently established' by God. In the final analysis, all he has is willed verbal relations.[5]

In such terms one hears anticipations of points that would be repeatedly at issue in early modern contentions about the sacraments, about history, authority, and representation.[6]

No stranger to considerations of representation and authority, Francis Bacon reflects on the perils of realism in his essays concerning the idols that haunt the human condition generally and the late scholastic mind in particular. One essay, 'Of Deformity', addresses an aspect of what might be called—in a dramatic context—character. Accepting the apparent truth

---

[3]See Steven Ozment, 'Mysticism, Nominalism, and Dissent', in Charles Trinkaus and Heiko A. Oberman (eds.), *The Pursuit of Holiness in Late Medieval and Renaissance Religion* (Leiden: Brill, 1974), 78. Cf. William J. Courtenay, 'Covenant and Causality in Pierre d'Ailly', *Speculum*, 46 (1971), 94-119.

[4]Ozment, 'Mysticism, Nominalism, and Dissent', 78.

[5]Ibid., 80.

[6]On these developments in relation to early modern theater generally, see James R. Siemon, *Shakespearean Iconoclasm* (Berkeley, CA: University of California Press, 1985). For an excellent analysis of *Richard III* in terms of the desacralization of the ritual order, see William C. Carroll, '"The Form of Law": Ritual and Succession in *Richard III*', in Linda Woodbridge and Edward Berry (eds.), *'True Rites and Maimed Rites': Ritual and Anti-Ritual in Shakespeare and His Age* (Urbana, IL: University of Illinois Press, 1992), 203-19.

of a well-established tradition of iconic thinking and representation while challenging its explanation of things, Bacon asks the reader to reconsider physical ugliness.[7] He admits physical ugliness to be linked to a state of being, but the essay reasons that this linkage has been misunderstood as a matter of 'necessity' rather than of social history and willed 'election'. Not a signifier inevitably bound to an evil being in the essential unity of a natural 'sign', bodily deformity instead should be considered as a socially determining 'cause' which induces certain specific kinds of elective behavior. Because deformity generally occasions contempt, the deformed person is said by Bacon to have a 'perpetual spur in himself to rescue and deliver himself from scorn'. Whether physical malformation ultimately causes an individual to reason and act virtuously or maliciously, the 'ground' upon which such elective reasoning and action are constructed is the same: 'still the ground is, they will, if they be of spirit, seek to free themselves from scorn; which must be either by virtue or malice'. Furthermore, Bacon goes on to describe a practical politics necessitated by physical deformity. The deformed person is said to be predisposed to be bold and industrious— especially in spying out 'the weakness of others'—and likely to excel in a reasoning capacity which is characterized as highly competitive. At the same time, those with whom the deformed person interacts are said to be, due to the effects of the deformity on their own perceptions, less given to jealousy (if superior in rank to the deformed person) or simply less attentive (if socially equal to the deformed person).

At this point, one could suggest obvious parallels between Bacon's analysis and Shakespeare's treatment of Richard in the opening soliloquy of *Richard III*. Richard details the features of his physical deformity and proclaims it the direct cause for his attitudes and subsequent behavior. Adapting lines from Lyly's *Campaspe* which oppose the activities of love ('soft noise of lyre and lute'; 'delicate tunes and amorous glances') to those of war ('warlike sound of drum and trump'; 'neighing of barbed steeds'), Shakespeare's Richard insists that he is not 'made to court an amorous looking-glass' but 'cheated of feature [...] | Deform'd, unfinish'd'.[8] '[T]herefore', he reasons, 'since [he] cannot prove a lover', he is 'determined to prove a villain' (1.1.1-30). Here, as in Bacon's analysis, physical attributes are treated as causes for, rather than as signs of, character. However, the fact that Richard's villainy is to a degree elective—'determined'

---

[7]Francis Bacon, *Works*, eds. James Spedding et al., vol. 6 (1870; repr. New York: Garrett, 1968), 480-1.

[8]Quotations are taken from the Arden edition of *King Richard III*, ed. Antony Hammond (London and New York: Methuen, 1981). Lyly's *Campaspe* is quoted from John Lyly, *'Campaspe' and 'Sappho and Phao'*, eds. G.K. Hunter and David Bevington (Manchester: Manchester University Press, 1991), 2.2.40-60; cf. 4.3.13-27 and 5.3.19-24.

by personal decision—rather than unavoidably 'determined' by nature or inevitably dictated by the physical circumstances of his embodiment will be clearly suggested by his subsequent demonstration of the capacity to be precisely the lover that his specious reasoning says he can never become.[9] Furthermore, Richard's opening soliloquy proclaims (and he later displays) a mode of villainy that parallels Bacon's practical politics of deformity. Richard will be industrious (renouncing 'idle pleasures' for active villainy), bold (eagerly pursuing 'inductions dangerous' against the highest authorities), and strategically rational ('subtle, false and treacherous'). His initial encounter with his brother Clarence, moreover, might be taken to represent the inattentiveness of a social equal in the presence of the deformed person.

I am not suggesting that Bacon modelled his essay on Shakespeare's representation of Richard. There are two important dimensions in which Shakespeare's play—and Shakespearean drama generally—goes further and also, paradoxically, less far than Bacon in suggesting a 'nominalistic' revision of the linkage between physical deformity and character. These dimensions may be compactly suggested by comparing Bacon's account of the social order and his employment of the term 'general habit' to Shakespeare's treatment of Richard's social environment, and, in turn, placing both in relation to Pierre Bourdieu's notion of habitus.

If nominalism tends to interpret the ontological as the linguistic, the natural as the contingently instituted, then Bacon's remarks might be said to be insufficiently nominalistic on one hand and overly nominalistic on the other. First, it is striking that an analysis which de-naturalizes the assumed, substantial linkage of physical deformity to evil—a traditional linkage common in early modern literary and dramatic representation, as well as in non-aesthetic contexts—should presume a natural uniformity of social formations at all times and places.[10] Thus, whatever its stress on the individual will as determining particular reactions to the stigma of deformity, and whatever its awareness that particular institutions such as court eunuchs are not universal, Bacon's essay assumes that in social and institu-

---

[9]The paradoxes arising from the ambiguous sense of 'determined' here are further explored in the final act of *Julius Caesar*. In a context heavily ironized by the manifest gap between his Roman rhetoric and his actual practice, Brutus discusses the extent to which he is 'determined' by a conscious ideological choice ('the rule of [stoic] philosophy' (5.1.100-1)), even as he exhibits characteristic self-blind vacillation and willfulness that discredit that philosophy in himself.

[10]For non-aesthetic linkage of deformity and evil nature, see Neil Rhodes, *The Elizabethan Grotesque* (London: Routledge & Kegan Paul, 1980), esp. 14. Compare Barnabe Googe, *The Spiritual Husbandrie* (London, 1570), which maintains, 'For sure the outward countenaunce doth declare the inwarde minde' and adds:
For sure these misshapen folkes vnto themselues or other men, Betoken harme, or else a signe of froward witte in them. (66v)

tional contexts as various as King Solomon's family, Aesop's Rome, sixteenth-century Peru, Socratic Athens 'and others', the problems, values, and potential strategies confronting the physically deformed person are the same. Everywhere and always, the deformed are said, above all, to yearn to be 'free' from the threat of 'scorn'. Furthermore, while perhaps inevitably hierarchical in organization, the social matrix Bacon imagines as containing the deformed person is characterized as comprised of changeable positions that offer 'possibilit[ies] for advancement', while spawning 'competitors and emulators'. Surprisingly, the essay does not suggest that any qualification such as possession of land, breeding, ancestry or ready income might have a role in determining who may enter this competition of advancement and emulation. The strategies assumed everywhere useful for self-advancement, moreover, are defined in rather narrow terms as 'spials and [...] whisperer[ing]', 'watch[ing] and observ[ing] the weakness of others'. Bacon's all-purpose human society—hierarchical yet permitting advancement to the bold (who need neither land, wealth, chivalric prowess, nor distinguished lineage to reinforce their boldness nor to enable their entry into the contest itself), competitive in nothing so much as in scorn, and productive of no profit nor product but strategy, spying, and emulation—sounds, as contemporaries realized, rather like the post-feudal, pre-industrial bureaucratic system that evolved under Robert Cecil. The relation between Bacon's essay and the recently deceased Cecil was noted by contemporaries such as John Chamberlain, who observes on 17 December 1612: 'Sir Fraunces Bacon hath set out new essayes, where in a chapter of deformitie the world takes notice that he paints out his late litle cousin to the life'.[11]

But if Bacon the essayist overlooks culture-specific differences of values, behavior, and social organization that Bacon the historian elsewhere recognizes, the essay also puts an interesting qualification on the notion of the 'free' individual consciousness that it otherwise assumes as normative. Bacon does assert a well-established difference between mind and body: 'there is in man an election touching the frame of his mind, and a necessity in the frame of his body'. Yet, in describing how 'all deformed persons are extreme bold', the essay suggests a realm in which the freedom of mental

---

[11] *The Letters of John Chamberlain*, ed. N.E. McClure, vol. 1 (Philadelphia: American Philosophical Society, 1939), 397. Bacon describes Cecil's state organization in a letter of 1616 to King James: '[I]n the time of the Cecils, the father and the son, able men were by design and of purpose suppressed' (see Alan G.R. Smith, *Servant of the Cecils: The Life of Sir Michael Hicks, 1543-1612* (Totowa, NJ: Rowman & Littlefield, 1977), 54). Robert Cecil suffered from curvature of the spine and developed a noticeable hump; he was small enough in stature, furthermore, to be nicknamed 'pigmy' by Queen Elizabeth (see Alan Haynes, *Robert Cecil, Earl of Salisbury, 1563-1612* (London: Peter Owen, 1989), 11-2).

election is less than complete: 'First, [they are bold] as in their own defence, as being exposed to scorn; but in process of time by a general habit'. The deformed person's 'bold' behavior, which is assumed to originate as a specific choice arising from the 'natural' need to resist the inevitable scorn of others, eventually becomes an automatism of 'general' application, regardless of particular situation or occasion. In this notion of the 'general habit', Bacon suggests a way to modify the either-or dilemma posed by a too rigidly opposed nominalism and realism. Habit, after all, not only brings the realms of bodily necessity and mental election, of nature and will, into mutually qualifying interaction with one another within the individual, but it also provides a means for reconceptualizing relations of general and particular in a broader sense. Since it leaves social context undifferentiated, Bacon's essay does not explore this broader potential of his argument. It is precisely this area of investigation that is usefully illuminated by the sociological analysis of Pierre Bourdieu and that is suggestively embodied in the dramatic semiotics represented in Shakespeare's *Richard III*.

Among the most distinctive aspects of Bourdieu's work is its struggle with all sorts of dualistic alternatives. Social analysis has been plagued, Bourdieu argues, with either-or dilemmas that affect virtually every level of enquiry—whether at the macro-level of class analysis or at the micro-level of local interactions among agents and interlocutors.[12] The primary means for overcoming such oppositions appear in his notion of an 'historicist ontology', which would replace such splits as that between individual and society or between subjective and objective with a 'double history' comprised of a bodily component—habitus—and an institutional component—field.[13] That is, Bourdieu argues that human existence ought to be understood in terms of an 'ontological complicity' between enduring, embodied, pre-reflective, socially produced dispositions in behavior and perception (the habitus) and the objectified history of specific institutions and social formations (the field).[14] Together, habitus and field constitute

---

[12]This dimension of Bourdieu's work is discussed in Loic Wacquant and Pierre Bourdieu, *An Introduction to Reflexive Sociology* (Chicago, IL: University of Chicago Press, 1992), 122; cf. the rejection of the 'ritual either/or choice between objectivism and subjectivism in which the social sciences have so far allowed themselves to be trapped' in Pierre Bourdieu, *Outline of a Theory of Practice*, tr. Richard Nice (Cambridge: Cambridge University Press, 1977), 4.

[13]For one statement of many concerning the double history of field and habitus, see Pierre Bourdieu, *In Other Words: Essays Towards a Reflexive Sociology*, tr. Matthew Adamson (Stanford, CA: Stanford University Press, 1990), 190.

[14]Bourdieu's notion of ontological complicity is mentioned in his 'Concluding Remarks' to Craig Calhoun, Edward LiPuma, and Moishe Postone (eds.), *Bourdieu: Critical Perspectives* (Chicago, IL: University of Chicago Press, 1993), esp. 273-4.

the grounds—neither strictly external nor internal—of 'being' as conceived in 'historicist ontology'.[15] Pursuit of an analysis conducted in such terms would neither do away with the nominalist recognition of particular will and contingent truth conditions nor with the realist sense of 'natural' and substantial identities that include more than the individual and his or her situated acts of will. Each notion has its—mutually qualifying and qualified—place in an account which conceives being as *social* being. Thus, in practice, any semiotics arising from such a conceptualization would leave one with neither the immutable stability of the natural sign nor, on the other hand, with merely the occasional and elective signifier. Any signifying practice would be the product of 'the whole social person'— an entity unthinkable apart from the particular historical context provided by 'the social conditions of the production and reproduction of the producers and receivers and of their relationship'.[16]

In *Richard III*, the modes of realist iconism—as chiefly instanced by the emphasis given to the meaning of Richard's various deformities—and nominalist semiotic voluntarism—as exemplified in the self-conscious theatricalism of Richard and others who repeatedly 'counterfeit'—are both contained within the play's representation of a larger matrix of culturally produced schemata that organize action and perception.

The importance I am suggesting for this social-contextual dimension of Shakespeare's play contrasts with emphases that have largely dominated representation and analysis of Richard's reign (and of Shakespeare's play) since the early modern period. The long-standing tendency has been to focus attention on the isolated figure of Richard himself in his two most typical embodiments—either as utterly consistent, natural born villain (the monster born with teeth) or as scheming, hypocritical actor (the smiling, ingratiating Machiavell). So, for example, on the one hand, the editorial commentators who compile one of Shakespeare's sources, *The Mirror for Magistrates*, assume that any and every aspect of the representation of Richard must of necessity reveal a quality of disorder inherent in the historical original: 'Seying than that kyng Rychard never kept measure in any of his doings [...] it were agaynst the *decorum* of his personage, to vse eyther good Meter or order'.[17] Here, the assumed standard is a restrictive, essentialized decorum that demands, quite independently of any particular concrete situation, a characteristic consistency of rough speech and be-

---

[15] Bourdieu writes of 'historicist ontology' in ibid., 273.
[16] Pierre Bourdieu, 'The Economics of Linguistic Exchanges', *Social Science Information*, 16 (1977), 645-68, esp. 650-3.
[17] *The Mirror for Magistrates*, ed. Lily B. Campbell (1938; repr. New York: Barnes & Noble, 1960), 371.

havior from a villain so well-established in his villainy by tradition.[18] Of course, it is exactly such predictable standards and notions of type that are both exploited and significantly challenged by the situational and dialogical dimensions of Shakespearean drama, as well as by early modern theatrical practice generally. On the other hand, a substantial line of interpretation which reaches back to Sir Thomas More's foundational account has stressed Richard's personal autonomy as a conscious, even hyper-conscious, role player—Richard's 'consummate acting', in A.P. Rossiter's phrase.[19] This assessment of Richard, while at least allowing that he may be a skillful individual in his use of seeming rather than a predictable, type-cast embodiment of disorder, simply makes another sort of monster out of Richard.

It may be granted that these two alternative interpretations do limited justice to the terms of self-presentation articulated in the final soliloquy of Shakespeare's Richard. In those last moments, Richard struggles with alternative frameworks in which to evaluate himself:

> What do I fear? Myself? There's none else by;
> Richard loves Richard, that is, I am I.
> Is there a murderer here? No. Yes, I am!
> Then fly. What, from myself? Great reason why,
> Lest I revenge? What, myself upon myself?
> [...]
> I am a villain—yet I lie, I am not!
>
> (5.3.183-92)[20]

Here the terms of identity that conflict with one another are the stage Machiavell's self-love, with its characteristic mixture of self-assertion and gloating pride in strategic deceptiveness, and a more iconic identity that conceives the murderer in the mode of the morality play—that is, as being essentially murderous regardless of situation. True to this type, he even threatens himself with murder when presented with no other victim upon which to exercise his murderousness.

---

[18] This view of decorum is to be contrasted with a prevalent Renaissance view that equated decorum with timeliness itself (cf. James R. Siemon, 'Sporting Kyd', *English Literary Renaissance*, 24 (1994), 553-82).

[19] Rossiter's phrasing is from *Angel With Horns and other Shakespeare Lectures*, ed. Graham Storey (New York: Theatre Arts Books, 1961); Rossiter's famous account describes a paradoxical composition consisting of a 'heavy handed justice' and a central character who is 'an early old masterpiece of the art of rhetorical stage-writing, a monstrous being incredible in any sober, historical scheme of things' (2). The most extreme statement of meta-theatrical interpretation is Thomas F. Van Laan's claim that 'The hero's play-acting forms the only real subject of at least the first three acts' (*Role Playing in Shakespeare* (Toronto: University of Toronto Press, 1978), 72).

[20] I have modified the Arden text here to follow the Folio reading of line 184, which has 'I am I' instead of Q1's 'I and I'.

What either of these alternatives overlooks is the important fact that Richard's victims are not really any more completely taken in by his acting of roles than he himself is in this passage. He may deny to himself as he denies to others the reality of his villainy, but, even as he does in these lines, he, like those who are his victims, sees what he is about: 'yet I lie', he says, recognizing his evil as evil even as he perpetrates it. As Robert C. Jones observes, it is a mistake to overemphasize Richard's success in fooling other characters; many do see through his acting, but still become his victims all the same.[21] Instead of simply relapsing into tautological terms and assuming that Richard equals Richard, the stage character simply replaying (or, at best, strategically modifying) a historical character already determined by inheritance from Sir Thomas More and the *Mirror* traditions; or instead of permitting the impressive meta-theatrical dimension of the play to rivet our fascinated attention on Richard 'himself alone', another question might be asked. What is it about the world that he inhabits and that inhabits him which both enables and limits Richard's corrupt actions?

Here, the 'double history' constituted by the play suggests a kind of answer through its representation of a mode of being that is produced by and also productive of a particular form of society. In this the play looks back to Shakespeare's innovative treatment of the unspoken assumptions underlying *romanitas* in *Titus Andronicus* and forward to the probing examination of the social reflexes of Roman republicanism in *Julius Caesar*. The characters of *Richard III*, as the substitutability of their names and their crimes suggests, are more like one another in perception and behavior than they are distinguished from one another.[22] The signs of such shared 'substantial' identity in spite of individual differences of degree, age, credo, or condition are everywhere apparent, with virtually everyone sharing aspects of Richard's ostensibly individualizing characteristics. Like the gems that bejewel the death's head in Clarence's dream (1.4.30-3), Richard himself not only creeps his way into ever more exalted positions and woos those who surround him, but he also *reflects* their common nature. Thus, resembling him, children and mothers lie and

---

[21]Robert C. Jones, *Engagement with Knavery* (Durham, NC: Duke University Press, 1986), 37. Cf. Donald G. Watson, *Shakespeare's Early History Plays: Politics at Play on the Elizabethan Stage* (Athens, GA: University of Georgia Press, 1990), 109-10.

[22]The epitome of substitution is reached in the famous duelling curses of Margaret and the Duchess of York:

Marg. I had an Edward, till a Richard kill'd him;
　　　I had a husband, till a Richard kill'd him:
　　　Thou hadst an Edward, till a Richard kill'd him;
　　　Thou hadst a Richard, till a Richard kill'd him.
Duch. I had a Richard too, and thou didst kill him:
　　　I had a Rutland too: thou holp'st to kill him. (4.4.40-5)

contend for mastery and revenge, victims struggle for status distinctions, clerics dissemble and equivocate, underlings strategically (mis)interpret their own crimes, and all displace responsibility for their actions onto others. Such phenomena are so widespread in the play that they might be interpreted as being naturally human rather than culturally specific—i.e. the propensity of what Hastings calls 'mortal men' (3.4.96). But this universalizing interpretation can be balanced by the Scrivener's nominalist formulation of the specific discursive conditions under which he and the others all suffer: 'Bad is the world', he observes, *when* corrupt power dictates that recognized wrong cannot be openly denounced—'When such ill-dealing must be seen in thought' (3.6.13-4). However, even though he speaks from the privileged position of choric observer, the Scrivener's assessment of the situation should not be taken as definitive because his claim that no one is so 'bold' as to speak out is belied by the play's abundant bold speech. Characters do see and do denounce evil—*in others*.

The classic instance of this general habit of displacement and its attendant semiotic appears in Margaret's lengthy evocation of everyone who surrounds her as merely signs, indexes, flags, dreams, flourishes—insubstantial refractions of a genuine being that she alone and always embodies and defines: 'The presentation of but what I was; | [...] | A sign of dignity; a breath, a bubble' (4.4.84-90). The egocentrism that defines the limits of any claim to 'justice' (4.4.105) pronounced on the basis of such a perspective is revealed by the fact that equivalent semiotic reflexes appear virtually everywhere and in almost everyone as instances of automatic, habitual symbolic violence rather than as credible testimony to the truth of things. So, for instance, although King Edward's attempts to bring everyone to Christian reconciliation might seem the exact opposite of Margaret's typical vindictiveness, his calls for divine 'justice', like hers, are accompanied by projections of his own guilt onto others. 'Who sued to me for him?' Edward demands of his courtiers, grotesquely blaming those who surround him for failing to remind him how much he owed his brother Clarence whom he has had killed (2.1.103-35). In other words, the character whose position as monarch gives him the best claim available on the Elizabethan stage to something resembling free agency proclaims himself a victim of compulsion by others.[23] A similarly surprising example of this sort of category violation occurs when the youthful victim of Richard's designs, the Duke of York, is made to resemble the consummate villain, his uncle Richard, while exhibiting something of the same reflex that marks Edward's displacements of his personal agency onto others. Employing terms that are remarkably close to those which Bacon uses to

---

[23]For an extremely insightful analysis of the monarch as agent, even in self-destruction, see Franco Moretti's chapter on Renaissance tragedy in *Signs Taken for Wonders*, tr. Susan Fischer, David Forgacs, and David Miller (London: NLB, 1983).

characterize the deformed person, Buckingham describes the 'bold, quick, ingenious' child and his impressive ability to heap gratuitous 'scorn' on Richard while seeming, through his acts of equivocation, to claim innocence for himself and to deny himself any personal agency in or responsibility for the verbal thrusts of his 'sharp-provided wit' (3.1.132-5). That this is a general habit in the child rather than his response to a specific situation of utterance is suggested by the fact that the same epithet —'a parlous boy'—is used to characterize both his conversation with his grandmother and his exchanges with Richard (2.4.35; 3.1.154), while similar forms of aggression, lying, and evasiveness mark his performance in both instances (see 2.4.32-5). A similarly striking instance of violated category expectations in matters of 'character' occurs when the otherwise pitiful orphans of Clarence deny pity to their adult relations, the bereaved Duchess of York and Queen Elizabeth, and offer in its place a brutally frank competition for distinction in having attained the highest degree of suffering (2.2). The unity that binds these characters together is a milieu that embraces them all; within it they exhibit similar behaviors—even when their practices and pursuits appear incapable of doing them any recognizable benefit.[24]

It may be true that Richard's distinctive bodily deformity is frequently treated by the play as a natural 'sign' of an innate, substantial being. And, it may also be true that, however perfunctorily, his appearance is often suggested as a particular 'cause' for his villainous perceptions and actions. But the larger context created by the nearly universal distribution of similar attitudes and practices argues that his mode of being is more like a 'general habit'. Of course, 'general' here means not only typical of Richard himself as an individual, but spread about among the whole body of his stage contemporaries. The play suggests that tyrant and courtly subjects inhabit a dynamic system which in-habits them—all shaped by and shaping the same 'double history'. The semiotic implications of this dramaturgy that threatens to make a mockery of such otherwise crucially distinct categories as Christian monarch and brutal tyrant, innocent child and hardened villain, professing Christian and bloody revenger, remain to be developed. Whether or not Shakespeare could be justifiably characterized as a 'political scientist' in writing *Richard III*, the possibility that what he does could in part be described as historical sociology deserves further consideration.[25]

---

[24]Here there is a resemblance to Marlowe's dramaturgy in *Tamburlaine* and *Jew of Malta* in that Marlowe's characters are shown to pursue behaviors—respectively boasting self-assertion and self-conscious 'politic' scheming—that take on a life of their own, spreading over the action and through the cast in ways that outrun their motivation by particular circumstances.

[25]Antony Hammond maintains (against Irving Ribner and Lily Campbell) that Shakespeare is no 'political scientist', and that in practice 'Shakespeare universalizes

True, this play, like *Richard II*, is short on non-aristocratic characters by which to gauge the precise social measure or borders of the phenomena Shakespeare represents. There's no Cade here as there had been in *2 Henry VI*, no Thump and Horner, nor any tavern world resembling that of the later Henriad to mock and reflect upon the values, epistemology, and behavior of the aristocratic characters. But what we do see in *Richard III* suggests that there may be some salient differences between the characters associated with the courtly milieu and some of those, like the Citizens, the Murderers, and the Scrivener, who approach that world from outside. At the very least, one may notice how the Citizens are surprisingly differentiated. If the courtiers often sound more alike than different despite their claims to ontological distinction by family and position, the Citizens of 2.3. are compactly differentiated: One is vaguely optimistic (offering, most tellingly, 'all will be well'); Two is filled with general, but largely undefined foreboding ('I fear, I fear, 'twill prove a giddy world.'); and Three is a very precise analyst of history, current events, and future likelihood. But what is truly striking about Citizen Three is not merely his ability precisely to differentiate past conditions from present circumstances, nor his capacity to assess the various degrees of 'emulation', 'danger', and 'haught' pride in each of the aristocratic contenders for ascendancy—including the hypocritical Richard—who threaten to render the realm 'sickly', but his mixture, unusual for this play, of clear-sighted analysis with a measured degree of self-accusation that is free of self-pity: 'All may be well; but if God sort it so | 'Tis more than we deserve, or I expect' (2.3.36-7). Unlike the courtly figures, he comes to this insight neither upon the moment of his own impending personal destruction nor with self-serving protestations upon his tongue (contrast Clarence on being the 'innocent' victim of King Edward's ingratitude (1.4.66-8; 170), or Rivers on his own status as 'guiltless' victim, 'unjustly' doomed (3.3.14; 23)).

As the non-aristocratic characters appear to be involved with the court, however, any capacity for clear vision is compromised according to a principle articulated by Brakenbury. When he is called upon to take steps

---

the historical detail' (*King Richard III*, 75), finding 'in the events of history and their interpretation a way of representing dynamic human conflict' (ibid., 119). I would suggest that there is a difference between Shakespeare's generalizing of detail to fit a particular context (i.e. the aristocratic (pre-Tudor?) court) and 'universalizing' to evoke a 'human' context (such an opposition would apply as well to views such as Kott's evocation of Richard in the context of the deterministic 'grand mechanism' of state power in *Shakespeare Our Contemporary*, tr. Boleslaw Taborski (Garden City, NY: Anchor Books, 1966)). As Barbara Hodgdon points out, such critical approaches can easily 'produce history as an endless recycling of the same narratives, though with changed players' (*The End Crowns All: Closure and Contradiction in Shakespeare's History* (Princeton, NJ: Princeton University Press, 1991), 79).

that will facilitate the murder of Clarence, Brakenbury chooses not to interpret the moral choice that confronts him, averting his gaze from his own complicity with the observation: 'I will not reason what is meant hereby, I Because I will be guiltless from the meaning' (1.4.93-4). Here, on the fringes of the courtly world, we witness a character's decision to choose blindness, but in this deliberate individual election there are detectable elements of the more automatic, largely habitual, socio-pathology discernible in those who surround Richard more nearly.

This line of enquiry makes the case of the murderers particularly interesting. Unlike the clerical aristocrat, the Cardinal, whose express convictions about the 'deep [...] sin' of violating 'blessed sanctuary' are simply and instantly overridden by reflexes that dictate deference to his social superiors (3.1.43), the play's vulgar murderers have a great deal of difficulty violating their own consciences, despite the orders of their king.[26] This makes for comedy in the case of the two would-be killers who waver back and forth before prosecuting Clarence's murder; but it also produces lyrical pathos in Tyrrel's description of the agonies that vex the guilt-stricken slaughterers of the young princes:

> Dighton and Forrest, who I did suborn
> To do this piece of ruthless butchery—
> Albeit they were flesh'd villains, bloody dogs—
> Melted with tenderness and mild compassion,
> Wept like two children, in their deaths' sad story.
> (4.3.4-8)

The fact that two such professional 'villain[s]' are said to have 'almost chang'd [their] mind' and to have been rendered speechless by 'conscience and remorse' (4.3.15; 20) that keep them from claiming their promised reward offers sharp contrast to the cruel insensitivity that characterizes the resolutely self-interested and overwhelmingly articulate world of the court. 'Bloody dogs' confronted by the horror of their own deeds can change enough to melt with tenderness, even coming to resemble their victims in experiencing a sympathy that provokes them to weep 'like two children'. If such uncharacteristic behavior suggests the possibility of radically beneficent transformation in character among the vulgar, then what is being implied about an aristocratic world that is routinely complicitous with a serial murderer who enlists general help under transparent pretenses of being a lover, a true friend, or 'a child, [to] go by thy direc-

---

[26]Here I differ from Richard Wheeler, who emphasizes the similarity of the murderers to Richard in their choice to violate 'internal restraint' rather than the great difference between them in the murderers' extended struggles of conscience ('History, Character and Conscience in *Richard III*', *Comparative Drama*, 5 (1972), 301-21, esp. 317).

tion' (2.2.153)? Or, even more tellingly, what is being said about a social order that reproduces itself by producing children who can boldly scorn the grief of their own family members with 'Our fatherless distress was left unmoan'd: I Your widow-dolour likewise be unwept' (2.2.64-5)?[27]

---

[27]The burden of this argument is in direct contrast to claims such as that by David Haley, *Shakespeare's Courtly Mirror: Reflexivity and Prudence in 'All's Well That Ends Well'* (Newark, DE: University of Delaware Press, 1993), which maintains that Shakespeare ordinarily 'presents [a] normative, aristocratic society without examining its ideological basis' (26).

DON QUIXOTE, HAMLET, FOUCAULT—
LANGUAGE, 'LITERATURE', AND THE LOSSES OF ANALOGISM

ANDREAS MAHLER

The Renaissance has quite adequately been termed an 'analogical yet transitional age',[1] an in-between 'early modern', or rather pre-modern, epoch still clinging to concepts like analogism, providence, authority yet witnessing their unrelenting disordering and final breakdown;[2] World and Word dissolved into worlds and words[3] and a predominantly realist *episteme* slowly disintegrated under the impact of an emergent nominalist critique.[4] One of the most influential reformulations of the premodern analogical world-view in recent times has been Michel Foucault's semiologically oriented account of a Renaissance *episteme* in his historical archaeology *Les mots et les choses*.[5] I will begin by giving a brief outline of Foucault's

---

[1]W.R. Elton, 'Shakespeare and the thought of his age', in *The Cambridge Companion to Shakespeare Studies*, ed. Stanley Wells (Cambridge: Cambridge University Press, 1986), 17-34, quote: 32.

[2]For a concise description of the Renaissance as an epoch of multiple 'crises', theological, philosophical, epistemological and semiological, see ibid., 24ff.

[3]For a view of early modern European culture as 'the site of the battle of signs which is the Reformation', see Kurt Tetzeli von Rosador, 'The Sacralizing Sign: Religion and Magic in Bale, Greene, and the Early Shakespeare', *Yearbook of English Studies*, 23 (1993). 30-45, quote: 30; for a discussion of early modern semiotic pluralization and rivalry, with special reference to Marlowe, see also Hugo Keiper, 'Ikarus im Labyrinth der Zeichen: Überlegungen zu einer Neuinterpretation des A-Textes von Marlowes *Doctor Faustus*', in Peter Csobádi et al. (eds.), *Europäische Mythen der Neuzeit: Faust und Don Juan*, 2 vols. (Wort und Musik, 18) (Anif/Salzburg: Verlag Müller-Speiser, 1993), vol. 2: 373-96.

[4]See Michael Randall, 'Reversed Analogy in Jean Molinet's *Chappelet des Dames*', in Richard J. Utz (ed.), *Literary Nominalism and the Theory of Rereading Late Medieval Texts: A New Research Paradigm* (Lewiston, NY: Edwin Mellen Press, 1995), 81-100.

[5]All quotes are to Michel Foucault, *Les mots et les choses: Une Archéologie des sciences humaines* (coll. tel, 166) (1966; repr. Paris: Editions Gallimard, 1992) (abbreviation used: *MC*).

version of a Renaissance semiotics and modify it by taking into closer account the roles of subject and language in the early modern acquisition of 'truth'; I will then illustrate the epistemological function of language by giving a non-literary example before I go on to discuss the literary thematization of its disintegration and loss in Cervantes' *Don Quixote* and Shakespeare's *Hamlet*.

I

Let me begin with Foucault. In the chapter significantly entitled 'La prose du monde', Foucault describes the *episteme* of the Renaissance as one predominantly grounded in analogies.[6]

> Jusqu'à la fin du XVIe siècle, la ressemblance a joué un rôle bâtisseur dans le savoir de la culture occidentale. C'est elle qui a conduit pour une grande part l'exégèse et l'interprétation des textes; c'est elle qui a organisé le jeu des symboles, permis la connaissance des choses visibles et invisibles, guidé l'art de les représenter. (*MC*, 32)

Renaissance thought ordered the world in terms of relations of resemblance, and resemblance itself was the guiding principle for the acquisition of knowledge.[7] In order to find 'truth', one would have to 'read' the world and, by establishing links of analogy and sympathy, interpret it.[8] For this, Foucault adds, it is of course necessary to know, or at least suspect, that such an order exists; it has to be signalized:

> Il faut que les similitudes enfouies soient signalées à la surface des choses; il est besoin d'une marque visible des analogies invisibles. [...] Il n'y a pas de ressemblance sans signature. (*MC*, 41)

---

[6]Foucault was, of course, not the first one to do so; for classical accounts of analogism and the function of similitude in medieval thought, see C.S. Lewis, *The Discarded Image: An Introduction to Medieval and Renaissance Literature* (1964; repr. Cambridge: Cambridge University Press, 1988), esp. 92ff.; E.M.W. Tillyard, *The Elizabethan World Picture* (1943; repr. Harmondsworth: Penguin, 1978), esp. 91ff.; Friedrich Ohly, 'Vom geistigen Sinn des Wortes im Mittelalter' [1958], in *Schriften zur mittelalterlichen Bedeutungsforschung* (Darmstadt: Wissenschaftliche Buchgesellschaft, 1977), 1-31, esp. 12ff.; for the more general background, see Arthur O. Lovejoy, *The Great Chain of Being: A Study of the History of an Idea* (1936; repr. Cambridge, MA: Harvard University Press, 1964). The main difference between these and Foucault, however, lies in the latter's epistemic approach.

[7]For a brief description of Foucault's view of the Renaissance, see also Gary Gutting, *Michel Foucault's Archaeology of Scientific Reason* (Modern European Philosophy) (Cambridge: Cambridge University Press, 1989), 140ff.

[8]For the cognitive metaphor of 'reading' the world as book, see also Hans Blumenberg, *Die Lesbarkeit der Welt* (stw, 592) (Frankfurt a.M.: Suhrkamp, 1986); for its medieval and Renaissance variants, see esp. 47ff.

The play of resemblances is thus twofold; it is substantial in the sense that the things of the world are related to each other in secret alliances, and it is functional in the sense that it gives hints 'on the surface' as to how these secret alliances can be discovered. That way, the semiological instrument of hinting at resemblances provides the clue to the hermeneutics of a world miraculously put together in endless mirrorings, analogies and sympathies by the Creator himself.

> Appelons herméneutique l'ensemble des connaissances et des techniques qui permettent de faire parler les signes et de découvrir leur sens; appelons sémiologie l'ensemble des connaissances et des techniques qui permettent de distinguer où sont les signes, de définir ce qui les institue comme signes, de connaître leurs liens et les lois de leur enchaînement: le XVIe siècle a superposé sémiologie et herméneutique dans la forme de la similitude. (*MC*, 44)

Resemblances, signatures and similitude form a model of Renaissance semiotics that can be called ternary; it is thus distinct from the binary model of arbitrary relation between signifier and signified that we have become used to from the classical period onwards.[9]

> Depuis le stoïcisme, le système des signes dans le monde occidental avait été ternaire, puisqu'on y reconnaissait le signifiant, le signifié et la 'conjoncture' [...]. A partir du XVIIe siècle, en revanche, la disposition deviendra binaire, puisqu'on la définira, avec Port-Royal, par la liaison d'un signifiant et d'un signifié. (*MC*, 57)[10]

This redefinition reduces the sign from an epistemological instrument of 'finding' truth to a mere ancillary instrument of 'representing' it; instead of indicating the path to truth and endlessly corroborating this truth, the sign is merely used to show a truth found elsewhere. Foucault suggests that this shift from a ternary conception of the sign as motivated essence to a binary

---

[9] For a more strictly linguistic account of medieval and Renaissance attitudes to language, see Roy Harris and Talbot J. Taylor, *Landmarks in Linguistic Thought: The Western Tradition from Socrates to Saussure* (London and New York: Routledge, 1989), esp. 75ff., and Robert Henry Robins, *A Short History of Linguistics* (London and New York: Longman, 3rd ed. 1990), 75ff.

[10] For a cogent critique of the largely unquestioned dualism inherent in the Western conception of words as 'signs' referring to something else, see Richard Waswo, *Language and Meaning in the Renaissance* (Princeton, NJ: Princeton University Press, 1987), 3ff.; observing that 'some very grave doubts about this model [...] became articulate and widely diffused in the culture of the fifteenth and sixteenth centuries' (5), Waswo describes a Renaissance shift 'from referential to relational semantics [...]: from the "model of the garment" (the cosmetic view) to "the model of the melody" (the constitutive view)' (60; the quotes within the quote are to Max Black).

model of arbitrariness can roughly be fixed at about 1600; this is the moment when the age of transparency begins:

> Dès lors, le texte cesse de faire partie des signes et des formes de la vérité; le langage n'est plus une des figures du monde, ni la signature imposée aux choses depuis le fond des temps. La vérité trouve sa manifestation et son signe dans la perception évidente et distincte. Il appartient aux mots de la traduire s'ils le peuvent; ils n'ont plus droit à en être la marque. Le langage se retire du milieu des êtres pour entrer dans son âge de transparence et de neutralité. (*MC*, 70)

II

Foucault's account of the Renaissance *episteme* has come in for criticism from various sides:[11]

1. Foucault's main interest lies in the era of Representation and he only uses the Renaissance as a kind of prelude or foil, which results in a reductionist and selective treatment of sources.[12]

2. His concept of the Renaissance is too monolithic as to explain the heterogeneity and pluralism of the epoch as an epoch of transition; what is more, there are no clear dividing lines between the *epistemai* of the Renaissance and/or the Middle Ages and/or Antiquity.[13]

3. Foucault falls prey to the anonymizationist tendencies of early structuralism—his basic model being a pre-pragmatic *langue/parole*-model within whose frame he is mainly concerned with *langue*—and, consequently, he does not take into account the role of the early modern subject as a subject of appropriation.[14]

---

[11] For the sake of brevity, I sum up the main points of criticism only; for a discussion in more detail, see the literature referred to in the notes.

[12] Waswo, *Language and Meaning in the Renaissance*, 69.

[13] Klaus W. Hempfer, 'Probleme traditioneller Bestimmungen des Renaissancebegriffs und die epistemologische "Wende"', in Klaus W. Hempfer (ed.), *Renaissance—Diskursstrukturen und epistemologische Voraussetzungen* (Text und Kontext, 10) (Stuttgart: Franz Steiner, 1993), 9-45, esp. 24ff.; Gerhard Regn, 'Mimesis und Episteme der Ähnlichkeit in der Poetik der italienischen Spätrenaissance', in Hempfer (ed.), *Renaissance—Diskursstrukturen*, 133-45, here 136ff., esp. 138. For a highly suggestive differentiation of the analogist *episteme* into four sub-periods—constitution in late antiquity, absolutist institutionalization in scholasticism, nominalist disintegration in the Renaissance, substantial loss in mannerism—see Joachim Küpper, *Diskurs-Renovatio bei Lope de Vega und Calderón: Untersuchungen zum spanischen Barockdrama. Mit einer Skizze zur Evolution der Diskurse in Mittelalter, Renaissance und Manierismus* (Romanica Monacensia, 32) (Tübingen: Narr, 1990), 18ff., and in more detail 230ff.

[14] Regn, 'Mimesis und Episteme der Ähnlichkeit', 137, note 16; Stephan Otto, *Das Wissen des Ähnlichen: Michel Foucault und die Renaissance* (Frankfurt a.M. et al.: Lang, 1992), 26, 63ff., and passim.

4. The underlying historical model concentrates too much on the aspect of discontinuity, neglecting undeniable processes of assimilation and accommodation.[15]

5. In his project of writing about the order of 'things', Foucault's description of Renaissance semiotics as a ternary model is largely based on 'things' that serve as 'signs', which results in an onto-semantic bias that does not do full justice to early modern linguistic practices.[16]

6. His interest in the anonymous framework of a Renaissance *episteme* causes him to neglect the dialectical nature of a linguistically guided, *topos*-oriented early modern epistemology which finds 'truth' by systematically investigating things *and* words (*res et verba*).[17]

I want to concentrate on the last two points of critique. At one point in his book, Foucault explicitly states:

> Le monde est couvert de signes qu'il faut déchiffrer, et ces signes, qui révèlent des ressemblances et des affinités, ne sont eux-mêmes que des formes de la similitude. Connaître sera donc interpréter: aller de la marque visible à ce qui se dit à travers elle, et demeurerait sans elle, parole muette, ensommeillé dans les choses. (*MC*, 47)

The main hermeneutic activity is thus to detect the semiological marks visibly imprinted on things and to relate them to similar things elsewhere. Foucault's examples illustrate this quite clearly; 'read' properly, the aconite signalizes its usefulness for the treatment of diseases of the eye by the affinity of the outward shape of its seeds with an eye covered by an eyelid, and the walnut indicates that it can be used to treat diseases of the skull or brain by its outward and inward forms (*MC*, 42).[18] The fruit of the walnut is thus a 'sign' for the brain, just as much as the aconite 'means' eye, and the structure of this kind of onto-semantics is ternary in the sense that the similitude between signifier and signified guarantees that the aconite is the signifier for the signified 'eye'. Foucault then takes this reading of 'la prose du monde' one step further by treating language in

---

[15] See Andreas Mahler, 'Jahrhundertwende, Epochenschwelle, epistemischer Bruch? England um 1600 und das Problem überkommener Epochenbegriffe', in Klaus Garber (ed.), *Europäische Barock-Rezeption*, 2 vols. (Wolfenbütteler Arbeiten zur Barockforschung, 20) (Wiesbaden: Harrassowitz, 1991), vol. 2: 995-1026.

[16] Otto, *Das Wissen des Ähnlichen*, 87ff.; see also Waswo, *Language and Meaning in the Renaissance*, 69ff.

[17] Otto, *Das Wissen des Ähnlichen*, 67ff., esp. 80ff.

[18] For a list of similar examples, more adequately taking into account the 'names' of 'things', see also Umberto Eco, *Kunst und Schönheit im Mittelalter*, tr. Günter Memmert (1991; repr. Munich: dtv, 1993), 209ff.; this chapter has not been included in the English version of the book, *Art and Beauty in the Middle Ages*, tr. Hugh Bredin (New Haven, CT, and London: Yale University Press, 1986).

exactly the same way. Words are meaningful because they are things that can be treated as signs.

> Dans son être brut et historique du XVIe siècle, le langage n'est pas un système arbitraire; il est déposé dans le monde et il en fait partie à la fois parce que les choses elles-mêmes cachent et manifestent leur énigme comme un langage, et parce que les mots se proposent aux hommes comme des choses à déchiffrer. [...] Le langage [...] doit être étudié lui-même comme une chose de nature. (*MC*, 49-50)

The problem with language, however, is that it is in disorder. After Babel, the similitude between signifier and signified has been lost, and it is only in some languages, such as Hebrew, that it can still be guessed. The verb '*hasas*', for example, which means 'rise', shows a marked affinity to the noun '*sus*', which means 'horse', and this similitude in the signifiers reveals the hidden affinities in the signifieds (*MC*, 51).[19]

Foucault's outline of a Renaissance semiotics has mainly been criticized precisely for this reductionist concentration on the semantics of things.[20] In discussing Foucault's account of the 'être brut et historique' of sixteenth-century language, Claude-Gilbert Dubois has called back into mind that, in the Biblical tradition, it is the Word that gives life to things by naming them; he concedes:

> Le langage est chose certes, mais il est aussi forme, au sens aristotélicien du terme, et comme tel participe activement à la mise en sens de l'univers. La réification des faits de langue [...] ne peut occulter le caractère fondateur de la Parole. [...] C'est le verbe de Dieu qui a crée les choses, qui les arrache par leur dénomination à leur inertie matérielle.[21]

But even though the original language, the Word of God, has been lost, there is still hope. Following the Judaeo-Christian scheme of original purity, fall and redemption, which consequently also applies to language, there is always hope for its rediscovery, and this justifies epistemological work with language.[22] The early modern concentration on the material side

---

[19] The reference is to Claude Duret.

[20] Foucault thus seems himself to fall prey to the dualist fallacy of a purely referential semantics; see again Waswo, *Language and Meaning in the Renaissance*, 3ff.

[21] Claude-Gilbert Dubois, *L'imaginaire de la Renaissance* (Paris: Presses Universitaires de France, 1985), 49.

[22] Ibid., 52; for the traditions of Cratylism, see Gérard Genette, *Mimologiques: Voyage en Cratylie* (coll. Poétique) (Paris: Editions du Seuil, 1976); for a detailed account of the idea of a perfect language, see Umberto Eco, *The Search for the Perfect Language*, tr. James Fentress (Oxford and Cambridge, MA: Blackwell, 1995), for the role of Hebrew and an account of the early modern *furor etymologicus*, see 73ff.

of language and its relations of analogy can thus be seen as an expression of the attempt to pursue traces and fragments of the 'promised language' in order to reconstruct it.[23] What is more, it is also a path to 'truth'.

In his long reply to Foucault's sketch of the Renaissance role of language, Stephan Otto has pointed out that words, not things, constitute the decisive hinge in Renaissance epistemology. Referring among others to Lorenzo Valla and Rudolph Agricola, he makes it quite clear that one of the basic humanist assumptions was to consider language the most important instrument in the acquisition of knowledge.[24] The early modern formula of '*res et verba*' thus indicates that in order to understand a thing one has to analyse the word attributed to it, and that it is only by realizing the difference between word and thing that one becomes aware of the thing itself: 'Allein durch Sprache wird Seiendes für den Menschen *wirklich*.'[25] The early modern path to truth leads through language, and the task of linguistic theory and rhetoric is to show how. Rudolph Agricola's *De inventione dialectica* (about 1480)[26] does precisely this; it offers a catalogue of *topoi*,[27] with the help of which it becomes possible to discover the nature of a thing (*res*) by systematically going through the corresponding word (*verbum*) and its affinities. This means that language is understood as a dialectical instrument of cognition; it is not an enigmatic part of an anonymous *episteme*, rather it is the central epistemological instrument for the early modern subject to find truth.

---

[23]Dubois, *L'imaginaire de la Renaissance*, 50-1: '[L]a réification du langage, qui s'établit chez les théoriciens du XVIᵉ siècle, renvoie à ce qu'on appellerait aujourd'hui sa *matérialité*.—'Le discours par analogies [...] était considéré au XVIᵉ siècle comme un type de raisonnement valide et conforme à l'ordre de réalité.' (54)

[24]Otto, *Das Wissen des Ähnlichen*, 79ff.; see also, without explicit reference to Foucault, Stephan Otto, *Renaissance und frühe Neuzeit* (Geschichte der Philosophie in Text und Darstellung, 3) (Stuttgart: Reclam, 1984), 108: 'mit der Formel "Wort und Sache" (*res et verbum*) [geht es] um die humanistische These, daß Seiendes dem Menschen nie bloß begrifflich, sondern erst mittels der Sprache zugänglich ist'.

[25]Otto, *Renaissance und frühe Neuzeit*, 112.

[26]Rodolphus Agricola, *De inventione dialectica libri III* (Cologne, 1523; repr. Frankfurt a.M.: Minerva, 1967). As Stephan Otto points out, this book can be regarded as an early modern 'bestseller'; it obtained up to sixty reprints in the Renaissance and soon became one of the rhetorical standard texts in the universities of Cambridge and Paris (see Otto, *Renaissance und frühe Neuzeit*, 126-7).

[27]For a list of all possible *topoi*, see Agricola, *De inventione dialectica*, 25; one of these *topoi* is similitude, which manages to establish a metaphorical link between two things, thus making them comparable (ibid., 142ff.). Consequently, their resemblance is not in the things themselves, but found through, and thematized by, language; see Otto, *Das Wissen des Ähnlichen*, 90.

III

In order to illustrate the early modern shift from regarding language as an epistemological instrument to using it as a quasi-transparent means of representation, I choose to take up an example which I have discussed in more detail elsewhere; it is the word and thing 'satire', and I will concentrate on a brief comparison of Drant's and Dryden's respective attempts to define it.[28]

In 1566, Thomas Drant published a translation of *Horace: His Arte of Poetrie, Pistles and Satyrs Englished*.[29] In the humanist project of appropriating new genres, this is one of the first English renderings of Roman satire and, as a consequence, Drant wants his readers to know what they should expect. He therefore adds a prefatory poem—'*Priscus Grammaticus de Satyra*'[30]—in which he tries to explain what the thing 'satire' is. In order to do this, he first of all concentrates on the word 'satire' and its possible analogies (1-24), before he goes on to corroborate his findings with reference to the authority of the Roman satirists themselves (25-30). His approach is thus topically organized inasmuch as he begins with the signifier of the word designating the thing to be analyzed, and makes use of the topos of similitude in order to transfer metaphorically meaning from similar phenomena to the phenomenon he is interested in. Since the signifier 'satire' is similar to the Persian word '*satr*', to the word for the satyr of the woods, to the word of the planet Saturn and to the Latin '*satur*', it becomes possible to extract from each similitude a portion of truth which adds up to the idea of what the thing 'satire' could be.[31]

Drant begins with the word '*satr*':

> A *Satyre* is a tarte, and carping kinde of verse,
>   An instrument to pynche the prankes of men,
> And for as much as pynching instrumentes do perce,
>   Yclept it was full well a Satyre then.
> A name of Arabic to it they gaue:
> For Satyre there doth signifye a glaue[.]
>
>   (1-6)

---

[28] See Andreas Mahler, *Moderne Satireforschung und elisabethanische Verssatire: Texttheorie, Epistemologie, Gattungsgeschichte* (Texte und Untersuchungen zur Englischen Philologie, 16) (Munich: Fink, 1992), 111ff.

[29] Thomas Drant, *Horace: His Arte of Poetrie, Pistles and Satyrs Englished*, ed. Peter E. Medine (Delmar, NY: Scholars' Facsimiles & Reprints, 1972); see also Marie Claire Randolph, 'Thomas Drant's Definition of Satire, 1566', *Notes and Queries*, 180 (1941), 416-8.

[30] Drant, *Horace*, 139; in my quotes, I have changed the long 's'.

[31] Drant thus follows the traces of (pseudo-)etymological similitude; see also Ernst Robert Curtius, 'Etymologie als Denkform', in *Europäische Literatur und lateinisches Mittelalter* (1948; Berne and Munich: Francke, 10th ed. 1984), 486-90.

A 'glaive', i.e. a sword, is very clearly an 'instrument to pinch'; the analogy between the signifiers '*satyre*' and '*satr*' not only reveals an important semantic trait of the thing to be explained, but also reaffirms the rightness of the chosen epistemological path thematized in the poem itself: 'Yclept it was full well a Satyre then'.

The next analogy that similitude enables us to see is based on the resemblance between '*satyre*' and the heathenish woodland deity:

> Or *Satyra*, of *Satyrus*, the mossye rude,
>   Unciuile god: for those that will them write,
> With taunting girds, & glikes, & gibes must vexe the lewde,
>   Strayne curtesy, ne recke of mortall spite.
>   Shrowded in mosse, not shrynkinge for a shower,
>   Deming of mosse as of a regall bower.
>   (7-12)

From the analogy to '*Satyr*', Drant manages to derive semantic elements such as rudeness, plainness, love of truth and lack of fear, which he then tries to use pragmatically for the conception of a satiric speaker eager to 'vexe the lewde'.

Drant's third analogy integrates a cosmological correspondence:

> Satyre of writhled waspyshe Saturne may be namde,
>   The Satyrist must be a waspe in moode,
> Testie, and wrothe with vice and hers, to see both blamde,
>   But courteous and frendly to the good,
>   As Saturne cuttes of tyme with equall sythe:
>   So this man cuttes down synne to coy, and blythe.
>   (13-8)

The resemblances between '*satyre*' and '*Saturne*' are manifold: first, he who is under the influence of Saturn tends to be moody and lightly irritated; second, in Elizabethan medical theory, Saturn is linked with the black choler, and hence responsible for the fits of melancholy a satirist from time to time falls prey to; third, the festivities held in the name of Saturn, the Saturnalia, constituted the institutionalized place for satire; and fourth, in his work for justice, the satirist proves to be as inexorable as Saturn, whose traits link him to Kronos/Chronos and thus to inexorable time.

Drant's last analogy finds the idea of *varietas* in the sense that the satirist himself must be well versed and skillful, otherwise no one will listen to him:

> Or *Satyr* of *Satur*, th'authors must be ful
>   Of frostred arte, infarst in balladse brest.
> To teach the worldlings wyt, whose witched braines are dul
>   The worst wyll pardie hearken to the best.
>   If that the Poet be not learnde in deede,
>   Muche may the [sic!] chatte, but fewe wyll marke his reede.
>   (19-24)

What Drant does in his introductory poem, then, is to go through possible analogies linked to the word '*satyre*' in order to find signifieds that can be truthfully attributed to the thing 'satire'. The satire is like a sword; this is why it is pungent. It is like the Satyr of the woods; this is why it is rude and humorous. It is like Saturn; this is why it is melancholic and irritable. It is like a hodge-podge[32] (*satur*); this is why it must be presented with art and wit. And since the speaker is like the poem, all these traits also apply to the satirist himself.

Drant is not worried about which etymology is the right one; he juxtaposes them as equally valid paths to truth and adds them up to a definition which must have been perfectly satisfactory for him and his contemporaries.[33] For Dryden, however, such an explanation is no longer acceptable. He is not interested in pluralizing interpretation; what he wants is the one and only truth. In Foucault's terms, the decisive change from the Renaissance to the Classical Age is a shift from interpretation to order— '[l]e rapport à l'*Ordre* est aussi essentiel pour l'âge classique que le fut pour la Renaissance le rapport à l'*Interprétation*' (*MC*, 71)—and this implies that time becomes an important factor: 'Le projet d'une science de l'ordre, tel qu'il fut fondé au XVIIe siècle impliquait qu'il soit doublé d'une genèse de la connaissance' (*MC*, 86). This explains why Dryden's 'Discourse concerning the Original and Progress of Satire' (1693) is obsessed with the correct etymology, the 'true' origin of the word and thing 'satire', in order to fix it eternally in a system of identities and differences.

> *Scaliger* [...] derives the word Satyre, from *Satyrus*, that mix'd kind of Animal, or as the Ancients thought him, Rural God, made up betwixt a Man and a Goat; with a Humane Head, Hook'd Nose, Powting Lips, a Bunch, or Struma under the Chin, prick'd Ears, and upright Horns; the Body shagg'd with hair, especially from the waste, and ending in a Goat, with the legs and feet of that Creature. But *Casaubon*, and his Followers, with reason, condemn this derivation; and prove that from *Satyrus*, the word *Satira*, as it signifies a Poem, cannot possibly descend. For *Satira* is not properly a Substantive, but an Adjective; to which the word *Lanx*, in *English* a Charger, or large Platter, is understood [...].[34]

---

[32]For this term, with reference to Lyly, see Robert Weimann, *Shakespeare und die Macht der Mimesis: Autorität und Repräsentation im elisabethanischen Theater* (Berlin and Weimar: Aufbau-Verlag, 1988), 138 and 161.

[33]Cf. also Ohly, 'Vom geistigen Sinn des Wortes', 16: 'Das Mittelalter treibt eine spekulative [...] Etymologie. [...] Es wäre töricht, solche Etymologie als unwissenschaftlich zu verlachen, wenn sie ihrer Zeit zu einer tieferen Sinndeutung des Wortes verhalf [...].'

[34]John Dryden, 'Discourse concerning the Original and Progress of Satire', in *The Poems of John Dryden*, 4 vols., ed. J. Kinsley (Oxford: Clarendon Press, 1958), vol. 2:

A little further on, Dryden again insists on the linearity of knowledge, deriving its authority from finding the origin of truth and representing it by using the word as an arbitrary signifier for a precisely defined signified.

> *Casaubon* judg'd better, and his Opinion is grounded on sure Authority; that *Satyre* was deriv'd from *Satura*, a *Roman* word, which signifies Full, and Abundant; and full also of Variety, in which nothing is wanting to its due Perfection. [...] According to this Derivation, from *Satur* comes *Satura*, or *Satira*: According to the new spelling; as *optumus* and *maxumus* are now spell'd *optimus* and *maximus*. ('Discourse', 628)

This also explains why Dryden is no longer occupied with the question of what satire is *like*, but with what it *is*, and his definition, following Heinsius, begins accordingly:

> *Satire is a kind of Poetry, without a Series of Action, invented for the purging of our Minds; in which Humane Vices, Ignorance, and Errors, and all things besides, which are produc'd from them, in every Man are severely Reprehended; partly Dramatically, partly Simply, and sometimes in both kinds of speaking; but for the most part Figuratively, and Occultly; consisting in a low familiar way, chiefly in a sharp and pungent manner of Speech; but partly, also, in a Facetious and Civil way of Jesting; by which, either Hatred, or Laughter, or Indignation is mov'd.* ('Discourse', 660)[35]

The best kind of satire, however, is the one in which language and contents, words and things, fall apart.

> How easie it is to call Rogue and Villain, and that wittily! But how hard to make a Man appear a Fool, a Blockhead, or a Knave, without using any of those opprobrious terms! [...] [T]here is [...] a vast difference betwixt the slovenly Butchering of a Man, and the fineness of stroak that separates the Head from the Body, and leaves it standing in its place. ('Discourse', 655)

Dryden refers to a linguistic practice in which the materiality of the signifier has disappeared; the words used in such a kind of satire are entirely transparent in the sense that even in the choice of words the aggressivity of the genre can no longer be recognized. Dryden's epistemological approach and his satirical practice are thus both based on the new, 'classical', *episteme* of transparency and representation.

601-70, here 621-2 (abbreviation used: 'Discourse'); the search for origins sets in before Dryden, and Dryden is right to point out that in the new paradigm of thinking, the exclusive derivation of 'satire' from 'Satyr' would, of course, be the wrong one. The idea of exclusivity, however, is incompatible with analogical thinking.

[35] Satire thus is 'pungent', on the one hand, like the sword, but 'civil', on the other, very unlike the Satyr.

IV

In our culture and knowledge, there is nothing, Foucault says, which reminds us of the ways and means of analogical thinking—

> [p]lus rien, sauf peut-être la littérature [...]. On peut dire en un sens que la 'littérature', telle qu'elle s'est constituée et s'est désignée comme telle au seuil de l'âge moderne, manifeste la réapparition, là où on ne l'attendait pas, de l'être vif du langage. (*MC*, 58)[36]

I would like to argue that it is not as late as the nineteenth century that such a 'contre-discours' (*MC*, 59) came into being, but that there has always been, even if distinctly marginal, a field for the imaginary compensation of worldly losses.[37] Foucault himself draws attention to this when he points out that in the early seventeenth century in certain fields such as art, the play of resemblances seems to have run wild:

> Au début du XVIIe siècle, en cette période qu'à tort ou à raison on a appelée baroque, la pensée cesse de se mouvoir dans l'élément de la ressemblance. La similitude n'est plus la forme du savoir, mais plutôt l'occasion de l'erreur [...]. L'âge du semblable est en train de se refermer sur lui-même. Derrière lui, il ne laisse que des jeux. [...] [P]artout se dessinent les chimères de la similitude, mais on sait que ce sont des chimères; c'est le temps privilégié du trompe-l'oeil, de l'illusion comique, du théâtre qui se dédouble, du quiproquo, des songes et visions; c'est le temps des sens trompeurs; c'est le temps où les métaphores, les comparaisons et les allégories définissent l'espace poétique du langage. (*MC*, 65)[38]

Such a 'poetical space of language' is addressed in Shakespeare's 'Will'-sonnets, for example, which constitute an ironic, if not disenchanted, echo to Petrarch's *l'aura/Laura*-sonnets and to all the other epistemologically meaningful names of Renaissance poetry. It is even more directly addressed in Cervantes' *Don Quixote* and Shakespeare's *Hamlet*. Both texts explicitly thematize the losses of analogism—*Don Quixote* by

---

[36] See also *MC*, 312ff. For a general discussion of the impact of Foucauldian thought on literary studies, see Simon During, *Foucault and Literature: Towards a Genealogy of Writing* (London and New York: Routledge, 1992); on literature, see 68ff., on knowledge 92ff.

[37] See Wolfgang Iser, *The Act of Reading: A Theory of Aesthetic Response* (Baltimore, MD: Johns Hopkins University Press, 1978), 83ff.; for a similar conception of early modern 'literature', see Hugo Keiper, '"I wot myself best how y stonde": Literary Nominalism, Open Textual Form and the Enfranchizement of Individual Perspective in Chaucer's Dream Visions', in Utz (ed.), *Literary Nominalism*, 205-34.

[38] For a rejection of the notion of an English 'baroque', see Mahler, 'Jahrhundertwende, Epochenschwelle, epistemischer Bruch?', esp. 1018ff.

placing an analogist character in an open world,[39] *Hamlet* by confronting analogical inauthenticity with a scepticist subject.[40] In order to illustrate this, I will concentrate on two aspects of early modern literary epistemology—on the role of names in *Don Quixote* and on the acquisition of knowledge in *Hamlet*.

Right at the beginning of the novel, Don Quixote undertakes a topically organized search for names adequate enough to designate himself and his horse in the adventures to come. In medieval romance, a name is a well chosen and interpretable signifier which clearly indicates what its bearer's semantic potential in the story will be: Amadís, Amatus, Amadeus.[41] Don Quixote, however, reverses the process; the names he is concerned with are not pre-existent, he chooses them himself. This means that instead of reading a world of analogies he creates one, and he does so by giving 'form' to things, instilling life by naming.

> Fue luego a ver su rocín [...]. Cuatro días se le pasaron en imaginar qué nombre le pondría; porque [...] no era razón que caballo de caballero tan famoso [...] estuviese sin nombre conocido; [...] y así, después de muchos nombres que formó, borró y quitó, añadió, deshizo y tornó a hacer en su memoria e imaginación, al fin le vino a llamar *Rocinante*, nombre, a su parecer, alto, sonoro y significativo de lo que había sido cuando fue rocín, antes de lo que ahora era, que era antes y primero de todos los rocines del mundo. (*DQ*, 1: 101-2)[42]

---

[39]Foucault interprets Cervantes' text as 'le négatif du monde de la Renaissance' (*MC*, 60ff.; the quote is on 61); for a detailed discussion of the role of the signs in *Don Quixote,* see Horst Weich, Don Quijote *im Dialog: Zur Erprobung von Wirklichkeitsmodellen im spanischen und französischen Roman (von* Amadís de Gaula *bis* Jacques le fataliste*)* (Passauer Schriften zu Sprache und Literatur, 3) (Passau: Rothe, 1989), 95ff.; for a synoptic Spanish version, see Horst Weich, 'El "Quijote" en diálogo', *Estudios de Investigación Franco-Española*, 4 (1991), 45-77.

[40]For the idea of early modern subjectivity, see Catherine Belsey, *The Subject of Tragedy: Identity and Difference in Renaissance Drama* (1985; repr. London and New York: Routledge, 1991), for a reference to *Hamlet,* see 41-2; Hamlet makes it quite clear right from the beginning that for him it is no longer the outward signs of similitude '[t]hat can denote me truly. These indeed seem, | For they are actions that a man might play; | But I have that within which passes show, | These but the trappings and the suits of woe.' (William Shakespeare, *Hamlet,* ed. Harold Jenkins (The Arden Shakespeare) (London and New York: Methuen, 1982), 1.2.83ff.) All quotes are to this edition (abbreviation used: *Ham.*).

[41]For further details, with reference to *Amadís de Gaula* and *Don Quixote,* see Weich, Don Quijote *im Dialog,* 45ff.

[42]All quotes are to Miguel de Cervantes, *El Ingenioso Hidalgo Don Quijote de la Mancha,* 2 vols., ed. John Jay Allen (Cátedra. Letras Hispánicas, 100-1) (Madrid: Cátedra, 1989) (abbreviation used: *DQ*).

Since, as accompaniment to a famous knight, the horse can neither remain nameless nor bear a name unknown, Don Quixote takes four days of intensive thought to find the adequate designation for him. When he finally calls him 'Rocinante', he does so precisely because Rocinante used to be an 'old nag' (*rocín*), 'before' (*antes*) he was imaginatively turned into a knight's companion, the 'horse before all horses' (*rocín antes de todos los rocines*). And the name seems rightly given, since, at least in Don Quixote's view ('a su parecer'), it is a worthy, well-sounding, and meaningful name ('alto, sonoro y significativo'). The same procedure repeats itself when it comes to his own name:

> Puesto nombre, y tan a su gusto, a su caballo, quiso ponérsele a sí mismo, y en este pensamiento duró otros ocho días, y al cabo se vino a llamar *don Quijote*; de donde, como queda dicho, tomaron ocasión los autores desta tan verdadera historia que sin duda se debía de llamar Quijada, y no Quesada, como otros quisieron decir. Pero acordándose que el valeroso Amadís no sólo se había contentado con llamarse Amadís a secas, sino que añadió el nombre de su reino y patria, por hacerla famosa, y se llamó Amadís de Gaula, así quiso, como buen caballero, añadir al suyo el nombre de la suya y llamarse *don Quijote de la Mancha* [...]. (*DQ*, 1: 102)

This time, Don Quixote needs twice as long but, in the end, he is just as pleased with his own name as with Rocinante's. With '*quijada*' meaning 'jaw'/'jawbone', with the Old French '*cuissot*' and the Catalan '*cuixot*' designating those parts of a knight's armour covering the thighs, and with '*mancha*' meaning 'stain' or 'spot', however, Don Quixote's name turns out to be just as ambiguous as Rocinante's, indicating his knighthood and denying it at the same time.[43] And the same applies again when it comes to finding an adequate name for his beloved:

> Llamábase Aldonza Lorenzo, y a ésta le pareció ser bién darle título de señora de sus pensamientos; y buscándole nombre que no desdijese mucho del suyo, y que tirase y se encaminase al de princesa y gran señora, vino a llamarla *Dulcinea del Toboso*, porque era natural del Toboso; nombre, a su parecer, músico y peregrino y significativo, como todos los demás que a él y a sus cosas había puesto. (*DQ*, 1: 103)

'Aldonza' is turned into the 'sweeter' ('*dulce*') anagrammatical equivalent of 'Dulcinea' and then further nobilitated by the topographical specifi-

---

[43]He is thus something like 'The Knight of the Stained Armour'; for a discussion of the names in *Don Quixote,* see Weich, Don Quijote *im Dialog,* 57ff.; cf. also Dominique Reyre, *Dictionnaire des noms des personnages du Don Quichotte de Cervantes: Suivi d'une analyse structurale et linguistique* (Paris: Editions hispaniques, 1980).

cation of 'del Toboso', which, in Don Quixote's view again, makes the coinage as well-sounding and as meaningful as the previous two.[44]

Don Quixote thus does not really find 'truth' through language; he uses language to suit his imagination.[45] He 'names' the world but it is his world only. He looks for analogies—'[t]out son chemin est une quête aux similitudes' (*MC*, 61)—and finds signifiers which seem significant ('nombres, a su parecer, significativos') because it is he who has invented them. In the novel's universe of discourse, language has lost its epistemological function of indicating the path to truth, and Don Quixote, as belated knight-errant, wanders about finding signs that are no longer 'really' there; he creates a path of chimeric similitudes that leads him into the realm of 'modern' fiction. This fiction of a by-gone analogical world ends with the end of the novel: 'yo no soy don Quijote de la Mancha, sino Alonso Quijano, a quien mis costumbres me dieron renombre de *Bueno*.' (*DQ*, 2: 574) When the 'curtain' comes down, the Renaissance 'idea' of resemblance finds itself relegated to a figural perspective, and its former epistemological truth is madness, fiction, play.

In his reading of *Hamlet*, Simon During concludes: 'In terms of Foucault's archaeological epistemes, we can see that Hamlet is doubly stranded—he belongs neither to the prose of the world, nor to a (Lockean and mimetic) grid of representations.'[46] The crucial epistemological stage of the play is reached at the point when the ghost pronounces his commandment to take revenge and to 'remember' him. Hamlet answers:

> [...] Remember thee?
> Ay, thou poor ghost, whiles memory holds a seat
> In this distracted globe. Remember thee?
> Yea, from the table of my memory
> I'll wipe away all trivial fond records,
> All saws of books, all forms, all pressures past
> That youth and observation copied there,
> And thy commandment all alone shall live
> Within the book and volume of my brain
> Unmix'd with baser matter.
>   (*Ham.*, 1.5.95-104)

---

[44] For a discussion of Sancho Panza as the only character not being given a *nom de guerre*, see Weich, Don Quijote *im Dialog*, 61-2.

[45] For an account of Don Quixote's semiological '*locura*' of attributing the semantics of knighthood to a contingent reality ('[d]en Signifikanten der Lebenswelt stülpt er die Signifikate der Ritterromanwelt über'), see Weich, Don Quijote *im Dialog*, 104ff., the quote is on 105.

[46] See During, *Foucault and Literature*, 208ff., the quote is on 215; During's choice of *Hamlet* seems just as little haphazard as Foucault's selection of *Don Quixote*, since both texts quite significantly point to what can be termed 'a threshold of modernity' (217).

Hamlet refers to the notion of 'artificial memory', to the 'book', or 'table', of the brain, which was considered to hold all 'records', 'saws', 'forms', 'pressures' once inscribed and which served as a major means of orientation. It can be conceived of as a basic analogical archive of knowledge organized according to verbal *topoi* and pictures (*'loci et imagines'*), as a topological storeroom to be activated in questions of cognition and epistemology.[47] The problem of 'judging' the ghost, however, is beyond the scope of the memory; since a ghost is no longer a 'thing' of the world it can neither be similar to any other 'thing' on earth: 'There are more things in heaven and earth, Horatio, | Than are dreamt of in our philosophy.' (1.5.174-5)[48] In 'wiping away' everything on record in his memory, Hamlet deliberately discards the past ways and means of topical reasoning, making room for new things to be 'copied there':

> My tables! Meet it is I set it down
> That one may smile, and smile, and be a villain—
> At least I am sure it may be so in Denmark.   [*Writes.*]
> So, uncle, there you are. [...]
>   (*Ham.*, 1.5.107ff.)

The first new 'saw' to be set down is the one that appearances can be deceptive. This seems to apply almost certainly to Claudius ('I'm sure it may be so'), but it also applies to the ghost. For a man who 'know[s] not "seems"' (1.2.76), the 'appearance' of a ghost cannot unquestionably constitute immediate proof; he is not in a position to simply 'believe'. Since neither topical reasoning nor the will to believe offer acceptable paths to 'truth', Hamlet resorts to the more 'modern' method of forming a hypothesis ('it may be so in Denmark'), which he then tries to verify or falsify; he resorts to rationalism and empiricism. Truth is thus found by means of experiment and observation; after strategically putting on 'an antic disposition' (1.5.180) and setting up the '*Mousetrap*' (3.2.232), Hamlet instructs Horatio to '[o]bserve my uncle', and it is by observation that the hypothesis of Claudius' 'occulted guilt' (3.2.80) is at last verified: 'O good Horatio, I'll take the Ghost's word for a thousand pound. Didst perceive?'

---

[47]The inner structure of the artificial memory has been most conclusively described in the *Rhetorica ad Herennium*: 'Constat igitur artificiosa memoria ex locis et imaginibus' (III, 16). I quote from Otto, *Das Wissen des Ähnlichen*, 94, where Otto also discusses this speech from *Hamlet*; for a somewhat different interpretation of the same speech, see During, *Foucault and Literature*, 213ff.

[48]For the two methodological steps of 'finding' a *topos* and of 'judging' it, or, in Ciceronian terms, of '*invenire*' and '*iudicare*', see Otto, *Das Wissen des Ähnlichen*, 88; for the inaccessibility of the ghost, see 95.

(3.2.280-1)[49] The method of experimental verification makes Hamlet eventually 'see' Claudius for what he really is, and language is only needed to express and to communicate this truth after it has been found: Claudius, Hamlet now knows for sure, *is* '[a] murderer and a villain', '[a] cutpurse of the empire and rule' (3.4.96 and 99).

Cervantes' *Don Quixote* and Shakespeare's *Hamlet* stage possible worlds in which language no longer serves as a convincing means of orientation. Words and things disintegrate. Don Quixote still uses language to build up a providentialist universe but the truth he finds remains unratified by his surroundings; Hamlet explicitly discards the topical knowledge of similitude in order to find truth outside language in empirical evidence. Looking back at the passing era of analogism, and foreshadowing the new age of transparency, both texts thus thematize the slow but conclusive early modern epistemological 'death' of language.

Epilogue

Let me conclude with a brief look at the early modern question of 'realism' vs. 'nominalism' and the divergent histories of England and Spain after *Hamlet* and *Don Quixote*. One of the major points of critique brought up against Foucault's epistemological archaeology has been that his Renaissance concept of a 'prose of the world' neglects the emergence of nominalism; his *episteme* of the Renaissance is a realist *episteme*.[50] Foucault thus seems to have restricted himself to what Raymond Williams in his description of social and cultural change has called 'the *dominant*'; but, as Williams points out, 'it is also the case that in cultural production both the *residual*—work made in earlier and often different societies and times, yet still available and significant—and the *emergent*—work of various new kinds—are often equally available *as practices*.'[51] The medieval rivalry between the emergent discourse of nominalism and the dominant discourse of realism articulates itself first and foremost in theological and philosophical text types;[52] yet whenever nominalist thought appears as a

---

[49]'La vérité trouve sa manifestation et son signe dans la perception évidente et distincte.' (*MC*, 70; see also quote at end of Section I above.)

[50]'Es steckt in der Sprache und im Sprachverständnis der Renaissance ein viel zu großes Erbe des Nominalismus, als daß da eine Rede von der Ähnlichkeit der Dinge, die sich in der Sprache "offenbart", überhaupt noch geführt werden dürfte.' (Otto, *Das Wissen des Ähnlichen*, 91)

[51]For a brief description of his categories of social and cultural change, see Raymond Williams, *Culture* (London: Fontana, 1981), 203ff.; the quotes are on 204.

[52]For the distinction between epistemologically conceived 'discourses' and generically defined 'text types', see Michael Titzmann, 'Kulturelles Wissen—Diskurs—Denksystem. Zu einigen Grundbegriffen der Literaturgeschichtsschreibung', *Zeitschrift für französische Sprache und Literatur*, 99 (1989), 47-61, esp. 50-1.

serious threat to the realist dominance, it finds itself excluded from the discursive fields of truth. One way out for nominalism, however, seems to have been 'literature'; in literary text types such as visions, dreams, or debates, nominalist ideas could be articulated without risking the immediate reproach of destabilizing the realist orthodoxy.[53] It is in the Renaissance that the fairly stable oscillation between 'nominalist emergence' and 'realist recuperation' is broken. In this, Renaissance Spain and Renaissance England show a fairly similar profile; after the period of *Hamlet* and *Don Quixote*, however, England moves on to 'Modernity', whereas Spain, under the successful monological impact of the Counter-Reformation, seems to have to undergo one more 'realist' loop.[54]

---

[53]As can be seen in *Don Quixote*'s celebration of the residual practice of analogism and in *Hamlet*'s pointing forward to the emergent practice of empirical proof, literature often eludes the dominant. For the postulation of a 'nominalist turn' in medieval and early modern literature, with special reference to Chaucer's dream poetry, see Keiper, "'I wot myself best how y stonde'"; for a more general description of a medieval 'literary nominalism', see Richard J. Utz, *Literarischer Nominalismus im Spätmittelalter: Eine Untersuchung zu Sprache, Charakterzeichnung und Struktur in Geoffrey Chaucers* Troilus and Criseyde (Frankfurt a.M. et al.: Lang, 1990).

[54]See Küpper, *Diskurs-Renovatio*, passim.

THE EMANCIPATION OF THE SIGN: THE CHANGING SIGNIFICANCE OF BEAUTY IN SOME ENGLISH RENAISSANCE ROMANCES

SUSANNE FENDLER

Over the centuries, the meaning and significance of beauty have been subject to a good deal of variation and change. The changes and developments discussed in this paper are historically situated at a point where, as is often claimed, the discovery and discussion of individuality and the individual became increasingly prominent topics in literature. Moreover, it has been argued that it was in the sixteenth century that signs were beginning to be used self-consciously, i.e., as Robert Weimann suggests, that they were more and more seen as constructs that are developed and used in specific historical, cultural and discursive contexts. As Weimann further points out, one might also assume that it was such heightened awareness of the historicity of signs which, in turn, brought about their reconsideration and re-evaluation in terms of temporal constructs, rather than as allegorical entities.[1] It seems plausible to assume, therefore, that such processes of re-evaluation would also entail a reconsideration of certain traditional, conventionalized conceptions of beauty, as well as of its uses and functions as a literary sign.

The following argument focuses on the re-evaluation of beauty in Renaissance prose romances in the tradition of Philip Sidney's *Arcadia*. In that tradition, originally, the conventional, allegorical meaning of beauty consists mainly in the fact that it signifies virtue. According to that conception of the sign, then, virtue functions as the signified, whereas the ultimate referent of the sign is God's perfection. In the final analysis, therefore, beauty is here seen as a reflection of God's perfection in human

---

[1] See Robert Weimann, *Shakespeare und die Macht der Mimesis: Autorität und Repräsentation im elisabethanischen Theater* (Berlin and Weimar: Aufbau-Verlag, 1988), esp. 36. The present contribution is an enlarged version of a paper that was presented at ISSEI's 1994 Graz conference (see Preface). I am much obliged to Hugo Keiper for substantial suggestions and help in revising the original version.

beings, and it is precisely that sort of reference which, from a realist point of view, marks the sign as 'complete'.

In his study on art and beauty in the Middle Ages, Umberto Eco cites Curtius to the effect that in scholasticism beauty is one of God's attributes.[2] In his further discussion of the Neoplatonic concept of beauty Eco points out that the experience of beauty can be employed as a means of direct contact with supernatural beauty.[3] Similarly, Leclercq states that '[t]he formula "love of beauty" [...] consists in loving [...] Beauty, that is the one who is the Beautiful [...] per excellence, namely God.'[4] Subsequent developments, however, some of which may be connected with the growing ascendancy of nominalist positions in late-medieval and early modern thinking, seem to indicate that certain conventionalized types of signs,[5] yet especially such culturally charged ones as beauty, were beginning to lose their original, established functions and that the existence of a transcendent referent, i.e. of a higher or hidden 'truth' behind earthly concepts, was increasingly questioned or even denied. Thus, for example, the exact nature of transcendent referents was a central concern of philosophers and schoolmen of the fourteenth century, especially as part of the argument between nominalists and realists. In late-medieval nominalism, as W.H. Watts and R.J. Utz point out in the introduction to their bibliographical essay on Chaucer's nominalism, 'universals [in this case God's beauty] have no substantial existence outside of the human mind'.[6] They go on to state that, according to some readings of Ockham,

> [...] there is no assurance that universal ideas and words bear any resemblance to the real world. And finally, if humans are incapable of knowing the contingent created world, they are no more capable of knowing the divine world of enduring truth. Humans cannot know God directly through intuitive cognition, nor can they know Him indirectly through an understanding of secondary causes since these causes are themselves subject to God's absolute power. In short, Ockham would seem to call into question humans' capacity to know anything, on earth or in heaven, with any certainty.[7]

---

[2] See Umberto Eco, *Kunst und Schönheit im Mittelalter*, tr. Günter Memmert (1991; repr. Munich: dtv, 1993), 17.

[3] See ibid., 206.

[4] Jean Leclerq, 'The Love of Beauty as a Means and an Expression of the Love of Truth', *Mittellateinisches Jahrbuch*, 16 (1981), 62-72, here: 62.

[5] For the relation between 'symbol' and 'sign', see Gerhart Ladner, 'Medieval and Modern Understanding of Symbolism: A Comparison', *Speculum*, 54 (1979), 223-56, esp. 224-5.

[6] William H. Watts and Richard J. Utz, 'Nominalist Perspectives on Chaucer's Poetry: A Bibliographical Essay', *Medievalia et Humanistica*, n.s. 20 (1993), 147-73, here: 148.

[7] Ibid., 149.

In the Renaissance, then, we may be witnessing the resurgence of comparable considerations, and generally a re-evaluation of 'nominalist' versus 'realist' positions which, among other things, is evident in English courtesy theory. It is in that tradition, at any rate, that David Kuchta discovers what he takes as the first signs of a dismantling, even destruction of the reference system that was traditionally aligned to beauty. 'In this discursive tradition', he states,

> dress and manners were not mere externals: they were manifestations of internal worth, graceful supplements to nobility [...]. In this semiotics of masculinity, the hypothetical 'true sign' consisted of an identity between outward beauty and inward goodness, between material signifier and social signified, between appearance and status.[8]

Here, however, we are already one step removed from the original concept of the sign as necessarily including a transcendent referent.

It is all the more interesting, therefore, that a specific sub-genre of English Renaissance romances should display a similar developmental dynamics and would thus, in a sense, appear to replay the earlier development from a traditional, 'realist' concept of beauty and its significance in the direction of 'nominalist' orientations. In these romances, the resurgence of the argument between realist and nominalist positions can be followed even more closely than in most other traditions, as this paper will attempt to demonstrate. In order to focus my comparison of these texts, I will begin with Sidney's *Arcadia* and then go on to discuss various imitations of that romance.

Myron Turner has argued that Sidney used the new *Arcadia* to illustrate his Neoplatonic faith that 'all this [i.e. the sensible world] is but "a faire Inn | Of fairer guestes, which dwell within"'.[9] She goes on to say:

> This notion takes its place within the more general Christian Humanist faith, which Renaissance Platonism shares, that the beauty, order, and functionalism of the universe reflect the divine wisdom, goodness and power.[10]

---

[8]David Kuchta, 'Semiotics of Masculinity in Renaissance England', in James Grantham Turner (ed.), *Sexuality and Gender in Early Modern Europe: Institutions, Texts, Images* (Cambridge: Cambridge University Press, 1993), 233-46, here: 235.

[9]Myron Turner, 'The Disfigured Face of Nature: Image and Metaphor in the Revised *Arcadia*', *English Literary Renaissance*, 2 (1972), 116-35, here: 122.

[10]Ibid., 122.

Here, then, beauty is seen as 'the "divine sparke" descended from heaven',[11] which is to inspire love. Love's aim, in turn, is to lead to virtuous action.[12] As W.R. Davis points out, however, the improvement of one's character through love is limited in Sidney's *Arcadia*, since in those plotlines of the text that deal with the topic of improvement through love, it remains restricted to love of a woman. The step required by Neoplatonism, though, would be that love of the beauty of one woman should lead to self-improvement and love of virtue (as the signified) in general. In this, Davis argues, Sidney parts from the Platonic conception.[13]

Yet there is one exception. In the opening scene of the new *Arcadia*,[14] the shepherds Claius and Strephon talk about the shepherdess Urania. They praise her beauty, but they also point out that her virtues are more noteworthy than her beauty. Claius compares the effect of her beauty to that of the rays of the sun, and just as the sun brings life to earth, so, he argues, Urania's beauty inspires him and Strephon to lead more virtuous lives (*Arc.*, 5). Maureen Quilligan sees the shepherds' self-awareness in this opening scene as 'the truest sign of humanist discourse—because it carries a sense of self-worth beyond class'.[15] At the beginning of the text, the reader is thus made aware of the fact that beauty is not merely the beauty of a face, but serves as mediator. Beauty, that is to say, is merely the outward manifestation of virtues that are a reflection of God's virtues in man. It has only the function to engender love, which in turn should lead to self-improvement. Beauty, then, is not to be valued for itself but is rather comparable to the rays of the sun and is, therefore, not the substance but only the part visible to others-i.e., it counts only as the signifier of inner qualities. Thus, beauty is that part of the sign that attracts others and which, eventually, is to bring out the best in them.

Sidney goes on to provide variations of this concept. In the story of Argalus and Parthenia, he further investigates the significance of beauty, and it is in this plot that he indicates the limitations of the sign's referent. Argalus falls in love with Parthenia's beauty (*Arc.*, 28). She, however, is

---

[11] Ibid., 117.

[12] See A.C. Hamilton, 'Sidney's *Arcadia* as Prose Fiction: Its Relation to Its Sources', *English Literary Renaissance*, 2 (1972), 29-60, esp. 49-50.

[13] See Walter R. Davis, 'A Map of Arcadia: Sidney's Romance in Its Tradition', in Walter R. Davis and R.A. Lanham (eds.), *Sidney's* Arcadia (Yale Studies in English, 158) (New Haven, CT, and London: Yale University Press, 1965), 1-180, here: 83.

[14] Throughout this essay, page references are to the following edition: Philip Sidney, *The Countess of Pembroke's Arcadia (The New Arcadia)*, ed. Victor Skretkowicz (Oxford: Clarendon Press, 1987) (abbreviation used: *Arc.*).

[15] Maureen Quilligan, 'Lady Mary Wroth: Female Authority and the Family Romance', in George M. Logan and Gordon Teskey (eds.), *Unfolded Tales: Essays on Renaissance Romance* (Ithaca, NY: Cornell University Press, 1989), 257-80, here: 260.

disfigured by a disappointed suitor (*Arc.*, 30). Pointing out that he loves her 'self', and not just her face, Argalus insists on marrying her. Parthenia, though, refusing to burden him, leaves the country and is finally restored to health (*Arc.*, 31-2). Later on, when she returns under a different name, she pretends to have been sent to Argalus by Parthenia as a substitute, since she resembles her so closely. Argalus passes this test as well and refuses her, protesting once more that he did not love Parthenia's face alone. As a consequence, Parthenia makes herself known and they are at last able to marry (*Arc.*, 44).

Sidney is here testing the notion of 'true' love—'true' in the sense that the object of love is not the outward signifier but the substance, the 'self'. In this, he already introduces a variation on the traditional concept of the sign, for Argalus does not insist on loving Parthenia's virtues but on loving her self. However, since Argalus passes his test—Parthenia's loss of beauty—in all respects, the story demonstrates that beauty is still seen to exist in order to evoke love. Having fulfilled this purpose, it is of no further use. Since Argalus has managed to go beyond the mere surface and love the 'essence', he proves that he is able to see virtue without having to rely on outward beauty.

Yet this is not a purely Platonic story. The emphasis is not on the referent of the sign, i.e. on the reflection of God's perfection in human virtues as signified in outward beauty, because Parthenia's former beauty and virtues are entirely her own. Argalus emphasizes her selfhood-that is, we find here traces of individuality, even if that aspect is not yet enlarged upon. This particular presentation of the sign thus also implies a reduction as compared to its former, traditional conception: part of it is still valid— beauty signifies virtue—but the Christian idea that sees meaning and reference beyond personal virtues, i.e. the referent, does not figure any longer. In Urania's story the complex sign still stands for higher virtues, for God's 'divine spark', whereas here it is a reduced sign which does not point beyond itself to any transcendent referent. According to Davis, this is owing to a development which made 'the transfer from moral to religious values [...] exceedingly difficult in the world of men'.[16] But a different meaning of beauty is included here as well. We know nothing more about Urania than the mere fact that she is virtuous, with matching beauty. The other characters, however, whose beauty is praised, are all aristocratic, i.e. beauty and virtuous behaviour together denote an aristocratic descendancy. The sign, therefore, is now embedded in a different, largely secularized system of reference. It loses the Christian background it had in Urania's case and gains a worldly significance instead, since in this case it is the social status of a character that becomes the sign's referent.

---

[16]Davis, 'A Map of Arcadia', 83.

This shift in the established reference system, it could be argued, is necessary to allow the introduction of individuality. Urania does not appear as a possible individual but is represented as a sign herself. Since, then, there is no 'substance' of its own to this character, it is quite in keeping that Urania does not even once appear in person in Sidney's *Arcadia*. She is described and talked about by the shepherds, but she does not actually enter the scene, nor is she shown 'in action'. Parthenia, on the other hand, is compared not to the sun, but only to other female characters in the romance and is thus presented as an 'ordinary character', i.e. as a figure that does not carry any transcendent associations. Accordingly, her beauty does not nurture virtue in others, as did Urania's—it is a 'worldly' beauty that may be admired by men, but which is still only outward beauty. Typically, then, Claius and Strephon are content to admire Urania from afar; love of her has improved them, and that is considered sufficient. Argalus, by contrast, is a different case entirely. As opposed to Claius and Strephon, he is not satisfied until he is reunited with Parthenia. For him, in other words, the good she might have worked on him is not enough, nor is he merely interested in some abstract improvement, because what he wants is this particular woman *qua* individual.

In the descriptions of Pamela and Philoclea we find further indications that Sidney, in this context, is indeed interested in the idea of the individual, which generally appears to have gained in importance during the sixteenth century. As Evelyn Vitz has pointed out, individuality comes in when a quality is differentiated in kind, not just in degree.[17] Pamela and Philoclea have the same beauty in degree, but they differ in kind. In order to establish a 'mere' Neoplatonic type of beauty it would be sufficient to mention that the two women are exceedingly beautiful. Sidney, however, makes a point of differentiating between them. Hence, Philoclea's beauty is described as softer and more yielding in nature, whereas Pamela is shown as majestical, 'threatening' and 'demanding' (*Arc.*, 17). In this way, we are made aware of a difference between the two, for even though they are still described in terms of their respective types of beauty, it is obviously their character and individuality, i.e. their 'selves', that we are introduced to. Telling of how they fall in love with the two princes, Musidorus and Pyrocles, the plot which follows goes on to demonstrate these differences. In accordance with her type of beauty, Pamela is revealed to be a demanding woman who is fully conscious of her role as a princess with duties to her country, while Philoclea, in turn, is shown to be mainly interested in love and is portrayed, through her behaviour, as the 'ideal' woman, i.e. as soft and yielding. Hence, the types of beauty represented by the two women have to be seen

---

[17]Evelyn Birge Vitz, 'Type et individu dans l'<autobiographie> médiévale: Etude d'Histoire Calamitatum', *Poétique*, 6 (1975), 426-45.

as the outward manifestations of their inner qualities. But as in Parthenia's case, the traditional referent of the sign, its ultimate pointing to and reference to God, is missing; instead, the social connotation is emphasized. In Sidney's *Arcadia*, then, the introduction of individual traits already leads to a first displacement in the tradition's semiotics of beauty, and even though the 'conventional' sign is not completely dismantled as yet—not, at least, as regards the relation between signifier and signified—it has nonetheless been wrenched from its original referent, or at any rate, that process has been set on its way.

Mary Wroth's *Urania*, one of the texts which took up central elements and features of Sidney's romance, was published in 1621.[18] Wroth's romance opens with the lament of Urania, who has just learnt that the shepherds who raised her are not her parents. Interestingly, Wroth applies the new connotations introduced by Sidney, i.e. the social status as referent, to the one character in *Arcadia* which, in its original context, is associated with the religious reference system. In Sidney's conception, as we have seen, Urania epitomized a perfect being, whereas Wroth turns her Urania's beauty and virtue into a mere sign of her higher birth, which at the beginning is unknown. If in Sidney's *Arcadia* Urania's function was to serve as a symbol of the shepherds' love, Wroth's Urania is a much more developed, individualized character, who is searching for her identity.[19] Wroth's Urania, of course, like her prototype, is still described as beautiful and virtuous (*Ur.*, 1; 17), but Wroth digresses from Sidney's treatment yet further. Thus, for example, her Urania is addressed as follows:

> Admired Shepherdes, and most worthy to bee so; since inward beauty of your mind so much excells the peereless excellency of your outward perfections, as vertue excels beauty [...]. (*Ur.*, 17)

In this passage, then, the comparison to the traditional conception of character is made, but simultaneously a difference is pointed out, too. Since Urania's 'inner beauty' is not only more important now than her outward beauty, but greater as well, the degree of her beauty is no longer a direct reflection or even a measure of the degree of her virtue. Thus, once again, the direct, immediately apparent link between virtue and beauty, and

---

[18] Throughout this essay, page references are to the following edition: Mary Wroth, *The Countesse of Mountgomery's Urania* (London, 1621) (MS No 26051) (abbreviation used: *Ur.*).

[19] For a discussion of Urania, see Quilligan, 'Lady Mary Wroth', and Naomi J. Miller, '"Not Much to be Marked": Narrative of the Woman's Part in Lady Mary Wroth's *Urania*', *Studies in English Literature*, 29 (1989), 121-37.

consequently the conventionalized conception of the sign, is called into question. Later in the text, Urania comments on that connection herself:

> [...] beautie is besides a vertue counted among men of that excellent worth, as it wil draw their hearts [...] beauty will sooner compasse ones desires in loue, then any other vertue, since that is the attractiue power, though worth is often made the glosse of their change [...]. (*Ur.*, 399)

Here, Urania names beauty as a virtue, but only as one among others. Hence, instead of being a mere signifier of virtues, beauty has now become one of them. As virtues and beauty now stand for themselves only, the traditional sign and its reference are challenged, and ultimately dissolved. Thus, the signifier 'beauty' no longer works as such, or in the ways it was originally seen to function, for beauty now stands only for beauty and does not in itself imply the existence of a virtuous character. Wroth here applies Renaissance courtesy theory, in so far as beauty and virtues are 'graceful supplement to nobility', but beauty and virtue are now on the same level. Indeed, virtues themselves have become of less value if beauty is the one among them that is the most valued. Wroth looks to it that this preference is not yet stated directly; moreover, her characters make a pretence of their continuing belief in higher values, and of their opting for them. In the second passage above, however, men are accused of opting for beauty alone and of using the conventional conception of worth that lies behind it as a mere excuse, and there is even a sense of bitterness here about the destruction of the traditional link. At the same time, though, women are also accused of loving only 'outward beauty' (cf. *Ur.*, 510), and in this much the same argument is used, namely that women pretend to love the virtues of men but, in fact, love beauty alone. As the narrator points out,

> she vsed his vertues but for a mask for her liking him,[20] or an excuse for her choice, when it should haue been a commendations for her vnderstanding, to find so much in the inward part, as to ouersee the ordinary way for womens loue, which is outward beauty, and that in some measure he had, that being ioyned with delicate apparell, being the most vsuall attractiue powers to their affections, as if rather they would loue Pictures, then the wisest or worthiest man in old cloathes, or ill made [...]. (*Ur.*, 510)

In Wroth's *Urania*, then, beauty is finally cut loose from its former system of reference. Its function is not any longer as the signifier of inner worth, which is meant to induce a love that betters the lover, but it is now placed on the same level as 'other vertues', even though it is still the one to command attention. Moreover, since the love beauty inspires is no more

---

[20] The male figure referred to in this passage is the Duke of Brunswick; 'she' is given no name but only introduced as the daughter of the 'lord of a castle in the desert'.

a reason to improve oneself, or to remain constant, love has been reduced to mere admiration of a picture that may be transferred elsewhere whenever an alternative turns up. Love, therefore, is no longer an incentive for self-improvement, but has rather become 'the Ruiner of beauty' (*Ur.*, 534).

Like Sidney's *Arcadia*, Wroth's version contains also a story about the loss of beauty, but if Sidney's Parthenia was suddenly disfigured, loss of beauty for Wroth comes about naturally—through the process of ageing, 'from beauty to decay' (*Ur.*, 45). Using precisely the same argument as Sidney's Argalus, who had insisted that in spite of Parthenia's loss of beauty he still loves her, Wroth's Perselina, the woman concerned, insists on still being the same person. It is significant, though, that she has to make this demand for herself, i.e. that she herself has to insist on being loved for her inner worth, whereas in Sidney it was Argalus's ability to do so that was doubtful to Parthenia. Perselina's lover, however, fails his test and turns to another, more beautiful woman. The difference between Argalus and Perselina's lovers thus lies in the kind of love they are able to give, for Perselina's lover turns not from one 'self' to another, but simply replaces a 'picture'. That is to say, he is interested in appearance only, not in essence.

Once again, this points to the loss in beauty's higher significance, which in this case clearly goes further than in *Arcadia*. In Wroth's *Urania* it is through outward beauty alone that love is inspired, and that kind of love, moreover, is a selfish love that cannot improve the lover and cannot, therefore, be retained as soon as the beloved's former beauty is lost. Once it has lost its referent, it seems that the sign itself, i.e. the connection between beauty as signifier and virtue as signified, is quickly destroyed. Virtues do not count any more, and beauty can exist without carrying any significance beyond itself. Thus, for example, the Queen of Bulgaria is introduced as 'a Lady of beautie sufficient, but of behauiour insolent' (*Ur.*, 342), which suggests that the Queen loves just herself and accepts others only when they adore her. However, the narrator refuses to look any further into the married life of this Queen. As this character is intent on outward show alone, her inner, private life is regarded as unimportant, obviously by narrator and character alike, as can be seen from the following passage, which excuses her from being civil to others—for the simple reason that this might damage her looks:

> [...] rather sure should all ciuilitie be laid aside, and the contrary excused, then beauty should suffer, and this, if the cause, who will that loues their faces [...] blame her, who neglects for these all others. This I take the Queenes case to bee, and thus I thinke I excuse her, especially being knowne to loue nothing but her selfe [...]. (*Ur.*, 463)

Not only has beauty become a value in its own right, but the process of dismantling the original idea(l) of beauty has been taken a step further:

beauty is now shown as the only value that counts, and this view is excused—if, perhaps, with ironical overtones. The narrator thus judges the character of a person on its own grounds and, in the Queen's case at least, beauty is accepted as the only important attribute even by the narrator, despite the fact that it is listed as one among several virtues.

Wroth, then, manages to point up several implications that result from dissolving the original sign. In Sidney's romance, the sign's established frame of reference was still largely 'intact'; beauty still signified virtue, even though it had already begun to lose its points of reference beyond the social context: for already here its reference to God's perfection and to the love of all perfection that is to follow love of human beauty had been dispensed with. In Wroth's romance, however, beauty is itself emancipated, its significance ranging from 'one virtue among others' to being 'the only one'. But Wroth goes still further than that and does away altogether with the social significance of beauty when—as opposed to princesses in the disguise of shepherdesses—she introduces 'true' shepherdesses into her story who are, potentially, more beautiful and virtuous than the Queen of Bulgaria, for example.[21]

Wroth thus constructs varying denials of even the secular connection between beauty, dress, and internal values. In Urania's case, the constituents of the conventional sign are still present, even though beauty and virtue are now given much the same importance, but with the Queen of Bulgaria one finds that only dress and beauty are left as pointers to her nobility; she can boast no corresponding inner values, however. As a further contrast to the Queen, moreover, we also encounter characters of beauty and virtue who are nonetheless of low social standing. The shepherdess Celina, for instance, is described as 'a Shepheardesse as *Vrania* was, and that is sufficient expression for her perfections' (*Ur.*, 541). Accordingly, she is beautiful and virtuous, but in spite of these characteristics she is a genuine shepherdess. In addition, Wroth establishes clear distinctions between various kinds of beauty, as well as between different characters' responses to beauty. As a consequence, beauty, like any other virtue, has become a quality or inherent property of the individual and can thus be used to turn former literary types into distinguishable, differentiated characters. Correspondingly, love can now range from love of the other 'self', via love of beauty alone, to complete self-love. The idea that love of beauty ought to lead to self-improvement has been dismissed, since love of beauty no longer implies love of virtues and, ultimately, of God's perfection. Some of the characters complain about that situation. They insist on being loved for their own sake—as individuals, not as beautiful objects—but hardly any of them succeed. The world of *Urania*, then, is a

---

[21]See, for instance, Celina's story (*Ur.*, 541-2).

disillusioned one in which outward appearance is the most important asset, especially in the eyes of men. As a corollary, the traditional sign is still further reduced to only one of its former components, i.e. the one which originally functioned as the signifier. Beauty, in other words, is now no longer valued for its connection with virtue but stands on its own; indeed, in some cases it remains the only characteristic of interest.

Let me briefly outline the further development of the tradition. Thirty years after Wroth's *Urania*, Anna Weamys took up the task of finishing Sidney's romance in her *Continuation of Sir Philip Sidney's Arcadia*.[22] Weamys selects some of Sidney's plotlines and provides the happy ending. The plot around Urania is one of those which Weamys chooses for her continuation. However, as opposed to *Arcadia*, where Urania was introduced only as the absent object of the shepherds' love, Urania does make an appearance in Weamys, just as in Wroth's version, though on the other hand—and here the parallel to Sidney's opening scene is preserved—she is still followed by Claius and Strephon. Claius introduces her as follows:

> [...] our Bride may equal yours in Beautie, though not in rich attire, and in noble virtues, though not in Courtly accoutrements [...]. (*CA*, 170)

In that way, Weamys establishes a clear difference between outward appearance and inner worth, but specifically she makes a distinction between clothes and beauty, rank and virtue. Beauty, however, is here not the signifier for virtue either, nor do Urania's beauty and virtue denote her as an aristocratic character, as in Wroth's romance. Rather, beauty and virtue are listed as possible characteristics of a woman that remain unconnected. Correspondingly, Claius and Strephon are presented as two different types of characters. In *Arcadia*, both of them strove for selfless love, insisting that their love helped to improve them and could therefore not cause any jealousy between them. In Weamys's text, likewise, they appear at first to continue in that tradition. This presentation of the two shepherds is undercut, however, when they appeal to Musidorus to decide who is to be the one to marry Urania, for at that point they begin to lament most selfishly. Instead of trying to compete in their mutual praise of Urania, they prefer to compete in complaining of what would become of them if the other one were to marry her. Claius, as the older man, threatens that such a disappointment would surely be his death. Strephon, for his part, insists that

---

[22]Throughout this essay, page references are to the following reprint edition: Anna Weamys, *A Continuation of Sir Philip Sidney's Arcadia* (London, 1651); reprint edition plus modernized version, ed. Patrick Colborn Cullen (Oxford: Oxford University Press, 1994), 107-96 (abbreviation used: *CA*).

Urania deserves a young husband. He stresses her virtues rather than her beauty, and even condemns himself for being so presumptuous as to desire her, but in the end he is quite willing to take Urania when Musidorus decides to give her to him. From *Arcadia*'s heights, these two characters have sunk deeply. As neither of them considers what might be best for the woman he wants to marry, Weamys presents them as utterly selfish. Urania, in turn, refuses to choose a husband for herself and thus ends up as a mere prize in the contest of the two men.

The last text I would like to discuss, John Reynolds's *The Flower of Fidelity* (publ. 1654),[23] goes yet a step further than that. For the greater part, it is true, Reynolds *seems* to share Sidney's position, for with the majority of characters their inward and outward beauty are made to correspond, even if that correspondence impresses the reader as more of a lip-service or a fulfilment of conventions on the author's part than as being actually connected to any deeper 'reality'. Simultaneously, outward beauty in this romance is mostly made to stand for aristocratic descendance. However, there is also a different kind of beauty—a loose appearance of sorts that agrees with the respective character's inner disposition, but which nonetheless is beauty. As such, it has the power to engender love, but love of that kind will eventually lead to self-destruction instead of improvement. Significantly, it is the main characters, two young princes, who represent that type of beauty. These two princes are initially characterized as handsome, courageous and virtuous (cf. *FF*, 2), but the subsequent development of the plot calls these apparent virtues into question. Far from being perfect, then, they turn out to have quite a lot of faults. So, for example, as soon as they turn their backs they do not keep the promises of help they have made, and are thus shown to be forgetful and selfish. When they run away with two princesses, one of them the daughter of the king they serve, the other one his prisoner, they are characterized as ungrateful and negligent of duty—a stark contrast to what their beauty had promised, which is described in entirely traditional terms at the very beginning of the romance. In the end, and in accordance with their faults, their love does not lead them to any more significant action than marriage. By contrast, we also encounter an old man who mourns for his love—a virtuous, beautiful woman—beyond her death and who is mocked by the young princes for this very constancy. But even in his case, the reader is led to realize that love has made him not wise but foolish, for his is a selfish love, intent only on cultivating his pain of loss.

---

[23]Throughout this essay, page references are to the following edition: John Reynolds, *The Flower of Fidelity* (London, 1654) (R 1304) (abbreviation used: *FF*).

In Reynolds's text, *Vertue* is personified and appears as an old woman to guide the princes (*FF*, 23ff.). Obviously, then, virtue is presented here not even as beautiful any more, but as merely old(-fashioned). *Vertue* advises the two princes not to pay attention to beauty, but rather to try and be virtuous themselves. Yet again, that advice is not heeded and they do nothing of this: they listen and promise to obey, but they forget about their commitment almost immediately. Virtue is thus shown not to count any longer, and even *Vertue* herself denies any connection between herself and beauty by warning the princes of beauty's effect: '*Gaze not on Beauty, lest it ingender repentance: but loath a lascivious Courtisan as the scourge of iniquity.*' (*FF*, 28)

In conclusion, it can be said that Sidney starts off his new *Arcadia* with a presentation of beauty that may yet be considered in terms of a sign 'complete' in itself, in the sense that beauty signifies virtue, which in turn refers to God's perfection. Then, in the same text, he begins to question the conventional system of signification. In those parts of *Arcadia* that develop this questioning stance, the improvement that is traditionally to be derived from love of beauty, and consequently from love of virtue, is problematized and shown to have lost its sway. Thus, moving away from the conventional concept of beauty, Sidney goes on to present and investigate the concept of love of an individual. In that context, beauty is still shown to signify virtue, but both qualities belong to the person thus described and, furthermore, are used to distinguish the respective character from others. Here, then, various kinds of beauty, as well as other virtues, are used to characterize individuals. Mary Wroth's *Urania*, in turn, introduces further developments, and altogether changes the significance of beauty and virtues. In her text, beauty stands for beauty alone, but nothing else. It can still be 'in good company', thus counting as one of a character's good qualities. Yet it can also stand entirely on its own, as the only indication of worth and justification of love. Love thus loses its capacity to stimulate self-improvement, which had still been indispensable in Sidney. Just as beauty can decay, love can be transferred from one object to another, without any substantial loss to the lover. Weamys and Reynolds, finally, introduce yet further, more radical variations on that theme. In their romances, love— even love of virtue—is of no avail against selfishness, but it is in Reynolds's version, specifically, that virtue has become old and faded, and is no longer beautiful; the implied rationale, then, is that virtue need not be heeded or sought for any longer.

The trends and developments discussed in this paper start off with a comparatively firm belief in a significance of beauty that stretches beyond external, earthly beauty, and they end with an emphasis on external appearance alone, at the expense of whatever may lie beyond. Such developments, moreover, might be seen as connected to the introduction of individualized characters, and generally of the idea of the individual, into the texts scrutinized. For obviously, ideas of individuality do not sit well with the almost allegorical quality of a figure like Sidney's Urania. Therefore, as different kinds of beauty are introduced and made to become characteristics that distinguish one character from another, beauty has to be freed from its religious connotations.

JOHN LOCKE AND THE TRADITION OF NOMINALISM

NICHOLAS HUDSON

The tradition of Medieval nominalism continued to exercise an important influence on philosophical and linguistic thought in the seventeenth and eighteenth centuries. But this influence is sometimes difficult to detect. The term 'nominalism' itself fell from ordinary usage, and the great controversy between nominalists and realists receded into history. Virtually every philosopher was a 'nominalist', insofar as he rejected belief in the real existence of 'universals'. But nominalism had mutated into radically new forms. William of Ockham himself would have been shocked to discover what strange and heretical doctrines had evolved from his first principles. Among the philosophers who developed nominalism in daring new directions, none is more important than John Locke. For Locke was a bridge between the past and the future. He was, until this century, among the last philosophers to deal explicitly with the scholastic problem of universals. But he was also widely recognised by later philosophers of the Enlightenment as the figure who had launched a new and vigorous movement in the study of language.

Strangely, Locke's background in the tradition of nominalism has been little studied. Philosophers have considered his linguistic thought almost solely in the light of twentieth-century developments: he has come virtually to incarnate a naive 'mentalistic' or 'psychologistic' theory of language discredited by Frege, Wittgenstein and the leaders of the 'linguistic turn' of the twentieth century.[1] Among historians and literary scholars, Locke is

---

[1] Fairly typical statements of this view of Locke include Ian Hacking, *Why Does Language Matter to Philosophy?* (Cambridge: Cambridge University Press, 1975), 51-2; Charles Landesman, 'Locke's Theory of Meaning', *Journal of the History of Philosophy*, 14 (1976), 23-35; Godfrey Vesey, 'Locke and Wittgenstein on Language and Reality', in H.D. Lewis (ed.), *Contemporary British Philosophy* (London: George Allen & Unwin, 1976), 253-73; Stephen K. Land, 'Locke's Theory: Idealism', in *The Philosophy of Language in Britain* (New York: AMS, 1986), 31-77. Some of the arguments of the following are more briefly presented in Nicholas Hudson, 'Locke's Nominalism and the "Linguistic Turn" of the Enlightenment', *The European Legacy*, 2.2 (1997), 223-8.

sometimes vaguely referred to as a 'nominalist'. But specialists in the eighteenth century generally show little knowledge of what 'nominalism' really means. Scholarship on Locke, or on the eighteenth century, pays little attention to that central principle of nominalism—that there are no 'universal' entities in the world or in the mind, for all existing things are individual.

Yet Locke himself attached great importance to this principle. It is an important premise of his discussion of 'general words' in Book 3 of *Essay Concerning Human Understanding* (1690),[2] his major philosophical work. Moreover, Locke's quite original extension of this principle would have a major impact on later philosophers. He maintained not only, like previous nominalists, that universals were mental 'signs' grouped under general names.[3] He also went on to insist that humans decided on the nature and extent of these general concepts. As Locke put it, 'the Boundaries of *Species*, are as Men, and not as Nature makes them' (bk. 3, ch. 6, §29, 457). Even more radically, Locke indicated that universals existed basically for the purposes of *language*, and were fashioned to serve the ends of communication. And in giving language this central role in the construction of universals, he inspired later and even more radical studies of the relationship between language and mind, as in the work of Condillac, Rousseau and Adam Smith.

Where, then, did Locke get his information on nominalism? As E.J. Ashworth has pointed out, Locke would have gained an intimate knowledge of texts in the scholastic tradition during his time as a student and don at Christ Church College, Oxford.[4] These works still formed the backbone of university logic courses. Ockham is not mentioned in the list of books used by Locke's students. Yet a new edition of Ockham's *Summa totius logicae* was published at Oxford in 1675, and this philosopher continued to be widely cited by logicians as the principal representative of

---

[2] John Locke, *An Essay Concerning Human Understanding*, ed. Peter H. Nidditch (Oxford: Clarendon Press, 1975). Page references in the text are to this edition.

[3] Throughout this essay, I will use the term 'nominalist' to refer to the whole tradition that rejected the realist claim that universals really existed, physically or metaphysically, in the world or the mind. I will not distinguish between 'nominalist' and 'conceptualist' doctrines. In this terminology, I follow the meaning of 'nominalism' accepted by all philosophers in history until our time. Renaissance and Enlightenment thinkers widely accepted Ockham as the founder of 'nominalism', yet Ockham himself placed universals in mental *concepts* not words. Indeed, no Medieval philosopher placed universals solely in names ('voces') except Roscelin, who was quickly refuted by Abelard. Among later philosophers, perhaps only Hobbes would qualify as a 'nominalist' in the narrow sense demanded by some historians.

[4] See E.J. Ashworth, '"Do Words Signify Ideas or Things?" The Scholastic Sources of Locke's Theory of Language', *Journal of the History of Philosophy*, 19 (1981), 299-326.

the nominalist tradition. Evidence in Locke's writing suggests, as well, that he both knew and strongly supported the major principles of nominalism as advanced by Ockham and developed by later authors such as Valla and Nizolius.

Let us turn to the arguments of nominalism that had the greatest impact on Western philosophy. Ockham replaced the realist conception of universals with a theory of mental signs. According to the 'moderate' realist position that dominated Medieval philosophy, general names such as 'homo' or 'equus' referred to 'essences' that truly existed in the world. These essences did not exist apart from individual objects, as believed by Plato; nor were they fully realised outside the intellect, which recognised the universal nature of species from information received by the senses. Nevertheless, this Aristotelian position assured that general statements about the world (such as 'homo est animal rationale') corresponded with the real nature of things as eternally established by God. For Ockham, on the contrary, the word 'homo' referred only to a mental 'sign'. Early in his career, he described this universal concept in ways that closely anticipated Locke's theory: the universal, wrote Ockham, is a mental 'image' (*fictum*) or 'pattern' (*exemplar*) which 'relates indifferently to all singular things outside the mind' (*indifferenter respiciens omnia singularia extra [mente]*).[5] He later abandoned this view for the position that the universal is 'an intention of mind' (*intentio animae*) that is 'identical with the act of understanding' (*ab actu intelligo non differt*).[6] In the cases of both the early and late theories, however, Ockham denied that individual objects contained 'essences' that were recognised by the intellect. The intellect merely abstracted what was common about individual 'homines' or 'equi' to form a general concept of these objects.

Ockham's fundamental charge against the realists was that they had absurdly confused words and things. They assumed that because we have a general name like 'homo', there must also be some entity in nature, the 'universal', corresponding to this word. According to Ockham, on the contrary, 'common names signify only particulars'.[7] The existence of universal concepts or universal words did not indicate the existence of any corresponding entity in nature, which consisted solely of individuals.

---

[5] William of Ockham, *Ordinatio*, in *Philosophical Writings*, tr. Philotheus Boehner, rev. F. Brown (Indianapolis, IN: Hackett Publishing, 1990), D. II, Q. viii, prima redactio, 41.

[6] William of Ockham, *Summa Logicae*, in *Ockham's Theory of Terms: Part I of the 'Summa Logicae'*, tr. Michael J. Loux (Notre Dame, IN, and London: University of Notre Dame Press, 1974), pars 1, cap. 15, 81. On the shift from Ockham's earlier to later theory of universals, see Marilyn McCord Adams, *William Ockham*, 2 vols. (Notre Dame, IN: University of Notre Dame Press, 1987), vol. 1: 73-107.

[7] Ockham, *Summa Logicae*, pars 1, cap. 17, 86.

Ockham also insisted that there was a gap between words and concepts. Words signify things only 'secondarily' through the medium of concepts, which denoted things 'primarily and naturally'.[8] Furthermore, many of the elements of language did not have an equivalent in the mind. Synonymous terms referred to only one mental 'intention'. Rhetorical flourishes, word gender, participles and perhaps pronouns contributed as well to a complexity in language that far exceeded the simple and logical formulations of thought.[9]

Ockham's critique of realism thus implied a radical separation of words, concepts and things. The importance of his making this division may not be clear to students of modern philosophy: in our time, philosophers who led 'the linguistic turn' have scorned the belief that words refer to mental images or any other results of mental operations.[10] But Ockham was arguing against a tradition that ordinarily made no careful distinction between words and reality. Although Aristotle asserted in an influential passage that words are only the symbols of mental experience,[11] his analysis of predication encouraged the belief among the whole scholastic tradition that Latin grammar provided a transparent mirror of the structure of the world. This was a confidence in language that Ockham discredited by, in part, denying the existence of real universals. And in doing so, he made possible later developments that would ultimately reintegrate language into the process of constructing 'reality' in the human mind.

In certain respects, moreover, Ockham anticipated the linguistic interests of our own time. Like Frege, Russell and the young Wittgenstein, he stressed the deficiencies of natural (i.e. ordinary) language, and sought to isolate a lucid and simple idiom for the use of philosophy. Ockham's work puts paid to the assumption that no author before our time recognised the centrality of language to understanding and solving the old problems of philosophy. In the nominalistic tradition that he did much to found, the major principles of scholastic thought were demystified into confusions of language. According to Lorenzo Valla, writing in the mid-fifteenth century, the scholastics had built their philosophy on what were fundamentally distinctions of grammar: that favourite scholastic concept of 'ens' or 'being', for example, was merely the participle of 'sum', and not the name of some actual substance. Similarly, 'humanitas' was no more a 'substance' in

---

[8] Ibid., pars 1, cap. 1, 50.

[9] See ibid., pars 1, cap. 3.

[10] See Frege's attack on the doctrine that words refer to some 'idea' in his famous essay 'On Sense and Meaning', in Gottlob Frege, *Collected Papers on Mathematics, Logic and Philosophy*, ed. Brian McGuiness (Oxford: Blackwell, 1984), 160.

[11] See Aristotle, *De interpretatione*, ed. W.D. Ross, tr. E.M. Edghill (= vol. 1 (1928) of *Works*, 12 vols. (Oxford: Clarendon Press, 1908-52)), 16a.

individual humans than 'platonitas' was a 'substance' in Plato.[12] A century later, Marius Nizolius made the same kind of charge against the realists at great length, contending that 'homo' was only a collective noun like 'exercitus' or 'populus', which obviously referred to individuals and not to some single entity.[13] In elucidating these problems, Valla and Nizolius found fresh interest in language, rhetoric and grammar. While accusing the scholastics of building their metaphysics on the shaky ground of words, Valla himself helped to launch the humanist interest in recovering a pure, classical Latin free from corruptions introduced in the Middle Ages. If language became suspect for its capacity to deceive philosophers, it also gained unprecedented importance as an activity worth studying for its own sake.[14]

It has even been claimed, by Richard Waswo, that the Renaissance marks a 'semantic shift' towards the view that language does not refer to some separate reality, but actually *constitutes* that reality. According to Waswo, Valla, Luther, Erasmus and others were, in effect, proto-Wittgensteins who set out to overturn the 'referential' theories of all previous thinkers. But Waswo's thesis leans heavily on sketchy and ambiguous evidence.[15] Most seriously for our purposes, he echoes the common but completely erroneous belief that philosophers after Descartes lost any sense of the importance of language to understanding or 'constituting' reality.[16] Indeed, it was in the seventeenth century that philosophers began to insist, in an explicit and unambigious way, that human knowledge was inseparable from the conventions of language. This insight, furthermore, represents a direct continuation of the logic of nominalism.

---

[12]Laurentius Valla, *Dialecticae disputationes*, in *Opera* (Basileae, 1540), 652-3.

[13]See Marius Nizolius, *De veris principiis et vera ratione philosophandi contra pseudophilosophos* (Parma, 1553), 50.

[14]On Valla's influence on the study of *eloquentia*, and on the rise of grammatical scholarship in the Renaissance, see G.H. Padley, *Grammatical Theory in Western Europe 1500-1700*, 2 vols. (Cambridge: Cambridge University Press, 1985-8), vol. 2: 5-85.

[15]See Richard Waswo, *Language and Meaning in the Renaissance* (Princeton, NJ: Princeton University Press, 1987). Waswo credits Valla with the 'brilliant insight that words and things are somehow identical' (109). Yet this assertion is based largely on a single passage from Valla's *Dialecticarum Disputationum* that Waswo himself admits is 'ambiguous' and 'nowhere [...] explicitly makes the epistemological point that words are necessary to bring objects into consciousness' (108). Waswo finds 'the spirit of the later Wittgenstein' in Valla's statement that 'the populace speaks better than the philosopher' (98). But Valla was not, like Wittgenstein, proposing a linguistic theory of 'usage' against theories of referentiality. He clearly had in mind the inanity of scholastic verbiage (such as I have indicated in the text), which he contrasted with the relative sanity of common speech. This is quite a different distinction from that which concerned Wittgenstein.

[16]See ibid., 293.

No thinker makes this legacy more obvious than Thomas Hobbes. Hobbes's radical extension of Ockham's nominalism was to deny that even *concepts* could be universal. Only words assured that we could make general statements about the world. In Hobbes's work, therefore, the difference between logic and grammar threatened to disappear completely. As he wrote in *The Elements of Philosophy*,

> this word *universal* is never the name of anything existent in nature, nor of any idea or phantasm found in the mind, but always of the name of some word or name; so that when a *living creature, a stone, a spirit*, or any other thing is said to be *universal*, it is not to be understood, that any man, stone, etc. ever was or can be universal, but only that these words, *living creature, stone*, etc. are *universal names*, that is, names common to many things; and the conceptions answering them in our mind are the images and phantasms of several living creatures, and other things.[17]

Hobbes's sceptical doctrine might, indeed, strike us as particularly far-reaching and 'modern'. Building on the basic principles of nominalism, he argued that definitions and propositions are equally as 'arbitrary' as the words that make them up. The proposition 'man is a living creature', for example, is true only because people have agreed to give the names 'man' and 'living creature' to the same objects. Moreover, as all knowledge concerns the general nature of things, and only names can be general, this knowledge is theoretically founded solely on the conventions of naming. Here was a bold extension of nominalism that distressed even nominalists. In a preface to an edition of Nizolius, for example, Leibniz called Ockham 'a man of great genius',[18] and endorsed his rejection of realism. But Hobbes, said Leibniz, was another matter. He was really a 'super-nominalist', for he contended that 'the truth of things itself consists of names'.[19]

Hobbes is a major predecessor to Locke in the development of nominalist theories. Nevertheless, it is Locke who finally produced the more coherent and the more influential argument concerning the relationship between language and general knowledge. Hobbes's thought on this subject is weakened, first, by serious contradictions. At times, he sounds like a seventeenth-century counterpart of Richard Rorty or Jacques Derrida, as in the passage cited above. But elsewhere Hobbes expressed a stolid confidence in the knowledge of the senses. When he turns to 'Physics, or the Phenomena of Nature' in Part 4 of *Elements of Philosophy*, the scepticism of early sections strangely evaporates. He insists that knowledge of

---

[17]Thomas Hobbes, *The Elements of Philosophy*, in *English Works*, 2 vols., ed. Sir William Molesworth (London: Bohn, 1839), vol. 1: 20.

[18]Gottfried Wilhelm Leibniz, *Philosophical Papers and Letters*, 2 vols., ed. Leroy E. Loemaker (Chicago, IL: University of Chicago Press, 1956), vol. 1: 198.

[19]Ibid., 199.

physical nature is *not* dependent on human definitions, but is grounded on principles 'placed in the things themselves by the Author of Nature'.[20] The same vacillation characterises his discussions of knowledge in *Leviathan*: sometimes he boldly claims that there is 'no Reasoning without Speech', but he just as often warns against the deluding qualities of language. 'Words are wise mens counters [...]', he warned, 'but they are the mony of fooles'.[21]

Hobbes's critics were not entirely wrong to accuse him of contradiction and illogic. As the Port-Royal authors pointed out, for instance, it does not follow that all truth is 'arbitrary' because definitions are made up of 'arbitrary' words. Presumably, the names 'man' and 'living creature' record real sensory experiences, and were not given to the same creature through some 'arbitrary' whim of the first speakers.[22] Indeed, Hobbes himself defines 'ratiocination' as 'when we add and substract [sic!] in our silent thoughts, without the use of words'.[23] Furthermore, Hobbes's arguments stir up some important questions which he fails to address. Why do humans make one kind of general term rather than another? What criteria do they bring to bear on the decision to group certain individuals under one universal, and other individuals under another?

These were the problems that most interested Locke. His discussion of general words may seem, superficially, less challenging and forward-looking than Hobbes's.[24] Locke's strongly psychological orientation—his primary interest in how general concepts are *made*—may strike many modern readers as irrelevant or at least outside the purview of real 'philosophy'. Nevertheless, Locke made his most influential contribution to nominalism in theorising about how and why we distinguish between 'species' and 'genera'. Unlike Hobbes, he did not dismiss all general knowledge as utterly conventional. But Locke did identify a considerable *degree* of arbitrariness in how we classify nature. Most important, while his arguments are not unmarred by inconsistency, he did not, like Hobbes,

---

[20] Hobbes, *Elements of Philosophy*, 388.

[21] Thomas Hobbes, *Leviathan*, ed. C.B. Macpherson (Harmondsworth: Penguin, 1968), pt. 1, ch. 4, 106.

[22] See Antoine Arnauld and Pierre Nicole, *La logique, ou l'art de penser*, ed. Pierre Clair and François Girbal (Paris: Presses Universitaires de France, 1965), 34-5.

[23] Hobbes, *Elements of Philosophy*, 3.

[24] Michael Ayers (*Locke*, 2 vols. (London and New York: Routledge, 1991), vol. 1: 253-4) has portrayed Locke as basically rejecting Hobbes's view that universals depend on language, though Locke does make some 'concessions' to this position. In the argument that follows, I will contend that Locke was led by his own logic to conclude that language did play a role in the construction of universals. His insights on this subject are not mere concessions to Hobbes. Indeed, it was Locke who advanced the more coherent analysis of traditional nominalistic problems.

make sweeping assertions about universals without a fully developed epistemology.

Locke most clearly recalls the claims of Medieval nominalism in Book 3 of *Essay Concerning Human Understanding*, 'Of Words'. Here he denies that species and genera are anything but 'the Workmanship of the Understanding'. The basis of all perception is single sensory impressions of particular objects, or what Locke calls 'simple ideas'. In our experience of the world, we find these simple ideas combined in 'complex ideas' of objects like individual humans, horses, and pieces of gold. But in order to achieve the universal concept of 'human', 'horse' or 'gold', we must abstract what is common to all the individual members of a species. By means of this abstraction, we form 'general ideas', which Locke describes as 'Patterns, or Forms' standing for all individual objects given a common name such as 'man' or 'gold' (bk. 3, ch. 3, §§12-3, 415).

Modern commentators frequently berate Locke for his doctrine of 'general ideas'. In this criticism, they follow Berkeley, who could not find any 'general' ideas in his visual memory and therefore insisted that even ideas must be particular. But Locke was only trying to explain what seems a plausible observation on human experience: we can form a general concept without presenting its name in our head at the same time. I can recognise a tree without quietly repeating the word 'tree' to myself. I can also understand the word 'tree' in a sentence without conjuring a mental picture of some individual tree: the general concept, as understood by Locke, need not be one that is sensible or visualised in the way demanded by Berkeley. Moreover, in distinguishing between general words and general concepts, Locke was only following a basic distinction in nominalist thought since Ockham. Like Ockham, Locke regarded *semeiotike* or '*the Doctrine of Signs*' (bk. 4, ch. 21, §4, 720) as a basis for understanding human perception and thought. Both words and 'ideas' (Locke's word for all perceptions and concepts) should be regarded as 'signs'. Ockham and Locke did not entirely agree about how we perceive individuals: Ockham argued that we begin with an 'intuitive cognition', by which he meant a full intellectual grasp of the object, not merely a collection of sensory impressions, as indicated by Locke. Moreover, Ockham did not descend to component perceptions or 'simple ideas' that make up individuals. But these philosophers did agree that the universal was the workmanship of the understanding achieved, through abstraction, after the experience of individual objects.

At this point, however, we should also notice some more significant disparities between Ockham's nominalism and the version of this doctrine developed by Locke. Ockham's nominalism by no means implied that our universal ideas were subjective or lacked a foundation in the order of nature. Nor did he believe that there was anything 'arbitrary' about how the mind formed universal concepts by means of abstraction. The universal concept of 'man', to cite his example, was no less a 'natural' sign of all men than 'weeping is a natural sign of grief'.[25] While denying the realist claim that the universal was an actual 'substance' existing outside the mind, Ockham maintained a firm foundation for the study of species and genera. In the words of Philotheus Boehner, 'there is something in nature, namely the individual essence or nature, not something or some nature different from the individuals, which is genuinely represented by these universal ideas'.[26]

Locke agreed with Ockham, and indeed the whole Medieval tradition, in insisting on the conventional or 'arbitrary' basis for words. Nevertheless, Locke did not conceive of 'general ideas' as 'natural' signs for an external reality. In his view, some general ideas were entirely human-made and lacked any object or 'archetype' in nature whatsoever: notable among such 'arbitrary' general ideas were the 'mixed modes' designated by ethical and religious terms such as 'justice', 'temperance', 'prodigality' (bk. 2, ch. 22, 288-95). These concepts were fashioned entirely by humans in accordance with prevailing needs and beliefs. For this reason, they varied greatly from nation to nation. But even our general ideas of 'substances' such as humans, horses or gold contained an important measure of arbitrariness and variability. In his chapter 'Of the Names of Substances', Locke argued at length that the 'Boundaries of *Species*, are as Men, and not as Nature makes them' (bk. 3, ch. 6, §29, 457). Citing the usual example of a species in Medieval philosophy, he denied that there was anything 'essential' about reason to the definition of 'man'. According to our normal ways of speaking, he pointed out, an irrational idiot or 'Changeling' is still a 'man' despite his or her lack of reason (bk. 4, ch. 4, §§13-6, 569-73). Similarly, theological uncertainty about whether to baptise highly deformed births revealed the lack of clear or objective criteria for qualifying or disqualifying individuals as 'men' (§26, 453-4).

Locke indicated as well that many of our ways of sorting the species are inconsistent and illogical. We distinguish 'water' from 'ice', but have no separate name for frozen 'Gelly' (§13, 447-8). We group a spaniel and a hound in the same species, despite a considerable disparity of size and appearance. Why then are hounds and elephants assigned to different species (§37, 463)? These inconsistencies indicated to Locke that the

---

[25]Ockham, *Summa Logicae*, pars 1, cap. 15, 78-9.

[26]Philotheus Boehner, 'The Realistic Conceptualism of William Ockham', in *Collected Articles on Ockham*, ed. Eligius M. Buytaert (St. Bonaventure, NY: The Franciscan Institute. 1958), 163. On Ockham's basic confidence in the correspondence between universal concepts and extramental reality, see also Stephen F. Brown, 'A Modern Prologue to Ockham's Natural Philosophy', in Jan P. Beckmann et al. (eds.), *Sprache und Erkenntnis im Mittelalter* (Berlin and New York: Walter de Gruyter, 1981), 107-29; Adams, *William Ockham*, vol. 1: 111-5.

'Schoolmen' (a term that he applied to the whole tradition of scholastic philosophy, stretching into the seventeenth century) had been wrong to assume that our general words correspond with a stable order of genera and species in nature. Relying largely on how general words are used in common speech (rather than in the language of philosophy),[27] Locke rejected not only realism, but also Ockham's nominalistic doctrine that universal concepts were 'natural' signs of genera and species existing in the world.

Locke's scepticism should not be exaggerated: he did believe that our mental formation of general ideas was roughly guided by the information of our senses. God had established a real order of species, each individual of a species sharing the same 'real essence'. But Locke's term 'real essence' should not be confused with some actual entity in nature, as believed by Medieval realists, or with some relation of matter and form mirrored in true definitions, as argued by St Thomas Aquinas. Rather, Locke was referring to the sub-sensible atomic structure of physical things that was the ultimate source of all sensible qualities. His consistent point was that 'real essences' were unknowable, and therefore irrelevant to how people actually sort things into genera and species. We sort these universals by forming 'nominal essences'—clusters of sensible qualities that we find consistently in a number of individual objects. And these 'nominal essences' can and do vary considerably depending on the nature of our individual experiences, on the care of our observations, and on our particular concerns and needs.

In insisting that our general ideas, formed by the mind, only vaguely reflect the real (and inaccessible) order of nature, Locke went further down the road of scepticism than Ockham or any Medieval nominalist. Furthermore, Locke's view implied a much more central role for conventional signs in the formation of universals. For it is no accident that Locke's major discussion of universals takes place in the chapters devoted to the issue of language. 'General ideas', in his view, were originally contrived specifically to facilitate speech with others. A language in which every object had a proper name would be vast and unwieldy. Primitive speakers thus formed ideas of species and genera with the objective of 'naming and comprehending them under general terms' (bk. 3, ch. 6, §30, 458). They sought above all to create a language that was short and convenient: '[...] Men, in making their general *Ideas*, seeking more the convenience of Language and quick dispatch, by short and comprehensive signs, than the true and

---

[27]Locke's use of ordinary language again distinguishes him from Ockham, who was critical of common locutions, and sought an 'Ideal' language that approximated mental discourse. See John Trentman, 'Ockham on Mental', *Mind,* 79 (1970), 583-90; Claude Panaccio, 'Langage ordinaire et langage abstrait chez Guillaume d'Occam', *Philosophiques,* 1 (1974), 37-60.

precise Nature of Things, as they exist, have, in the framing their abstract *Ideas*, chiefly pursued that end, which was, to be furnished with store of general, and variously comprehensive Names' (§32, 459-60).

This position in the *Essay* is, in my view, of major and largely unrecognised significance.[28] Departing from the nominalist tradition that he carried on in other respects, Locke contended that the formation of general words was the major purpose for forming general concepts. The understanding of general concepts was, by implication, almost inseparable from the examination of language. As Locke argued, '*general Truths*' are '*seldom apprehended, but as conceived and expressed in Words*' (bk. 4, ch. 6, §2, 579). In contrast with Ockham, who had confirmed the ancient distinction between mental and verbal discourse, Locke became convinced that no study of the understanding could avoid discussion of how language influenced even our ways of thinking about the world.

For it is naming, in Locke's view, that gives ideas real clarity, distinctness and stability.[29] Ideas that 'have not had names given to them pass [...] not for Species' (bk. 2, ch. 18, §7, 226), and are hardly noticed among the innumerable impressions and objects of sensory experience. Moreover, general ideas vary between different communities and professions according to their particular needs of communication. A chemist, a smith and a brewer all use special terms such as '*Coltshire, Drilling, Filtration, Cohobation*' and so forth to denote distinctions that are virtually meaningless to others (225-6). Whereas some nations lack even a word for 'horse', European jockeys and equestrian trainers give names to subtle variations of pedigree (bk. 2, ch. 28, §2, 350). We have a complex system for classifying the family relations of humans—father, son, aunt, uncle, cousin, and so forth—but no such system for classifying analogous relations between animals (349). We have names for certain shades of colour, but none for others (bk. 2, ch. 18, §§4-6, 224-5). The reason for these differences, Locke observed repeatedly, is closely linked to the ends of speech: different communities and professions make use of different classifications in order to express their mutual concerns and objectives. It is the requirements of speech, and not the 'reality' of nature, that largely determines how we name and even how we perceive the world:

---

[28]Land, 'Locke's Theory', 53, briefly describes 'a weak form of linguistic relativism' in the *Essay*, but maintains that this by no means undermines Locke's assurance in the universality of ideas or the autonomy of ideation from speech. See also Ayers's observations on Locke's 'concessions' to Hobbesian conventionalism (Ayers, *Locke*, vol. 1: 253-4).

[29]On the importance of names in keeping ideas distinct and clear, see Locke, *Essay*, bk. 2, ch. 29, §6, 364-5; bk. 4, ch. 5, §4, 575.

> This [...] may give us some light into the different state and growth of Languages, which being suited only to the convenience of Communication, are proportioned to the Notions Men have, and the commerce of Thoughts familiar amongst them; and not to the reality or extent of Things, nor to the various Respects might be found among them. (bk. 2, ch. 28, §2, 349)

Locke thus made two major and interrelated changes to traditional nominalism. First, he strongly questioned the belief of Medieval nominalists that our universal concepts correspond by 'natural' signification to real species and genera in the extramental world. Second, he narrowed and blurred the distinction between mental and verbal signs, pointing to the integral psychological function of words in all our ways of thinking. In summary,

> I find, that there is so close a connexion between *Ideas* and Words; and our abstract *Ideas*, and general Words, have so constant a relation one to another, that it is impossible to speak clearly and properly and distinctly of our Knowledge, which all consists in Propositions, without considering, first, the Nature, Use, and Signification of Language (bk. 2, ch. 33, §19, 401)

This position does not seem consistent with the modern reading of Locke as a 'mentalist' who insisted on the absolute independence and primacy of mental discourse. Yet it is a recurring thesis in Locke's work, and is prominent even in the earliest extant draft of the *Essay* from 1671.[30] Moreover, Locke's emphasis on language in his treatment of general ideas was immediately noticed and attacked by contemporary opponents such as Stillingfleet and Leibniz.[31] Nor was the novelty and significance of Locke's linguistic insights lost on his admirers later in the eighteenth century. Let us examine how Locke's thought inspired a wave of interest in general terms, and in the interrelations between language and reason.

The pivotal figure here is the Enlightenment *philosophe* Etienne Bonnot, Abbé de Condillac. In the introduction of *Essai sur l'origine des connaissances humaines* (1746), this philosopher applauded Locke for seeing 'that the consideration of words, and of our manner of using them, might give

---

[30] See R.I. Aaron and Jocelyn Gibb (eds.), *An Early Draft of Locke's* Essay (Oxford: Clarendon Press, 1936), 44-5.

[31] Edward Stillingfleet, Bishop of Worcester, believed that a realist account of species and genera was necessary to protect belief in the Trinity. See his attack on Locke in *A Discourse in Vindication of the Doctrine of the Trinity* (London, 1697), 254-8. Gottfried Wilhelm Leibniz assailed Locke's chapter on 'General Terms' in a long chapter of his *Nouveaux essais sur l'entendement humaine* (written c. 1703-5; published 1765), bk. 3, ch. 3.

some light into the principle of our ideas'.[32] But Condillac also alleged that Locke had not capitalised on the potential richness of his own inspirations. As we have seen, for example, Locke argued that words were essential to the creation of ethical and religious concepts: a word like 'justice' acted as a mental bond that united all the various simple ideas that made up the corresponding concept. But Locke failed to perceive that, for similar reasons, a word was necessary to bind the component ideas of a substance. He took for granted that we could form the concept of gold without the word 'gold'. The source of this error, argued Condillac, was Locke's assumption that because substances were unified in the world, they would also be unified in the mind. Blinded by this confusion between the world and the mind, he did not remember that the complex idea of gold was just a loose assemblage of ideas like the complex idea of justice. A clearer perception of this fact would have led Locke to the conclusion drawn by Condillac: the word for a substance, such as 'gold', served a no less essential role than the word 'justice' as the mental glue of our complex ideas (see ibid., pt. 1, sec. 4, ch. 2, 135-6).

Building on Locke's partial insights, therefore, Condillac brought language into the very midst of ordinary thinking. He set out to show that words were necessary to form not just moral terms, but all complex ideas whatsoever. Here as well, he believed, lay the root of Medieval realism, with all its delusions. Because the schoolmen discovered that they could not even think about substances such as 'gold' or 'humans' without the corresponding word, they supposed that this word referred to some real 'essence' or 'quiddity' in things—a 'goldness' or 'humanity' shared by all objects of the same class (see ibid., pt. 1, sec. 5, 146-52). Indeed, this error is virtually unavoidable in ordinary thinking. We normally suppose that our words refer not just to collections of ideas or abstractions, but to actual entities (see ibid., 149). But Condillac insisted that modern philosophers must be more scrupulous. They should realise that general terms were necessary to thinking only because of the limited capacity of human brains. This argument, we might note, is a revealing alternative to a position that we have considered in Locke's *Essay*. Locke maintained general words are necessary to simplify *language*, for the first speakers could not invent an individual name for every object. Condillac's emphasis, on the contrary, lay on the necessity of simplifying *thinking*. Mortals need to arrange individuals into groups because they are overwhelmed by the multiplicity of particular objects. Not so the omnipotent intelligence of God: the divine mind contemplates all the particulars of the universe without recourse to species, genera or universals of any kind (see ibid., pt. 1, sec. 5, 139).

---

[32]Etienne Bonnot, Abbé de Condillac, *An Essay on the Origin of Human Knowledge*, tr. Thomas Nugent (London, 1756; facs. repr. Gainesville, FL: Scholars' Facsimiles and Reprints, 1971), introduction, 9.

General terms, then, are the expedient of feeble mortal brains. They do not reflect the real order of things in nature: 'we must observe that it is less in regard to the nature of things, than to our manner of knowing them, that we determine their genus or species' (ibid.). If we possessed keener senses, we would find that our classifications were erroneous, for things that now seem similar would suddenly appear quite distinct. Thus, Condillac went much further than Locke in questioning the existence of species and genera. Locke did not, like Condillac, deny the existence of species and genera, but only the capacity of humans to know their boundaries exactly. Condillac, by contrast, denied the very existence of species and genera. Nevertheless, it is inaccurate to portray Condillac as refuting or contradicting Locke. As his numerous citations from Locke's *Essay* show, he was consciously building on the English philosopher's discussion of general terms. Condillac seems, indeed, to have had only the scantiest first-hand knowledge of the Medieval debate between nominalists and realists: Locke had become for Condillac, as he would for many other philosophers of the Enlightenment, a major source of information on the issue of nominalism. Nor did Condillac's work merely eclipse the quite independent value and originality of Locke's *Essay*. Condillac did not, for instance, develop Locke's interesting observations on how cultural factors (such as the professions and general habits of a people) shape what humans notice about the world and how they form classes.

It was Condillac, however, who brought Locke's linguistic insights into the mainstream of Enlightenment thought. When Rousseau observed that 'general ideas can enter the Mind only with the help of words' he was thinking of Condillac, whom he cited in his *Discours sur l'origine de l'inégalité* (1754).[33] Condillac's analysis of mind and language also led the scientist Buffon to conclude that 'only individuals truly exist in nature and [...] genera, orders and classes exist only in our imagination' ('il n'existe reéllement dans la Nature que des individus, & [...] les genres, les ordres

---

[33] Jean-Jacques Rousseau, *Discourse on Inequality*, in *The First and Second Discourses, together with Replies to Critics*, tr. Victor Gourevitch (New York: Perennial, 1986), 156. Rousseau acknowledges that it was Condillac who first suggested his own speculations on the origin of language (see 153). But Rousseau was not without criticisms of Condillac. He denied, in particular, that any society could have existed before the invention of language, as Condillac assumes when he traces the origin of language to the dialogue of a hypothetical couple, 'two children', in the state of nature. For Rousseau, the interdependency of language and society left philosophers with the following paradox: '[W]hich was the more necessary, an already united Society for the institution of Languages, or already invented Languages for the establishment of Society?' (157-8). This problem fascinated later authors such as Herder, who also criticised certain aspects of Condillac's theory.

& les classes n'existent que dans notre imagination').[34] The legacy of Condillac was most obviously displayed by the *idéologues* of the early nineteenth century: Destutt de Tracy and Degérando acknowledged their debt to Condillac in recognising the interdependence of language and reason.[35] In Germany too, as Hans Aarsleff has so well shown, Condillac exercised a crucial influence on the linguistic thought of Süßmilch, Herder, and Wilhelm von Humboldt.[36] Here, indeed, is the flourishing heritage of the nominalist tradition. These Enlightenment philosophers have in common a basically nominalist conviction that nature consists solely of individuals, and that only words are truly 'general'. This position was the foundation of their shared conviction in the centrality of language to thinking and to the examination of all philosophical problems.

The philosophy of Locke, in brief, inaugurated the 'linguistic turn' of the Enlightenment. In inviting this comparison between linguistic thought in the eighteenth century and in our time, I run the risk, admittedly, of blurring some important differences. Modern philosophers of language have not generally concerned themselves with the psychological role of language. They have argued instead that philosophy must focus on problems of language in order to understand and, if possible, resolve the traditional questions of their discipline. Early in this century, this mission gave rise to attempts to form an ideal logical language. More recently, it has led to profound scepticism concerning the possibility of ever isolating some 'truth' beyond the conventions of language. For philosophers of the Enlightenment, on the contrary, the construction of an ideal logical or philosophical language was of minor interest (though it had been a central concern of many philosophers in the seventeenth century).[37] Nor did the linguistic interests of the Enlightenment foment scepticism of a modern sort: the insight that language plays a central role in thinking did not

---

[34]Georges-Louis Leclerc, Comte de Buffon, *Histoire naturelle*, 'Premier Discours', in *Oeuvres philosophiques*, ed. Jean Piveteau (Paris: Presses Universitaires de France, 1954), 19.

[35]This debt to Condillac is most obvious in Degérando's *Des signes et de l'art de penser considérés dans leurs rapports mutuels* (1800), and Destutt de Tracy's *Eléments d'idéologie* (1804-15).

[36]See 'The Tradition of Condillac: The Problem of the Origin of Language in the Eighteenth Century and the Debate in the Berlin Academy before Herder', in Hans Aarsleff, *From Locke to Saussure: Essays on the Study of Language and Intellectual History* (Minneapolis, MN: University of Minnesota Press, 1982), 146-209. A strong defender of Locke's stature as a linguistic thinker, Aarsleff discusses the influence of Locke on Condillac in 'The History of Linguistics and Professor Chomsky' (*From Locke to Saussure*, 107-9).

[37]I have not had room here to discuss seventeenth-century plans to form an ideal philosophical language, though these projects dealt directly with the problems of classification that preoccupied philosophers from Ockham to Locke. Umberto Eco has

induce the conclusion that all truth was therefore relative, or that certainty must be abandoned to an endless play of signification.

Even in our time, the question of 'universals' has remained a minor, though fairly vigorous sub-discipline. But the debate has moved to a level of sophistication not found in the Enlightenment. It has been rightly pointed out that previous philosophers, such as Locke, were preoccupied with the general nature of nouns, and virtually ignored the similarly 'universal' nature of verbs, prepositions and other parts of speech. They tended to imagine the first speakers as giving names to things, and then extending the same name to various similar objects. What this account ignores, according to recent commentators, is that 'resemblance' is itself a subjective and universalised relationship. It is this issue of resemblance that has absorbed much modern interest in universals. Most famously, Wittgenstein pointed out that two members of the same class (such as 'games') may in fact have nothing in common whatsoever. Two individuals may be related only by a 'family resemblance'—a mutual relation to some other particular.[38]

But does this account of universals really depart so drastically from the line of inquiry begun in the Enlightenment? Indeed, Locke's own reflections on problems of 'resemblance' differ less from more recent ideas than has been claimed. A main contention of Book 3 in Locke's *Essay* is that humans decide what counts as 'similar' and what does not. Generality, he argued, is a relation governed ultimately by the needs of speakers, and not by 'nature' or by any standard separate from the ends of communication. Locke did not, it is true, exploit the full potential of his insights into the

---

recently commented that nominalism had the effect of removing the 'aura of sacrality' from language, which was regarded by the language planners not as divine gift but as merely an instrument of communication, open to change and improvement (see Umberto Eco, *The Search for the Perfect Language*, tr. James Fentress (Oxford and Cambridge, MA: Blackwell, 1995), 87). Other scholarship on the language planners has presented these authors—including Francis Lodwick, George Dalgarno and John Wilkins—as carrying on the moderate realism of Aristotle and the schools. Scholars have also argued that Locke's rebuttal of this realism helped to cause the marked decline of interest in these plans during the eighteenth century. On the Aristotelian roots of language reform, see M.M. Slaughter, *Universal Languages and Scientific Taxonomy in the Seventeenth Century* (Cambridge: Cambridge University Press, 1982). Slaughter also discusses Locke's impact on these authors (194-202), as does Lia Formigari, *Language and Experience in 17th-Century British Philosophy* (Amsterdam and Philadelphia, PA: John Benjamins, 1988), 99-131.

[38] Wittgenstein's discussion of universals is in *The Blue and Brown Books*, but is perhaps best known from Renford Bambrough's 'Universals and Family Resemblance' [1960], repr. in Michael J. Loux (ed.), *Universals and Particulars* (Notre Dame, IN, and London: Notre Dame University Press, 1976), 106-24. Bambrough argues that 'Wittgenstein solved what is known as "the problem of universals"' (106). On the relation of 'resemblance', see also Farhang Zabeeh, *Universals: A New Look at an Old Problem* (The Hague: Martinus Nijhoff, 1966), 38-49.

mental role of language. This extension of his insights was undertaken by philosophers like Condillac who were acute enough to see the importance of his work. Nevertheless, in seeing that problems of classification could not, in fact, be separated from problems of human language, it was Locke who opened a debate on the relationship between language and thought, and on the nature of universals, that still continues today.

A MODERN DEBATE OVER UNIVERSALS?
CRITICAL THEORY VS. 'ESSENTIALISM'

CHRISTOPH BODE

I

The two-part anecdote that Stanley Fish uses both to open his essay 'Is There a Text in This Class?' and to close his collection of the same title is, I gather, by now a familiar one. It goes like this: On the first day of a new semester, a colleague of Professor Fish's at Johns Hopkins University is asked by a student whether there is a text in his class, to which he answers, 'Yes; it's the *Norton Anthology of Literature*', upon which the student, evidently an acolyte of radical Fishean demystification of 'the text', mends her speech by rejoining, 'No, no, I mean in this class do we believe in poems and things, or is it just us?'

Already at this stage, Fish's colleague stands demasked as a relatively naive teacher who mistakes a critical question for a practical one, but it is only some 65 pages later that Fish, with theatrical aplomb, deals him the final blow by letting us know his colleague's self-destructing retort to this readerly challenge: 'Yes, there *is* a text in this class; what's more, it has meanings and I am going to tell you what they are.'[1]

This happened, if it happened at all, many years ago, and yet the anecdote epitomizes almost ideally (that is, after all, the reason why Fish made it so central in his book) the oppositions in a critical debate that has been raging for some decades now and which—if one thinks, to give but two examples, of the exchanges following Anthony Easthope's plea for critical theory and cultural studies in the *Times Literary Supplement* of May 25th, 1994, or those following the publications of Graham Brad-

---

[1] Stanley Fish, *Is There a Text in This Class? The Authority of Interpretive Communities* (Cambridge, MA: Harvard University Press, 1980), 305; 371. The present essay is a revised, updated version of the paper I presented at ISSEI's 1994 Graz conference (see Preface). An abridged version has been published, under the same title, in the selected workshop proceedings in *The European Legacy*, 2.2 (1997), 229-37.

shaw's *Misrepresentations: Shakespeare and the Materialists*[2] and of Brian Vickers' *Appropriating Shakespeare: Contemporary Critical Quarrels*[3]—shows no sign of abating.

The battle is about texts and their meanings. On the one hand, there are those who hold that texts carry meanings, that meanings reside, as it were, *in* the text and that if you want to know what a text means, you have to enter it, preferably under the guidance of a knowledgeable and trustworthy Cicerone, in order to encounter the meaning which has been placed there by an author and which awaits the coming of a dear reader like Sleeping Beauty. It is already there, whether you get there or not, whether you are the real prince or just a fumbling dilettante. Its being is in no way dependent upon your kissing it or your bringing it about, and even if you have awakened it to life there is no doubt that its existence precedes yours and your reading and that the ultimate source and haunt of this meaning is 'the text'.

According to this idea, concrete readings are only more or less partial realizations or instantializations of 'a something given' that is not only richer but also somehow more real than its various actualizations. It goes without saying, therefore, that access to the arcana of the text can only be gained if the reader submits to the authority of the text. Even hermeneutists who generally see the text-reader relationship in terms of a dialogue and grant that the level and fertility of the exchange are largely determined by what the reader brings with himself ('Unto every one that hath shall be given...') will insist that *submission* is the key virtue in the reading process. Hans-Georg Gadamer, for example, points out that 'auf den Text hören und horchen', which might still be interpreted as respectful attentiveness to the text, also entails 'dem Text *ge*horchen'[4]—which does make sense if you believe that meaning is there and present, and if you want to learn it and not fall victim to your own delusory projections. After all, a textual encounter is only profitable in so far as you respect the text as an Other, as alterity. One can only become another by reading if that otherness of the text is appropriated *as such*. The paucity and predictability of many ostentatiously 'projectionist' readings would be a pragmatic argument for the basic soundness of this view of the text and its meaning: lack of acknowledgement of the meaning of the text as being something

---

[2]Graham Bradshaw, *Misrepresentations: Shakespeare and the Materialists* (Ithaca, NY, and London: Cornell University Press, 1993).

[3]Brian Vickers, *Appropriating Shakespeare: Contemporary Critical Quarrels* (New Haven, CT, and London: Yale University Press, 1993). For a discussion of Bradshaw's and Vickers' monographs, see my review article 'Eigentumsfragen', *Shakespeare Jahrbuch*, 132 (1996), 226-33.

[4]Thus in an unpublished paper he read at the 'Saving the Text' symposium, Heidelberg, June 11th-14th, 1991.

different from my subjective gropings for it need not be sanctioned from outside; readings based upon such disrespect are inevitably self-confining and self-impoverishing practices.

Semiotically, this view of the text and its meaning could be termed 'essentialist' since it presupposes a stable meaning—meaning as an essence—that is not subject to change, time, and history and is miraculously unaffected by human practices such as power relations or interpretive strategies or moves. This stability of the sign can, of course, only be guaranteed if there is, on the other side of the semiotic relationship, as an implicitly postulated ideal, an ahistorical addressee, a transhistorical, absolute and autonomous subject that reads literature in order to find answers to eternal human problems or is habitually looking for manifestations of never-changing 'human nature', 'human essence'. Such a subject could by no means be a historically concrete reader, because such a one would reintroduce a dynamic variable into the semiotic relationship, but it would be a *construct* or *postulate*, much like Kant's 'regulative Ideen', to whose condition the concrete reader can only aspire, but which, upon closer inspection, without fail turns out to be anything but an ahistorical entity, but is rather very much a product of his or her respective times, only hypostasized as atemporal and ordained with 'essential humanism'.

Essentialist approaches see reading as the discovery of a meaning that is already there, in the text. Eclipsing the temporal and historical dimension of literature and minimizing the role of the reader, essentialist approaches privilege the general above the concrete, the universal above the particular, the purportedly eternal above the historically concrete, that which is given above that which is made. Philosophically, therefore, it would not seem to be unfair to regard essentialists as *realists of meaning*.

In the opposite camp, we find a rainbow coalition of deconstructionists, new historicists, cultural materialists, feminists, some reader-response critics and critical hermeneutists. Notwithstanding their at times considerable differences of opinion and emphasis they can be, I believe, and indeed they are lumped together under the tag of 'critical theory', the material reason for this being that they all subscribe to an idea of text and meaning that is diametrically opposed to the one just sketched. For critical theorists, meaning is never simply there, unmediated and unchanging. Quite the contrary, for them meaning is always the outcome of concrete, historically differentiated semiotic practices, the variable value of a function.

This view dynamizes and historicizes the text-reader relationship. The text is seen as a historically situated section of a force field of discourses and counterdiscourses, marked and riven by strains, contradictions and irresolvable paradoxes that ultimately stem from the futile attempt to impose closure upon language—be it for ideological or systematic reasons. The reader, in this view, is somebody whose activity brings meaning about. There is no meaning without human beings for whom something is meaningful, and therefore there is no meaning outside time and human practice. Wherever meaning may occur, it is not 'in' the text, but it can either be seen as the outcome of a dialectical encounter between reader and text, or, more radically, as the realization of certain interpretive strategies *on the occasion of* a given text or artefact.

Since neither text nor reader are seen as unified, homogenous wholes and since the historicity of the former can only be discerned from the viewpoint of the latter, which is equally and unavoidably historical—there is no privileged standpoint outside time—it follows a) that 'meaning' can only be something made, constructed, projected in ever new attempts to relate oneself to a text and b) that such constructed meanings are inevitably marked by the same kind of heterogenous forces that already went into the construction of the artefact. Meanings are temporary traces of our endeavour to make sense. Consequently, critical theorists poke fun at the idea that 'the' meaning is purveyed, as it were ready-made, by the text or by the author. Alluding to the information which used to be given in theatrical programmes, Terry Hawkes ridicules his opponents as simpletons who believe that in the same way as cigarettes were provided by Abdullah, 'Costumes by Motley, Music by Mendelssohn', so was 'Meaning by Shakespeare'.[5]

There is no such thing and there can be no such thing as *the* meaning of a text because as long as texts are read new meanings will proliferate. Even a conservative hermeneutist like Gadamer says that the meaning of a text evolves and realizes itself in time. Its ultimate meaning—if such a thing exists—is something to be found in the future, and not by going back to an original 'source' that holds the *potential* only but which is by no means exempt from standing in need of interpretation itself. There is no uninterpreted, unmediated 'original' meaning of a text, for there is no meaning outside understanding, and that is synonymous with no meaning outside language, time and interpretation. Interpretation—reading in the strong sense of the word—is not something that is recklessly super-imposed upon a text that already contains its Sleeping-Beauty meaning, but interpretation is the mode in which meaning comes into being. The meaning of a text depends on the reader, and it does so in the most basic sense: without him or her, it simply would not exist.

Now, it cannot be denied that extremists in this camp who give absolute sovereignty to the reader and deny that the text by itself has any meaning whatsoever run into some difficulties when they are asked what their interpretations are interpretations *of*. The same problem crops up again when we ask ourselves whether all readings of a text are equally good or

---

[5]Terence Hawkes, *Meaning by Shakespeare* (London and New York: Routledge, 1992), 3.

at least equally acceptable and whether we should not regard 'the text as such' as some sort of point of reference when disagreements occur (as a colleague once remarked, 'Whatever *King Lear* may be about, it is not about Manchester United.'). This is not the time and place to refute these objections, but I believe they can be and indeed have been countered with sufficient force and acumen, for instance in Fish's above-mentioned *Is There a Text in This Class?*[6]

Here it is more to the purpose to underline that critical theory seems to deal successfully with the problem of the historicity and temporality of text, meaning and reader. Seeing meaning as originating in the act of reading—so that historically we are given whole strings of meanings in the reception history of a text (which is not the history of its survival but the history of its coming into being/meaning), or on a socio-historical plane we find historically differentiated, collectively amalgamated ideas of 'the meaning' of, say, *Hamlet*, whose origin is nevertheless in (collective) semiotic practices—critical theory evidently favours the concrete above the general, the particular above the universal, the historically concrete above the purportedly eternal, that which is made above that which is given. Philosophically, critical theory can be said to have a *nominalist* conception of meaning, because it denies that the meaning of a text has any reality outside concrete acts of human thinking, understanding and language.

It looks, therefore, as if we are witnessing a modern debate over universals, a replay of the realist vs. nominalist controversy of the European Middle Ages. And I would hold that the similarity is not merely a superficial one, for exactly as in the first bout the real issue is not some scholastic quibble but the conflict is one of incompatible epistemologies, incompatible ontologies, incompatible methodologies and incompatible ideologies, with far-reaching consequences and wide-ranging repercussions. And the very incompatibility of the positions—each denying the basic premises of the other—may explain some of the fierceness and the anger with which the debate is fought out.

Can we learn something from history? If this is not merely superficially reminiscent of the debate over universals, not merely a farcical rehash of a historical debate, but much rather *a conspicuous structural analogue*, can we not, in retrospect, position ourselves historically, today, with the benefit of hindsight and find (or construct) for ourselves a valuable meaning in the classical debate of yesterday?

---

[6]See also Christoph Bode, *Ästhetik der Ambiguität: Zu Funktion und Bedeutung von Mehrdeutigkeit in der Literatur der Moderne* (Konzepte der Sprach- und Literaturwissenschaft, 43) (Tübingen: Niemeyer, 1988), 340-79, and *Den Text? Die Haut retten! Bemerkungen zur 'Flut der Interpretationen' und zur institutionalisierten Literaturwissenschaft* (Graz: Droschl, 1992).

II

The classical texts make fascinating reading. Plato, Aristotle, Porphyry, Boethius, St. Augustine, John Scotus Erigena, Anselm of Canterbury, Roscelin, William of Champeaux, Abelard, Hugh of St. Victor, Thomas Aquinas, Duns Scotus, William of Ockham—they all are like so many pieces of an intriguing mosaic, but one that has something of a picture puzzle whose changing *Gestalten* and protean configurations transcend static dichotomies.

What is the ontological status of general terms? Do universals have a real existence of their own, preceding that of particulars? Do they reside in particulars? Or are they 'only' in the mind? According to the established definition, a realist in these matters is somebody who holds that universals have a real existence. Realism is—in spite of the Stoa—the dominant conviction of classical antiquity and—up to the 14th century—that of the Christian Middle Ages. The debate that was initiated by Boethius' comments on the Neoplatonist Porphyry's *Isagoge* was mainly between the extreme realism of the Platonic-Augustinian tradition (*universalia ante rem*) on the one hand and the moderate kind that traces its origin to Aristotle (*universalia in re*) on the other. Thus, the first historically relevant opposition is not between realism and nominalism, but *within* the realist camp.

Nominalism—holding that universals have no real, independent being but are rather formed by thinking and language after the experience of things (*universalia post rem*) and that they exist only in the mind (*universalia in intellectu*)—is a minority position and a latecomer. It takes some time for 'our' dichotomy to develop, and, as will be seen, some cannot wait to explain it away. Of the above-mentioned philosophers only two are traditionally known as nominalists and even their status as nominalists is now uncertain: Of Roscelin, we have no original statement as to the question of universals but only the reactions of his opponents. According to them, he seems to have held somewhat extreme views, like universals are merely words and nothing else (*flatus vocis*). But did he really say that?

And William of Ockham? How can it be contested that he who held that universals existed in the mind only was a nominalist—as some recent studies, encyclopedias and handbooks do?[7] The mechanics of the inter-

---

[7] See for example the *Encyclopaedia Britannica, Fifteenth Edition*, vol. 10 (Micropaedia) (Chicago, IL: Encyclopaedia Britannica, 1983), s.v. 'universal', 278; Philotheus Boehner, 'The Realistic Conceptualism of William Ockham', *Traditio*, 4 (1946), 307-35; Gordon Leff, *William of Ockham: The Metamorphosis of Scholastic Discourse* (Manchester: Manchester University Press, 1975), 95; *Historisches Wörterbuch der Philosophie*, eds. Joachim Ritter and Karlfried Gründer, vol. 6 (Darmstadt: Wissenschaftliche Buchgesellschaft, 1984), 879.

pretive move are most interesting. It seems to me that the very extremity of Roscelin's alleged tenet is used to shift Ockham towards a middle position on the spectrum because in Ockham universals undeniably function as concepts: they exist *in the mind only* but they do *exist* there and they are *useful*. This is enough, some believe, to make him a *conceptualist*, i.e. somebody who believes that universals are names and mental concepts but that there is, at the same time, something in the particulars that forms the basis for their making, viz. the similarity of certain aspects that allows abstraction into general terms. Such a position was held by Abelard (and Hugh of St. Victor) and its proximity to the moderate realism of Aristotle (*universalia in re*) is often pointed out.

So, as the result of a policy of historical interpretation that might be seen as the equivalent of a *Nineteen Eighty-four*-style rewriting of the past, we are left with a medieval dispute over universals without the participation of a single nominalist. The debate, we are led to believe, was between realists and conceptualists, and since at least some forms of conceptualism— e.g. Abelard's—can be regarded as versions of moderate realism, so the tale goes, the debate was basically about shades of realism. Q.E.D., I suppose. That this line of reasoning, resulting in the virtual elimination of philosophical nominalism from this period of European thought, is by no means an accident can be inferred from the fact that some of those who doubt that there were any medieval nominalists will not stop before they have proved that nominalism is a logical impossibility. Not only did it not exist, it never *could have* existed in any logically coherent way either![8] A very curious argument, I think, since the history of European thought seems to be riddled with ideas that are logically untenable...

On the inclined—if not to say tilted—plane of such a historical representation, all (*vulgo*) 'nominalist' philosophies slip and slide to the right, realist side—a kind of philosophical red shift, as we move on in time, that virtually ignores Albertus Magnus' 13th century summing up that identified a third party in addition to the long-established dyad of absolute vs. moderate realism. What are we to make of that? And what good does it hold?

Granted that 'the dispute about universals was in fact very confused',[9] that 'the position of Nominalism is difficult to distinguish from some

---

[8]Cf. Wolfgang Stegmüller, 'Das Universalienproblem einst und jetzt', *Archiv für Philosophie*, 6 (1956), 192-225, and 7 (1957), 45-81, repr. in *Glaube, Wissen und Erkennen. / Das Universalienproblem einst und jetzt* (Darmstadt: Wissenschaftliche Buchgesellschaft, 1965); *Encyclopaedia Britannica*, vol. 10 (Micropaedia), s.v. 'universal', 278; A.D. Woozley, 'Universals', in *The Encyclopedia of Philosophy*, ed. Paul Edwards, vol. 8 (New York and London: Macmillan, 1967), 194-206.

[9]*Encyclopaedia Britannica*, vol. 12 (Macropaedia), s.v. 'Metaphysics', 16.

forms of Conceptualism',[10] that 'the position of Conceptualism is extremely difficult to distinguish from some versions of Nominalism on the one hand, and from moderate Realism on the other',[11] so that consequently 'the distinction is sometimes so fine between Nominalist and Conceptualist, or between Conceptualist and Moderate Realist, that the distinctions are not very useful'[12]—granted all that, three points should and can be stated with sufficient clarity:

1. Extreme nominalism is by no means an absurd position. *Pace* Russell, one can argue that universals refer only conventionally to groups or classes of individual things without having to accept the notion of 'similarity' as a 'real' universal. To see two things as similar does not necessarily bind me to presuppose the 'real' existence of such a thing as 'similarity'.

2. When a nominalist says that universals do not exist this is shorthand for 'they do not exist as substances', i.e. he answers Porphyry's first question whether genera and species are substances or set in the mind alone. This anti-realist statement entails and acknowledges as a matter of course the existence and use of universals as *mental concepts*. Therefore, the invention of a philosophical position called 'conceptualism'—and be it merely because Roscelin and others had given nominalism a bad name[13]—is not, at least not at this stage, systematically compelling (it may be for later stages of Rationalism, Kantianism etc.).

3. Therefore, Abelard, sometimes passed off as a 'moderate realist',[14] was appropriately described by his successors as a nominalist.[15] When he says that universality can only be attributed to *words* as meaningful sound (*sermo*) and that abstraction issues from the isolation and generalization of an aspect that our mind has selected, he emphasizes that the general is not 'real' but a necessary and useful fiction, something that we have created through and in language.[16] As stated above, the idea that this making of

---

[10]William L. Reese, *Dictionary of Philosophy and Religion: Eastern and Western Thought* (Atlantic Highlands, NJ, and Hassocks, Sussex: Humanities, 1980), 393.

[11]Ibid., 100. See also Jan P. Beckmann, 'Nominalismus', in *Lexikon des Mittelalters*, eds. Robert-Henri Bautier, Robert Auty et al., vol. 6 (Munich and Zurich: Artemis & Winkler Verlag, 1993), cols. 1222-7, here 1223: '[Es] läßt sich keine allgemein anerkannte Definition des Nominalismus geben[.]'

[12]Reese, *Dictionary*, 597.

[13]Cf. Kurt Flasch, *Das philosophische Denken im Mittelalter: Von Augustin zu Machiavelli* (Stuttgart: Reclam, 1986), 216: 'Man nannte diese Position [Abelard's] "nominalistisch"; um die Unterschiede zwischen Abaelard und dem Nominalismus des 14. Jahrhunderts nicht zu verwischen, erfand man eigens für Abaelards Theorie das Etikett "Konzeptualismus"'.

[14]See Andrew B. Schoedinger (ed.), *The Problem of Universals* (New Jersey and London: Humanities, 1992), 23.

[15]See Woozley, 'Universals', 203; see also Flasch, *Denken,* 216.

[16]See Kurt Flasch (ed.), *Geschichte der Philosophie in Text und Darstellung, Vol. 2: Mittelalter* (Stuttgart: Reclam, 1982), 216; 217.

concepts is based upon observed similarities is by no means alien to or irreconcilable with nominalism, not even of the most radical kind. According to Abelard, universals are products of our mind, features of our understanding, not of existence, 'they are characteristic of the way we think, not of the way things exist.'[17] It is true that Abelard in the end puts similarity down to God's creating individuals according to the same divine idea but it is typical of Abelard that he does not even attempt to declare that these divine ideas are universals. Universals, he says unequivocally, are words and concepts and in the mind alone. Therefore it can hardly be denied that the seeming proximity of Abelard's 'conceptualism' to the moderate realism of Aristotle is at best one of epistemological convergence[18]—ontologically they have nothing in common. Abelard is uncompromisingly anti-realist.

If we now turn to William of Ockham[19] it becomes at once evident in which respect he went beyond Abelard and why the *via moderna* that is so intimately connected with his name could eventually undermine the established epistemologies and ontologies of the Middle Ages. For Ockham, 'universals are in no way substances', they are a 'mental content',[20] 'a thing in the mind', 'the result of the mind's activity'.[21] When spoken or written down, they form parts of sentences; 'proposition[s are] composed of universals',[22] and propositions assert a relation between *signs*. They are conventional signs, not images, the semiotic chips we habitually use to make sense of extra-mental reality, which is, however, distinct from the world in our heads. Ockham insists that science and knowledge is not about *things*, it is about the terms we 'suppose' for things.[23] Truth is the truth of sentences.[24]

---

[17]Abelard in Schoedinger (ed.), *Universals*, 31.

[18]Cf. *Philosophielexikon: Personen und Begriffe der abendländischen Philosophie von der Antike bis zur Gegenwart*, eds. Anton Hügli and Poul Lübcke (Hamburg: Rowohlt, 1991), 586.

[19]For a splendid new introduction to Ockham's ideas, see Jan P. Beckmann, *Wilhelm von Ockham* (Beck'sche Reihe, 533) (Munich: Beck, 1995). A more formal discussion is presented by Marilyn McCord Adams, *William Ockham*, 2 vols. (Notre Dame, IN: University of Notre Dame Press, 1987).

[20]Ockham in Schoedinger (ed.), *Universals*, 56.

[21]Leff, *Ockham*, 100; 123.

[22]Ockham in Schoedinger (ed.), *Universals*, 56.

[23]Cf. Wilhelm von Ockham, *Texte zur Theorie der Erkenntnis und der Wissenschaft: Lateinisch/Deutsch*, ed. and tr. Ruedi Imbach (Stuttgart: Reclam, 1984), 86ff.; Ockham in Flasch (ed.), *Geschichte*, 472. Cf. also Beckmann, *Ockham*, 130: 'Der einzige Weg, Metaphysik in ihrer Identität zu bewahren und ihren Wissenschaftscharakter sicherzustellen, ist nach Ockham derjenige, sie nicht als Sach-, sondern als Satzwissenschaft zu konzipieren.'

[24]Cf. Ockham, *Texte*, 94ff. See also Matthias Kaufmann, *Begriffe, Sätze, Dinge: Referenz und Wahrheit bei Wilhelm von Ockham* (Studien und Texte zur Geistesgeschichte des Mittelalters, 40) (Leiden: Brill, 1994); Oliver Leffler, *Wilhelm von Ockham: Die sprachphilosophischen Grundlagen seines Denkens* (Franziskanische Forschungen, 40) (Werl, Westf.: Dietrich-Coelde-Verlag, 1995).

Cognition, consequently, is the understanding of the meaning of sentences.[25] This is not the place to go into the intricacies of 'intuitive' and 'abstractive' cognition in Ockham. The decisive point is that in Ockham the problem of universals is transferred to a *linguistic plane*. Again: *Cognition is the understanding of the meaning of sentences*. And if that is so, all metaphysical propositions can be subjected to logical and linguistic criticism. One of his findings will be that theology is not a science.[26]

If nominalism and the *via moderna* are rightly said to have been highly implemental in the transformation of the ideological landscape of medieval Europe, I would argue that this is not only due to the changes in methodology it introduced to logic, mathematics and the natural sciences, not only due to the primacy it ceded to the individual and the concrete,[27] not only due to its 'modern' note of scepticism[28] or its affinity to a philosophy of the contingent,[29] but maybe ultimately to something that underlies all these phenomena and impressive manifestations of a major shift of paradigm—namely, *Ockham's linguistic turn*. In Ockham, epistemology is redefined as *criticism of language*, and since we can only talk about the existence of that which we know, ontology follows suit. The battle was about texts and meaning, and Ockham pointed the way that Hobbes, Berkeley and Wittgenstein were to explore later on: *the meaning is the usage*—and therefore it can only be *made*, and it's not *there*, and it's not *stable*. It is the trace of our endeavours.

III

The above reading of the historic role of nominalism is, of course, highly suspicious and amusingly self-contradictory. Of unmistakable nominalist leaning, it presents a philosophical controversy as a struggle between the forces of light and darkness, the victory of the former heralding the advent of the modern age, progress, enlightenment. It is a 'Whig' reading of the history of ideas, and what is more, while it officially subscribes to one set of ideas and celebrates its prevalence, it understands itself in terms of quite another, viz. in those of the supposedly subdued one. Committed to nominalism, it should be averse to or at least sceptical of general and reified concepts like 'the course of history', 'the march of reason', 'the dawning of modern man', and yet when it speaks of itself and its history it

---

[25]Ockham, *Texte*, 125ff.; Ockham in Flasch (ed.), *Geschichte*, 470; Otl Aicher, Gabriele Greindl, and Wilhelm Vossenkuhl, *Wilhelm von Ockham: Das Risiko modern zu denken* (Munich: Callwey, 2nd ed. 1987), 123; 125.
[26]Cf. Ockham, *Texte*, 123ff.
[27]Cf. *Historisches Wörterbuch*, eds. Ritter and Gründer, vol. 6: 876; 877.
[28]Cf. Flasch, *Denken*, 451; 453.
[29]Cf. Ockham, *Texte*, 97; Aicher et al., *Wilhelm von Ockham*, 125.

clandestinely takes recourse to a *grand récit*. The very idea of a 'change of paradigm' conjures up—in spite of Kuhn's disclaimers—the concomitant idea that something better is substituted for something not so good, or not so good *any more*. Progress. The script for this dramatic movie is a *realist* one, the message that you can't keep a good nominalist down because the forces of History and Progress are on his side. Paradoxically the self-image of nominalism victorious is an inherently realist one. And even the petty cantankerousness that tries to recapture for nominalism a philosopher several hundred years dead betrays a dubious preoccupation with tags and labels—as if they were more than just that. At last, the insinuation that the forces of yesteryear in a kind of desperate rearguard action are still trying to undermine the otherwise indubitable historical triumph of nominalism by deviously explaining it away marks the ultimate victory of the parasite discourse of realism over its host discourse of nominalism. For we have left behind even the sphere of reified concepts like History and Progress and are now into full-blown mythology: The story of nominalism vs. realism is replayed day by day, forever and ever, in an eternal now. Transforming particulars into universals, myth knows no historical time. In mythologizing itself and its mission, nominalism contains its Other—in more than just one way.

What would a realist reading of the classical debate and its aftermath look like? There are, I think, two roads open. Taking the first, easily recognizable one, one could conjure up absurdly silly versions of nominalism, then declare that, in order to avoid confusion, more sensible versions of it should be called conceptualism and finally try to show that conceptualism is really a weak variety of moderate realism. The results of that manoeuvre would be a) that, as seen above, you end up with a medieval dispute over universals without any nominalist (except for the bogeyman Roscelin)—and b) that your idea of moderate realism would be virulently infected with nominalist essentials, in other words: in the attempt to minimize the relevance or import of nominalism, you'd have accepted, in practice, the basic soundness of nominalist doctrine.

Taking the other road, realists could admit defeat in the historical dispute, but then point out that forms of realism do of course reappear in Idealism (in Hegel, for example) or that Rationalism and Kantianism are unthinkable without the idea of *a priori* universals, which seems to vindicate the realist tenet, if somewhat refashioned. They could then adduce the modern, twentieth-century debate over universals in mathematics and logic[30] as evidence for a continuing relevance of the realist approach, admittedly radically overhauled. In short, these realists, after

---

[30]Cf. Wolfgang Stegmüller (ed.), *Das Universalienproblem* (Darmstadt: Wissenschaftliche Buchgesellschaft, 1978).

having lost and conceded the day, would be free to look into particular cases of similar configurations, free to elaborate without blinkers the differences and specificities of later manifestations. Indeed, it could well be that since they have an idea of the general at the back of their minds, they would be especially apt to bring out the *differentia specifica* in each individual case. In practice, the realist would be a magnificent nominalist, indeed would almost inevitably have to be one. In practice—since the continuous re-statement of the universal is a drab and futile affair—realism as a meaningful, productive methodological approach survives in that it contains its Other.

That this is not only a logical postulate is borne out—and this brings us back to literary studies—by the example of August Wilhelm Schlegel, whose basic distinction of 'the classical' and 'the romantic' sounds as realist as realist can be. But what a wealth of insights and acute observations when, on the basis of this dichotomy, he turns to their particular manifestations and examines their historical specificity! The ahistorical realism of his dichotomy is dissolved in concrete differentiation, the blunt instrument of 'either-or' is sharpened in meticulous dissecting practice, and as he wields his bisecting tool, it is always pointed, as it should be, *towards the object*. The function of concepts is to make themselves forgotten.

It seems therefore that each of the possible accounts of the medieval debate over universals—and it should be clear that the second realist option is of course as much of an account as the others are practical reactions, the distinctions being highly specious—not only has swallowed up its opposite but has been inwardly taken over by its Other and allows its parasite discourse to influence if not govern its metabolism and critical practice. What does that mean with regard to the question whether it makes sense to see the contemporary dispute between critical theory and essentialism in the light of the medieval debate over universals? If our view and understanding of the historical controversy is a function of our own theoretical (especially ontological and epistemological) presuppositions and predispositions, our attempts to position ourselves historically and systematically by trying to assess 'the meaning of it all', for us, inevitably result in a discourse that is largely *auto-referential* and instantiates itself *as a self-validating practice*. Readings and practices of that self-validating and more or less auto-referential kind have the *primary* function of allowing ourselves to demonstratively position ourselves in (historical) time and (mental) space and thereby to constitute ourselves as scholars in our interpretive community through acts of *ascription* that are just as much acts of self-description, or, since they inform instances of our practice, *acts of performance* that *primarily* point to themselves and mean themselves.

But if each discourse—and it could be shown quite easily that critical theory and essentialism are no exceptions—already contains its opposite, and not only contains it but likens itself to it with a kind of unintentional, inadvertent complimentary gesture, this curious incorporation and embodiment of the Other might well be regarded as the saving grace for otherwise circular auto-referentiality. For it could be argued that only because the Other is *aufgehoben* do our critical discourses, when they speak about themselves, escape the fatal standstill of absolute self-identity.

The meaning and the message, not of the medieval dispute over universals 'as such', *but of our sketch of the moves to extract some from it*, of the reciprocal containment and preservation of the submerged Other, could therefore be that our critical discourses are defined by the way in which they take cognizance of the share of the Other in themselves.

The message and the meaning of our self-contradictory attempts to retrieve and appropriate the legacy, to salvage the goods of the history of thought might be that respect for the Other is possibly the highest form of self-respect, and that the traces of our endeavours, the meanings we make and cherish and defend, are like footprints on the shore.

BIBLIOGRAPHY

I. Sources

Abelard, Peter. *Abelard's Christian Theology,* tr. J. Ramsey McCallum (Oxford: Blackwell, 1948).

Agricola, Rodolphus. *De inventione dialectica libri III* (Cologne, 1523; repr. Frankfurt a.M.: Minerva, 1967).

Altensteig, Johannes. *Opusculum de amicicia* (Hagenau: Anshelm, 1519).

———. *Vocabularius theologie complectens vocabulorum descriptiones, [...] compilata a Joanne Altenstaig Mindelhaimensi [...]* (Hagenau: Henricus Gran, 1517).

Anselm of Canterbury. *Proslogion,* ed. with parallel English translation by M.J. Charlesworth (Oxford: Clarendon Press, 1965).

Aquinas, Saint Thomas. *Summa Theologiae,* ed. and tr. Timothy McDermott (vol. 2 in the Blackfriars series) (London: Blackfriars, 1964).

Aristotle. *De interpretatione,* ed. W.D. Ross, tr. E.M. Edghill (= vol. 1 (1928) of *Works,* 12 vols. (Oxford: Clarendon Press, 1908-52)).

Arnauld, Antoine, and Pierre Nicole. *La logique, ou l'art de penser,* ed. Pierre Clair and François Girbal (Paris: Presses Universitaires de France, 1965).

Augustine, Saint. *Confessions,* tr. R.S. Pine-Coffin (New York: Penguin, 1961).

———. *Confessions,* tr. Henry Chadwick (Oxford: Oxford University Press, 1992).

———. *De doctrina christiana,* in *Patrologiae cursus completus,* vol. 34 (Paris: Migne, 1841).

———. *In Ioannis evangelium,* in *Patrologiae cursus completus,* vol. 35 (Paris: Migne, 1841).

Awdeley, John. *The Fraternitye of Vacabondes* [1561], in Edward Viles and F. J. Furnivall (eds.), *The Rogues and Vagabonds of Shakspere's Youth* (London: New Shakspere Society, 1880), 1-16.

Bacon, Francis. *Works,* eds. James Spedding et al., vol. 6 (1870; repr. New York: Garrett, 1968).

Biblia Sacra cum Glossa Ordinaria, vol. 5 (Antwerp, 1617).

Bonaventure, Saint. *Doctoris Seraphici S. Bonaventurae S.R.E. Episcopi Cardinalis Opera Omnia, iussu et auctoritate R.mi P. Bernardini a Portu Romatino totius ordinis minorum S. P. Francisci Ministri Generalis edita studio et curia P.P. Collegii S. Bonaventurae,* vol. 2 (Ad Claras Aquas (Quaracchi): Ex Typographia Collegii S. Bonaventurae, 1885).

Borges, Jorge Luis. 'From Allegories to Novels', in *Borges: A Reader*, eds. Emir Rodriguez Monegal and Alastair Reid (New York: Dutton, 1981), 230-2.

Breviarium ad usum insignis ecclesie eboracensis: Vol. 1, ed. Stephen W. Lawley (Surtees Society, 71) (Durham: Surtees Society, 1880).

Buffon, Georges-Louis Leclerc, Comte de. *Oeuvres philosophiques*, ed. Jean Piveteau (Paris: Presses Universitaires de France, 1954).

Castelvetro, Lodovico. *Poetica d'Aristotele vulgarizzata e sposta*, ed. Werther Romani (Rome and Bari: Laterza, 1978).

Cervantes, Miguel de. *El Ingenioso Hidalgo Don Quijote de la Mancha*, 2 vols., ed. John Jay Allen (Cátedra. Letras Hispánicas, 100-1) (Madrid: Cátedra, 1989).

Chamberlain, John. *The Letters of John Chamberlain*, 2 vols., ed. N.E. McClure (Philadelphia, PA: American Philosophical Society, 1939).

Chaucer, Geoffrey. *The Riverside Chaucer*, gen. ed. Larry D. Benson (Boston, MA: Houghton Mifflin, 1987; Oxford: Oxford University Press, 1988).

Chettle, Henry. *Kind-Hartes Dreame (1592)*, ed. G.B. Harrison (London: John Lane, 1923).

Chrétien de Troyes. *Le Chevalier au Lion*, ed. Mario Roques (Paris: Champion, 1982).

———. *Le Chevalier de la Charrette*, ed. Mario Roques (Paris: Champion, 1983).

———. *Cligés*, ed. Alexandre Micha (Paris: Champion, 1982).

———. *Erec et Enide*, ed. Mario Roques (Paris: Champion, 1983).

———. *Le Roman de Perceval ou le Conte du graal*, ed. William Roach (Paris: Librairie Minard, and Genève: Librairie Droz, 1959).

Condillac, Etienne Bonnot, Abbé de. *An Essay on the Origin of Human Knowledge*, tr. Thomas Nugent (London, 1756; facs. repr. Gainesville, FL: Scholars' Facsimiles and Reprints, 1971).

Dante Alighieri. *Tutte le opere: edizione del centenario*, ed. Fredi Chiappelli (Milan: Mursia, 7th ed. 1969).

Dekker, Thomas. *O per se O* (London: 1612).

Drant, Thomas. *Horace: His Arte of Poetrie, Pistles and Satyrs Englished*, ed. Peter E. Medine (Delmar, NY: Scholars' Facsimiles & Reprints, 1972).

Dryden, John. *The Poems of John Dryden*, 4 vols., ed. J. Kinsley (Oxford: Clarendon Press, 1958).

Duns Scotus, John. *Philosophical Writings: A Selection*, ed. and tr. Allan Wolter (Edinburgh: Nelson, 1962).

English Historical Documents, vol. 5 (1485-1558), ed. C.H. Williams (London: Eyre & Spottiswoode, 1967).

Erasmus, Desiderius. *Opera omnia*, 10 vols. (Loudun: Petrus Vander Aa, 1703-6).

———. *The Colloquies of Erasmus*, tr. Craig R. Thompson (Chicago, IL: University of Chicago Press, 1965).

———. *De ratione studii*, in *Opera omnia*, vol. 1.2., ed. Jean-Claude Margolin (Amsterdam: North Holland Publishing Company, 1971).

Frege, Gottlob. *Collected Papers on Mathematics, Logic and Philosophy*, ed. Brian McGuiness (Oxford: Blackwell, 1984).

Googe, Barnabe. *The Spiritual Husbandrie* (London, 1570).

Heinrich von Neustadt. *Apollonius von Tyrland: Nach der Gothaer Handschrift*, ed. Samuel Singer (Berlin: Weidmann, 1906).

Hobbes, Thomas. *English Works*, 2 vols., ed. Sir William Molesworth (London: Bohn, 1839).

———. *Leviathan*, ed. C.B. Macpherson (Harmondsworth: Penguin, 1968).

Holcot, Robert. *In Librum Sapientiae Regis Salomonis: Praelectiones CCXIII* (Basel, 1586).

Holinshed, Raphael. *Holinshed's Chronicles*, 6 vols., ed. Henry Ellis (London: J. Johnson, 1807-8).

Lefèvre d'Etaples, Jacques. *Commentarii initiatorii in quatuor evangelia* (Meaux: Simon de Colines, 1522).

Leibniz, Gottfried Wilhelm. *Philosophical Papers and Letters*, 2 vols., ed. Leroy E. Loemaker (Chicago, IL: University of Chicago Press, 1956).

Locke, John. *An Essay Concerning Human Understanding*, ed. Peter H. Nidditch (Oxford: Clarendon Press, 1975).

Ludolphus de Saxonia. *Vita Jesu Christi*, 4 vols., ed. L.M. Rigollot (Paris: Victorem Palme, and Brussels: G. Lebrocquy, 1878).

Lyly, John. *'Campaspe' and 'Sappho and Phao'*, eds. G.K. Hunter and David Bevington (Manchester: Manchester University Press, 1991).

Milne, A.A. *Winnie-the-Pooh* (1926; repr. London: Methuen, 1965).

The Mirror for Magistrates, ed. Lily B. Campbell (1938; repr. New York: Barnes & Noble, 1960).

The New Oxford Annotated Bible with the Apocrypha (Revised Standard Edition), eds. Herbert G. May and Bruce M. Metzger (New York: Oxford University Press, 1977).

Nizolius, Marius. *De veris principiis et vera ratione philosophandi contra pseudophilosophos* (Parma, 1553).

Ockham, Wilhelm von. *Texte zur Theorie der Erkenntnis und der Wissenschaft: Lateinisch/Deutsch*, ed. and tr. Ruedi Imbach (Stuttgart: Reclam, 1984).

Ockham, William of. *Philosophical Writings*, ed. and tr. Philotheus Boehner (Indianapolis, IN: Hackett, 1957; rev. ed. by F. Brown: Hackett, 1990).

———. *Ockham's Theory of Terms: Part I of the 'Summa Logicae'*, tr. Michael J. Loux (Notre Dame, IN, and London: University of Notre Dame Press, 1974).

Peter Lombard. *Sententiae in IV libris distinctae*, 3rd ed., 2 vols. (Grottoferrata (Rome): Collegium S. Bonaventurae ad Claras Aquas, 1971-81).

Philip Julius, Duke of Stettin-Pomerania. 'Diary of the Journey of Philip Julius, Duke of Stettin-Pomerania, through England in the Year 1602', ed. G. von Bulow, *Transactions of the Royal Historical Society*, n.s. 6 (1892), 1-67.

Plato. *Cratylus*, ed. and tr. H.N. Fowler (Loeb Classical Library) (London: Heinemann, 1926).

Platter, Thomas. *Thomas Platter's Travels in England 1599*, tr. Clare Williams (London: Jonathan Cape, 1937).

Rabelais, François. *Gargantua and Pantagruel*, tr. J.M. Cohen (Penguin Classics) (Harmondsworth: Penguin, 1955).

———. *Pantagruel*, ed. Gérard Defaux (Paris: Librairie Générale Française, 1994).

Reynolds, John. *The Flower of Fidelity* (London, 1654).

Rousseau, Jean-Jacques. *The First and Second Discourses, together with Replies to Critics*, tr. Victor Gourevitch (New York: Perennial, 1986).

Shakespeare, William. *Hamlet*, ed. Harold Jenkins (The Arden Shakespeare) (London and New York: Methuen, 1982).

———. *King Richard III*, ed. Antony Hammond (The Arden Shakespeare) (London and New York: Methuen, 1981).

Sidney, Philip. *The Countess of Pembroke's Arcadia (The New Arcadia)*, ed. Victor Skretkowicz (Oxford: Clarendon Press, 1987).

Star Trek VI: The Undiscovered Country (Paramount Pictures, 1991).

Stillingfleet, Edward, Bishop of Worcester. *A Discourse in Vindication of the Doctrine of the Trinity* (London, 1697).

Swift, Jonathan. *Gulliver's Travels*, eds. Peter Dixon and John Chalker (Penguin Classics) (1967; repr. Harmondsworth: Penguin, 1985).

Texte zum Universalienstreit, 2 vols., ed. and tr. Hans-Ulrich Wöhler: *Band 1—Vom Ausgang der Antike bis zur Frühscholastik: Lateinische, griechische und arabische Texte des 3.-12. Jahrhunderts*; *Band 2—Hoch- und Spätmittelalterliche Scholastik: Unter Einschluß von zwei erstmals kritisch edierten Texten W. Burleys und J. Buridans* (Berlin: Akademie-Verlag, 1992-4).

The Towneley Plays, 2 vols., eds. Martin Stevens and A.C. Cawley (Oxford: Oxford University Press, 1994).

Tolkien, J.R.R. *The Lord of the Rings* (London: Allen & Unwin, 1968).

Tudor Economic Documents, 3 vols., eds. R.H. Tawney and Eileen Power (London: Longmans, 1924).

Valla, Laurentius. *Opera* (Basileae, 1540).

Weamys, Anna. *A Continuation of Sir Philip Sidney's Arcadia* (London, 1651); reprint edition plus modernized version, ed. Patrick Colborn Cullen (Oxford: Oxford University Press, 1994).

Whetstone, George. *The Censure of a loyall Subject* (London: 1587).

Wroth, Mary. *The Countesse of Mountgomery's Urania* (London, 1621).

Wyclif, John. *De Logica*, 3 vols., ed. M.H. Dziewicki (London: Trubner, 1899).

———. *De Veritate Sacrae Scripturae*, 3 vols., ed. Rudolf Buddensieg (London: Trubner, 1905-7).
York: Records of Early English Drama, 2 vols., eds. Alexandra F. Johnston and Margaret Rogerson (Toronto: University of Toronto Press, 1979).
The York Plays, ed. Richard Beadle (London: Arnold, 1982).

II. Critical Reference

Aaron, R.I., and Jocelyn Gibb (eds.). *An Early Draft of Locke's* Essay (Oxford: Clarendon Press, 1936).
Aarsleff, Hans. *From Locke to Saussure: Essays on the Study of Language and Intellectual History* (Minneapolis, MN: University of Minnesota Press, 1982).
Adams, Marilyn McCord. *William Ockham*, 2 vols. (Notre Dame, IN: University of Notre Dame Press, 1987).
Adorno, Theodor W. *Noten zur Literatur* (Frankfurt a.M.: Suhrkamp, 1977).
Aicher, Otl, Gabriele Greindl, and Wilhelm Vossenkuhl. *Wilhelm von Ockham: Das Risiko modern zu denken* (Munich: Callwey, 2nd ed. 1987).
Allen, Judson B. *The Friar as Critic: Literary Attitudes in the Later Middle Ages* (Nashville, TN: Vanderbuilt University Press, 1971).
Amos, Flora Ross. *Early Theories of Translation* (New York: Columbia University Press, 1920).
Ariès, Philippe. 'Introduction', in *A History of Private Life*, gen. eds. Ariès and Georges Duby, Vol. III: *Passions of the Renaissance*, ed. Roger Chartier, tr. Arthur Goldhammer (Cambridge, MA, and London: Harvard University Press, 1989), 1-11.
Armstrong, D.M. *Universals and Scientific Realism I: Nominalism and Realism* (Cambridge: Cambridge University Press, 1978).
Arthur, Ross. *Medieval Sign Theory and* Sir Gawain and the Green Knight (Toronto: University of Toronto Press, 1987).
Ashley, Kathleen M. 'Divine Power in Chester Cycle and Late Medieval Thought', *Journal of the History of Ideas*, 39 (1978), 387-404.
———. 'Chester Cycle and Nominalist Thought', *Journal of the History of Ideas*, 40 (1979), 477.
Ashworth, E.J. '"Do Words Signify Ideas or Things?" The Scholastic Sources of Locke's Theory of Language', *Journal of the History of Philosophy*, 19 (1981), 299-326.
———. 'Analogy and Equivocation in Thirteenth-Century Logic: Aquinas in Context', *Mediaeval Studies*, 54 (1992), 94-135.
Assunto, Rosario. *Die Theorie des Schönen im Mittelalter* (1963; repr. Cologne: Dumont, 1982).
Auerbach, Erich. *Mimesis: Dargestellte Wirklichkeit in der abendländischen Literatur* (Berne and Munich: Francke, 3rd ed. 1964).

Aydelotte, Frank. *Elizabethan Rogues and Vagabonds* (1913; repr. New York: Barnes & Noble, 1967).

Ayers, Michael. *Locke*, 2 vols. (London and New York: Routledge, 1991).

Baier, Walter. *Untersuchungen zu den Passionsbetrachtungen in der Vita Christi des Ludolf von Sachsen*. 3 vols. (Salzburg: Institut für Englische Sprache und Literatur, 1977).

Baird, Lorrayne Y. *A Bibliography of Chaucer, 1964-1973* (Boston, MA: G.K. Hall, 1977).

Baird-Lange, Lorraine Y., and Hildegard Schnuttgen. *A Bibliography of Chaucer, 1974-1985* (Hamden, CT: Archon Books, and Cambridge: D.S. Brewer, 1988).

Baker, Denise. 'From Plowing to Penitence: *Piers Plowman* and Fourteenth-Century Theology', *Speculum*, 55 (1980), 715-25.

Bakhtin, Mikhail. *The Dialogic Imagination*, ed. Michael Holquist, tr. Caryl Emerson and Michael Holquist (Austin, TX: University of Texas Press, 1981).

Balducelli, P. Ruggero. *Il concetto teologico di carità attraverso le maggiori interpretazioni patristiche e medievali di I ad Cor. XIII* (Washington, DC: Catholic University of America Press, 1951).

Baldwin, Anna. '"The Man of Law's Tale" as a Philosophical Narrative', *Yearbook of English Studies*, 22 (1992), 181-9.

Baldwin, C.P. *Medieval Rhetoric and Poetic* (New York: Macmillan, 1928).

Bambrough, Renford. 'Universals and Family Resemblance' [1960], repr. in Michael J. Loux (ed.), *Universals and Particulars* (Notre Dame, IN, and London: Notre Dame University Press, 1976), 106-24.

Bannet, Eve Tavor. *Postcultural Theory: Critical Theory after the Marxist Paradigm* (London: Macmillan, 1993).

Barr, Helen. *Signes and Sothe in the* Piers Plowman *Tradition* (Cambridge: D.S. Brewer, 1994).

Barry, Peter. *Beginning Theory: An Introduction to Literary and Cultural Theory* (Manchester: Manchester University Press, 1995).

Barthes, Roland. 'The Death of the Author', in *Image-Music-Text*, tr. Stephen Heath (London: Fontana, 1977), 142-8.

———. 'From Work to Text', in *Image-Music-Text*, tr. Stephen Heath (London: Fontana, 1977), 155-64.

Baudrillard, Jean. *Simulations* (New York: Semiotext(e), 1983).

Baxter, Timothy M.S. *The 'Cratylus': Plato's Critique of Naming* (Leiden: Brill, 1992).

Beardsley, Monroe C. *Aesthetics from Classical Greece to the Present: A Short History* (New York: Macmillan, 1966).

Beckett, Sister Wendy. *The Story of Painting* (London: Dorling Kindersely, 1994).

Beckmann, Jan P. 'Nominalismus', in *Lexikon des Mittelalters*, eds. Robert-Henri Bautier, Robert Auty et al., vol. 6 (Munich and Zurich: Artemis & Winkler Verlag, 1993), cols. 1222-7.

———. *Wilhelm von Ockham* (Beck'sche Reihe, 533) (Munich: Beck, 1995).

Beier, A.L. *Masterless Men: The Vagrancy Problem in England 1560-1640* (London: Methuen, 1985).

Belsey, Catherine. *The Subject of Tragedy: Identity and Difference in Renaissance Drama* (1985; repr. London and New York: Routledge, 1991).

Bennett, J.A.W. *Chaucer at Oxford and Cambridge* (Toronto: University of Toronto Press, 1974).

Blanch, Robert, and Julian Wasserman. 'The Current State of *Sir Gawain and the Green Knight* Criticism', *Chaucer Review*, 27 (1993), 401-12.

Bloch, R. Howard. 'Genealogy as Medieval Mental Structure and Textual Form', in *La littérature historiographique des origines à 1500* (= vol. 11/1 of *Grundriß der Romanischen Literaturen des Mittelalters*, eds. Hans Ulrich Gumbrecht et al.) (Heidelberg: Winter, 1986), 135-56.

Blofeld, John. *Mantras: Secret Words of Power* (London: Unwin Paperbacks, 1977).

Bloomfield, Morton W. 'Distance and Predestination in *Troilus and Criseyde*', *PMLA*, 72 (1957), 14-26.

Blumenberg, Hans. 'Paradigma, grammatisch' [1971], in *Wirklichkeiten in denen wir leben: Aufsätze und eine Rede* (Stuttgart: Reclam, 1981), 157-62.

———. *The Legitimacy of the Modern Age*, tr. Robert M. Wallace (Cambridge, MA, and London: MIT Press, 1981).

———. *Die Lesbarkeit der Welt* (stw, 592) (Frankfurt a.M.: Suhrkamp, 1986).

Bode, Christoph. *Ästhetik der Ambiguität: Zu Funktion und Bedeutung von Mehrdeutigkeit in der Literatur der Moderne* (Konzepte der Sprach- und Literaturwissenschaft, 43) (Tübingen: Niemeyer, 1988).

———. *Den Text? Die Haut retten! Bemerkungen zur 'Flut der Interpretationen' und zur institutionalisierten Literaturwissenschaft* (Graz: Droschl, 1992).

———. 'Eigentumsfragen', *Shakespeare Jahrbuch*, 132 (1996), 226-33.

———. *John Keats: Play On* (Anglistische Forschungen, 242) (Heidelberg: Winter, 1996).

———. 'A Modern Debate over Universals? Critical Theory vs. "Essentialism"', *The European Legacy*, 2.2 (1997), 229-37.

Boehner, Philoteus. 'The Realistic Conceptualism of William Ockham', *Traditio*, 4 (1946), 307-35, repr. in *Collected Articles on Ockham*, 156-74.

———. 'Ockham's Theory of Supposition and the Notion of Truth', *Franciscan Studies*, 6 (1946), 261-92, repr. in *Collected Articles on Ockham*, 232-67.

———. 'The Metaphysics of William Ockham', *Review of Metaphysics*, 1.4 (1947-8), 59-86, repr. in *Collected Articles on Ockham*, 373-97.

———. *Collected Articles on Ockham*, ed. Eligius M. Buytaert (St. Bonaventure, NY: The Franciscan Institute, 1958).

———. 'The *Notitia Intuitiva* of Non-Existents According to William of Ockham', in *Collected Articles on Ockham*, 268-300.
Borghesi, Pietro. *Boccaccio and Chaucer* (Bologna: N. Zanichelli, 1903).
Boucher, Holly Wallace. 'Nominalism: The Difference for Chaucer and Boccaccio', *Chaucer Review*, 20 (1986), 213-20.
Bourdieu, Pierre. 'The Economics of Linguistic Exchanges', *Social Science Information*, 16 (1977), 645-68.
———. *Outline of a Theory of Practice*, tr. Richard Nice (Cambridge: Cambridge University Press, 1977).
———. *Homo academicus* (Paris: Editions de Minuit, 1984).
———. *In Other Words: Essays Towards a Reflexive Sociology*, tr. Matthew Adamson (Stanford, CA: Stanford University Press, 1990).
———. 'Concluding Remarks', in Craig Calhoun, Edward LiPuma, and Moishe Postone (eds.), *Bourdieu: Critical Perspectives* (Chicago, IL: University of Chicago Press, 1993), 263-75.
Boyer, Robert H. 'Chaucer and Thomas', in Michael B. Lukens (ed.), *Conflict and Community: New Studies in Thomistic Thought* (New York et al.: Lang, 1992), 103-24.
Bradshaw, Graham. *Misrepresentations: Shakespeare and the Materialists* (Ithaca, NY, and London: Cornell University Press, 1993).
Breuer, Rolf. 'Christian Tragedy/Tragedy of Christianity', in Uwe Böker, Manfred Markus, and Rainer Schöwerling (eds.), *The Living Middle Ages: Studies in Mediaeval English Literature and its Tradition—A Festschrift for Karl Heinz Göller* (Stuttgart: Belser, 1989), 183-95.
Brown, Carleton. 'The Author of the *Pearl*, considered in the Light of his Theological Opinions', *PMLA*, 19 (1904), 115-53.
Brown, Stephen F. 'A Modern Prologue to Ockham's Natural Philosophy', in Jan P. Beckmann et al. (eds.), *Sprache und Erkenntnis im Mittelalter* (Berlin and New York: Walter de Gruyter, 1981), 107-29.
Bumke, Joachim. *Die Wolfram von Eschenbach Forschung seit 1945: Bericht und Bibliographie* (Munich: Fink, 1970).
Burnley, J.D. *Chaucer's Language and the Philosophers' Tradition* (Cambridge: D.S. Brewer, and Totowa, NJ: Rowman & Littlefield, 1979).
Bursill-Hall, Geoffrey. *Speculative Grammars of the Middle Ages* (The Hague: Mouton, 1971).
Calhoun, Craig, Edward LiPuma, and Moishe Postone (eds.). *Bourdieu: Critical Perspectives* (Chicago, IL: University of Chicago Press, 1993).
The Cambridge Dictionary of Philosophy, ed. Robert Audi (Cambridge: Cambridge University Press, 1995).
The Cambridge History of Later Medieval Philosophy: From the Rediscovery of Aristotle to the Disintegration of Scholasticism, 1100-1600, eds. Norman Kretzmann et al. (Cambridge: Cambridge University Press, 1982).

Cardini, Franco, and M.T. Fumagalli Beonio-Brocchieri. *Universitäten im Mittelalter: Die europäischen Stätten des Wissens*, tr. Annemarie Seling (Munich: Südwest Verlag, 1991).
Carlson, Marvin. 'Theatre and Performance', *Semiotica*, 92 (1992), 99-105.
Carré, Meyrick H. *Realists and Nominalists* (Oxford: Oxford University Press, 1946).
Carroll, William C. '"The Base Shall Top Th'Legitimate": The Bedlam Beggar and the Role of Edgar in *King Lear*', *Shakespeare Quarterly*, 38 (1987), 426-41.

———. '"The Form of Law": Ritual and Succession in *Richard III*', in Linda Woodbridge and Edward Berry (eds.), *'True Rites and Maimed Rites': Ritual and Anti-Ritual in Shakespeare and His Age* (Urbana, IL: University of Illinois Press, 1992), 203-19.

———. *Fat King, Lean Beggar: Representations of Poverty in the Age of Shakespeare* (Ithaca, NY, and London: Cornell University Press, 1996).

———. 'Semiotic Slippage: Identity and Authority in the English Renaissance', *The European Legacy*, 2.2 (1997), 212-6.
Carswell, Catherine. 'Lollius Myn Autour', *TLS*, Dec. 28, 1935, 899.
Cawley, A.C., et al. *The Revels History of Drama in English: Vol. 1: Medieval Drama* (London and New York: Methuen, 1983).
Chomarat, Jacques. *Grammaire et rhétorique chez Erasme* (Paris: Belles Lettres, 1981).
Clark, David W. 'William of Ockham on Right Reason', *Speculum*, 48 (1973), 13-36.
Coleman, Janet. Piers Plowman *and the 'Moderni'* (Rome: Edizioni di storia e letteratura, 1981).
Colish, Marcia. *The Mirror of Language: A Study in the Medieval Theory of Knowledge* (New Haven, CT: Yale University Press, 1968; Lincoln, NE, and London: University of Nebraska Press, rev. ed. 1983).
Copeland, Rita. 'Rhetoric and the Politics of the Literal Sense in Medieval Literary Theory', in Piero Boitani and Anna Torti (eds.), *Interpretation Medieval and Modern* (Cambridge: D.S. Brewer, 1993), 1-23.
Copleston, Frederick. *A History of Philosophy, Vol. 3: Ockham to Suarez* (Westminster, MD: The Newman Press, 1953).
Cornilliat, François. *'Or ne mens': Couleurs de l'éloge et du blâme chez les 'Grands Rhétoriqueurs'* (Paris: Champion, 1994).
Coulton, George G. *Chaucer and His England* (London: Methuen, 1908).
Courtenay, William J. 'Covenant and Causality in Pierre d'Ailly', *Speculum*, 46 (1971), 94-119, repr. in *Covenant and Causality*, (IX) 94-119.

———. 'The King and the Leaden Coin: The Economic Background of "Sine Qua Non" Causality', *Traditio*, 28 (1972), 185-209.

———. 'Nominalism and Late Medieval Religion', in Trinkaus and Oberman (eds.), *The Pursuit of Holiness*, 26-59, repr. in *Covenant and Causality*, (XI) 26-59.

———. 'Late Medieval Nominalism Revisited: 1972-1982', *Journal of the History of Ideas*, 64 (1983), 159-64.

———. *Covenant and Causality in Medieval Thought: Studies in Philosophy, Theology and Economic Practice* (London: Variorum Reprints, 1984).

———. 'The Dialectic of Divine Omnipotence', in *Covenant and Causality*, (IV) 1-37.

———. *Schools and Scholars in Fourteenth-Century England* (Princeton, NJ: Princeton University Press, 1987).

———. *Capacity and Volition: A History of the Distinction of Absolute and Ordained Power* (Bergamo: Lubrina, 1990).

Crafton, John Michael. 'Emptying the Vessel: Chaucer's Humanistic Critique of Nominalism', in Utz (ed.), *Literary Nominalism*, 117-34.

Cramer, Thomas. '*Solus Creator est Deus*: Der Autor auf dem Weg zum Schöpfertum', *Daphnis*, 15 (1986), 261-76.

Crystal, David. *The Cambridge Encyclopedia of Language* (Cambridge: Cambridge University Press, 1987).

Cummings, Hubertis M. *The Indebtedness of Chaucer's Works to the Italian Works of Boccaccio* (Cincinnati, OH: University of Cincinnati, 1916).

Curry, Walter Clyde. *Chaucer and the Mediaeval Sciences* (New York: Barnes & Noble, 2nd ed. 1960).

Curtius, Ernst Robert. *Europäische Literatur und lateinisches Mittelalter* (Berne and Munich: Francke, 4th ed. 1963); English translation: *European Literature and the Latin Middle Ages*, tr. Willard R. Trask (Bollingen Series, 36) (Princeton, NJ: Princeton University Press, 1983).

Davidson, Clifford. 'The Realism of the York Realist and the York Passion', *Speculum*, 50 (1975), 270-83.

Davis, Walter R. 'A Map of Arcadia: Sidney's Romance in Its Tradition', in Walter R. Davis and R.A. Lanham (eds.), *Sidney's* Arcadia (Yale Studies in English, 158) (New Haven, CT, and London: Yale University Press, 1965), 1-180.

Delany, Sheila. 'Undoing Substantial Connection: The Late Medieval Attack on Analogical Thought', *Mosaic*, 5.4 (1972), 33-52, repr. in *Medieval Literary Politics*, 19-41.

———. *Medieval Literary Politics: Shapes of Ideology* (Manchester: Manchester University Press, 1990).

———. *Chaucer's 'House of Fame': The Poetics of Sceptical Fideism* (Chicago, IL: University of Chicago Press, 1972; repr. Gainesville, FL: University Press of Florida, 1994).

Delasanta, Rodney. 'Chaucer and the Problem of the Universal', *Mediaevalia*, 9 (1986), 145-63.

———. 'Chaucer and Strode', *Chaucer Review*, 26 (1991), 205-18.
A Dictionary of Philosophy, eds. Antony Flew et al. (Pan Reference Books) (London: Pan, 1979).
Diedrick, James. 'Heteroglossia', in *Encyclopedia of Contemporary Literary Theory: Approaches, Scholars, Terms*, ed. Irena R. Makaryk (Toronto: University of Toronto Press, 1993), 551-2.
Diekstra, Frans. 'The Language of Equivocation: Some Chaucerian Techniques', *Dutch Quarterly Review*, 11 (1981), 267-77.
Diller, Hans-Jürgen. *The English Mystery Play: A Study in Dramatic Speech and Form*, tr. Frances Wesels (Cambridge: Cambridge University Press, 1992).
Donaldson, E. Talbot. *Speaking of Chaucer* (New York: Norton, 1970).
———. 'Chaucer's Three "P"s: Pandarus, Pardoner, Poet', *Michigan Quarterly Review*, 14 (1975), 282-301.
Dronke, Peter. *Fabula* (Leiden: Brill, 1974).
Dubois, Claude-Gilbert. *L'imaginaire de la Renaissance* (Paris: Presses Universitaires de France, 1985).
Duggan, Joseph P. 'Oral Performance of Romance in Medieval France', in Norris J. Lacy and Gloria Torrini-Roblin (eds.), *Continuations: Essays on Medieval French Literature and Language in Honor of John L. Grigsby* (Birmingham, AL: Summa Publications, 1989), 51-61.
Dunne, John. 'St. Thomas' Theology of Participation', *Theological Studies*, 18 (1957), 487-512.
During, Simon. *Foucault and Literature: Towards a Genealogy of Writing* (London and New York: Routledge, 1992).
Duval, Edwin M. *The Design of Rabelais's* Pantagruel (New Haven, CT: Yale University Press, 1992).
East, W.G. 'Lollius', *English Studies*, 58 (1977), 396-8.
Eco, Umberto. *Das Offene Kunstwerk*, tr. Günter Memmert (Frankfurt a.M.: Suhrkamp, 1977).
———. 'The Return of the Middle Ages', in *Travels in Hyperreality*, tr. William Weaver (London: Pan, 1987), 59-85.
———. *Kunst und Schönheit im Mittelalter*, tr. Günter Memmert (Munich: Hanser, 1991; repr. Munich: dtv, 1993); English translation: *Art and Beauty in the Middle Ages*, tr. Hugh Bredin (New Haven, CT, and London: Yale University Press, 1986).
———. *The Search for the Perfect Language*, tr. James Fentress (Oxford and Cambridge, MA: Blackwell, 1995).
Eldredge, Laurence. 'Chaucer's *House of Fame* and the *Via Moderna*', *Neuphilologische Mitteilungen*, 71 (1970), 105-19.
———. 'Poetry and Philosophy in the *Parlement of Foules*', *Revue de l'Université d'Ottawa*, 40 (1970), 441-59.
———. 'Boethian Epistemology and Chaucer's *Troilus and Criseyde* in the Light of Fourteenth-Century Thought', *Mediaevalia*, 2 (1976), 49-75.

———. 'The Concept of God's Absolute Power at Oxford in the Later Fourteenth Century', in D.L. Jeffrey (ed.), *By Things Seen: Reference and Recognition in Medieval Thought* (Ottawa and Grand Rapids, MI: University of Ottawa Press, 1979), 211-26.

Elton, W.R. 'Shakespeare and the thought of his age', in *The Cambridge Companion to Shakespeare Studies*, ed. Stanley Wells (Cambridge: Cambridge University Press, 1986), 17-34.

Encyclopædia Britannica, Fifteenth Edition (Chicago, IL: Encyclopædia Britannica, 1988).

The Encyclopedia of Philosophy, 8 vols., ed. Paul Edwards (New York and London: Macmillan, 1967).

Epstein, Hans J. 'The Identity of Chaucer's Lollius', *Modern Language Quarterly*, 3 (1942), 391-400.

Falk, W. 'Wolframs Kyot und die Bedeutung der "Quelle" im Mittelalter', *Literaturwissenschaftliches Jahrbuch*, n.s. 9 (1968), 1-63.

Feckes, Carl. *Die Rechtfertigungslehre des Gabriel Biel und ihre Stellung innerhalb der nominalistischen Schule* (Münster, Westf.: Aschendorff, 1925).

Felperin, Howard. *Beyond Deconstruction: The Uses and Abuses of Literary Theory* (Oxford: Clarendon Press, 1985).

Ferré, Frederick. 'Analogy in Theology', in *The Encyclopedia of Philosophy*, ed. Edwards, vol. 1: 94-7.

Feyerabend, Paul. *Against Method: Outline of an Anarchistic Theory of Knowledge* (1975; repr. London: Verso, 1978); enlarged German edition: *Wider den Methodenzwang: Skizze einer anarchistischen Erkenntnistheorie* (Frankfurt a.M.: Suhrkamp, 1976).

———. *Wissenschaft als Kunst* (Frankfurt a.M.: Suhrkamp, 1984).

Fichte, Joerg O. 'Man's Free Will and the Poet's Choice: The Creation of Artistic Order in Chaucer's Knight's Tale', *Anglia*, 93 (1975), 335-60.

———. '*Quha wait gif all that Chauceir wrait was trew—Auctor* and *auctoritas* in 15th Century English Literature', in Walter Haug and Burghart Wachinger (eds.), *Traditionswandel und Traditionsverhalten* (Tübingen: Niemeyer, 1991), 61-76.

Finlayson, John. 'The Knight's Tale: The Dialogue of Romance, Epic, and Philosophy', *Chaucer Review*, 27 (1992), 126-49.

Fischer, Walther. [Review of Hertha Korten, *Chaucers literarische Beziehungen zu Boccaccio: Die künstlerische Konzeption der* Canterbury Tales *und das Lolliusproblem* (Rostock: Hinstorff, 1920)], *Die Neueren Sprachen*, 20 (1921), 172-3.

Fish, Stanley. *Is There a Text in This Class? The Authority of Interpretive Communities* (Cambridge, MA: Harvard University Press, 1980).

Flasch, Kurt (ed.). *Geschichte der Philosophie in Text und Darstellung, Vol. 2: Mittelalter* (Stuttgart: Reclam, 1982).

―――. *Das philosophische Denken im Mittelalter: Von Augustin zu Machiavelli* (Stuttgart: Reclam, 1986).
Fleming, John V. *Classical Imitation and Interpretation in Chaucer's Troilus* (Lincoln, NE, and London: University of Nebraska Press, 1990).
Formigari, Lia. *Language and Experience in 17th-Century British Philosophy* (Amsterdam and Philadelphia, PA: John Benjamins, 1988).
Foucault, Michel. *Les mots et les choses: Une Archéologie des sciences humaines* (coll. tel, 166) (1966; repr. Paris: Editions Gallimard, 1992); English translation: *The Order of Things: An Archaeology of the Human Sciences* (New York: Vintage, 1973).
―――. 'Qu'est-ce qu'un auteur?', *Bulletin de la Société Française de philosophie*, 63.3 (1969), 73-104; English translation: 'What is an Author?', tr. J.V. Harari, in Josue V. Harari (ed.), *Textual Strategies: Perspectives in Post-Structuralist Criticism* (Ithaca, NY: Cornell University Press, 1979), 141-60.
―――. *The Archeology of Knowledge*, tr. A.M. Sheridan Smith (London: Tavistock Publications, 1972).
―――. *Discipline and Punish: The Birth of the Prison*, tr. Alan Sheridan (New York: Vintage, 1979).
Frappier, Jean. *Chrétien de Troyes: l'homme et l'œuvre* (Paris: Hatier-Boivin, 1957).
Freccero, John. *Dante: The Poetics of Conversion*, ed. Rachel Jacoff (Cambridge, MA: Harvard University Press, 1986).
―――. 'Introduction to *Inferno*', in *The Cambridge Companion to Dante*, ed. Rachel Jacoff (Cambridge: Cambridge University Press, 1993), 172-91.
Freeman, Michelle A. *The Poetics of 'Translatio Studii' and 'Conjointure': Chrétien de Troyes' Cligés* (Lexington, KY: French Forum Publishers, 1979).
Fried, Johannes (ed.). *Schulen und Studium im sozialen Wandel des hohen und späten Mittelalters* (Sigmaringen: Thorbecke, 1986).
Funkenstein, Amos. *Theology and the Scientific Imagination from the Middle Ages to the Seventeenth Century* (Princeton, NJ: Princeton University Press, 1986).
Furr, Grover C. 'Nominalism in the *Nun's Priest's Tale*: A Preliminary Study', in Utz (ed.), *Literary Nominalism*, 135-46.
Fyler, John. 'The Fabrications of Pandarus', *Modern Language Quarterly*, 41 (1980), 115-30.
Gadamer, Hans-Georg. *Truth and Method*, tr. Garret Barden and William G. Doerpel (New York: Seabury Press, 1975).
Gál, Gedeon. 'Petrus de Trabibus on the Absolute and Ordained Power of God', in R.S. Almagno and C.L. Harkins (eds.), *Studies Honoring Ignatius Charles Brady, Friar Minor* (St. Bonaventure, NY: The Franciscan Institute, 1976), 283-92.

Genette, Gérard. *Mimologiques: Voyage en Cratylie* (coll. Poétique) (Paris: Editions du Seuil, 1976).

Ginsberg, Warren. 'Place and Dialectic in *Pearl* and Dante's *Paradiso*', *Journal of English Literary History*, 55 (1988), 731-53.

Ginzburg, Carlo. *The Cheese and the Worms: The Cosmos of a Sixteenth-Century Miller*, tr. John and Anne Tedeschi (1980; repr. Harmondsworth: Penguin, 1992).

Gleick, James. *Chaos: Making a New Science* (New York: Viking, 1987).

Goffin, R.C. 'Chaucer's Lollius', *TLS*, Aug. 26, 1926, 564.

———. 'Chaucer's Lollius', *TLS*, April 21, 1927, 280.

Grennen, Joseph. 'Science and Sensibility in Chaucer's Clerk', *Chaucer Review*, 6 (1971), 81-93.

Griffin, Salatha Marie. *Chaucer's 'Troilus' from the Perspective of Ralph Strode's 'Consequences'*, PhD diss. University of Nebraska, 1978.

Gutting, Gary. *Michel Foucault's Archaeology of Scientific Reason* (Modern European Philosophy) (Cambridge: Cambridge University Press, 1989).

Guyer, Foster Erwin. *Chrétien de Troyes: Inventor of the Modern Novel* (New York: Bookman Associates, 1957).

Hacking, Ian. *Why Does Language Matter to Philosophy?* (Cambridge: Cambridge University Press, 1975).

Haley, David. *Shakespeare's Courtly Mirror: Reflexivity and Prudence in 'All's Well That Ends Well'* (Newark, DE: University of Delaware Press, 1993).

Hamilton, A.C. 'Sidney's *Arcadia* as Prose Fiction: Its Relation to Its Sources', *English Literary Renaissance*, 2 (1972), 29-60.

Hammond, Eleanor P. 'Two Chaucer Cruces', *Modern Language Notes*, 22 (1907), 51-2.

———. *Chaucer: A Bibliographical Manual* (New York: Macmillan, 1908).

Hardison, O.B., Jr. et al. (eds.). *Medieval Literary Criticism: Translations and Interpretations* (New York: Frederick Ungar, 1974).

Harris, Roy, and Talbot J. Taylor. *Landmarks in Linguistic Thought: The Western Tradition from Socrates to Saussure* (London and New York: Routledge, 1989).

Hathaway, Charles. 'Chaucer's Lollius', *Englische Studien*, 44 (1911), 158-63.

Hawkes, Terence. *Meaning by Shakespeare* (London and New York: Routledge, 1992).

Hawthorn, Jeremy. *A Concise Glossary of Contemporary Literary Theory* (London: Arnold, 1992).

Hayles, N. Katherine. *Chaos Bound: Orderly Disorder in Contemporary Literature and Science* (Ithaca, NY: Cornell University Press, 1990).

Haynes, Alan. *Robert Cecil, Earl of Salisbury, 1563-1612* (London: Peter Owen, 1989).

Heer, Friedrich. *Mittelalter: Vom Jahr 1000 bis 1350, Teil 2* (= vol. 10 of *Kindlers Kulturgeschichte Europas*) (1961; rev., expanded ed. 1977; repr. Munich: dtv, 1983).
Hempfer, Klaus W. 'Probleme traditioneller Bestimmungen des Renaissancebegriffs und die epistemologische "Wende"', in Klaus W. Hempfer (ed.), *Renaissance—Diskursstrukturen und epistemologische Voraussetzungen* (Text und Kontext, 10) (Stuttgart: Franz Steiner, 1993), 9-45.
Hindman, Sandra. *Sealed in Parchment: Rereadings of Knighthood in the Illuminated Manuscripts of Chrétien de Troyes* (Chicago, IL: University of Chicago Press, 1994).
Historisches Wörterbuch der Philosophie, 9 vols. (A to St), eds. Joachim Ritter and Karlfried Gründer (Darmstadt: Wissenschaftliche Buchgesellschaft, 1971-95).
History of Linguistics, 2: Classical and Medieval Linguistics, ed. Giulio Lepschy (London: Longman, 1994).
Hocke, Gustav René. *Manierismus in der Literatur: Sprach-Alchimie und esoterische Kombinationskunst* (Rowohlts Deutsche Enzyklopädie, 82-3) (Reinbek: Rowohlt, 1959).
Hodgdon, Barbara. *The End Crowns All: Closure and Contradiction in Shakespeare's History* (Princeton, NJ: Princeton University Press, 1991).
Hofmann, Werner. *Zauber der Medusa: Europäische Manierismen*, ed. Wiener Festwochen (Vienna: Löcker Verlag, 1987).
Holley, Linda Tarte. 'Medieval Optics and the Framed Narrative in Chaucer's *Troilus and Criseyde*', *Chaucer Review*, 21 (1986), 26-44.
Holmes, Urban Tigner. *Chrétien de Troyes* (New York: Twayne Publishers, 1970).
Holmes, Urban Tigner, and Sister M. Amelia Klenke, O.P. *Chrétien, Troyes, and the Grail* (Chapel Hill, NC: University of North Carolina Press, 1959).
Hornstein, Lillian Herlands. 'Petrarch's Laelius, Chaucer's Lollius?', *PMLA*, 63 (1948), 64-84.
Howard, Donald. *Chaucer: His Life, His Works, His World* (New York: E.P. Dutton, 1987).
Hudson, Nicholas. 'Locke's Nominalism and the "Linguistic Turn" of the Enlightenment', *The European Legacy*, 2.2 (1997), 223-8.
Huizinga, Johan. *The Waning of the Middle Ages: A Study of the Forms of Life, Thought and Art in France and the Netherlands in the Fourteenth and Fifteenth Centuries*, tr. Frederick Jan Hopman (London: Arnold, 1924).
Hult, David F. 'Reading it Right: The Ideology of Text Editing', *Romanic Review*, 79 (1988), 74-88.
Hunt, Tony. 'The Rhetorical Background to the Arthurian Prologue: Tradition and the Old French Vernacular Prologues', *Forum for Modern Language Studies*, 6.1 (1970), 1-23.

———. 'The Prologue to Chrestien's *Li Contes del Graal*', *Romania*, 92 (1971), 362-79.
Imbach, Ruedi. 'Vorwort', in Wilhelm von Ockham, *Texte zur Theorie der Erkenntnis und der Wissenschaft: Lateinisch/Deutsch*, ed. and tr. Ruedi Imbach (Stuttgart: Reclam, 1984), 5-10.
Imelmann, Rudolf. 'Chaucers *Haus der Fama*', *Englische Studien*, 45 (1912), 406-9.
Iser, Wolfgang. *The Act of Reading: A Theory of Aesthetic Response* (Baltimore, MD: Johns Hopkins University Press, 1978).
Iserloh, Erwin. *Gnade und Eucharistie in der philosophischen Theologie des Wilhelm von Ockham: Ihre Bedeutung für die Ursachen der Reformation* (Wiesbaden: Steiner, 1956).
Jameson, Frederick. *Postmodernism: Or the Cultural Logic of Late Capitalism* (Durham, NC: Duke University Press, 1991).
Jauß, Hans Robert. 'Literaturgeschichte als Provokation', in *Literaturgeschichte als Provokation* (Frankfurt a.M.: Suhrkamp, 1977), 144-207.
———. 'The Alterity and Modernity of Medieval Literature', *New Literary History*, 10 (Winter 1979), 181-230.
Jefferson, B.L. *Chaucer and the Consolation of Philosophy of Boethius* (Princeton, NJ: Princeton University Press, 1965).
The Johns Hopkins Guide to Literary Theory and Criticism, eds. Michael Groden and Martin Kreiswirth (Baltimore, MD, and London: Johns Hopkins University Press, 1994).
Jones, Robert C. *Engagement with Knavery* (Durham, NC: Duke University Press, 1986).
Jordan, Robert M. 'The Narrator of Chaucer's *Troilus*', *English Literary History*, 25 (1958), 237-57.
———. *Chaucer's Poetics and the Modern Reader* (Berkeley, CA: University of California Press, 1987).
Joseph, John E. 'The End of Languages as We Know Them', *Anglistik*, 8.2 (1997), 31-46.
Jurschak, Gertrud Mary. *Chaucer and Fourteenth-Century Thought*, PhD diss. Loyola University of Chicago, 1972.
Käsmann, Hans. '*I wold excuse hir yit for routhe*: Chaucers Einstellung zu Criseyde', in Arno Esch (ed.), *Chaucer und seine Zeit: Symposion für Walter F. Schirmer* (Tübingen: Niemeyer, 1968), 97-122.
Kaufmann, Matthias. *Begriffe, Sätze, Dinge: Referenz und Wahrheit bei Wilhelm von Ockham* (Studien und Texte zur Geistesgeschichte des Mittelalters, 40) (Leiden: Brill, 1994).
Keiper, Hugo. 'Ikarus im Labyrinth der Zeichen: Überlegungen zu einer Neuinterpretation des A-Textes von Marlowes *Doctor Faustus*', in Peter Csobádi et al. (eds.), *Europäische Mythen der Neuzeit: Faust und Don Juan*, 2 vols. (Wort und Musik, 18) (Anif/Salzburg: Verlag Müller-Speiser, 1993), vol. 2: 373-96.

———. '"I wot myself best how y stonde": Literary Nominalism, Open Textual Form and the Enfranchizement of Individual Perspective in Chaucer's Dream Visions', in Utz (ed.), *Literary Nominalism*, 205-34.

———. 'Introduction: "Poohness", or Of Universals, Paradigms, and Literature', *The European Legacy*, 2.2. (1997), 199-205.

Kelly, F. Douglas. *The Art of Medieval French Romance* (Madison, WI: University of Wisconsin Press, 1992).

Kelly, Henry Ansgar. 'Chaucer and Shakespeare on Tragedy', *Leeds Studies in English*, 20 (1989).

Kennedy, Leonard. 'Philosophical Scepticism in England in the Mid-Fourteenth Century', *Vivarium*, 21 (1983), 35-57.

———. 'Late-Fourteenth-Century Philosophical Scepticism at Oxford', *Vivarium*, 23 (1985), 124-51.

———. 'Osbert of Pickenham, O.Carm. (fl. 1360) on the Absolute Power of God', *Carmelus*, 35 (1988), 178-225.

Kenny, Anthony. *Wyclif* (Oxford: Oxford University Press, 1985).

Kirk, Elizabeth. 'Nominalism and the Dynamics of the *Clerk's Tale*: Homo Viator as Woman', in C. David Benson and Elizabeth Robertson (eds.), *Chaucer's Religious Tales* (Cambridge: D.S. Brewer, 1990), 111-20.

Kiser, Lisa. *Truth and Textuality in Chaucer's Poetry* (Hanover, NH, and London: University Press of New England, 1991).

Kittredge, George Lyman. 'Chaucer's Lollius', *Harvard Studies in Classical Philology*, 28 (1917), 47-132.

Knapp, Peggy. 'Robyn the Miller's Thrifty Work', in Wasserman and Roney (eds.), *Sign, Sentence, Discourse*, 294-308.

———. *Chaucer and the Social Contest* (New York: Routledge, 1990).

Knight, Stephen. 'Chaucer—A Modern Writer?', *Balcony*, 2 (1965), 37-43.

Knopp, Sherron E. 'The Narrator and His Audience in Chaucer's *Troilus and Criseyde*', *Studies in Philology*, 79 (1981), 323-40.

Knowles, David. *The Evolution of Medieval Thought* (London: Longman, 1962).

Kobusch, Theo, and Burkhard Mojsisch (eds.). *Platon in der abendländischen Geistesgeschichte: Neue Forschungen zum Platonismus* (Darmstadt: Wissenschaftliche Buchgesellschaft, 1997).

Koch, John. 'Ein Beitrag zur Kritik Chaucers', *Englische Studien*, 1 (1877), 249-93.

Koeppel, Emil. 'Chaucer and Cicero's *Laelius de Amicitia*', *Archiv*, 126 (1911), 180-2.

Kolve, V.A. *The Play Called Corpus Christi* (Stanford, CA: Stanford University Press, 1966).

Korten, Hertha. *Chaucers literarische Beziehungen zu Boccaccio: Die künstlerische Konzeption der* Canterbury Tales *und das Lolliusproblem* (Rostock: Hinstorff, 1920).

Kott, Jan. *Shakespeare Our Contemporary*, tr. Boleslaw Taborski (Garden City, NY: Anchor Books, 1966).

Kreuzer, James R. 'An Alleged Crux in Chaucer', *Notes & Queries*, n.s. 4 (1957), 409.

Kristeller, Paul Oskar. *Renaissance Thought and the Arts* (Princeton, NJ: Princeton University Press, 1964; expanded ed. 1990).

Kristeva, Julia. *Le Texte du roman: approche sémiologique d'une structure discursive transformationelle* (The Hague: Mouton, 1970); English translation (excerpt): 'From Symbol to Sign', tr. Seán Hand, in *The Kristeva Reader*, ed. Toril Moi (Oxford: Blackwell, 1986), 63-73.

Kuchta, David. 'Semiotics of Masculinity in Renaissance England', in James Grantham Turner (ed.), *Sexuality and Gender in Early Modern Europe: Institutions, Texts, Images* (Cambridge: Cambridge University Press, 1993), 233-46.

Kuhl, Ernest P. 'Some Friends of Chaucer', *PMLA*, 29 (1914), 270-6.

Kuhn, Thomas S. *The Structure of Scientific Revolutions* (1962; Chicago, IL: University of Chicago Press, 2nd ed. 1970).

Küpper, Joachim. *Diskurs-Renovatio bei Lope de Vega und Calderón: Untersuchungen zum spanischen Barockdrama. Mit einer Skizze zur Evolution der Diskurse in Mittelalter, Renaissance und Manierismus* (Romanica Monacensia, 32) (Tübingen: Narr, 1990).

Ladner, Gerhart. 'Medieval and Modern Understanding of Symbolism: A Comparison', *Speculum*, 54 (1979), 223-56.

Laird, Edgar. 'Cosmic Law and Literary Character in Chaucer's *Knight's Tale*', in Utz (ed.), *Literary Nominalism*, 101-15.

Lambert, Malcolm D. *Medieval Heresy: Popular Movements from Bogomil to Hus* (London: Arnold, 1977).

Land, Stephen K. *The Philosophy of Language in Britain* (New York: AMS, 1986).

Landesman, Charles. 'Locke's Theory of Meaning', *Journal of the History of Philosophy*, 14 (1976), 23-35.

Lange, Hugo. 'Chaucers "Myn Auctour Called Lollius" und die Datierung des *Hous of Fame*', *Anglia*, 42 (1918), 345-51.

Langer, Ullrich. *Divine and Poetic Freedom in the Renaissance: Nominalist Theology and Literature in France and Italy* (Princeton, NJ: Princeton University Press, 1990).

Laqueur, Thomas. 'Crowds, Carnival and the State in English Executions, 1604-1868', in A.L. Beier, David Cannadine, and James Rosenheim (eds.), *The First Modern Society* (Cambridge: Cambridge University Press, 1989), 305-55.

Latham, R.G. 'Chaucer', *The Athenaeum*, Oct. 3, 1868, 433.

Leclerq, Jean. 'The Love of Beauty as a Means and an Expression of the Love of Truth', *Mittellateinisches Jahrbuch*, 16 (1981), 62-72.

Leff, Gordon. *Bradwardine and the Pelagians* (Cambridge: Cambridge University Press, 1957).

―――. *Medieval Thought from Saint Augustine to Ockham* (London: Merlin, 1959).

———. *Richard Fitzralph* (Manchester: Manchester University Press, 1963).

———. *William of Ockham: The Metamorphosis of Scholastic Discourse* (Manchester: Manchester University Press, 1975).

Leffler, Oliver. *Wilhelm von Ockham: Die sprachphilosophischen Grundlagen seines Denkens* (Franziskanische Forschungen, 40) (Werl, Westf.: Dietrich-Coelde-Verlag, 1995).

Leonard, E.M. *The Early History of English Poor Relief* (1900; repr. New York: Barnes & Noble, 1965).

Levy, M.L. 'As myn Auctour Seith', *Medium Aevum*, 12 (1943), 25-9.

Lewis, C.S. *The Discarded Image: An Introduction to Medieval and Renaissance Literature* (1964; repr. Cambridge: Cambridge University Press, 1988).

Lindberg, David C. *The Beginnings of Western Science: The European Scientific Tradition in Philosophical, Religious, and Institutional Context, 600 B.C. to A.D. 1450* (Chicago, IL, and London: University of Chicago Press, 1992).

Lockhart, Adrienne. 'Semantic, Moral, and Aesthetic Degeneration in *Troilus and Criseyde*', *Chaucer Review*, 8 (1973), 100-18.

Lofmark, C. 'Die Interpretationen der Kyotstellen im *Parzival*', *Wolfram Studien*, 4 (1977), 33-70.

Lord, Albert B. *The Singer of Tales* (Cambridge, MA, and London: Harvard University Press, 1960).

Lorenz, Edward. *The Essence of Chaos* (1993; repr. Seattle, WA: University of Washington Press, 1995).

Lovejoy, Arthur O. *The Great Chain of Being: A Study of the History of an Idea* (1936; repr. Cambridge, MA: Harvard University Press, 1964).

Lowes, John L. 'Chaucer's "Etik"', *Modern Language Notes*, 25 (1910), 87-9.

Lukens, Michael B. (ed.). *Conflict and Community: New Studies in Thomistic Thought* (New York: Lang, 1992).

Lumianski, Robert M. 'Chaucer's *Parlement of Foules*: A Philosophical Interpretation', *Review of English Studies*, 24 (1948), 81-9.

Luscombe, D. 'Trivium, Quadrivium and the Organisation of Schools', *Miscellanea del centro di studi medioevali*, 12 (1989), 81-100.

Luttrell, Claude. 'The Prologue to Crestien's *Li Contes del Graal*', *Arthurian Literature*, 3 (1983), 1-25.

Machan, Tim William. 'Robert Henryson and Father Aesop: Authority in the *Moral Fables*', *Studies in the Age of Chaucer*, 12 (1990), 193-214.

Mahler, Andreas. 'Jahrhundertwende, Epochenschwelle, epistemischer Bruch? England um 1600 und das Problem überkommener Epochenbegriffe', in Klaus Garber (ed.), *Europäische Barock-Rezeption*, 2 vols. (Wolfenbütteler Arbeiten zur Barockforschung, 20) (Wiesbaden: Harrassowitz, 1991), vol. 2: 995-1026.

———. *Moderne Satireforschung und elisabethanische Verssatire: Texttheorie, Epistemologie, Gattungsgeschichte* (Texte und Untersuchungen zur Englischen Philologie, 16) (Munich: Fink, 1992).

Maierù, Alfonso. 'The Philosophy of Language', in *History of Linguistics, 2: Classical and Medieval Linguistics*, ed. Giulio Lepschy (London: Longman, 1994), 272-306.

Man, Paul de. 'The Resistance to Theory', *Yale French Studies*, 63 (1982), 3-20.

Mann, Jill. *Chaucer and Medieval Estates Satire* (Cambridge: Cambridge University Press, 1973).

Marrone, John. 'The Absolute and Ordained Powers of the Pope. A Quodlibetal Question of Henry of Ghent', *Mediaeval Studies*, 36 (1974), 7-27.

Maturana, Humberto R. *Erkennen: Die Organisation und Verkörperung von Wirklichkeit*, tr. Wolfram K. Köck (1982; Braunschweig and Wiesbaden: Vieweg, 2nd ed. 1985).

McGrath, Alistir E. *Iustitia Dei: A History of the Christian Doctrine of Justification, Vol. 1: From the Beginnings to 1500* (Cambridge: Cambridge University Press, 1986).

———. *The Intellectual Origins of the European Reformation* (Oxford: Blackwell, 1987).

McHale, Brian. *Postmodernist Fiction* (New York and London: Methuen, 1987).

———. *Constructing Postmodernism* (London and New York: Routledge, 1992).

McNamara, John F. *Responses to Ockhamist Theology in the Poetry of the 'Pearl'-Poet, Langland, and Chaucer*, PhD diss. Louisiana State University, 1968.

Meech, B. Sandford. *Design in Chaucer's* Troilus (Syracuse, NY: Syracuse University Press, 1959).

Mensching, Günther. *Das Allgemeine und das Besondere: Der Ursprung des modernen Denkens im Mittelalter* (Stuttgart: Metzler, 1992).

Meredith, Peter. 'The Towneley Cycle', in *The Cambridge Companion to Medieval English Theatre*, ed. Richard Beadle (Cambridge: Cambridge University Press, 1994), 134-62.

Mertens-Fonck, Paule. '*The Canterbury Tales*: New Proposals of Interpretation', *Atti della Accademia Peloritana dei Pericolanti*, 69 (1993), 5-29.

———. 'Le nominalisme de Geoffrey Chaucer dans *Troilus and Criseyde*: A propos d'un ouvrage récent', *Le Moyen Age*, 101 (1995), 314-8.

Meyer, Matthias. '"Sô dunke ich mich ein werltgot": Überlegungen zum Verhältnis Autor-Erzähler-Fiktion im späten Artusroman', in Volker Mertens and Friedrich Wolfzettel (eds.), *Fiktionalität im Artusroman* (Tübingen: Niemeyer, 1993), 185-202.

Miezkowski, Gretchen. 'The Reputation of Criseyde', *Transactions Published by the Connecticut Academy of Arts and Sciences*, 43 (1971), 71-153.

Miller, Jaqueline T. *Poetic License: Authorship and Authority in Medieval and Renaissance Contexts* (New York and Oxford: Oxford University Press, 1986).

Miller, Naomi J. '"Not Much to be Marked": Narrative of the Woman's Part in Lady Mary Wroth's *Urania*', *Studies in English Literature*, 29 (1989), 121-37.

Millett, Bella. 'Chaucer, Lollius, and the Medieval Theory of Authorship', *Studies in the Age of Chaucer*, 1 (1984), 93-103.

Mills, David. 'Religious Drama and Civic Ceremonial', in A.C. Cawley et al., *The Revels History of Drama in English: Vol. 1: Medieval Drama* (London and New York: Methuen, 1983), 152-206.

Minnis, Alastair J. '"Authorial Intention" and "Literal Sense" in the Exegetical Theories of Richard Fitzralph and John Wyclif', *Proceedings of the Royal Irish Academy*, 75 (1975), 1-31.

———. *Medieval Theory of Authorship: Scholastic Literary Attitudes in the Later Middle Ages* (London: Scolar Press, 1984; Philadelphia, PA: University of Philadelphia Press, 2nd ed. 1988).

———. with V.J. Scattergood and J.J. Smith. *Oxford Guides to Chaucer: The Shorter Poems* (Oxford: Oxford University Press, 1995).

———. and Tim William Machan. 'The Boece as Late-Medieval Translation', in Alastair J. Minnis (ed.), *Chaucer's Boece and the Medieval Translation of Boethius* (Cambridge: D.S. Brewer, 1993), 167-91.

———. and A.B. Scott (eds.). *Medieval Literary Theory and Criticism c.1100-c.1375* (Oxford: Oxford University Press, 1986).

Mittelstraß, Jürgen. 'Versuch über den sokratischen Dialog', in Karlheinz Stierle and Rainer Warning (eds.), *Das Gespräch* (Poetik und Hermeneutik, 11) (Munich: Fink, 1984), 11-27.

Moody, Ernest A. *The Logic of William of Ockham* (London: Sheed & Ward, 1935).

———. 'A Quodlibetal Question of Robert Holkot, O.P., on the Problem of the Objects of Knowledge and Belief', *Speculum*, 39 (1964), 53-74.

———. 'Ockhamism', in *The Encyclopedia of Philosophy*, ed. Edwards, vol. 5: 533-4.

Moonan, Lawrence. *Divine Power: The Medieval Power Distinction up to its Adoption by Albert, Bonaventure, and Aquinas* (Oxford: Clarendon Press, 1994).

Morel, W. 'An Alleged Crux in Chaucer', *Notes & Queries*, n.s. 4 (1957), 238-9.

Moretti, Franco. *Signs Taken for Wonders*, tr. Susan Fischer, David Forgacs, and David Miller (London: NLB, 1983).

Morley, Henry. *English Writers: An Attempt Towards a History of English Literature*, vol. 5.2 (London: Cassell, 1890).

Morse, J. Mitchell. 'The Philosophy of the Clerk of Oxenford', *Modern Language Quarterly*, 19 (1958), 3-20.

Morse, Ruth. *Truth and Convention in the Middle Ages: Rhetoric, Representation, and Reality* (Cambridge: Cambridge University Press, 1991).

Murphy, James J. 'A New Look at Chaucer and the Rhetoricians', *The Review of English Studies*, n.s. 15 (1964), 1-20.

Myles, Robert. *Chaucerian Realism* (Woodbridge: D.S. Brewer, 1994).

Nash, Christopher. 'Foreword', in Christopher Nash (ed.), *Narrative in Culture: The Uses of Storytelling in the Sciences, Philosophy, and Literature* (Warwick Studies in Philosophy and Literature) (London and New York: Routledge, 1994), xi-xiv.

The New Princeton Encyclopedia of Poetry and Poetics, eds. Alex Preminger and T.V.F. Brogan (Princeton, NJ: Princeton University Press, 1993).

Nichols, Stephen G. (ed.). *The New Philology* (special issue of *Speculum*, 65 (1990)).

Normore, Calvin G. 'The Tradition of Mediaeval Nominalism', in John F. Wippel (ed.), *Studies in Medieval Philosophy* (Studies in Philosophy and the History of Philosophy, 17) (Washington, DC: Catholic University of America Press, 1987), 201-17.

Norris, Christopher. *Derrida* (London: Fontana, 1987).

———. *Truth and the Ethics of Criticism* (Manchester: Manchester University Press, 1994).

Oakley, Francis. *The Political Thought of Pierre d'Ailly: The Voluntarist Tradition* (New Haven, CT: Yale University Press, 1964).

———. *Omnipotence, Covenant, and Order* (Ithaca, NY, and London: Cornell University Press, 1984).

Oberman, Heiko A. 'Some Notes on the Theology of Nominalism with Attention to its Relation to the Renaissance', *Harvard Theological Review*, 53 (1960), 47-76.

———. 'Facientibus Quod in Se Est Deus Non Denegat Gratiam: Robert Holcot, O.P. and the Beginnings of Luther's Theology', *Harvard Theological Review*, 55 (1962), 317-42.

———. *The Harvest of Medieval Theology: Gabriel Biel and Late Medieval Nominalism* (Cambridge, MA: Harvard University Press, 1963; Durham, NC: Labyrinth Press, 3rd ed. 1983).

———. 'The Shape of Late Medieval Thought: The Birthpangs of the Modern Era', in Trinkaus and Oberman (eds.), *The Pursuit of Holiness*, 3-25.

———. 'Fourteenth-Century Religious Thought: A Premature Profile', *Speculum*, 53 (1978), 80-93.

Ohly, Friedrich. 'Vom geistigen Sinn des Wortes im Mittelalter' [1958], in *Schriften zur mittelalterlichen Bedeutungsforschung* (Darmstadt: Wissenschaftliche Buchgesellschaft, 1977), 1-31.

O'Mara, Philip F. 'Robert Holcot's "Ecumenism" and the Green Knight', *Chaucer Review*, 26 (1992), 329-42, and 27 (1992), 97-106.

Otto, Stephan. *Renaissance und frühe Neuzeit* (Geschichte der Philosophie in Text und Darstellung, 3) (Stuttgart: Reclam, 1984).

———. *Das Wissen des Ähnlichen: Michel Foucault und die Renaissance* (Frankfurt a.M. et al.: Lang, 1992).
The Oxford Companion to Philosophy, ed. Ted Honderich (Oxford: Oxford University Press, 1995).
Ozment, Steven. *Mysticism and Dissent: Religious Ideology and Social Protest in the Sixteenth Century* (New Haven, CT: Yale University Press, 1973).
———. 'Mysticism, Nominalism, and Dissent', in Trinkaus and Oberman (eds.), *The Pursuit of Holiness*, 67-92.
———. *The Age of Reform 1250-1500: An Intellectual and Religious History of Late Medieval and Reformation Europe* (New Haven, CT: Yale University Press, 1980).
Padley, G.H. *Grammatical Theory in Western Europe 1500-1700*, 2 vols. (Cambridge: Cambridge University Press, 1985-8).
Panaccio, Claude. 'Langage ordinaire et langage abstrait chez Guillaume d'Occam', *Philosophiques*, 1 (1974), 37-60.
Panofsky, Erwin. *Gothic Architecture and Scholasticism* (New York: New American Library, and Latrobe, PA: The Archabbey Press, 1951).
———. *Early Netherlandish Painting: Its Origins and Character* (1953; repr. Cambridge, MA: Harvard University Press, 1964).
Paris, Gaston. '[Cligés]', in Mario Roques (ed.), *Mélanges de littérature française du moyen âge*, 2 vols. (Paris: Champion, 1912), vol. 1: 252-60.
Patch, Howard A. 'Troilus on Determinism', *Speculum*, 6 (1931), 225-43.
Patterson, Lee. 'On the Margin: Postmodernism, Ironic History, and Medieval Studies', in Stephen G. Nichols (ed.), *The New Philology* (special issue of *Speculum*, 65 (1990)), 87-108.
———. *Chaucer and the Subject of History* (Madison, WI: University of Wisconsin Press, 1991).
Payne, Robert O. *The Key of Remembrance: A Study of Chaucer's Poetics* (New Haven, CT: Yale University Press, 1963).
Pearsall, Derek. *The Life of Geoffrey Chaucer* (Oxford: Blackwell, 1992).
Peck, Russel. 'Chaucer and the Nominalist Questions', *Speculum*, 53 (1978), 745-60.
Perron, Paul. 'Semiotics', in *The Johns Hopkins Guide to Literary Theory and Criticism*, eds. Michael Groden and Martin Kreiswirth (Baltimore, MD, and London: Johns Hopkins University Press, 1994), 658-65.
Petersen, Kate O. *On the Sources of the 'Nonnes Preestes Tale'* (Radcliffe College Monographs, 10) (Boston: Radcliffe College, 1892).
Pétré, Hélène. *Caritas: Etude sur le vocabulaire latin de la charité chrétienne* (Louvain: Spicilegium sacrum lovaniense, 1948).
Pfister, Manfred. *The Theory and Analysis of Drama*, tr. John Halliday (Cambridge: Cambridge University Press, 1988).
Philosophielexikon: Personen und Begriffe der abendländischen Philosophie von der Antike bis zur Gegenwart, eds. Anton Hügli and Poul Lübcke (Hamburg: Rowohlt, 1991).

Pollard, Sidney. *The Idea of Progress: History and Society* (1968; repr. Harmondsworth: Penguin, 1971).
Popper, Karl R. *The Poverty of Historicism* (London: Routledge & Kegan Paul, 2nd corr. ed. 1961).
Powicke, Frederick. *The Medieval Books of Merton College* (Oxford: Clarendon Press, 1931).
Pratt, Robert. 'A Note on Chaucer's Lollius', *Modern Language Notes*, 65 (1950), 183-7.
———. 'A Note on Chaucer and the *Policraticus* of John of Salisbury', *Modern Language Notes*, 65 (1950), 243-6.
———. 'Some Latin Sources of the Nonnes Preest on Dreams', *Speculum*, 52 (1977), 538-70.
Preston, Raymond. *Chaucer* (London: Sheed and Ward, 1952).
Pulsiano, Phillip. 'Redeemed Language and the Ending of *Troilus and Criseyde*', in Wasserman and Roney (eds.), *Sign, Sentence, Discourse*, 153-74.
Purdon, Liam. 'Chaucer's *Lak of Stedfastnesse*: A Revalorization of the Word', in Wasserman and Roney (eds.), *Sign, Sentence, Discourse*, 144-52.
Quilligan, Maureen. 'Lady Mary Wroth: Female Authority and the Family Romance', in George M. Logan and Gordon Teskey (eds.), *Unfolded Tales: Essays on Renaissance Romance* (Ithaca, NY: Cornell University Press, 1989), 257-80.
Randall, Michael. 'Reversed Analogy in Jean Molinet's *Chappellet des dames*', in Utz (ed.), *Literary Nominalism*, 81-100.
———. *Building Resemblance: Analogical Imagery in the Early French Renaissance* (Baltimore, MD: Johns Hopkins University Press, 1996).
Randi, Eugenio. 'Il rasoio contro Ockham? Un sermone inedito di Giovanni XXII', *Medioevo*, 9 (1983), 179-98.
———. 'La vergine e il papa. *Potentia Dei absoluta* e *plenitudo potestatis* papale nel XIV secolo', *History of Political Thought*, 5 (1984), 425-45.
———. 'Potentia Dei conditionata. Una questione di Ugo di saint-Chér sull'onnipotenza divina (Sent. I, 42, q. 1)', *Rivista di storia della filosofia*, n.s. 1 (1984), 521-36.
———. '*Lex est in potestate agentis*. Note per una storia dell'idea scotista di *potentia absoluta*', in M. Beonio-Brocchieri Fumagalli (ed.), *Sopra la volta del mondo: Onnipotenza e potenza assoluta di Dio tra medioevo e età moderna* (Bergamo: Lubrina, 1986), 129-38.
———. *Il sovrano e l'orologiaio: Due immagini di Dio nel dibattito sulla 'potentia absoluta' fra XIII e XIV secolo* (Firenze: Cionini, 1987).
Randolph, Marie Claire. 'Thomas Drant's Definition of Satire, 1566', *Notes and Queries*, 180 (1941), 416-8.
Réau, Louis. *Iconographie de l'art Chrétien*, 3 vols. (Paris: Presses Universitaires de France, 1956; repr. Nendeln and Liechtenstein: Kraus, 1979).

Reese, William L. *Dictionary of Philosophy and Religion: Eastern and Western Thought* (Atlantic Highlands, NJ, and Hassocks, Sussex: Humanities, 1980).

Regn, Gerhard. 'Mimesis und Episteme der Ähnlichkeit in der Poetik der italienischen Spätrenaissance', in Klaus W. Hempfer (ed.), *Renaissance— Diskursstrukturen und epistemologische Voraussetzungen* (Text und Kontext, 10) (Stuttgart: Franz Steiner, 1993), 133-45.

Reichl, Karl. 'Chaucer's *Troilus*: Philosophy and Language', in Piero Boitani (ed.), *The European Tragedy of 'Troilus'* (Oxford: Clarendon Press, 1989), 133-52.

Reiss, Edmund. 'Ambiguous Signs and Authorial Deceptions in Fourteenth-Century Fictions', in Wasserman and Roney (eds.), *Sign, Sentence, Discourse*, 113-37.

Reyre, Dominique. *Dictionnaire des noms des personnages du Don Quichotte de Cervantes: Suivi d'une analyse structurale et linguistique* (Paris: Editions hispaniques, 1980).

Rhodes, Neil. *The Elizabethan Grotesque* (London: Routledge & Kegan Paul, 1980).

Robertson, D.W. 'Some Medieval Literary Terminology, with Special Reference to Chrétien de Troyes', *Studies in Philology*, 48 (1951), 669-92.

———. *A Preface to Chaucer* (Princeton, NJ: Princeton University Press, 1962).

Robins, Robert Henry. *A Short History of Linguistics* (London and New York: Longman, 3rd ed. 1990).

Roney, Lois. *Chaucer's Knight's Tale and Theories of Scholastic Psychology* (Tampa, FL: University of South Florida Press, 1990).

Rooney, Anne. *Geoffrey Chaucer: A Guide through the Critical Maze* (State of the Art series) (Bristol: The Bristol Press, 1989).

Rossiter, A.P. *Angel With Horns and other Shakespeare Lectures*, ed. Graham Storey (New York: Theatre Arts Books, 1961).

Royse, James R. 'Nominalism and Divine Power in the Chester Cycle', *Journal of the History of Ideas*, 40 (1979), 475-6.

Ruffolo, Lara. *Unison and Cacophony: Reflections of Skepticism in Fourteenth-Century English Poetry*, PhD diss. University of California at Irvine, 1993.

Rusch, Gebhard. *Erkenntnis, Wissenschaft, Geschichte: Von einem konstruktivistischen Standpunkt* (Frankfurt a.M.: Suhrkamp, 1987).

Ruud, Jay. 'Chaucer and Nominalism: the *Envoy to Bukton*', *Mediaevalia*, 10 (1984), 199-212.

———. *'Many a Song and Many a Lecherous Lay': Tradition and Individuality in Chaucer's Lyric Poetry* (New York: Garland, 1992).

———. 'Julian of Norwich and the Nominalist Questions', in Utz (ed.), *Literary Nominalism*, 31-49.

Saenger, Paul. 'Silent Reading: Its Impact on Late Medieval Script and Society', *Viator*, 13 (1982), 367-414.

Salgado, Gamini. *The Elizabethan Underworld* (London: J.M. Dent, 1977).
Saussure, Ferdinand de. *Cours de linguistique générale*, ed. Charles Bally and Albert Sechehaye (Paris: Bibliothèque Scientifique, 1955).
Scase, Wendy. Piers Plowman *and the New Anticlericalism* (Cambridge: Cambridge University Press, 1989).
Schoedinger, Andrew B. (ed.). *The Problem of Universals* (New Jersey and London: Humanities, 1992).
Schwartz, Jerome. 'Scatology and Eschatology in Gargantua's Androgyne Device', *Etudes rabelaisiennes*, 14 (1977), 265-75.
Screech, Michael A. *Rabelais* (London: Duckworth, 1980).
Sheldrake, Rupert. *The Presence of the Past: Morphic Resonance and the Habits of Nature* (1988; repr. London: Harper-Collins, 1994).
Shepherd, Geoffrey. 'Religion and Philosophy in Chaucer', in Derek S. Brewer (ed.), *Geoffrey Chaucer* (Writers and Their Background) (London: Bell, 1974), 262-89.
Shippey, T.A. *The Road to Middle Earth* (1982; London: Grafton, 2nd ed. 1992).
Siegel, Marsha. 'What the Debate Is and Why It Founders in Fragment A of *The Canterbury Tales*', *Studies in Philology*, 82 (1985), 1-24.
Siemon, James R. *Shakespearean Iconoclasm* (Berkeley, CA: University of California Press, 1985).
——. 'Sporting Kyd', *English Literary Renaissance*, 24 (1994), 553-82.
——. 'Sign, Cause or General Habit? Towards an "Historicist Ontology" of Character on the Early Modern Stage', *The European Legacy*, 2.2 (1997), 217-22.
Slack, Paul. 'Poverty and Politics in Salisbury 1597-1666', in Peter Clark and Paul Slack (eds.), *Crisis and Order in English Towns 1500-1700* (London: Routledge & Kegan Paul, 1972), 164-203.
Slaughter, M.M. *Universal Languages and Scientific Taxonomy in the Seventeenth Century* (Cambridge: Cambridge University Press, 1982).
Smalley, Beryl. *English Friars and Antiquity in the Early Fourteenth Century* (Oxford: Blackwell, 1960).
——. *Medieval Exegesis of Wisdom Literature*, ed. Roland E. Murphy (Atlanta, GA: Scholars Press, 1986).
Smith, Alan G.R. *Servant of the Cecils: The Life of Sir Michael Hicks, 1543-1612* (Totowa, NJ: Rowman & Littlefield, 1977).
Spitzer, Leo. 'Note on the Poetic and the Empirical "I" in Medieval Authors', *Traditio*, 4 (1946), 414-22.
Stackmann, Karl. 'Neue Philologie?', in Joachim Heinzle (ed.), *Modernes Mittelalter: Neue Bilder einer populären Epoche* (Munich: Insel Verlag, 1994), 398-427.
Stegmüller, Wolfgang. 'Das Universalienproblem einst und jetzt', *Archiv für Philosophie*, 6 (1956), 192-225, and 7 (1957), 45-81, repr. in *Glaube*,

Wissen und Erkennen. / *Das Universalienproblem einst und jetzt* (Darmstadt: Wissenschaftliche Buchgesellschaft, 1965).

———. (ed.). *Das Universalienproblem* (Darmstadt: Wissenschaftliche Buchgesellschaft, 1978).

Steiner, George. *After Babel: Aspects of Language and Translation* (Oxford: Oxford University Press, 1975).

Steinmetz, David. 'Late Medieval Nominalism and the *Clerk's Tale*', *Chaucer Review*, 12 (1977), 38-54.

Stepsis, Robert. '*Potentia absoluta* and the *Clerk's Tale*', *Chaucer Review*, 10 (1975), 129-46.

Stevens, Martin. 'The Performing Self in Twelfth-Century Culture', *Viator*, 9 (1978), 193-212.

———. *Four Middle English Mystery Cycles* (Princeton, NJ: Princeton University Press, 1987).

Stock, Brian. '*Antiqui* or *Moderni*?', *New Literary History*, 10 (Winter 1979), 391-401.

———. 'History, Literature, and Medieval Textuality', in Kevin Brownlee and Stephen G. Nichols (eds.), *Images of Power: Medieval History/Discourse/Literature* (special issue of *Yale French Studies,* 70 (1986)), 7-20.

Tachau, Katherine H. *Vision and Certitude in the Age of Ockham: Optics, Epistemology, and the Foundations of Semantics, 1250-1345* (Leiden: Brill, 1988).

Tatarkiewicz, Wladyslaw. *Geschichte der Ästhetik, vol. II: Die Ästhetik des Mittelalters* (Basel and Stuttgart: Schwabe, 1980).

Taylor, Barry. *Vagrant Writing: Social and Semiotic Disorders in the English Renaissance* (Toronto: University of Toronto Press, 1991).

Taylor, Charles. *Sources of the Self: The Making of the Modern Identity* (Cambridge, MA: Harvard University Press, 1989).

Taylor, Karla. *Chaucer Reads the* Divine Comedy (Stanford, CA: University of California Press, 1989).

Taylor, P.B. 'Chaucer's *Cosyn to the Dede*', *Speculum*, 57 (1982), 315-27.

Ten Brink, Bernhard. *Chaucer: Studien zur Geschichte seiner Entwicklung und zur Chronologie seiner Schriften* (Münster, Westf.: Russell, 1870).

Tetzeli von Rosador, Kurt. 'The Sacralizing Sign: Religion and Magic in Bale, Greene, and the Early Shakespeare', *Yearbook of English Studies*, 23 (1993), 30-45.

Thomas, Mary Edith. *Medieval Scepticism and Chaucer* (New York: William Frederick Press, 1950).

Thomson, Patricia. 'The *Canticus Troili*: Chaucer and Petrarch', *Comparative Literature*, 11 (1959), 313-28.

Tillich, Paul. *The Courage to Be* (New Haven, CT: Yale University Press, 1952).

———. *A History of Christian Thought: From its Judaic and Hellenistic Origins to Existentialism*, ed. Carl E. Braaten (New York: Simon & Schuster, 1967).

Tillyard, E.M.W. *The Elizabethan World Picture* (1943; repr. Harmondsworth: Penguin, 1978).
Titzmann, Michael. 'Kulturelles Wissen—Diskurs—Denksystem. Zu einigen Grundbegriffen der Literaturgeschichtsschreibung', *Zeitschrift für französische Sprache und Literatur*, 99 (1989), 47-61.
Todorov, Tzvetan. *Theories of the Symbol*, tr. Catherine Porter (Oxford: Blackwell, 1982).
Topsfield, L.T. *Chrétien de Troyes: A Study of the Arthurian Romances* (Cambridge: Cambridge University Press, 1981).
Trentman, John. 'Ockham on Mental', *Mind*, 79 (1970), 583-90.
Trinkaus, Charles, and Heiko A. Oberman (eds.). *The Pursuit of Holiness in Late Medieval and Renaissance Religion* (Leiden: Brill, 1974).
Turner, Myron. 'The Disfigured Face of Nature: Image and Metaphor in the Revised *Arcadia*', *English Literary Renaissance*, 2 (1972), 116-35.
Ussery, Huling E. 'Fourteenth-Century English Logicians: Possible Models for Chaucer's Clerk', *Tulane Studies in English*, 18 (1970), 1-15.
Utz, Richard J. *Literarischer Nominalismus im Spätmittelalter: Eine Untersuchung zu Sprache, Charakterzeichnung und Struktur in Geoffrey Chaucers* Troilus and Criseyde (Frankfurt a.M. et al.: Lang, 1990).
―――. 'Negotiating the Paradigm: Literary Nominalism and the Theory and Practice of Rereading Late Medieval Texts', in Utz (ed.), *Literary Nominalism*, 1-30.
―――. (ed.), *Literary Nominalism and the Theory of Rereading Late Medieval Texts: A New Research Paradigm* (Lewiston, NY: Edwin Mellen Press, 1995).
―――. '*For all that comth, comth of necessitee*: Chaucer's Critique of Fourteenth-Century Boethianism in *Troilus and Criseyde* IV, 957-958', *Arbeiten aus Anglistik und Amerikanistik*, 21 (1996), 29-31.
―――. 'Literary Nominalism in Chaucer's Late-Medieval England', *The European Legacy*, 2.2 (1997), 206-11.
―――. 'Zu Funktion und Epistemologie des Sprichwortes bei Geoffrey Chaucer', *Das Mittelalter: Perspektiven mediävistischer Forschung*, 2.2 (1997) (forthcoming).
Van Laan, Thomas F. *Role Playing in Shakespeare* (Toronto: University of Toronto Press, 1978).
Vance, Eugene. '*Mervelous Signals*: Poetics, Sign Theory, and Politics in Chaucer's *Troilus*', *New Literary History*, 10 (Winter 1979), 293-337.
―――. *Mervelous Signals: Poetics and Sign Theory in the Middle Ages* (Lincoln, NE, and London: University of Nebraska Press, 1986).
Vesey, Godfrey. 'Locke and Wittgenstein on Language and Reality', in H.D. Lewis (ed.), *Contemporary British Philosophy* (London: George Allen & Unwin, 1976), 253-73.
Vickers, Brian. *Appropriating Shakespeare: Contemporary Critical Quarrels* (New Haven, CT, and London: Yale University Press, 1993).

Vitz, Evelyn Birge. 'Type et individu dans l'<autobiographie> médiévale: Etude d'Histoire Calamitatum', *Poétique*, 6 (1975), 426-45.

———. 'Chrétien de Troyes: Cler ou ménestrel. Problèmes des traditions orale et littéraire dans les cours de France au XIIe siècle', *Poétique*, 8 (1990), 23-42.

Wacquant, Loic, and Pierre Bourdieu. *An Introduction to Reflexive Sociology* (Chicago, IL: University of Chicago Press, 1992).

Wallace, David. 'Chaucer's *Ambages*', *American Notes and Queries*, 23 (1984), 1-4.

———. *Chaucer and the Early Writings of Boccaccio* (Woodbridge: D.S. Brewer, 1985).

Waltz, Matthias. *Ordnung der Namen—Die Entstehung der Moderne: Rousseau, Proust, Sartre* (Frankfurt a.M.: Fischer, 1993).

Wasserman, Julian, and Lois Roney (eds.). *Sign, Sentence, Discourse: Language in Medieval Thought and Literature* (Syracuse, NY: Syracuse University Press, 1989).

Waswo, Richard. 'The Narrator of *Troilus and Criseyde*', *English Literary History*, 50 (1983), 1-25.

———. *Language and Meaning in the Renaissance* (Princeton, NJ: Princeton University Press, 1987).

Watson, Donald G. *Shakespeare's Early History Plays: Politics at Play on the Elizabethan Stage* (Athens, GA: University of Georgia Press, 1990).

Watts, William H., and Richard J. Utz. 'Nominalist Perspectives on Chaucer's Poetry: A Bibliographical Essay', *Medievalia et Humanistica*, n.s. 20 (1993), 147-73.

Weich, Horst. Don Quijote *im Dialog: Zur Erprobung von Wirklichkeitsmodellen im spanischen und französischen Roman (von* Amadís de Gaula *bis* Jacques le fataliste*)* (Passauer Schriften zu Sprache und Literatur, 3) (Passau: Rothe, 1989).

———. 'El "Quijote" en diálogo', *Estudios de Investigación Franco-Española*, 4 (1991), 45-77.

Weimann, Robert. *Shakespeare und die Macht der Mimesis: Autorität und Repräsentation im elisabethanischen Theater* (Berlin and Weimar: Aufbau-Verlag, 1988).

Wells, John E. *A Manual of the Writings in Middle English* (New Haven, CT: Yale University Press, 1916).

Wetherbee, Winthrop. 'Some Intellectual Themes in Chaucer's Poetry', in George D. Economou (ed.), *Geoffrey Chaucer* (New York: McGraw-Hill, 1975), 75-91.

———. *Chaucer and the Poets: An Essay on 'Troilus and Criseyde'* (Ithaca, NY: Cornell University Press, 1984).

Wheeler, Richard. 'History, Character and Conscience in *Richard III*', *Comparative Drama*, 5 (1972), 301-21.

Williams, Raymond. *Keywords: A Vocabulary of Culture and Society* (1976; London: Flamingo-Fontana, rev. and expanded ed. 1983).
———. *Marxism and Literature* (Oxford: Oxford University Press, 1977).
———. *Culture* (London: Fontana, 1981).
Wilson, Richard. *Will Power: Essays on Shakespearean Authority* (New York et al.: Harvester Wheatsheaf, 1993).
Windeatt, Barry. *Oxford Guides to Chaucer: Troilus and Criseyde* (Oxford: Clarendon Press, 1992).
Wippel, John F. 'Thomas Aquinas and Participation', in John F. Wippel (ed.), *Studies in Medieval Philosophy* (Studies in Philosophy and the History of Philosophy, 17) (Washington, DC: Catholic University of America Press, 1987), 117-58.
Wolf, Werner. 'The Language of Feeling between Transparency and Opacity', in Wilhelm G. Busse (ed.), *Anglistentag 1991 Düsseldorf: Proceedings* (Tübingen: Niemeyer, 1992), 108-29.
Woolf, Rosemary. *The English Mystery Plays* (London: Routledge & Kegan Paul, 1972).
Woozley, A.D. 'Universals', in *The Encyclopedia of Philosophy*, ed. Edwards, vol. 8: 194-206.
Wrightson, Keith. *English Society 1580-1680* (New Brunswick, NJ: Rutgers University Press, 1982).
Zabeeh, Farhang. *Universals: A New Look at an Old Problem* (The Hague: Martinus Nijhoff, 1966).
Zimbardo, Rose. 'Creator and Created: The Generic Perspective of Chaucer's *Troilus and Criseyde*', *Chaucer Review*, 11 (1977), 283-98.
Zink, Michel. 'Une mutation de la conscience littéraire: Le langage romanesque à travers des exemples français du XIIe siècle', *Cahiers de Civilisation Médiévale,* 24 (1981), 3-27.
———. *De la subjectivité littéraire* (Paris: Presses Universitaires de France, 1985).
Zumthor, Paul. *Speaking of the Middle Ages*, tr. Sarah White (Lincoln, NE, and London: University of Nebraska Press, 1986).
———. *La lettre et la voix* (Paris: Editions du Seuil, 1987).

CONTRIBUTORS

Christoph Bode is Professor of English and American Literature at Otto-Friedrich-Universität Bamberg, Germany. His publications include: *William Wordsworth und die Französische Revolution* (1977); *Intellektualismus und Entfremdung: Das Bild des Intellektuellen in den frühen Romanen Aldous Huxleys* (1979); *Lyrik und Methode: Propädeutische Arbeit mit Gedichten* (1983); *Aldous Huxley, 'Brave New World'* (1985); *'Ein Lehrer des langsamen Lesens': Anglistische Studien 1980-1986* (1987); *Ästhetik der Ambiguität: Zu Funktion und Bedeutung von Mehrdeutigkeit in der Literatur der Moderne* (1988); *Den Text? Die Haut retten! Bemerkungen zur 'Flut der Interpretationen' und zur institutionalisierten Literaturwissenschaft* (1992); *'And what were thou...?': Essay über Shelley und das Erhabene* (1992); *John Keats: Play On* (1996); *West Meets East: Klassiker der britischen Orient-Reiseliteratur* (1997).

William C. Carroll is Professor of English at Boston University. He is the author of *Fat King, Lean Beggar: Representations of Poverty in the Age of Shakespeare* (Cornell, 1996), *The Metamorphoses of Shakespearean Comedy* (Princeton, 1985), *The Great Feast of Language in 'Love's Labour's Lost'* (Princeton, 1976), and editor of Thomas Middleton's *Women Beware Women* (New Mermaid, 1994). He is currently editing *The Two Gentlemen of Verona* for the Arden 3 Series.

William J. Courtenay is the Charles Homer Haskins Professor of Medieval History at the University of Wisconsin-Madison. He is the author of several books in medieval intellectual history, including *Covenant and Causality in Medieval Thought* (1984), *Schools and Scholars in Fourteenth-Century England* (1987), and *Capacity and Volition: A History of the Distinction of Absolute and Ordained Power* (1990). He is presently completing a book on the University of Paris in the early fourteenth century.

Susanne Fendler received her PhD from Passau University and is currently an Assistant Professor and lecturer in English at the University of Würzburg, Germany. Her doctoral thesis (publ. 1996) deals with the emergence and presentation of individuality in English Renaissance romances by Gervase Markham, Mary Wroth, Anna Weamys and John Reynolds. She has co-edited a collection of articles on women's contributions to English literary history (1996). At present, she is at work on an extended study of fragmentation in eighteenth-century English literature and co-editing an anthology on the idea of Europe in literature.

Nicholas Hudson is Professor of English at the University of British Columbia. He is the author of *Samuel Johnson and Eighteenth-Century Thought* (Oxford, 1988), *Writing and European Thought 1600-1830* (Cambridge, 1994), and of many essays on eighteenth-century literature and thought. He is currently finishing *The Nominalist Revolution: Language, Mind and Nature from Ockham to the Enlightenment*.

Hugo Keiper is a lecturer in English and 'Assistenzprofessor' at Karl-Franzens-Universität Graz, Austria. He has written a book on the representation and aesthetics of dramatic space in Marlowe (Essen, 1988) and co-edited *Anglistentag 1994 Graz: Proceedings* (Tübingen, 1995). His articles include studies on various aspects in Chaucer, Marlowe, and Shakespeare. He is presently preparing an annotated edition and translation into German of Marlowe's *Doctor Faustus*, and an extended study of Late-Medieval English dream poetry.

Ullrich Langer is Professor of French at the University of Wisconsin-Madison. He is the author, most recently, of *Perfect Friendship: Studies in Literature and Moral Philosophy from Boccaccio to Corneille* (Geneva: Droz, 1994) and *Divine and Poetic Freedom in the Renaissance: Nominalist Theology and Literature in France and Italy* (Princeton: Princeton University Press, 1990). Currently he is completing a book on rhetoric, literature, and the theory of the virtues in Renaissance France.

Andreas Mahler is a lecturer in English at the University of Munich. He has written a book-length study on the relation between satirical discourse and Elizabethan verse satire and is the author of several articles on comedy, satire, and the problem of early modern epistemology.

William F. Munson is Associate Professor of English at the University of Alabama in Huntsville. He has published articles on *Everyman* and on English mystery plays in *The Chaucer Review*, *Mediaevalia*, *Comparative Drama*, and *Research Opportunities in Renaissance Drama*. He is interested especially in the bearing of liturgical and theological contexts on literary works in respect to issues of self.

Stephen Penn is a research student in the Department of English and Related Literature at the University of York, England. He is currently preparing a doctoral dissertation on theories of symbol and allegory in the writings of John Wyclif, and has a strong interest in the development of nominalist thinking in the later Middle Ages.

Gerald Seaman received his PhD from Stanford University and is Director of the French Program at the University of Evansville. He has published and presented a number of papers on Chrétien de Troyes and has been a Guest Lecturer in Old French at an NEH Summer Institute on Medieval Romance. His other research interests include Old French Hagiography and the relationship of myth to literature.

James R. Siemon is Professor of English at Boston University. He is the author of *Shakespearean Iconoclasm* (Berkeley, 1985) and the editor of Christopher Marlowe's *The Jew of Malta* (London, 1994). He is currently completing *Word Against Word: Shakespeare's 'Richard II' as Bakhtinian Utterance* and is editing *Richard III* for the new Arden series.

Richard J. Utz is Associate Professor of Early English Literature at the University of Northern Iowa and currently teaches Old and Middle English language and literature at the University of Tübingen. He is editor of *Literary Nominalism and the Theory and Practice of Rereading Late-Medieval Texts* (1995), author of *Literarischer Nominalismus im Spätmittelalter* (1990), and has published essays on the correspondences between nominalism and literature in late-medieval and twentieth-century texts. He is also co-editor of *Disputatio: An International Transdisciplinary Journal of the Late Middle Ages* and of *Prolepsis: The Tübingen Review of English Studies*.

William H. Watts is Assistant Professor of English at Butler University, where he teaches courses in composition, medieval literature, and the history of the English language. He has written articles on Boethius, Chaucer, the *Pearl*-Poet and William Langland, and is at work on an extended study of *Troilus and Criseyde*.

INDEX OF MAJOR REFERENCES
(COMPILED BY HUGO AND ANITA KEIPER)

Aarsleff, Hans, 297
Abelard, Peter, 6, 94, 106, 116, 171, 284, 306; anti-realist philosophy of, 95, 309; conceptualist-nominalism of, 96; nominalism of, 95-6, 109; 'scripta poetae', 109
absolutes, 49
abstraction(s), 66, 95, 97, 285, 290, 307-8
abstractive cognition, 159, 310. *See also:* intuitive cognition
Ackroyd, Peter: *Hawksmoor*, 51
aconite, 255
action, 191, 199, 207, 215; psychological, 213; virtuous, 272
actualization, 302
aesthetic(s), 133; advanced, 52; incongruous, 51; medieval 174; Platonic, 162; revolutionary, 52; nominalist, 37; realist, 37. *See also:* literary aesthetic(s)
aesthetic: experience, 90, 96; modes, 53; sensibility, 64
aetiological myth, 200
affinity, 255-7; natural, 237
agency, 192, 194, 199, 208; autonomy and efficacy of human, 211; double, 207; free, 246; natural, 160; personal, 246-7
agent(s), 198; function of, 224. *See also:* man
Agricola, Rudolph, 257-8
Ailly, Pierre d', 116, 132
Albertus Magnus, 113, 307
allegorization, 187
allegory, 22, 26, 87, 182, 187-8, 282; and analogy, 185; Chaucerian, 185; decline of, 185; scriptural, 184. *See also:* realist
alliances (secret), 253
allusion, 20
Altensteig, Johannes, 132, 219
alterity, 36. *See also:* Other

alternatives, 245; dualistic, 242
ambiguity, 137, 162, 170-1, 174-6, 179
anagrammatical equivalent, 264
analogia: nominum, 183; *rerum*, 183
analogical: archive, 266; decline, 186; forms of literature, 133; inauthenticity, 263; thinking, 262; view of universe, 184; world-view, 251
analogism, 251-2; era of, 267; losses of, 262
analogue(s), 129, 146, 305
analogy, 22, 120, 182-4, 186, 251-3, 257-9, 265; epistemological, 133; literary, 186; of proportionality, 184; of things, 183; of words, 183; structural, 128; theory of, 182
analysis: literary-critical, 44; logical, 237; semiotic, 56; social, 237
angel(s), 193, 195, 198, 200, 212; as token(s), 200, 214
anonymity, 93
Anselm of Canterbury, 306
anthropology: non-Augustinian, 210; of *via moderna*, 211. *See also:* Augustinian
Antiquity, 6, 44
apocalypse, 108
appearance(s), 266, 277, 279
appropriation, 137
Aquinas, Saint Thomas, 4, 95, 113, 116, 173, 175, 183-4, 205, 292, 306; *Summa Theologiae*, 183. *See also:* Thomism, Thomist synthesis, Thomists
arbitrariness, 96, 139, 288-9; of general ideas, 291
archetype *ante rem*, 159
Ariès, Philippe, 70
aristocratic: descendance, 273, 280; setting, 98
Aristotelianism, 88, 205, 222, 285; Franciscan reaction to, 205
Aristotle, 6, 94, 164, 166, 182, 202, 286,

298, 306; formal causes of, 9; *De interpretatione*, 286; *Poetics*, 224
Arnauld, Antoine, 289
Arthurian writers, 132. *See also:* romance
artifact(s), 3; aesthetic, 43; cultural, 104
artifex, 130; as fabricator of fiction, 135
artificer, 3
arts of poetry (medieval), 88
ascription (acts of), 312
Ashley, Kathleen M., 112, 116, 162
Ashworth, E.J., 284
Assunto, Rosario, 13
Astralabius, 95
attribute(s), 220-2, 226; individual, 222; marked, 222
attribution, 93-4
auctor(es), 94, 125, 131
auctoritas, 94
auctour, 123, 138-9, 142; fictional, 140
audience, 130, 136, 140, 213-6; general, 143-4. *See also:* reader(s)
Augustine, Saint, 4, 6, 94, 103, 113, 146, 150, 162, 173, 176-7, 183-4, 217-9, 220, 306; *Confessions*, 103
Augustinian, 95, 202; anthropology, 194; dichotomies, 103; inwardness, 201; realism, 88
authentication, 98, 140
author(s), 1-3, 88, 90-1, 93, 96-8, 120, 128, 132, 141-4, 170, 302, 304; absence of, 93; absolute power of, 137; arbitrary, 143; as compiler(s), 131; as translator(s), 131; biography of, 88; late-medieval, 129; medieval, 128; name of, 91-2; of nature, 289; omnipotence of, 123; status of, 3, 92
author-text transactions, 55
authorities: judicial, 228, 233; Tudor, 234
authority, 1-3, 11, 22, 88, 93-4, 125, 127, 139-40, 143, 145, 150, 160, 185, 228, 230, 258; creative, 136; gendering of, 3; of the text, 302; problem of, 27. *See also: auctor(es), auctoritas*
authorizing strategies, 22
authorship, 22, 74, 88-9, 91, 94, 97-8, 101-2, 104-9, 128, 144; concepts of, 50; definitions of, 99; jongleuresque, 88-93, 98-9; masks of, 131; roman-esque, 88-93
auto-referentiality, 312

autonomy, 134; of the sign, 170; of *texte*, 90. *See also: in se*
Autrecourt, Nicholas d', 132
Ayers, Michael, 289

Babel, 256
Babington Plot, 229
Bacon, Francis, 237; 'Of Deformity', 238-42, 246-7, 249 ('boldness', 240-2, 246-7, 249; 'competition', 241, 247; 'contempt', 239; 'general habit', 240, 242, 247; 'idols', 238; 'jealousy', 239; 'scorn', 239, 241-2, 247, 249)
Bacon, Roger, 175
badging (of licensed beggars), 231
Bakhtin, Mikhail, 55-6, 171-2
Bakhtinian: methodologies, 188; readings, 171
Bambrough, Renford, 298
baptism, 193-4, 212-3, 215; agency of, 195; of Christ (Jesus) by John, 192; power of, 195. *See also:* John the Baptist, Towneley, York
baptismal water, 195-6
Barney, Stephen A., 127
Barth, John, 58
Barthes, Roland, 4, 55-6
Baudrillard, Jean, 234
beauty, 269-82; allegorical meaning of, 269-70; and virtue, 269-82; as mediator, 272; as signifier, 269-82; conceptions of, 269-71; experience of, 270; inward, 275, 280; kinds of, 280; loss of, 277; outward, 280; realist concept of, 271
beggar(s), 229-35; counterfeiting, 230, 233; licensed, 230; sturdy, 229-30, 232; true, 230; unlicensed, 231. *See also:* badging
being: human, 218; human and divine, 184; innate, 247; modes of, 183; social, 243; substantial, 247. *See also:* chain of being, God
Benoît de Sainte Maure, 98-9, 106; *Roman de Troie*, 99, 106
Berkeley, George, 290, 310
Bible, 100, 102, 105; Authorized Version of, 1; exegesis of, 193
biblical drama (English), 202. *See also:* morality play(s), mystery play(s)

Index   351

biblical echoes, 100, 104
Biel, Gabriel, 113, 132, 208, 220
Bloom, Harold, 171
Blumenberg, Hans, 13, 134
Boccaccio, Giovanni, 124-5, 135, 162; *Il Filostrato*, 125, 135
Bode, Christoph, 73-4, 83
body, 231, 233. *See also:* Christ
Boehner, Philotheus, 168, 291
Boethian: material, 145; realism, 178
Boethius, 6, 113, 146, 149, 162, 164, 176-7, 180-2, 306; *Consolation of Philosophy*, 178. *See also:* Chaucer (Geoffrey)
Bonaventure, Saint, 113, 132
book of nature/creation, 3, 131
Borges, Jorge Luis, 7, 204
Boucher, Holly Wallace, 162-3, 165, 167, 169-71, 176-7
Bourdieu, Pierre, 237, 240, 242. *See also:* double history, field, habitus, historicist ontology
Bradshaw, Graham, 301-2
Bradwardine, Thomas, 119, 145, 149-51, 173; *De causa dei*, 151-2
branding, 232-3
Brooke-Rose, Christine, 51
Buckingham, Thomas, 149
Buffon, Georges-Louis Leclerc, Comte de: *Histoire naturelle*, 297
Buridan, Jean, 133
Burnley, J.D., 146
Burroughs, William, 58

Carlson, Marvin, 228
carnival, 228. *See also:* Chaucer (Geoffrey)
Carré, Meyrick, 158
Carroll, Lewis, 16-7
Carroll, William C., 74, 79-80
Castelvetro, Lodovico, 224
categories (as distinct), 221
categorization (historical), 56; of texts, 54, 57; typological, 56-7
category violation, 246-7
Cato: *Distiches*, 152
causal fertility, 67-8
causality, 207, 212; covenantal, 207; covenantal conception of, 205; interactive, 208; ontological, 207; primal, 102
causation, 45-6; primary, 160

cause(s), 114, 239, 247; doctrine of primary and secondary, 160. *See also:* Creator, *prima causa efficiens*
Cecil, Robert, Earl of Salisbury, 241
certainty, 49, 114, 166, 298
Cervantes, Miguel de: *Don Quixote*, 262-5, 267
chain of being, 205
Chalcidius, 176, 180
Chamberlain, John, 241
Chanson de Roland, 99
chaos theory, 84
character(s), 74, 120, 134, 154, 224, 237-8, 240, 274-5, 278; analogist, 263; aristocratic, 279; as sign of the real, 172; conception of, 22, 275; different types of, 279; differentiated, 278; individualized, 275, 282; ordinary, 274
characteristics (individualizing), 245
characterization, 215, 237, 281
charity, 104, 196, 218; as mimetic relationship, 217; Christian, 100, 217; object of Christian, 221; refusal of, 226; relationship of, 217; sameness of, 221-2
Charles V., 126
Chaucer, Geoffrey, 3, 62, 64, 71, 113, 117, 123, 127, 129, 134-5, 141, 143, 145-6, 148, 153, 162, 171, 174-7, 179-80; allegory in, 185; and nominalism, 129; and philosophical disputes, 154; anti-essentialist features in, 63; as affirmative author, 61; as deconstructionist, 61; as icon of cultural/national identity, 60-1; as ironist, 61; as orthodox Christian writer, 61-3; as partisan in the philosophical debate, 146, 155; as representative of Merry Old England, 61; awareness of nominalism, 155; carnivalesque dimension in, 63; clerks in, 19; dream visions of, 50, 130; epistemological implications in, 146; images of, 60-1; interrogative tendencies in, 63; nominalistic realism in, 187; philosophical approaches to, 146; philosophical interpretation of, 150; philosophical issues in, 145; philosophical re-evaluation of, 147; readings of, 61-4; realist epistemology of, 149; representations of philoso-

phizing clerks in, 145, 148, 152-5; subversion in, 61, 63-4; *Boece*, 145; *The Canterbury Tales*, 174: 'Canon's Yeoman's Prologue', 154; 'Clerk's Tale', 116-7, 147; 'Franklin's Tale', 153-5; 'General Prologue', 153, 180; 'Knight's Tale', 147, 171-3; 'Manciple's Tale', 180; 'Miller's Tale', 153, 171-3, 175; 'Nun's Priest's Tale', 150-2, 154; 'Pardoner's Tale', 181; 'Reeve's Tale', 153; 'Retractatio', 142; 'Summoner's Tale', 175; *Envoy to Bukton*, 165; *House of Fame*, 16, 24, 123, 125-6, 130, 178; *Lak of Stedfastnesse*, 180-1; *Treatise on the Astrolabe*, 131; *Troilus and Crisyede*, 123, 125, 127, 129-30, 134-8, 140-2, 145, 148, 154-5, 177-9

Chaucer, Lewis, 148-9

Chettle, Henry: *Kind-Hartes Dreame*, 233

Chrétien de Troyes, 72, 87, 94, 96-105, 107-9; and Christianity, 99; Christian figure(s) of, 87-8, 104, 108; Christian isotopy in, 99, 108; figure of the seed in, 100-1, 103, 105-9; good seed ('bone semence') in, 101, 108; name of, 92-3; poetics of authorship and exclusion of, 108; prologues of, 87-8, 97-109; seed of poetry in, 103; status as author of, 104; status as vernacular poet of, 88; *Le Chevalier au Lion*, 92, 108; *Le Chevalier de la charrette*, 92, 108; *Cligés*, 92, 98, 108; *Le Conte du graal*, 87, 92, 100-2, 105, 107; *Erec et Enide*, 88, 92, 97-9, 107-8. *See also*: poetics, romance

Christ, 210, 218; as Logos, 195; body of, 218-9, 226; brothers in, 219; disciple of, 102; membership in body of, 220; parables of, 107-8. *See also*: baptism, Logos, parable

Christian figure(s): *see*: Chrétien de Troyes

Christian-Pagan opposition, 99

Christocentrism, 194

Church (universal), 194, 196-7

Church Fathers, 182

Cicero, 97. *See also*: Tullius

class struggles, 34

class(es), 296, 298

Classicism (age of), 260

classification, 92, 293, 297; of nature, 289

clerks: *see*: Chaucer (Geoffrey)

closure, 47, 303

clothing, 234

codes, 104

cognition: *see*: abstractive cognition, intuitive cognition

Coleman, Janet, 112

commonplaces, 146

communication, 11, 284, 294, 298

compiler, 137, 139. *See also*: author

concepts, 284, 288, 307, 309; and signification, 164; and words, 164; ethical, 295; normative 49; reified, 310; religious, 295. *See also*: *ficta*, general, mental, universal

conceptualism, 5, 307-8; as term, 284

conceptualist-nominalism, 94. *See also*: Abelard

Condillac, Etienne Bonnot, Abbé de, 284, 294-7, 299

construction: of difference(s), 224; of the individual, 223; of universals, 284, 289. *See also*: history

constructivism, 21, 170

context(s): cultural, 14; extra-literary, 42, 44; institutional, 240-1; non-aesthetic, 240; non-literary, 44; philosophical, 74, 111; theological, 74, 119

contingency, 11, 74, 120, 131, 134, 137, 211-2; of creation, 120; of entities, 203; of literary universe, 144; of sacraments, 206, 211; of verbal relationships, 239; of world(s), 141; of sacraments as causes, 205. *See also*: philosophy, sacrament(s), truth(s), world

contradiction(s), 227, 288-9, 303

convention(s), 289; discursive, 41; generic, 41, 52; literary, 41, 52. *See also*: naming

correspondence(s), 183, 259, 280, 292, 294

cosmology, 4

Counter-Reformation (monological impact of), 268

counterdiscourse(s), 72-3, 262, 303

counterfeiting, 230-3, 243; of vagrants, 233

court, 98, 113, 248-9
Courtenay, William J., 74-6, 81, 132-3, 146, 152, 158-60, 188
courtesy theory (English), 271
covenant, 103, 115, 205, 207-8, 238; God's relation to nature as, 120; Scotist emphasis on, 205. *See also:* God, world
Crafton, John Michael, 155, 170, 176-7
creation *ex nihilo*, 130
creator(s): of fiction, 137; of story, 136. *See also:* literary fiction
Creator, 1-3, 253; Christian 142; omnipotent, 121, 143. *See also: prima causa efficiens*, 130
creature(s) of God, 220-4; essential sameness of, 222
crisis: age of, 35; and paradigm shifts, 12; of authority, 227; of the sign, 227, 234
criterion, 289, 291; of exclusion, 26, 30; of inclusion, 30, 44
critical: debate(s), 301; practice, 312; theory, 32, 167, 182, 301, 303-5, 312
Crucifixion, 115
cultural: change, 34, 70, 185; codes, 235; configurations, 26, 44; constituents, 14, 39, 44, 134; contexts, 14; evolution, 59; factors, 296; generalized, 34; historians, 9; meaning, 15, 65; negotiations, 14, 27-8, 37, 45; studies, 63; theory, 167; transformation, 7, 14; transition, 51
culture (dominant), 230. *See also:* dominant
Curry, Walter Clyde, 145-7

Dante Alighieri, 162, 171, 178-9; *Divina Commedia*, 163; *La Vita Nuova*, 163
Davidson, Clifford, 185
death, 99
debate over universals, 8, 42, 217, 312; after-effects of, 8-9; continuity of, 73; discursive dynamics of, 42; discursive properties of, 42; general awareness of, 29; general development of, 9; historical development of, 33; historical parameters of, 9; history of, 6-7; implications of, 13; in cultural studies, 8; in linguistics, 8-9; in mathematics, 8; in philosophy, 8; inherent dynamics of, 33; intrinsic development of, 39; issues of, 26; medieval, 6-7, 27, 296, 307; philosophical, 42; privileging of, 42; theological, 42; twentieth-century, 305, 311. *See also:* literary debate over universals
deceit, 229
decidability, 51
decorum, 243-4
defamiliarization, 215
Defaux, Gérard, 225
definition(s), 288-9; true, 292
deformity, 240-1, 247. *See also:* Bacon (Francis)
deistic 'leap of faith', 63. *See also:* fideism
Dekker, Thomas: *O per se O*, 231
Delany, Sheila, 33-4, 38, 133, 185, 187
Delasanta, Rodney, 117, 149, 171, 174, 177, 181-2, 187
demystification, 286
dependability, 115, 120, 212. *See also:* reliability, reliabilism
Derrida, Jacques, 3-4, 8, 32, 171, 288
Descartes, René, 287
descent, 229
designation (adequate), 264. *See also:* name(s)
determination, 240-1, 248
deus absconditus, 134
deviousness, 154
difference(s), 248, 257, 260, 274-5, 279; between creatures, 221; between groups, 221
differentia specifica, 312
discontinuity, 255
discourse(s), 39, 88, 162, 167, 174, 303, 311; as term, 38; critical, 312; dialectics of, 37; difference(s) between, 41; dominant, 171-2, 267; emergent, 267; hierarchical order of, 42; mental, 292-3; mental and verbal, 293; of authority, 87, 109; of the Church, 104; parasite, 312; parasitical, 42; patristic, 61, 188; philosophical, 15, 145, 148; referential, 20; secondary, 42; scientific, 15; theological, 129; type(s) of, 38-41. *See also:* dominant, literary discourse, nominalist
discovery (procedures of), 60
discursive: conditions, 237, 246; domains,

14; function(s), 55, 92; levels, 40; strategies, 47; tradition(s), 271
disease, 229
disguise, 229
disorder, 230
dissembling, 230, 246
dissemination, 105
dissimulation (Baudrillard), 234
distinction of absolute and ordained power of God, 113, 118; canonist interpretation of, 118-9; history of, 114; theological (traditional), 119-20; two definitions of, 119. *See also:* power of God
distinction(s), 227, 247, 281-2, 290-1, 293, 312; ethical, 222; of grammar, 286
divine: action (forms of), 116; capacity, 118, 120; grace, 101, 115, 195, 197, 201-2, 209; idea(s), 184, 309; immediacy, 211; intervention, 114, 120; legislator, 132; logos, 104; names, 179; nature, 120; omnipotence, 111, 123, 130; omniscience, 151; order, 163; plan, 120; power, 118, 159; power as absolute, 112; power as ordained, 112; spark, 272-3; transcendence, 120; truths, 177; volition, 116, 118; will, 200; will as beneficent, 119; Word, 103, 195. *See also:* God, Logos, power of God, Word
dominant (vs. emergent vs. residual), 68, 267
Donaldson, E. Talbot, 154-5
Donatus, 97
double history (Bourdieu), 242, 247
drama, 208, 213; meta-theatrical dimension of, 245. *See also:* biblical drama
dramatic presentation, 215
Drant, Thomas: *Horace: His Arte of Poetrie, Pistles and Satyrs Englished*, 258-60
dressing, 233
Dryden, John: *Discourse concerning the Original and Progress of Satire*, 260-1
dualism, 253
Dubois, Claude-Gilbert, 256
Duns Scotus, John, 119, 145, 157, 161, 171, 306
During, Simon, 265

early modern: context, 72; period, 217; situation, 71
Easthope, Anthony, 301
Eco, Umberto, 55-6, 255, 270, 297-8
egocentrism, 246
Einstein, Albert, 31-2
either-or: dilemma, 242; choice, 242; dichotomy, 312; quandary, 59
Eldredge, Laurence, 112, 117, 177
election, 239, 241-2, 249
Elton John, 8
embedding, 57. *See also:* framing
emblem, 87
embodiment, 99, 103-4, 108, 243-4, 246
empiricism, 180, 266
encoding, 104; literary modes of, 15
England, 72, 267-8; early modern, 227-35
Enlightenment, 283, 310; philosophers, 297
entities, 96; as actual in nature, 285, 292; distinct, 203; separate, 94; single, 287; volitional, 211
enunciations (multiple), 95
epilogue, 92
epiphany, 50
episteme, 252; analogist, 254; archaeological, 265; as term, 13; 'classical', 261; Foucault's concept of, 13; medieval, 89. *See also:* realist, Renaissance
epistemology, 11, 96, 162-3, 178-9, 185, 202, 204, 238, 255, 265-6, 290, 309; as criticism of language, 310; linguistic, 183; sceptical, 160, 166; theories of, 182; topos-oriented, 255. *See also:* nominalist, Renaissance
Epstein, Hans J., 125
equivocation, 174-5, 246-7
Erasmus, Desiderius, 217-23, 287; *De ratione studii*, 222; *Enchiridion militis christiani*, 217-8
Erigena, John Scotus, 306
Eschenbach, Wolfram von, 124
essence(s), 95, 184, 196, 211, 226, 253, 273, 277, 285, 291, 295; nominal, 292; real, 292. *See also:* human
essentialism, 8, 312. *See also:* reading
essentialization, 243
Essex, Earl of, 229
eternal (vs. temporal), 172

eternity, 105
etymology, 65; correct, 260
Eurocentrism, 8
Europe, 8; modern, 7
European cultural history, 7, 13; (re-)construction of, 14. *See also:* history
European: history of ideas, 6; intellectual history, 62-3
Evangelists, 101. *See also:* Gospel(s)
Evanthius, 96
evil, 240, 245
evolution: aesthetic, 56; in history, 67; literary, 56
ex puris naturalibus, 209
exegetical approach, 188. *See also:* Robertson
exemplarism, 196
existence, 184; extra-mental, 291; mental, 95-6; objective, 94; of real universals, 286; of universal(s), 177; real, 308. *See also:* God, universals
exordium, 100
experience, 290; sensory, 289-90, 293
experiences (individual), 292

facere quod in se (est), 115, 209
facienti quod in se (est), 208-9
faith, 133-4, 213-4; affirmation of, 215-6; and reason, 115
family resemblance (Wittgenstein), 298
Feckes, Carl, 114
Felperin, Howard, 9
feminist studies, 8
Fendler, Susanne, 74, 82
Feyerabend, Paul, 12
ficta (figmenta), 163, 168. *See also:* mental
fiction, 96, 109, 131, 142, 144, 169; allegorical, 184; and the issue of universals, 17; modern, 265; Old French, 88; self-authenticating illusion of, 96; writers of, 17. *See also:* literary discourse, literary fiction, literary text(s)
fictional world, 16; interpretation of, 50
fictionalizer(s), 137; hierarchy of, 141
fideism, 158
field (Bourdieu), 242
figure(s): *see:* Chrétien de Troyes
first speakers (the), 295, 298
Fish, Stanley, 301

flatus vocis (Roscelin), 306
foregrounding, 46, 53
Forms (Ideas), 6, 95. *See also:* Plato
Foucauldian methodologies, 188
Foucault, Michel, 14, 91-3, 228; *Les mots et les choses*, 251-2, 255-7, 262
Foullechat, Denis, 126
fragmentation, 63, 93
framing, 47, 58
Frege, Gottlob, 283, 286
Freud, Sigmund, 31
Furr, Grover C., 187
Fyler, John, 135

Gadamer, Hans-Georg, 90, 302, 304
Gawain-poet, 170, 174
genera, 289-90, 295-6, 308
general habit: *see:* Bacon (Francis)
general: concepts, 284, 289-90, 293, 310; ideas, 290, 292, 294, 296; knowledge, 289; names, 284-5, 293; statements, 285, 288; terms, 289, 292, 296, 306; words, 284, 289-90, 292-4
generality, 298
generalization(s), 9, 212, 308
gentlemen, 233-4
genus: *see:* genera
Gilson, Etienne, 116
Glossa Ordinaria, 193
God, 1-2, 119, 132, 160, 169, 184, 194, 205, 220; absolute otherness of, 212; absolute power of, 132; agency of, 211; arbitrariness of, 120; arbitrary intervention of, 141; as conceptual and linguistic reference, 95; as First Cause, 207; as individual, 205; as legislator, 120-1; as omnipotent and unknowable, 158; attributes of, 270; Being of, 206; existence of, 160, 173; existence of (proofs), 161; free will of, 129, 133; freedom of, 115; grace of, 115, 193-5, 197, 201-2, 208-9; hidden, 134; image of, 220; indwelling action of, 208; law of, 118, 199, 211; mind of, 95; normal action of, 120; omnipotence of, 115, 141, 160; perfection of, 269, 273, 281; Person of, 206; power of, 11, 193; will of, 161, 194, 198-9, 210; willed covenant of, 206. *See also:* creature(s), *deus*

absconditus, covenant, indwelling, nominalist, power of God, presence, self/selves, Trinity, *visibilia/invisibilia*
gods (Greek), 135
Googe, Barnabe: *The Spiritual Husbandrie*, 240
Gorgias, 6
Gospel(s), 101, 105, 108; according to John, 1-2, 102, 195; according to Luke, 101, 105; according to Mark, 101, 105; according to Matthew, 101-2, 107, 192-3
government (organs of), 229
Gower, John, 143; 'moral', 148
grace: *see:* divine, God
grammar, 10, 176, 286-8; speculative, 175
grammarians, 164; preceptive, 175
grand récit, 65, 311
Gregory of Rimini, 116
Grosseteste, Robert, 173
Guido delle Colonne, 127

habitus (Bourdieu), 240, 242
Hammond, Antony, 247
Hammond, Eleanor P., 125
Harrison, William, 234
Hathaway, Charles, 124
Hawkes, Terence, 304
Hebrew, 256
Heer, Friedrich, 13
hegemony, 14. *See also:* dominant
Heinrich von dem Türlin, 131
Henry of Ghent, 118
Herder, Johann Gottfried von, 296-7
heretics, 173
hermeneutic: activity, 255; circle/spiral, 60; limits, 88
hermeneutics, 253, 302, 304; orthodox tradition of, 61-2
heterogeneity, 254
heteroglossia, 55-6
hierarchy, 230
historians, 158, 167; of philosophy, 31, 62
historical: accounts, 9; actuality, 69; analysis, 58, 157; configurations, 26; consciousness, 90; constructions, 69; continuity, 71; definition, 158; depth, 72; dynamics, 14; evolution, 67-8; experience, 66; facts (as significant), 65-6, 68; interpretation, 31, 36, 70, 116, 307; methodology, 187; periodization, 70; presence, 96; representation, 307; significance, 73; situation, 35; transition, 63; turning points, 68, 70-1; validity, 59; watersheds, 68, 70-1
historical change, 68; laws of, 67; patterns of, 84
historical development(s), 58-9, 69; as linear, 67; large-scale, 69; stages of, 68
historical reconstruction(s), 5, 9-10, 34, 37, 59-60, 67; types of, 69
historicist ontology (Bourdieu), 237, 243
historicity, 36, 59, 147, 303-4; of criticism, 64; of interpretive approaches, 59. *See also:* Lollius, signs
historiographical: analysis, 120; problems, 182
historiography: epistemological scepticism in, 67; narrative in, 67; problems of, 67; relativism in, 67; shifts in, 114
history, 59-61, 65, 90, 96, 304; and progress, 311; as contingent, 67, 69; as discursive phenomenon, 65-6; as narrative, 65-6; causality in, 66-7; constructions of, 60; directedness in, 67; discovery of coherence in, 66; early modern, 14; 'Edenist' visions of, 67; functions of, 69; interpretations of, 9; irreversibility in, 69, 71; nature of, 66; of ideas, 310; production of coherence in, 66; readings of, 36; selection in, 66; significance of, 66, 69; speculative systems of, 67; reading(s) of, 66; teleology in, 67. *See also:* causal fertility, double history, European, European cultural history
histrionics, 230
Hobbes, Thomas, 284, 288-9, 310; as 'super-nominalist', 288; sceptical doctrine of, 288; *Elements of Philosophy*, 288; *Leviathan*, 289
Holcot, Robert, 119, 145, 147, 149, 151-2, 167, 187, 207-8; necessity in, 207; *Sapientia (Wisdom Commentary)*, 151-2, 207
holistic thinking, 8
Holmes, Urban Tigner, and Sister M. Amelia Klenke, 87
Holy Spirit/Ghost, 95, 193, 195-6, 210; descent of, 197; indwelling, 197, 210

Homer, 127
homogeneity (of cultural settings), 64
homology, 34; between nominalism and literary discourse, 29
Horace: *Epistolae*, 125-6
Hornstein, Lillian Herlands, 125
Hudson, Nicholas, 73, 82-3
Hugh of St. Victor, 306
Huizinga, Johan, 185
human: essence, 303; nature, 147, 194, 196-7, 303; practice, 304
humanism, 257-8, 287; evangelical, 218, 222
Humboldt, Wilhelm von, 297
humility, 201; as humble service, 192, 194; obedient, 199
Hunt, Tony, 87, 100

iconic thinking, 239
iconism (realist), 243
iconoclasm, 28, 49
iconography, 200
idea(s), 163-4, 183, 290; abstract, 293-4; complex, 290, 295; component, 295; in the mind, 164-65; Plato's theory of, 10; platonic, 9; simple, 295. *See also:* Forms, Plato, universal
idealism, 168, 311; conceptual, 168; linguistic, 169. *See also:* nominalist
identities and differences (system of), 260
identity, 183-4, 201, 230; authorial, 92; iconic, 244; modern, 203; paradigmatic, 88; participatory, 205, 210; substantial, 243. *See also:* self-identity, similarity
identity criterion, 203
ideological upheaval, 51
idéologues, 297
idols: *see:* Bacon (Francis)
image(s), 288, 309. *See also:* mental
imagination, 130
Imbach, Ruedi, 133
imitation, 193, 195, 224; sophistic, 225. *See also:* mimesis
immediacy, 198
immortality, 106
immutability, 63, 105
impious (the), 218
implication(s), 20
in se, 209; autonomy, 210

Incarnation, 106, 115, 132, 179; meaning of, 104. *See also:* Word
incommensurability, 60. *See also:* paradigm(s)
incompatibility, 60, 221, 305. *See also:* paradigm(s)
inconclusiveness, 154
independence (ontological), 203
indistinguishability, 234
individual, 95; minds, 204; objects, 285, 290, 292; things, 284, 308
individual (the), 27, 49, 192, 203, 240, 269, 274, 278, 282, 290, 292, 310; in late-medieval England, 132
individualism, 192
individuality, 22, 221, 269, 274
individuals, 159, 237, 278, 287, 289-91, 297, 309
indwelling, 210; by God, 197; presence, 194. *See also:* God, Holy Spirit/Ghost, Word
influence, 45-6, 146, 171, 173, 176-7, 181, 187-8; nominalist, 30; Ockhamist, 30; of Derrida, 32. *See also:* nominalist
insecurity, 63
instability, 120
intellect, 285
intentio animae, 285
inter-modality, 89
interaction, 197-9; with God, 207, 214; with Jesus, 201. *See also:* causality, relation(s), salvation
interpretation, 59-60, 87, 112, 114, 158, 260, 304; historically adequate, 36; of literary texts, 116; pluralizing, 260; universalizing, 246. *See also:* readings
interpretive: categories, 60; frameworks, 65-6; strategies, 303-4. *See also:* New Philologists
intertext (non-literary), 42
intertextuality, 49
intervention (supernatural), 159. *See also:* divine, God
intuitive cognition, 159, 290, 310; of a non-existent, 114, 132, 144, 160-1. *See also:* abstractive cognition
irresolution, 154
Iserloh, Erwin, 114

358   Index

Jameson, Frederick, 8
Jean de Meun, 180. *See also: Roman de la Rose*
Jean Molinet, *Chappellet des dames*, 186
Jesus Christ, 102, 105, 191, 193. *See also:* Towneley, York
Johannes Baptista: see: Towneley
John of Salisbury: *Policraticus*, 125-7
John the Baptist, 191. *See also:* Towneley, York
Jones, Robert C., 245
jongleur, 89-90, 96-7, 99; as system of signs, 89. *See also:* authorship
Jordan, Robert M, 175
Jurschak, Gertrud Mary, 150

Kantianism, 311
Keats, John: *Endymion*, 51
Kelly, F. Douglas, 88
Kelly, Henry Ansgar, 149
Kennedy, Leonard, 114
Kenny, Anthony, 173
Kirk, Elizabeth, 147
Kittredge, George Lyman, 123-8, 137
Knapp, Peggy, 171, 173, 176-7, 186, 188
knowledge, 289, 294, 309; acquisition of, 263; disciplines of, 4; empirical, 178; fields of, 4, 43; kinds of, 166; medieval system of, 176; of the senses, 288; sceptical conception of, 158; textually-based tradition of, 109; transcendent, 178. *See also:* epistemology, truth(s)
Knowles, David, 116, 158
Kolve, V.A., 202
Kristeva, Julia, 14
Kuchta, David, 271
Kuhn, Thomas S., 12
Küpper, Joachim, 254

Laird, Edgar, 173
Lamb (Towneley), 200; as handed over to John, 197, 214; as interactive sign, 214; as token (of God), 200-1, 205; of God, 209, 212, 214
Langer, Ullrich, 38, 72, 74, 78-9, 130-1
Langland, William, 174, 177
language, 161, 163, 257, 265, 284, 289, 292, 294, 297; acquisition (innateness of), 8; aesthetic uses of, 20; and mind, 284; and reason, 292, 294, 297; anxiety about, 179; as contingent, 48; as epistemological instrument, 253, 257; as epistemological path, 259; as isomorphic with reality, 18; as means of representation, 257; as vehicle for truth, 179; confusions of, 286; disintegration of, 59; efficacy of, 172; elements of, 286; epistemological function of, 252, 265; examination of, 293; games, 167; human, 103; ideal, 292; ideal logical/philosophical, 297; in itself, 176; invention of, 296; medieval theory of, 172; mental role of, 299; myth of true, 18; natural, 286; of philosophy, 292; of the divine, 103; ordinary, 292; original, 2, 256; planners, 298; psychological role of, 297; psychologistic theory of, 283; recuperation through, 49; in relation to truth, 177; status of poetic, 179; study of, 283; system, 165, 168; temporal, 103-4; theory, 167; true nature and function of, 18. *See also:* literary
langue, 254
Laqueur, Thomas, 228
late-medieval thought, 113; nominalist, 144. *See also:* nominalism, realism
Latham, R.G., 125
Latin, 287
laws: Elizabethan sumptuary, 228; of nature, 114; Tudor sumptuary, 227. *See also:* divine, God
Leclercq, Jean, 270
Lefèvre d'Etaples, Jacques, 220
Leff, Gordon, 113-4, 116, 158
Leibniz, Gottfried Wilhelm, 288, 294
Leigni, Godefroi de, 92
light metaphysics, 194
Light, 196, 201, 211. *See also:* Logos, Word
linguistic turn: Ockham's, 310; Ockhamist, 238; of Enlightenment, 297; of twentieth century, 283, 286
linguistic: decline, 181; diversity, 171; fidelity, 181; games, 20; play, 168-70
linguistics, 4; systematic, 4
linguists, 3
linkage: non-aesthetic, 240; substantial, 240

literacy, 88, 91
literary: composition, 101; creation, 128, 143; critics, 15; discourse, 129; epistemology, 263; evangelism, 102; historians, 15; history, 171; language, 177; meaning, 15; modes, 88; paradigm(s), 88-9, 108-9; performance, 89; practice, 187; production, 55; reception, 55; semiosis, 85; significance, 92; studies, 63; subjectivity, 92-4; theorists, 2, 15; tradition(s), 57; triumphalism, 98. *See also:* mimesis, paradigm(s), readings, representation
literary aesthetic(s): approaches to, 55; development of, 85; historical evolution of, 69; modernist, 56; nominalist, 37, 43, 47-50, 53-4; realist, 37, 43, 47-8, 53-4; traditional, 56
literary debate over universals, 24, 38, 42-3; definition of, 46-7; development of, 53; discursive dimension of, 42; historical unfolding of, 44; history of, 69
literary discourse, 14, 41, 46, 85; aesthetic side of, 74; and philosophy, 19; and scholastic theology, 19; as representing human experience, 18-9; nominalist and realist, 46; transparency of, 53; typologies of, 53-7. *See also:* literary nominalism, literary nominalism and realism, literary realism, literary text(s), semiosis, text(s)
literary fiction, 224; as mimesis, 224; creation of, 129
literary genre(s), 41, 44, 57-8; intrinsic evolution of, 44. *See also:* literary sub-genres
literary nominalism, 27-8, 37, 43, 188; aesthetic component of, 37; approaches to, 27-37, 157-8, 162-89; as counter-discourse, 72; as late medieval phenomenon, 43; as term, 35; history of, 84; marker(s) of, 46. *See also:* literary aesthetic(s), literary text(s), text(s)
literary nominalism and realism, 40-7; as discourses *sui generis*, 39, 73; as functional categories, 55; as master categories, 55; as terms, 85; historical reconstruction of, 72; key issues of, 74; specificity of, 46; study of, 73; typological approach to, 58

literary realism, 27-8, 37; aesthetic component of, 37. *See also:* literary aesthetic(s), literary text(s), text(s)
literary semiotics, 74; history of, 85
literary sub-genres, 41, 44, 58, 271; intrinsic evolution of, 44
literary text(s), 15-24, 40, 43, 52; aesthetic conception of, 52, 55; aesthetically advanced, 51; analysis of, 14; and cultural transformation, 14; and philosophical discourse, 32-3; as classified in terms of nominalism/realism, 20, 50-4; as *fictum*, 4; as verbal artifact, 52; categorization of, 51; composition of, 16; epigonic, 52; experimental, 51; fundamental (semiotic) position of, 53; historical functions of, 57-8; historical position of, 57; metafictional dimension of, 21, 26; metafictional strategies of, 49; overall aesthetic conception of, 53; sceptical epistemology of, 30; sceptical ontology of, 30; semiotic orientation of, 57; structural levels of, 47; trivial, 52. *See also:* literature, semiosis, text(s)
literary theory, 4; current, 167; medieval, 188; post-modern(ist), 170
literature, 109, 268; and nominalism/realism, 29; as different from other types of discourse, 15; as symbolic mode of signification, 14; courtly, 97; English, 71; French, 72; high medieval, 72; late medieval, 33, 35, 71; Middle English, 112-3, 120. *See also:* literary discourse, literary nominalism, literary realism, literary text(s), vernacular
Liturgy, 193
localization, 198, 213; concrete (Towneley), 202; of signs, 214; strong, 203. *See also:* sign(s)
localized: contact, 199; events, 66. *See also:* nominalism and realism, readings
loci et imagines, 266
Locke, John, 4, 283-5, 288-99; as 'mentalist', 294; *Essay Concerning Human Understanding,* 283-5, 288-99
logic, 10, 159, 165-6, 176, 284, 287-8, 311
logicians, 164, 284
Logos, 1, 105, 162, 168, 196, 203-4, 206. *See also:* Light, Word

Lollius, 123-28, 135-6, 138-44; historicity of, 125-7; identity of, 124-7
London, 230
Lounsberry, T.R., 125
love, 272, 277; as representation of the other, 226; improvement through, 272; of beauty, 278, 281; of God, 224; of individual, 220; of one person for another, 217; of oneself, 226; of sinner(s), 220; of neighbour, 218; of virtue, 272, 281; selfish, 277, 280; selfless, 279. *See also:* self-love
Ludolphus the Carthusian (= Ludolphus de Saxonia): *Vita Christi*, 195-6
Lull, Raymond, 125
Luther, Martin, 287
Luttrell, Claude, 100-1
Lyly, John: *Campaspe*, 239
Lyotard, Jean-François, 171

Machiavell (stage), 243-4
Mahler, Andreas, 74, 81
Man, Paul de, 176
man: as agent, 201; as creature of God, 192; as sacramental vessel, 207; as sinner, 192; autonomous might of, 194, 212; capacity of, 202; deeds of, 193; effort of, 193; fallen, 201-2; natural, 202, 210-1; power of, 212; role in salvation of, 192; will of, 198. *See also:* human, universal, vessel, will
mannerism, 43
mantras, 2
manuscripts, 126
marginality (as a role), 234
marking: judicial, 234; of beggars, 231-4; of cultural record, 102; policy of, 233. *See also:* authorship, badging, branding, mutilation
Marlowe, Christopher, 247; *Doctor Faustus*, 16-7, 51
Marrone, John, 117-8
Marsilius of Padua, 133
Mary Wroth: *Urania*, 275-9, 281
mathematics, 8, 311
matière antique, 98
McGrath, Alistir, 208
meaning(s), 201, 301-2, 304; aesthetic modes of creating, 22; as essence, 303; as usage, 310; cultural, 65; nominalist conception of, 305; of texts, 60, 65; proliferation of, 105, 304; stable, 303; surface, 104; ultimate, 304. *See also:* reading, readings, realism, realist(s), signified(s), signifier(s)
mediators, 140
medieval studies, 28
medievalists, 35, 60. *See also:* New Philologists
memory (artificial), 266
mental: concept(s), 308; image(s), 95, 97, 285-6, 288; intention, 286; picture(s), 290. *See also:* discourse(s), existence, language, sign(s)
mentalités, 70, 112
mentality: late medieval, 33; universalized, 34
merit, 161, 208
meritum: condignum, 208; *de congruo*, 208
Merton College, 149-50
metafiction: *see:* drama, literary text(s), *mise-en-abyme*
metaphysics: *see:* light metaphysics, nominalist
Middle Ages, 72; Christian, 306; historical view of, 62
milieu, 248; intellectual, 128
Milne, A.A., 3; *Winnie-the-Pooh*, 16, 19-20
mimesis, 181, 224; anti-ethical, 225; principles of, 165. *See also:* charity, representation
Minnis, Alastair J., 186
miracles, 120, 142
Mirror for Magistrates, 243-5
mise-en-abyme, 58
misrepresentation(s), 71-2
model-building, 11
modern, 266, 288; age, 310; European thinking, 13; world picture, 13. *See also:* fiction
moderni, 6, 28, 31
modernism, 50-1
modernity, 72, 268
modernization, 34
modistae, 164
Moody, E.A., 237
morality play(s), 244

Index

More, Thomas, 244-5
Morse, J. Mitchell, 117, 157
Mr Spock, 71
multiplication: of forms, 105; of parts, 202-3
multiplicity, 203, 295
Munson, William H., 74, 78
Murdoch, Iris, 58
mutability, 63
mutilation, 229, 234. *See also:* semiotic
mystery play(s), 213. *See also:* Towneley, York
mysticism, 46, 194
mystifications, 9
myth, 311

name(s), 92, 245, 263-5, 288-9; adequate, 264; as epistemologically meaningful, 262; as indicating substantial connection, 17; as interpretable signifier(s), 263; as stories, 17; common, 284-5, 288, 290; giving of, 17; giving of (to things), 298; of things, 255; true, 17; true nature and function of, 18. *See also:* proper name(s), universal
naming, 256, 292-3; conventions of, 288-9; life by, 263
narrative, 224; Chaucerian, 16; fictional, 177; late medieval, 27. *See also:* historiography, history
narrative strategies, 130, 172
narrator, 130, 135-42, 179-80, 277-8; and author, 137; subjective tendencies of, 138; unreliable, 140, 142
narratorial: comment, 16; commentaries, 138; voice, 135
natural and divine realms, 184
nature, 3, 284; and supernature, 202; common, 237; divine and human, 159; singular, 287; theories of, 288. *See also:* book of nature/creation, human, nominalist
necessity, 11, 74, 239; unfailing, 212. *See also:* Holcot, non-necessity
Neoplatonism, 6, 177-8, 194, 196, 271-2. *See also:* Renaissance
New Age thinking, 8
New Philologists, 129
Nicholas of Lyra, 193
Nicole, Pierre, 289

Nizolius, Marius, 285, 287-8
nobility, 278
nominalism, 93, 102, 109, 111, 146, 157-8, 165, 202-3, 284, 306-8; and literature, 188; as coeval philosophical superstratum, 29, 33-36; as culturally transformative momentum, 63; as defined as theory of universals, 10; as direct source, 29-32; as emergent paradigm, 28; as historical reassertion, 29-30, 36-7; as influence on commentators/ exegetes, 188-9; as logical impossibility, 307; as part of inclusive systems of thought, 10-1; as science of terms, 165; as seen as historical episode, 62; as (semiotic) paradigm, 12; as term, 8, 35, 283; as transforming factor, 62; as unified/coherent system of thought, 158; ascendancy of, 7, 13, 62; 'conceptual' and 'predicate', 164; conceptualist (of Abelard), 88; emergence of, 62, 268; extreme, 159, 308; growing interest in, 63; historical, 237; historical development of, 3-8; historical dimension of, 5; historical forms of, 25-6; historical reconstruction of, 5; ideological correlates of, 172; late medieval, 115, 270; logic of, 287; medieval, 105, 169, 173, 290, 294; moderate, 158-9; modern, 158; philosophical, 4, 192, 202; radical, 309; revised view of, 117, 158; rise of, 7; rise to cultural hegemony of, 71; sceptical, 167, 174, 176; sceptical interpretation of, 162; sceptical version of, 178; tradition of, 107, 283; traditional, 294; typological definition of, 5; valuation of, 63; versions of, 158-61. *See also:* conceptualism, conceptualist-nominalism, constructivism, literary nominalism, terminism
nominalism and realism, 3-8; as (semiotic) paradigms, 9-12; as twin paradigms, 50; dialectics between, 59; early modern question of, 267; historical description of, 84; historical evolvement of, 67, 72; localized readings of, 83; mutual determination of, 50. *See also:* nominalism/realism-complex

nominalism/realism-complex, 1-8, 15, 41, 69, 74; aesthetic response(s) to, 16; and literary fictions, 22; development of, 41; discursive manifestations of, 40; engagement with, 53; experiental dimension of, 20; explicit literary response(s) to, 15-21, 23-27; implicit literary response(s) to, 16, 21-7; literary representation of, 16; literary response(s) to, 15-6, 25; thematization of, 16; transdiscursive dimension of, 40
nominalist: as term, 8, 284; criticism, 177; critique, 251; discourse, 162, 172, 174; epistemology, 185; features of God, 131; frame of reference, 47; idealism, 168; ideologemes, 62; influence, 171, 173, 176-7, 181, 188; influence on literature, 27-32; language theory, 167; metaphysics, 170; methods of argumentation, 31; paradigm, 39; philosophy, 159; poetic paradigm, 106; poetics, 96, 104; readings, 147, 157, 167, 187; refusal, 226; semiotics, 171, 174, 180; separation, 210, 213; sign theory, 158, 162, 174; texts, 57; theology, 115; theories of nature, 288; theory, 134; theory of universals, 109; tradition(s), 179, 285-6, 293, 297; turn, 57
nominalist orientations, 62; ascendancy of, 72; emergence of, 71; evolution of, 71
nominalist(s), 5, 8-9, 149, 178, 311; as radical sceptics, 62; as term, 6; radical late medieval, 62; status as, 306
non-contradiction, 132
non-individuality, 222
non-necessity, 207; of created order, 159
non-reference, 175
nouns, 298; collective, 287

Oakley, Francis, 114, 117
obedience, 194, 198, 202, 211-5; unawed, 194, 198. *See also:* humility
Oberman, Heiko A., 112-3, 115, 205
Ockham's razor, 187, 202
Ockham, William of, 4, 6, 26, 28-31, 62, 116, 119, 121, 132, 145-7, 149, 151, 157, 159-60, 163-6, 173, 178, 182, 184, 187, 208, 270, 286, 288, 290-3, 306-7; as reliabilist, 30; as sceptical thinker, 30; conceptualism of, 168; epistemology of, 166; impact of, 7; individual logic of, 163; rejection of analogy in, 185; revised interpretation of, 30; semiological and linguistic theory of, 159; separation between theology and philosophy in, 10; theology of, 161; theory of signification of, 163-4; *Ordinatio*, 285; *Quodlibeta*, 160; *Summa logicae*, 159, 164, 284-5, 291
Ockhamism, 165. *See also: via moderna*
Ockhamist: 119, 185, 191, 202, 237-8; epistemology of vision, 204; philosophy, 186; theologians, 192, 206; theology, 184, 202; *via moderna*, 212
œuvre, 89-90, 97. *See also: texte*
omnipotence: *see:* Creator, creator, divine, God
onto-semantics, 255
ontology, 11, 163, 238, 309; metaphysical, 206. *See also:* historicist ontology
oral vs. written, 89
oral-formulaic theory, 89
order, 252, 260; created, 159, 183-4; of nature, 114, 290, 292; of salvation, 114; of signification, 162; of things, 255; social, 240; stable, 133, 292
ordinata-absoluta distinction, 161. *See also:* distinction of absolute and ordained power of God, power of God
Oresme, Nicholas, 133
origin, 260; of language, 296; of truth, 261
orthodoxy (Christian), 173
Other (the), 90, 302, 311, 313; as alterity, 302; containment of, 312; embodiment of, 313; submerged, 313
other-exclusion, 227
otherness, 302; of Holy Spirit, 196. *See also:* God
Otto, Stephan, 257
Oxford, 119, 148, 150, 284
Ozment, Steven, 133, 238

pact, 115, 211. *See also:* covenant
Panofsky, Erwin, 13, 203
papal power, 118
parable: of harvest, 108; of mustard seed, 107; of the sower, 87, 102, 105, 107

Index 363

paradigm(s), 9, 40, 68, 88, 124; anti-realist poetic, 106; as conceptual grid(s), 11; as dynamic system(s) of reference, 39; as evolving system(s) of reference, 39; as term, 13; change of, 311; constraints of, 11; critical, 36, 54, 85; definition of, 11-3; dialectics between, 40; incommensurability of, 12; incompatibility of, 12; interpretive, 65; nominalist/realist, 47; of medieval vernacular literature, 87; of semiosis, 9; prevalent, 51; research, 54; semiotic, 55, 58; vernacular, 104. *See also:* nominalism, nominalism and realism, nominalist, poetic, realism, realist, Renaissance
paradigm shift(s), 63, 158, 310
paradigmatic unity/closure, 73
parody, 26, 143
participation, 183, 192, 194, 196, 206; doctrine of, 184. *See also:* identity
particular objects, 290, 295
particular(s), 5, 94, 97, 163, 165, 178, 181, 242, 285, 290, 295, 298, 303, 305-6; correct meaning of sensory, 198
particularity, 198
Patrington, Stephen, 119
patronage, 101
Pauline evangelical thought, 218
Pearsall, Derek, 148
Peck, Russell, 146, 151
Pelagian vs. Augustinian, 202
penal: semiotic program, 234; spectacles, 228. *See also:* punishment, semiotics
Penn, Stephen, 77-8, 81
Pentecost hymn, 197
perception, 4, 290, 293
perfection, 181
performance, 88, 90-1
Peter de Trabibus, 118
Peter Lombard, 32-3, 218
Petersen, Kate O., 151
Petrarch, Francis, 125, 262
Philip Julius, Duke of Stettin-Pomerania, 229
Philip of Flanders, 87
philosopher(s): and authors, 170; as nominalists, 11; as realists, 11; position of, 10; post-medieval, 8; post-Renaissance, 8; scholastic, 6; writings of, 32

philosophical: reconstruction, 9-10, 31; systems, 10; theory and literary practice, 157
philosophy, 4, 145-55; ancient Greek, 6, 159; as 'handmaiden of theology', 10; medieval, 174; moral, 217; of the contingent, 310; scholastic, 5, 188. *See also:* nominalism, nominalist, realism
Plato, 3, 6-7, 94, 145, 176-7, 180-3, 285, 287, 306; dialectical method of, 10; theory of Ideas of, 10; *Cratylus*, 177
Platonic ideal, 180
Platonism, 95, 162, 181. *See also:* Renaissance
Platter, Thomas, 228
play (as sign), 214. *See also:* drama
plot, 134
pluralism, 254; metaphysical 203
poeta-theologus, 129
poetic: 'Christ', 103; paradigm, 106; phenomena, 88; strategy, 128; word, 109. *See also:* paradigm, word
poetics, 4, 93, 96, 104; medieval romance, 95; of authorship, 98; of authorship and exclusion, 96; of exclusion, 94, 97-9; of the proper name, 92; of the seed, 107. *See also:* Chrétien de Troyes, nominalist, romance
poetry (relationship to truth), 163, 180. *See also:* entries under literary
poets, 3; and storytellers, 186; explicit statements of, 180
polysemy, 105
poor relief, 231
Popper, Karl R., 8
Porphyry: *Isagoge*, 306
Port-Royal (authors), 253, 289
post-colonial studies, 8
post-modernism, 21, 26, 50-1
post-modernist writing, 57
post-structuralists, 8, 13-4
potentia (dei) absoluta: see: power of God
potentia (dei) ordinata: see: power of God
power of God, 11; (as) absolute, 114-5, 117-8, 128-9, 132-3, 159; (as) absolute and ordained, 114; (as) ordained, 115-6, 132, 159; dialectic of (as absolute

and ordained), 111-20, 211-2. *See also:* distinction of absolute and ordained power of God, divine, God
Powicke, Frederick, 150
Pratt, Robert, 126-7, 151-2
precursorism, 182
predestination, 76, 154
predication, 286. *See also:* universal
preface(s), 16
presence, 198, 214; absolute, 211; full, 201; of God, 208; of God as the Word, 199; of God within man, 198; physical, 200; verbal, 95. *See also:* universal
prima causa efficiens, 130, 135, 143. *See also:* cause(s), Creator
professions, 293
progress, 67, 84, 310
prologue(s), 16, 87-8, 96-8, 100-5, 108. *See also:* Chrétien de Troyes, romance
proper name(s), 292
propositions, 166, 288, 294, 309; existential, 166; truth-value of, 166
proverbs, 135, 152
Prudentius: *Psychomachia*, 185
psychology, 4; faculty, 147; Freudian, 31
Pulsiano, Phillip, 179
punishment, 233, 235; as public execution, 228; as public penal spectacle, 228; public, 228; schemes of, 234. *See also:* beggar(s), semiotic(s)
puns, 174. *See also:* language, linguistic
Purdon, Liam, 181

Queste del Sainte Graal, 163
quiddity, 295
Quidort, Jean, 133
Quilligan, Maureen, 272
Quintilian, 97

Rabelais, François, 26, 72, 143, 218, 222-6; *Gargantua*, 25, 217-8, 222; *Pantagruel*, 217-8, 223-6. *See also:* charity, mimesis, relationship(s)
radicalism, 161
Randall, Michael, 186-7
Randi, Eugenio, 118
Rationalism, 311
readability, 74. *See also:* reading
reader(s), 90, 139, 302, 304; actual, 143; as active participant(s), 50; as passive receptacle(s), 50; attention of, 23; common, 3; concrete, 302; ideal, 64; informed, 64; modern, 91; role of, 50
readerly challenge, 301. *See also:* text(s)
reading, 176; act of, 305; essentialist approaches to, 303; negative, 176; the world as book, 252. *See also:* book of nature/creation
readings of history: constructivist, 69; essentialist, 69; nominalist, 69; realist, 69
readings, 60, 147, 157, 167, 187, 303; historically faithful, 60; incommensurability of, 60; incompatibility of, 60; literary, 174; localized, 70; projectionist, 302. *See also:* nominalist
realism, 93, 146, 306, 312; absolute vs. moderate, 307; and literature, 28; and orthodoxy, 173; as defined as theory of universals, 10; as part of inclusive systems of thought, 10-1; as (semiotic) paradigm, 12; critique of, 286; defeat of, 13; extreme, 149; historical dimension of, 5; historical forms of, 25-6; historical reconstruction of, 5; medieval, 57, 173, 295; moderate, 149, 285, 307-8; of meaning, 303; philosophical, 4, 171, 176, 192; sceptical, 176; shades of, 307; typological definition of, 5. *See also:* essentialism, nominalism, nominalism and realism
realism: mimetic, 52; representational, 52. *See also:* Chaucer (Geoffrey), realistic detail
realist: as term, 8; counterdiscourse(s), 73; *episteme*, 267; frame of reference, 47; influence on literature, 27; paradigm, 39; perspective, 217, 270; recuperation, 268; scepticism, 177; semiotics, 182; text(s), 174; theory of universals, 94; tradition(s), 28, 177, 179; turn, 57; view of allegory, 121
realist(s), 5, 9, 149, 306, 309, 311-2; of meaning, 303
realistic detail, 185
reality, 3, 163, 167; actual structure of, 47; constitution of, 287; construction of, 11, 286; essentialist view of, 48; external, 291; extra-linguistic, 4; extra-mental, 4, 291, 309; hetero-

glossic, 49; intensified perception of, 52; intractable, 49; of nature, 293; ontological, 104; perception of, 11; prevalent constructions of, 52; scheme of, 163; transparent concept of, 49; universalizing view of, 48
reason, 133, 291; and faith, 158
reception history, 305
redemption, 194, 210
reference, 95, 226, 273, 275; common, 95-6; disintegration of, 59; mental, 96; system of, 271, 273-6. *See also:* non-reference, self-reference
referent(s) (*res*), 45, 96, 162, 164-6, 170, 269, 273, 275, 277; external, 166, 169; stable, 169; transcendent, 270-1, 273. *See also:* sign(s), universals, word(s)
referential quality, 109
referentiality (theories of), 287
Reformation, 7
reification, 49, 121
reinterpretation, 60, 147, 158
Reiss, Edmund, 170-1
relation(s): arbitrary, 253; as interactive with God, 208; family, 293; homological, 34; non-participatory, 204; of language to truth, 177; of man to God, 238
relationship(s): between God and His creatures, 159; between Pantagruel and Panurge, 223-6; between philosophical and literary discourse, 28-35, 37-44, 186; causal, 42; interdiscursive, 41. *See also:* charity, Rabelais, text-reader relationship
relativism, 50, 163, 174; in historiography, 67: linguistic, 162; nominalistic, 181
reliabilism, 31
reliability: distrust in, 49; of divine nature, 120
Renaissance, 50, 72, 251, 260; as historical watershed, 70; as threshold to modernity, 70; authors, 131; conduct books, 227; courtesy theory, 276; English, 227-8, 235; *episteme*, 254-5; epistemology, 257; Neoplatonism, 57; paradigms, 72; Platonism, 7, 271; prose romances, 269-82; semiotics, 252-3, 255-6; studies, 28, 60

representation, 4, 11, 213, 215, 234, 238-9, 253, 261; dramatic, 211; literary, 134, 217; mimetic, 223; mimetic model of, 226; naturalized practices of, 52; of charitable relationships, 223; of persons, 222. *See also:* Chaucer (Geoffrey), literary discourse, mimesis
repression, 230
res et verba, 257. *See also:* referent(s), thing(s), word(s)
res-conceptus-vox, 164. *See also:* concepts, referent(s), thing(s), *vox*
resemblance(s), 222, 225-6, 252, 259, 265, 298; ethical, 225; functional, 253; play of, 262; substantial, 253. *See also:* family resemblance
resolution, 155
resurrection, 99
revelation, 49, 134
Reynolds, John: *The Flower of Fidelity*, 280-1
rhetoric, 10, 46, 104, 136, 169, 174-6, 287; principles of, 175; treatises on, 227. *See also:* tradition(s)
Ricardian period, 188
Robertson, D.W., 104, 188; exegetical approach of, 61-3
Robertsonian criticism, 63
rogues, 234
roles (acting of), 245-6
Roman de la Rose, 145, 180, 185
Roman de Thèbes, 99, 106
romance, 271; Arthurian, 97, 100; author, 99; authorship, 94, 101-2, 106; composer(s), 109; composition, 88-9; medieval, 94, 96, 106, 263; Old French, 87; poetics, 107; prologues, 89; secular word of, 105; writer(s), 92. *See also:* Chrétien de Troyes, poetics, prologue(s), Renaissance
romanitas, 245
romans antiques, 98, 107
Roney, Lois, 147
Rorty, Richard, 4, 288
Roscelin, 6, 159, 284, 306-8, 311; adversaries of, 7
Rossiter, A.P., 244
Rousseau, Jean-Jacques, 284, 296; *Discours sur l'origine de l'inégalité*, 296
Russell, Bertrand, 308
Ruud, Jay, 117, 151, 165-7

sacrality, 298
sacrament(s), 199, 206, 209; as contingent vehicles, 202; as vessels for universals, 202; as vessels of God, 196; dependability of, 212; fulfillment of, 199; intrinsic power of, 206; of baptism, 196. See also: man, Towneley, vessel(s), York
Sallust, 180
salvation, 115, 161, 194, 201, 206-8; causality of, 207; interaction, 210; process, 202, 205; process (as interactive), 202; theology, 191; theory (medieval), 192, 208. See also: agency, man, Towneley, vessel(s), York
satire, 257-61; as thing, 260; as word, 258; Roman, 258
satirist, 259-60; Roman, 258
Saturn, 259-60
Satyr, 260
Saussure, Ferdinand de, 4, 165
scepticism, 50, 149, 159, 167, 175, 177-80, 288, 292, 297, 310; late medieval, 35; linguistic, 177; medieval 182; philosophical 182; radical, 161. See also: nominalism, realism, realist
Schlegel, August Wilhelm, 312; the 'classical' in, 312; the 'romantic' in, 312
scholastic: philosophy, 5; synthesis, 173
scholasticism, 33, 165; beauty in, 270; fourteenth-century, 26; late, 113; semiotics of, 174. See also: semiotic(s), tradition, universals
scholastics, 217, 219; earlier, 160
schoolmen, 6, 295
science(s), 165-6; observational, 204
Scotists, 163. See also: tradition(s)
Script, 2
Seaman, Gerald, 72, 74-5
self-affirmation, 192
self-awareness, 201, 211-12
self-deconstruction, 49
self-discovery, 215
self-identification, 227
self-identity, 313
self-improvement, 272, 277-8
self-love, 278
self-reference (discursive), 49
self-referentiality, 66. See also: terms

self-validating practice(s), 312
self-validation, 65
self-will, 201
self/selves, 90, 191-2, 194, 202, 207, 209-12; as interacting with God, 201; autonomous, 216; in relation to God, 192; in relation to others, 192; medieval, 192; reflective, 216
selfhood (early modern), 192
semantics (of things), 256
semeiotike, 290
semiological marks, 255
semiologists, 170
semiosis, 4; implicit, 47; indirect, 47; literary, 85; naturalized practices of, 52; paradigm(s) of, 9; textual, 48, 55, 59
semiotic: analysis, 233; clarity, 228; confinement, 235; devices, 104; enquiry (limits of), 11; implications of dramaturgy, 247; intention(s), 228; mutilation, 232; orientation(s), 11; program, 233; reception, 228; reflexes, 246; relationship, 303; scheme, 232; slippage, 46, 227-35; systems, 227
semiotic(s), 4, 11, 162, 171, 180, 182, 242-3; as independent field of enquiry, 10; binary model of, 253-4; dramatic, 242; of beauty, 275; of clothing, 227; penal, 228, 234; propedeutic function of, 10; scholastic, 174; ternary model of, 253; theories of, 167. See also: nominalist, realist
semioticians, 3
Seneca, 145
sense (spiritual), 184
sensible qualities, 292
sensory impressions, 290. See also: experience
sentence(s), 290, 309-10
separation, 210, 213, 216; in space and time, 203; of truth, 134; of words, concepts and things, 286. See also: nominalist
sfumato, 138
Shakespeare, William, 3, 58, 237, 240, 247, 262; *Hamlet*, 262-3, 265-7; *Julius Caesar*, 240; *Richard III*, 239-40, 243-9; *Romeo and Juliet*, 16, 21
Sheldrake, Rupert, 9
Shippey, T.A., 18

Sidney, Philip: *The New Arcadia*, 269, 271-75, 277-82
Siemon, James R., 74, 80-1
sign(s), 45, 159, 161-2, 165, 167, 180, 191, 201, 213, 215, 232, 239, 253, 255, 265, 272-3, 281; and reality (*res* and referent), 163; arbitrariness of, 234, 254; as 'complete', 270; as constitutive of 'reality', 162; as elements in-between, 204; as 'intact', 278; as tokens, 202; conventional, 292, 309; differential nature of, 167; function of, 11; historical politics of, 74; historicity of, 269; in Ockham, 169; interactive, 202, 215; juridical, 228; linguistic, 164; localized, 202; mental, 285; modern and medieval conceptions of, 164; natural, 159, 243, 247, 291-2; nature of, 11; Ockhamist concept of, 46; properties of, 188; reception of, 228; relation between, 309; stability of, 174, 303; status of, 4, 14, 228; status of verbal, 4; system, 169; ternary conception of, 253; voluntary institution of, 238; war of, 229. *See also:* autonomy, crisis, readability, split sign, token(s)
sign theory, 158, 162, 174, 182; literary analysis of nominalist, 157; literary aspects of medieval, 170; medieval, 157, 162, 165; of Augustine, 179. *See also:* nominalism, nominalist, realism, realist, universals
signature (of author), 101; discursive role of, 91
signatures, 253
signification, 4, 11, 161, 183; as contingent, 48; crises of, 35; culture as web of, 3; disintegration of, 59; historical politics of, 74; natural, 294; play of, 298; problems of, 51; process of, 49; purity of, 230; social, 234; system of, 281; texts as dynamic systems of, 53
signified(s), 162, 165, 167-8, 227, 253, 255-6, 260-1, 269; deconstruction of, 167; transcendent, 168-9; transcendental, 48
signifier(s), 90, 162, 165, 167, 169, 227, 239, 253, 255-6, 258-9, 265, 272, 276; arbitrary, 261; elective, 243; having power over signified, 18; infinitely regressing, 169; materiality of, 261; regressive, 169; 'satire' as, 258; sliding of, 168-9; transcendental, 48
signifier(s) and signified(s), 163-4, 171-2, 174, 180; drifting apart of, 45; relation of, 230; similitude between, 256; split between, 162-3. *See also: res-conceptus-vox*, split sign, *vox*
signifying: correspondences, 227; power of words, 2; practice(s), 3, 14, 227, 243; substance, 89; systems, 234
similarity, 183-4, 222, 224, 307-8; vs. identity, 203
similitude(s), 130, 252-3, 255, 258-9; chimeric, 265
simulation (Baudrillard), 234
sin, 195, 209
singularity, 223, 225-6; substantial, 221
Smalley, Beryl, 151
Smith, Adam, 284
socio-semiotic control, 228
Socrates (Platonic), 10
Sophistst, 6
soteriology, 194, 210. *See also:* salvation
sound (original), 2
source(s), 126, 129, 131-2, 136-8, 140, 142-3, 146, 151-2, 181-2, 195; Boethian, 180; editing of nominalist, 5; historical, 66; Platonic, 180; ultimate, 49
Spain, 267-8
Spark, Muriel, 58
speakers: *see:* first speakers
species, 237, 289-90, 295, 308; and genera, 291; boundaries of, 291; real, 294; real order of, 292. *See also:* genera, universal
specificity (historical), 312
spectacle, 215; admonitory, 228: *See also:* punishment
speech: common, 292; parts of, 298
Speght, Thomas, 125
split sign, 164, 167, 171-2; epistemology of, 182
statements (generalizing), 4
Stein, Gertrude, 51
Steinmetz, David, 112, 117, 147
Stepsis, Robert, 112, 116, 147, 162
Sterne, Laurence: *Tristram Shandy*, 50
Stillingfleet, Edward, Bishop of Worcester, 294

Stoa, 306
Stoics, 165
Strode, Ralph, 117, 130, 143, 148-51, 154-5, 187; 'philosophical', 148-50
structuralism, 254
structuralists, 165
subject, 22, 303; early modern, 254; historical, 37; independent psychological, 204; scepticist, 263; willing, 192. *See also:* self/selves, selfhood
subjection, 194
subjectivism, 203
subjectivity, 11, 74, 92, 135, 201; personal 203; psychological, 201; radical, 95. *See also:* literary
substance(s), 121, 274, 286-7, 291, 295, 309
substantial connection, 133. *See also:* name(s)
substitutability, 245
substitution, 245
subversion, 49, 172-3, 230. *See also:* Chaucer (Geoffrey), text(s)
supernatural effects, 160
superstructure, 35
supposition (*suppositio*), 166, 309; material, 169; simple, 169; theory of, 175
Swift, Jonathan: *Gulliver's Travels,* 16, 25, 50
symbol, 22, 179. *See also:* word(s)
sympathy (sympathies), 252-3

Taylor, Charles, 203
Taylor, P.B., 180
temporal (vs. eternal), 172
Ten Brink, Bernhard, 125
terminism, 175
terms: equivocal (theory of), 174; moral, 295; self-referential, 169; special, 293; status of, 166; synonymous, 286
text(s), 96, 301-3; as act(s) of signification, 48; closed, 48; composition of, 23; constitution of, 41; fictional, 20; imposing property on, 93; interrogative, 53, 61; meaning of, 302-3; monologic, 48; monologic vs. polyphonic, 53, 55-6; open vs. closed, 53, 55-6; religious, 99; status of, 104; typologies of, 54; writerly vs. readerly, 53, 55-6. *See also:* entries under literary, semiosis

text types, 39, 267-8; referential, 16
text-reader: relationship, 302; transactions, 55
texte, 89-90, 96. *See also: œuvre*
texte-oeuvre dichotomy, 91, 94, 109
textual: analysis, 54; communities, 88; elements, 24; integrity, 92; perspective, 22, 47; strategies, 23-4, 47, 57; transmission (modes of), 98; universe, 16
textual meaning, 60; construction of, 50
textuality, 96, 104-5; concepts of, 50
theatricalism, 243
thematics (evangelical), 217
theologians, 3
theological systems, 10
theology, 4, 115, 310; medieval, 202; of man's power, 195; Scotist, 212. *See also:* nominalist, realist
thing(s), 163-4, 183, 255-7, 309; and words (*res et verba*), 255; as particulars, 5; nature of, 178, 288, 293; real, 166; real nature of, 285; reality of, 294; semantic trait(s) of, 259; singular, 285. *See also: res et verba, res-conceptus-vox*
thisness, 49. *See also:* quiddity
Thomas, Mary Edith, 117
Thomism, 185
Thomist synthesis, 133
Thomists, 163
Tillich, Paul, 192
token(s), 199, 215, 232; contingent, 211-2. *See also:* angel(s), sign(s)
Tolkien, J.R.R., 3, 19; *Lord of the Rings,* 16-8
topical: knowledge of similitude, 267; organization, 263; reasoning, 266
topos (*topoi*), 106-7, 255, 257-8, 266; of similitude, 258
Tosettis, Lellus Pietri Stephani de, 125
touch, 199-200
Towneley: mystery play cycle, 191; theology of, 211; *Johannes Baptista,* 191-5, 197-201, 205, 207-16. *See also:* Lamb, sacrament(s), salvation, token(s)
tradition(s), 285-6, 293, 297; cultural, 41; Eastern, 2; English literary, 16; epistemological, 96, 101; exegetical,

61, 87, 205; Judeo-Christian, 2; Platonic-Augustinian, 306; rhetorical, 87, 96-7; scholastic, 158, 284, 292; Scotistic, 119; the English, 60. *See also:* discursive, hermeneutics, nominalism, nominalist, realist, vernacular
tragedy, 21; pagan, 142
transcendence, 178; shift to immanence, 134
transcoding, 45
transdiscursivity, 38
transition (epoch of), 254; from medieval to early modern, 36
transitional phase, 71; late Middle Ages as, 28
translation, 40-1, 140
translator, 130, 137
transparency, 74, 261, 286; age of, 254, 267; of literary discourse, 53. *See also:* readability
trickster, 224
Trinity, 94-5, 155, 179, 200, 294
trivium, 10, 176
trope(s), 105; and figures, 175. *See also:* Chrétien de Troyes
Troy (matter of), 126-7, 143
truth(s), 95-6, 163, 178-80, 238, 252, 257-8, 260, 268, 270, 288, 309; analogical representation of a higher, 184; authoritative, 48; conditions, 237, 243; contingent (secular), 134; epistemological, 265; essential, 48; finding of, 253; general, 293; guaranteed, 48, 50; higher degree of, 47; immutable, 163; levels of, 134; of fiction, 96; of philosophy, 96; path to, 260, 265-6; reliable, 50; religious, 134; stable, 48, 162; transcendent, 48, 162. *See also:* epistemology, knowledge
Tullius (Cicero): in Chaucer, 145
Turks, 223
Turner, Myron, 271

uncertainty, 291
unemployment, 230
union (hypostatic), 200
uniqueness, 212
unity (substantial), 203
universal (the), 192, 303, 305
universal: concepts, 285, 292, 294; ideas, 181, 290-1; man, 195; names, 288; nature of species, 285; predication, 164; presences, 204. *See also:* Church, words
universalia: *ante rem*, 306; *in intellectu*, 306; *in re*, 306; *post rem*, 306. *See also:* universals
universalism (of Christianity), 222
universality, 198
universalization, 247-8, 298
universals, 94, 96-7, 109, 121, 159, 162-3, 179, 270, 284-5, 288, 292, 306-7, 309; *a priori*, 309, 311; *ante rem*, 6; as categorial concepts within the mind, 5; as mental signs, 284; as mere names, 5; as physical entities, 97; as products of mind, 309; as quality, 5; as singulars, 159; *in re*, 6; in things, 95; logic of, 159; medieval inquiry on, 94; nature of, 4, 163, 299; ontological status of, 163; problem of, 42, 159; question of, 298; real (substantial) existence of, 5, 308; reference of, 308; scholastic problem of, 283; status of, 6, 14, 164, 204; theory of, 109, 285. *See also:* nominalist, realist
universe, 1-2; textual, 16
univocity, 184, 186
Ur-Text, 2
utopian society, 222
Utz, Richard J., 29, 33, 62, 74, 76, 112, 117. *See also:* Watts, William H., and Richard J. Utz

vagabondage, 231
vagabonds, 232-3
vagrancy, 232-3
vagrants, 229, 232-4; statute against, 232
validation (procedures of), 60
Valla, Lorenzo, 257, 285-7; *Dialecticae disputationes*, 287
Vance, Eugene, 104, 174
variability, 291
varietas, 259
Veni Creator, 197
vernacular: literature, 97, 188; Old French, 96; poet(s), 103, 140; poetry, 105; tradition(s), 109; writers, 124; writing, 88. *See also:* Chrétien de Troyes, paradigm(s), romance

vessel(s), 206, 210; metaphor of, 196; of the Spirit, 103
via antiqua, 178
via moderna, 178, 192, 209-12, 309-10; theologians, 206; theology, 208. *See also:* Ockham, Ockhamist
Vickers, Brian, 302
victims, 245-6
villain(s), 246, 249
virtue(s), 269, 272, 275-6, 281; as signifier(s), 277
visibilia/invisibilia, 133
Vitz, Evelyn Birge, 274
vocations, 234
volition, 207. *See also:* entity, will
voluntarism, 161; semiotic, 243
vox: and *conceptus*, 163-4; and *verbum,* 177. *See also:* name(s)

Wakefield, 191
Warton, Thomas, 125
Waswo, Richard, 253, 287
Watts, William H., 77
Watts, William H., and Richard J. Utz, 172, 181, 270
Weamys, Anna: *A Continuation of Sir Philip Sidney's Arcadia*, 279-81
Weimann, Robert, 269
Wheeler, Richard, 249
Whetstone, George, 229
will, 161, 185-6, 243; free, 151, 154. *See also:* divine, God, self-will
William of Auxerre, 116
William of Champeaux, 306
William of Ockham: *see:* Ockham, William of
Williams, Raymond, 68, 267
wisdom, 107
Wittgenstein, Ludwig, 283, 286-7, 310
Woodham, Adam of, 149
Woolf, Rosemary, 193
Word (of God), 102; eternal, 103, 105; incorrect interpretation of, 105

word(s), 1-3, 96, 101, 103, 105, 162-5, 169, 180-1, 183, 199, 215, 256-7, 288-9; and concepts, 286; and deed(s), 180-2; and reality, 286; and referent, 172; and thing(s), 180-2, 261, 267, 285-7; as body and soul, 177; as epistemological instrument, 257; as meaningful sound *(sermo)*, 308; as sign(s), 4, 290; as symbol(s), 286; corrupted, 99; games, 162; of poet(s), 103, 105; original, 2; psychological function of, 294; secular (romance), 105; status of, 4; universal, 285; written, 90. *See also:* puns
Word (the), 1-3, 101-2, 106, 179, 196; incarnate, 196; indwelling, 210; made flesh, 104. *See also:* divine, God, Light, Logos
world, 2; contingent character of, 133, 160; covenantal character of, 160; empirical, 203; fictional, 129, 131, 134, 137, 141; of ideas, 171; of language and logic, 164; of things, 164, 171; real, 165; structure of, 286. *See also:* interpretation, readability, reading
writerly, 53, 55-6; modes, 98; romance autorship, 99; romance paradigm, 91. *See also:* text(s)
writing (secular), 105-6, 109
Wroth, Mary: *Urania*, 275-9, 281
Wyclif, John, 145, 149, 173, 189; *De Veritate Sacrae Scripturae*, 174

York, 191; *Memorandum Book*, 191; Passion Plays, 185; Play on the Baptism of Christ (York Baptism), 191-7, 199, 201, 207-8, 210-11; *The York Plays*, 191

Zeitgeist: late medieval, 29, 33, 35; universalized, 34
Zink, Michel, 92, 109
Zumthor, Paul, 88-9

Dalkey Archive Press

The Complete Fiction
W. M. Spackman

$16.95 paperback
$44.95 cloth

"Elegant, witty, and urbane, Spackman's fiction presents achingly beautiful and never less than scintillating depictions of the psychology of love and sexual attraction." —*Booklist*

"A welcome gathering of the work of one of the most idiosyncratic, provocative, and intensely stylish American writers of recent decades." —*Kirkus Reviews*

"A sensuous delight... Like Jane Austen, he exposes savage passions lurking beneath civilized exteriors." —*Publishers Weekly*

Available at better bookstores or visit our website for the catalog at: www.cas.ilstu.edu/english/dalkey/dalkey.html

Dalkey Archive Press

Pack of Lies

Gilbert Sorrentino
$14.95 paperback

Odd Number
Rose Theatre
Misterioso

Gilbert Sorrentino

"The work of a sophisticated, meticulous artist with a gift for comedy, a perfect-pitch ear for American speech."
—*Hudson Review*

"A literary game which imitates, parodies, satirizes and elaborates upon the fantasies, pleasures, surprises, and disappointments of American life."
—*Los Angeles Times*

Available at better bookstores or visit our website for the catalog at: www.cas.ilstu.edu/english/dalkey/dalkey.html

Dalkey Archive Press

Palinuro of Mexico Fernando del Paso

$14.95 paperback

"Dreamlike and fantastic, filled with sensuous, poetic language, a positively orgiastic love of life, bubbling humor and a special brand of literary alchemy. . . . Enormous fun to read."

—*Los Angeles Times*

Available at better bookstores or visit our website for the catalog at: www.cas.ilstu.edu/english/dalkey/dalkey.html

Dalkey Archive Press

Killoyle

Roger Boylan
$13.95 paperback

"A virtuoso performance . . . with truly funny turns of phrase and events."
—*Publishers Weekly*

"Pleasure awaits in this hilarious Irish farce . . . Boylan's wacky tale is deftly fleshed out with dense footnotes addressed directly to the reader—a clever technique that, in the hands of this skilled writer, helps provide for heaps of hearty laughter."
—*Library Journal*

Available at better bookstores or visit our website for the catalog at: www.cas.ilstu.edu/english/dalkey/dalkey.html

Dalkey Archive Press

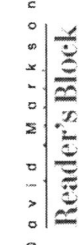

Reader's Block

David Markson

$12.95 paper

"Exhilarating, sorrowful and amazing. Indeed, a minor masterpiece."
—*Washington Post*

"Not only is this a compelling novel, it is a fascinating history of a collective cultural past."
—*Rain Taxi*

"A novel often dreamed about by the avant-garde but never seen . . . utterly fascinating."
—*Publishers Weekly*

Available at better bookstores or visit our website for the catalog at: www.cas.ilstu.edu/english/dalkey.html

differences

A Journal of Feminist Cultural Studies, edited by Naomi Schor and Elizabeth Weed, focuses on how concepts and categories of difference—notably but not exclusively gender—operate within culture.

On Violence

Avital Ronell: *The Uninterrogated Question of Stupidity*

Pamela Haag: *"Putting Your Body on the Line": The Question of Violence, Victims, and the Legacies of Second Wave Feminism*

Timothy Melley: *"Stalked by Love": Female Paranoia and the Postmodern Stalker Novel*

Naomi E. Morgenstern: *Mother's Milk and Sister's Blood: Trauma and the Neoslave Narrative*

David Savran: *The Sadomasochist in the Closet: White Masculinity and the Culture of Victimization*

Sarah Currie: *The Killer Within: Christianity and the Invention of Murder in the Roman World*

Vol. 8, No. 2 $14.95

Love, Anger, and the Body

Henrietta Moore: *Sex, Symbolism, and Psychoanalysis*

Willy Apollon: *Nothing Works Anymore!*

Renata Salecl: *The Sirens and Feminine Jouissance*

Neil Hertz: *The Scene Came Alive: Autobiography and Anger*

Claire Kahane: *Gender and Patrimony*

Xiaoying Wang: *Postmodernism and the Amnesia of its Origins*

Vol. 9, No. 1 $14.95

Journals Division,
Indiana University Press,
601 N. Morton,
Bloomington, IN 47404

Phone: 800-842-6796
Fax: 812-855-8507

E-Mail: Journals@Indiana.Edu
http://www.indiana.edu/~iupress/journals

Subscriptions (3 issues)

Individuals: $32.00
Institutions: $65.00
Surface post outside the USA: $10.00

Single Issues:

Add $3.00 postage and handling for the first and $1.00 each additional

INDIANA UNIVERSITY PRESS

differences

*A Journal of Feminist Cultural Studies,
edited by Naomi Schor and Elizabeth Weed, focuses on how concepts and
categories of difference—notably but not exclusively gender—
operate within culture.*

More Gender Trouble: Feminism Meets Queer Theory

Introduction: Against Proper Objects
by Judith Butler

Interview: Feminism by Any Other Name by Rosi Braidotti with Judith Butler

Interview: Sexual Traffic by Gayle Rubin with Judith Butler

Extraordinary Homosexuals and the Fear of Being Ordinary by Biddy Martin

Black (W)holes and the Geometry of Black Female Sexuality by Evelynn Hammonds

Camp, Masculinity, Masquerade by Kim Michasiw

Melancholic Modernity: The Hom(m)osexual Symptom and the Homosocial Corpse by Trevor Hope

Passing, Narcissism, Identity, and Difference by Carole-Anne Tyler

The More Things Change by Elizabeth Weed

The Labors of Love, Analyzing Perverse Desire: An Interrogation of Teresa de Lauretis's The Practice of Love by Elizabeth Grosz

Responses by Rosi Braidotti, Trevor Hope, and Teresa de Lauretis

Price: $14.95

Volume 7, Number 3

Baby Killers by Jonathan Crewe

How to Do Things with Fetishism by E.L. McCallum

(Dis)figuring the Nation: Mother, Metaphor, Metonymy by Sandhya Sheety

The Hollow Women: Modernism, The Prostitute, and Commodity Aesthetics by Laurie Teal

Reconstructions: Prosthetics and the Rehabilitation of the Male Body in World War I France by Roxanne Panchasi

Mechanizing the Female: Discourse and Control in the Industrial Economy by Katherine Stubbs

Price: $10.00

Subscriptions (3 issues)
Individuals: $32.00
Institutions: $65.00
Surface post outside the USA: $10.00

Single Issues:
Add $3.00 postage and handling for the first and $1.00 each additional

*Journals Division,
Indiana University Press,
601 N. Morton, Bloomington, IN 47404*

Phone: 812-855-9449
Fax: 812-855-8507

E-Mail: Journals@Indiana.Edu
http://www.indiana.edu/~iupress

LIT
Literature Interpretation Theory

Edited by
Lee A. Jacobus
and
Regina Barreca
University of Connecticut
Storrs, Connecticut
USA

Current Subscription:
Volume 7 (1996)
4 issues per volume
ISSN 1043-6928
Base List Rate for individuals:
US$82/ ECU 66
Special society rate
available to individual members of the
Modern Language Association:
US$38/ ECU 35

"**LIT** *has so far been exciting and diverse, current in its topics, and even fashionable in the methodologies it foregrounds. It is a tough-minded journal with lean prose and lots of hard thinking in its pages. It is one of the journals I look forward to reading.*"
—**Robert Con Davis**, *University of Oklahoma, Norman, OK, USA; Co-editor of the Oklahoma Project for Discourse & Theory*

Lit: Literature Interpretation Theory aims to publish readable, smart essays interpreting literature from a strong theoretical viewpoint. Its goal is to broaden the critical base of literary studies while assuring that the work produced is clear, sensible, and bound to make an impact on the field. Special issues on Hélène Cixous, horror, popular culture, illustrated books, and women's fiction have all received favorable notice. Future issues on Margaret Atwood and travel literature complement the scheduled regular issues which offer important essays on works from several nationalities and periods.

To order:
North/South America:
International Publishers Distributor, PO Box 27542, Newark, NJ 07101-8742, USA
Tel: +1 (800) 545-8398 · Fax: +1 (215) 750-6343
Europe/Middle East/Africa:
International Publishers Distributor c/o PO Box 90, Reading, Berkshire, RG1 8JL, UK
Tel: +44 (0) 1734 568316
Fax: +44 (0) 1734 568211
Australia/New Zealand: Fine Arts Press, PO Box 480, Roseville NSW 2069, Australia · Tel: (02) 417 1033
Fax: (02) 417 1045 · Email: info@gbhap.com.au
Asia: International Publishers Distributor, Kent Ridge, PO Box 1180, Singapore 911106 · Tel: +65 741 6933
Fax: +65 741 6922
Customers in Japan should contact our exclusive agent for a separate yen price: Yohan (Western Publications Agency), 3-14-9, Okubo, Shinjuku-ku, Tokyo 169, Japan.

E-mail (info@gbhap.com)
Gordon and Breach

Piercing Social Analysis

Some behaviors scream. But what do people hear? How do they judge? What's real?

In other words, how do stereotypes and language skills affect perceptions of intelligence, social class and behavior?

We make snap judgements all the time.

But, if you're looking for penetrating insights about everyday life, individuals and societies large and small around the globe, there are two places to start.

Sociological Abstracts (SA) and *Social Planning/ Policy & Development Abstracts* (SOPODA).

Our data are drawn from more than 2,000 serials from 35 countries, along with books, conference papers, book and other media reviews and dissertations.

You'll find the piercing social analysis that gets beneath the fashion and under the skin.

sociological abstracts

P.O. Box 22206 San Diego, CA 92192-0206
619/695-8803 Fax: 695-0416
Internet socio@cerfnet.com
User Assistance: 800/752-3945

The SAI family of services: *Sociological Abstracts* (SA) • *Social Planning/Policy & Development Abstracts* (SOPODA) • *sociofile* (SA and SOPODA on CD-ROM) • Products are available in print; online from Knight-Ridder, DIMDI, OCLC, and Ovid; on CD-ROM from SilverPlatter, EBSCO and Ovid; on magnetic tape via SAI direct. Document delivery available via SOCIOLOGY*Express*: 800/313-9966; 415/259-5013; Fax 415/259-5058; email: socabs@ebscodoc.com

Editor: James M. Mellard
Publisher: Northern Illinois University

Style

A quarterly journal of aesthetics, poetics, stylistics, and interpretation of film and literature

Next in *Style*:
Rhetoric and Poetics
Volume 30, Number 2, Summer 1996

James I. Wimsatt. Rhyme, the Icons of Sound, and the Middle English *Pearl*

Rodney Stenning Edgecombe. Ways of Personifying

Michael Simpson. Who Didn't Kill Blake's Fly: Moral Law and the Rule of Grammar in "Songs of Experience"

Manfred Jahn. Windows of Focalization: Deconstructing and Reconstructing a Narratological Concept

Richard Badenhausen. Representing Experience and Reasserting Identity: The Rhetoric of Combat in the British Literature of World War I

Gerald Doherty. The Art of Appropriation: The Rhetoric of Sexuality in D. H. Lawrence

Kai Mikkonen. Theories of Metamorphosis: From Metatrope to Textual Revision

Jane Frazier. Writing Outside the Self: The Disembodied Narrators of W. S. Merwin

Joyce Wexler. Speaking Out: Dialogue and the Literary Unconscious

---

Information on Subscriptions and Sales:
Style is now accepting new subscriptions and renewals to volume 30 (1996):
Institutions $40; Individuals $28;
Students $18; *all add $4 for foreign postage*
Current single numbers $10; *add $1 for foreign postage*

Attention Librarian and Collectors: Back volumes of *Style* may be purchased at $12 per volume for volumes 1-16 (plus $4 per volume for foreign postage) or at $180 for all 16 volumes (plus $20 for domestic postage and $30 for foreign postage). Volumes 17 to the present volume may be purchased at $24 per volume. Add $4 per volume for foreign postage. Inquire for single issue prices. Address orders to: Associate Editor for Business Affairs, *Style*, Department of English, Northern Illinois University, DeKalb, Illinois 60115-2863.

Please enter my subscription to *Style* for Volume 30 (1996).

Number 1: *Reading Style, Reading Fiction*
Number 2: *Rhetoric and Poetics*
Number 3: *Narrating the Multicultural*
Number 4: *Essays, Bibliographies, and Bibliographical Surveys*

Please make checks payable to *Style* in U.S. dollars and send to: Associate Editor for Business Affairs, *Style*, Department of English, Northern Illinois University, DeKalb, Illinois 60115-2863.

Name _____ Address _____

City _____ State _____ Zip _____

My check in the amount of $ _____ is enclosed.

New Payment Option: *Style* now accepts Visa and MasterCard from subscribers purchasing a minimum two-year subscription. To pay for a two-year subscription by credit card, complete the above form and provide in the space below the full name of the cardholder as it appears on the credit card, the card number, and the expiration date.

Name _____ Card Number _____ Exp. _____

A forum for interdisciplinary and international dialogue in the fields of philosophy of culture, philosophy and epistemology of cultural anthropology, methodological problems of history of culture, phenomenological theory of culture, analytical philosophy of humanities, cultural hermeneutics, methodology of cross-cultural studies, naturalistic models of culture, sociology of culture.
Biannual: Spring and Autumn. Papers come out in English, German or French.
Editor: Dimitri Ginev, University of Sofia.

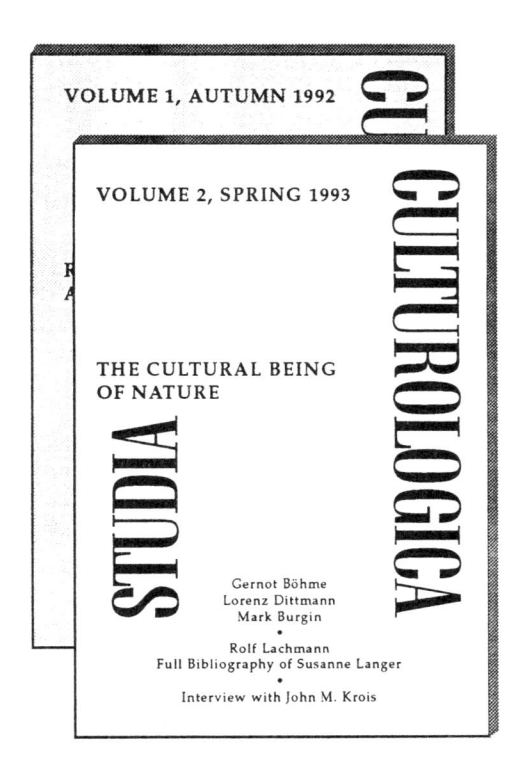

VOLUME 1, AUTUMN 1992

VOLUME 2, SPRING 1993

STUDIA CULTUROLOGICA

THE CULTURAL BEING OF NATURE

Gernot Böhme
Lorenz Dittmann
Mark Burgin
•
Rolf Lachmann
Full Bibliography of Susanne Langer
•
Interview with John M. Krois

ALREADY APPEARED:
VOLUME 1, SPRING 1992
Special Issue Dedicated to the 60th Anniversary of Nikolai Genchev
VOLUME 1, AUTUMN 1992
Rationality and Life-World
VOLUME 2, SPRING 1993
The Cultural Being of Nature
VOLUME 3, SPRING–AUTUMN 1994
Interculturality/ Sociocultural Reality/ Human Studies at the End of Modernity
VOLUME 4, SPRING–AUTUMN 1996
Modernity and its Legitimation Strategies

ISSN–0861–6329.
Address: Center for Culturology, University of Sofia, 15 Tzar Osvoboditel Blvd., Sofia 1000, Bulgaria.

Critical*Review*

An interdisciplinary journal focusing on the effects of market and state on human well-being.

"A miracle: a genuinely interesting, civilized publication." **Robert Heilbroner**

"One of the more interesting journals these days because it is scholarly, quirky, and unpredictable." **Daniel Bell**

"An excellent publication." **Anthony Giddens**

"Gives every sign of becoming the place where scholars working in very different modes actually conduct useful discussions with each other." **Bertell Ollman**

IN RECENT ISSUES (back issues available):
Rational Choice Theory and Political Science (DOUBLE ISSUE)
15 leading political scientists debate the empirical validity of *Pathologies of Rational Choice Theory*, by Don Green and Ian Shapiro. Green and Shapiro reply.

Consumerism
Colin Campbell, Robert E. Lane, James Q. Wilson on consumerism and happiness; plus Cass Sunstein in defense of government regulation and a debate on the causes of financial crises.

Communitarianism
Brenda Almond, Ronald Beiner, Jeffrey Friedman, Will Kymlicka, James Hudson, Paul Rosenberg, Peter Simpson, Charles Taylor, John Tomasi on community, communitarianism, and liberalism.

FORTHCOMING:
- P. J. Boettke, Stephen Holmes, David Johnston, Seymour Martin Lipset, Steven Lukes, Alan Ryan on **F. A. Hayek**
- Benedict Anderson, Shlomo Avineri, Liah Greenfeld, Leszek Kolakowski, Eugen Weber, Bernard Yack on **nationalism**
- special issue on **Christopher Lasch**
- special issue on **public opinion formation in mass democracies**
- **art and capitalism**
- special issue on Tibor Scitovsky's **Joyless Economy** after 20 years
- Karl Polanyi's **The Great Transformation** after 50 years

MANUSCRIPT SUBMISSION GUIDE AND BACK ISSUE LIST AVAILABLE UPON REQUEST

Single issues $10, double issues $20. 1-year (4-issue) subscriptions: $29 U.S., $35 foreign, $15 students with copy of ID, $54 institutions; add $15 for air mail. Send check, money order, or Visa/MC number and expiration date to: CRITICAL REVIEW, P.O. BOX 1254, Dept. 4, Danbury, CT 06813, or fax credit card information to (203) 794-1007, or e-mail critrev@aol.com.
(issn 0891-3811)

The Red Shoes and Other Tattered Tales

a novel by Karen Elizabeth Gordon

"Sensual and surreal . . . to be relished *comme une coupe de plaisir.*"—Rikki Durconet

$12.95 paper

Storytown

stories by Susan Daitch

"It is always a delight to discover a new voice as strong as Susan Daitch's."—Salman Rushdie

$12.95 paper

Palinuro of Mexico

a novel by Fernando del Paso

"Grotesque, macabre and Dionysiac . . . del Paso is a great and unorthodox writer."—*Le Monde*

$14.95 paper

Nobodaddy's Children

a trilogy by Arno Schmidt

"A truly innovative and witty writer. . . . Beautifully translated."
—*Chicago Tribune*

$13.95 paper

The Corpus in the Library

stories and novellas by Alf Mac Lochlainn

"The finest style I have encountered in any Irish writer in recent years."—John Banville

$11.95 paper

DALKEY ARCHIVE PRESS

Illinois State University, Campus Box 4241, Normal, IL 61790-4241

Critical Quarterly

Edited by Colin McCabe

'This is the only journal to remain faithful to the original spirit of cultural studies. It mixes 'high' and 'low' culture, criticism and creative writing without losing sight of political and social questions.'
Rosalind Coward

Critical Quarterly has been at the forefront of literary criticism since the 1960's and in the last ten years it has established an international reputation for its unique blend of fiction, criticism and poetry which mix together to reflect contemporary issues.

ORDER FORM   CRITICAL QUARTERLY

Subscription Rates, Volume 38, 1996   ISSN 0011-1562

Institutional Rates, £57.00 (UK-Europe), $99.00 (N. America*), £64.00 (Rest of World)

Personal Rates, £31.00 (UK-Europe), $58.00 (N. America*), £37.00 (Rest of World)

Published in: April, July, October and December   *Canadian customers please add 7% GST

❑ Please enter my subscription/send me a sample copy

❑ I enclose a cheque/money order payable to Blackwell Publishers

❑ Please charge my American Express/Diners Club/Mastercard/Visa account

Card Number . . . . Expiry Date . . . .

Signature . . . . Date . . . .

Name . . . .

Address . . . .

. . . .

. . . . Postcode . . . .

Payment must accompany orders
Please return this form to: Journals Marketing, Blackwell Publishers, 108 Cowley Road, Oxford, OX4 1JF, UK.
Or to: Journals Marketing, CRIQ, Blackwell Publishers, 238 Main Street, Cambridge, MA 02142, USA.

Internet
Full details of Blackwell Publishers books and journals are available on the internet.
To access use a WWW browser such as Netscape or Mosaic, and the following URL:
http://www.blackwellpublishers.co.uk

APPLY FOR YOUR FREE SAMPLE COPY BY E-MAIL!
jnlsamples@blackwellpublishers.co.uk

The Centennial Review
Edited by R. K. Meiners

The Centennial Review is committed to reflection on intellectual work, particularly as set in the University and its environment. We are interested in work that examines models of theory and communication in the physical, biological, and human sciences; that re-reads major texts and authoritative documents in different disciplines or explores interpretive procedures; that questions the cultural and social implications of research in a variety of disciplines.

Special Section   *Spring 1996*

From Kansas University's symposium on:

Reconsidering Graduate Education: Pressures, Practices, Prospects

Edited by Iris L. Smith

With keynote speeches by **Michael Bérubé** and **Herbert Lindenberger**

Please begin my *CR* subscription with Spring 1996

☐ $12/year (3 issues)   ☐ $18/two years (6 issues)   ☐ $6 single issue
(Add $4.50 per for mailing outside the US)

Name_____
Address_____
State/Country_____Zip _____

Please make your check payable to *The Centennial Review*. Mail to *The Centennial Review*, 312 Linton Hall, Michigan State Univ. E. Lansing, MI 48824-1044.

in *Twentieth Century Literature*

Volume 21, No. 1 (Winter, 1997)

A journal devoted to literary theory and practical criticism

A Special Issue on
Contemporary German Poetry
James Rolleston, Guest Editor

Contributors include:

Nora M. Alter ... und Fried ... und ...: The Poetry of Erich Fried and the Structure of Contemporaneity

Amy Colin Writings from the Margins: German-Jewish Women Poets from the Bukovina

Christine Cosentino "An Affair on Uncertain Ground": Sarah Kirsch's poetry Volume *Erlking's Daughter* in the Context of Her Prose After the "Wende"

Neil H. Donahue The Intimacy of Internationalism in the poetry of Joachim Sartorius

Elke Erb Fundamentally Grounded

Erk Grimm Mediamania? Contemporary German Poetry in the Age of New Information Technologies: Thomas Kling and Durs Grünbein

Barbara Mabee Footprints Revisited or "Life in the Changed Space that I don't Know": Elke Erb's Poetry Since 1989

Charlotte Melin Improved Versions: Feminist Poetics and Recent Work by Ulla Hahn and Ursula Krechel

Jonathan Monroe Between Ideologies and a Hard Place: Hans Magnus Enzensberg's Utopian Pragmatist Poetics

Leonard Olschner A Poetics of Place: Günter Kunert's Poem Sequence "Herbstanbruch in Arkadien"

James Rolleston Modernism and Metamorphosis: Karin Kiwus' *Das Chinesische Examen*

and **New Poetry** by **Gerhard Falkner** and **Günter Kunert**

Also in preparation: *Illness and Disease in Twentieth-Century Literature*—Sander L. Gilman, Guest Editor

Subscriptions: Douglas Benson email: bensonml@ksu.ksu.edu

MSS in French and German—Marshall Olds, Editor: molds@unlinfo.unl.edu
MSS in Spanish and Russian—Silvia Sauter, Editor: silviae@ksu.ksu.edu

Women in French Studies

Women in French Studies, the annual journal of **Women in French**, an allied organization of the Modern Languages Association, publishes articles in both English and French on any aspect of women in French-speaking literatures or cultures. WIF members, men and women who work in these areas, may submit articles for consideration. **Women in French Studies** also sponsors an annual prize for the best essay submitted by a graduate student. Essays should be sent to the editor, Adele King, Department of Modern Languages and Classics, Ball State University, Muncie, IN 47306.

The annual subscription is $8 for the U.S. and $12 for Canada and $15 overseas (payable in U.S. dollars, postage included). Checks or money orders, made out to **Women in French**, should be sent to the managing editor, and president of **Women in French**: Colette Hall, Ursinus College, Collegeville, PA 19426.

For membership forms, contact Barbara Klaw, Department of Literature and Language, Northern Kentucky University, Highland Heights, KY 41099-1500. Membership is $25 ($35 Canadian) for full and associate professors, $15 ($21 Canadian) for others. Membership includes two newsletters and a copy of **Women in French Studies**.

Women in French Studies is indexed in the MLA Bibliography, and is a member of the Council of Editors of Learned Journals.

symplokē

editor-in-chief
Jeffrey R. Di Leo

associate editor
Christian Moraru

advisory board
Charles Altieri
Michael Bérubé
Ronald Bogue
Matei Calinescu
Edward Casey
Gilbert Chaitin
Albert Cook
Stanley Corngold
Robert Con Davis
Eugene Eoyang
Henry Giroux
Karen Hanson
Phillip Brian Harper
Peter C. Herman
Oscar Kenshur
Candace Lang
Vincent B. Leitch
Paisley Livingston
Donald Marshall
Michael L. Morgan
Marjorie Perloff
Mark Poster
Gerald Prince
Joseph Ricapito
Robert Scholes
Alan Schrift
Tobin Siebers
Hugh Silverman
John H. Smith
Paul M. Smith
Henry Sussman
Mark Taylor
S. Tötösy de Zepetnek
Joel Weinsheimer
Jeffrey Williams

subscriptions
editor, symplokē, school of literature, communication and culture, georgia institute of techology, atlanta, ga, 30332-0165
email jeffrey.dileo@lcc.gatech.edu
fax (404)-894-1287 phone (404)-894-2730

a journal for the intermingling of literary, cultural and theoretical scholarship

symplokē is a comparative literature and theory journal. Our aim is to provide an arena for critical exchange between established and emerging voices in the field. We support new and developing notions of comparative literature, and are committed to interdisciplinary studies, intellectual pluralism, and open discussion. We are particularly interested in scholarship on the interrelations among philosophy, literature, culture criticism and intellectual history, though will consider articles on any aspect of the intermingling of discourses and disciplines.

forthcoming special issues
REFIGURING EUROPE
PRACTICING DELEUZE & GUATTARI

past special issues
THE NEXT GENERATION
WITTGENSTEIN AND ART
PHILOSOPHY AND LITERATURE
RHETORIC & THE HUMAN SCIENCES
THE HISTORIES OF MICHEL FOUCAULT

some past & future contributors
Peter Baker on deconstruction and violence
Michael Bernard-Donals on liberatory pedagogy
Ronald Bogue on minor literature
Matei Calinescu on modernity and modernization
Joseph Carroll on evolution and literary theory
Peter Caws on sophistry and postmodernity
Alina Clej on translation and modernism
Albert Cook on virtual subjectivities and periodization
Sandra Corse on the fetish character of art
Frank M. Farmer on the superaddressee
William Franke on dante and the poetics of religion
Elizabeth Grosz on the future in deleuze
James Guetti on wittgenstein, conrad and the darkness
Candace Lang on robbe-grillet
Richard Lanigan on foucault's science of rhetoric
John Mowitt on queer resistance
Linda Myrsiades on constituting resistance
Richard Nash on gorilla rhetoric
Sharon O'Dair on working class cultural choices
David Palumbo-Liu on asian america and the imaginary
John Smith on queering the will
Allen Stoekl on the holocaust
Allen Weiss on the erosion of thought
Jeffrey Williams on the posttheory generation
Ewa Ziarek on foucault's ethics

please enter my one-year subscription (two issues) to *symplokē*
☐ Individuals: $15   ☐ Institutions: $30   Add $5 for subscriptions outside the U.S.

Name

Address   Apt.

City   State   Zip

CULTURAL POLITICS AND POLITICAL CULTURE IN POSTMODERN EUROPE

Ed. by J. Peter Burgess

Amsterdam/Atlanta, GA 1997. 451 pp.
(Postmodern Studies 24)
ISBN: 90-420-0327-8   Bound Hfl. 180,-/US-$ 94.50
ISBN: 90-420-0317-0   Paper Hfl. 60,-/US-$ 31.50

The present volume assembles essays from a broad cultural and professional spectrum around the question of European cultural identity. The heterogeneity of the contributors — their differing points of departure and methods — attests to a tension in intellectual communities which today is more intense than ever. Europe's identity crisis is not merely an empirical matter. It reflects a far deeper, and far older, *discursive* crisis. The mandate of Europe's traditional intellectual institutions to preserve and police their own cultural heritage has proved incapable of evolving in a manner sufficient to account for the mutation in its object: European culture. It is not merely that Europe's identity, like any identity in the flux of history, has changed. Rather, the notion of identity, the very basis of any questions of who we are, where we are going, and the appropriate political forms and social institutions for further existence, all rely on a logic of identity which has, at best, become extremely problematic. It is this problematization which provides the common thread unifying the following essays. Each contributor, in his/her own way and with respect to his/her own research object, confronts the adequacy of the concept of cultural identity. The hidden presuppositions of this concept are indeed remarkable, and the logic of cultural identity prescribes that they remain undisclosed.

NEW PERSPECTIVES ON DUBLINERS

Ed. by Mary Power and Uli Schneider

Amsterdam/Atlanta, GA 1997. 298 pp.
(European Joyce Studies 7)
ISBN: 90-420-0385-5   Bound Hfl. 150,-/US-$ 78.50
ISBN: 90-420-0375-8   Paper Hfl. 45,-/US-$ 23.50

Contents: Introduction. Fritz SENN: Dynamic Adjustments in *Dubliners*. Fritz SENN: *Dubliners*: Renewed Time after Time. Wolfgang KARRER: Gnomon and Triangulation: The Stories of Childhood. William JOHNSEN: Joyce's Many Sisters and the Demodernization of *Dubliners*. Laurent MILESI: Joyce's Anamorphic Mirror in "The Sisters". Wolfgang WICHT: Eveline and/as "A Painful Case": Paralysis, Desire, Signifiers. Margot NORRIS: Narrative Bread Pudding: Joyce's "The Boarding House". John GORDON: "A Little Cloud" as a Little Cloud. Carol SCHLOSS: Money and Other Rates of Exchange: Commercial Relations and "Counterparts". Jana GILES: The Craft of "A Painful Case": A Study of Revisions. Mary POWER: The Stories of Public Life. Marie-Dominique GARNIER: From Paralysis to Para-lire: Another Reading of "A Mother". Yvonne STUDER: "Grace" after Piers Plowman: A Comparison of "Grace" and the Medieval Allegory of Glotoun. Ulrich SCHNEIDER: Cruxes and Grace Notes: A Hermeneutic Approach to "Grace".

Editions Rodopi B.V.

USA/Canada: 2015 South Park Place, Atlanta, GA 30339, Tel. (770) 933-0027, *Call toll-free* (U.S.only) 1-800-225-3998, Fax (770) 933-9644

All Other Countries: Keizersgracht 302-304, 1016 EX Amsterdam, The Netherlands. Tel. + + 31 (0)20 6227507, Fax + + 31 (0)20 6380948

E-mail: orders-queries@rodopi.nl — http://www.rodopi.nl